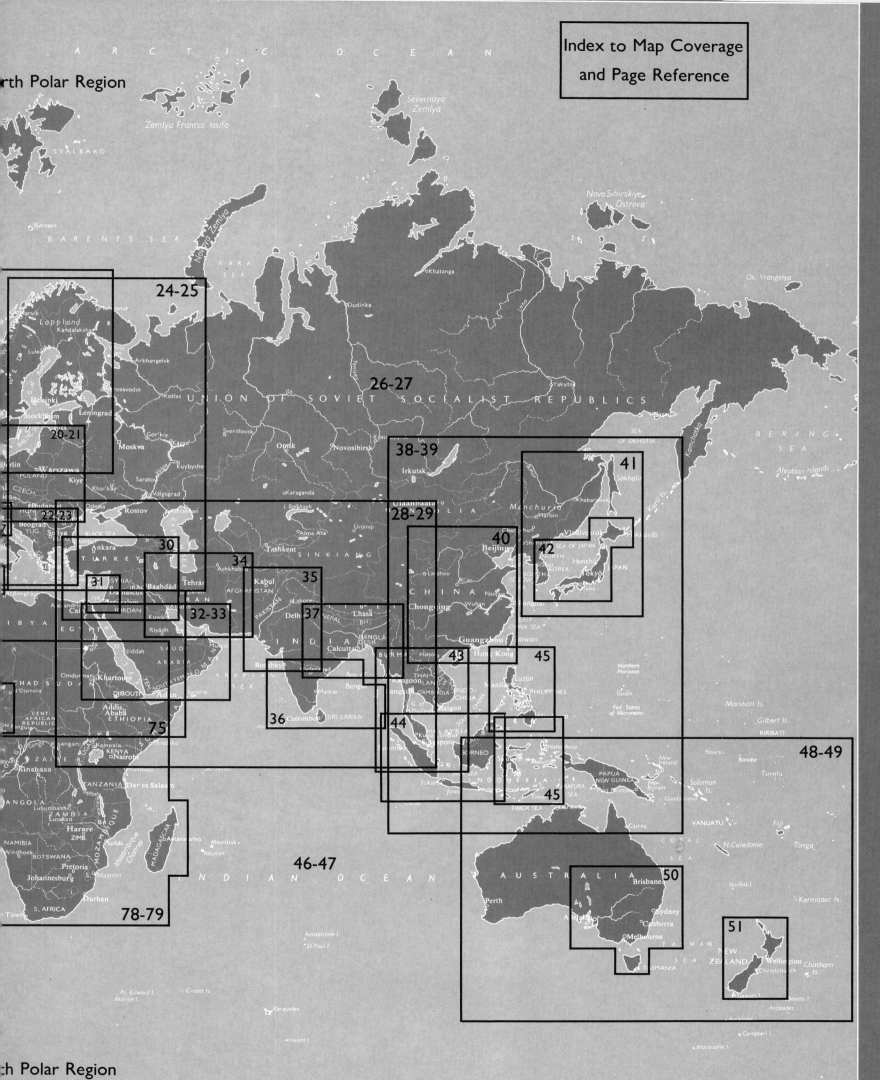

Index to Map Coverage
and Page Reference

North Polar Region

South Polar Region

BARTHOLOMEW
ATLAS
OF THE
WORLD

BARTHOLOMEW
ATLAS
OF THE
WORLD

CONTENTS

Photographs from space

HALF-TITLE Planet Earth: Africa, Arabia and (at bottom) Antarctica partly obscured by cloud systems.
(Robert Harding Picture Library)

TITLE SPREAD A view south-eastwards across the Nile valley and Red Sea towards Saudi Arabia. The Egyptian city of Qena is at the apex of the bend in the Nile seen below the jetstream clouds; at the extreme right the dark areas are the lakes above the Aswan High Dam.
(Colorific Photo Library)

LEFT The eastern half of Pelopónnisos, Greece. Near the top centre the blue line of the Corinth canal cuts through the isthmus; at the extreme top right are Athens and its port, Piraiévs; the large dark area on the right of the picture is the Mirtoan Sea.
(Colorific Photo Library)

First published in 1983 by
Octopus Books Limited
59 Grosvenor Street London W1

© 1983 Hennerwood Publications Limited

ISBN 0 86273 075 9

Printed in Spain by
Artes Graficas Toledo, S.A.

DL To-1192-1983

All cartographic material in this atlas was designed and produced by John Bartholomew and Son Limited. Map pages 10-80 are © 1983 John Bartholomew and Son Limited and are published here with permission.

Abad *(Persian)*, town.

Ada *(Turkish)*, island.

Aiguille *(French)*, needle; hence, mountain peak.

Ain, bir *(Arabic)*, well or spring.

Akaba *(Arabic)*, pass.

Alf, älv, elf, elv *(Swedish and Norse)*, river.

Alluvium, fine sand or silt deposited, largely during flood periods, by streams and rivers.

Anticline, an arch of stratified rocks on both sides of which the layers dip downwards.

Anticyclone, a high-pressure system occurring in the zone of the 'Westerlies', usually accompanied by fine weather. Wind tends to move outwards in clockwise direction in the Northern Hemisphere, anticlockwise in the Southern.

Antipodes, that part of the earth diametrically opposite to our feet, on the same meridian, but with latitude and seasons reversed; thus, New Zealand is the antipodes of Great Britain.

Arctic Circle, constituted by the parallel 66°32′N., separating North Temperate and North Frigid zones. North of this at mid-summer the sun does not set during the 24 hours, while at mid-winter it does not rise. In the Southern Hemisphere the same conditions apply south of the **Antarctic Circle**, 66°32′S.

Arroyo *(Spanish)*, a **creek** or water-carved channel in an arid region.

Artesian well, a water supply obtained by tapping porous rock strata from which the water rises by natural pressure. The name was derived from Artois in France.

Atoll, a circular coral reef enclosing a central lagoon connected with the outside sea by an opening. Found mostly in the Pacific Ocean.

Avalanche, a mass of loosened snow and ice mixed with earth and stone, precipitated with destructive force down a mountain side.

Axis, the imaginary line running from pole to pole through the centre of the Earth and about which it revolves.

Bahia *(Portuguese and Spanish)*, bay.

Bahr *(Arabic)*, sea, lake, river.

Bal, bally, baile *(Celtic)*, town, village.

Ban *(Siamese)*, village.

Bandar, nagar, pura *(Indian)*, town.

Bar, gravel, sand or mud deposited across the mouth of a river by currents or wave action.

Bas *(French)*, low, low-lying.

Basin, area of land drained by a river and its tributaries.

Basin of inland drainage, an area of land which has no surface-drainage outlet to the sea.

Batang *(Malay)*, river.

Beach, raised, a small platform of land, formerly sea shore, now left dry through a rise of the land level.

Beaufort Scale, a scale of 13 symbols used in weather maps to portray the force of the wind from calm to more than 120km/h (75 mph).

Beled *(Arabic)*, country, village.

Ben, beinn *(Celtic)*, mountain.

Bender *(Persian)*, harbour, landing-place.

Black earth, fertile soil in southern Russia and parts of Romania and Hungary on which heavy grain crops are grown; known also as chernozem.

Bora, a cold, dry, northerly wind blowing in winter and spring along the Dalmatian coast of the Adriatic Sea.

Bore or **eagre**, a tidal wave arising in the estuaries of certain rivers.

Boulder clay, a glacial deposit consisting of boulders of various sizes embedded in finer material laid down under a glacier or ice cap; often found at great depth in glaciated valleys.

Brdo *(Czech.)*, hill.

Brunn *(German)*, spring, well.

Bugt, bukt *(Danish and Swedish)*, bay.

Buran, snow blizzards of winter occurring in Russia and Siberia.

Burun *(Turkish)*, cape, promontory.

Bush, interior uncultivated scrubland.

Butte *(French and Amer.)*, isolated hill or peak.

Cabo *(Portuguese and Spanish)*, cape.

Campo *(Italian and Spanish)*, plain.

Campos, grasslands of south-east Brazil.

Cañon or **canyon** *(Spanish)*, a deep gorge or ravine with lofty sides, formed by rapid erosion of the softer strata in a dry region.

Catingas, open forest lands on the plateaux of eastern Brazil, north of 15°s. Drier and warmer than the adjoining **Cerrados**.

Cerrados, semi-dry plateaux of south-east Brazil covered with grass and trees of stunted growth.

Chinook, a warm, dry west wind blowing down the eastern slopes of the Rocky Mountains.

Chott *(Arabic)*, salt lake or marsh in Algeria and Tunisia.

Chow *(Chinese)*, town of the second rank.

Cidade *(Portuguese)*, town.

Cima, pizzo *(Italian)*, mountain peak.

Città *(Italian)*, town, city.

Ciudad *(Spanish)*, city, town.

Climate, the generalisation of day-to-day weather conditions.

Col *(French)*, **colle** *(Italian)*, pass or neck.

Cold front, the sloping boundary between an advancing mass of cold air and warmer air under which the cold air forms a wedge.

Continental shelf, a sea-covered platform extending from the coast-line of all continents. It varies in width and the edge is usually marked by the **isobath** for 100 fathoms.

Contour, a line on a map joining all points which are at the same height above sea-level.

Cordillera *(Spanish)*, mountain range.

Crater, the cup-shaped cavity forming the mouth of a volcano.

Creek *(Amer.)*, stream or small river.

Crevasse, rent or fissure in a glacier or ice sheet.

Cycle of erosion, the development of landscape by the processes of **denudation** from

the youthful stage, after a period of instability and mountain building, through maturity, until the surface has been reduced to a **peneplane**.

Cyclone, a low pressure system, or **depression**, generally associated with stormy or wet weather. Winds blow inwards in anticlockwise direction in Northern Hemisphere; clockwise in Southern.

Daban *(Mongolian)*, a **pass**.

Dagh *(Turkish)*, mountain.

Dal *(Norwegian, Swedish)*, valley.

Dar'ya *(Persian)*, sea, stream, river.

Date Line, International, this follows approximately the 180° **meridian** from Greenwich, and marks the point where according to international convention the day begins. A ship crossing this line eastwards goes back a day, while westward it goes forward a day.

Declination, the deviation of the compass needle from True North.

Deke *(Japanese)*, mountain, range.

Delta, a triangular or finger-shaped tract of mud and detritus deposited by a river at its mouth when it no longer has sufficient speed to keep them in suspension.

Denudation, the slow process or laying bare and levelling down the physical features of the Earth's surface by natural forces.

Depression, a localised and mobile low-pressure system occurring in the zone of the 'Westerlies' associated with rain and stormy weather.

Derbend *(Persian, Turkish)*, pass.

Desert, a barren area of land, practically devoid of rainfall or vegetation.

Dip, the angle between the downward slope of a stratum of rock and the horizontal.

Doldrums, nautical term for a region of calms and baffling winds near the **Equator** between the N.E. and S.E. **Trade winds**.

Dolina *(Slav.)*, a large hollow or basin caused by the dissolving of limestone.

Donga *(Afrikaans)*, ravine, gulley.

Dorp *(Dutch)*, **Dorf** *(German)*, village.

Dunes, mounds formed by wind-blown sand.

Earthquake, disturbance of the Earth's surface generally occurring along faults or lines of weakness in the Earth's crust.

Eiland *(Dutch)*, island.

Ennis *(Irish)*, island.

Equator, imaginary line circumscribing the globe midway between the poles and at its greatest circumference, 40 075.82km (24 901.96 miles). It constitutes the zero from which latitudes N. and S. are calculated.

Equinox, one of the two times of the year when day and night are of equal duration owing to the sun's crossing the Equator: 20-1 March and 22-3 September.

Erosion, the wearing away of surface features of the Earth by the action of wind, water or ice.

Escarpment, the steep face of a

hill or range which on the other side slopes gently.

Estuary, the lower reaches of a river affected by the tides.

Falu *(Hungarian)*, village.

Fault, a break or crack in the Earth's surface.

Fell *(Norwegian, **fjeld**; Swedish, **fjell**)*, mountain.

Fen *(Anglo-Saxon)*, swampy or boggy land.

Fiume *(Italian)*, river.

Fjord, old glacial valley filled by the sea. Sides often steepened by faulting.

Flood plain, the generally flat area in the bottom of a valley which is covered by water when the river draining it is in flood.

Föhn, a dry warm wind in the valleys of the Alps, blowing in winter from the south.

Fork, the junction of two streams or rivers of approximately the same size.

Fu *(Chinese)*, town of importance.

Ganga *(Indian)*, river.

Gawa, kawa *(Japanese)*, river.

Gebel, jebel, jabal *(Arabic)*, rock, mountain.

Geyser, intermittently spouting hot spring associated with volcanic activity.

Glacier, river of ice originating in snowfields, and moving slowly down a valley until it melts, or on reaching the sea breaks off as an **iceberg**.

Gol, song *(Mongolian)*, river.

Gora *(Slav.)*, mountain.

Gorod, grad *(Slav.)*, town.

Great circle, a circle on the Earth's surface whose plane passes through the centre of the Earth. In aviation, a Great Circle route represents the shortest distance between two points.

Guba *(Russian)*, bay.

Gulch *(Amer.)*, narrow, deep ravine.

Gulf, an area of ocean or sea partly enclosed by land.

Gulf Stream, a great warm-water current originating in the Gulf of Mexico and flowing across the Atlantic Ocean to north-western Europe.

Gunung *(Malay)*, mountain.

Hachures, closely drawn lines used on some maps to denote ground relief. They follow the direction of slope and vary in intensity with the gradient.

Haf *(Swedish)*, sea.

Hai, hu *(Chinese)*, sea or lake.

Hamn *(Swedish)*, harbour.

Harmattan, a hot dry wind laden with clouds of reddish dust from the Sahara desert blowing over the lands of the Gulf of Guinea in December, January and February. It is an extension of the north-east **Trade winds**.

Havn *(Danish)*, **havre** *(French)*, port, harbour.

Hegy *(Hungarian)*, mountain.

Height of land *(Amer.)*, a watershed or divide.

Hinterland, region lying inland from a coast.

He *(Chinese)*, river.

Hoek *(Dutch)*, cape.

Höhe *(German)*, height, hill.

Horse latitudes, regions of calms and variable winds between 25° and 40° N. and S. on the polar margins of the **Trade winds**.

Horst, a block of rock left upstanding by the down faulting of rocks on either side. Exact opposite of **rift valley**.

Hsi (*Chinese*), west.

Hsien (*Chinese*), town of the third class.

Humidity, the concentration of water vapour in the air. Relative humidity is percentage of moisture contained as compared with that contained in air completely saturated at the given temperature.

Hurricane or **typhoon,** a violent tropical cyclone which occasionally blows in the Gulf of Mexico and in the China Sea in August, September or October.

Iceberg, a detached mass of ice floating in the polar seas, carried along by ocean currents. Originates from a **glacier.**

Inch, innis (*Celtic*), island.

Irmak (*Turkish*), river.

Isla (*Spanish*), **isola** (*Italian*), island.

Isobar, line connecting points having the same barometric pressure at a given time.

Isobath, line connecting points of the ocean of equal depths.

Isohyet, line connecting points with equal rainfall over given period.

Isotherm, line connecting points of equal temperature at a given time.

Jaur, javr, järvi (*Finnish*), lake.

Jesero (*Serbian*), lake.

Jiang (*Chinese*), river.

Joch (*German*), mountain ridge; pass.

Joki (*Finnish*), river.

Jug (*Serbian*), south.

Kampong (*Malay*), village.

Karst, the porous limestone region of the Dinaric Alps north-east of Adriatic Sea. Also applied to similar types of country in other lands where the river system disappears underground.

Kato (*Greek*), under.

Khali (*Arabic*), desert.

Khamsin (*Arabic*, 'fifty'), name given to **Sirocco** in lower Egypt where it blows for 50 days between April and June.

Kopje (*Afrikaans*), small hill.

Kuh (*Persian*), mountain.

Kul (*Turkish*), lake.

Kum or **qum** (*Turkish*), sand.

La (*Tibetan*), pass.

Lac (*French*), **lacul** (*Romanian*), lake.

Lago (*Italian, Portuguese, Spanish*), lake.

Lande (*French*), heath or wasteland.

Latitude, the angular distance of a place north or south of the Equator measured on its meridian. Each degree represents 60 geographical or nautical miles, equal to 111.322km or 69.172 statute miles.

Levante (*Italian*), east.

Levee, embankment erected along the bank of a river to prevent flooding.

Llanos, grasslands of the north-western Orinoco basin (South America).

Loch, lough (*Celtic*), lake.

Loess, a post-glacial wind-blown soil of great fertility; found in the North European Plain and in the Huang He valley of China.

Longitude, the angular distance of any place on the globe eastwards or westwards from a standard **meridian,** as in Great Britain that of Greenwich. Each degree of longitude represents 4 minutes of time; 15° of longitude represent an hour.

Mallee, type of Australian scrub growing in the Murray-Darling basin and other areas, characterised by low-growing eucalyptus and other gum trees.

Marais (*French*), marsh.

Mean annual rainfall, the average amount of rain which falls in a year. The average is deduced from observations taken over a considerable period.

Meander, the winding about of a river in its flood plain.

Medine (*Arabic*), town.

Mer (*French*), **Meer** (*German*), sea.

Meridian, an imaginary line represented by a portion of a circle passing through the Earth's two poles and on which all places have noon at the same time.

Mesa (*Spanish*), a usually isolated hill with a level top and steep sides.

Miasto (*Polish*), village.

Mile (geographical) = 1 minute of latitude (1.85km or 1.15 statute miles).

Millibar, a standard unit of barometric pressure. Average pressure is approximately 1013 millibars or 29.91 inches of mercury.

Mistral, a violent, dry, cold wind blowing in winter down the Rhône valley (France).

Monsoon, seasonal winds blowing over the south-eastern half of Asia. General direction October to March from north-east, April to September from south-west.

Mont (*French*), **monte** (*Italian*), mount.

Montagna (*Italian*), mountain range.

Moraine, the waste material deposited by a glacier.

More (*Russian*), sea.

Muang (*Siamese*), town.

Myo (*Burmese*), town.

Nagar (*Indian*), town.

Nahr (*Arabic*), river.

Najd (*Arabic*), high plain.

Nam (*Siamese*), river.

Nan (*Chinese*), south.

Näs (*Scandinavian*), cape.

Neap tides, period of lowest tide-range, when sun and moon are at right angles, as seen from the Earth.

Negri (*Malay*), town.

Nor (*Mongol.*), lake.

Nos (*Russian*), cape.

Oasis, fertile spot in a desert owing its existence to a spring or well.

Ola (*Mongolian*), mountain range.

Ostrov (*Russian*), island.

Oxbow lake, remains of a pronounced **meander** which has been short circuited by the river cutting through its neck.

Ozero (*Russian*), lake.

Pack ice, sea ice which has drifted from its original position. It takes the form of floes of various sizes, loosely or tightly packed.

Pampa (*Argentina*), expanse of treeless grass plain and salt **steppe,** lat. 30° to 40° S., between the Andes and the Atlantic Ocean.

Pampero, a cold south-westerly wind that sweeps over the **pampas** in central South America.

Pass, a depression or gap in a mountain range which serves as way for communication between the lands on either side.

Peneplane, the almost level surface which, if the normal course of **denudation** is undisturbed, results from the erosion of a landscape by running water. The gradient of a river draining a peneplane is just great enough for water flow to be maintained.

Pizzo (*Italian*), peak.

Plain, an area of flat or undulating ground usually at low altitude.

Planina (*Bulg.*), mountain range.

Plateau, an area of relatively flat ground at considerable altitude, sometimes called a tableland.

Polder, land recovered from the sea in Holland, and protected by dykes.

Ponente (*Italian*), evening, west.

Pont, ponte (*French, Spanish, Italian*), bridge.

Potomos (*Greek*), river.

Prairie, a series of grassy plains stretching eastwards from the Rocky Mountains in Canada and United States.

Pristan (*Russian*), port, harbour.

Projection, the process of transferring the outline of the features on the Earth's spherical surface on to a flat surface in order to produce a map.

Pueblo (*Spanish*), village.

Pulo (*Malay*), island.

Puna, a high **plateau** between the eastern and western Andes in Bolivia and Peru.

Pur, pura (*Indian*), town.

Ras (*Arabic*), cape.

Reef, a ridge of rock or coral, generally covered by sea, but exposed at low tide.

Representative fraction, a fraction representing a distance of unit length on a map over its corresponding length on the Earth's surface.

Ria, river valley drowned by the sea owing to a fall in the land level.

Rieka (*Slav.*), river.

Rift valley, valley with steep walls caused by the sinking of land between two parallel faults.

Rio (*Portuguese, Spanish*), river.

River capture, process by which one river, having more rapid powers of erosion than another, cuts into the head waters of the latter and steals certain of its tributaries.

Roaring Forties, nautical name of steady north-westerly winds between lat. 40° and 60° S. Equivalent to **Westerlies** of Northern Hemisphere.

Ross (*Celtic*), promontory.

Saki (*Japanese*), cape.

Sargasso Sea, an area of calms and floating seaweed in the North Atlantic, east of the Bahamas and the Antilles Current.

Savanna, grassland of the subtropics.

Sea level, the mean level of the sea between high and low tides.

Selo (*Russian*), village.

Selva (*Portuguese*), forest. The name Selvas is given to the rain forests of the Amazon basin.

Shan (*Chinese*), mountain range.

Sierra (*Spanish*), **serra** (*Portuguese*), mountain range.

Silt, material, finer than sand, often carried in suspension by rivers and deposited by them on flood plains and **deltas.**

Sirocco, a hot southerly wind blowing off Africa in southern Mediterranean countries.

Sjö (*Swedish*), lake.

Slieve (*Irish*), mountain.

Snow line, the lower limit in altitude of a highland region which is never free from snow.

Spring tides, period of highest tides at new or at full-moon time, *i.e.* when sun and moon are pulling in line with the Earth.

Stad, Stadt (*Dutch, Swedish, German*), town.

Steppe, large expanses of grassland as in European Russia and south-western Siberia.

Strait, a narrow water passage connecting two larger bodies of water.

Strath (*Celtic*), broad valley of a river.

Sudd, large floating islands of vegetable matter which impede navigation on the upper White Nile.

Syd (*Danish-Norwegian*), south.

Sziget (*Hungarian*), island.

Taiga, coniferous-forest belt near the edge of the **tundra.**

Tanjong (*Malay*), cape.

Tind (*Norwegian*), peak.

Trade winds, regular steady winds in the tropics, between latitudes 30° N and 30° S, blowing to the Equator from north-east in the Northern Hemisphere and south-east in the Southern.

Tributary, a river or stream which flows into and thus becomes part of a larger river.

Tropics, the parallels 23½° N. **Tropic of Cancer,** and 23½° S., **Tropic of Capricorn,** are 'turning points' in the apparent seasonal movements of the sun. On 22 June at noon it is vertically above all points on the Northern Tropic; on 22 December at noon it is vertically above all points on the Southern Tropic.

Tundra, treeless plains in Arctic and Antarctic regions: hard-frozen in winter, and only partly thawed in summer; scanty vegetation of lichens and mosses.

Tung (*Chinese*), east.

Ula (*Mongol.*), mountain.

Vatn (*Norwegian*), lake.

Veld, grassy plain in South Africa.

Volcano, a vent in the Earth's crust through which molten rock, ashes and steam are ejected from the hot interior.

Wadi, oued (*Arabic*), a watercourse.

Warm front, the sloping boundary in the atmosphere between an advancing mass of warm air and colder air over which the warm air rises.

Watershed, a land-form separating head streams of two river systems flowing away from one another. Also known as waterparting or divide.

Westerlies, predominantly westerly winds in the Northern and Southern hemispheres N. of 30° N. and S. of 30° S.

Zee (*Dutch*), sea.

Zeliv (*Russian*), gulf.

Zemlya (*Russian*), land.

STATE	AREA sq km	AREA sq miles	POPULATION (estimate 1980)
EUROPE			
Albania	28 748	11 100	2 730 000
Andorra	453	175	30 000
Austria	83 849	32 374	7 510 000
Belgium	30 513	11 781	9 860 000
Bulgaria	110 912	42 823	8 860 000
Czechoslovakia	127 870	49 371	15 320 000
Denmark	43 069	16 629	5 120 000
Faeroes	1 373	530	40 000
Finland	337 032	130 128	4 780 000
France	549 430	212 135	53 710 000
Germany, East	108 173	41 766	16 740 000
Germany, West	248 533	95 959	61 560 000
Gibraltar	6	2.3	30 000
Greece	131 944	50 944	9 600 000
Hungary	93 030	35 919	10 710 000
Iceland	103 000	39 768	230 000
Ireland, Rep. of	68 893	26 600	3 310 000
Italy	301 224	116 303	57 040 000
Liechtenstein	160	61.8	30 000
Luxembourg	2 586	999	360 000
Malta	316	122	360 000
Monaco	15	5.8	30 000
Netherlands	40 893	15 789	14 140 000
Norway	324 219	125 181	4 090 000
Poland	312 700	120 734	35 580 000
Portugal	92 082	35 553	9 930 000
Romania	237 500	91 699	22 270 000
San Marino	61	23.6	20 000
Spain	504 748	194 883	37 430 000
Sweden	449 793	173 665	8 310 000
Switzerland	41 288	15 941	6 370 000
Union of Soviet Socialist Republics	22 400 00	8 648 640	265 000 000
United Kingdom	230 608	89 038	56 150 000
Vatican City	0.4	0.15	1 000
Yugoslavia	255 804	98 766	22 340 000
ASIA & OCEANIA			
Afghanistan	657 500	253 861	15 500 000
Australia	7 686 900	2 967 912	14 620 000
Bahrain	598	231	360 000
Bangladesh	142 776	55 126	88 660 000
Bhutan	46 600	17 992	1 295 000
Brunei	5 765	2 226	190 000
Burma	678 034	261 789	32 910 000
China	9 560 975	3 691 492	956 850 000
Cyprus	9 255	3 573	630 000
Fiji	18 272	7 055	620 000
Hong Kong	1 032	399	5 070 000
India	3 287 593	1 268 340	663 600 000
Indonesia	1 904 334	735 263	151 890 000
Iran	1 648 180	636 362	37 450 000
Iraq	438 446	169 284	13 080 000
Israel	20 700	7 992	3 870 000
Japan	372 077	143 659	116 780 000
Jordan	97 740	37 737	3 190 000
Kampuchea (Cambodia)	181 035	69 898	8 870 000
Kiribati	728	281	70 000
Korea, North	127 158	49 096	17 910 000
Korea, South	98 431	38 004	38 200 000
Kuwait	16 000	6 176	1 360 000
Laos	236 800	91 429	3 720 000
Lebanon	10 400	4 015	3 160 000

STATE	AREA sq km	AREA sq miles	POPULATION (estimate 1980)
Macao	16	6	275 000
Malaysia	333 507	128 767	13 440 000
Mongolia	1 565 000	604 247	1 670 000
Nepal	141 400	54 595	14 010 000
New Zealand	268 680	103 737	3 100 000
Oman	212 000	81 853	890 000
Pakistan	803 994	310 422	82 440 000
Papua-New Guinea	461 700	178 262	3 080 000
Philippines	299 400	115 598	48 400 000
Qatar	11 000	4 247	220 000
Saudi Arabia	2 263 600	873 976	8 370 000
Singapore	581	224	2 391 000
Solomon Islands	29 785	11 500	220 000
Sri Lanka	65 610	25 332	14 740 000
Syria	185 680	71 691	8 980 000
Taiwan	35 961	13 885	15 300 000
Thailand	514 000	198 455	46 460 000
Turkey	780 576	301 380	45 360 000
Tuvalu	158	61	10 000
United Arab Emirates	83 660	32 301	800 000
Vanuatu	14 763	5 700	110 000
Vietnam	329 650	127 278	52 300 000
Yemen	195 000	75 290	5 930 000
Yemen, South	160 300	61 892	1 970 000
NORTH AMERICA & CARIBBEAN			
Antigua	442	171	75 000
Bahamas	11 400	4 402	240 000
Barbados	430	166	250 000
Belize	22 963	8 866	160 000
Bermuda	53	21	60 000
Canada	9 976 169	3 851 799	23 940 000
Costa Rica	50 900	19 653	2 250 000
Cuba	114 524	44 218	9 830 000
Dominica	751	290	80 000
Dominican Republic	48 442	18 704	5 430 000
El Salvador	21 393	8 260	4 810 000
Greenland	2 175 600	840 000	50 000
Grenada	344	133	98 000
Guadeloupe	1 779	687	334 000
Guatemala	108 889	42 042	7 260 000
Haiti	27 750	10 714	5 010 000
Honduras	112 088	43 277	3 690 000
Jamaica	11 525	4 450	2 190 000
Martinique	1 102	426	327 000
Mexico	1 967 183	759 529	71 910 000
Netherlands Antilles	1 019	393	270 000
Nicaragua	148 000	57 143	2 700 000
Panama	75 650	29 209	1 840 000
Puerto Rico	8 891	3 433	3 440 000
St Lucia	616	238	120 000
St Vincent	388	150	122 000
Trinidad & Tobago	5 128	1 980	1 140 000
United States of America	9 363 353	3 615 191	227 640 000
SOUTH AMERICA			
Argentina	2 778 412	1 072 745	27 060 000
Bolivia	1 098 580	424 162	5 600 000
Brazil	8 511 965	3 286 470	123 030 000
Chile	756 945	292 257	11 100 000

STATE	AREA		POPULATION
	sq km	sq miles	(estimate 1980)
Colombia	1 138 914	439 735	27 520 000
Ecuador	281 341	108 626	8 350 000
Falkland Islands	11 961	4 618	1 950
French Guiana	91 000	35 135	60 000
Guyana	214 970	83 000	880 000
Paraguay	406 752	157 047	3 070 000
Peru	1 285 215	496 222	17 780 000
Suriname	17 400	6 718	390 000
Uruguay	186 926	72 172	2 900 000
Venezuela	912 050	352 143	13 910 000
AFRICA			
Algeria	2 381 730	919 586	18 600 000
Angola	1 246 700	481 351	7 080 000
Benin	112 600	43 475	3 570 000
Botswana	600 000	231 660	820 000
Burundi	27 834	10 747	4 510 000
Cameroon	475 500	183 591	8 500 000
Cape Verde	4 033	1 557	320 000
Central African Republic	623 018	270 547	2 220 000
Chad	1 284 000	495 752	4 520 000
Congo	342 000	132 046	1 540 000
Djibouti	23 000	8 880	120 000
Egypt	1 000 253	386 198	42 000 000
Equatorial Guinea	28 051	10 831	360 000
Ethiopia	1 221 900	471 776	31 070 000
Gabon	267 000	103 089	550 000
Gambia	11 295	4 361	600 000
Ghana	238 539	92 100	11 450 000
Guinea	245 857	94 925	5 010 000
Guinea-Bissau	36 125	13 948	570 000
Ivory Coast	322 463	124 503	7 970 000
Kenya	582 600	224 942	16 400 000
Lesotho	30 340	11 714	1 340 000
Liberia	111 000	42 857	1 860 000
Libya	1 759 540	679 358	2 980 000
Madagascar	594 180	229 413	8 720 000
Malawi	126 338	48 779	5 970 000
Mali	1 240 000	478 764	6 910 000
Mauritania	1 030 700	397 953	1 630 000
Mauritius	1 865	720	960 000
Morocco	458 730	177 116	20 240 000
Mozambique	784 961	303 073	10 470 000
Namibia	824 283	318 256	880 000
Niger	1 267 000	489 189	5 310 000
Nigeria	923 773	356 669	77 080 000
Rwanda	26 330	10 166	5 050 000
São Tomé & Príncipe	964	372	85 000
Senegal	197 161	76 124	5 660 000
Seychelles	278	107	62 150
Sierra Leone	73 326	28 311	3 470 000
Somalia	637 660	246 201	3 640 000
South Africa	1 221 042	471 444	29 290 000
Sudan	2 505 813	967 494	18 690 000
Swaziland	173 400	66 950	550 000
Tanzania	939 700	362 818	17 980 000
Togo	56 000	21 622	2 470 000
Tunisia	164 150	63 378	6 360 000
Uganda	236 037	91 134	13 200 000
Upper Volta	274 122	105 839	6 910 000
Zaire	2 345 409	905 562	28 290 000
Zambia	752 262	290 448	5 830 000
Zimbabwe	389 361	150 332	7 360 000

KEY TO THE MAPS

This key explains the meanings of the principal symbols that appear in the maps, the type-sizes used for the names of the largest cities and towns, and the colours that indicate heights and depths. Bar scales are provided at the bottom of the map pages.

BOUNDARIES

International
International under dispute
Cease fire line
Autonomous or federal
Administrative
Maritime (national)
International date line

COMMUNICATIONS

Motorway
Major highway
Other highway
Road tunnel
Car ferry
Main railway
Other railway
Rail tunnel
Canal
Rail ferry
⊕ International airport
✦ Other airport

LANDSCAPE FEATURES

Marsh, swamp
Sand desert, dunes
Glacier, ice cap

LAKE FEATURES

Saltwater
Freshwater

OTHER FEATURES

River
Pass, gorge
Aqueduct
Reef
▲4231 Summit, peak
·217 Spot height, depth
△ Oil field
▲ Gas field
Gas/Oil Oil/natural gas pipeline

TOWNS AND CITIES

Square symbols denote capital cities — Population

■ ● **New York** over 5 000 000
■ ● **Montréal** over 1 000 000
□ ○ Ottawa over 500 000
▪ • Québec over 100 000
□ ○ St John's over 50 000

Built-up-area

MAP COLOURS

Height
6000m
5000m
4000m
3000m
2000m
1000m
500m
200m
0 — Sea level
200m
2000m
4000m
6000m
8000m
Depth

Scale according to Latitude
Nautical Miles

Nautical Miles

Ellesmere

Island

QUEEN

ELIZABETH

ISLANDS

G R E E N L A N D

Melville I.

Devon I.

BEAUFORT

SEA

Banks I.

Victoria
I.

B a f f i n
I.

BAFFIN

BAY

Upernavik

Scoresbysund

Jan Mayen I.
(To Nor.)

oBarrow

oAklavik

Godhavn

Angmagssalik

Denmark Strait

Arctic Circle

Nome

oFairbanks

Dawson

Gt. Bear L.

Repulse Bay

Davis
Str.

Godthåb

ICELAND

Reykjavik

Faeroerne

St. Lawrence I.

ALASKA

Yukon

Anchorage
Cordova

Whitehorse

Hay River

Gt. Slave L.

Mackenzie

Chesterfield Inlet

Churchill

HUDSON

BAY

Julianehåb

Seward

Skagway
Juneau
Sitka

Prince Ruperto

CANADA

Scheffervilleo

UNITED KINGDOM OF
GT. BRITAIN & N. IRELAND

NO.
Aberde

Glasgow
Edinbur
Belfasto
Newca

Kodiak

Dutch Harbor

Edmonton

Calgary
Saskatoon

Regina

Winnipeg

Moosonee

Sept Iles
Port
Alfred

Goose Bay

Newfoundland

St. Johns

REP.
OF IRELAND

Dublin
Liverool
Cork

London

Southampton
Cherbourg

Vancouver
VictoriaoSeattle

Minneapolis

Superior

Sudbury
Québec

Saint
John

Portland

Michigan

Huron

Toronto
Detroit

Erie

Ottawa

Buffalo
Cleveland

Montreal
Halifax

Boston

Bordeaux

FRA

Bilbao

San Francisco

Salt Lake
City

Kansas
City

St.
Louis

Missouri

Chicago

Washington

Philadelphia
Baltimore
New York

Porto
PORT.
Lisboa

Madrid

SPAIN

UNITED   STATES

Azores
(To Port.)

Tanger
Gibraltar

Los Angeles

Oklahoma
City

Memphis

Norfolk

Madeira
(To Port.)

Marrakech

Rabat
Casablanca

El Paso
San Antonio

Rio
Grande

MEXICO

Galveston

New
Orleans

Tampa

Charleston

Bermuda
(To U.K.)

N O R T H   A T L A N T I C

Is. Canarias
(To Sp.)

MOROCCO

ALGE

Adrar

Mazatlán

Monterrey

GULF OF
MEXICO

Miami

Habana

THE BAHAMAS

O C E A N

Dakhla

SA

Tropic of Cancer

Midway I.
(To U.S.A.)

Hawaiian Is.
(To U.S.A.)

HonoluluoHawaii

Guadalajara

Mexico

Tampico

Veracruz

CUBA

Hispaniola

P.R.

MAURITANIA

oSt. Louis

Tombou
MALI

Acapulco

GUAT.

BELIZE
Belmopan

JAMAICA

Pt. au Prince
Kingston

Leeward Is.

Cape Verde

Dakar
SENEGAL

Banjul

Clipperton I.
(To Fr.)

Guatemala
San Salvador

HOND.
Tegucigalpa

NIC.

CARIBBEAN SEA

Windward Is.

Barbados

Bissau
GUINEA BISSAU

Bamako
GUINEA

UPPER
VOLTA
IVORY

P A C I F I C   O C E A N

C.R.
San José

PANAMA

Panama

Barranquilla
Colón
Maracaibo

VENEZUELA

Caracas

Trinidad

Georgetown

GUYANA

Paramaribo
SURINAME
Cayenne
FR.
GUIANA

Freetown
Monrovia

COAST

BEN
Accra
LIB.

Takorad

Buenaventurao

COLOMBIA

Bogotá

Orinoco

Gulf of

Islas Galapagos
(To Ecuador)

Quito

ECUAD.

Manaus

Amazon

Belém

Equator

Phoenix Is.

Guayaquil

Paita

Sao
Luis

Fortaleza

Fernando de
Noronha (To Braz.)

Ascension
(To U.K.)

Marquesas
(To Fr.)

PERU

Callao
Lima

Cuzco

B R A Z I L

Pto
Velho

Recife

Samoa

Society Is.
(To Fr.)

Tahiti

Tuamotu
(To Fr.)

La Paz

BOLIVIA

Mollendo
Arica

Sucre

Brasília

Goiânia

Salvador

Belo Horizonte

S O U T H   A T L A N T I C

St. Helena
(To U.K.)

Cook Is.
Rarotonga (To N.Z.)

Tropic of Capricorn

Iquique

Antofagasta

PARAGUAY

S. Paulo

Rio de Janeiro

Santos

O C E A N

Pitcairn I.
(To U.K.)

Sala y Gomez
(To Chile)

Easter I.

Coquimbo

Asunción
Tucumán

Paraná

Florianopolis

Valparaiso

Juan Fernandez
(To Chile)

Santiago

Talcahuano

Rosario

Uruguay

URUG.

Rio
Grande

Buenos
Aires

Montevideo

Tristan da Cunha
(To U.K.)

Concepción

ARGENTINA

Bahia Blanca

Gough I.
(To U.K.)

Pto Montt

Comodoro
Rivadavia

Falkland Is.(To U.K.)

Stanley

Sth. Georgia
(To U.K.)

Punta Arenas

C. Horn

D r a k e   S t r a i t

Sth.Orkneys

Sth. Shetlands

Deception I.

A R C T I C   O C E A N

Severnaya Zemlya

Zemlya Frantsa Iosifa

SVALBARD

80°

B A R E N T S   S E A

Bjørnøya (To Nor.)

Hammerfest

75°

KARA SEA

Novaya Zemlya

Lagernoye

Tromsø

Narvik

Lappland

Kandalaksha

Pechenga

Murmansk

White Sea

Arkhangelsk

Nordvik

Os. Vrangelya (Wrangel I.)

70°

Kotlas

N. Dvina

Salekhard

Turukhansk

Khatanga

Tiksi

Tornio

Umeå

Luleå

Bottnia

Vaasa

FINLAND

Petrozavodsk

Ob

Yenisey

Dudinka

Zhigansk

Verkhoyansk

Lena

Gävle

Helsinki

EST.

Leningrad

Yaroslavl'

Kirov

UNION OF SOVIET SOCIALIST REPUBLICS

Yakutsk

Okhotsk

60°

Magadan

Kamchatka

BERING SEA

Stockholm

Göteborg

BALTIC SEA

Riga

Pskov

LAT.

LITH.

Moskva

Gor'kiy

Kazan'

Sverdlovsk

Omsk

Tomsk

Krasnoyarsk

SEA OF OKHOTSK

Nikolayevsk na Amure

Petropavlovsk Kamchatskiy

Aleutian Islands

Malmö

Klaipeda

Tula

Novosibirsk

Sakhalin

Berlin

Warszawa

WHITE RUSSIA

Kursk

Kuybyshev

Orenburg

Petropavlovsk

Szczecin

Gdansk

POLAND

Kraków

Lvov

Kiyev

Khar'kov

Saratov

Semipalatinsk

Irkutsk

Chita

Blagoveshchensk

Khabarovsk

Wakkanai

Hokkaidō

45°

CZECH.

Odessa

UKRAINE

Volgograd

K A Z A K H

Karaganda

Ulan Ude

Skovorodino

Amur

Vladivostok

Hakodate

AUS.

Budapest

HUN.

ROMANIA

Rostov

Gur'yev

L. Balkhash

Ulaanbaatar

Manchuria

Changchun

SEA OF JAPAN

Trieste

Beograd

Bucuresti

Astrakhan'

Aral Sea

Kzyl Orda

MONGOLIA

Shenyang

Harbin

NORTH

Honshū

JAPAN

YUG.

Sevastopol

Sofiya

BULG.

BLACK SEA

CASPIAN SEA

Nukus

UZBEK

Alma Ata

KIRGHIZ

Ürümqi

Beijing

Luda

Sendai

KOREA

Tōkyō

Venezia

Ankara

AZER.

Tbilisi

Batumi

Krasnovodsk

Tashkent

TADZHIK

SINKIANG

Tianjin

SOUTH KOREA

Sŏul

Yokohama

Messina

Athinai

TURKEY

Izmir

Baku

Tabriz

TURKMEN

Ashkhabad

Dushanbe

Lanzhou

Xi'an

YELLOW SEA

Kōbe

Osaka

Napoli

Malta

Crete

CYPRUS

Beirut

SYRIA

Halab

Mosul

Tehran

Herat

Kabul

Peshawar

C H I N A

Wuhan

Nanjing

Shanghai

Nagasaki

MEDITERRANEAN SEA

Benghazi

LEB.

Damascus

IRAQ

Baghdad

IRAN

Esfahan

AFGHANISTAN

Kandahar

Lahore

Chongqing

Changsha

EAST CHINA SEA

Okinawa

30°

Tripoli

Haifa

Jerusalem

ISR.

JORDAN

Basra

Abādān

Quetta

PAKISTAN

Delhi

Agra

NEPAL

Lhasa

Kunming

Alexandria

Cairo

Port Said

Kuwait

Bandar Abbas

Karachi

Lucknow

Patna

BANGLADESH

Guangzhou

Taiwan (Formosa)

LIBYA

EGYPT

Medina

Aswān

Riyadh

The Gulf

Muscat

T I B E T

I N D I A

Mandalay

Hanoi

Haiphong

Hong Kong (To U.K.)

15°

Wadi Halfa

SAUDI ARABIA

Nagpur

BURMA

Chiang Mai

Port Sudan

Jiddah

Mecca

Bombay

Calcutta

Hue

Luzon

Northern Marianas

CHAD

SUDAN

El Obeid

Omdurman

Khartoum

Massawa

ARABIA

ARABIAN SEA

Hyderabad

Bay of Bengal

THAI.

Rangoon

Bangkok

INDOCHINA

Manila

Guam (To U.S.A.)

Marshall Is. (To U.S.A.)

N'Djamena

Massawa

SOUTH YEMEN

OMAN

Madras

CAMBODIA

Saigon

PHILIPPINES

Fed. States of Micronesia

Gilbert Is.

CENT. AFRICAN REPUBLIC

Bangui

DJIBOUTI

Adan

Socotra

Mangalore

G. of Thailand

SOUTH CHINA SEA

Mindanao

KIRIBATI

Addis Ababa

ETHIOPIA

Juba

Colombo

SRI LANKA

George Town

MALAYSIA

SABAH

CELEBES SEA

Halmahera

Banaba

Nauru

ZAIRE

Kisangani

Kampala

UGANDA

KENYA

Nairobi

Maldives

Kuala Lumpur

Singapore

SAR.

BORNEO

Sulawesi

Moluccas

Ambon

PAPUA NEW GUINEA

New Ireland

Brazzaville

Kindu

Mombasa

Sumatera

Padang

JAVA SEA

Ujung Pandang

New Britain

Solomon Is.

Kinshasa

Kalémié

Kigoma

TANZANIA

Zanzibar

Dar es Salaam

Jakarta

Surabaya

I N D O N E S I A

ARAFURA SEA

Port Moresby

Guadalcanal

Tuvalu

Kamina

ANGOLA

Lubumbashi

Mtwara

Seychelles

Jawa

Timor

Darwin

Fiji

Huambo

ZAMBIA

Zambezi

TIMOR SEA

VANUATU

15°

Lusaka

Mahajanga

MADAGASCAR

Cocos (Keeling Is.) (To Aust.)

Derby

Birdum

Cairns

Townsville

CORAL SEA

N. Caledonie (To Fr.)

Tonga

Marama

Harare

ZIMB.

Toamasina

Antananarivo

Mauritius

Onslow

Alice Springs

Rockhampton

NAMIBIA

Bulawayo

MOZAMBIQUE

Réunion (To Fr.)

Sofala

A U S T R A L I A

Brisbane

Norfolk I. (To Aust.)

30°

Windhoek

BOTSWANA

Maputo

Mozambique Channel

I N D I A N   O C E A N

Geraldton

Newcastle

Kermadec Is. (To N.Z.)

Johannesburg

Pretoria

Kimberley

Bloemfontein

Durban

Perth

Fremantle

Albany

Adelaide

Sydney

Canberra

Auckland

Cape Town

S. AFRICA

East London

Port Elizabeth

Cape of Good Hope

Amsterdam I.

St. Paul I. (To Fr.)

Melbourne

TASMAN SEA

NEW ZEALAND

Nelson

Wellington

Christchurch

Chatham Is. (To N.Z.)

Pr. Edward I.

Marion I. (To S.A)

Crozet Is. (To Fr.)

Hobart

TASMANIA

Invercargill

Dunedin

Stewart I.

Antipodes

Bounty I.

Kerguelen (To Fr.)

Auckland I. (To N.Z.)

Campbell I.

Heard I. (To Aust.)

Macquarie I. (To Aust.)

60°

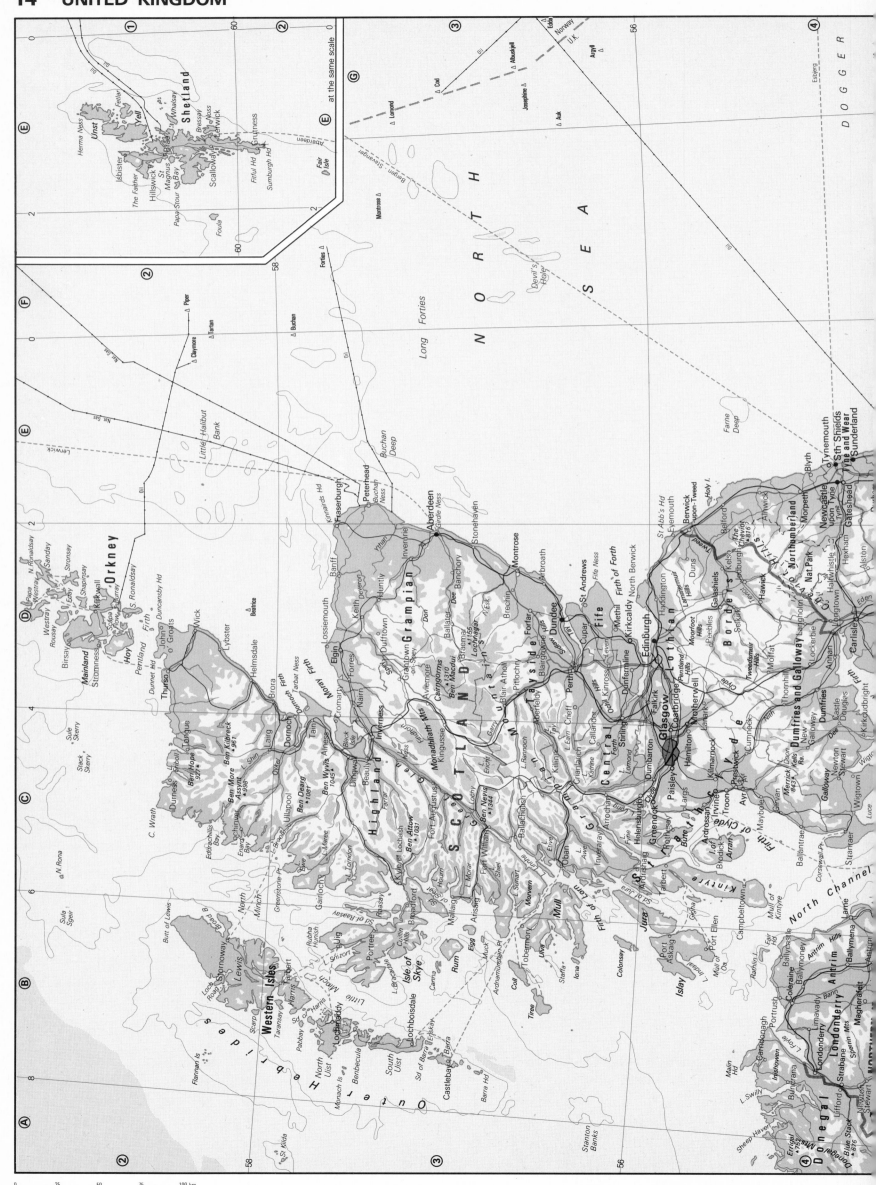

at the same scale

Shetland

Herma Ness
Unst
Isbister
The Father
Hillswick
St Magnus Bay
Papa Stour
Scalloway
Foula
Yell
Whalsay
Bressay
Lerwick
Gruness
Fitful Hd
Sumburgh Hd
Fair Isle

Orkney

Papa Westray
N Ronaldsay
Westray
Rousay
Sanday
Stronsay
Eday
Shapinsay
Birsay
Mainland
Stromness
Kirkwall
Scapa Flow
Hoy
S Ronaldsay
Duncansby Hd

NORTH SEA

DOGGER

Norway
U.K.
Argyll
Cod
Albuskjell
Josephine
Auk
Lomond
Montrose
Stavanger
Bergen
Forties
Devil's Hole
Long Forties
Piper
Tartan
Claymore
Buchan
Nat Gas
Nat Gas

Esbjerg

Little Halibut Bank
Buchan Deep

Lewrick

Kinnaird's Hd
Fraserburgh
Buchan Ness
Peterhead

Aberdeen
Girdle Ness
Stonehaven

Farne Deep
Farne Is
Holy I.
Bamburgh
Blyth
Tynemouth
Newcastle upon Tyne
Sth Shields
Tyne and Wear
Gateshead
Sunderland

SCOTLAND

C. Wrath
Durness
Eddrachillis Bay
Lochinver
Enard Bay
Ben More Assynt 998
Ben Hope 927
Ben Kilbreck 961
Ben Klibreck
Tongue
Loch Eriboll
Loch Naver
Stack Skerry
Sule Skerry
N. Rona
Sula Sgeir
Butt of Lewis

Sule Stack

Wick
Lybster
Helmsdale
Brora
Golspie
Dornoch
Dornoch Firth
Tarbat Ness
Tain
Ben Wyvis 1045
Dingwall
Cromarty
Beauly
Inverness
Moray Firth
Nairn
Forres
Elgin
Lossiemouth

Thurso
John o'Groats
Dunnet Hd
Pentland Firth

Loch Shin
Lairg
Loch Maree
Gairloch
Greenstone Pt
Ullapool
Rubha Reidh
Torridon
Ben Attow 1031
Loch Hourn
Kyle of Lochalsh
Broadford
Fort Augustus
Loch Ness
Loch Oich
Loch Lochy
Monadhliath Mts
Kingussie
Aviemore
Cairngorms 1310
Ben Macdui
Grantown-on-Spey
Dufftown
Keith
Huntly
Banff
Deveron
Spey
Don
Ythan
Inverurie
Grampian

HIGHLAND

Lewis
Stornoway
Loch Roag
Broad B.
North Harris
Harris
Tarransay
Scalpay
Sd. of Harris
Scarp
Flannan Is
St Kilda
Western Isles

Pabbay
Berneray
Lochmaddy
North Uist
Benbecula
Monach Is
Loch Boisdale
South Uist
Eriskay
Barra
Castlebay
Barra Hd
Sd of Barra

Outer Hebrides

Little Minch
The Minch
North Minch

Rubha Hunish
Uig
Portree
Raasay
Sd of Raasay
L. Snizort
Isle of Skye
Cuillin Hills
Broadford
Camasunary
Rum
Eigg
Muck
Canna
Mallaig
Arisaig
Morar
Ardnamurchan Pt
Coll
Tiree
Tobermory
Staffa
Iona
Mull
Ulva
Colonsay

Loch Morar
Loch Shiel
Fort William
Ben Nevis 1344
Glen Coe
Loch Etive
Loch Linnhe
Morvern
Sunart
L. Sunart
Loch Leven
Ballachulish
Oban
Firth of Lorn

Sd. of Jura
Jura
Port Askaig
Islay
Port Ellen
Gigha
Oa
Mull of Oa
Rathlin
Rathlin I.

Loch Awe
Loch Fyne
Inveraray
Arrochar
Helensburgh
L. Long
Dumbarton
L. Lomond
Crianlarich
Killin
L. Earn
L. Tay
Aberfeldy
Pitlochry
Blair Atholl
Braemar
Ballater
Banchory
Lochnagar
Brechin
Forfar
Dee
Esk
Montrose
Arbroath
Tayside

Rannoch
Loch Rannoch
Loch Tummel
Crieff
Callander
Dunblane
Stirling
Doune
Perth
Cupar
St Andrews
Fife Ness
North Berwick
Firth of Forth
Methil
Kirkcaldy
Dunfermline
L. Leven
Kinross
Loch Katrine
Falkirk
Grangemouth
Clyde
Glasgow
Coatbridge
Motherwell
Hamilton
Paisley
Lanark
Ochil Hills
CENTRAL
Fife
Leven
Methven
Dundee
Blairgowrie
Sidlaw Hills
Kinnoull

Strathclyde
Kintyre
Mull of Kintyre
Campbeltown
Machrihanish
Tarbert
Ardrishaig
Bute
Firth of Clyde
Rothesay
Arran
Brodick
Lamlash
Fairlie
Largs
Greenock
Gourock
Ayr
Irvine
Kilmarnock
Prestwick
Troon
Ardrossan
Saltcoats
Maybole
Girvan
Ballantrae
Deer
Cumnock
Sanquhar
New Galloway
Kells
Merrick 843
Rhinns of Kells
Newton Stewart
Wigtown
Whithorn
Galloway
Mull of Galloway
Corsewall Pt
Stranraer
Luce B.
Loch Ryan

Lothian
Edinburgh
Haddington
Dunbar
St Abb's Hd
Eyemouth
Pentland Hills
Peebles
Moorfoot Hills
Lammermuir Hills
Galashiels
Selkirk
Borders
Duns
Berwick-upon-Tweed
Kelso
Jedburgh
Hawick
Tweed
Tweedsmuir Hills
Cheviot 816
Cheviot Hills
Langholm
Newcastleton
Lockerbie
Moffat
Annan
Dumfries and Galloway
Dumfries
Castle Douglas
Kirkcudbright
Solway Firth

Alnwick
Rothbury
Morpeth
Northumberland
Nat Park
Hexham
Haltwhistle
Longtown
Carlisle
Eden
Cumbria

NORTH CHANNEL

Donegal
Londonderry
Londonderry
Portrush
Coleraine
Portstewart
Ballycastle
Ballymoney
Antrim
Antrim Hills
Ballymena
Magherafelt
Limavady
Dungiven
Strabane
Sperrin Mts
Omagh
Newtownstewart
Lifford
Buncrana
Inishowen
L. Foyle
L. Swilly
Malin Hd
Sheep Haven
Errigal 752
Derryveagh Mts
Donegal Mts
Blue Stack Mts 676
Ballybofey
Letterkenny
Larne
Carnlough

Stanton Banks

Scale
0   25   50   75   100 km
0   25   50 mls

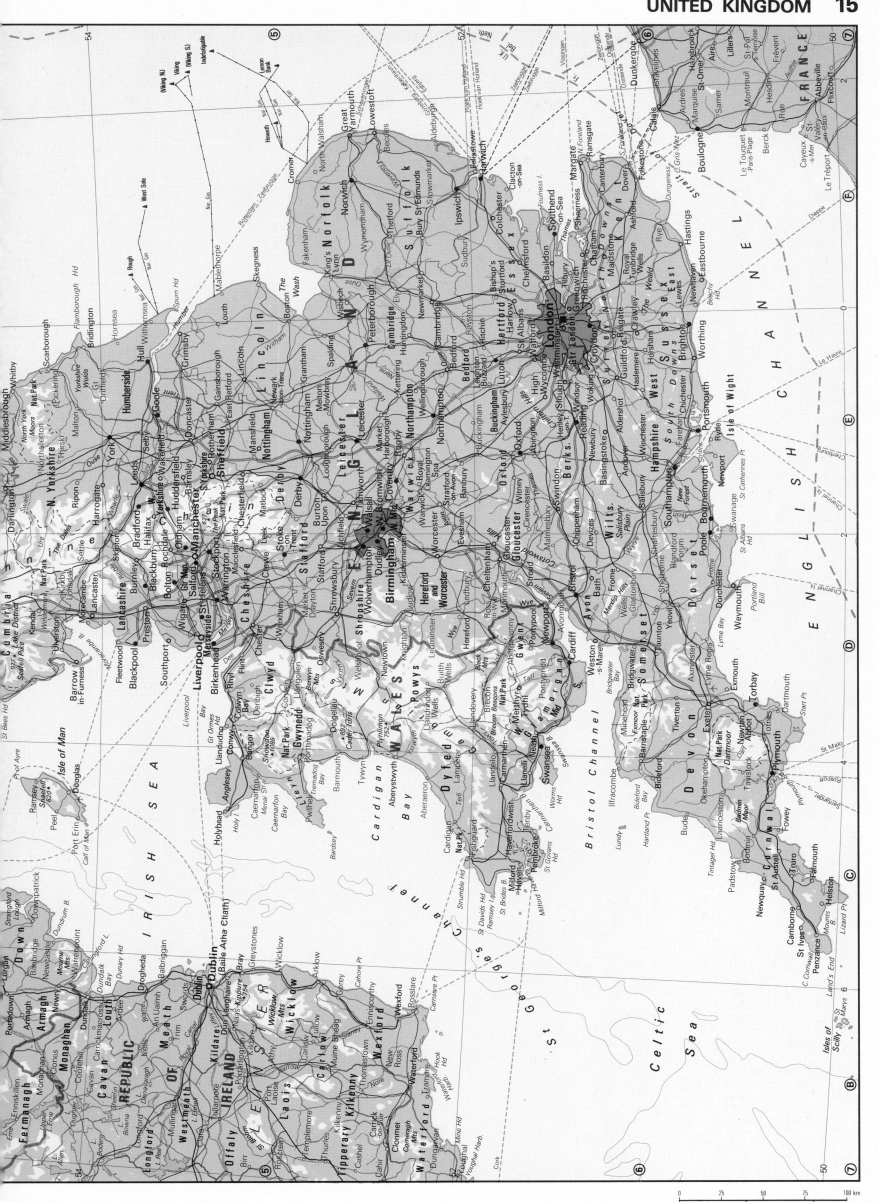

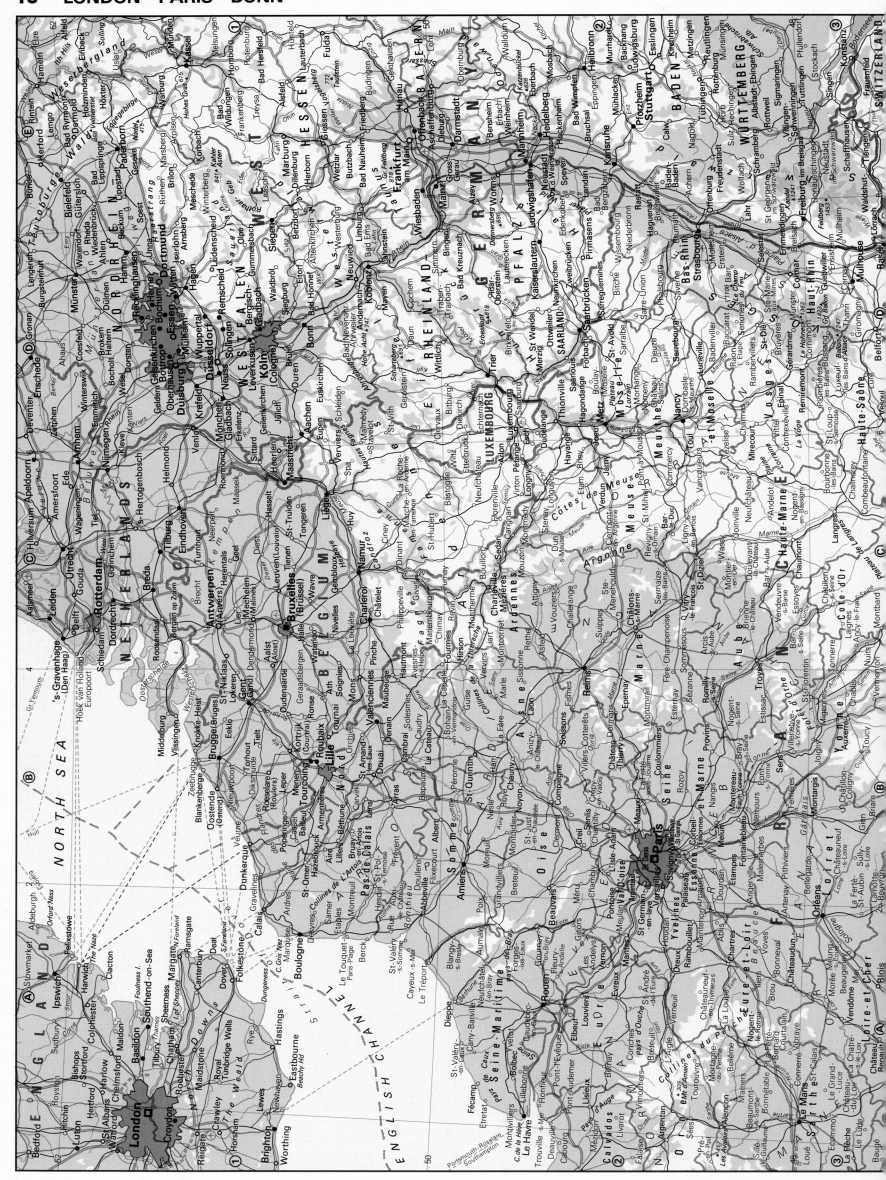

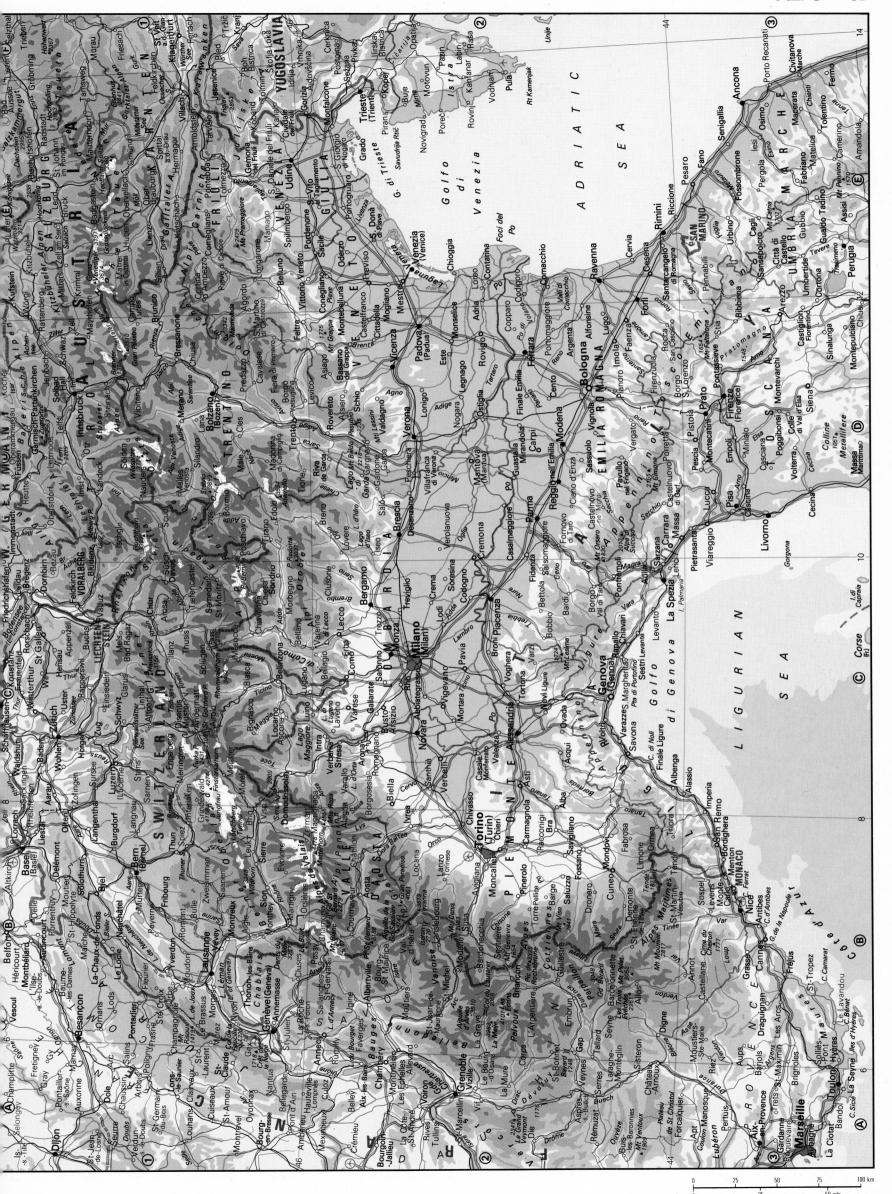

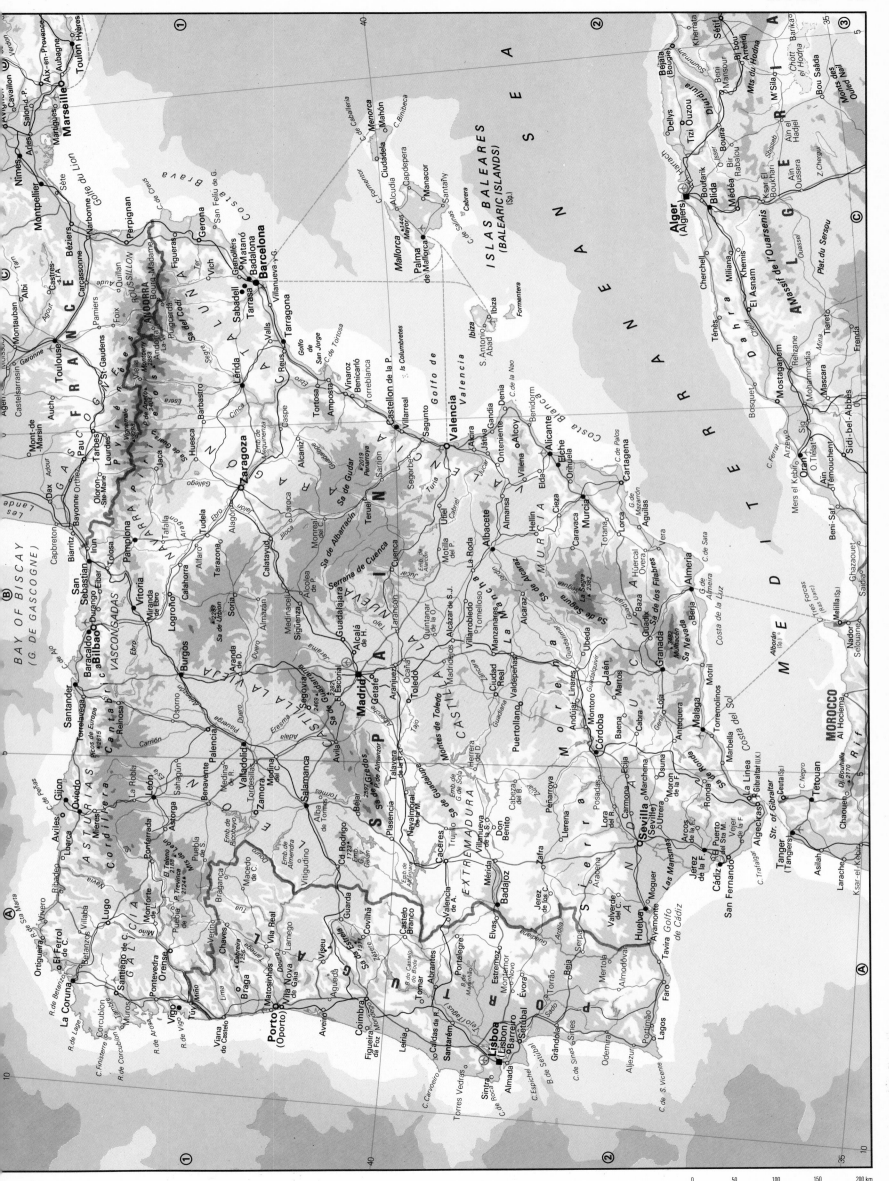

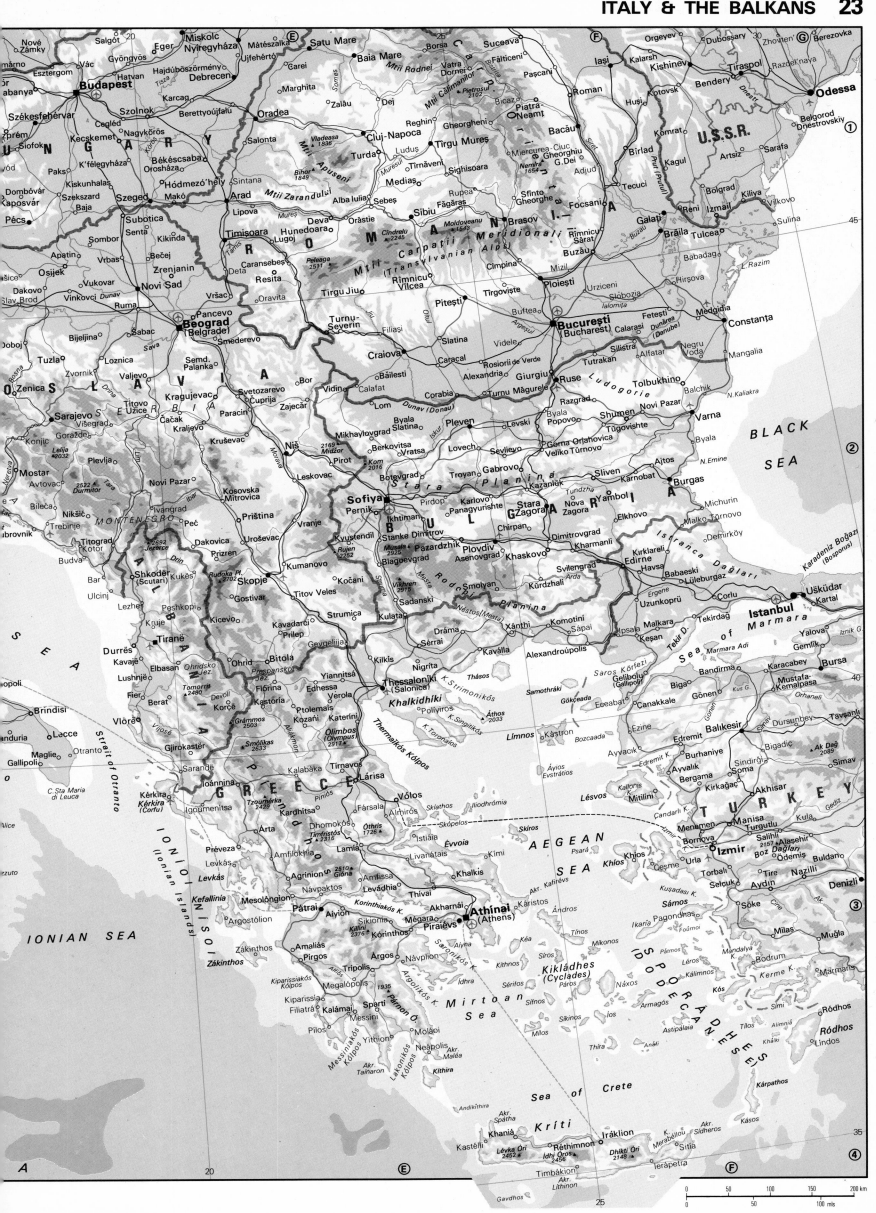

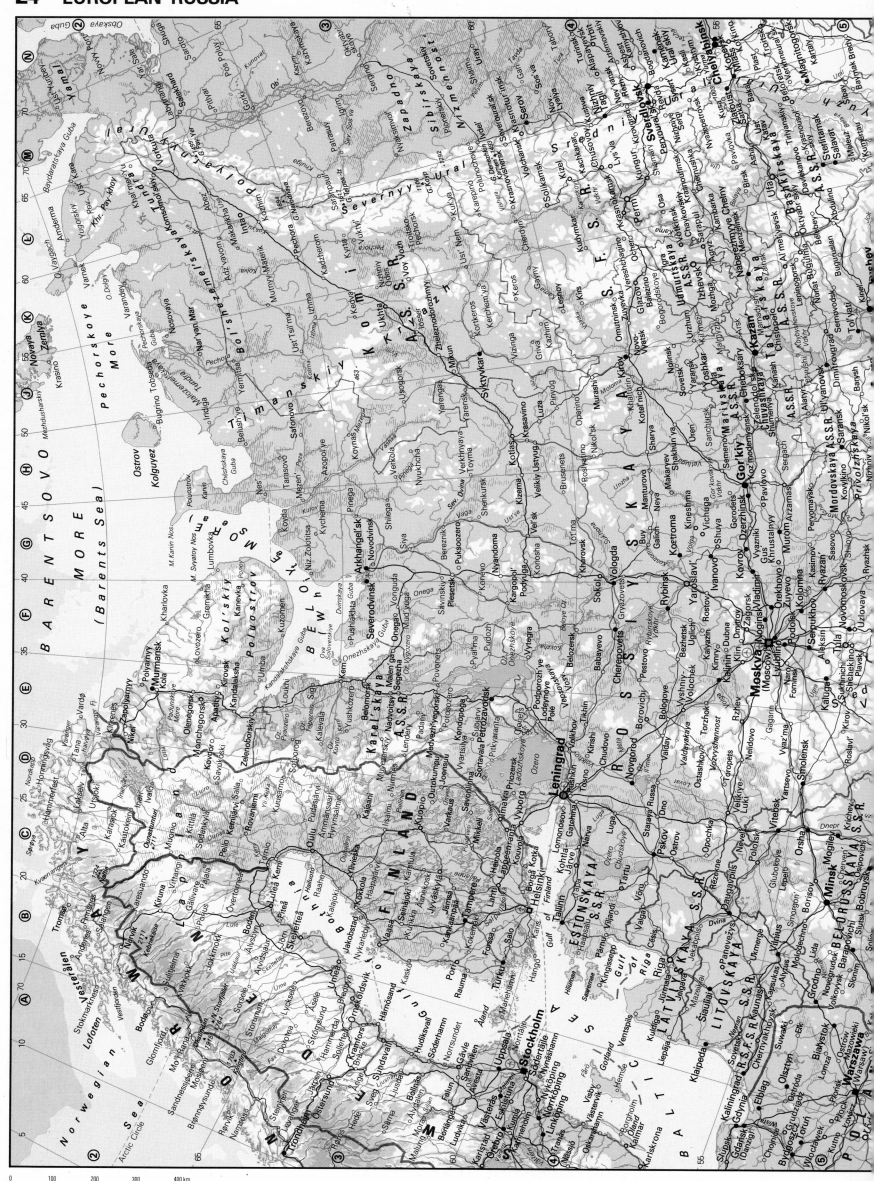

0 100 200 300 400 km
0 100 200 mls

CASPIAN SEA

BLACK SEA

Azovskoye More

Mediterranean Sea

Sea of Crete

Aegean Sea

1 Severo-Osetinskaya A.S.S.R.
2 Adzharskaya A.S.S.R.
3 Checheno-Ingushskaya A.S.S.R.
4 Kabardino-Balkarskaya A.S.S.R.
5 Nakhichevanskaya A.S.S.R.

0   100   200   300   400 km
0   100   200 mls

R.S.F.S.R.
1 Chuvashkaya A.S.S.R.
2 Checheno-Ingushskaya A.S.S.R.
3 Severo-Osetinskaya A.S.S.R.
4 Kabardino-Balkarskaya A.S.S.R.
GRUZINSKAYA S.S.R.
5 Abkhazskaya A.S.S.R.
6 Adzharskaya A.S.S.R.
AZERBAYDZHANSKAYA S.S.R.
7 Nakhichevanskaya A.S.S.R.

0   200   400   600   800 km
0   200   400 mls

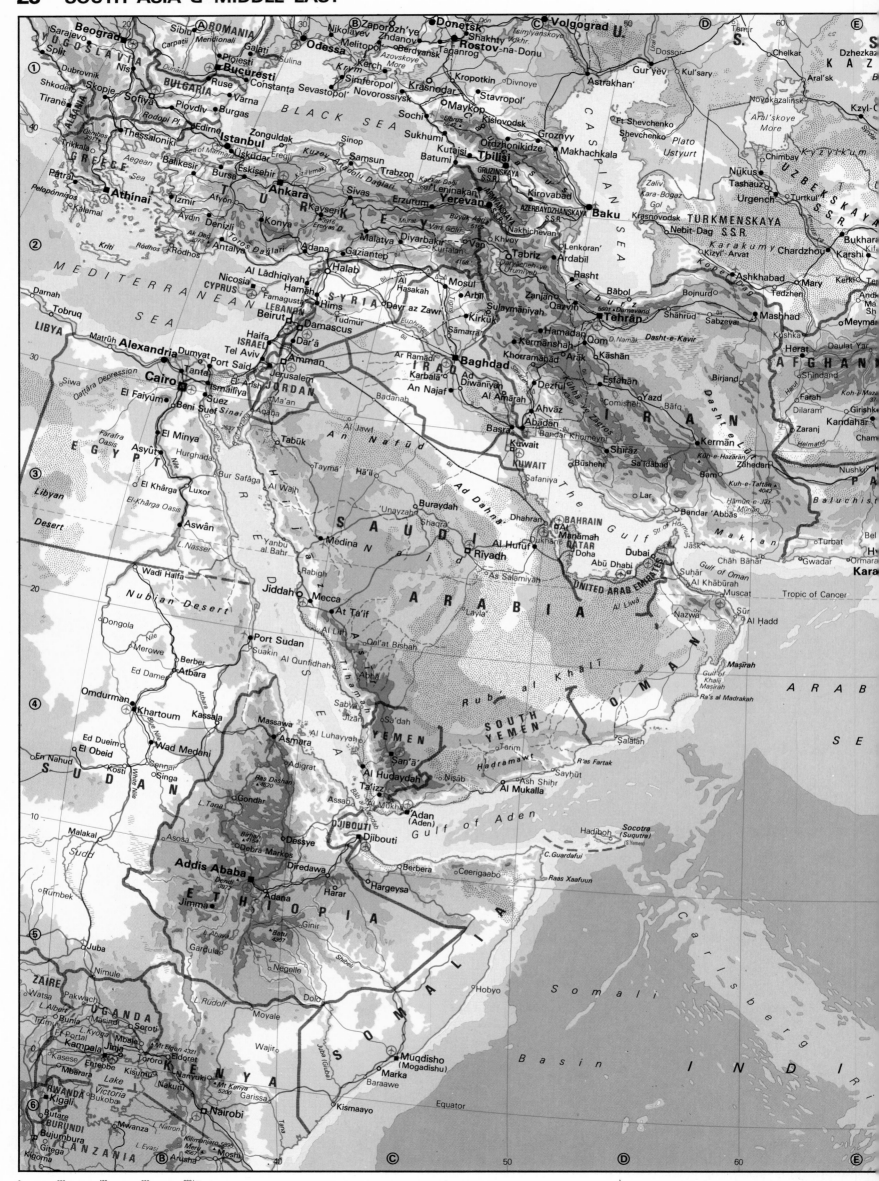

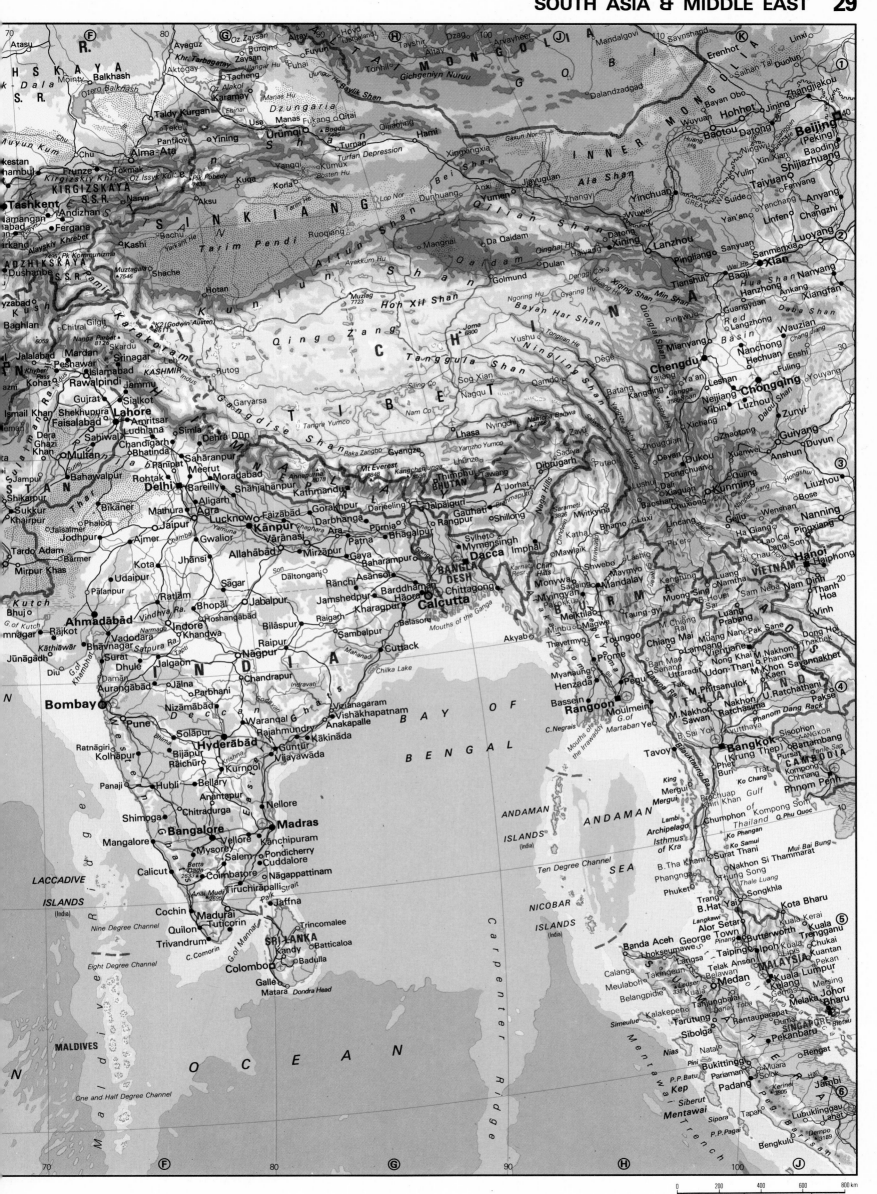

BLACK SEA

U.S.S.R.

I R A N

I R A Q

S Y R I A

TURKEY

GREECE

CYPRUS

LEBANON

ISRAEL

JORDAN

SAUDI ARABIA

EGYPT

KUWAIT

Mediterranean Sea

Gulf of Aqaba

Gulf of Suez

Sea of Marmara

Major cities and places:

Bakú, Sumgait, Tbilisi, Rustavi, Yerevan, Leninakan, Kirovabad, Kars, Erzurum, Van, Tabriz, Urumiyeh, Ardabil, Zanjan, Hamadan, Kermanshah, Khorramabad, Dezful, Ahváz, Abadan, Basra, Kuwait, Al Ahmadi

Trabzon, Samsun, Sivas, Kayseri, Ankara, Eskişehir, Konya, Istanbul, İzmit, Bursa, Balıkesir, İzmir, Denizli, Antalya, Mersin, Adana, Iskenderun, Antakya

Mosul, Arbil, Kirkük, Sulaymaniyah, Baghdad, Al Kut, Al Amárah, An Nasiríyah, Ad Diwaniyah, Karbalá, An Najaf, Al Hillah, Sámarrá, Ar Ramadi, Falüjah

Halab (Aleppo), Hamáh, Hims, Tartus, Al Ládhiqiyah, Ar Raqqah, Dayr az Zawr, Tudmur, Damascus (Dimashq)

Beirut (Beyrouth), Tripoli (Tarabulus esh Sham), Saida, Tyr

Haifa, Tel Aviv Yafo, Jerusalem, Gaza, Beersheba, Nazareth, Nablus, Hebron

Amman, Irbid, Zarqa, Ma'an, Aqaba

Nicosia, Famagusta, Limassol, Larnaca

Cairo (El Qâhira), Alexandria (El Iskandariya), Port Said (Bur Said), Suez (El Suweis), Ismailiya, El Mansura, Tanta, El Giza, Helwân, Beni Suef, El Faiyúm, El Minya

Tabük

SINAI

Euphrates, Tigris, Nile

Scale:
0   100   200   300 km
0   50   100   150 mls

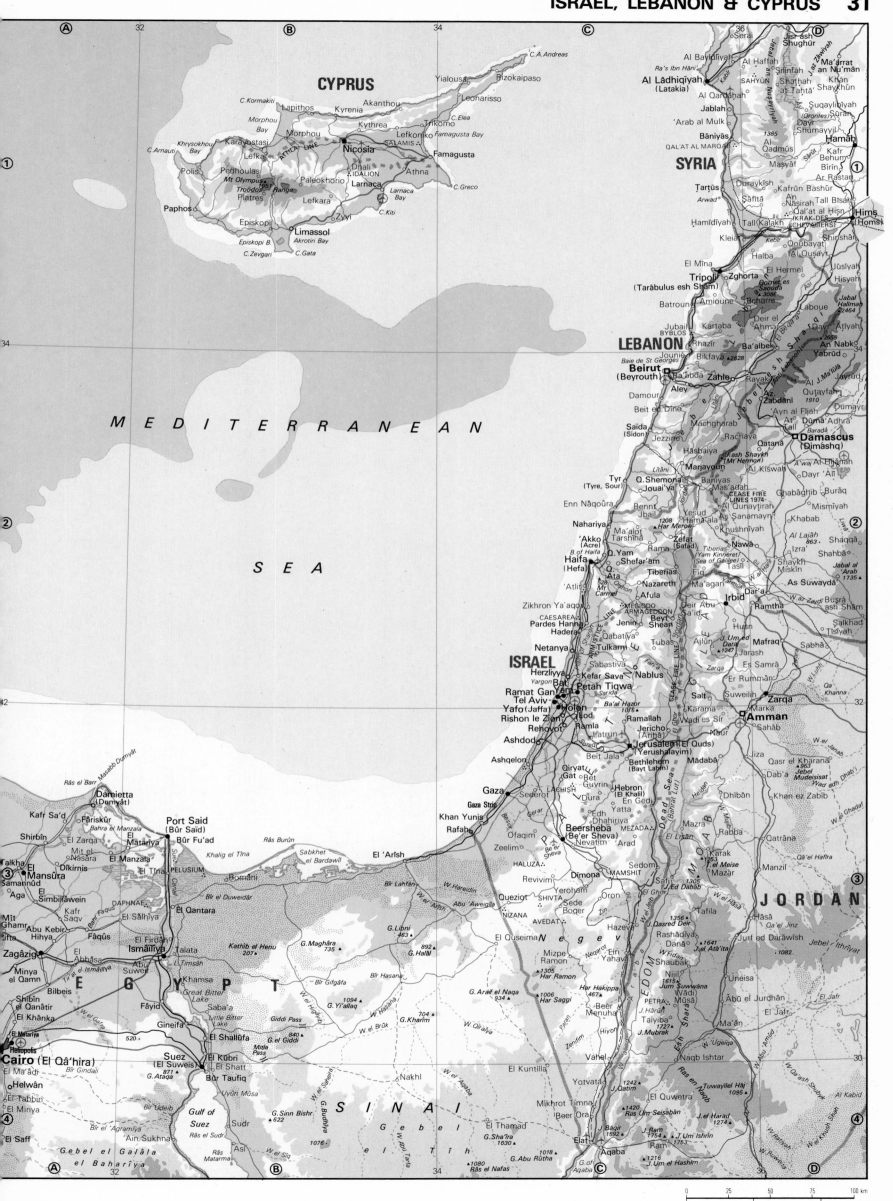

CYPRUS

C.A.Andreas
Yialousa
Rizokalpaso
Lapithos
Kyrenia
C.Kormakiti
Akanthou
Leonarisso
C.Elea
Morphou
Kythrea
Trikomo
Bay
Lefkoniko
Famagusta Bay
Khrysokhou
Karavostasi
ATHLA LINE
SALAMIS
Bay
Lefka
Nicosia
Famagusta
Pedhoulas
Dhali
C.Arnauti
Polis
IDALION
Athna
Paleokhorio
C.Greco
Mt Olympus
Panga
Larnaca
Troodos
Platres
Lefkara
Larnaca
Paphos
Zyyi
Bay
C.Kiti
Episkopi
Limassol
Akrotiri Bay
Episkopi B.
C.Zevgari
C.Gata

SYRIA

Serai
Jisr ash Shughūr
Al Baylūnīyah
Ma'arrat
Al Haffah
an Nu'mān
Ra's Ibn Hāni'
Silinfah
Khān
Shaykhūn
Al Lādhiqīyah
SAHYŪN
Shaṭhah
al Taḥtā
(Latakia)
Al Qardāḥah
Suqaylibīyah
Jablah
(Orontes)
Dayr
Sūrān
Shumayyil
'Arab al Mulk
Bāniyās
QAL'AT AL MARQAB
1385
Al Qadmūs
Hamāh
Kafr
Behum
Tarṭūs
Durayksh
Kafrūn Bashūr
Birīn
Arwad
Āafītā
An
Ar Rastan
Nāṣirah Tall Bīsah
Qal'at al Hisn
(KRAK-DES
Hims
Ḥamīdīyah
Tall Kalakh
CHEVALIERS)
(Homs)
Kleiat
El Hermel
Halba
Qoubayāt
Al Ouāayr
El Mīna
Shinshār

LEBANON

Tripoli
Zghorta
Jūsīyah
(Tarābulus esh Sham)
Qornet es
Hisyah
Saouda
3086
Batroun
Amioune
Bcharre
Laboue
Deir el
Ahmar
Dayr 'Aṭīyah
Jubail
Kartaba
2659
BYBLOS
Jabal
Rhazir
Ba'albek
Halīmah
2464
An Nabk
Jounié
Bikfaya
2628
Yabrūd
Beirut
Ba'abda
Zahle
Al J. Ma'lūla
Jayrūd
(Beyrouth)
Aley
Rayak
Qutayfah
Baie de St Georges
Az
1910
Zabdāni
Damour
Beit ed Dine
Dūmā 'Adhra
'Ayn al Fijah
Machgharab
Tall
Barādā
Damascus
Saïda
Rachaiya
(Dimāshq)
(Sidon)
Jezzine
Qatana
Hāsbaiya
J. ash Shaykh
Al Hijānah
Marjayoun
(Mt Hermon)
Al Kiswah
Tyr
Q. Shemona
Baniyas
A'waj Al Hijānah
(Tyre, Sour)
Jouai'ya
Mas'adah
Dayr 'Alī
Enn Nâqoûra
CEASE FIRE
Ghabāghib
Burāq
LINES 1974
Hama'ala As Sanamayn
Nahariya
Ma'alot
1208
Yesud
Al Qunayṭirah
Mismīyah
Tarshiha
Har Meron
Khushnīyah
'Akko
Zefat
Nawā
Al Lajāh
Khabab
(Acre)
(Safad)
863
Shaqqā
Q. Yam
Rama
Tiberias
Jabal al
Izra
Shefar'am
(Yam Kinneret)
Fiq
'Arab
Haifa
Q. Ata
(Sea of Galilee)
Tasil
Shaykh
1735
(Hefa)
526
Tiberias
Miskīn
Shahbā
Mt
Nazareth
Ma'agan
Dar'a
'Atlit
Carmel
Afula
Irbid
Ramtha
Zikhron Ya'aqo
MEGIDDO
Deir Abu
W ar Zayd
CAESAREA
ARMAGEDDON
Sa'id
ash Sham
Pardes Hanna
Jenin
Beyt
Husn
Salkhad
Haderao
Qabatiya
Shean
Tisiyah
ISRAEL
Tubas
Ajlūn
J. Um ed
Netanya
Tulkarm
Fārs
Dara
Mafraq
Sabastiya
1247
Jarash
Sabhā
Herzliyya
Kefar Sava
Es Samrā
Bat Yam
Nablus
Er Rummān
Ramat Gan
Petah Tiqwa
Zarqa
Qa
Tel Aviv
Sarida
Khanna
Yafo (Jaffa)
Holon
Ba'al Hazor
Salt
Suweilih
Zarqā
Rishon le Ziyon
1016
Karama
Rehovot
Lod
Ramallah
Wadi es Sir
Marka
Amman
Ashdod
Ramla
Jericho
Naur
Sahāb
Latrun
(Ariha)
Beit Jala
Jerusalem (El Quds)
Mādabā
Ashqelon
(Yerushalayim)
Jiza
Qasr el Kharana
Qiryat
Bethlehem
Dāb'a
Gat
Bet
(Bayt Lahm)
Mudeisisat
Guvrin
Wad edh Dhab'a
LACHISH
Dura
En Gedi
Khan ez Zabib
Gaza
Gerar
Hebron
Yatta
Dhībān
Gaza Strip
(El Khalil)
Edh
Khan Yunis
Besor
Dhahiriya
Rafah
Sederot
Mazra
Rabba
Ofaqim
Beersheba
MEZADA
El Lisan
Qatrāna
Zeelim
(Be'er Sheva)
Sedom
Be'er
Nevatim
Arad
M
Sheva
HALUZA
O
Kerak
1253
Dimona
MAMSHIT
Safi
T. el Meise
Mazār
Manzil
Revivim
MASHIT
Ed Dabab
Yeroham
SHIVTA
El Ghor
Qeziot
Sede
Zin
Rashādīya
Qā'el Hafira
NIZANA
Boqer
Tafila
Oron
Danā
AVEDAT
1356
Hāsā
El Quseima
Mizpe
J.Qasred Deir
Ramon
1641
J.el Atā'ita
Jurf ed Darāwīsh
Negarot
El Jafr
Ein
Jebel Ithrīyet
G.Araif el Naga
Yahav
Shaubāk
934
Har Ramon
1082
Beer
PETRA
1727
Menuha
J. Hārūn
J.Mubark
Taiyiba
Abū el Jurdhān
El Jafr
Naqb Ishtar

EGYPT

Rās el Barr
Masabb Dumyāt
Damietta
(Dumyāt)
Kafr Sa'd
Fāriskūr
Bahra el Manzala
Port Said
Shirbîn
El Zarqa
(Būr Said)
El Mataria
Būr Fu'ad
Mit el
Khalig el Tina
Nasāra
El Manzala
Rās Burūn
Talkha
El Tîna
PELUSIUM
Dîkirnis
El Qantara
Sabkhet
El 'Arîsh
El Mansūra
el Bardawîl
Samannûd
DAPHNAE
Rōmâni
Bîr Lahfān
Aga
El Sālhîya
Bîr el Duweidâr
W. el Arîsh
Abu Aweigîla
Mît
El Firdân
Ismâilîya
Abu
Ghamr
Kafr
Faqûs
Aweigîla
Sede
Zagāzig
Saqr
L. Timsâh
Kathîb el Henu
G.Libni
Boqer
Minya
El Abbâsa
207
463
G.Yi'allaq
892
Quseima
el Qamn
Abu
Talata
Bîr Gifgâfa
G.Halâl
Bilbeis
Hammad
Khamsa
892
704
Shibîn
Great Bitter
Bîr Hasana
G.Khārîm
W. el Bruk
el Qanāter
Lake
520
Gineifa
Giddi Pass
1094
El Khānka
Fâyid
Little Bitter
840
G.Yi'allaq
G.Araif el Naga
El Matariya
Lake
G.el Giddi
Negarot
Heliopolis
El Shallûfa
Mitle
G.Maghâra
Har Ramon
Cairo (El Qâ'hira)
Suez
El Kûbri
Pass
735
1006
Har Hakippa
El Ma'âdi
(El Suweis)
Būr Taufiq
G.Sinn Bishr
Nakhl
W. el Hasana
G.Saggi
Helwân
Bîr Gindali
622
W. el Giddi
El Minya
G.Ataqa
Gulf of
Sûdr
W. el Brûk
El Kuntilla
El Thamad
El Saff
Bîr 'Agramîya
Suez
Rās Matarma
Asl
W.el Saheira
Mikhrot Timna
Ain Sukhna
1076
G.Sha'îra
Beer Ora
1420
Rās Um Seisaban
Gebel el Galâla
Rās el Gindi
1630
G.Abu Rútha
1242
el Baharîya
1080
Rās en Nafas
J.Qatim
SINAI
Gebel el Tîh
Yotvata
1095
J.el Harad
J.Um Ishrin
1274
1216
1592
J.Ram
J. Bâgir
1754
Elat
1753
J. Um el Hashim
Mikhrot Timna
Aqaba
Beer Ora

JORDAN

MEDITERRANEAN SEA

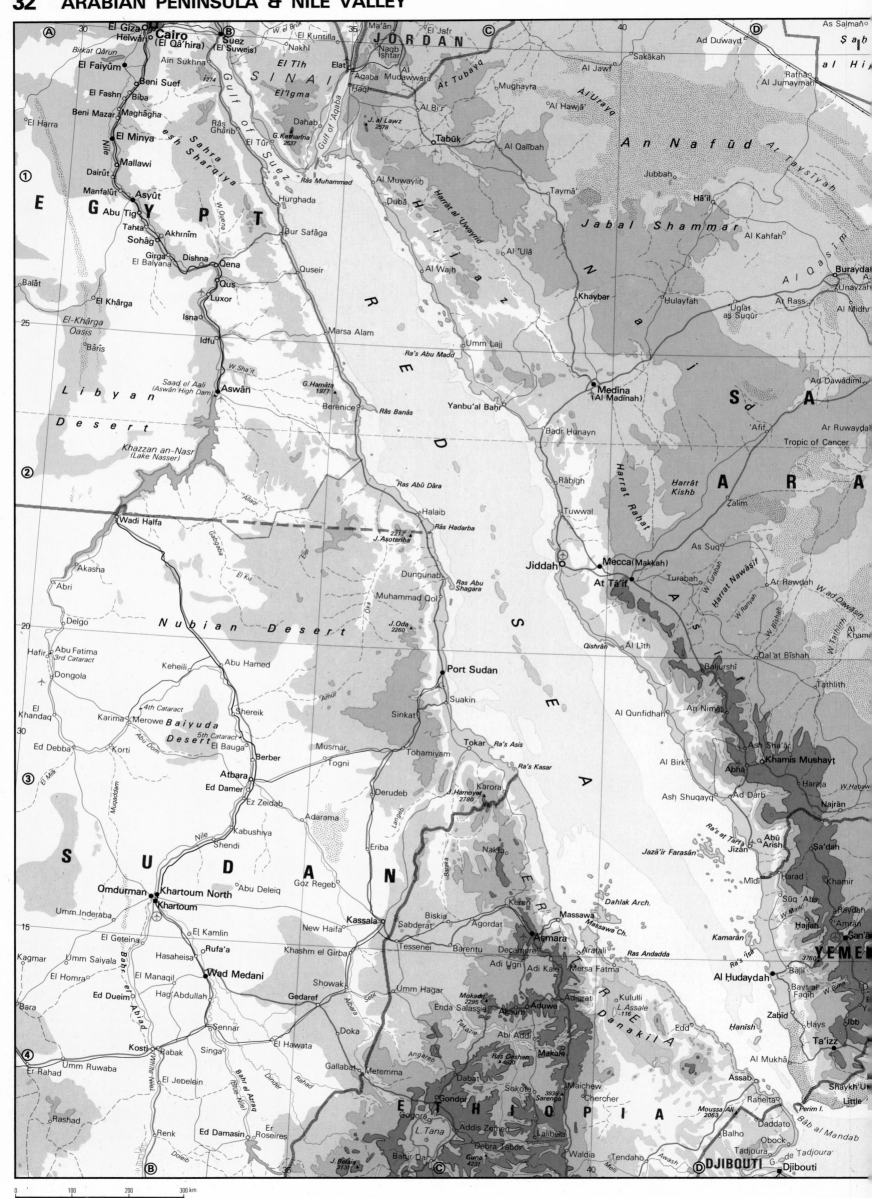

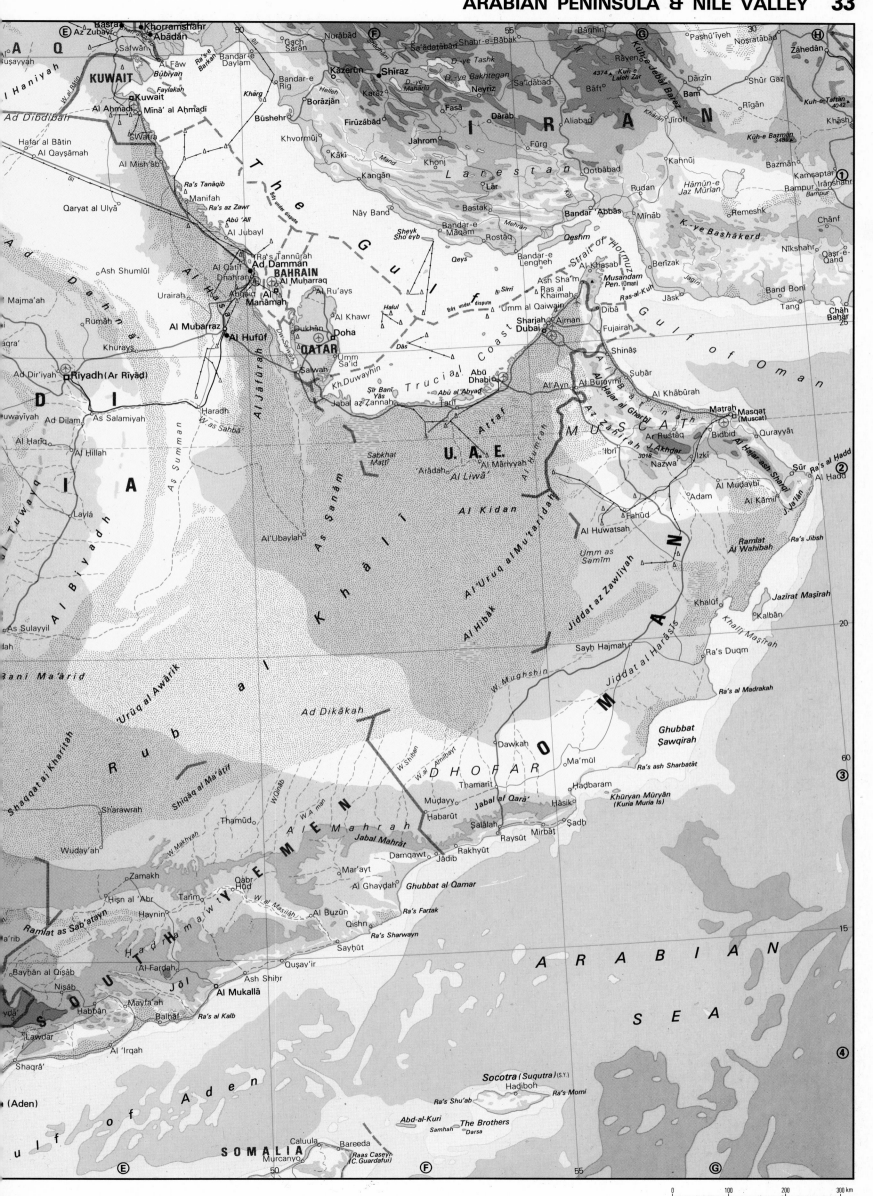

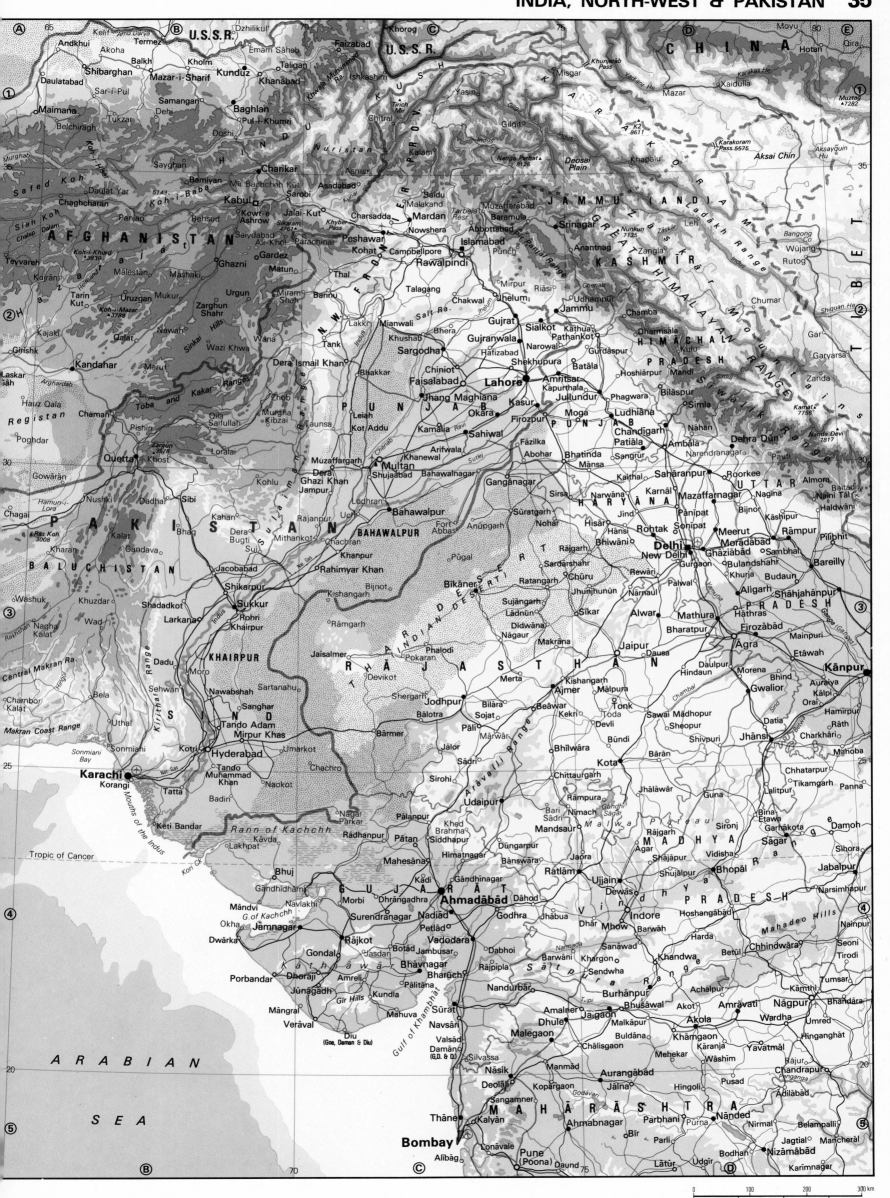

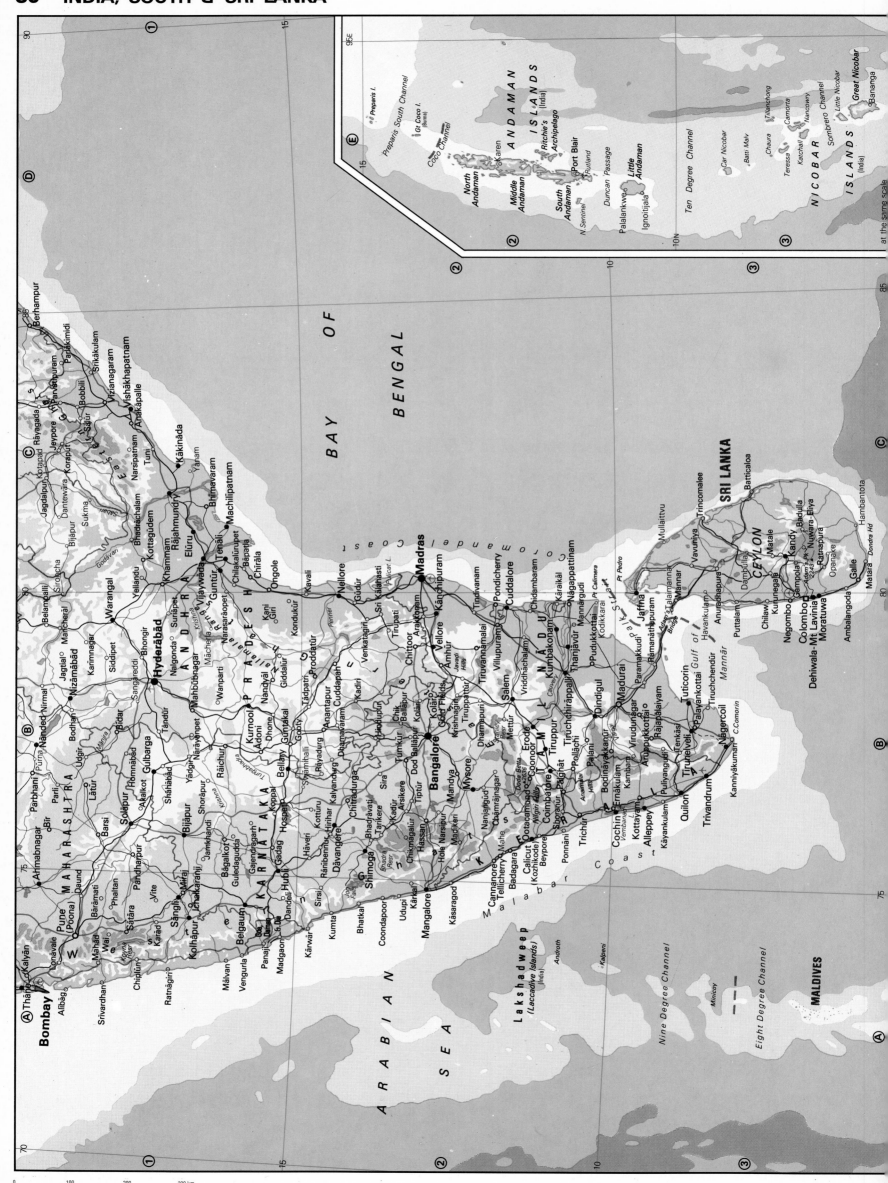

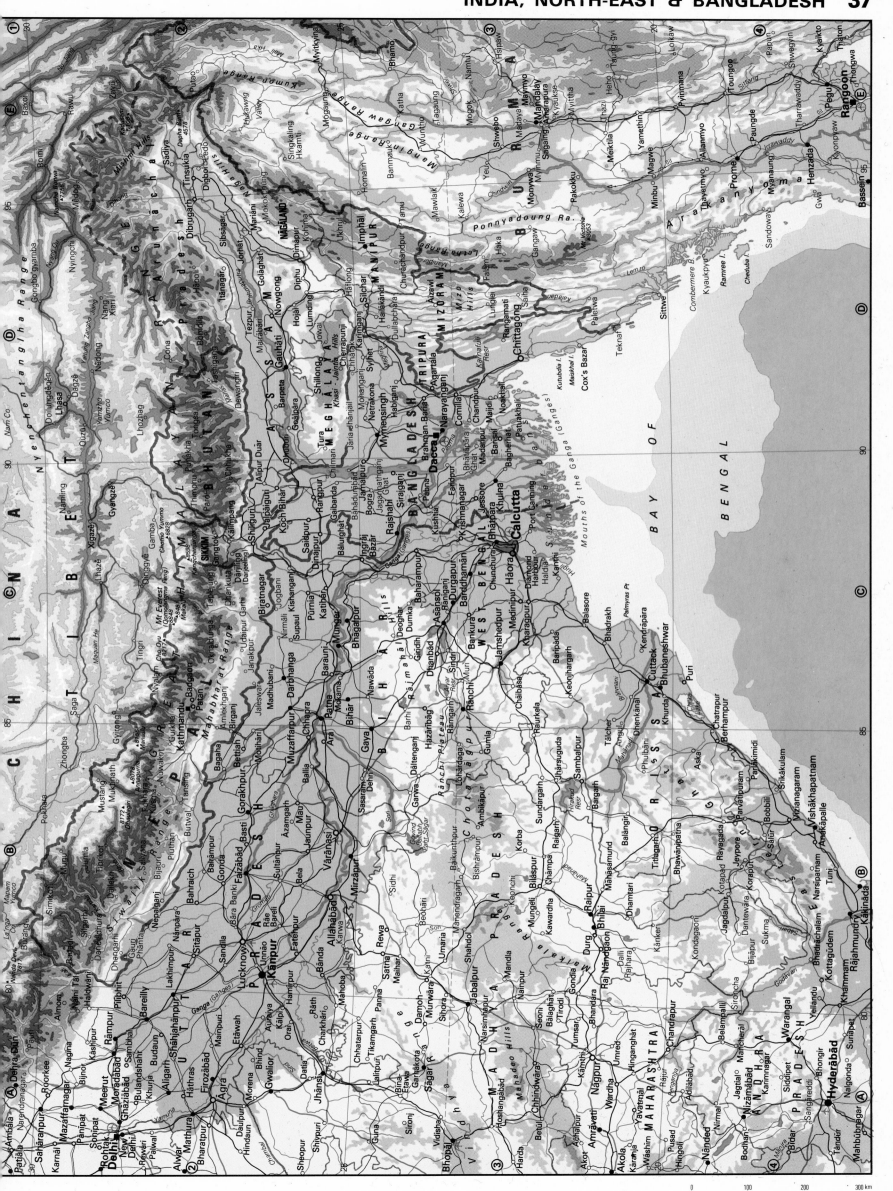

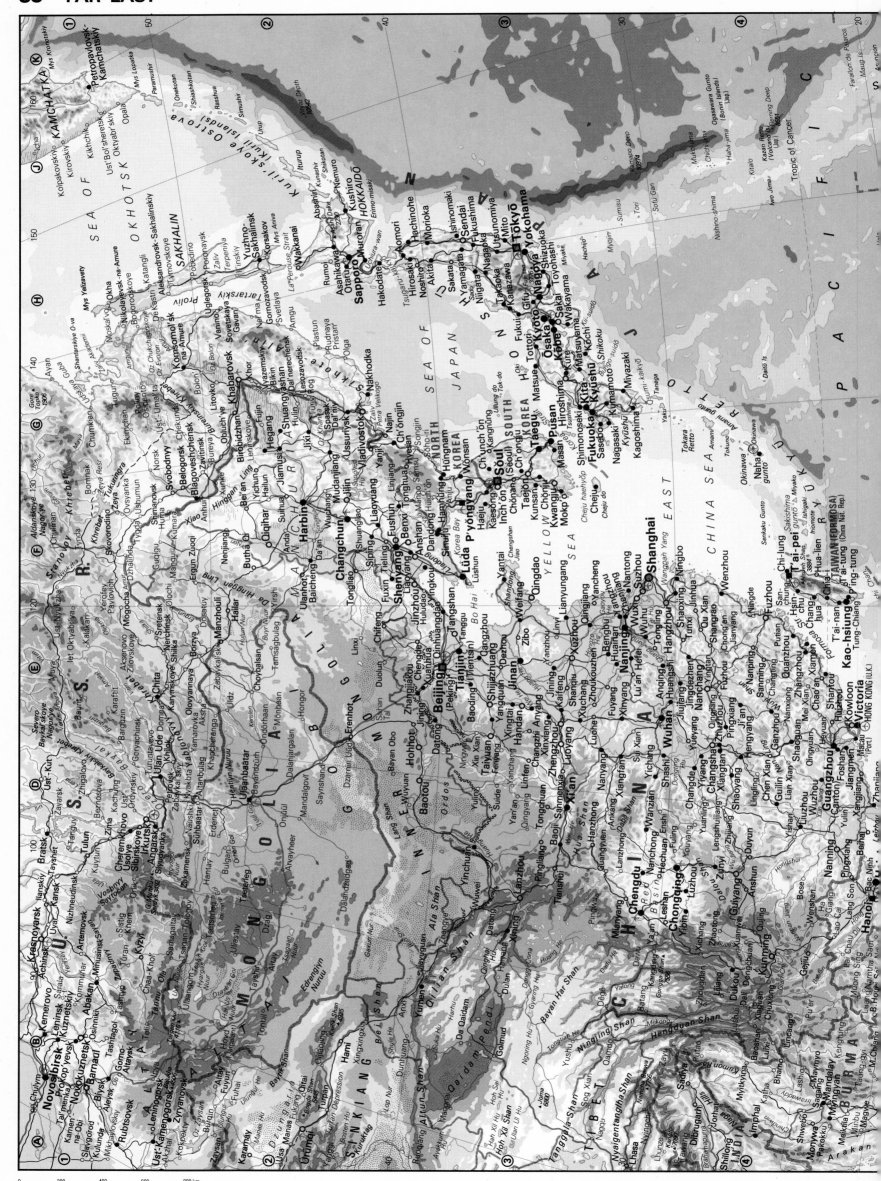

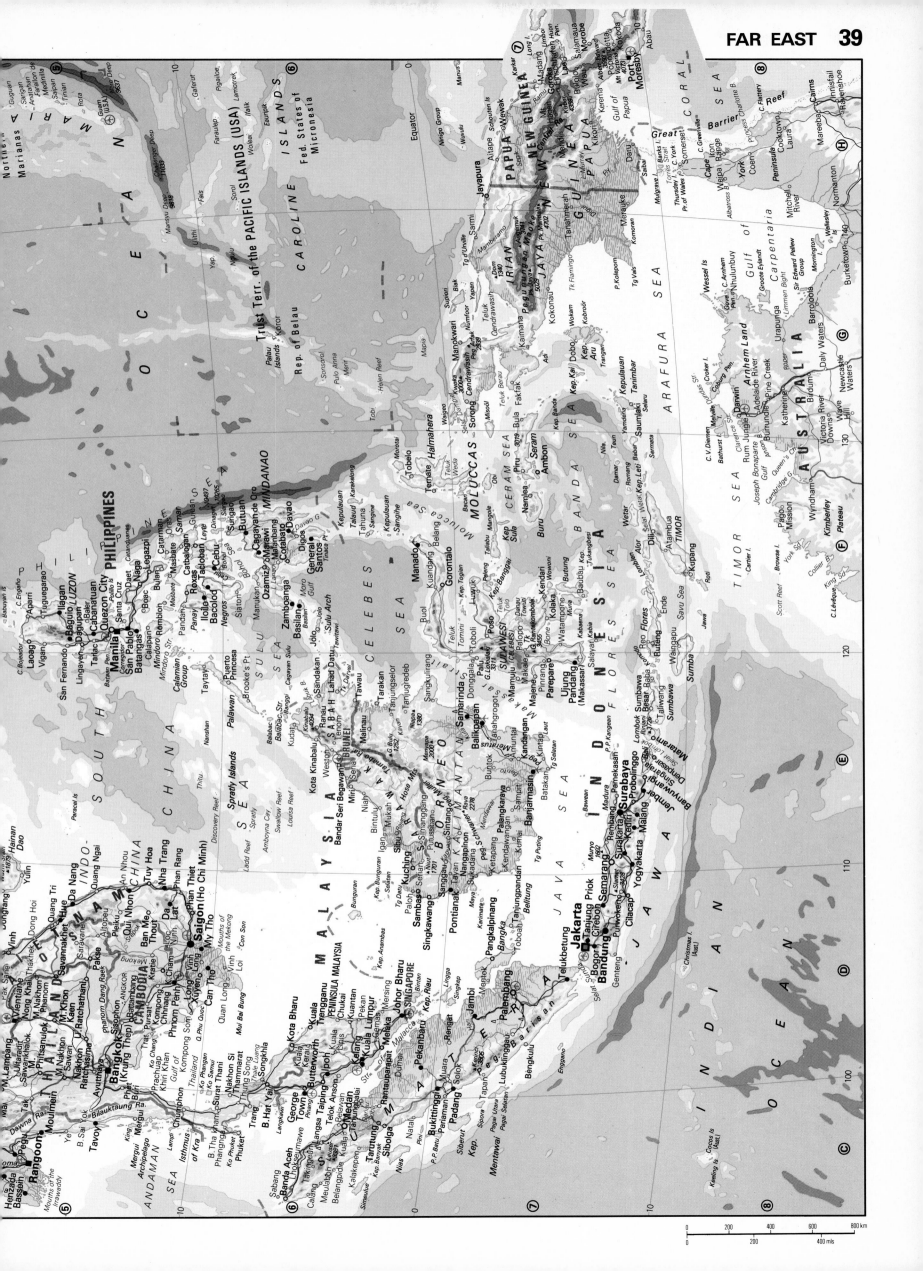

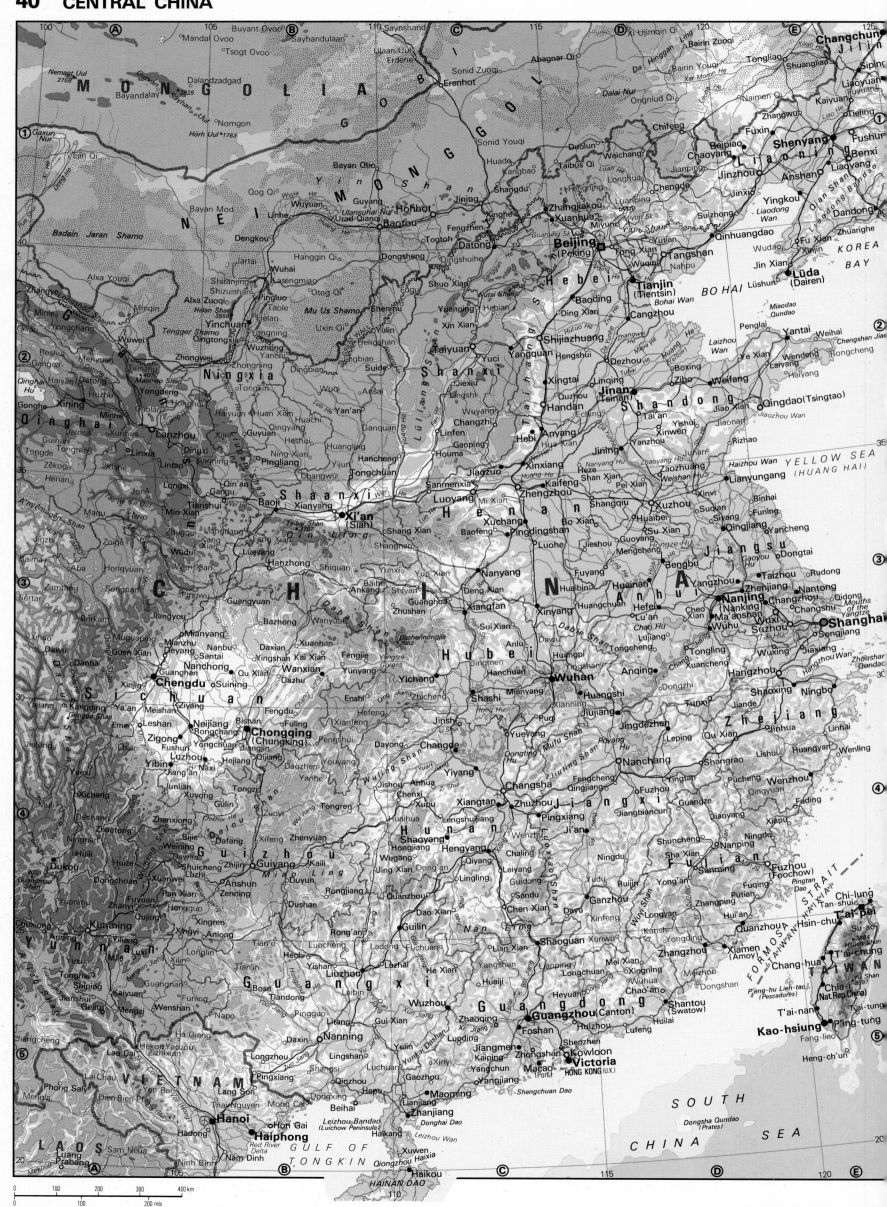

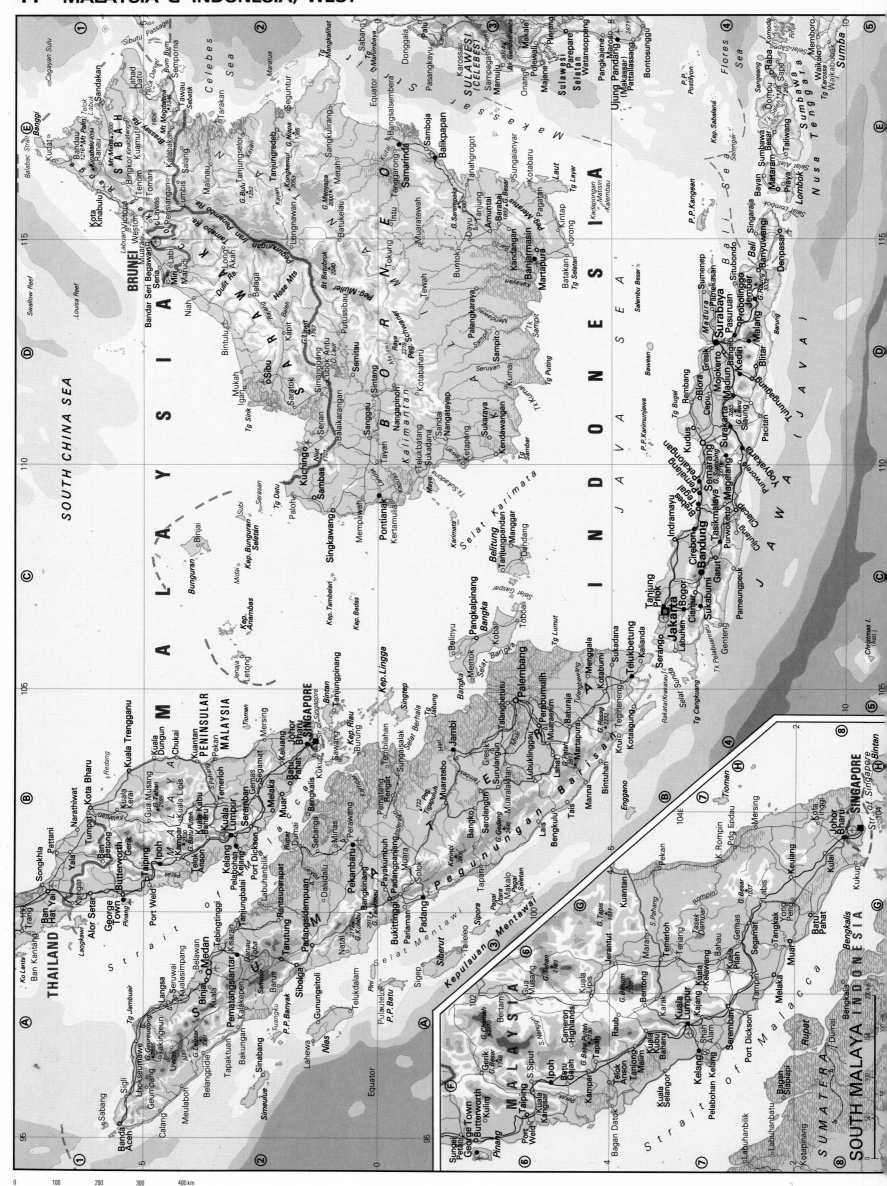

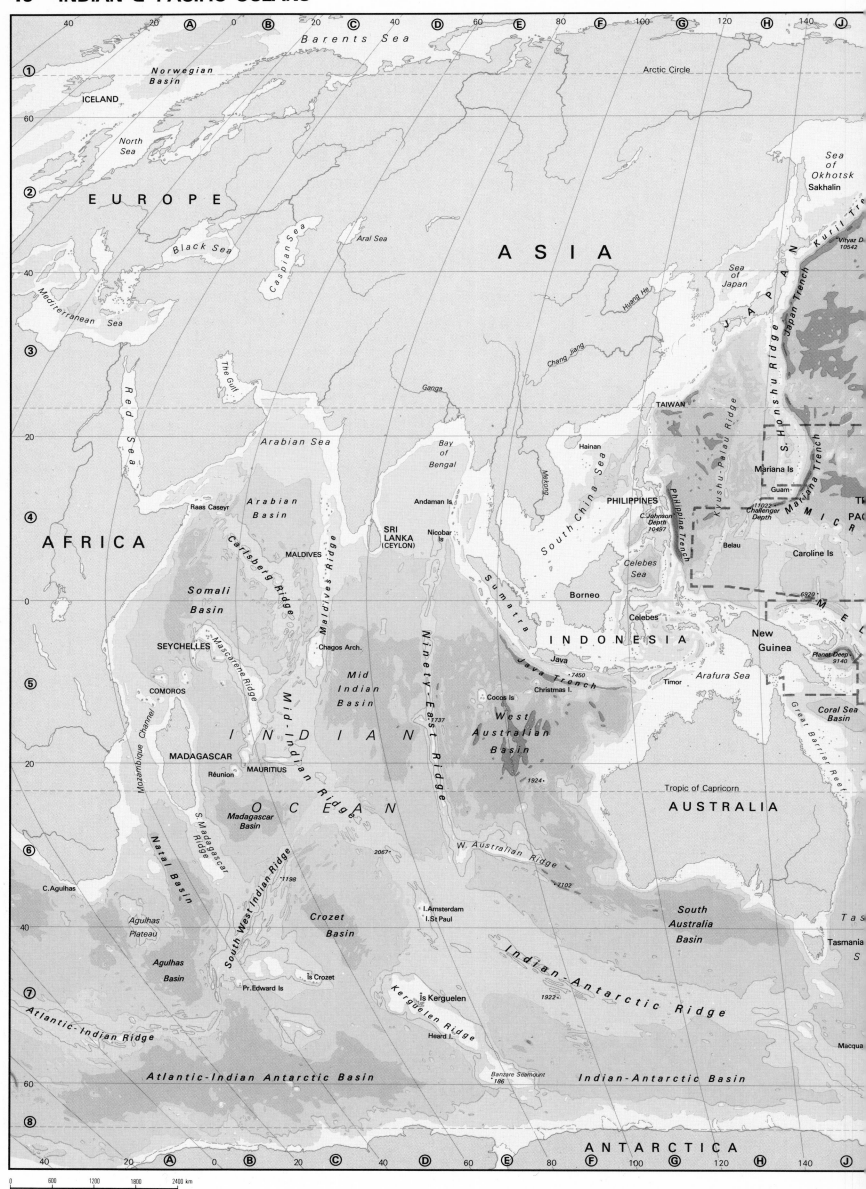

ICELAND

Norwegian Basin

Barents Sea

Arctic Circle

North Sea

E U R O P E

A S I A

Black Sea

Caspian Sea

Aral Sea

Sea of Okhotsk

Sakhalin

Sea of Japan

Mediterranean Sea

Huang He

Chang Jiang

Red Sea

The Gulf

Ganga

Arabian Sea

Bay of Bengal

TAIWAN

Hainan

J A P A N

Kuril Trench

S. Honshu Ridge

Japan Trench

Vityaz D. 10542

A F R I C A

Raas Caseyr

Arabian Basin

MALDIVES

SRI LANKA (CEYLON)

Andaman Is

Nicobar Is

Mekong

South China Sea

PHILIPPINES

C.Johnson Depth 10497

Mariana Is

Guam

Challenger Depth 11022

Mariana Trench

M I C

PAC

R

Somali Basin

Carlsberg Ridge

Maldives Ridge

Chagos Arch.

Ninety-East Ridge

Sumatra

Borneo

Celebes

Celebes Sea

Belau

Caroline Is

6920

SEYCHELLES

Mascarene Ridge

I N D O N E S I A

New Guinea

Planet Deep 9140

M

E

L

COMOROS

Mid Indian Basin

Java

Java Trench 7450

Christmas I.

Cocos Is

West Australian Basin

Timor

Arafura Sea

Coral Sea Basin

Great Barrier Reef

Mozambique Channel

MADAGASCAR

Réunion

MAURITIUS

Mid-Indian Ridge

1737

I N D I A N

1924

Tropic of Capricorn

A U S T R A L I A

S. Madagascar Ridge

Madagascar Basin

O C E A N

2067

W. Australian Ridge

7102

Natal Basin

C.Agulhas

South West Indian Ridge

1198

I.Amsterdam

I.St Paul

South Australia Basin

Tas

Agulhas Plateau

Crozet Basin

Indian-Antarctic Ridge

Tasmania

S

Agulhas Basin

Îs Crozet

Pr.Edward Is

Îs Kerguelen

1922

Macqua

Atlantic-Indian Ridge

Kerguelen Ridge

Heard I.

Banzare Seamount 186

Atlantic-Indian Antarctic Basin

Indian-Antarctic Basin

A N T A R C T I C A

Ⓚ 180 Ⓛ 160 Ⓜ 140 Ⓝ 120 Ⓞ 100 Ⓟ 80 Ⓠ 60 Ⓡ 40 Ⓢ 20 0

ic Ocean

GREENLAND

To enhance the ocean features, the 3000m contour has been added, and over 5000m is shown by an extra tint.

ICELAND ①

Bering Sea

Hudson Bay

C.Farewell

Labrador Basin 60

Aleutian Is

Atlantic

Newfoundland ②

7822

Aleutian Trench

Ocean

Grand Banks

Emperor Seamount Chain

NORTH

AMERICA 40

2926·

Mendocino Seascarp

North American

Bermuda ③

18·

104·

Midway Is

Murray Seascarp

Basin

Gulf of Mexico

1477·

d-Pacific Mountains

Hawaiian Islands

Tropic of Cancer

C.Falso

CUBA

West Indies 20

Cayman Tr.

P

Clarion Fracture Zone

Is Revilla Gigedo

Middle America Trench

Caribbean Sea ④

OF NDS

O

PACIFIC

Is

East Pacific Rise

Cocos Ridge

L

Marshall Is

Line Is

Equator

Is Galápagos

SOUTH

0

NAURU

Y

O

AMERICA

KIRIBATI

Phoenix Is

N

C

E

A

N

Ís Marquises

⑤

SOLOMON ISLANDS

TUVALU

Tokelau

American Samoa

F

R

French Polynesia

East Pacific Ridge

6150·

UATU

Wallis & Futuna

Wrn Samoa

E

Samoa

Ís de la Société

Ís Tuamotu

Peru Basin

S.W. Peru or Nasca Ridge

FIJI

TONGA

Tahiti

N

Peru-Chile Trench

Nouvelle Calédonie

Niue

Cook Is

C

S

Ís Tubuai

Ís Gambier

·8066 20

S. Fiji Basin

Horizon Depth 10882

Tonga Trench

A

Pitcairn

·1344

5537

S.Ambrosio

S.Félix

Sala y Gómez

Kermadec Trench

Norfolk I.

Norfolk I. Ridge

10047

INTERNATIONAL DATE LINE

I.de Pascua

Is Juan Fernández

⑥

N.Cape

NEW ZEALAND

South West Pacific Basin

40

New Zealand Plateau

Chatham Is

Argentine Basin

Falkland Is ⑦

kland Is

6240·

Campbell I.

732·

Pacific-Antarctic Ridge

N.Scotia Ridge

S.Georgia

C.Horn

Scotia Sea

S.Sandwich Is

S.Sandwich Trench

South East Pacific Basin

Drake Passage

5486·

S.Orkney Is

60

leny Is

Scott Is

Antarctic Circle

Antarctic Peninsula

Weddell Sea ⑧

Ⓚ 180 Ⓛ 160 Ⓜ 140 Ⓝ 120 Ⓞ 100 Ⓟ 80 Ⓠ 60 Ⓡ 40 Ⓢ 20 0

0 600 1200 1800 2400 km

0 600 1200 mls

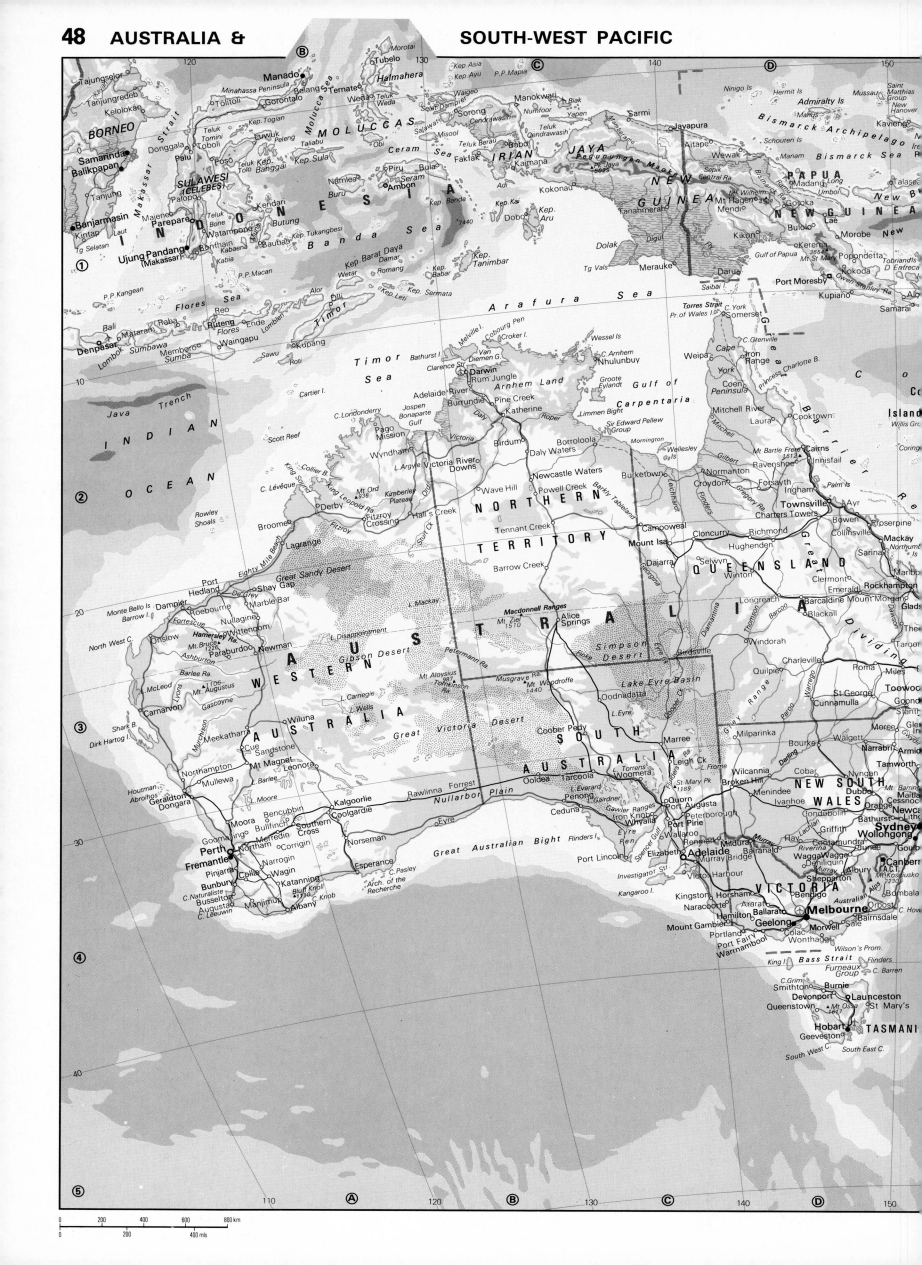

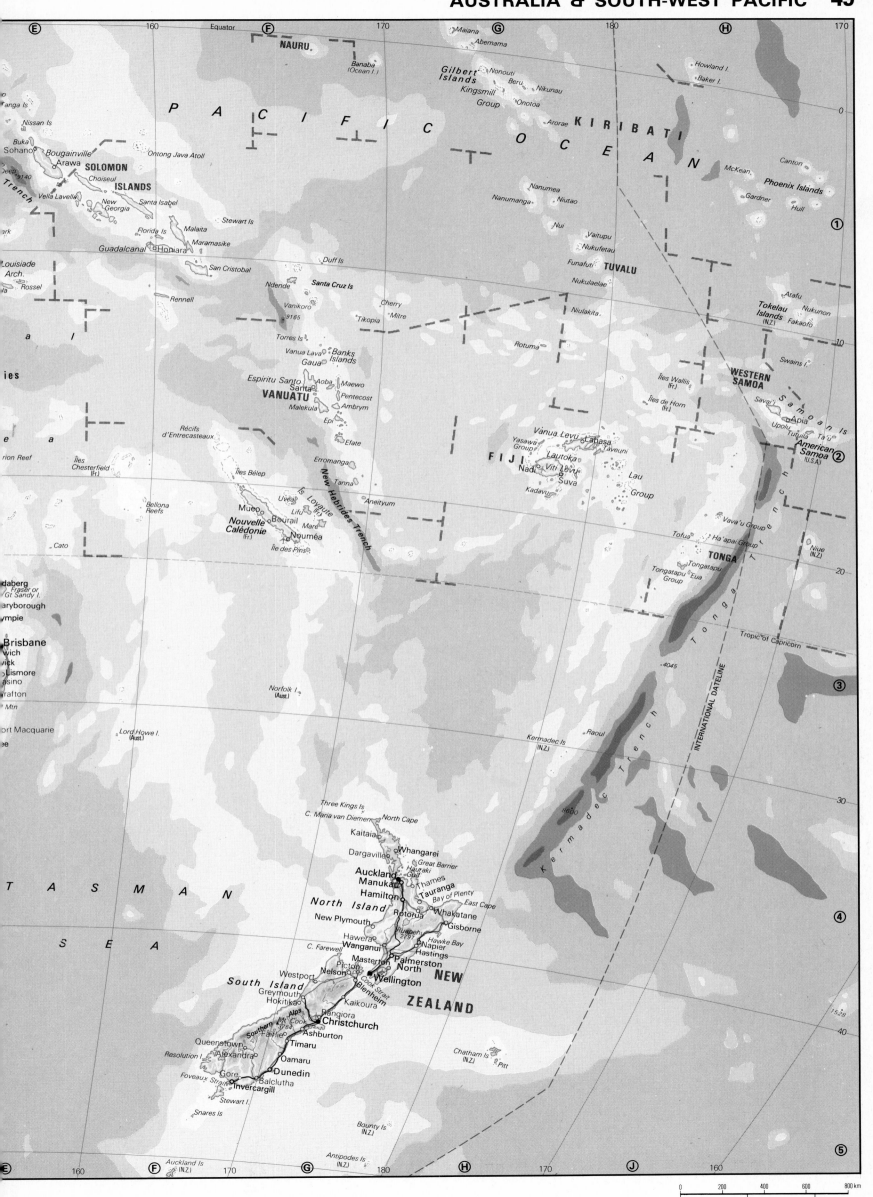

PACIFIC OCEAN

KIRIBATI

NAURU

Gilbert Islands

Nissan Is
Buka
Sohano
Bougainville
Arawa
SOLOMON
Choiseul
ISLANDS
Vella Lavella
Santa Isabel
New Georgia
Florida Is
Malaita
Maramasike
Guadalcanal
Honiara
San Cristobal
Rennell

Howland I.
Baker I.

McKean
Canton
Phoenix Islands
Gardner
Hull

Maiana
Abemama
Nonouti
Beru
Nikunau
Kingsmill Group
Onotoa
Arorae

Nanumea
Niutao
Nanumanga
Nui
Vaitupu
Nukufetau
Funafuti
TUVALU
Nukulaelae

Tokelau Islands (N.Z.)
Atafu
Nukunon
Fakaofo
Swains I.

WESTERN SAMOA
Savai'i
Apia
Upolu
Tutuila
Ta'u
American Samoa (U.S.A.)

Duff Is
Santa Cruz Is
Ndende
Vanikoro
9165
Torres Is
Vanua Lava
Gaua
Banks Islands
Espiritu Santo
Santo
Aoba
Maewo
VANUATU
Pentecost
Malekula
Ambrym
Epi
Efate
Erromanga
Tanna
Aneityum

Cherry
Tikopia
Mitre
Rotuma

Îles Wallis (Fr.)
Îles de Horn (Fr.)

Niulakita

FIJI
Vanua Levu
Yasawa Group
Labasa
Taveuni
Lautoka
Nadi
Viti Levu
Suva
Kadavu
Lau Group

Vava'u Group
Tofua
Ha'apai Group
Niue (N.Z.)
TONGA
Tongatapu
Eua
Tongatapu Group

Récifs d'Entrecasteaux
Îles Bélep
Mueo
Uvéa
Lifu
Loyauté Is
Bourail
Maré
Nouvelle Calédonie (Fr.)
Nouméa
Île des Pins

New Hebrides Trench

Tropic of Capricorn

-4045

INTERNATIONAL DATELINE

Kermadec Trench

Tonga Trench

-8600

Kermadec Is (N.Z.)
Raoul

Three Kings Is
C. Maria van Diemen
North Cape
Kaitaia
Whangarei
Dargaville
Great Barrier
Auckland
Hauraki Gulf
Manukau
Thames
Hamilton
Tauranga
Bay of Plenty
East Cape
North Island
Rotorua
Whakatane
New Plymouth
Gisborne
Ruapehu 2797
Hawera
Hawke Bay
Wanganui
Napier
C. Farewell
Masterton
Hastings
Westport
Nelson
Palmerston North
Picton
Wellington
Greymouth
Blenheim
NEW ZEALAND
Hokitika
Kaikoura
South Island
Alps
Rangiora
Mt Cook 3764
Christchurch
Fairlie
Ashburton
Queenstown
Timaru
Resolution I.
Alexandra
Oamaru
Gore
Dunedin
Foveaux Strait
Balclutha
Invercargill
Stewart I.
Snares Is

TASMAN SEA

Bundaberg
Fraser or Gt Sandy I.
Maryborough
Gympie
Brisbane
wich
wick
Lismore
Casino
Grafton
Mtn
ort Macquarie
ree

Lord Howe I. (Aust.)

Norfolk I. (Aust.)

Chatham Is (N.Z.)
Pitt

1528

Bounty Is (N.Z.)

Auckland Is (N.Z.)
Antipodes Is (N.Z.)

Equator

Banaba (Ocean I.)

Louisiade Arch.
Rossel

Trench
Deep 9140

Ontong Java Atoll

Stewart Is

ies
a l
ies
e a

Chesterfield (Fr.)

Bellona Reefs
Cato

ion Reef

| 0 | 200 | 400 | 600 | 800 km |
| 0 | | 200 | | 400 mls |

Three Kings Is

C. Maria
van Diemen
North Cape
Rangaunu B.
Ninety Mile Beach
Doubtless B.
Ahipara B.
Tauroa Pt
Kaitaia
Bay of Islands
C. Brett
Russell
Kaikohe
Kawakawa
Hokianga Har.
Hikurangi
Whangarei
Hen & Chickens Is
Bream B.
Dargaville
Little Barrier I.
Great Barrier I.
Kaipara Har.
Wellsford
C. Colville
Hauraki Gulf
Coromandel Peninsula
Maple
Takapuna
Mercury Is
Mercury Bay
Auckland
Manukau
Papatoetoe
Papakura
Pukekohe
Thames
Coromandel Ra.
Waiuku
Mayor I.
Paeroa
Waihi
NORTH
Glen Afton
Huntly
Te Aroha
Matakana I.
Tauranga Har.
White I.
C. Runaway
Hicks Bay
Ngaruawahia
Morrinsville
Tauranga
Bay of Plenty
East C.
ISLAND
Hamilton
Cambridge
Te Puke
Te Awamutu
Putaruru
Rotorua
Whakatane
Opotiki
Kawhia
Kawerau
Tauaatua
Otorohanga
Waitomo
Rotorua
Tarawera
Raukumara Ra.
Te Kuiti
Mangakino
L. Taupo
Tokomaru Bay
Taupo
Kaimanawa Mts
Makorako 1727
Mohaka
N. Taranaki Bight
Ohura
Taumarunui
Mt Ngauruhoe 2291
Tolaga Bay
Waitara
Mt Makorako
Gisborne
New Plymouth
Inglewood
Mt Ruapehu 2797
Tarawera
Wairoa
Poverty Bay
C. Egmont
Mt Egmont 2518
Stratford
Raetihi
Ohakune
Waikaremoana
Hawke Bay
Opunake
Eltham
Eskdale
Mahia Peninsula
Hawera
Ohakea
Waiouru
Taradale
Napier
Portland I.
S. Taranaki Bight
Patea
Taihape
Hastings
C. Kidnappers
Wanganui
Havelock North
Marton
Waipukurau
Feilding
Dannevirke
Palmerston N.
Woodville
C. Farewell
Farewell Spit
Foxton
Pahiatua
Herbertville
Collingwood
Golden Bay
Levin
Eketahuna
C. Turnagain
Rocks Pt
Takaka
Separation Pt
Otaki
COOK
Tasman Mts
C. Stephens
Paraparaumu
Masterton
The Twins 1826
D'Urville I.
Carterton
Karamea
Tasman Bay
Motueka
C. Jackson
Porirua
Upper Hutt
Martinborough
Karamea Bight
Motueka
Picton
Tawa
Lower Hutt
Seddonville
Nelson
Richmond
Wellington
Mt Ross 983
Westport
Murchison
Richmond Ra.
Wairau
Blenheim
Palliser Bay
C. Palliser
C. Foulwind
Buller
L. Rotoroa
STRAIT
Reefton
L. Rotoiti
Awatere
C. Campbell
Victoria Ra.
Mt Travers 2338
Kaikoura Ra.
Tapuaenuku 2885
Spenser Mts
Runanga
Grey
Lewis Pass
Clarence
Kaikoura
Greymouth
Hanmer Springs
Kaikoura Pen.
Waiau
Hokitika
L. Brunner
Waiau
Ross
L. Sumner
Culverden
PEGASUS
Arthurs Pass
Hurunui
Cheviot
Abut Hd
Puketeraki
Waipara
SOUTH
Franz Josef Gl.
Whataroa
Rangiora
Pegasus Bay
Coleridge
Waimakariri
Kaiapoi
Mt Cook 3764
Hornby
Christchurch
ISLAND
Mt Sefton 3157
Methven
Lyttelton
Hermitage
Lincoln
Banks Peninsula
Rakaia
Akaroa
Jackson Hd
Tekapo
Geraldine
Ellesmere
Cascade Pt
Pollux 2542
Pukaki
Ashburton
Awarua Pt
Lake Fairlie
Canterbury Bight
Mt Aspiring 3027
Ohau
Temuka
Mt Pyramid 2326
Wanaka
L. Benmore
Timaru
Milford Sd
Homer Tunnel
Hawea
George Sd
Omarama
Caswell Sd
Arrowtown
L. Aviemore
Waimate
Queenstown
Cromwell
Kurow
Waitaki
Secretary I.
Wakatipu
Clyde
Te Anau
Fiordland
Alexandra
Oamaru
Doubtful Sd
Manapouri
Kingston
Ranfurly
Nat. Park
Mt Ward 1718
Roxburgh
Hampden
Breaksea Sd
Lumsden
Palmerston
Resolution
Ohai
Heriot
Waikouaiti
Dusky Sd
Hauroko
Winton
Mataura
Port Chalmers
Puysegur Pt
Tuatapere
Te Waewae Bay
Gore
Lawrence
Otago Peninsula
Riverton
Edendale
Milton
Dunedin
Cameron Mts
Ohai
Clutha
Mosgiel
Solander I.
Riversdale
Balclutha
Kaitangata
Owaka
Invercargill
Bluff
Foveaux Strait
Codfish I.
Oban
Paterson Inlet
Stewart Island
Mt Allen 730
Shelter Pt
Port Pegasus

TASMAN SEA

PACIFIC OCEAN

0 50 100 150 200 km
0 50 100 mls

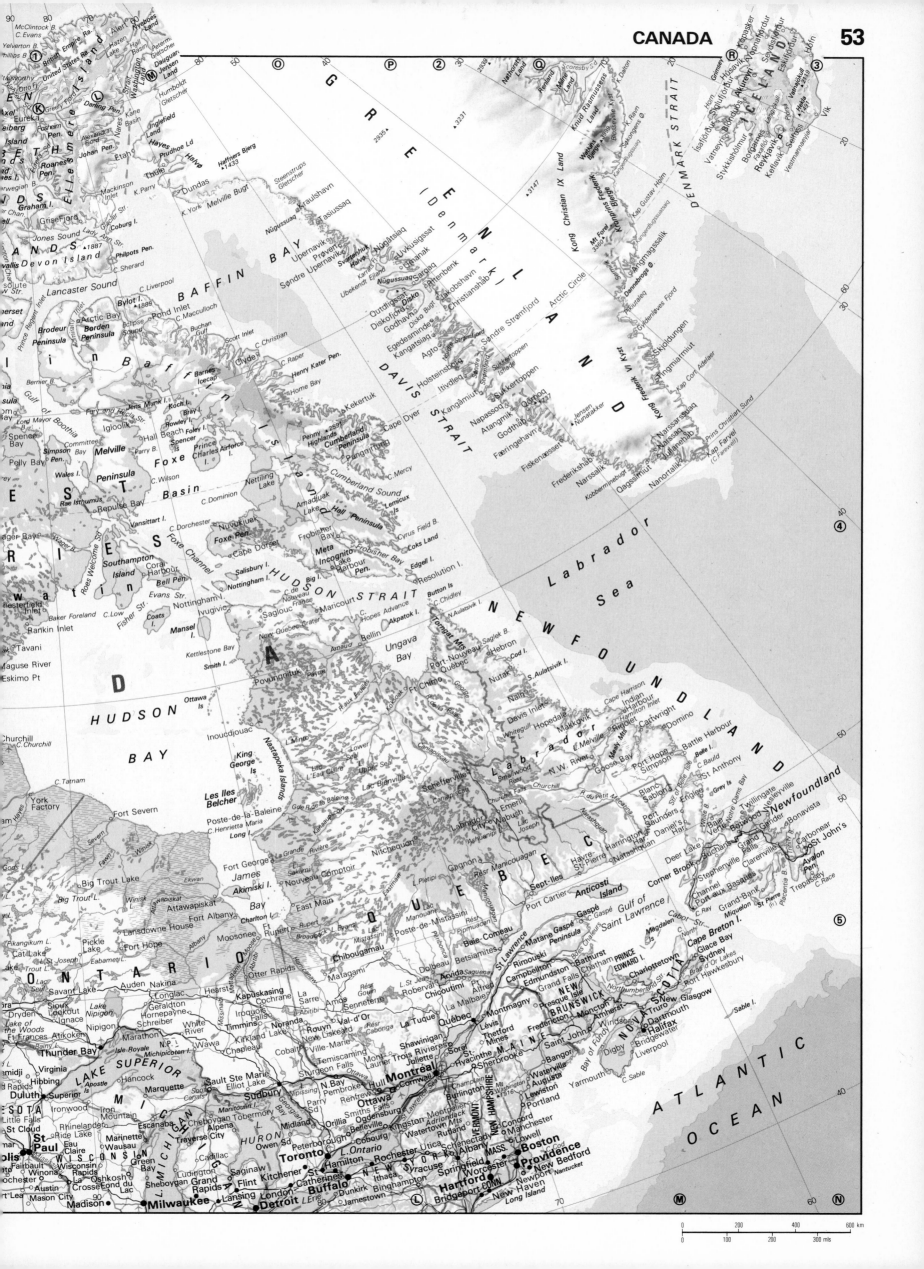

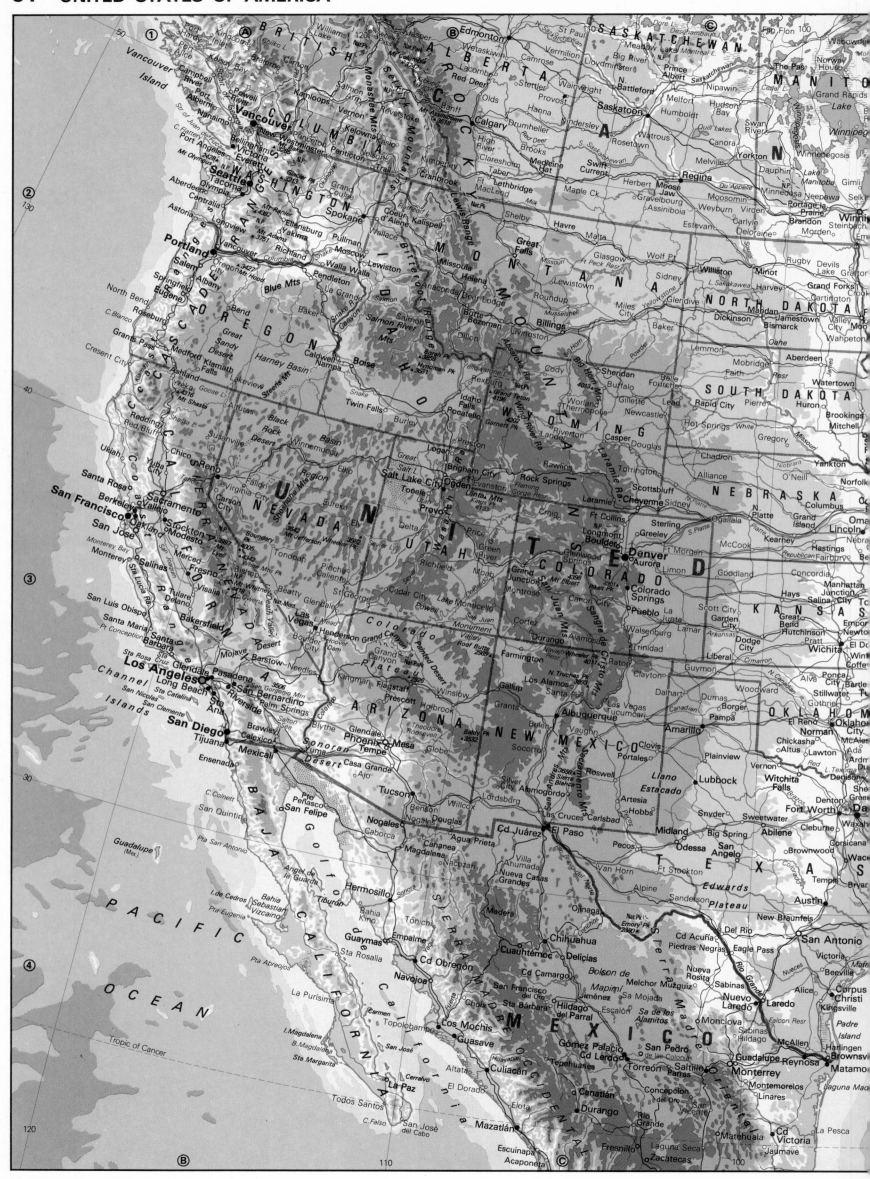

KEY TO THE MAPS

This key explains the meanings of the principal symbols that appear in the maps, the type-sizes used for the names of the largest cities and towns, and the colours that indicate heights and depths. Bar scales are provided at the bottom of the map pages.

BOUNDARIES

▬▬▬	International
▬ ▬ ▬	International under dispute
▪ ▪ ▪ ▪ ▪	Cease fire line
▬▬▬	Autonomous or federal
▬▬▬	Administrative
▬ ▬ ▬	Maritime (national)
─ ─ ─	International date line

COMMUNICATIONS

▬▬▬	Motorway
▬▬▬	Major highway
───	Other highway
═╪═╪═	Road tunnel
─ ─ ─	Car ferry
────	Main railway
───	Other railway
→----←	Rail tunnel
─┴─┴─	Canal
─ ─ ─	Rail ferry
⊕	International airport
✦	Other airport

LANDSCAPE FEATURES

	Marsh, swamp
	Sand desert, dunes
	Glacier, ice cap

LAKE FEATURES

	Saltwater
	Freshwater

OTHER FEATURES

∿∿	River
≍	Pass, gorge
→------←	Aqueduct
∿∿∿∿	Reef
▲ *4231*	Summit, peak
·*217*	Spot height, depth
△	Oil field
▲	Gas field
─Gas / Oil─	Oil / natural gas pipeline

TOWNS AND CITIES

Square symbols denote capital cities   *Population*

■	●	**New York**	over 5 000 000
■	●	**Montréal**	over 1 000 000
▫	○	Ottawa	over 500 000
■	•	Québec	over 100 000
▫	○	St John's	over 50 000
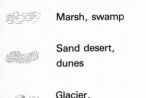			Built-up-area

MAP COLOURS

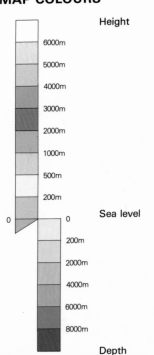

Height

6000m
5000m
4000m
3000m
2000m
1000m
500m
200m

0   0   Sea level

200m
2000m
4000m
6000m
8000m

Depth

MAP ABBREVIATIONS

Arch.	archipelago
A.S.S.R.	Autonomous Soviet Socialist Republic
B.	bay
Bj.	fort, cliff (Arab. *bordj*)
Bol.	big (Russ. *bol'shoy*)
Br.	1 bridge
	2 cape (Turk. *burun*)
C.	cape
Can.	canal
Cd.	town (Span. *ciudad*)
Ch.	salt lake (Arab. *chott*)
Chan.	channel
Ck.	creek
Cord.	mountain range (Span. *cordillera*)
Cuch.	hill, ridge (Span. *cuchilla*)
D.	mountain, range (Pers. *dag*, Turk. *dagi*, Jap. *dake*)
Dj.	mountain (Arab. *djebel*)
E.	east
Eil.	island(s) (Dutch *eiland,-en*)
Emb.	reservoir (Span. *embalse*)
Estr.	strait (Span. *estrecho*)
F.	firth (estuary)
Fj.	1 fjord
	2 mountain (Norw. *fjell*)
Ft.	fort
G.	1 gulf (Russ. *guba*)
	2 lake (Turk. *göl*)
	3 mountain (Arab. *gebel*, Malay *gunung*, Russ. *gora*)
	4 oasis (Arab. *ghedir*)
	5 river (Jap. *gawa*)
Gd., Gde	grand (Fr. *grande*)
Geb.	mountain range (Ger. *Gebirge*)
Gez.	island (Arab. *gezira*)
Ghub.	bay (Arab. *ghubba*)
Gl.	glacier
Gr.	great (Dutch *groot*, Ger. *gross*)
Gt., Gtr.	great, greater
H.	1 high (Ger. *hoch*)
	2 lake (Arab. *hawr*)
	3 mountain(s) (Czech. *hora*, *hory*)
Har.	harbour
Hd.	head
Hwy.	highway
I., Is.	island, islands
Isth.	isthmus
J.	1 glacier (Icel. *jökull*)
	2 lake (Fin. *jaure*)
	3 mountain (Arab. *jabal*)
Jct.	junction
K.	1 bay (Malay *kusia*)
	2 cape (Dutch *kaap*, Dan. *kap*, Norw. *kapp*)
	3 channel, strait (Jap. *kalkyo*)
	4 gulf (Gk. *kolpos*)
	5 lake (Jap. *ko*)
	6 mountain (Pers. *koh, kuh*)
	7 peak (Ger. *Kopf*)
	8 reef (Malay. *karang*)
Kan.	canal (Ger. *Kanal*)
Kep.	islands (Indones. *kepulauan*)
Kg.	1 river-bank (Indo-Chin. *kompong*)
	2 village (Malay *kampong*)
Kh.	wadi, river (Arab. *khawr*)
Khr.	mountain range (Russ. *khrebet*)
Kör.	gulf, bay (Turk. *körfez*)
L.	lake
Lag.	lagoon
Ld.	land
Lit.	little
M.	1 cape (Russ. *mys*)
	2 sea, lake (Dutch *meer*)
Mt., Mte	mountain (Ital. *monte*)
Mtn., Mts.	mountain, mountains
N.	1 cape (Russ. *nos*)
	2 new (Ger. *neu*)
	3 north
	4 south (Kor. *nam*)
Nat. Pk.	national park
Ndr.	lower (Dutch *neder*, Ger. *nieder*)
N.E.	north-east
Nizh.	lower (Russ. *nizhniy*)
Nizn.	lowland (Russ. *nizmennost*)
N.M.	national monument
N.O.	north-east (Dutch *noord oost*, Ger. *nord ost*)
Nov.	new (Russ. *novyy*)
N.P.	national park
N.W.	north-west
O.	1 east (Dutch *oost*, Ger., Swed. *ost*)
	2 island (Norw. *øy*, Russ. *ostrov*)
	3 old
Or.	mountain(s) (Gk. *óri, óros*)
Orm.	bay (Gk. *órmos*)
Ova.	islands (Russ. *ostrova*)
Oz.	lake (Russ. *ozero*)
P.	1 island (Malay *pulau*)
	2 pass
	3 peak
Pass.	passage
Peg.	mountains (Indones. *pegunungan*)
Pen.	peninsula
Pk.	1 park
	2 peak
Pl.	mountain range (Czech. *planinski*; Bulg. *planina*)
Plat.	plateau
Pov.	peninsula (Russ. *poluostrov*)
Pr.	1 cape (Pol. *przyladek*)
	2 strait (Russ. *proliv*)
Pt.	1 bridge (Fr. *pont*)
	2 point
	3 small (Fr. *petit*)
Pta.	point (Ital. *punta*, Span. *ponta*)
Pzo.	peak (Ital. *pizzo*)
Q.	1 mountain (Arab. *qàlat*)
	2 peak, fortress (Pers. *qala*)
R.	river
Ra.	range
Rap.	rapids
Res.	reservation
Resr.	reservoir
Rge.	ridge
Rly.	railway
R.S.F.S.R.	Russian Soviet Federated Socialist Republic
S.	1 lake (Norw. *sjö*)
	2 river (Malay. *sung*)
	3 saint (Span. *san*, Port. *sao*)
	4 salt marsh (Span. *salar*, *salina*)
	5 sea, lake (Ger. *See*)
	6 south
	7 strait (Jap. *seto*)
Sa.	mountain range (Port. *serra*, Span. *sierra*)
Sab.	salt flat (Arab. *sabkat*)
Sd.	sound
S.E.	south-east
Sev.	north (Russ. *sever*, *severnaya*)
Sh.	1 island (Jap. *shima*)
	2 ravine (Arab. *sh'aib*)
	3 river (Arab. *shatt*)
Sp.	peak (Ger. *Spitze*)
St., Sta., Ste.	saint (Ital. *santa*, Fr. *sainte*)
Sten.	pass, strait (Gk. *stenon*, *stenos*)
Str.	strait
Sty.	old (Czech. *staryy*)
Sv.	holy (Pol. *svaty*, Czech. *sveti*)
S.W.	south-west
T.	1 hill, mountain (Arab. *tall*, Hebr. *tel*)
	2 peak, hill (Turk. *tepe*)
Tg.	cape (Malay *tanjong*)
Tk.	bay (Indones. *téluk*)
Tr.	trench
Tun.	tunnel
U.	water-course (Arab. *uad*)
Ug.	cape (Malay *ujung*)
Unt.	lower (Ger. *unter*)
Upr.	upper
V.	1 lake (Icel., Norw. *vatn*)
	2 town (Fr. *ville*)
	3 valley
	4 west (Swed. *vastor*, Dan. *vest*, Norw. *vester*)
Vdkhr.	reservoir (Russ. *vodokhranilishche*)
Verkh.	upper (Russ. *verkhniy*)
Vol.	volcano
Vost.	eastern (Russ. *vostochnyy*)
W.	1 forest (Ger. *Wald*)
	2 gulf, bay (Chin. *wan*)
	3 wadi, water-course
	4 water
	5 well
	6 west
Y.	south (Russ. *yuzhnyy*)
Z.	1 gulf, bay (Russ. *zaliv*)
	2 intermittent lake (Arab. *zahrez*)
Zap.	western (Russ. *zapadnyy*)
Zem.	land, country (Russ. *zemlya*)

0   100   200   300   400 km
0   100   200 mls

ONTARIO

MANITOBA

SASKATCHEWAN

MINNESOTA

WISCONSIN

IOWA

NORTH DAKOTA

SOUTH DAKOTA

NEBRASKA

MONTANA

WYOMING

L. SUPERIOR

Lake of the Woods

Lake Winnipeg

Lake Manitoba

Lake Sakakawea

Lake Oahe

Badlands

Black Hills

Bighorn Mts

Laramie Mts

Medicine Bow Mtn. 3661

Cloud Peak 4016

White Butte 1016

Elk Mtn. 3400

Thunder Bay

Winnipeg

Regina

Moose Jaw

Brandon

Duluth

Superior

St Paul

Minneapolis

Bloomington

Bismarck

Mandan

Fargo

Grand Forks

Sioux City

Sioux Falls

Rapid City

Des Moines

Dubuque

Davenport

Rock Island

Cedar Rapids

Eau Claire

La Crosse

Rochester

Mason City

Aberdeen

Pierre

Fort Pierre

Watertown

Huron

Mitchell

Yankton

Norfolk

Scottsbluff

Casper

Missouri

Mississippi

Red

Yellowstone

Little Missouri

Belle Fourche

Cheyenne

White

Niobrara

N. Platte

0 50 100 150 200 km
0 50 100 mls

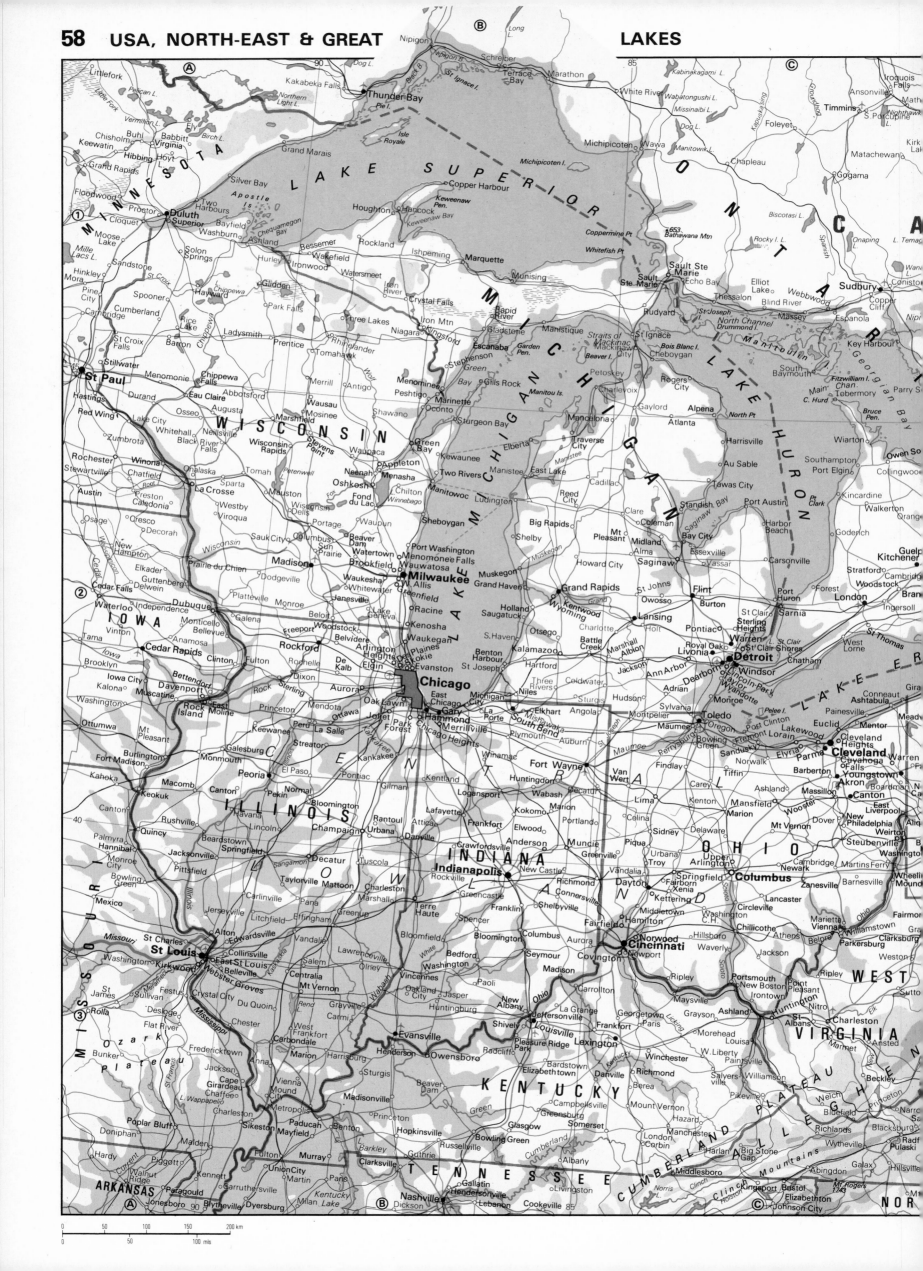

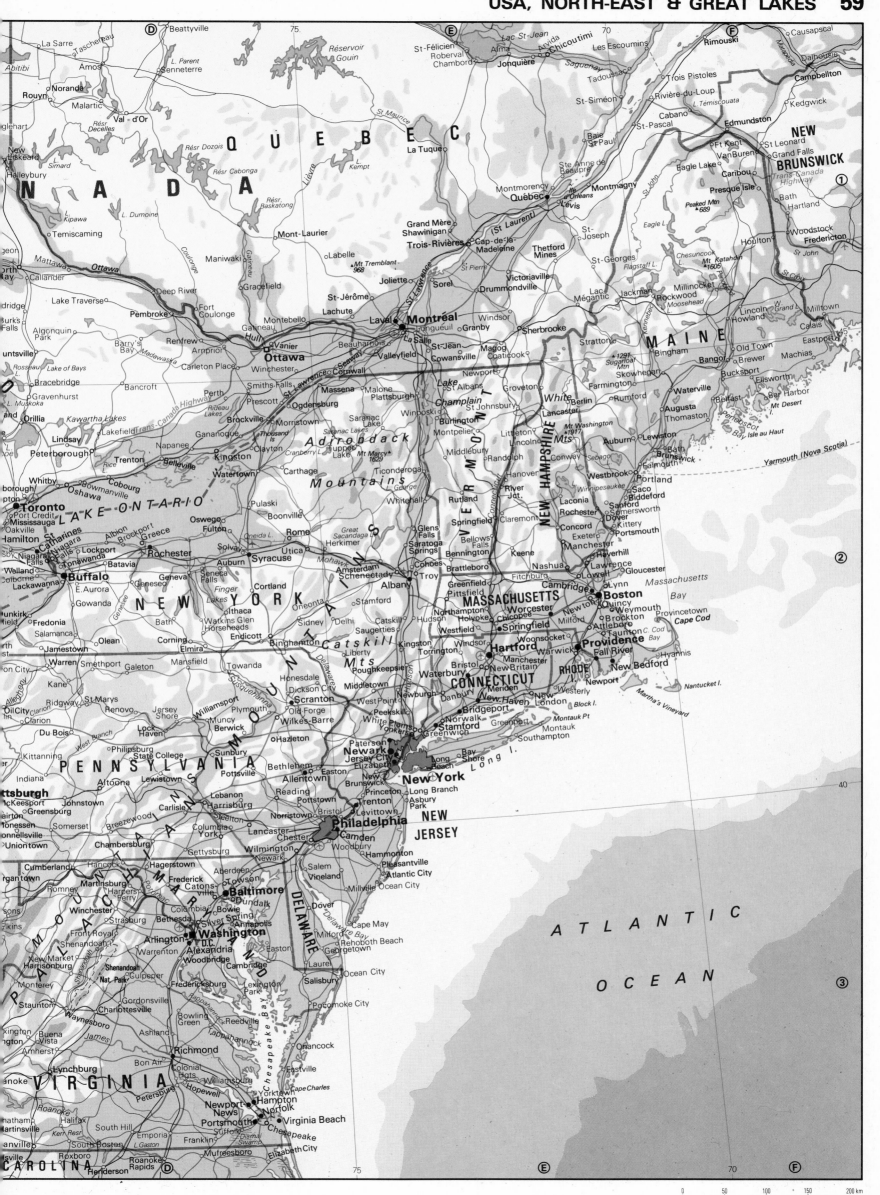

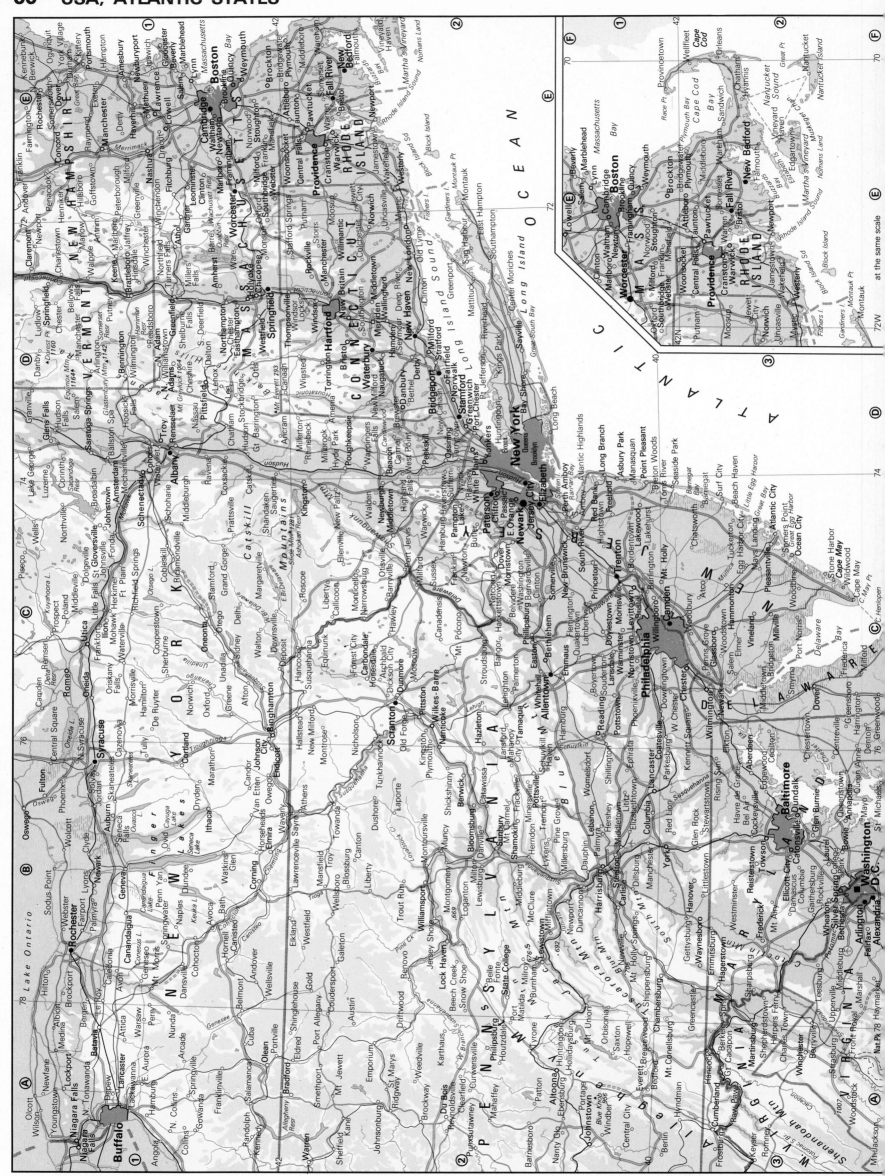

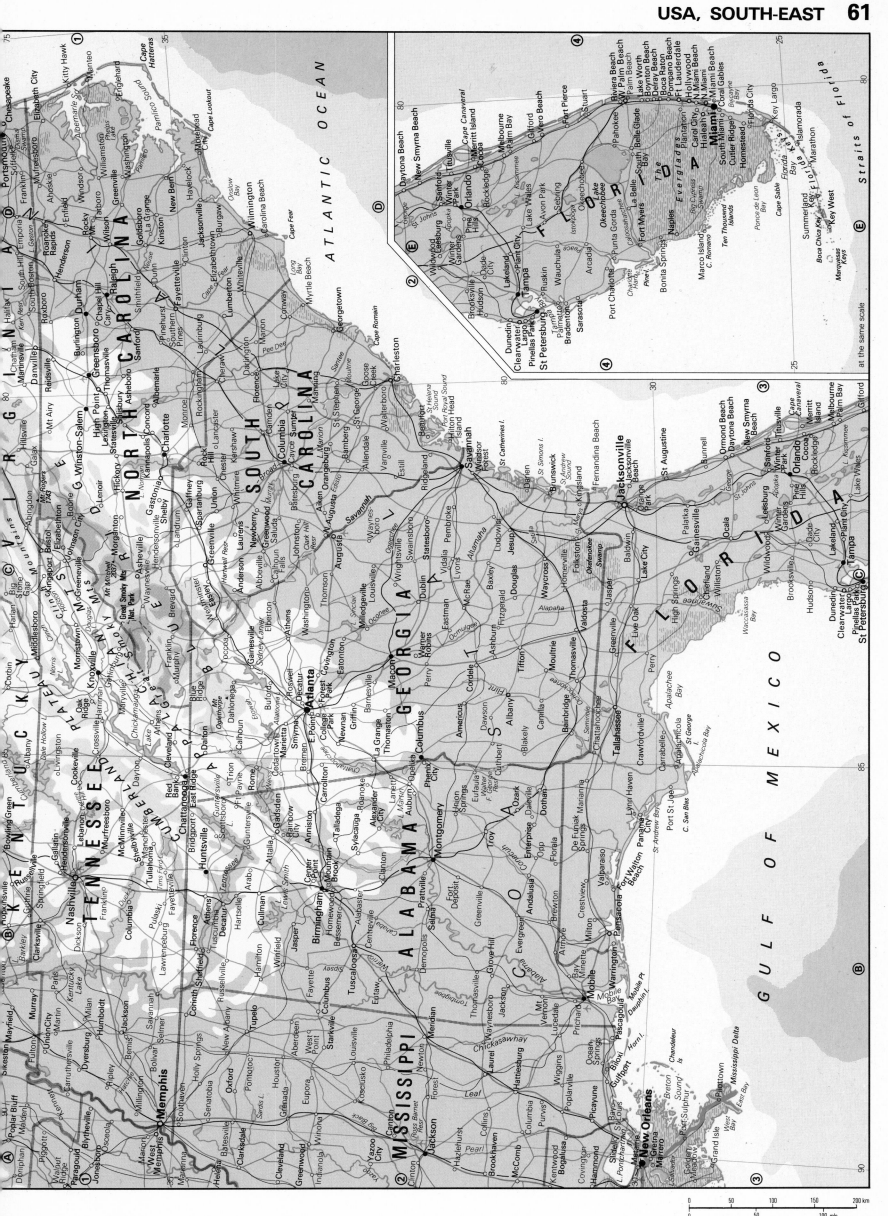

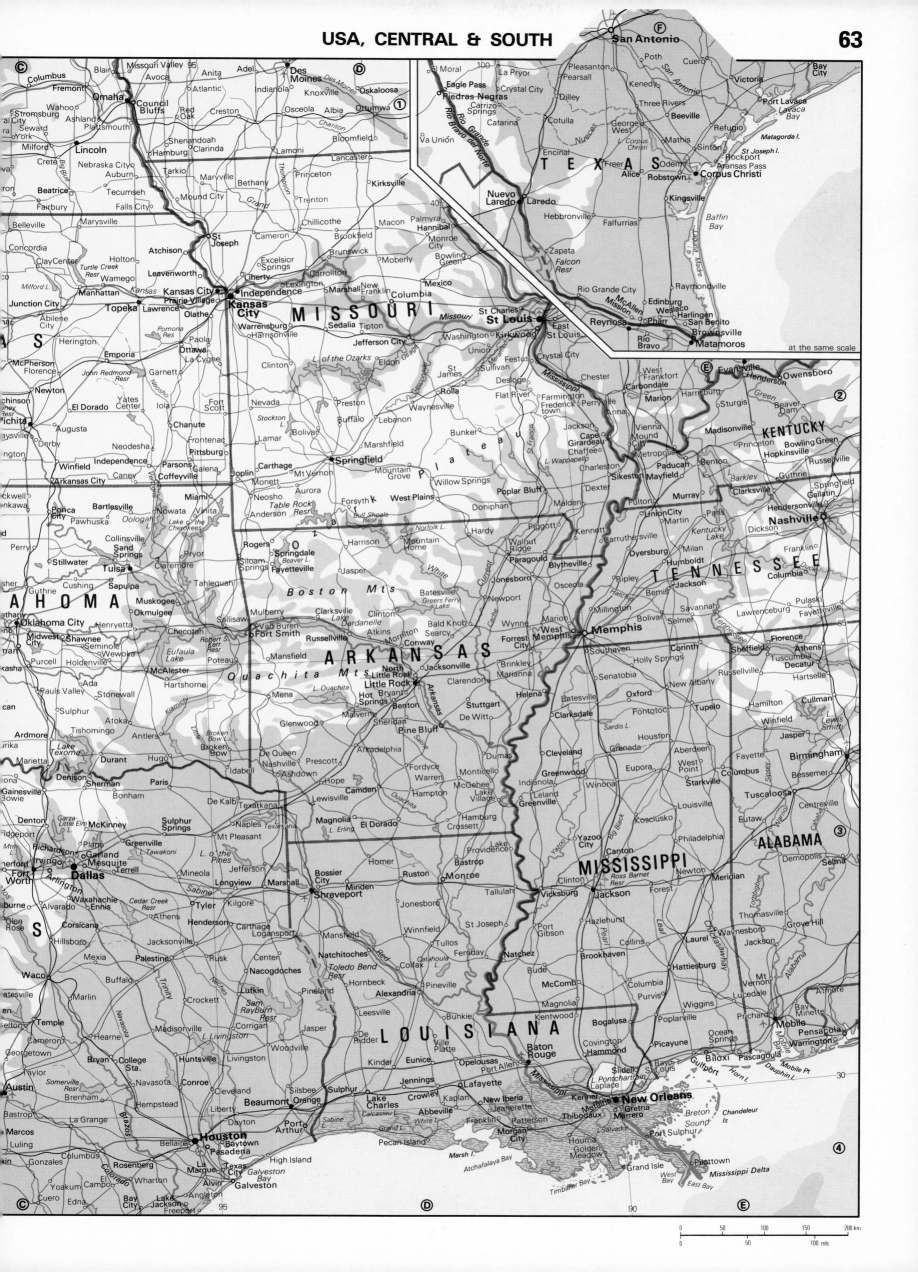

at the same scale

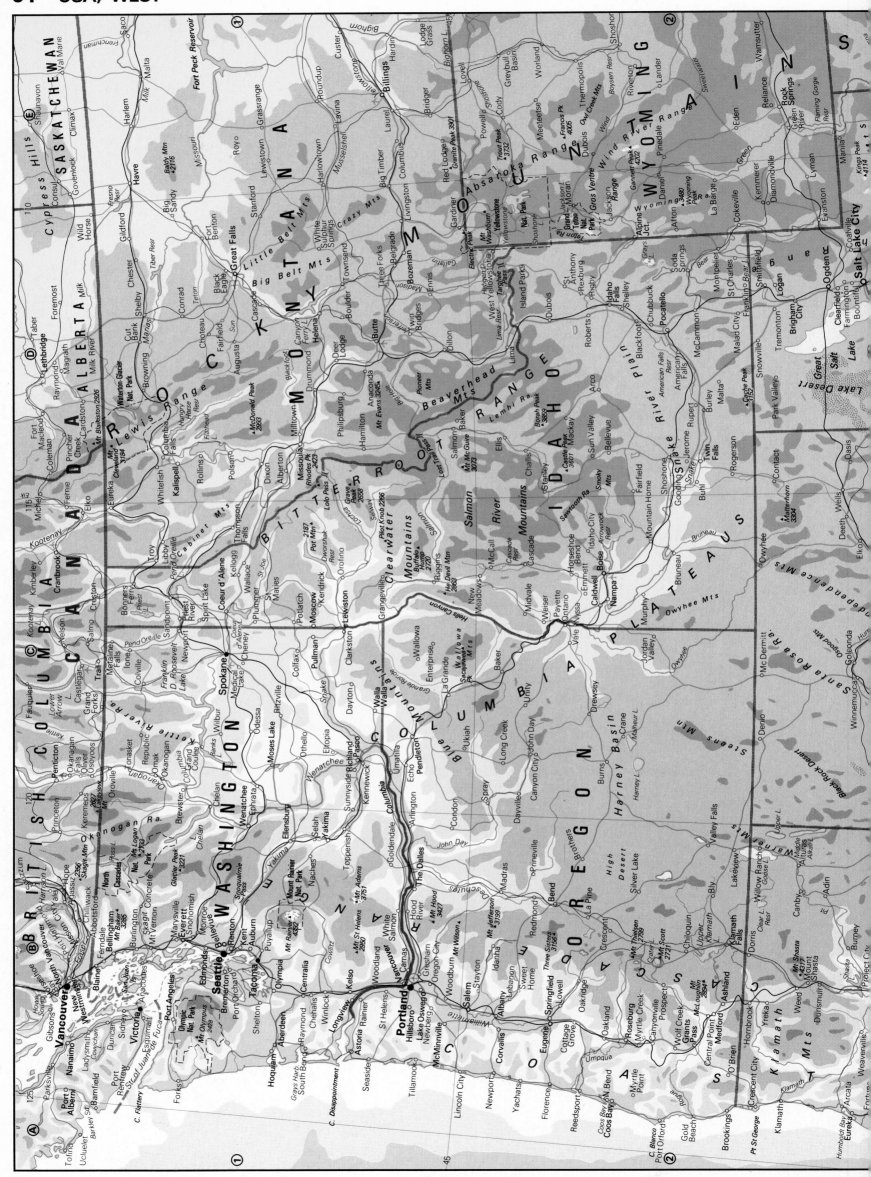

E

D

C

B

③ ④

Grand Valley
Mack Fruita
Uncompahgre Plateau
Grand Junction ③
Roan Plateau
Grand Mesa
Uravan
Duchesne
Price
Green River
Green
Dolores
Dove Creek
Cortez
Shiprock
Trohatchi
Gallup
Zuni
Quemado
Alpine
Springerville
McNary
St Johns
Clifton
Glenwood
Bowie
Willcox
Chiricahua Peak 2986
Agua Prieta
Douglas
Bisbee
Tombstone
110
Nogales

COLORADO
Castle Dale
Ephraim
Manti
Moab
Brendel
Monticello
Abajo Mts
Blanding
Bluff
Mexican Hat
Monument Valley
San Juan
Kayenta
Ganado
opalocca
Joseph City
Petrified Forest Nat. Park
Holbrook
Snowflake
Show Low
Globe
San Carlos
Kearny
Hayden
Safford
Mt Graham 3265
Mammoth
Benson
Sierra Vista
Mt Wrightson 2879

UTAH
Mt Pleasant
Gunnison
Salina
Richfield
Mt Marvine 3540
Bicknell
Mt Ellen 3540
Escalante
Lake Powell
Page
Tuba City
Winslow
Flagstaff
Humphreys Peak 3826
Cottonwood
Camp Verde
Black Canyon City
Miami
Superior
Florence
Coolidge
Eloy
Marana
Catalina
Tucson
Green Valley
NOGALES

Eureka
Nephi
Mt Nebo
Ephraim
Holden
Fillmore
Delta
Beaver
Junction
Mt Dutton 3621
Panguitch
Henrieville
Kanab
Marble Canyon
Grand Canyon Nat. Park
Grand Canyon
Williams
Sedona
Prescott
Mayer
Wickenburg
El Mirage
Glendale
Avondale
Buckeye
Gila Bend Mts
Gila Bend
ARIZONA
Ajo
Lukeville
Sonoita
SONORA

Granite Peak
Sevier Desert
Sevier L.
Delano Peak 3712
Cedar City
Parowan
Virgin
St George
Kaibab Plat.
Shivwits Plat.
Mt Trumbull 2449
Peach Springs
Bagdad
Scottsdale
Tempe Mesa
Chandler
Casa Grande
Phoenix
Sonora
Puerto Peñasco

GREAT
Wheeler Peak 4011
Schell Creek Range
Egan Range
Washington
Overton
Mesquite
Grand Canyon
Hualapai Peak 2519
Yucca
Kingman
Topock
Lake Havasu City
Parker
Quartzsite
Gila
Gadsden
Yuma
Gran Desierto
El Golfo de Santa Clara
G. de California

Roberts Creek Mtn
McGill
Ely
Ruth
Pioche
Panaca
Caliente
Alamo
Black Mts
Searchlight
Mohave L.
Earp
Blythe
Ehrenberg
Colorado
BAJA CALIFORNIA NORTE
MEXICO
Pto. Peñasco

NEVADA
Eureka
Austin
Summits Mtn 3188
Mt Jefferson 3642
Warm Springs
Tonopah
Goldfield
Hiko
Indian Springs
Las Vegas
Paradise
Henderson
Boulder City
Lake Mead
Needles
Patagonia
Desert Center
Niland
Calipatria
Brawley
El Centro
Calexico
Mexicali
San Luis

Wildcat Pk 3303
Monitor Range
Shoshone Mts
Gabbs
Coaldale
Boundary Peak 4005
Spring Mts
Charleston Peak 3631
Sloan
Nipton
Clark Mtn 2403
Baker
Ludlow
Barstow
Twentynine Palms
San Bernardino Mts
Palm Springs
Coachella
Mecca
Salton Sea
Imperial Valley
Tecate
Descanso
El Sauzal
Ensenada

Lovelock
Carson Sink
Fallon
Schurz
Walker L.
Hawthorne
Mina
Piper Pk 2880
White Mtn Peak 4342
Bishop
Big Pine
Death Valley
Panamint Range
Telescope Peak 3368
Shoshone
Johannesburg
Victorville
San Antonio San Bernardino
Redlands
Beaumont
San Jacinto Peak 3291
Palomar Mtn 1871
Ramona
Escondido
Vista
Oceanside
Carlsbad
San Clemente
Santo Tomas
Bahía de Todos Santos
Cabo Punta Banda

Pyramid L.
Fernley
Sparks
RENO
Virginia City
Silver City
Carson City
Stewart
Yerington
Bridgeport
Mono L.
Mt Grant 3426
Benton
Owens L.
Keeler
Lone Pine
Independence
Owens
Inyokern
Mojave
Lancaster
Arvin
Tehachapi Mts
Fillmore
Santa Paula
Ventura
Oxnard
Oildale
Bakersfield
Wasco
Delano
Santa Maria
Lompoc
Pt Conception
Santa Barbara
Santa Barbara Chan
Santa Cruz
Santa Rosa
San Miguel
San Nicholas I.
Channel Islands
Santa Catalina
Santa Monica
Beverly Hills
Burbank
Glendale
Pasadena
LOS ANGELES
Pomona
Riverside
Anaheim
Santa Ana
Long Beach
Huntington Beach
Laguna Beach
San Clemente
Gulf of Santa Catalina
La Mesa
El Cajon
National City
Chula Vista
SAN DIEGO
Tijuana

Stillwater Range
Eastgate
Carson
S. Lake Tahoe
Mt Whitney 4418
Kings Canyon Nat. Park
Sequoia Nat. Park
Pine Flat Res.
Exeter
Visalia
Porterville
Earlimart
Tulare
McFarland
Shafter
PACIFIC OCEAN

SIERRA NEVADA
Quincy
Feather R.
Donner Pass
Tahoe L.
Colfax
Auburn
Placerville
Sutter Creek
Jackson
Sonora
San Andreas
Oakdale
Modesto
Turlock
Merced
Madera
Fresno
Hanford
Lemoore
Coalinga
Kings River
Paso Robles
San Luis Obispo
Santa Margarita
Grover City
Pt Arena

CALIFORNIA
Chico
Paradise
Oroville
Marysville
Yuba City
Grass Valley
Roseville
SACRAMENTO
Galt
Lodi
Stockton
Lathrop
Manteca
Gustine
Los Banos
San Joaquin
Diablo Range
King City
Salinas
Gonzales
Soledad
Santa Lucia Range
Morro Bay

Red Bluff
Willows
Williams
Woodland
Davis
Vacaville
Fairfield
Antioch
Concord
Walnut Creek
Livermore
San Jose
Santa Clara
Sunnyvale
Gilroy
Watsonville
Santa Cruz
Monterey
Pt Pinos
Monterey Bay

Clear L.
Lakeport
Healdsburg
Santa Rosa
Petaluma
Napa
Sonoma
Vallejo
San Rafael
Berkeley
OAKLAND
Alameda
Hayward
SAN FRANCISCO
Daly City
San Mateo
Redwood City
San Carlos
Los Gatos

Fort Bragg
Ukiah
Russian R.
Bodega Head
Pt Reyes

Cummings
Willits

Sacramento Valley
Sacramento R.

③ ④

0   50   100   150   200 km
0   50   100 mls

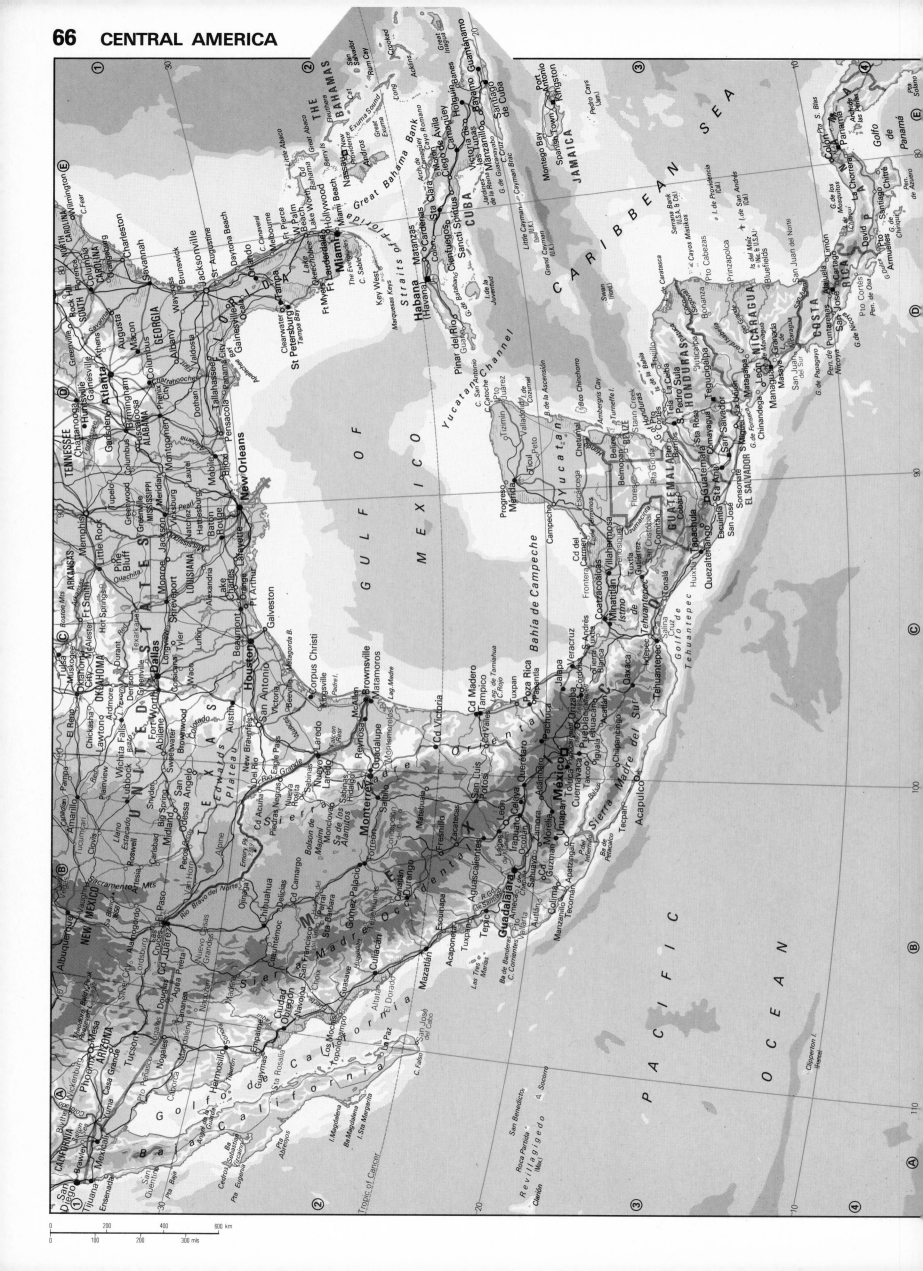

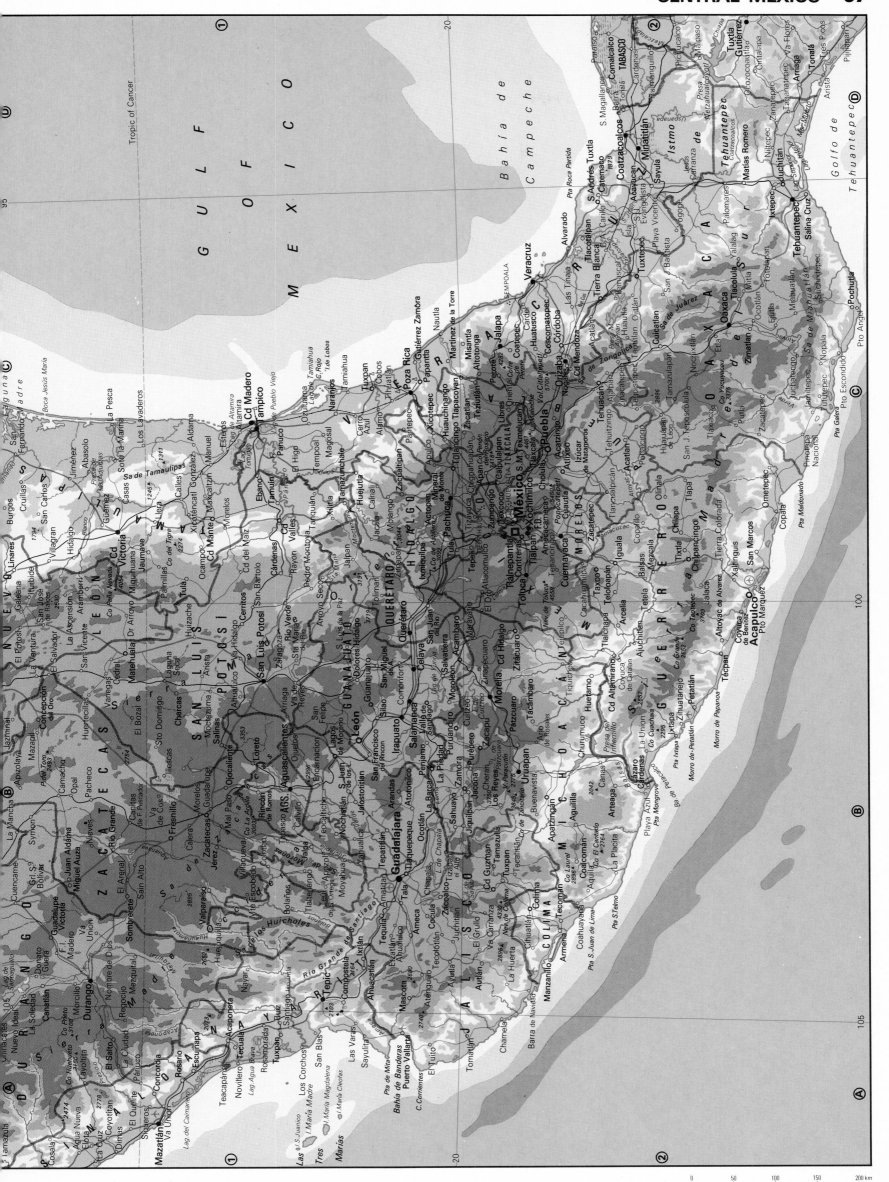

Tropic of Cancer

G U L F   O F   M E X I C O

Bahía de Campeche

Golfo de Tehuantepec

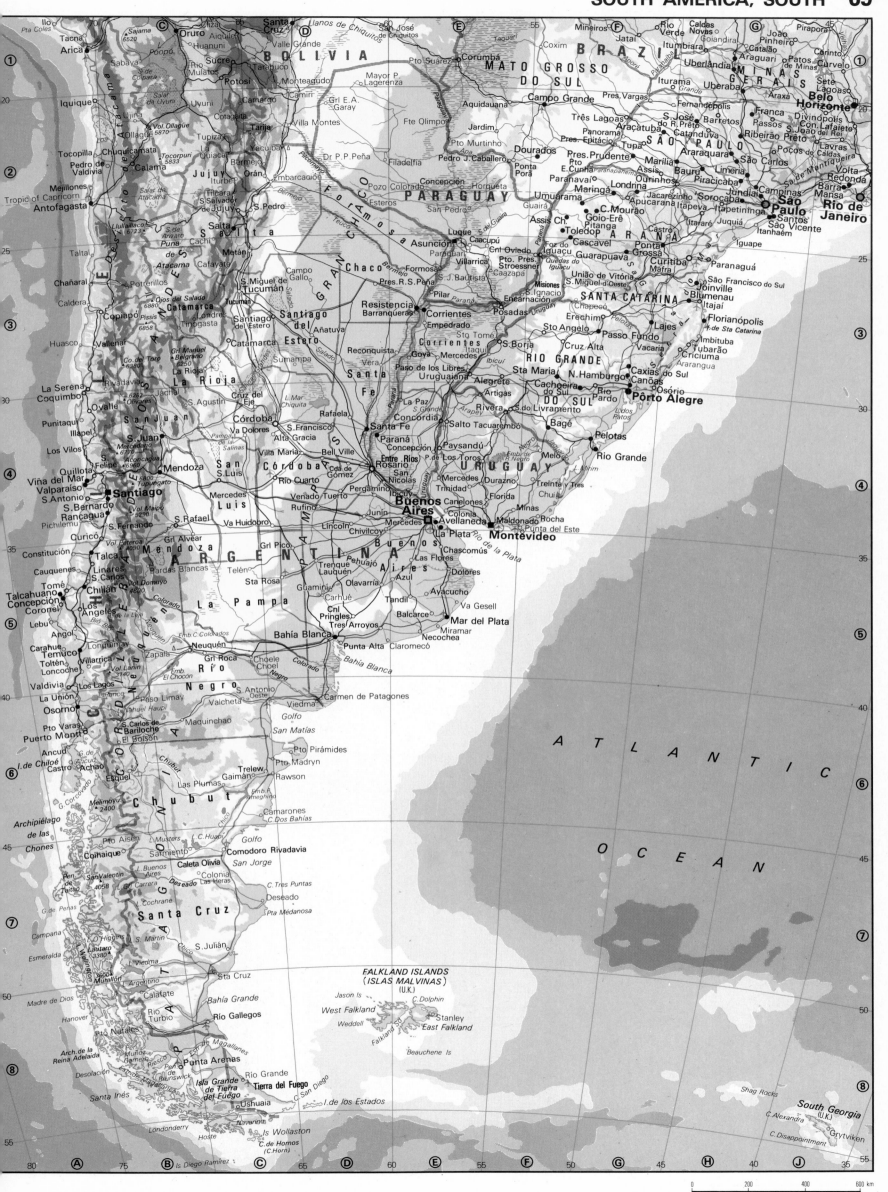

Countries: NICARAGUA, COSTA RICA, PANAMA, COLOMBIA, VENEZUELA, ECUADOR, PERU, BOLIVIA, CHILE, ARGENTINA, AMAZONAS, RORAIMA, RONDÔNIA, ACRE

Oceans/Seas: PACIFIC OCEAN

Selected place names:

Siguatepeque, Comayagua, Tegucigalpa, San Miguel, Somoto, Choluteca, Chinandega, Esteli, Matagalpa, León, La Unión, Managua, Masaya, Granada, Bluefields, Rivas, S. Carlos, L. de Nicaragua, Pto Cabezas, I. de Providencia (Col.), I. de San Andrés (Col.), I. de Perlas

San José, Cartago, Heredia, Limón, Alajuela, Puntarenas, Pen. de Nicoya, G. de Nicoya, B. de Coronado, Pto Armuelles, David, Santiago, Chitré, Pen. de Azuero, Colón, Panamá, La Chorrera, La Palma, G. de Panamá, Arch. de las Perlas, G. de Chiriqui, I. Coiba, Pta Mariato

Sta Marta, Ciénaga, Barranquilla, Cartagena, Ríohacha, Maicao, Valledupar, S. Jacinto, Sincelejo, Magangué, Montería, Caucasia, El Banco, Ocaña, Turbo, G. de Urabá, Quibdó, Yarumal, Pto Berrío, Bello, Barbosa, Medellín, Itagüí, Manizales, Pereira, Cartago, Armenia, Bogotá, Tuluá, Ibagué, Buga, Girardot, Villavicencio, Buenaventura, Palmira, Cali, Granada, Santander, Neiva, Popayán, Vol. Puracé, Pto Rico, Tumaco, El Divisio, Pasto, Florencia, Belén, S. Lorenzo, Ipiales, Mocoa, Pto Asis, Esmeraldas, Ibarra, Tulcán, Otavalo, Cojimies, Quito, Coca, Lago Agrio, Leguizamo, Jama, Chone, Cotopaxi, Tena, Napo, Manta, Ambato, Chimborazo, Guaranda, Riobamba, Guayaquil, Bebahoyo, Milagro, Macas, La Libertad, Azogues, Playas, Cuenca, Gualaceo, I. Puná, Machala, Tumbes, Zaruma, Loja, Zamora, Talara, Negritos, Sullana, Paita, Piura, Chulucanas, Catacaos, Huancabamba, Jaén, Yurimaguas, Moyobamba, Tarapoto, Lambayeque, Ferreñafe, Chachapoyas, Chiclayo, Chepén, Cajamarca, Pacasmayo, Cajabamba, Huamachuco, Pucallpa, Trujillo, Otusco, Pomabamba, Tingo María, Huallanca, Huascarán, Chimbote, Huaraz, La Unión, Casma, Huánuco, Huarmey, Oxapampa, La Merced, Pativilca, Cerro de Pasco, Barranca, Tarma, Huacho, La Oroya, Jauja, Acobamba, Ancón, Callao, Huancayo, Lima, Huancavelica, Machu Picchu, Chincha Alta, Ayacucho, Cuzco, Pisco, Andahuaylas, Ica, Abancay, Sicuani, Nazca, Ayaviri, Chala, Juliaca, Sta Ana, Coropuna, Puno, Coroico, Camaná, Arequipa, Misti, Juli, L. Titicaca, Ancohuma, La Paz, Matarani, Moquegua, Mollendo, Tacna, Sajama, Oruro, Huanuni, Cochabamba, Santa Cruz, Quillacollo, Arica, Poopó, Sucre, Potosí, Iquique, Salar de Uyuni, Uyuni, Tarija, Tocopilla, Chuquicamata, Calama, Pedro de Valdivia, Mejillones, Antofagasta, S. Salvador de Jujuy, Jujuy, Salta

Maracaibo, Cabimas, Machiques, Cd Ojeda, Trujillo, Valera, Coro, Pto Fijo, G. de Venezuela, Pen. de Paraguaná, Aruba, Curaçao, Bonaire, Willemstad, Neth. Antilles, Is Los Roques, La Tortuga, Valencia, Maracay, Caracas, Maiquetia, Pto Cabello, Barquisimeto, Acarigua, San Juan, Cumaná, Barcelona, Pto la Cruz, Anaco, El Tigre, Barinas, Guanare, V. de la Pascua, Zárara, Bucaramanga, Pamplona, Cúcuta, San Cristóbal, Mérida, Bolívar, Arauca, Apure, San Fernando, Pto Carreño, Pto Ayacucho, Meta, Vichada, Orocué, Calamar, Mitú, Vaupés, Inírida, Guainía, Guaviare, Yari, Caquetá, Iquitos, Leticia, Tabatinga, Caxias, Elvira, Cruzeiro do Sul, Feijó, Sena Madureira, Rio Branco, Brasiléia, Cobija, Porvenir, Pto Heath, Riberalta, Guajará-Mirim, Porto Velho, Humaitá, Lábrea, Tefé, Manacapuru, La Asunción, Carúpano, Güiria, Maturín, Barrancas, Cd Guayana, Cd Bolívar, Upata, El Dorado, Sta Elena, Boa Vista, Cucui, Içana, Tapurucuara, Negro, Branco, Orinoco, Caroní, Emb. de Gurí

Islands (insets):

ISLAS GALÁPAGOS (ARCHIPIÉLAGO DO COLÓN) (Equ.) — Culpepper, Wenman, Pinta, Marchena, Genovesa, Fernandina, Isabela, Santa Cruz, San Cristóbal, San Salvador, Baquerizo Moreno, Santa Maria, Española

Islas Juan Fernández (Chile) — Alejandro Selkirk, Robinson Crusoe, Sta Clara

Fort-de-France, Martinique (Fr.), Roseau, ST LUCIA, Castries, ST VINCENT, Kingstown, The Grenadines, GRENADA, St George's

Scale: 0 200 400 600 km / 0 100 200 300 mils

at the same scale

Tropic of Capricorn

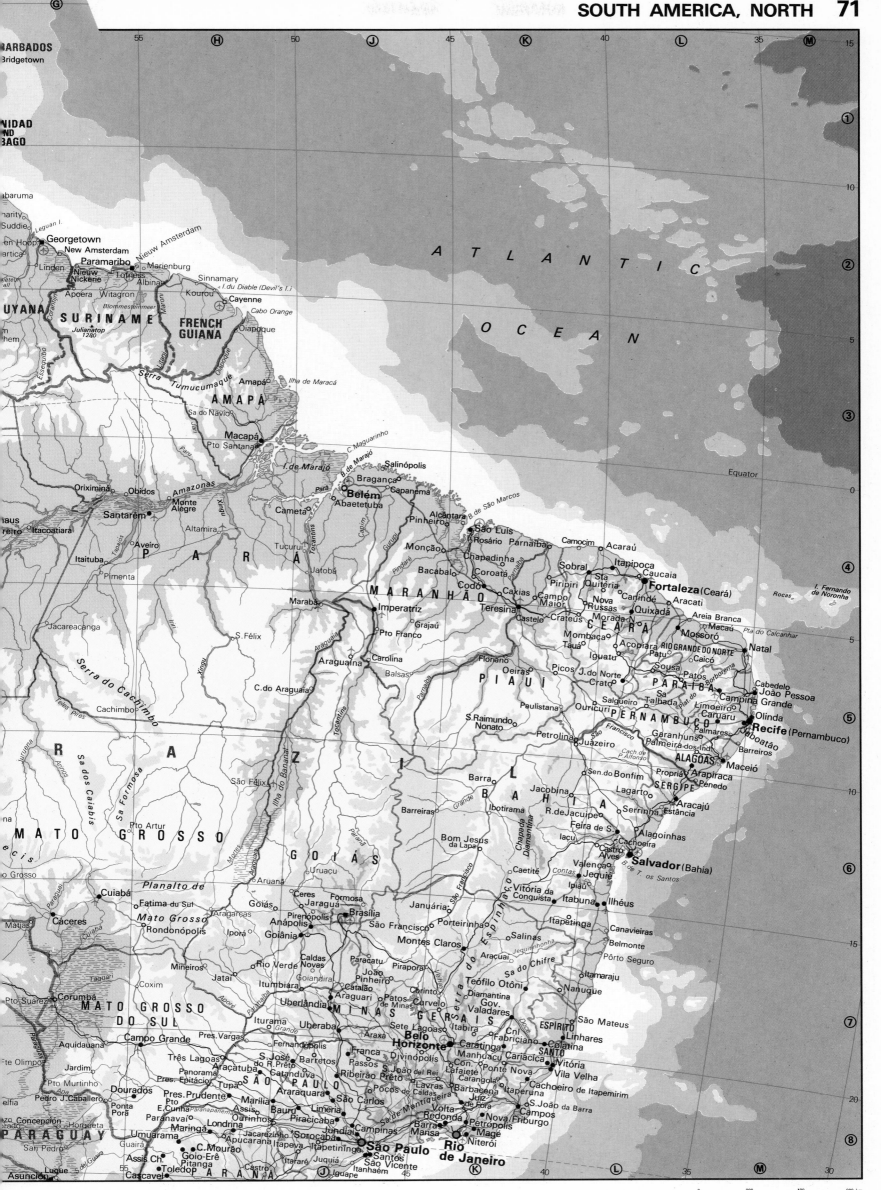

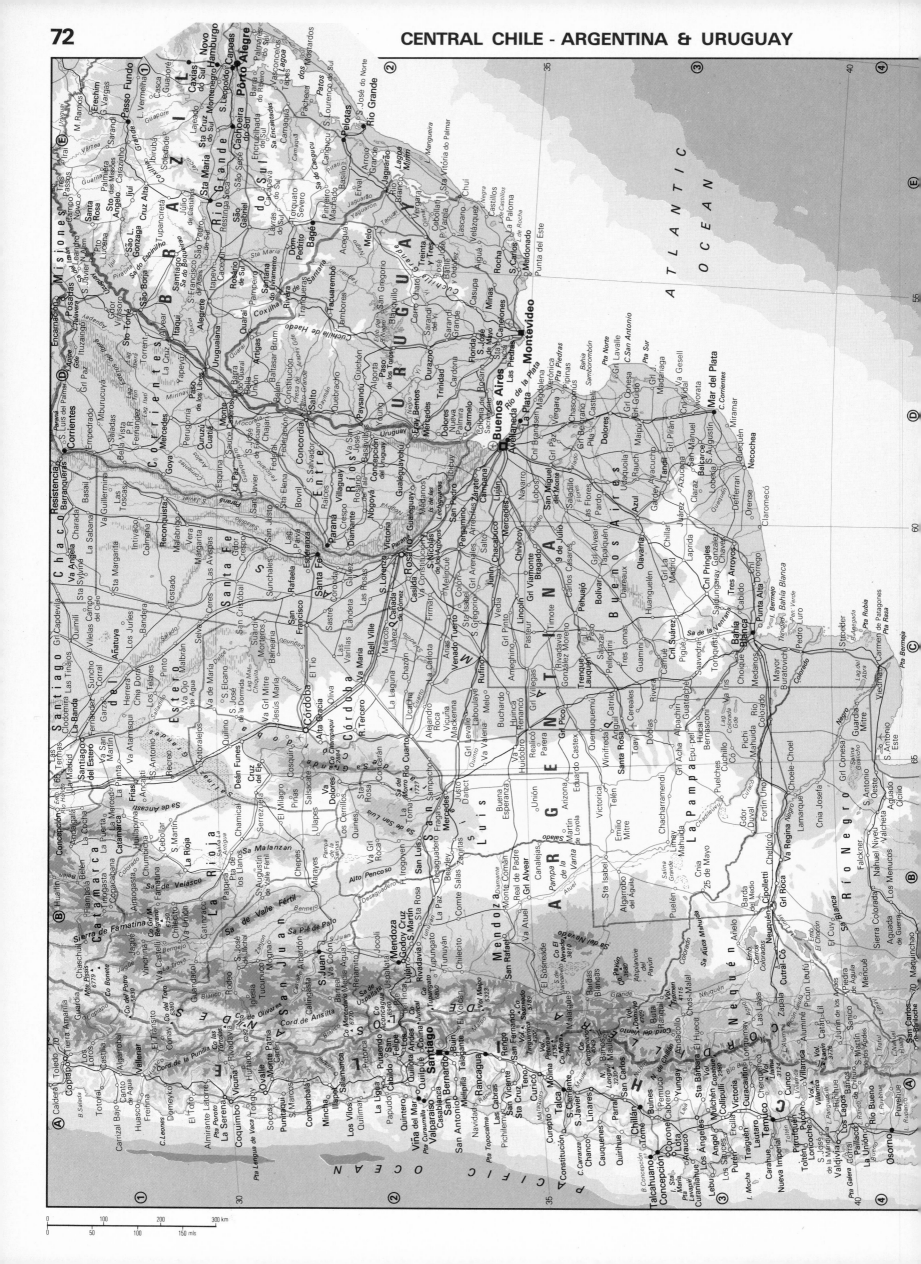

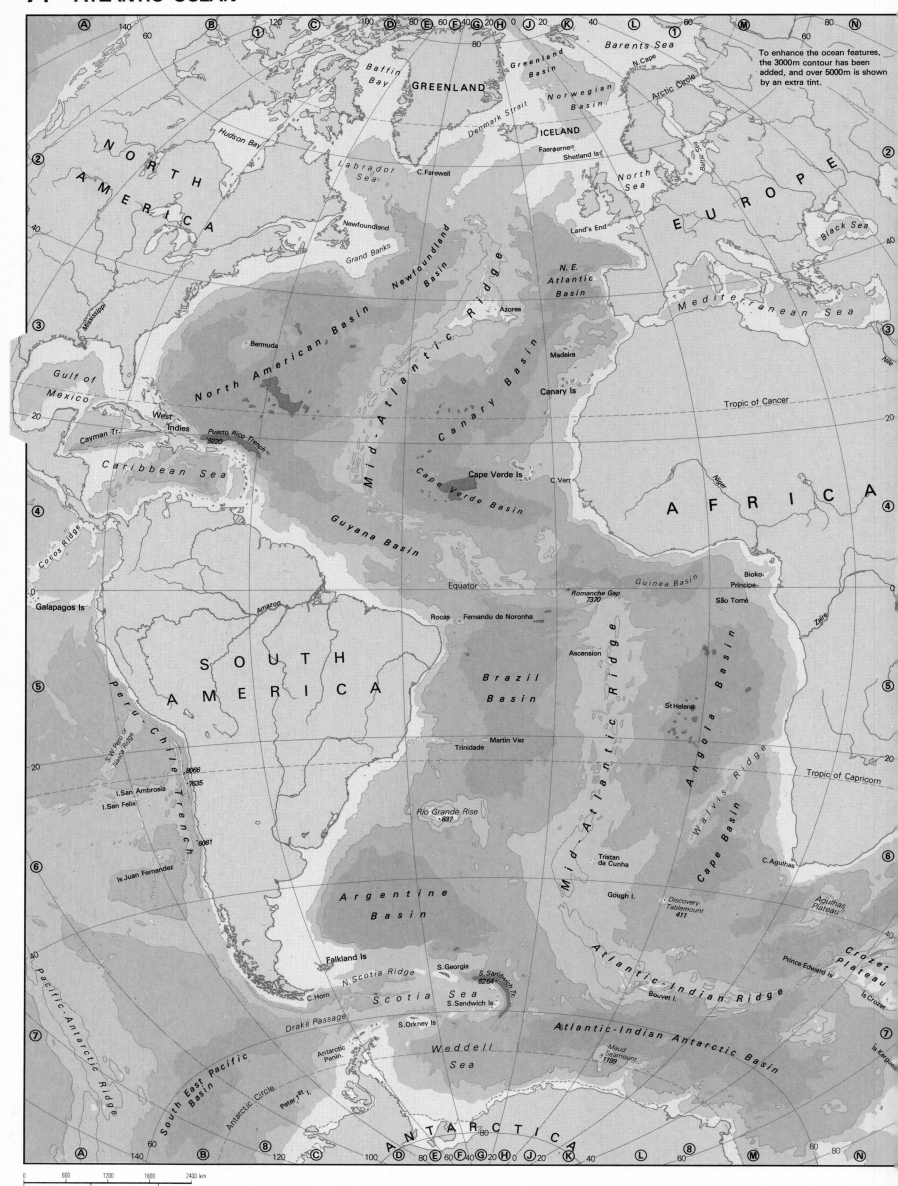

To enhance the ocean features, the 3000m contour has been added, and over 5000m is shown by an extra tint.

NORTH AMERICA

EUROPE

AFRICA

SOUTH AMERICA

ANTARCTICA

Baffin Bay

GREENLAND

Greenland Basin

Barents Sea

N.Cape

Norwegian Basin

Arctic Circle

Denmark Strait

ICELAND

Hudson Bay

Labrador Sea

C.Farewell

Faerøerne

Shetland Is

North Sea

Land's End

Black Sea

Newfoundland

Grand Banks

Newfoundland Basin

N.E. Atlantic Basin

Mediterranean Sea

Bermuda

North American Basin

Azores

Mid-Atlantic Ridge

Canary Basin

Madeira

Canary Is

Tropic of Cancer

Gulf of Mexico

Mississippi

West Indies

Puerto Rico Trench
·9220

Cayman Tr.

Caribbean Sea

Cape Verde Is

Cape Verde Basin

C.Vert

Guyana Basin

Cocos Ridge

Galapagos Is

Equator

Guinea Basin

Romanche Gap
7370

Bioko
Príncipe

São Tomé

Niger

Zaïre

Amazon

Rocas

Fernando de Noronha

Brazil Basin

Ascension

St Helena

Angola Basin

Peru or Chile Trench

S.W. Peru or Nasca Ridge

I.San Ambrosia
I.San Felix

·8066
·7635

·6081

Is Juan Fernández

Mid-Atlantic Ridge

Martin Vaz
Trinidade

Rio Grande Rise
·637

Tropic of Capricorn

Walvis Ridge

Cape Basin

Tristan da Cunha

Gough I.

Discovery Tablemount
411

C.Agulhas

Agulhas Plateau

Argentine Basin

Falkland Is

N.Scotia Ridge

S.Georgia

S.Sandwich Tr.
8264

C.Horn

Scotia Sea

S.Sandwich Is

S.Orkney Is

Atlantic-Indian Ridge

Prince Edward Is

Bouvet I.

Crozet Plateau

Is Crozet

Pacific-Antarctic Ridge

Drake Passage

Antarctic Peninsula

Weddell Sea

Atlantic-Indian Antarctic Basin

Maud Seamount
1199

Is Kerguel

Antarctic Circle

Peter 1st I.

South East Pacific Basin

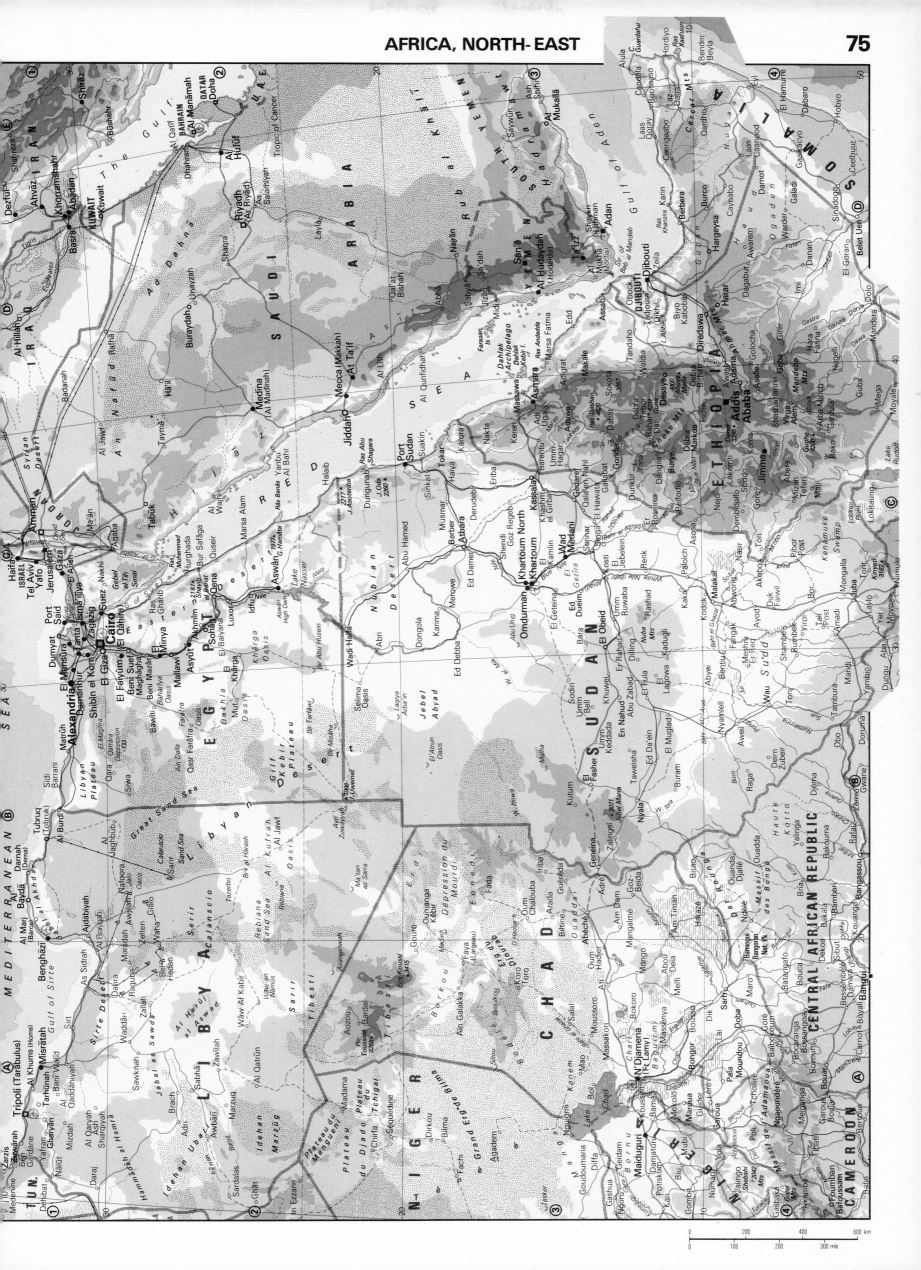

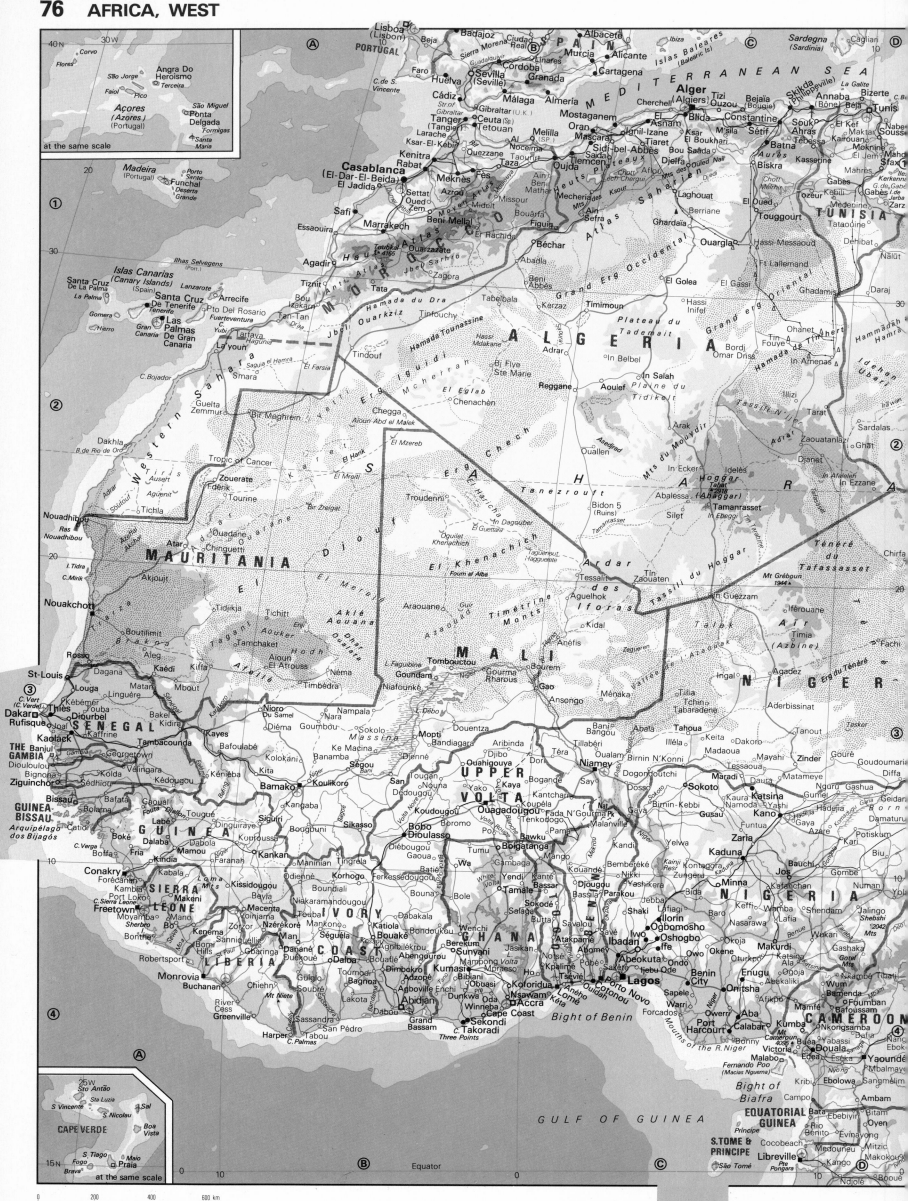

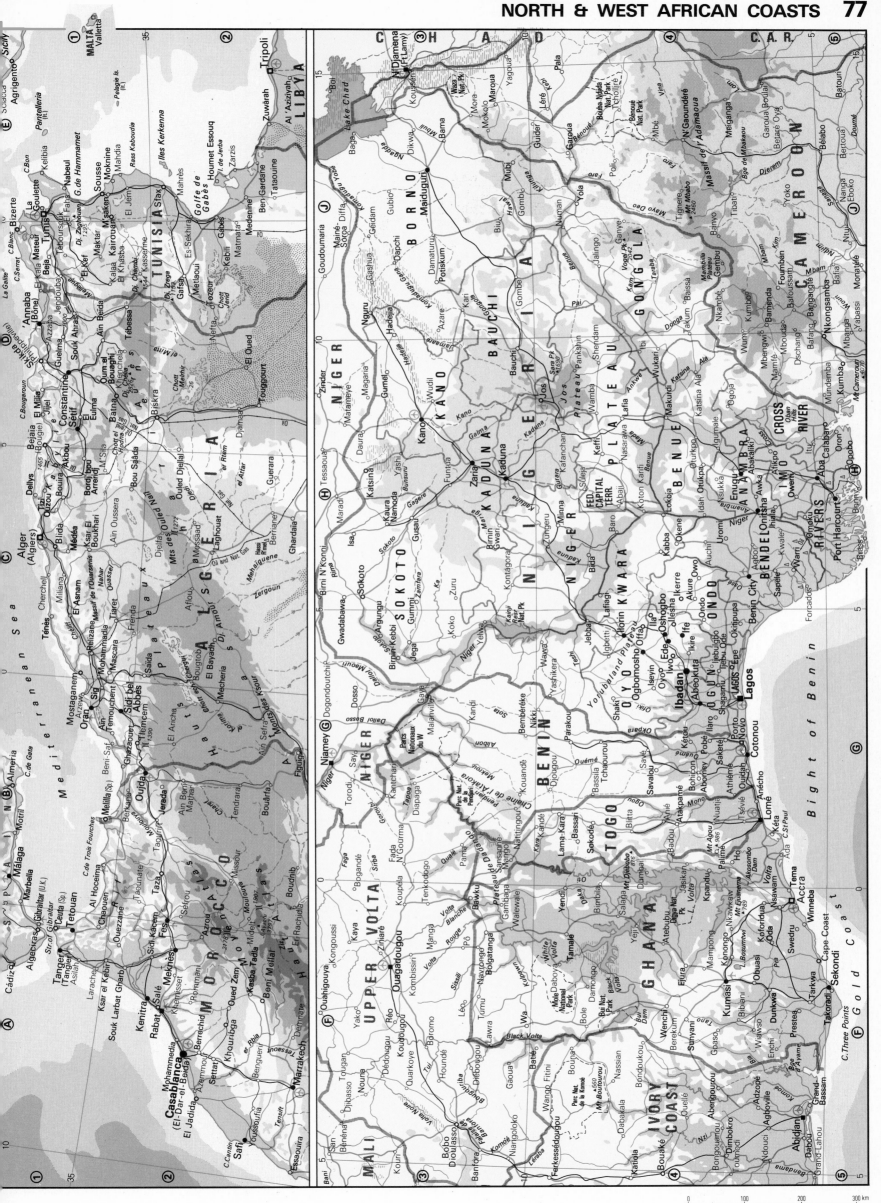

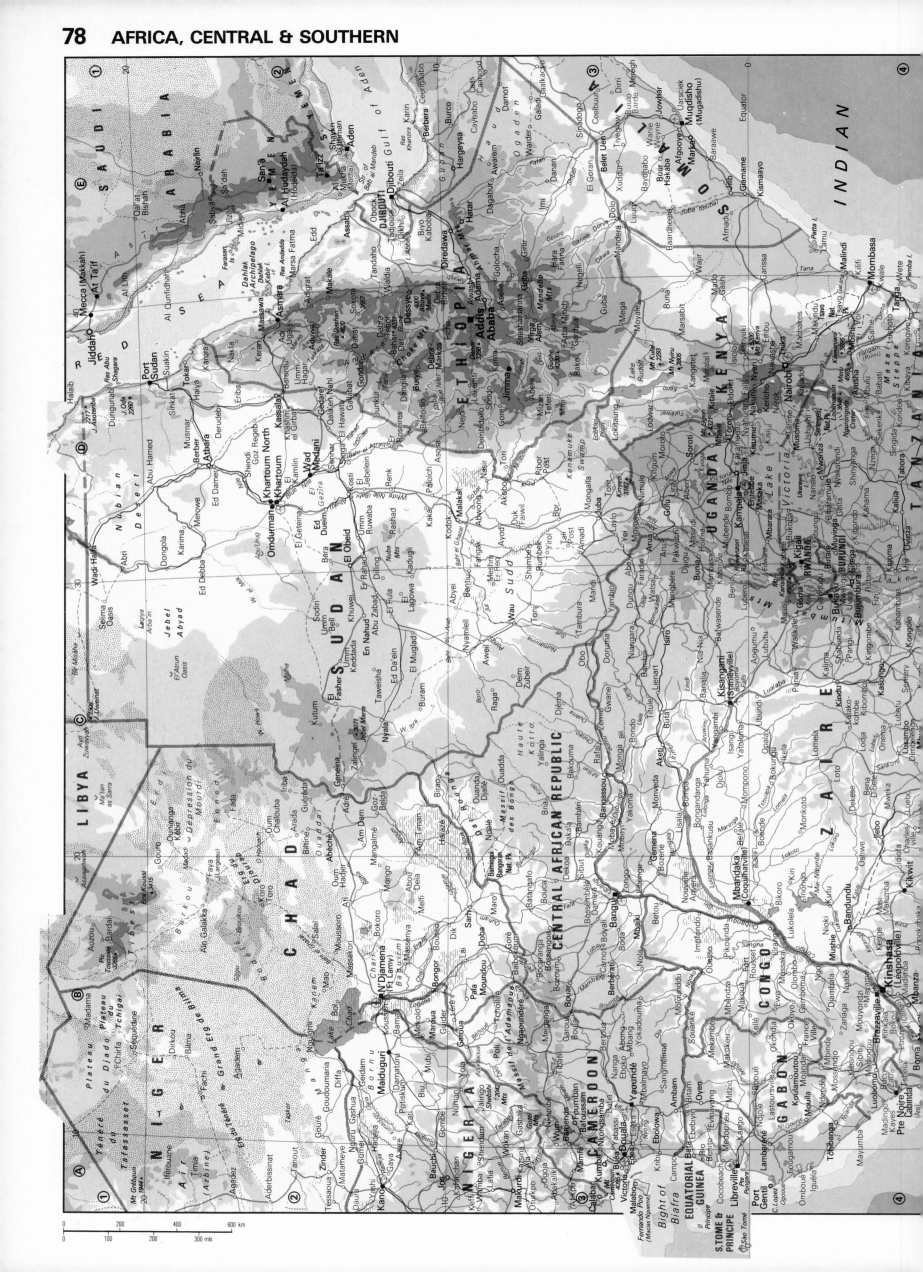

OCEAN

SEYCHELLES

COMOROS

Moroni

ATLANTIC OCEAN

INDIAN OCEAN

Mozambique Channel

MADAGASCAR (MALAGASY REP.)

Antananarivo (Tananarive)

MADAGASCAR (MALAGASY REP.)
at the same scale 50

MAURITIUS
Port Louis
Round I.

Réunion (Fr.)
St Denis.
at the same scale

ANGOLA

Luanda
Lobito
Benguela
Novo Redondo
Moçâmedes (Mossâmedes)

ZAMBIA

Lusaka
Ndola
Kitwe
Chingola
Chililabombwe
Mufulira
Luanshya
Kabwe
Lubumbashi
Elisabethville
Likasi

MALAWI

Blantyre
Zomba
Lilongwe

MOZAMBIQUE

Nampula
Quelimane
Beira
Sofala (Beira)
Maputo
Lourenço Marques

ZIMBABWE

Harare
Salisbury
Bulawayo
Gweru
Mutare

BOTSWANA

Gaborone
Francistown
Kalahari Desert

NAMIBIA (S.W. AFRICA)

Windhoek
Walvis Bay
Swakopmund
Lüderitz
Namib Desert

SOUTH AFRICA

TRANSVAAL
Pretoria
Johannesburg

ORANGE FREE STATE
Bloemfontein

CAPE PROVINCE
Cape Town
Cape of Good Hope
Port Elizabeth
East London
Kimberley

LESOTHO
Maseru

SWAZILAND
Manzini

Durban
Pietermaritzburg

Tropic of Capricorn

Scale:
0 — 200 — 400 — 600 km
0 — 100 — 200 — 300 mls

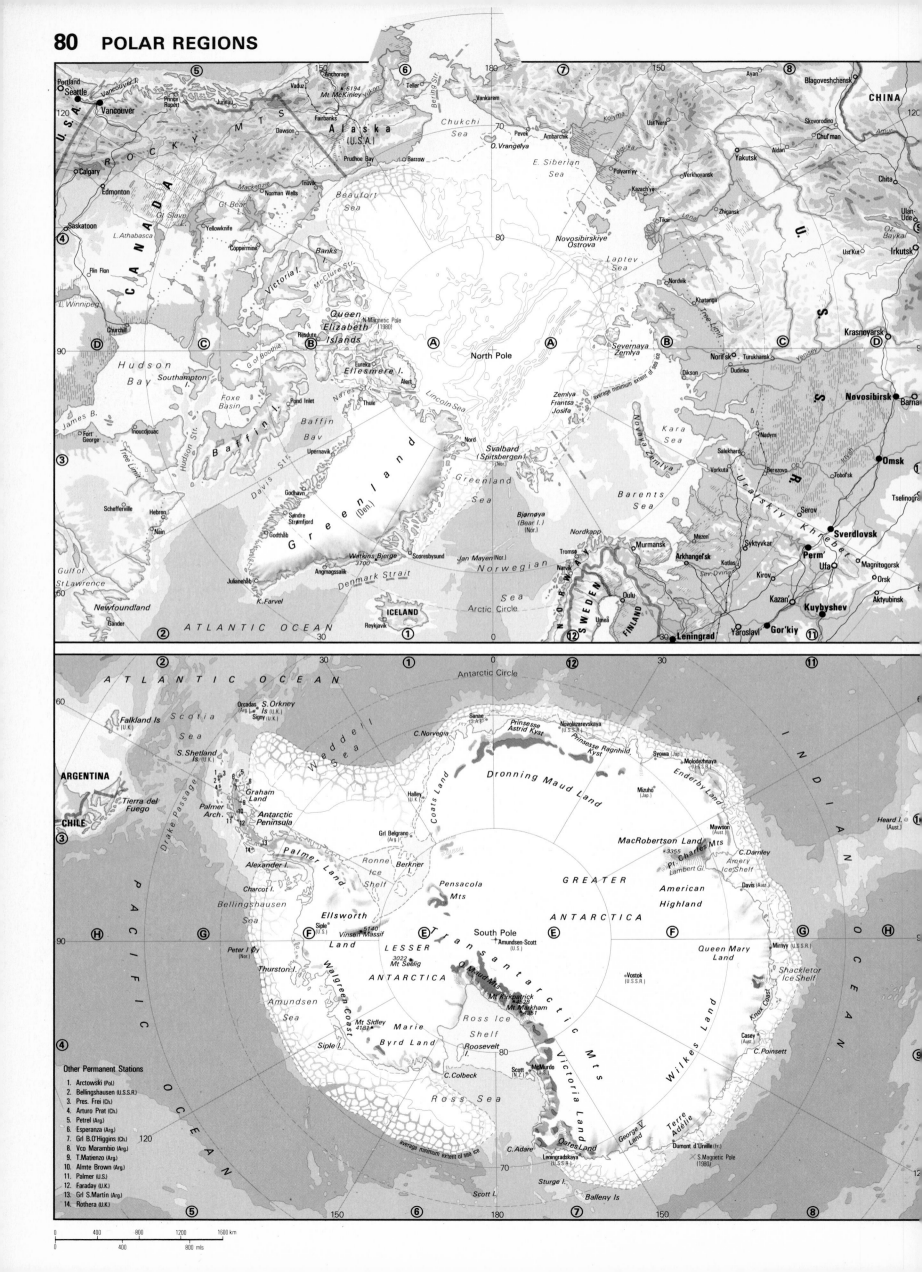

Index

Introduction to the index

In the index, the first number refers to the page, and the following letter and number to the section of the map in which the index entry can be found. For example, Paris 18C2 means that Paris can be found on page 18 where column C and row 2 meet.

Abbreviations used in the index

Afghan	Afghanistan	Hung	Hungary	Pol	Poland	Arch	Archipelago
Alb	Albania	Ind	Indonesia	Port	Portugal	B	Bay
Alg	Algeria	Irish Rep	Ireland	Rom	Romania	C	Cape
Ant	Antarctica	N Ire	Ireland, Northern	S Arabia	Saudi Arabia	Chan	Channel
Arg	Argentina	Leb	Lebanon	Scot	Scotland	Gl	Glacier
Aust	Australia	Lib	Liberia	Sen	Senegal	I(s)	Island(s)
Bang	Bangladesh	Liech	Liechtenstein	S Africa	South Africa	Lg	Lagoon
Belg	Belgium	Lux	Luxembourg	S Yemen	South Yemen	L	Lake
Bol	Bolivia	Madag	Madagascar	Switz	Switzerland	Mt(s)	Mountain(s)
Bulg	Bulgaria	Malay	Malaysia	Tanz	Tanzania	O	Ocean
Camb	Cambodia	Maur	Mauritania	Thai	Thailand	P	Pass
Can	Canada	Mor	Morocco	Turk	Turkey	Pass	Passage
CAR	Central African Republic	Mozam	Mozambique	USSR	Union of Soviet Socialist	Pen	Peninsula
Czech	Czechoslovakia	Neth	Netherlands		Republics	Plat	Plateau
Den	Denmark	NZ	New Zealand	USA	United States of America	Pt	Point
Dom Rep	Dominican Republic	Nic	Nicaragua	U Volta	Upper Volta	Res	Reservoir
E Germ	East Germany	Nig	Nigeria	Urug	Uruguay	R	River
El Sal	El Salvador	Nor	Norway	Ven	Venezuela	S	Sea
Eng	England	Pak	Pakistan	Viet	Vietnam	Sd	Sound
Eq Guinea	Equatorial Guinea	PNG	Papua New Guinea	W Germ	West Germany	Str	Strait
Eth	Ethiopia	Par	Paraguay	Yugos	Yugoslavia		
Fin	Finland	Phil	Philippines	Zim	Zimbabwe		

A

Aachen W Germ	20B2
Aalst Belg	16C1
Äänekoski Fin	12K6
Aarau Switz	17C1
Aare R Switz	17B1
Aba China	40A3
Aba Nig	77H4
Aba Zaïre	78D3
Abādān Iran	34B2
Ābādeh Iran	34C2
Abadla Alg	76B1
Abaeté Brazil	73C2
Abaeté R Brazil	73C2
Abaetetuba Brazil	71J4
Abagnar Qi China	40D1
Abaji Nig	77H4
Abajo Mts USA	65E3
Abakaliki Nig	77H4
Abakan USSR	27L4
Abala Niger	76C3
Abalessa Alg	76C2
Abancay Peru	70D6
Abarqū Iran	34C2
Abashiri Japan	41E3
Abashiri-wan B Japan	41E3
Abasolo Mexico	67C1
Abau PNG	39H7
Abaya L Eth	78D3
Abbai R Eth	78D2
Abbe L Eth	78E2
Abbeville France	18C1
Abbeville Louisiana USA	63D4
Abbeville S Carolina USA	61C2
Abbiategrasso Italy	17C2
Abbotsford Can	64B1
Abbotsford USA	58A2
Abbottabad Pak	35C2
Abd-al-Kuri I S Yemen	33F4
Abdulino USSR	24J5
Abéché Chad	78C2
Abengourou Ivory Coast	77F4
Åbenrå Den	12F7
Åbenra Den	20B1
Abeokuta Nig	77G4
Abera Eth	78D3
Aberaeron Wales	15C5
Aberdeen Maryland USA	59D3
Aberdeen Mississippi USA	61B2
Aberdeen S Africa	79C7
Aberdeen Scot	14D3
Aberdeen S Dakota USA	54D2
Aberdeen Washington USA	54A2
Aberdeen L Can	52J3
Aberfeldy Scot	14D3
Abergavenny Wales	15D6
Aberystwyth Wales	15C5
Abez' USSR	24L2
Abhā S Arabia	32D3
Abhar Iran	34B1
Abi Addi Eth	32C4
Abidjan Ivory Coast	77F4
Abilene USA	62C3
Abilene City USA	63C2
Abingdon Eng	15E6
Abingdon USA	58C3
Abitibi R Can	53K4
Abitibi,L Can	53L5
Abkhazskaya Republic USSR	25G7
Ablis France	16A2

Abohar India	35C2
Abomey Benin	77G4
Abong Mbang Cam	78B3
Aborlan Phil	45E9
Abou Deïa Chad	78B2
Abqaiq S Arabia	33E1
Abrantes Port	19A2
Abri Sudan	78D1
Abrolhos Is Aust	48A3
Absaroka Range Mts USA	54B2
Abū al Abyad I UAE	33F2
Abū 'Ali I S Arabia	33E1
Abū Arish S Arabia	32D3
Abu Deleiq Sudan	32B3
Abū Dhabi UAE	33F2
'Abu Dom Watercourse Sudan	32B3
Ābū el Jurdhān Jordan	31C3
Abu Fatima Sudan	32B3
Abu Hamed Sudan	78D2
Abu Kebir Hihya Egypt	31A3
Abunã Brazil	70E5
Abuna R Bol	70E6
Abú Sukhayr Iraq	30D3
Abu Suweir Egypt	31B3
Abut Head C NZ	51B2
Abu Tig Egypt	32B1
Abu'Urug Well Sudan	78D2
Abuye Meda Mt Eth	78D2
Abu Zabad Sudan	78C2
Abwong Sudan	78D3
Åby Den	20B1
Aby 'Aweigîla Well Egypt	31C3
Abyei Sudan	78C3
Acambaro Mexico	66B2
Acandi Colombia	68B5
Acaponeta Mexico	66B2
Acapulco Mexico	66B3
Acaraú Brazil	71L4
Acarigua Ven	70E2
Acatlán Mexico	66C3
Acatlan Mexico	67C2
Acatzingo Mexico	67C2
Acayucan Mexico	67D2
Accra Ghana	77F4
Aceguá Urug	72E2
Achalpur India	35D4
Achao Chile	69B6
Acheng China	41B2
Achensee L Austria	17D1
Achern W Germ	16E2
Achill I Irish Rep	13A3
Achinsk USSR	27L4
Ackley USA	57D3
Acklins I Caribbean	68C2
Acobamba Peru	70D6
Aconcagua Mt Chile	69B4
Acopiara Brazil	71L5
Acqui Italy	17C2
Acraman,L Aust	50A2
Acre = 'Akko	
Acre State Brazil	70D5
Actopan Mexico	67C1
Ada Ghana	77G4
Ada USA	63C3
Adaja R Spain	19B1
Adak I USA	56C6
Adam Oman	33G2
Adama Eth	78D3
Adamantina Brazil	73B3
Adamaoua Region Nig/Cam	78B3

Adamello Mt Italy	17D1
Adam's Bridge India/Sri Lanka	36B3
Adams,Mt USA	54A2
Adam's Peak Mt Sri Lanka	36C3
'Adan S Yemen	33E4
Adana Turk	25F8
Adapazari Turk	25E7
Adarama Sudan	32B3
Adare,C Ant	80F7
Adaut Indon	45D4
Adavale Aust	50B1
Adda R Italy	17C2
Ad Dahna' Region S Arabia	33E1
Ad Damman S Arabia	33F1
Ad Darb S Arabia	32D3
Ad Dawādimī S Arabia	32D2
Ad Dibdibah Region S Arabia	33E1
Ad Dikākah Region S Arabia	33F3
Ad Dilam S Arabia	33E2
Ad Dir'iyah S Arabia	33E2
Addis Ababa Eth	78D3
Addis Zeman Eth	32C4
Ad Dīwānīyah Iraq	30D3
Ad Dīī' S Yemen	32D4
Ad Duwayd S Arabia	30D3
Adel USA	57D3
Adelaide Aust	48C4
Adelaide Pen Can	52J3
Adelaide River Aust	39G8
Aden = 'Adan	
Aden,G of Yemen/Somalia	28C4
Aderbissinat Niger	76C3
Adhra Syria	31D2
Adi I Indon	39G7
Adige R Italy	22C1
Adigrat Eth	78D2
Adi Kale Eth	32C4
Adilābād India	35D5
Adin USA	64B2
Adirondack Mts USA	59E2
Adi Ugai Eth	78D2
Adiyaman Turk	30C2
Adjud Rom	23F1
Admiralty B USA	56G1
Admiralty I USA	52E4
Admiralty Inlet B Can	53K2
Admiralty Is PNG	48D1
Adonara I Indon	45B4
Adoni India	36B1
Adour R France	18B3
Adra Spain	19B2
Adrano Italy	17E2
Adrar Region Maur	76A2
Adrar Mts Alg	76C2
Adrar Soutouf Region Mor	76A2
Adré Chad	78C2
Adri Libya	75A2
Adria Italy	17E2
Adrian Michigan USA	58C2
Adrian Texas USA	62B2
Adriatic S Italy/Yugos	22C2
Aduwa Eth	78D2
Adycha R USSR	27P3
Adzopé Ivory Coast	77F4
Adz'va R USSR	24K2
Adz'vavom USSR	24K2
Aegean S Greece	23E3
Afghanistan Republic Asia	28E2
Afgooye Somalia	78E3
'Afif S Arabia	32D2
Afikpo Nig	77H4
Åfjord Nor	12G6

Aflou Alg	77C2
Afmadu Somalia	78E3
Afollé Region Maur	76A3
Afton New York USA	60C1
Afton Wyoming USA	64D2
Afula Israel	31C2
Afyon Turk	25E8
Aga Egypt	31A3
Agadem Niger	78B2
Agadez Niger	76C3
Agadir Mor	76B1
Agar India	35D4
Agartala India	37D3
Agassiz Can	64B1
Agattu I USA	56A6
Agattu Str USA	56A5
Agbor Nig	77H4
Agboville Ivory Coast	77F4
Agdam USSR	30E1
Agematsu Japan	42C3
Agen France	18C3
Agha Jārī Iran	34B2
Ağn Turk	25G8
Agno R Italy	17D2
Agordat Eth	32C3
Agordo Italy	17E1
Agou,Mt Togo	77G4
Agout R France	18C3
Àgra India	35D3
Ağri Turk	30D2
Agri R Italy	22D2
Agrigento Italy	22C3
Agrínion Greece	23E3
Agrio R Chile	72A3
Agropoli Italy	22C2
Agryz USSR	24J4
Agto Greenland	53N3
Agua Clara Brazil	73B3
Aguada de Guerra Arg	72B4
Aguadilla Puerto Rico	68D3
Aguado Cicilio Arg	72B4
Aguanava R Mexico	67B1
Aguapey R Arg	72D1
Agua Prieta Mexico	66B1
Aguaray Guazu Par	73A3
Aguascalientes Mexico	66B2
Aguascalientes State Mexico	67B1
Aguas Formosas Brazil	73D2
Agueda Port	19A1
Aguelhok Mali	76C3
Aguenit Well Mor	76A2
Aguilas Spain	19B2
Aguililla Mexico	67B2
Agulhas Basin Indian O	46C7
Agulhas,C S Africa	79C7
Agulhas Plat Indian O	46C6
Agusan R Phil	45G9
Ahaggar = Hoggar	
Ahar Iran	25H8
Ahipara B NZ	51B1
Ahlen W Germ	16D1
Ahmadābād India	35C4
Ahmadnagar India	36A1
Ahmar Mts Eth	78E3
Ahoskie USA	61D1
Ahr R W Germ	16D1
Ahrgebirge Region W Germ	16D1
Ahuacatlán Mexico	67B1
Ahualulco Mexico	67B1
Åhus Sweden	12G7
Ahvān Iran	34C1

Ahvāz Iran	34B2
Aiajuela Costa Rica	68A4
Aigle Switz	17B1
Aiguá Urug	72E2
Aiguille d'Arves Mt France	17B2
Aiguille de la Grand Sassière Mt France	17B2
Aihui China	41B1
Aikawa Japan	42C3
Aiken USA	61C2
Ailao Shan Upland China	40A5
Aimogasta Arg	72B1
Aimorés Brazil	73D2
Ain R France	17A1
Aïn el Beïda Alg	77D1
Ain Beni Mathar Mor	77B2
Ain Dalla Well Egypt	75B2
Aïn el Hadjel Alg	19C2
Aïn Galakka Chad	78B2
Aïn Oussera Alg	77C1
Aïn Sefra Alg	77B2
'Ain Sukhna Egypt	30B4
Ainsworth USA	57C3
Aïn Temouchent Alg	77B1
Aioi Japan	42B4
Aioun Abd el Malek Well Maur	76B2
Aïoun El Atrouss Maur	76B3
Aiquile Bol	70E7
Aïr Desert Region Niger	76C3
Aire France	16B1
Aire R Eng	15E5
Aire R France	16C2
Airforce I Can	53L3
Airolo Switz	17C1
Aishihik Can	52E3
Aishihik L Can	56L3
Aisne Department France	16B2
Aisne R France	18C2
Aitape PNG	48D1
Aiviekste R USSR	21F1
Aixa Zuogi China	40B2
Aix-en-Provence France	18D3
Aix-les-Bains France	17A2
Aiyar Res India	37C3
Aívion Greece	23E3
Aíyna I Greece	23E3
Āïzawl India	37D3
Aizeb R Namibia	79B6
Aizu-Wakamatsu Japan	41E3
Ajaccio Corse	22B2
Ajalpan Mexico	67C2
Ajdabiyah Libya	75B1
Ajdovščina Yugos	17E2
Ajigasawa Japan	41E3
Ajlūn Jordan	31C2
Ajman UAE	33G1
Ajmer India	35C3
Ajo USA	65D4
Ajtos Bulg	23F2
Ajuchitan Mexico	67B2
Ak R Turk	23F3
Akabira Japan	42D2
Akaishi-sanchi Mts Japan	42C3
Akalkot India	36B1
Akanthou Cyprus	31B1
Akaroa NZ	51B2
Akasha Sudan	32B2
Akashi Japan	42B4
Akbou Alg	77C1
Akbulak USSR	25K5
Akçakale Turk	30C2
Akchar Watercourse Maur	76A2

Ak Dağ Andikíthira

Ak Dağ Mt Turk 23F3
Akelamo Indon 45C2
Aketi Zaïre 78C3
Akhalkalaki USSR 30D1
Akhalsikhe USSR 30D1
Akharnái Greece 23E3
Akhiok USA 56H4
Akhisar Turk 30A2
Akhiste USSR 21F1
Akhmîm Egypt 75C2
Akhtubinsk USSR 25H6
Akhtyrka USSR 25E6
Aki Japan 42B4
Akimiski I Can 53K4
Akita Japan 41E4
Akjoujt Maur 76A3
'Akko Israel 31C2
Aklavik Can 56L2
Aklé Aouana Desert Region Maur 76B3
Akobo Sudan 78D3
Akobo R Sudan 78D3
Akoha Afghan 35B1
Akola India 35D4
Akosombo Dam Ghana 77G4
Akot India 35D4
Akpatok I Can 53M3
Ákra Kafirévs C Greece 23E3
Ákra Líthinon C Greece 23E4
Ákra Maléa C Greece 23E3
Akranes Iceland 12A2
Ákra Sídheros C Greece 23F3
Ákra Spátha C Greece 23E3
Ákra Taínaron C Greece 23E3
Akron USA 55E2
Akrotiri B Cyprus 31B1
Aksai Chin Mts China 35D1
Aksaray Turk 25E8
Aksay USSR 25J5
Aksayquin Hu L China 35D1
Akşehir Turk 30B2
Akseki Turk 30B2
Aksenovo Zilovskoye USSR 27N4
Aksha USSR 38E1
Aksu China 29G1
Aksu USSR 26J5
Aksum Eth 32C4
Aktogay USSR 26J5
Aktumsyk USSR 25K6
Aktyubinsk USSR 26G4
Akure Nig 77H4
Akureyri Iceland 12B1
Akutan USA 56E5
Akutan I USA 56E5
Akutan Pass USA 56E5
Akzhal USSR 26K5
Alabama State USA 55E3
Alabama R USA 61B2
Alabaster USA 61B2
Ala Dağlari Mts Turk 30C2
Alagir USSR 25G7
Alagna Italy 17B2
Alagoas State Brazil 71L5
Alagoinhas Brazil 71L6
Alagón Spain 19B1
Al Ahmadi Kuwait 30E4
Alajuela Costa Rica 66D3
Alakanuk USA 56F3
Alakurtti USSR 12L5
Al Amārah Iraq 30E3
Alameda USA 65B3
Alamo Mexico 67C1
Alamo USA 65C3
Alamogordo USA 62A3
Alamo Heights USA 62C4
Alamosa USA 62A2
Åland I Fin 12H6
Alanya Turk 25E8
Alapaha R USA 61C2
Alapayevsk USSR 26H4
Alas R Indon 44A2
Alaşehir Turk 30A2
Ala Shan Mts China 38D3
Alaska State USA 52C3
Alaska,G of USA 52D4
Alaska Pen USA 56G4
Alaska Range Mts USA 52C3
Alassio Italy 22B2
Alássio Region Italy 17C3
Alatna R USA 56H2
Alatyr USSR 24H5
Alawoona Aust 50B2
Al'Ayn UAE 33G2
Alayskiy Khrebet Mts USSR 29F2
Alazeya R USSR 27R3
Al'Azīzīyah Libya 77E2
Alba Italy 18D3
Al Bāb Syria 30C2
Albacete Spain 19B2
Alba de Tormes Spain 19A1
Al Badi Iraq 30D2
Alba Iulia Rom 23E1
Albania Republic Europe 23D2
Albany Aust 48A4
Albany Georgia USA 61C2
Albany Kentucky USA 58B3
Albany New York USA 59E2
Albany Oregon USA 54A2
Albany R Can 53K4
Albara R Sudan 32C4
Albardón Arg 72B2
Al Batinah Region Oman 33G2
Albatross B Aust 39H8
Al Baydā Libya 75B1
Al Baydā' Yemen 33E4
Al Baylūlīyah Syria 31C1
Albemarle USA 61C1
Albemarle Sd USA 61D1
Albenga Region Italy 17C2
Alberche R Spain 19B1
Alberga Aust 50A1
Albert France 16B1
Alberta Province Can 52G4
Albert Edward Mt PNG 39H7
Albert,L Uganda/Zaïre 78D3
Albert Lea USA 55D2
Albert Nile R Uganda 78D3
Alberton USA 64D1
Albertville France 18D2
Albi France 18C3
Albia USA 63D1
Albina Suriname 71H2
Albion Michigan USA 58C2
Albion Nebraska USA 57C3
Albion New York USA 59D2
Al Bi'r S Arabia 30C4
Al Birk S Arabia 32D3
Al Biyadh Region S Arabia 33E2
Alborán I Spain 19B2
Ålborg Den 12G7
Al Brayqah Libya 75A1
Albstadt-Ebingen W Germ 16E2
Al Bū Kamāl Syria 30D3
Albula R Switz 17C1
Albuquerque USA 54C3
Al Buraymi Oman 33G2
Al Burdī Libya 75B1
Albury Aust 48D4
Al Buşayyah Iraq 30E3
Albuskjell Oilfield N Sea 14G3
Al Buzūn S Yemen 33F3
Alcalá de Henares Spain 19B1
Alcamo Italy 22C3
Alcaniz Spain 19B1
Alcântara Brazil 71K4
Alcaraz Spain 19B2
Alcázar de San Juan Spain 19B2
Alcira Spain 19B2
Alcobaça Brazil 73E2
Alcolea de Pinar Spain 19B1
Alcoy Spain 19B2
Alcudia Spain 19C2
Aldama Mexico 62A4
Aldama Mexico 67C1
Aldan USSR 27O4
Aldan R USSR 27P4
Aldanskoye Nagor'ye Upland USSR 27O4
Aldeburgh Eng 15F5
Alderney I UK 18B2
Aldershot Eng 15E6
Aleg Maur 76A3
Alegre R Brazil 73A2
Alegrete Brazil 69E3
Alejandro Roca Arg 72C2
Aleksandrovsk Sakhalinskiy USSR 27Q4
Alekseyevka USSR 26J4
Aleksin USSR 24F5
Älem Sweden 20D1
Além Paraíba Brazil 73D3
Alençon France 18C2
Aleppo = Ḩalab
Alert Can 53M1
Alès France 18C3
Alessandria Italy 22B2
Ålesund Nor 26B3
Aleutian Is USA 56B5
Aleutian Range Mts USA 56G4
Aleutian Trench Pacific O 47L2
Alexander Arch USA 52E4
Alexander Bay S Africa 79B6
Alexander City USA 61B2
Alexander I Ant 80G3
Alexandra NZ 51A3
Alexandra,C South Georgia 69J8
Alexandra Fjord Can 53L2
Alexandria Egypt 75B1
Alexandria Louisiana USA 55D3
Alexandria Minnesota USA 55D2
Alexandria Virginia USA 55F3
Alexandroúpolis Greece 23F2
Aley Leb 31C2
Aleysk USSR 26K4
Al Fallūjah Iraq 30D3
Al Fardah S Yemen 33E4
Alfaro Spain 19B1
Alfatar Bulg 23F2
Al Fāw Iraq 30E3
Alfeld W Germ 16E1
Alfensas Brazil 73C3
Alfiós R Greece 23E3
Alfonsine Italy 17D2
Alfonzo Cláudio Brazil 73D3
Alfredo Chaves Brazil 73D3
Al Furūthi S Arabia 33E1
Alga USSR 25K6
Algarrobal Chile 72A1
Algarrobo del Águila Arg 72B3
Algeciras Spain 19A2
Alger Alg 77C1
Algeria Republic Africa 76B2
Al Ghaydah S Yemen 33F3
Alghero Sardegna 22B2
Algiers = Alger
Algona USA 57D3
Algonquin Park Can 59D1
Algorta Urug 72D2
Al Hadd Oman 33G2
Al Hadithah Iraq 30D3
Al Hadithah S Arabia 30C3
Al Haḑr Iraq 30D2
Al Haffah Syria 31D1
Al Hajar al Gharbī Mts Oman 33G2
Al Hajar ash Sharqī Mts Oman 33G2
Al Hamad Desert Region Jordan/S Arabia 30C3
Al Haniyah Desert Region Iraq 30E4
Al Harīq S Arabia 33E2
Al Harrah Desert Region S Arabia 30C3
Al Harūj al Aswad Upland Libya 75A2
Al Hasa Region S Arabia 33E1
Al Hasakah Syria 30D2
Al Hawjā' S Arabia 30C4
Al Hayy Iraq 30E3
Al Hibāk Region S Arabia 33F2
Al Hījānah Syria 31D2
Al Hillah Iraq 30D3
Al Hillah S Arabia 33E2
Al Hoceima Mor 77B1
Al Hudaydah Yemen 32D4
Al Hufūf S Arabia 33E1
Al Humrah Region UAE 33F2
Al Huwatsah Oman 33G2
Aliābad Iran 34B1
Aliabad Iran 34D3
Aliákmon R Greece 23E2
Alī al Gharbī Iraq 30E3
Alībāg India 36A1
Alibori R Benin 77B3
Alicante Spain 19B2
Alice USA 54D4
Alice Springs Aust 48C3
Alicudi I Italy 22C3
Aligarh India 35D3
Aligūdarz Iran 34B2
Ali-Khel Afghan 35B2
Alimniá I Greece 23F3
Alīpur Duār India 37C2
Aliquippa USA 58C2
Al'Irqah S Yemen 33E4
Al' Īsawiyah S Arabia 30C3
Aliwat North S Africa 79C7
Al Jaghbūb Libya 75B2
Al Jālamīd S Arabia 30D3
Al Jawf Libya 75B2
Al Jawf S Arabia 30C4
Al Jazīrah Syria 25G8
Al Jazīrah Desert Region Syria/Iraq 30D2
Aljezur Port 19A2
Al Jubayl S Arabia 33E1
Al Kabid Desert Jordan 31D4
Al Kahfah S Arabia 32D1
Al Kāmil Oman 33G2
Al Khābūr R Syria 30D2
Al Khābūrah Oman 33G2
Al Khālis Iraq 30D3
Al Khamāsīn S Arabia 32D2
Al Khasab Oman 33G1
Al Khawr Qatar 33F1
Al Khums Libya 75A1
Al Kidan Region S Arabia 33F2
Al Kiswah Syria 31D2
Alkmaar Neth 20A2
Al Kufrah Oasis Libya 75B2
Al Kūt Iraq 30E3
Al Lādhiqīyah Syria 30C2
Allahābād India 37B2
Al Lajāh Mt Syria 31D2
Allakaket USA 56H2
Allanmyo Burma 43B2
'Allaqi Watercourse Egypt 32B2
Allatoona L USA 61C2
Allegheny R USA 59D2
Allegheny Mts USA 55F3
Allegheny Res USA 60A2
Allendale USA 61C2
Allen,Mt NZ 51A3
Allentown USA 59D2
Alleppey India 36B3
Aller R France 18C2
Allgäu Mts W Germ 17D1
Alliance USA 57B3
Al Līth S Arabia 32D2
Al Liwā Region UAE 33F2
Allora Aust 50D1
Allos France 17B2
Alma Can 59E1
Alma Michigan USA 58C2
Alma Nebraska USA 62C1
Alma Ata USSR 29F1
Almada Port 19A2
Al Madinah = Medina
Almagan I Pacific O 39H5
Al Mahrah Region S Yemen 33F3
Al Majma'ah S Arabia 33E1
Al Manāmah Bahrain 33F1
Al Ma'nīyah Iraq 30D3
Almanor,L USA 65B2
Almansa Spain 19B2
Al Māriyyah UAE 33F2
Al Marj Libya 75B1
Almazán Spain 19B1
Alme R W Germ 16E1
Almenara Brazil 73D2
Almeria Spain 19B2
Almes R Brazil 73C2
Al'met'yevsk USSR 24J5
Älmhult Sweden 20C1
Al Midhnab S Arabia 32D1
Al Miqdādīyah Iraq 30E3
Almirante Brown Base Ant 80G3
Almirante Latorre Chile 72A1
Almirós Greece 23E3
Al Mish'ab A Arabia 33E1
Almodôvar Port 19A2
Almora India 35D3
Al Mubarraz S Arabia 33E1
Al Mudawwara Jordan 30C4
Al Mudaybi Oman 33G2
Al Muharraq Bahrain 33F1
Al Mukallā S Yemen 33E4
Al Mukhā Yemen 32D4
Al Musayyib Iraq 30D3
Al Muwaylih S Arabia 32C1
Alness Scot 14C3
Al Nu'mānīyah Iraq 30E3
Alnwick Eng 14E4
Alor I Indon 45B4
Alor Setar Malay 43C4
Alost = Aalst
Alotau PNG 48E2
Aloysius,Mt Aust 48B3
Alpachiri Arg 72C3
Alpe di Succiso Mt Italy 17D2
Alpena USA 58C1
Alpes du Valais Mts Switz 17B1
Alpes Maritimes Mts France 17B2
Alpi Carniche Mts Italy 17E1
Alpi Dolomitiche Mts Italy 22C1
Alpi Graie Mts Italy 17B2
Alpine Arizona USA 65E4
Alpine Texas USA 62B3
Alpine Junction USA 64D2
Alpi Orobie Mts Italy 17C1
Alpi Penine Mts Italy 17B2
Alpi Retiche Mts Switz 17C1
Alpi Venoste Mts Italy 17D1
Alps Mts Europe 22B1
Al Qaddāhiyah Libya 75A1
Al Qadmūs Syria 31D1
Al Qā'im Iraq 30D3
Al Qalībah S Arabia 30C4
Al Qāmishlī Syria 30D2
Al Qardāhah Syria 31D1
Al Qaryah Ash Sharqiyah Libya 75A1
Al Qaryatayn Syria 30C3
Al Qasim Region S Arabia 32D1
Al Qātif S Arabia 33E1
Al Qatrūn Libya 75A2
Al Qaysāmah S Arabia 33E1
Al Quatayfah Syria 31D2
Al Qunayţirah Syria 30C3
Al Qunfidhah S Arabia 32D3
Al Qurnah Iraq 30E3
Al Quşayr Syria 31D1
Al Qutayfah Syria 30C3
Al Quwayīyah S Arabia 33E2
Als I Den 20B1
Alsace Region France 18D2
Alsfeld W Germ 20B2
Alston Eng 14D4
Alta Nor 12J5
Alta Gracia Arg 69D4
Altagracia de Orituco Ven 68D5
Altai Mts Mongolia 38B2
Altamaha R USA 61C2
Altamira Brazil 71H4
Altamira Mexico 67C1
Altamura Italy 22D2
Altanbulag Mongolia 38D1
Altandulag USSR 27M5
Altape PNG 39H7
Altata Mexico 66B2
Altay China 26K5
Altay Mongolia 27L5
Altay Mts USSR 26K5
Altdorf Switz 17C1
Altenkirchen W Germ 16D1
Altiplanicie del Payún Plat Arg 72B3
Altkirch France 17B1
Alto Araguaia Brazil 73B2
Alto Molócue Mozam 79D5
Alton USA 58A3
Altoona USA 59D2
Alto Pencoso Mts Arg 72B2
Alto Sucuriú Brazil 73B2
Altotonga Mexico 67C2
Altoyac de Alvarez Mexico 67B2
Altun Shan Mts China 29G2
Alturas USA 64B2
Altus USA 62C3
Al'Ubaylah S Arabia 33F2
Al'Ulā S Arabia 32C1
Alula Somalia 75E3
Aluminé Arg 72A3
Al Urayq Desert Region S Arabia 30C4
Al'Uruq al Mu'taridah Region S Arabia 33F2
Alva USA 62C2
Alvarado Mexico 67C2
Alvarado USA 63C3
Älvdalen Sweden 12G6
Alvear Arg 72D1
Alvin USA 63C4
Alvsbyn Sweden 12J5
Al Wajh S Arabia 32C1
Alwar India 35D3
Al Widyān Desert Region Iraq/S Arabia 30D3
Alxa Yougi China 40A2
Alyat USSR 30E2
Alytus USSR 12J8
Alytus USSR 24C5
Alzey W Germ 16E2
Amacuzac R Mexico 67C2
Amadi Sudan 78D3
Amādīyah Iraq 30D2
Amadjuak L Can 53L3
Amahai Indon 45C3
Amakusa-shotō I Japan 41B5
Åmål Sweden 12G7
Amalat R USSR 27N4
Amaliás Greece 23E3
Amalner India 35C4
Amambai Brazil 73A3
Amambai R Brazil 73B3
Amami I Japan 38F4
Amami gunto Arch Japan 38F4
Amanzimtoti S Africa 79D7
Amapá Brazil 71H3
Amapá State Brazil 71H3
Amarapura Burma 37E3
Amarillo USA 62B2
Amasya Turk 25F7
Amatitan Mexico 67B1
Amaulipas Mexico 67C1
Amazonas = Solimões
Amazonas Brazil 71H4
Amazonas State Brazil 70E4
Ambāla India 35D2
Ambalangoda Sri Lanka 36C3
Ambalavao Madag 79E6
Ambam Cam 78B3
Ambanja Madag 79E5
Ambarchik USSR 27S3
Ambato Ecuador 70C4
Ambato-Boeny Madag 79E5
Ambatolampy Madag 79E5
Ambatondrazaka Madag 79E5
Amber B USA 56G4
Amberg W Germ 20C3
Ambergris Cay I Belize 66D3
Ambérieu France 17A2
Ambikāpur India 37B3
Ambilobe Madag 79E5
Amboasary Madag 79E6
Ambodifototra Madag 79E5
Ambohimahasoa Madag 79E6
Ambon Indon 45C3
Ambon I Indon 45C3
Ambositra Madag 79E6
Ambovombe Madag 79E6
Amboy USA 60C2
Ambriz Angola 79B4
Ambrym I Vanuatu 49F2
Amchitka USA 56B6
Amchitka I USA 56B6
Amchitka Pass USA 56C6
Am Dam Chad 78C2
Amderma USSR 26H3
Ameca Mexico 66B2
Ameca R Mexico 67A1
Amecacameca Mexico 67C2
Ameghino Arg 72C2
Ameland I Neth 20B2
Amenia USA 60D2
American Falls USA 64D2
American Falls Res USA 64D2
American Fork USA 65D2
American Highland Upland Ant 80F10
American Samoa Is Pacific O 47L5
Americus USA 61C2
Amery USA 57D2
Amery Ice Shelf Ant 80G10
Ames USA 57D3
Amesbury USA 60E1
Amfilokhía Greece 23E3
Amfissa Greece 23E3
Amga USSR 27P3
Amgal R USSR 27P3
Amgu USSR 41D2
Amguema R USSR 56C2
Amgun' R USSR 41D1
Amhara Region Eth 78D2
Amherst Can 53M5
Amherst Massachusetts USA 60D1
Amherst Virginia USA 59D3
Amhūr India 36B2
Amiens France 18C2
Amino Japan 42C3
Amioune Leb 31C1
Amistad Res Mexico 62B4
Amlekhgan Nepal 37C2
Amlia I USA 56D6
Amman Jordan 30C3
Ämmänsaario Fin 12K6
Ammersfoort Neth 20B2
Amnyong-dan C N Korea 42A3
Amoda'ya R USSR 28E1
Amol Iran 34C1
Amos Can 53L5
Amoy = Xiamen
Ampana Indon 45B3
Ampanihy Madag 79E6
Amparo Brazil 73C3
Amposta Spain 19C1
Amrān Yemen 32D3
Amrāvati India 35D4
Amreli India 35C4
Amritsar India 35C2
Amsterdam Neth 20A2
Amsterdam USA 59E2
Am Timan Chad 78C2
Amukta I USA 56D6
Amukta Pass USA 56D6
Amund Ringes I Can 53J2
Amundsen G Can 52F2
Amundsen S Ant 80F4
Amundsen-Scott Base Ant 80E
Amuntai Indon 44E3
Amur R USSR 27O4
Amur Watercourse Sudan 32C3
Amurang Indon 45B2
Amursk USSR 41D1
Amurskiy Liman Str USSR 41E1
Amurzet USSR 41C2
Anabar R USSR 27N2
Anaco Ven 70F2
Anaconda USA 54B2
Anacortes USA 64B1
Anadarko USA 62C2
Anadyr' USSR 27T3
Anadyr' R USSR 27T3
Anadyrskiy Zaliv S USSR 27U3
Anadyrskoye Ploskogor'ye Plat USSR 27T3
Anáfi I Greece 23F3
Anagé Brazil 73D1
'Ānah Iraq 30D3
Anaheim USA 65C4
Anaimalai Hills India 36B2
Anakāpalle India 36C1
Anaktuvuk P USA 56J2
Analalaya Madag 79E5
Anambra State Nig 77H4
Anambra R Nig 77H4
Anamosa USA 58A2
Anamur Turk 25E8
Anan Japan 42B4
Anantapur India 36B2
Anantnag India 35D2
Anápolis Brazil 71J7
Anār Iran 34D2
Anārak Iran 34C2
Anardara Afghan 34E2
Anatahan I Pacific O 39H5
Añatuya Arg 69D3
Anbyŏn N Korea 41B4
Ancasti Arg 72B1
Anchorage USA 52D3
Ancohuma Mt Bol 70E7
Ancón Peru 70C6
Ancona Italy 22C2
Ancram USA 60D1
Ancud Chile 69B6
Ancy-le-Franc France 16C3
Anda China 41B2
Andabuaylas Peru 70D6
Andacollo Arg 72A3
Andado Aust 50A1
Andagalá Arg 72B1
Andalsnes Nor 12F6
Andalucia Region Spain 19A2
Andalusia USA 61B2
Andaman Is Burma 29H4
Andaman S Burma 29H4
Andamooka Aust 50A2
Andaraí Brazil 73D1
Andee Irish Rep 15B5
Andelot France 16C2
Andenes Nor 12H5
Andermatt Switz 17C1
Andernach W Germ 20B2
Anderson Indiana USA 58B2
Anderson Missouri USA 63D2
Anderson S Carolina USA 61C2
Anderson R Can 52F3
Andhra Pradesh State India 36B1
Andikíthira I Greece 23E3

Andizhan
Athens

Andizhan *USSR* **26J5**
Andkhui *Afghan* **26H6**
Andong *S Korea* **41B4**
Andorra Principality *SW Europe* **19C1**
Andorra-La-Vella *Andorra* **19C1**
Andover *Eng* **15E6**
Andover New Hampshire *USA* **60E1**
Andover New York *USA* **60B1**
Andradina *Brazil* **73B3**
Andreafsky *USA* **56F3**
Andreanof Is *USA* **56C6**
Andreapol' *USSR* **21G1**
Andreas,C *Cyprus* **30B2**
Andrews *USA* **62B3**
Andria *Italy* **22D2**
Andros I *Bahamas* **55F4**
Ándros I *Greece* **23E3**
Androth I *India* **36A2**
Andújar *Spain* **19B2**
Andulo *Angola* **79B5**
Anécho *Togo* **77G4**
Anéfis *Mali* **76C3**
Aneityum I *Vanuatu* **49F3**
Añelo *Arg* **72B3**
Angareb Watercourse *Eth* **32C4**
Angarsk *USSR* **27M4**
Ånge *Sweden* **24A3**
Angel de la Guarda I *Mexico* **66A2**
Angeles *Phil* **45F7**
Angelholm *Sweden* **12G7**
Angellala Creek R *Aust* **50C1**
Angemuk Mt *Indon* **39G7**
Angers *France* **18B2**
Angerville *France* **16B2**
Angkor Hist Site *Camb* **43C3**
Anglesey I *Wales* **13C3**
Angleton *USA* **63C4**
Angmagssalik *Greenland* **53P3**
Angoche *Mozam* **79E5**
Angol *Chile* **69B5**
Angola Indiana *USA* **58C2**
Angola New York *USA* **60A1**
Angola Republic *Africa* **79B5**
Angola Basin *Atlantic O* **74J5**
Angoon *USA* **56M4**
Angoulême *France* **18C2**
Angra do Heroismo *Açores* **76A1**
Angra dos Reis *Brazil* **73D3**
Anguil *Arg* **72C3**
Anguilla I *Caribbean* **68E3**
Anguilla Cays Is *Caribbean* **68B2**
Angul *India* **37C3**
Angumu *Zaïre* **78C4**
Anholt I *Den* **20C1**
Anhua *China* **40C4**
Anhui Province *China* **40D3**
Anhumas *Brazil* **73B2**
Anhŭng *S Korea* **42A3**
Aniak *USA* **56G3**
Anicuns *Brazil* **73C2**
Anié *Togo* **77G4**
Animas R *USA* **62A2**
Animas Peak Mt *USA* **62A3**
Anita *USA* **57D3**
Anizy-le-Château *France* **16B2**
Anjak *USA* **52C3**
Anjou Republic *France* **18B2**
Anjouan I *Comoros* **79E5**
Anjozorobe *Madag* **79E5**
Anju *N Korea* **41B4**
Ankang *China* **40B3**
Ankara *Turk* **25E8**
Ankaratra Mt *Madag* **79E5**
Ankazoabo *Madag* **79E6**
Ankazobe *Madag* **79E5**
Ankeny *USA* **57D3**
Anklam *E Germ* **20C2**
Ankwe R *Nig* **77H4**
An Loc *Viet* **43D3**
Anlong *China* **40B4**
Anlu *China* **40C3**
Anna *USA* **58B3**
'Annaba *Alg* **77D1**
An Nabk *S Arabia* **30C3**
An Nabk *Syria* **30C3**
Anna Creek *Aust* **50A1**
An Najaf *Iraq* **30D3**
Annan *Scot* **14D4**
Annapolis *USA* **59D3**
Annapurna Mt *Nepal* **37B2**
Ann Arbor *USA* **58C2**
An Nāsirah *Syria* **31D1**
An Nāsirīyah *Iraq* **30E3**
Annecy *France* **17B2**
Annemasse *France* **17B1**
An Nhon *Viet* **43D3**
An Nimās *S Arabia* **32D3**
Anning *China* **40A5**
Anniston *USA* **61B2**
Annonay *France* **18C2**
Annot *France* **17B3**
Annotto Bay *Jamaica* **68J1**
Anqing *China* **40D3**
Ansai *China* **40B2**
Ansbach *W Germ* **20C3**
Anse d'Hainault *Haiti* **68C3**
Anshan *China* **40E1**
Anshun *China* **40B4**
Ansley *USA* **62C1**
Anson *USA* **62C3**
Anson B *Aust* **39F8**
Ansongo *Mali* **76C3**
Ansonville *Can* **58C1**
Ansted *USA* **58C3**
Antakya *Turk* **25F8**
Antalaha *Madag* **79F5**
Antalya *Turk* **25E8**
Antalya Körfezi B *Turk* **25E8**
Antananarivo *Madag* **79E5**
Antarctic Circle *Ant* **80G1**
Antarctic Pen *Ant* **80G3**
Antequera *Spain* **19B2**
Anthony *USA* **62A3**
Anti-Atlas Mts *Mor* **76B1**
Antibes *France* **17B3**
Anticosti I *Can* **53M5**
Antigo *USA* **58B1**
Antigua I *Caribbean* **68E3**
Anti Lebanon = Jebel esh Sharqi
Antioch *USA* **65B3**
Antipodes Is *NZ* **49G5**
Antlers *USA* **63C3**
Antofagasta *Chile* **69B2**
Antonina *Brazil* **73C4**
Antonito *USA* **62A2**
Antrim County *N Ire* **14B4**
Antrim *N Ire* **14B4**
Antrim *USA* **60E1**
Antrim Hills *N Ire* **14B4**
Antseranana *Madag* **79E5**
Antsirabe *Madag* **79E5**
Antsohiny *Madag* **79E5**
An Tuc *Viet* **43D3**
Añtuya *Arg* **72C1**
Antwerpen *Belg* **16C1**
An Uaimh *Irish Rep* **15B5**
Anui *S Korea* **42A3**
Anupgarh *India* **35C3**
Anuradhapura *Sri Lanka* **36C3**
Anvers = Antwerpen
Anvik *USA* **52B3**
Anvil Pk Mt *USA* **56B6**
Anxi *China* **27L5**
Anyang *China* **40C2**
A'nyêmaqên Shan Upland *China* **40A3**
Anyuysk *USSR* **27S3**
Anza R *Italy* **17C2**
Anzhero-Sudzhensk *USSR* **26K4**
Anzio *Italy* **22C2**
Aoba I *Vanuatu* **49F2**
Aomori *Japan* **41E3**
Aosta *Italy* **22B1**
Aoukar Desert Region *Maur* **76B3**
Aoulef *Alg* **76C2**
Aozou *Chad* **78B1**
Apa R *Brazil/Par* **69E2**
Apalachee B *USA* **55E4**
Apalachicola *USA* **61C3**
Apalachicola B *USA* **61B3**
Apan *Mexico* **67C2**
Apaporis R *Colombia* **70D3**
Aparecida do Taboado *Brazil* **73B3**
Aparri *Phil* **45F7**
Apatin *Yugos* **23D1**
Apatity *USSR* **24E2**
Apatzingan *Mexico* **66B3**
Apeldoorn *Neth* **20B2**
Apia *Western Samoa* **49H2**
Apiai *Brazil* **73C3**
Apizolaya *Mexico* **67B1**
Apoera *Surinam* **71G2**
Apollo Bay *Aust* **50B3**
Apo,Mt Mt *Phil* **45G9**
Apopka,L *USA* **61C3**
Aporé R *Brazil* **71H7**
Apostle Is *USA* **58A1**
Apostle L *USA* **55D2**
Apozol *Mexico* **67B1**
Appalachian Mts *USA* **55E3**
Appenino Tosco-Emiliano Mts *Italy* **17D2**
Appennino Abruzzese Mts *Italy* **22C2**
Appennino Ligure Mts *Italy* **22B2**
Appennino Lucano Mts *Italy* **22D2**
Appennino Napoletano Mts *Italy* **22D2**
Appennino Tosco-Emilliano Mts *Italy* **22C2**
Appennino Umbro-Marchigiano Mts *Italy* **22C2**
Appenzell *Switz* **17C1**
Appleby *Eng* **15D4**
Appleton Minnesota *USA* **57C2**
Appleton Wisconsin *USA* **58B2**
Apsheronskiy Poluostrov Pt *USSR* **25J7**
Apt *France* **17A3**
Apucarana *Brazil* **69F2**
Apulco *Mexico* **67C1**
Apure R *Ven* **70E2**
Apurimac R *Peru* **70D6**
'Aqaba *Jordan* **30C4**
'Aqaba,G of *Egypt/S Arabia* **30B4**
'Aqdā *Iran* **34C2**
Aqidauana *Brazil* **71G8**
Aqua Nueva *Mexico* **67A1**
Aquidabán R *Par* **73A3**
Aquidauana *Brazil* **69E2**
Aquidauana R *Brazil* **73A2**
Aquila *Mexico* **67B2**
Ara *India* **37B2**
Arab *USA* **61B2**
'Arab al Mulk *Syria* **31C1**
Arabian S *Asia/Arabian Pen* **28E4**
Arabian Basin *Indian O* **46E4**
Aracajú *Brazil* **71L6**
Aracanguy,Mts de *Par* **73A3**
Aracati *Brazil* **71L4**
Aracatu *Brazil* **73D1**
Araçatuba *Brazil* **71H8**
Aracena *Spain* **19A2**
Araçuai *Brazil* **71K7**
Arad *Israel* **31C3**
Arad *Rom* **25C6**
Arada *Chad* **78C2**
'Arādah *UAE* **33F2**
Arafura S *Indon/Aust* **48C1**
Aragarças *Brazil* **71H7**
Aragats Mt *USSR* **25G7**
Aragón Region *Spain* **19B1**
Aragon R *Spain* **19B1**
Araguaçu *Brazil* **73C1**
Araguaia R *Brazil* **71H6**
Araguaína *Brazil* **71J5**
Araguari *Brazil* **71J7**
Araguari R *Brazil* **73C2**
Arai *Japan* **42C3**
Arak *Alg* **76C2**
Arāk *Iran* **34B2**
Arakan Yoma Mts *Burma* **43A2**
Arakkonam *India* **36B2**
Araks R *USSR* **30E2**
Aral'sk *USSR* **26H4**
Aral'sk *USSR* **28E1**
Aral'skoye More S *USSR* **26G5**
Aramberri *Mexico* **67C1**
Aran I *Irish Rep* **13B2**
Aran Is *Irish Rep* **13B3**
Aranda de Duero *Spain* **19B1**
Arandas *Mexico* **67B1**
Aranjuez *Spain* **19B1**
Aransas Pass *USA* **63F4**
Arao *Japan* **42B4**
Araouane *Mali* **76B3**
Arapahoe *USA* **62C1**
Arapey R *Urug* **69E4**
Arapey Grande R *Urug* **72D2**
Arapiraca *Brazil* **71L6**
Araporgas *Brazil* **73B3**
Ararangua *Brazil* **69G3**
Araraquara *Brazil* **71J8**
Araras *Brazil* **73C3**
Ararat *Aust* **48D4**
Ararat *USSR* **30D2**
Aras R *Turk* **30D1**
Aras R *USSR* **25H8**
Aratali *Eth* **32C3**
Arato *Japan* **42D3**
Arauca R *Ven* **70E2**
Arauco *Chile* **72A3**
Arauea *Colombia* **70D2**
Arāvalli Range Mts *India* **35C3**
Arawa *PNG* **49E1**
Araxá *Brazil* **71J7**
Araxes R *Iran* **25G8**
Arba Minch *Eth* **78D3**
Arbatax *Sardegna* **22B3**
Arbīl *Iraq* **25G8**
Arbois *France* **17A1**
Arbrå *Sweden* **12H6**
Arbroath *Scot* **14D3**
Arc R *France* **17A3**
Arc R *France* **17B2**
Arcachon *France* **18B3**
Arcade *USA* **60A1**
Arcadia *USA* **61E4**
Arcata *USA* **64B2**
Arcelia *Mexico* **67B2**
Archbald *USA* **60C2**
Archipiélago de Camaguey Arch *Cuba* **68B2**
Archipiélago de la Reina Adelaida Arch *Chile* **69B8**
Archipiélago de las Chones Arch *Chile* **69B6**
Archipiélago de las Perlas Arch *Panama* **70C2**
Arcis-sur-Aube *France* **16C2**
Arco *USA* **64D2**
Arcos *Brazil* **73C3**
Arcos de la Frontera *Spain* **19A2**
Arc Senans *France* **17A1**
Arctic Circle **80C1**
Arctic Red *Can* **52E3**
Arctic Red R *Can* **52E3**
Arctic Village *USA* **52D3**
Arctowski Base *Ant* **80G2**
Arda R *Bulg* **23F2**
Ardabīl *Iran* **25H8**
Ardahan *Turk* **25G7**
Ardar des Iforas Upland *Alg/Mali* **76C2**
Ardekān *Iran* **34C2**
Ardel *Nor* **12F6**
Ardennes Department *France* **16C2**
Ardennes Region *Belg* **20B2**
Ardestan *Iran* **34C2**
Ardh es Suwwan Desert Region *Jordan* **30C3**
Ardila R *Port* **19A2**
Ardlethan *Aust* **50C2**
Ardmore *USA* **54D3**
Ardnamurchan Pt *Scot* **14B3**
Ardres *France* **15F6**
Ardres *France* **16A1**
Ardrishaig *Scot* **14C3**
Ardrossan *Scot* **14C4**
Arecibo *Puerto Rico* **68D3**
Areia Branca *Brazil* **71L4**
Arena,Pt *USA* **65B3**
Arendal *Nor* **12F7**
Arequipa *Peru* **70D7**
Arezzo *Italy* **22C2**
Argens R *France* **17B3**
Argenta *Italy* **22C2**
Argentan *France* **18C2**
Argenteuil *France* **16B2**
Argentine Basin *Atlantic O* **74F7**
Argenton-sur-Creuse *France* **18C2**
Argeşul R *Rom* **23F2**
Arghardab R *Afghan* **35B2**
Argolikós Kólpos G *Greece* **23E3**
Argonne Region *France* **16C2**
Árgos *Greece* **23E3**
Argostólion *Greece* **23E3**
Argungu *Nig* **77G3**
Argyle,L *Aust* **48B2**
Argyll Oilfield *N Sea* **14G3**
Århus *Den* **20C1**
Ariamsvlei *Namibia* **79C6**
Arian zón R *Spain* **19B1**
Arias Venado *Arg* **72C2**
Aribinda *Upper Volta* **76B3**
Arica *Chile* **69B1**
Arifwala *Pak* **35C2**
Arihā = Jericho
Arikaree R *USA* **62B2**
Arima *Trinidad* **68L1**
Arinos *Brazil* **73C2**
Arinos R *Brazil* **71G6**
Ario de Rosales *Mexico* **67B2**
Aripo,Mt *Trinidad* **68L1**
Aripuana *Brazil* **70F5**
Aripuanã R *Brazil* **70F5**
Arisaig *Scot* **14C3**
Ariskere *India* **36B2**
Arista *Mexico* **67B1**
Arista *Mexico* **67D2**
Arizona *Arg* **72B3**
Arizona State *USA* **54B3**
Årjäng *Sweden* **12G7**
Arka *USSR* **27Q3**
Arkadak *USSR* **25G5**
Arkadelphia *USA* **63D3**
Arkalya *USSR* **26H4**
Arkansas State *USA* **55D3**
Arkansas R *USA* **55D3**
Arkansas City *USA* **63C2**
Arkhangel'sk *USSR* **24G3**
Arkhara *USSR* **41C2**
Arkipelag Nordenshelda Arch *USSR* **27K2**
Arklow *Irish Rep* **13B3**
Arlberg P *Austria* **17D1**
Arles *France* **18C3**
Arlington S Dakota *USA* **57C3**
Arlington Texas *USA* **63C3**
Arlington Virginia *USA* **59D3**
Arlington Washington *USA* **64B1**
Arlington Heights *USA* **58B2**
Arlon *Belg* **20B3**
Armageddon = Megido
Armagh County *N Ire* **15B4**
Armagh *N Ire* **15B4**
Armagós I *Greece* **23F3**
Armançon R *France* **16B3**
Armavir *USSR* **25G7**
Armenia *Mexico* **67B2**
Armenia *Colombia* **70C3**
Armidale *Aust* **48E4**
Armu R *USSR* **41D2**
Armyanskaya SSR Republic *USSR* **26F5**
Arnaud R *Can* **53L3**
Arnauti C *Cyprus* **30B2**
Arnett *USA* **62C2**
Arnhem *Neth* **20B2**
Arnhem,C *Aust* **48C2**
Arnhem Land *Aust* **48C2**
Arno R *Italy* **17D3**
Arnoldstein *Austria* **17E1**
Arnprior *Can* **59D1**
Arnsberg *W Germ* **16E1**
Arolsen *W Germ* **16E1**
Arona *Italy* **17C2**
Aropuk L *USA* **56F3**
Arorae I *Kiribati* **49G1**
Arosa *Switz* **22B1**
Arpajon *France* **16B2**
Arquipélago dos Abrolhos Arch *Brazil* **73E2**
Arquipélago dos Bijagós Arch *Guinea-Bissau* **76A3**
Arraias *Brazil* **73C1**
Ar Ramādī *Iraq* **30D3**
Arran I *Scot* **14C4**
Ar Raqqah *Syria* **30C2**
Arras *France* **18C1**
Ar Rass *S Arabia* **32D1**
Ar Rastan *Syria* **31D1**
Ar Rawdah *S Arabia* **32D2**
Arrecife *Canary Is* **76A2**
Arrecifes *Arg* **72C2**
Arriaga *Mexico* **67B1**
Arriaga *Mexico* **67D2**
Ar Rifā't *Iraq* **30E3**
Ar Rihāb Desert Region *Iraq* **30E3**
Ar Riyād = Riyadh
Arrochar *Scot* **14C3**
Arroio Grande *Brazil* **72E2**
Arrojado R *Brazil* **73C1**
Arrowrock Res *USA* **64C2**
Arrowtown *NZ* **51A2**
Arroyo Seco *Mexico* **67C1**
Ar Ru'ays *Qatar* **33F1**
Ar Rustaq *Oman* **33G2**
Ar Rutbah *Iraq* **30D3**
Ar Ruwaydah *S Arabia* **32D2**
Arsen'yev *USSR* **41C3**
Arsiero *Italy* **17D2**
Arsizio *Italy* **18D2**
Arsk *USSR* **24H4**
Árta *Greece* **23E3**
Arteaga *Mexico* **67B2**
Artem *USSR* **41C3**
Artemovsk *USSR* **27L4**
Artemovskiy *USSR* **27N4**
Artenay *France* **16A2**
Artesia *USA* **54C3**
Arthurs P *NZ* **51B2**
Årthus *Den* **12G7**
Artic Bay *Can* **53K2**
Artigas *Urug* **69E4**
Artigas *Urug* **72D2**
Artillery L *Can* **52H3**
Artois Region *France* **18C1**
Artsiz *USSR* **21F3**
Arturo Prat Base *Ant* **80G2**
Artvin *Turk* **25G7**
Aru *Zaïre* **78D3**
Aruanã *Brazil* **71H6**
Aruba I *Caribbean* **68C4**
Arun R *Nepal* **37C2**
Arunāchal Pradesh Union Territory *India* **37D2**
Arun He R *China* **41A2**
Arun Qi *China* **41A2**
Aruppukkottai *India* **36B3**
Arusha *Tanz* **78D4**
Aruwimi R *Zaïre* **78C3**
Arvada *USA* **62A2**
Arvayheer *Mongolia* **38D2**
Arvayheer *USSR* **27M5**
Arve R *France* **17B2**
Arvida *Can* **53L5**
Arvidsjaur *Sweden* **12H5**
Arvidsjaur *Sweden* **24B2**
Arvika *Sweden* **12G7**
Arvin *USA* **65C3**
Arwad I *Syria* **31C1**
Arwala *Indon* **45C4**
Arzamas *USSR* **24G4**
Arzew *Alg* **77B1**
Asadabad *Afghan* **35C2**
Asahi R *Japan* **42B4**
Asahi dake Mt *Japan* **41E3**
Asahikawa *Japan* **41E3**
Asan-man B *S Korea* **42A3**
Asansol *India* **37C3**
Asawanwah Well *Libya* **75A2**
Asbest *USSR* **24L4**
Asbury Park *USA* **59E2**
Ascension I *Atlantic O* **74H5**
Aschaffenburg *W Germ* **20B3**
Aschersleben *E Germ* **20C2**
Ascoli Piceno *Italy* **22C2**
Ascona *Switz* **17C1**
Asedjirad Upland *Alg* **76C2**
Åsele *Sweden* **12H6**
Aselle *Eth* **78D3**
Asenovgrad *Bulg* **23E2**
Asfeld *France* **16C2**
Asha *USSR* **24K4**
Ashburn *USA* **61C2**
Ashburton *NZ* **49G5**
Ashburton R *Aust* **48A3**
Ashdod *Israel* **30B3**
Ashdown *USA* **63D3**
Asheboro *USA* **61D1**
Asheville *USA* **55E3**
Ashford *Aust* **50D1**
Ashford *Eng* **15F6**
Ash Fork *USA* **65D3**
Ashibetsu *Japan* **42D2**
Ashikaga *Japan* **41D4**
Ashizuri-misaki Pt *Japan* **42B4**
Ashkhabad *USSR* **26G6**
Ashland Kansas *USA* **62C2**
Ashland Kentucky *USA* **55E3**
Ashland Montana *USA* **57A2**
Ashland Nebraska *USA* **63C1**
Ashland Ohio *USA* **58C2**
Ashland Oregon *USA* **54A2**
Ashland Virginia *USA* **59D3**
Ashland Wisconsin *USA* **57D2**
Ashley *Aust* **50C1**
Ashley *USA* **57C2**
Ashokan Res *USA* **60C2**
Ashqelon *Israel* **31C3**
Ash Shabakh *Iraq* **30D3**
Ash Sha'm *UAE* **33G1**
Ash Sh'ār *S Arabia* **32D3**
Ash Sharqāt *Iraq* **30D2**
Ash Shatrah *Iraq* **30E3**
Ash Shihr *S Yemen* **33E4**
Ash Shumlul *S Arabia* **33E1**
Ash Shuqayq *S Arabia* **32D3**
Ashtabula *USA* **58C2**
Ashuanipi L *Can* **53M4**
Asi R *Syria* **25F8**
Asiago *Italy* **17D2**
Asilah *Mor* **77A1**
Asinara I *Medit S* **22B2**
Asino *USSR* **26K4**
Asir Region *S Arabia* **32D2**
Aska *India* **37B4**
Aşkale *Turk* **30D2**
Askersund *Sweden* **12G7**
Asl *Egypt* **31B4**
Asmar *Afghan* **35C1**
Asmara *Eth* **78D2**
Aso *Japan* **42B4**
Asosa *Eth* **78D2**
Aspermont *USA* **62B3**
Aspiring,Mt *NZ* **51A2**
Aspres-sur-Buëch *France* **17A2**
Assab *Eth* **78E2**
As Sabkhah *Syria* **30C2**
As Salamiyah *S Arabia* **33E2**
As Salamīyah *Syria* **30C2**
Assale,L *Eth* **32D4**
As Salmañ *Iraq* **30D3**
Assam State *India* **37D2**
As Samāwah *Iraq* **30E3**
As Şanām Region *S Arabia* **33F2**
As Sanamayn *Syria* **31D2**
Asse R *France* **17B3**
Assen *Neth* **20B2**
Assens *Den* **20C1**
As Sidrah *Libya* **75A1**
Assiniboia *Can* **52H5**
Assiniboia *USA* **57A2**
Assiniboine R *Can* **57C2**
Assiniboine,Mt *Can* **52G4**
Assis *Brazil* **71H8**
Assis *Brazil* **71H8**
Assissi *Italy* **17E3**
As Sukhnah *Syria* **30C3**
As Sulayyil *S Arabia* **33E2**
As Summan Region *S Arabia* **33E2**
Assumption I *Seychelles* **79E4**
As Suq *S Arabia* **32D2**
As Suwaydā' *Syria* **30C3**
As Suwayrah *Iraq* **30D3**
Astara *USSR* **30E2**
Asti *Italy* **22B2**
Astipálaia I *Greece* **23F3**
Astorga *Spain* **19A1**
Astoria *USA* **54A2**
Astrakhan' *USSR* **25H6**
Asturias Region *Spain* **19A1**
Asunción *Par* **69E3**
Aswa R *Uganda* **78D3**
Aswân *Egypt* **32B2**
Aswân High Dam *Egypt* **75C2**
Asyût *Egypt* **75C2**
As Zilaf *Syria* **30C3**
Atafu I *Tokelau Is* **49H1**
Atakpamé *Togo* **77G4**
Atambua *Indon* **45B5**
Atangmik *Greenland* **53N3**
Atapupu *Indon* **45B4**
Atar *Maur* **76A2**
Atasu *USSR* **26J5**
Atauro I *Indon* **45C4**
Atbara *Sudan* **78D2**
Atbasar *USSR* **26H4**
Atchafalaya B *USA* **55D4**
Atchison *USA* **55D3**
Atco *USA* **60C3**
Atebubu *Ghana* **77F4**
Atenguillo *Mexico* **67B1**
Atessa *Italy* **22C2**
Ath *Belg* **16B1**
Athabasca *Can* **52G4**
Athabasca R *Can* **52G4**
Athabasca L *Can* **52H4**
Athens = Athínai
Athens Alabama *USA* **61B2**
Athens Georgia *USA* **55E3**

Athens Banská Bystrica

Athens Ohio *USA* 58C3
Athens Pennsylvania *USA* 60B2
Athens Tennessee *USA* 61C1
Athens Texas *USA* 63C3
Athiémé *Benin* 77G4
Athínai *Greece* 23E3
Athlone *Irish Rep* 13B3
Athna *Cyprus* 31B1
Athol *USA* 60D1
Áthos Mt *Greece* 23E2
Athy *Irish Rep* 15B5
Ati *Chad* 78B2
Atikoken *Can* 53J5
Atka *USSR* 27R3
Atka I *USA* 56D6
Atkarsk *USSR* 25G5
Atkins *USA* 63D2
Atlacomulco *Mexico* 67C2
Atlanta Georgia *USA* 55E3
Atlanta Michigan *USA* 58C2
Atlantic *USA* 63C1
Atlantic City *USA* 55F3
Atlantic Highlands *USA* 60C2
Atlantic Indian Basin *Atlantic O* 74H8
Atlantic Indian Ridge *Atlantic O* 74H7
Atlas Saharien Mts *Alg* 76C1
Atlin *Can* 52E4
Atlin L *Can* 52E4
'Atlit *Israel* 31C2
Atlixco *Mexico* 67C2
Atmore *USA* 55E3
Atofinandrahana *Madag* 79E6
Atognak I *USA* 56H4
Atoka *USA* 63C3
Atotonilco *Mexico* 67B1
Atoyac R *Mexico* 67C2
Atrato R *Colombia* 70C2
Attaf Region *UAE* 33F2
At Tā'if *S Arabia* 32D2
At Tall *Syria* 31D2
Attalla *USA* 61B2
Attauapiskat *Can* 53K4
Attauapiskat R *Can* 53K4
At Taysīyah Desert Region *S Arabia* 30D3
Attica Indiana *USA* 58B2
Attica New York *USA* 60A1
Attigny *France* 16C2
Attila Line *Cyprus* 31B1
Attleboro Massachusetts *USA* 59E2
Attopeu *Laos* 43D3
Attu *USA* 56A5
Attu I *USA* 56A5
At Tubayq Upland *S Arabia* 30C4
Atuel R *Arg* 72B3
Atvidaberg *Sweden* 12H7
Aubagne *France* 18D3
Aube Department *France* 16C2
Aube R *France* 16C2
Aubenas *France* 18C3
Aubry L *Can* 56N2
Auburn Alabama *USA* 61B2
Auburn California *USA* 65B3
Auburn Indiana *USA* 58B2
Auburn Maine *USA* 59E2
Auburn Nebraska *USA* 63C1
Auburn New York *USA* 59D2
Auburn Washington *USA* 64B1
Auch *France* 18C3
Auchi *Nig* 77H4
Auckland *NZ* 49G4
Auckland Is *NZ* 47K7
Aude R *France* 18C3
Auden *Can* 53K4
Audincourt *France* 17B1
Audubon *USA* 57D3
Augathella *Aust* 50C1
Augsburg *W Germ* 20C3
Augusta *Aust* 48A4
Augusta Georgia *USA* 55E3
Augusta Kansas *USA* 63C2
Augusta Maine *USA* 55G2
Augusta Montana *USA* 64D1
Augusta Wisconsin *USA* 58A2
Augustine I *USA* 56H4
Augustow *Pol* 21E2
Augustus,Mt *Aust* 48A3
Auk Oilfield *N Sea* 14G3
Aulla *Italy* 17C2
Aumale *France* 16A2
Auponhia *Indon* 45C3
Aups *France* 17B3
Auraiya *India* 35D3
Aurangābād *India* 35D5
Aurès Mts *Alg* 77D1
Aurillac *France* 18C3
Aurora Colorado *USA* 54C3
Aurora Illinois *USA* 58B2
Aurora Indiana *USA* 58C3
Aurora Mississippi *USA* 63D2
Aurora Nebraska *USA* 63C1
Aus *Namibia* 79B6
Au Sable *USA* 58C2
Ausert Well *Mor* 76A2
Austin Minnesota *USA* 55D2
Austin Nevada *USA* 65C3
Austin Pennsylvania *USA* 60A2
Austin Texas *USA* 54D3
Australian Alps Mts *Aust* 48D4
Authie R *France* 16A1
Autlán *Mexico* 66B3
Autun *France* 18C2
Auvergne Region *France* 18C2
Auxerre *France* 18C2
Auxi-le-Château *France* 16A1
Auxonne *France* 17A1
Avallon *France* 18C2
Avalon Pen *Can* 53N5
Avalos R *Arg* 72D1
Avaré *Brazil* 73C3
Avaz *Iran* 34E2
Avedat Hist Site *Israel* 31C3
Aveíro *Brazil* 71G4
Aveiro *Port* 19A1
Avellaneda *Arg* 69E4
Avellino *Italy* 22C2
Avesnes-sur-Helpe *France* 16B1
Avesta *Sweden* 12H6
Avezzano *Italy* 22C2
Aviemore *Scot* 14D3
Aviemore,L *NZ* 51B2
Avigliana *Italy* 17B2
Avignon *France* 18C3
Avila *Spain* 19B1
Aviles *Spain* 19A1
Avisio R *Italy* 17D1
Avoca Iowa *USA* 57C3
Avoca New York *USA* 60B1
Avoca R *Aust* 50B3
Avon County *Eng* 15D6
Avon *USA* 60B1
Avon R Dorset *Eng* 15E6
Avon R Warwick *Eng* 15E5
Avondale *USA* 65D4
Avonmouth *Wales* 15D6
Avon Park *USA* 61E4
Avre R *France* 16B2
Avtovac *Yugos* 23D2
A'waj R *Syria* 31D2
Awaji-shima B *Japan* 41D5
Awarem *Eth* 78E3
Awarua Pt *NZ* 51A2
Awash *Eth* 78E3
Awash R *Eth* 78E3
Awa-shima I *Japan* 42C3
Awatere R *NZ* 51B2
Awbārī *Libya* 75A2
Aweil *Sudan* 78C3
Awjilan *Libya* 75B2
Awka *Nig* 77H4
Awuna R *USA* 56G2
Axel *Can* 53J1
Axminster *Eng* 15D6
Ayabe *Japan* 42C3
Ayacucho *Arg* 69E5
Ayacucho *Colombia* 68C5
Ayacucho *Peru* 70D6
Ayaguz *USSR* 26K5
Ayakkum Hu L *China* 29G2
Ayamonte *Spain* 19A2
Ayan *USSR* 27P4
Ayauiri *Peru* 70D6
Aydin *Turk* 25D8
Áyios Evstrátios I *Greece* 23F3
Aykhal *USSR* 27N3
Aylesbury *Eng* 15E5
'Ayn al Fījah *Syria* 31D2
Ayn Zālah *Iraq* 30D2
Ayn Zuwayyah Well *Libya* 75B2
Ayod *Sudan* 78D3
Ayr *Aust* 48D2
Ayr *Scot* 14C4
Ayr R *Scot* 14C4
Ayre,Pt of *Eng* 15C4
Aytthaya *Thai* 43C3
Ayutla *Mexico* 67B1
Ayvacik *Turk* 23F3
Ayvalik *Turk* 23F3
Āzamgarh *India* 37B2
Azaouad Desert Region *Mali* 76B3
Azare *Nig* 77J3
A'Zāz *Syria* 30C2
Azbine = Aïr
Azeffal Watercourse *Maur* 76A2
Azemmour *Mor* 77A2
Azerbaydzhanskaya SSR Republic *USSR* 26F5
Azogues *Ecuador* 70C4
Azopol'ye *USSR* 24H2
Azores = Açores
Azoum R *Chad* 78C2
Azovskoye More S *USSR* 25F6
Azrou *Mor* 77A2
Aztec *USA* 62A2
Azucena *Arg* 72D3
Azuero,Pen de *Panama* 70B2
Azúl *Arg* 69E5
Azzaba *Alg* 77D1
Az-Zabdānī *Syria* 31D2
Az Zāhirah Mts *Oman* 33G2
Az Zilfi *S Arabia* 32D1
Az Zubayr *Iraq* 30E3

B

Baa *Indon* 45B5
Ba'abda *Leb* 31C2
Ba'albek *Leb* 30C3
Ba'al Hazor Mt *Israel* 31C3
Baardheere *Somalia* 78E3
Babadag *Rom* 23F2
Babaeski *Turk* 30A1
Bāb al Mandab Str *Djibouti/S Yemen* 32D4
Babanoyo *Ecuador* 70C4
Babar I *Indon* 45C4
Babati *Tanz* 78D4
Babayevo *USSR* 24F4
Babbitt *USA* 57D2
Baberton *USA* 58C2
Babine L *Can* 52F4
Babo *Indon* 48C1
Bābol *Iran* 34C1
Babuyan Chan *Phil* 45F7
Babuyan Is *Phil* 45F7
Bacabal *Brazil* 71J4
Bacan I *Indon* 45C3
Bačau *Rom* 25D6
Bac Can *Viet* 43D1
Baccarat *France* 16D2
Bacchus Marsh *Aust* 50B3
Bachu *China* 29F2
Back R *Can* 52J3
Backbone Ranges Mts *Can* 56N3
Backnang *W Germ* 16E2
Bac Ninh *Viet* 43D1
Bacolod *Phil* 45F8
Baco,Mt *Phil* 45F8
Badagara *India* 36B2
Badain Jaran Shamo Desert *China* 40A1
Badajoz *Spain* 19A2
Badalona *Spain* 19C1
Badanah *S Arabia* 30D3
Bad Aussee *Austria* 17E1
Bad Bergzabern *W Germ* 16E2
Bad Ems *W Germ* 16D1
Baden Region *W Germ* 18D2
Baden *Switz* 17C1
Baden-Baden *W Germ* 20B3
Badenviller *France* 16D2
Baden-Württemberg State *W Germ* 20B3
Badgaon *Nepal* 37C2
Badgastein *Austria* 20C3
Bad-Godesberg *W Germ* 20B2
Bad Hersfeld *W Germ* 20B2
Bad Honnef *W Germ* 16D1
Badin *Pak* 35B4
Bad Ischl *Austria* 22C1
Badiyat ash Sham Desert Region *Jordan/Iraq* 30C3
Bad-Kreuznach *W Germ* 20B3
Badlands *USA* 57B2
Bad Lippspringe *W Germ* 16E1
Bad Nauheim *W Germ* 16E1
Bad Nevenahr-Ahrweiler *W Germ* 16D1
Badou *Togo* 77G4
Bad Ragaz *Switz* 17C1
Badr Hunayn *S Arabia* 32C2
Bad Ryrmont *W Germ* 16E1
Bad Tolz *W Germ* 20C3
Badulla *Sri Lanka* 36C3
Bad Wildungen *W Germ* 16E1
Bad Wimpfen *W Germ* 16E2
Badzhal'skiy Khrebet Mts *USSR* 41C1
Baena *Spain* 19B2
Bafang *Cam* 77J4
Bafatá *Guinea-Bissau* 76A3
Baffin B *Greenland/Can* 53L2
Baffin B *USA* 63F4
Baffin I *Can* 53L2
Bafia *Cam* 78B3
Bafing R *Mali* 76A3
Bafoulabé *Mali* 76A3
Bafoussam *Cam* 78B3
Bāfq *Iran* 34D2
Bafra Burun Pt *Turk* 25F7
Bāft *Iran* 34D3
Bafwasende *Zaïre* 78C3
Baga *Nig* 77J3
Bagaha *India* 37B2
Bāgalkot *India* 36B1
Bagamoyo *Tanz* 79D4
Bagan Datok *Malay* 44F7
Bagan Siapiapi *Indon* 44F7
Bagdad *USA* 65D4
Bagé *Brazil* 69F4
Baggs *USA* 62A1
Baghdād *Iraq* 30D3
Bagherhat *Bang* 37C3
Bāghīn *Iran* 34D2
Baghlan *Afghan* 35B1
Bagley *USA* 57C2
Bagnoa *Ivory Coast* 76B4
Bagnols-sur-Cèza *France* 18C3
Bagoé R *Mali* 76B3
Baguio *Phil* 45F7
Bāhādurābād *India* 37C2
Bahamas,The Is *Caribbean* 55F4
Baharampur *India* 37C3
Bahar Dar *Eth* 78D2
Baharīya Oasis *Egypt* 30A4
Bahau *Malay* 44G7
Bahawahpur Province *Pak* 35C3
Bahawalpur *Pak* 35C3
Bahawathagar *Pak* 35C3
Bahia = Salvador
Bahia State *Brazil* 71K6
Bahia Anegada *Arg* 72C4
Bahía Blanca *Arg* 69D5
Bahía Blanca B *Arg* 69D5
Bahía Concepción B *Chile* 72A3
Bahia da Ilha Grande B *Brazil* 73D3
Bahía de Banderas B *Mexico* 66B2
Bahía de Campeche B *Mexico* 66C2
Bahía de Corando B *Costa Rica* 70B2
Bahía de la Ascension B *Mexico* 66D3
Bahía de Petacalco B *Mexico* 66B3
Bahía de Rio de Oro B *Mor* 76A2
Bahia de Sepetiba B *Brazil* 73D3
Bahiá de Todos Santos B *Mexico* 65C4
Bahía Grande B *Arg* 69C8
Bahía Kino *Mexico* 54B4
Bahía Magdalena B *Mexico* 66A2
Bahía Salada B *Chile* 72A1
Bahía Samborombon B *Arg* 72D3
Bahía Sebastia Vizcaino B *Mexico* 66A2
Bahir Dar *Eth* 32C4
Bahrael Manzala L *Egypt* 31A3
Bahraich *India* 37B2
Bahrain Sheikdom *Arabian Pen* 28D3
Bahr al Milh L *Iraq* 30D3
Bahr Aouk R *Chad/CAR* 78C3
Bahrat Lut = Dead S
Bahr el Abiad = White Nile
Bahr el Abiad R *Sudan* 32B4
Bahr el Arab Watercourse *Sudan* 78C3
Bahr el Azraq = Blue Nile
Bahr el Azraq R *Sudan* 32B4
Bahr el Ghazal R *Sudan* 78D3
Bahr el Ghazal Watercourse *Chad* 78B2
Bahr Fāqûs R *Egypt* 31A3
Bāhū-Kalāt *Iran* 34E3
Bahumbelu *Indon* 45B3
Baia de Marajó B *Brazil* 71J4
Baiá de Pemba B *Mozam* 79E5
Baia de São Marcos B *Brazil* 71K4
Baia de Setúbal B *Port* 19A2
Baia de Todos os Santos B *Brazil* 71L6
Baia dos Tigres *Angola* 79B5
Baiá Guaratuba *Brazil* 73C4
Baia Mare *Rom* 25C6
Baïbokoum *Chad* 78B3
Baicheng *China* 41A2
Baie Antongila B *Madag* 79F5
Baie-Comeau *Can* 53M5
Baie de Bombetoka B *Madag* 79E5
Baie de Mahajamba B *Madag* 79E5
Baie de St Augustin B *Madag* 79E6
Baie de St Georges B *Leb* 31C2
Baie des Chaleurs B *Can* 55G2
Baie St Paul *Can* 59E1
Baihe *China* 40B3
Bai He R *China* 40C3
Ba'ījī *Iraq* 30D3
Baikunthpur *India* 37B3
Baile Atha Cliath = Dublin
Băilesti *Rom* 23E2
Bailleul *France* 16B1
Baillie Is *Can* 56N1
Baima *China* 40A3
Bainbridge *USA* 61C2
Baing *Indon* 45B5
Baiquan *China* 41B2
Baird Inlet *USA* 56F3
Baird Mts *USA* 52B3
Bairin Youqi *China* 40D1
Bairin Zuoqi *China* 40D1
Bairnsdale *Aust* 48D4
Bais *Phil* 45F9
Baissa *Nig* 77J4
Baitadi *Nepal* 37B2
Baiyuda Desert *Sudan* 32B3
Baja *Hung* 23D1
Baja California State *Mexico* 54B3
Baja California Pen *Mexico* 66A1
Baja California Norte *Mexico* 65C4
Bajawi *Indon* 45B4
Bājil *Yemen* 32D4
Bajo *Indon* 45B2
Bakal *USSR* 24K4
Bakala *CAR* 78C3
Bakel *Sen* 76A3
Baker California *USA* 65C3
Baker Montana *USA* 54C2
Baker Oregon *USA* 54B2
Baker *USA* 52G5
Baker Foreland Pt *Can* 53J3
Baker L *Can* 52J3
Baker Lake *Can* 52J3
Baker,Mt *USA* 54A2
Bakersfield *USA* 54B3
Bakharden *USSR* 34D1
Bakhardok *USSR* 34D1
Bakhmach *USSR* 25E5
Bakkaflói B *Iceland* 12C1
Bako *Eth* 78D3
Bakouma *CAR* 78C3
Baku *USSR* 25H7
Bakudek I *Indon* 45B3
Bakungan *Indon* 44A2
Balâ *Turk* 30B2
Balabac I *Phil* 45E9
Balabac Str *Malay* 44E1
Bālaghāt *India* 37B3
Balaikarangan *Indon* 44D2
Balaklava *Aust* 50A2
Balakovo *USSR* 25H5
Bala Murghab *Afghan* 34E1
Balāngīr *India* 37B3
Balashov *USSR* 25G5
Balasore *India* 37C3
Balât *Egypt* 32A1
Balaton L *Hung* 23D1
Balbriggan *Irish Rep* 15B5
Balcarce *Arg* 69E5
Balchik *Bulg* 23F2
Balclutha *NZ* 49F5
Bald Knob *USA* 63D2
Baldwin *USA* 61C2
Baldwin Pen *USA* 56F2
Baldy Mt *USA* 64E1
Baldy Peak Mt *USA* 54C3
Balearic Is = Islas Baleares
Baleh R *Malay* 44D2
Baler *Phil* 45F7
Balezino *USSR* 24J4
Balhāf *S Yemen* 33E4
Balho *Djibouti* 32D4
Bali I *Indon* 48A1
Balıkesir *Turk* 30A2
Balīkh R *Syria* 30C2
Balikpapan *Indon* 44E3
Balintang Chan *Phil* 45F7
Bali S *Indon* 44D4
Baliza *Brazil* 73B2
Baljurshī *S Arabia* 32D3
Balkh *Afghan* 35B1
Balkhash *USSR* 26J5
Ballachulish *Scot* 14C3
Ballantrae *Scot* 14C4
Ballantyne Str *Can* 52G2
Ballapur *India* 36B2
Ballarat *Aust* 48D4
Ballater *Scot* 14D3
Balleny Is *Ant* 80F7
Ballia *India* 37B2
Ballina *Aust* 50D1
Ballina *Irish Rep* 13B3
Ballinger *USA* 62C3
Ballon d'Alsace Mt *France* 16D3
Ballston Spa *USA* 60D1
Ballycastle *N Ire* 14B4
Ballymena *N Ire* 14B4
Ballymoney *N Ire* 14B4
Ballyshannon *Irish Rep* 15A4
Balmoral *Aust* 50B3
Balmorhea *USA* 62B3
Balnearia *Arg* 72C2
Balombo *Angola* 79B5
Balonn R *Aust* 50C1
Balotra *India* 35C3
Balrāmpur *India* 37B2
Balranald *Aust* 48D4
Balsas *Brazil* 71J5
Balsas *Mexico* 67C2
Balsas R *Mexico* 66B3
Balta *USSR* 25D6
Baltasar Brum *Urug* 72D2
Baltic S *N Europe* 12H7
Baltîm *Egypt* 30B3
Baltimore *USA* 55F3
Baluchistan Region *Pak* 35B3
Bālurghāt *India* 37C2
Balykshi *USSR* 25J6
Bam *Iran* 34D3
Bama *Nig* 78B2
Bamako *Mali* 76B3
Bambari *CAR* 78C3
Bamberg *USA* 61C2
Bamberg *W Germ* 20C3
Bambili *Zaïre* 78C3
Bambui *Brazil* 73C3
Bamenda *Cam* 78B3
Bamingui R *CAR* 78B3
Bamingui Bangoran National Park *CAR* 78B3
Bamiyan *Afghan* 35B2
Bampur *Iran* 34E3
Bampur R *Iran* 34E3
Banaba I *Kiribati*
Banalia *Zaïre* 78C3
Banamba *Mali* 76B3
Bananga *Nicobar Is* 36E3
Ban Aranyaprathet *Thai* 43C3
Ban Ban *Laos* 43C2
Ban Betong *Thai* 43C4
Banbridge *N Ire* 15B4
Banbury *Eng* 15E5
Banchory *Scot* 14D3
Banco Chinchorro Is *Mexico* 66D3
Bancroft *Can* 59D1
Bānda *India* 37B2
Banda Aceh *Indon* 44A1
Bandama R *Ivory Coast* 76B4
Bandar Abbās *Iran* 34D3
Bandar Anzalī *Iran* 25H8
Bandar-e Daylam *Iran* 34C3
Bandar-e Lengheh *Iran* 34C3
Bandar-e Māqām *Iran* 34C3
Bandar-e Rig *Iran* 34C3
Bandar-e Torkoman *Iran* 25J8
Bandar Khomeynī *Iran* 34B2
Bandar Seri Begawan *Brunei* 44D2
Banda S *Indon* 39F7
Bandau *Malay* 44E1
Band Bont *Iran* 34D3
Bandeira Mt *Brazil* 73D3
Bandera *Arg* 72C1
Banderantes *Brazil* 73B1
Bandiagara *Mali* 76B3
Band-i-Baba Upland *Afghan* 34E2
Bandirma *Turk* 25D7
Band-i-Turkestan Mts *Afghan* 34E1
Bandol *France* 17A3
Bandundu *Zaïre* 78B4
Bandung *Indon* 44C4
Baneh *Iran* 25H8
Banermo *Indon* 45C2
Banes *Cuba* 66E2
Banff *Scot* 14D3
Banff R *Can* 52G4
Banfora *U Volta* 77F3
Bangalore *India* 36B2
Bangangté *Cam* 77J4
Bangassou *CAR* 78C3
Banggi I *Malay* 44E1
Bang Hieng R *Laos* 43D2
Bangka I *Indon* 44C3
Bangkinang *Indon* 44B2
Bangko *Indon* 44B3
Bangkok *Thai* 43C3
Bangladesh Republic *Asia* 29H3
Bangong Co L *China* 35D2
Bangor Maine *USA* 55G2
Bangor *N Ire* 14B4
Bangor Pennsylvania *USA* 60C2
Bangor *Wales* 15C5
Bangsalsembera *Indon* 44E3
Bang Saphan Yai *Thai* 43B3
Bangued *Phil* 45F7
Bangui *CAR* 78B3
Bangweulu L *Zambia* 79D5
Ban Hat Yai *Thai* 43C4
Ban Hin Heup *Laos* 43C2
Ban Houei Sai *Laos* 43C1
Ban Hua Hin *Thai* 43B3
Bani R *Mali* 76B3
Bani Bangou *Niger* 76C3
Banī Ma'arid Region *S Arabia* 33E3
Banī Walīd *Libya* 75A1
Bāniyās *Syria* 30C2
Baniyas *Syria* 31C2
Banja Luka *Yugos* 22D2
Banjarmasin *Indon* 44D3
Banjul *The Gambia* 76A3
Ban Kantang *Thai* 43B4
Ban Khemmarat *Laos* 43D2
Ban Khok Kloi *Thai* 43B4
Banks Is *Vanuatu* 49F2
Banks I *Aust* 39H8
Banks I British Columbia *Can* 52E4
Banks I Northwest Territories *Can* 52F2
Banks L *USA* 64C1
Banks Pen *NZ* 51B2
Banks Str *Aust* 50E3
Bankura *India* 37C3
Ban Mae Sariang *Thai* 43B2
Ban Mae Sot *Thai* 43B2
Banmauk *Burma* 37E3
Ban Me Thuot *Viet* 43D3
Bann R *N Ire* 14B4
Ban Na San *Thai* 43B4
Bannu *Pak* 35C2
Baños de Chihuio *Chile* 72A4
Baños Maule *Chile* 72A3
Ban Pak Neun *Laos* 43C2
Ban Pak Phanang *Thai* 43C4
Ban Ru Kroy *Camb* 43D3
Ban Sai Yok *Thai* 43B3
Ban Sattahip *Thai* 43C3
Banská Bystrica *Czech* 21D3

Bānswāra Berkovitsa

Bānswāra India 35C4
Bantaeng Indon 45B4
Ban Tha Kham Thai 43B4
Ban Thateng Laos 43D2
Ban Tha Tum Thai 43C2
Bantry Irish Rep 13B3
Bantry B Irish Rep 13A3
Ban Ya Soup Viet 43D3
Banyo Cam 77J4
Banyuwangi Indon 44D4
Banzare Seamount Indian O 46E7
Baofeng China 40C3
Bao Ha Viet 43C1
Baoji China 40B3
Bao Loc Viet 43D3
Baoqing China 41C2
Baoshan China 38C4
Baotou China 40C1
Bāpatla India 36C1
Bapaume France 16B1
Ba'Qūbah Iraq 30D3
Bar Yugos 23D2
Bara Indon 45C3
Bara Sudan 78D2
Baraawe Somalia 78E3
Barabai Indon 44E3
Bāra Banki India 37B2
Barabinsk USSR 26J4
Barabinskaya Step Steppe USSR 26J4
Baracaldo Spain 19B1
Baracoa Cuba 68C2
Baradá R Syria 31D2
Baradine Aust 50C2
Baraka Watercourse Eth 32C3
Bārāmati India 36A1
Baramula Pak 35C2
Bārān India 35D3
Barangas Phil 45F8
Baranof I USA 52E4
Baranovichi USSR 24D5
Baratta Aust 50A2
Barauni India 37C2
Barbacena Brazil 71K8
Barbados I Caribbean 68F4
Barbastro Spain 19C1
Barbezieux France 18B2
Barbôsa Colombia 70D2
Barbuda I Caribbean 68E3
Barcaldine Aust 48D3
Barce = Al Marj
Barcellona Italy 22D3
Barcelona Spain 19C1
Barcelona Ven 70F1
Barcelonnette France 17B2
Barcoo R Aust 48D3
Barda del Medio Arg 72B3
Bardai Chad 78B1
Bardas Blancas Arg 69C5
Barddhamān India 37C3
Bardejov Czech 21E3
Bardi Italy 17C2
Bardonecchia Italy 17B2
Bardsey I Wales 15C5
Bardstown USA 58B3
Bareeda Somalia 33F4
Bareilly India 35D3
Barentsovo More S USSR 24F1
Barentsøya I Barents S 26D2
Barents S = Barentsovo More
Barentu Eth 78D2
Bargarh India 37B3
Barge Italy 17B2
Barguzin USSR 27N4
Barguzin R USSR 27N4
Bar Harbour USA 59F2
Barhi India 37C3
Bari Italy 22D2
Barika Alg 19D2
Barinas Ven 70D2
Baripāda India 37C3
Bārîs Egypt 32B2
Bari Sādri India 35C4
Barisal Bang 37D3
Barito R Indon 44D3
Barjols France 17B3
Barjuj Watercourse Libya 75A2
Barkam China 40A3
Barkley,L USA 58B3
Barkley,L USA 63E2
Barkly East S Africa 79C7
Barkly Tableland Mts Aust 48C2
Bar-le-Duc France 16C2
Barlee,L Aust 48A3
Barlee Range Mts Aust 48A3
Barletta Italy 22D2
Barmer India 35C3
Barmera Aust 50B2
Barmouth Wales 15C5
Barnard Castle Eng 15E4
Barnaul USSR 26K4
Barnegat USA 60C3
Barnegat B USA 60C3
Barnesboro USA 60A2
Barnes Icecap Can 53L2
Barnesville Georgia USA 61C2
Barnesville Ohio USA 58C3
Barnhart USA 62B3
Barnsley Eng 15E5
Barnstaple Eng 15C6
Baro Nig 77H4
Barpeta India 37D2
Barquisimeto Ven 70E1
Barr France 16D2
Barra Brazil 71K6
Barra I Scot 14B3
Barraba Aust 50D2
Barra da Estiva Brazil 73D1
Barra de Navidad Mexico 67B2
Barra de Piraí Brazil 73D3
Barra de Tonalá Mexico 67D2
Barra do Bugres Brazil 73A2
Barra do Garças Brazil 73B2
Barra do Quaraí Brazil 72D2
Barra do Ribeiro Brazil 72E2
Barrage d'Ayama Ivory Coast 77F4
Barrage de Mbakaou Dam Cam 77J4
Barragem do Castelo do Bode Res Port 19A2
Barragem do Maranhão Port 19A2
Barra Head Pt Scot 14B3
Barra Mansa Brazil 71K8
Barranca Peru 70C6
Barrancabermeja Colombia 70D2
Barrancas Ven 70F2
Barranqueras Arg 85E3
Barranquilla Colombia 70D1
Barra,Sound of Chan Scot 14B3
Barre USA 60D1
Barreal Arg 72B2
Barreiras Brazil 71K6
Barreiro Port 19A2
Barreiros Brazil 71L5
Barren,C Aust 48D5
Barren Is USA 56H4
Barretos Brazil 71J8
Barrie Can 59D2
Barrier Range Mts Aust 50B2
Barrington,Mt Aust 48E4
Barro Alto Brazil 73C2
Barroloola Aust 39G8
Barron USA 58A1
Barrouaillie St Vincent 68N2
Barrow USA 52C2
Barrow R Irish Rep 13B3
Barrow R Irish Rep 15B5
Barrow Creek Aust 48C3
Barrow I Aust 48A3
Barrow-in-Furness Eng 15D4
Barrow,Pt USA 52C2
Barrow Str Can 53J2
Barry's Bay Can 59D1
Barryville USA 60C2
Barsi India 36B1
Barstow USA 54B3
Bar-sur-Aube France 18C2
Bar-sur-Seine France 16C2
Bartica Guyana 71G2
Bartın Turk 30B1
Bartle Frere,Mt Aust 48D2
Bartlesville USA 54D3
Bartlett USA 57C3
Bartolomeu Dias Mozam 79D6
Bartoszyce Pol 21E2
Barung I Indon 44D4
Barus Indon 44A2
Barwāh India 35D4
Barwāni India 35C4
Barwon R Aust 50C1
Barysh USSR 24H5
Basail Arg 72D1
Basankusu Zaïre 78B3
Basavilbas Arg 72D2
Basco Phil 45F6
Basel France 16D3
Basel Switz 22B1
Basento R Italy 22D2
Bashi Chan Phil 45F6
Bashkirskaya ASSR Republic USSR 24J5
Basiano Indon 45B3
Basilan I Phil 45F9
Basildon Eng 15F6
Basilio Brazil 72E2
Basin USA 64E2
Basingstoke Eng 15E6
Basin Region USA 54B2
Basra Iraq 30E3
Bas-Rhin Department France 16D2
Bassac R Camb 43D3
Bassano Italy 22C1
Bassano del Grappa Italy 17D2
Bassari Togo 77G4
Bassas da India I Mozam Chan 79D6
Bassein Burma 43A2
Basse Terre Guadeloupe 68E3
Bassett USA 57C3
Bassila Benin 77G4
Bass Str Aust 48D5
Båstad Sweden 12G7
Bastak Iran 34C3
Basti India 37B2
Bastia Corse 22B2
Bastogne Belg 20B3
Bastrop Louisiana USA 63D3
Bastrop Texas USA 63C3
Bata Eq Guinea 78A3
Batakan Indon 44D3
Batala India 35D2
Batang China 38C3
Batangafo CAR 78B3
Batan Is Phil 45F6
Batanta I Indon 45D3
Batatais Brazil 73C3
Batavia USA 59D2
Batemans Bay Aust 50D3
Batesburg USA 61C2
Batesville Arkansas USA 63D2
Batesville Mississippi USA 63E3
Bath Can 59F1
Bath Eng 15D6
Bath Maine USA 59F2
Bath New York USA 59D2
Batha R Chad 78B2
Bathawana Mt Can 58C1
Bathurst Aust 48D4
Bathurst Can 53M5
Bathurst,C Can 52F2
Bathurst I Aust 48C2
Bathurst I Can 52H2
Bathurst Inlet B Can 52H3
Batié U Volta 77F4
Bātlāq-e-Gavkhūnī Salt Flat Iran 34C2
Batlow Aust 50C3
Batman Turk 30D2
Batna Alg 77D1
Baton Rouge USA 55D3
Batroun Leb 31C1
Battambang Camb 43C3
Batticaloa Sri Lanka 36C3
Batti Malv I Indian O 36E3
Battle Creek USA 55E2
Battle Harbour Can 53N4
Battle Mountain USA 64C2
Batu Gajah Malay 44F6
Batukelau Indon 44E2
Batumi USSR 25G7
Batu Pahat Malay 43C5
Baturaja Indon 44B3
Bat Yam Israel 31C2
Baubau Indon 48B1
Bauchi Nig 77H3
Bauchi State Nig 77H3
Baudette USA 57D2
Bauges Mts France 17B2
Bauld,C Can 53N4
Baumes-les-Dames France 17B1
Baunt USSR 27N4
Bauru Brazil 71J8
Baus Brazil 73B2
Bautzen E Germ 20C2
Baween I Indon 44D4
Bawîti Egypt 75B2
Bawku Ghana 77F3
Bawlake Burma 43B2
Bawlen Aust 50A2
Baxley USA 61C2
Baxoi China 37E1
Bayamo Cuba 66E2
Bayan China 41B2
Bayan Indon 44E4
Bayandalay Mongolia 40A1
Bayandzürh Mongolia 38D2
Bayandzürh USSR 27M5
Bayan Har Shan Mts China 38C3
Bayan Mod China 40A1
Bayan Obo China 40B1
Bayard Nebraska USA 57B3
Bayard New Mexico USA 62A3
Bayard P France 17B2
Bayard,Mt Can 56N4
Baybay Phil 45F8
Bayburt Turk 30D1
Bay City Michigan USA 55E2
Bay City Texas USA 63C4
Bay Dağlari Turk 30B2
Baydaratskaya Guba B USSR 26H3
Baydhabo Somalia 78E3
Bayeaux France 18B2
Bayerische Alpen Mts W Germ 17D1
Bayern State W Germ 20C3
Bayfield USA 58A1
Bayhan al Qisāb S Yemen 33E4
Bāyir Jordan 30C3
Baykalskiy Khrebet Mts USSR 38D1
Baykit USSR 27L3
Baylik Shan Mts China/ Mongolia 27L5
Baymak USSR 24K5
Bay Minette USA 61B2
Bayombang Phil 45F7
Bayonne France 18B3
Bayram Ali USSR 34E1
Bayreuth W Germ 20C3
Bay St Louis USA 63E3
Bay Shore USA 59E2
Bays,L of Can 59D1
Bayt al Faqīh Yemen 32D4
Baytik Shan Mts China 38B2
Bayt Lahm = Bethlehem
Baytown USA 63D4
Baza Spain 19B2
Bazaliya USSR 21F3
Bazar-Dyuzi USSR 25H7
Bazas France 18B3
Bazhong China 40B3
Bazmān Iran 34E3
Bcharre Leb 31D1
Beach USA 57B2
Beach Haven USA 60C3
Beachy Head Eng 15F6
Beacon USA 60D2
Bealanana Madag 79E5
Bear R USA 64D2
Beardstown USA 58A2
Bear I = Bjørnøya
Bear L USA 64D2
Beatrice USA 54D2
Beatrice Oilfield N Sea 14D2
Beatton River Can 52F4
Beatty USA 54B3
Beattyville Can 59D1
Beauce Region France 16A2
Beauchene Is Falkland Is 69E8
Beaudesert Aust 50D1
Beaufort S Can 80B5
Beaufort West S Africa 79C7
Beaugeney France 16A3
Beauharnois Can 59E1
Beauly Scot 14C3
Beaumont California USA 65C4
Beaumont Texas USA 55D3
Beaumont-sur-Sarthe France 16A2
Beaune France 18C2
Beausejour Can 57C2
Beauvais France 18C2
Beaver Alaska USA 56J2
Beaver Utah USA 65D3
Beaver Creek Can 52D3
Beaver Creek USA 56J2
Beaver Dam Kentucky USA 58B3
Beaver Dam Wisconsin USA 58B2
Beaverhead Mts USA 64D1
Beaver I USA 58B1
Beaver L USA 63D2
Beawar India 35C3
Beazley Arg 72B2
Bebedouro Brazil 73C3
Beccles Eng 15F5
Bečej Yugos 23E1
Béchar Alg 76B1
Becharof L USA 56G4
Bechevin B USA 56F4
Beckley USA 55E3
Beckum W Germ 16E1
Bedford County Eng 15E5
Bedford Eng 15E5
Bedford Indiana USA 58B3
Bedford Pennsylvania USA 60A3
Bedford Pt Grenada 68M2
Beech Creek USA 60B2
Beechey Pt USA 52D2
Beechworth Aust 50C3
Beenleigh Aust 50D1
Beer Menuha Israel 31C3
Beer Ora Israel 31C4
Beersheba Israel 30B3
Beèr Sheva = Beersheba
Beér Sheva R Israel 31C3
Beeville USA 54D4
Befale Zaïre 78C3
Befandriana Madag 79E5
Bega Aust 50C3
Behbehān Iran 34C2
Behm Canal Sd USA 56M4
Behshahr Iran 34C1
Behsud Afghan 35B2
Bei'an China 41B2
Beihai China 40B5
Beihai China 43D1
Beijing China 40D2
Beiliu China 43E1
Beipan Jiang R China 40B4
Beipiao China 40E1
Beira = Sofala
Beirut Leb 30C3
Bei Shan Mts China 38C2
Beit ed Dîne Leb 31C2
Beit Jala Israel 31C3
Beja Port 19A2
Beja Tunisia 77D1
Bejaïa Alg 77D1
Béjar Spain 19A1
Bejestān Iran 34D2
Békéscsaba Hung 21E3
Bekily Madag 79E6
Bela India 37B2
Bela Pak 35B3
Belaga Malay 44D2
Bel Air USA 60B3
Belamoalli India 36B1
Belang Indon 45B2
Belangpidie Indon 44A2
Belau Republic Pacific O 39G6
Belau I Pacific O 46H4
Bela Vista Mozam 79D6
Béla Vista Par/Brazil 73A3
Belawan Indon 44A2
Belaya R USSR 24K4
Belaya Tserkov USSR 21G3
Belcher Chan Can 53J2
Belchiragh Afghan 35B1
Belebey USSR 24J5
Belém Brazil 71J4
Belén Arg 72B1
Belén Colombia 70C3
Belén Par 73A3
Belén Urug 72D2
Belen USA 54C3
Belén R Arg 72B1
Belet Uen Somalia 78E3
Belfast N Ire 14B4
Belfast Lough Estuary N Ire 14B4
Belfield USA 57B2
Belfodio Eth 78D2
Belford Eng 14E4
Belfort France 18D2
Belgaum India 36A1
Belgium Kingdom N W Europe 20A2
Belgorod USSR 25F5
Belgorod Dnestrovskiy USSR 25E6
Belgrade = Beograd
Belgrade USA 64D1
Bel Hedan Libya 75A2
Belinyu Indon 44C3
Belitung I Indon 44C3
Belize Belize 66D3
Belize Republic C America 66D3
Bellac France 18C2
Bella Coola Can 52F4
Bellagio Italy 17C2
Bellaire USA 63C4
Bellano Italy 17C1
Bellary India 36B1
Bellata Aust 50C1
Bella Union Urug 72D2
Bella Vista Arg 72D1
Belledonne Mts France 17B2
Belle Fonte USA 60B2
Belle Fourche USA 54C2
Belle Fourche R USA 57B3
Bellegarde France 18D2
Belle Glade USA 61E4
Belle I Can 53N4
Belle-Ile I France 18B2
Belle Isle,Str of Can 53N4
Bellême France 16A2
Belleville Can 53L5
Belleville Illinois USA 58B3
Belleville Kansas USA 63C2
Bellevue Idaho USA 64D2
Bellevue Iowa USA 58A2
Bellevue Washington USA 64B1
Belley France 17A2
Bellin Can 53L3
Bellingen Aust 50D2
Bellingham USA 54A2
Bellingshausen Base Ant 80G2
Bellingshausen S Ant 80G3
Bellinzona Switz 22B1
Bello Colombia 70C2
Bellona Reefs Nouvelle Calédonie 49E3
Bellows Falls USA 59E2
Bell Pen Can 53K3
Belluno Italy 22C1
Bell Ville Arg 69D4
Belmont USA 60B1
Belmonte Brazil 71L7
Belmopan Belize 66D3
Belogorsk USSR 41B1
Beloha Madag 79E6
Belo Horizonte Brazil 71K7
Beloit Kansas USA 62C2
Beloit Wisconsin USA 55E2
Belomorsk USSR 26E3
Beloretsk USSR 24K5
Belorusskaya SSR Republic USSR 24D5
Belo-Tsiribihina Madag 79E5
Beloye More S USSR 26E3
Beloye Ozero L USSR 24F3
Belozersk USSR 24F3
Belpre USA 58C3
Beltana Aust 50A2
Belton USA 63C3
Bel'tsy USSR 21F3
Belukha Mt USSR 26K5
Belush'ye USSR 24H2
Belvidere Illinois USA 58B2
Belvidere New Jersey USA 60C2
Bembe Angola 79B4
Bembéréke Benin 77G3
Bemidji USA 55D2
Bemis USA 61B1
Bena Nor 12G6
Bena Dibele Zaïre 78C4
Benalla Aust 50C3
Ben Attow Mt Scot 14C2
Benavente Spain 19A1
Benbecula I Scot 14B3
Bencubbin Aust 48A4
Bend USA 54A2
Ben Dearg Mt Scot 14C3
Bendel State Nig 77H4
Bender Beyla Somalia 75E3
Bendery USSR 25D6
Bendigo Aust 48D4
Benedery USSR 21F3
Bénéna Mali 77F3
Benešov Czech 20C3
Benevento Italy 22C2
Bengal,B of Asia 29G4
Ben Gardane Libya 75A1
Ben Gardane Tunisia 77E2
Bengbu China 40D3
Benggai I Indon 45B3
Benghāzī Libya 75B1
Bengkalis Indon 44B2
Bengkulu Indon 44B3
Benguela Angola 79B5
Benguerir Mor 77A2
Benha Egypt 30B3
Ben Hope Mt Scot 14C2
Beni Zaïre 78C3
Béni R Bol 70E6
Beni Abbes Alg 76B1
Benicarló Spain 19C1
Benidji USA 53J5
Benidorm Spain 19B2
Beni Mansour Alg 19C2
Beni Mazar Egypt 75C2
Beni Mellal Mor 77A2
Benin Republic Africa 76C4
Benin City Nig 77H4
Beni-Saf Alg 77B1
Beni Suef Egypt 75C2
Benkelman USA 62B2
Ben Kilbreck Mt Scot 14C2
Ben Lawers Mt Scot 13C2
Ben Lomond Mt Aust 50E3
Ben Macdui Mt Scot 14D3
Ben More Assynt Mt Scot 14C2
Benmore,L NZ 51B2
Ben Nevis Mt Scot 14C3
Bennington USA 59E2
Bennt Jbail Leb 31C2
Bénoué R Cam 78B3
Bénoué Nat Pk Cam 77J4
Bensheim W Germ 16E2
Benson Arizona USA 54B3
Benson Minnesota USA 57C2
Bentiu Sudan 78C3
Bento Gomes R Brazil 73A2
Benton Arkansas USA 63D3
Benton Kentucky USA 58B3
Benton Harbour USA 58B2
Benue State Nig 77H4
Benue R Nig 77H4
Ben Wyvis Mt Scot 14C3
Benxi China 40E1
Beo Indon 45C2
Beograd Yugos 23E2
Beohāri India 37B3
Beppu Japan 41C5
Berat Alb 23D2
Berber Sudan 78D2
Berbera Somalia 78E2
Berbérati CAR 78B3
Berck France 16A1
Berdichev USSR 21F3
Berdichev USSR 25D6
Berdyansk USSR 25F6
Berea USA 58C3
Berebere Indon 45C2
Berekum Ghana 77F4
Berenice Egypt 32C2
Berens R Can 52J4
Berens River Can 52J4
Beresford Aust 50A1
Beresford USA 57C3
Berettyoújfalu Hung 21E3
Bereza USSR 21F2
Berezhany USSR 21E3
Berezina R USSR 21F2
Bereznik USSR 24G3
Berezniki USSR 26G4
Berezovka USSR 25E6
Berezovo USSR 26H3
Berezovyy USSR 41D1
Bergama Turk 30A2
Bergamo Italy 22B1
Bergen Nor 12F6
Bergen USA 60B1
Bergen op Zoom Neth 16C1
Bergerac France 18C3
Bergisch-Gladbach W Germ 16D1
Berhampur India 36C1
Bering Gl USA 56K3
Beringovskiy USSR 27U3
Bering S USSR/USA 47K2
Bering Str USSR/USA 80C6
Berīzak Iran 34D3
Berja Spain 19B2
Berkane Mor 77B2
Berkeley USA 54A3
Berkeley Spring USA 60A3
Berkner I Ant 80F2
Berkovitsa Bulg 23E2

Berkshire Bornholm

Berkshire County Eng 15E6
Berkshire Hills USA 60D1
Berlin E Germ 20C2
Berlin New Hampshire USA 59E2
Berlin Pennsylvania USA 60A3
Bermejo Bol 70F8
Bermejo R Arg 69E3
Bern Switz 22B1
Bernalillo USA 62A2
Bernardo de Irigoyen Arg 73B4
Bernardsville USA 60C2
Bernasconi Arg 72C3
Bernay France 16A2
Bernburg E Germ 20C2
Berner Orberland Mts Switz 17B1
Bernier B Can 53K2
Berounka R Czech 20C3
Berrechid Mor 77A2
Berri Aust 50B2
Berriane Alg 77C2
Berry Region France 18C2
Berry Is Bahamas 55F4
Berryville USA 60B3
Bertam Malay 44F6
Berthoud P USA 62A2
Bertoua Cam 78B3
Beru I Kiribati 49G1
Berwick USA 59D2
Berwick-upon-Tweed Eng 14D4
Berwyn Mts Wales 15D5
Besalampy Madag 79E5
Besançon France 18D2
Beskidy Zachodnie Mts Pol 21E3
Besni Turk 30C2
Besor R Israel 31C3
Bessemer Alabama USA 61B2
Bessemer Michigan USA 58B1
Betafo Madag 79E5
Betanzos Spain 19A1
Betaré Oya Cam 77J4
Bet Guvrin Israel 31C3
Bethanie Namibia 79B6
Bethany Missouri USA 63D1
Bethany Oklahoma USA 63C2
Bethel Alaska USA 52B3
Bethel Connecticut USA 60D2
Bethel Park USA 58C2
Bethesda USA 59D3
Bethlehem Israel 31C3
Bethlehem S Africa 79C6
Bethlehem USA 59D2
Bethnal S Africa 79C6
Bethune France 18C1
Béthune R France 16A2
Betioky Madag 79E6
Betoota Aust 50B1
Betou Congo 78B3
Betpak Dala Steppe USSR 29E1
Betroka Madag 79E6
Betsiamites Can 53M5
Bettendorf USA 58A2
Bettiah India 37B2
Bettles USA 56H2
Béttola Italy 17C2
Betul India 35D4
Betuwe Province Neth 16C1
Betwa R India 35D3
Betzdorf W Germ 16D1
Beverley,L USA 56G4
Beverly USA 60E1
Beverly Hills USA 65C4
Beyla Guinea 76B4
Beypore India 36B2
Beyrouth = Beirut
Beyşehir Turk 30B2
Beysehir Gölü L Turk 25E8
Beyt Shean Israel 31C2
Bezan Austria 17C1
Bezhetsk USSR 24F4
Béziers France 18C3
Bezmein USSR 34D1
Beznosova USSR 38D1
Bhadrāchalam India 36C1
Bhadrakh India 37C3
Bhadra Res India 36B2
Bhadrāvati India 36B2
Bhag Pak 35B3
Bhāgalpur India 37C2
Bhakkar Pak 35C2
Bhamo Burma 37E3
Bhandāra India 35D4
Bharatpur India 35D3
Bharūch India 35C4
Bhātiāpāra Ghat Bang 37C3
Bhatinda India 35C2
Bhatkal India 36A2
Bhātpāra India 37C3
Bhāvnagar India 35C4
Bhawānipatna India 37B4
Bhera Pak 35C2
Bheri R Nepal 37B2
Bhilai India 37B3
Bhīlwāra India 35C3
Bhīmavaram India 36C1
Bhind India 35D3
Bhiwāni India 35D3
Bhongir India 36B1
Bhopāl India 35D4
Bhubaneshwar India 37C3
Bhuj India 35B4
Bhusāwal India 35D4
Bhutan Kingdom Asia 29H3
Bia R Ghana 77F4
Biak I Indon 39G7
Biala Podlaska Pol 21E2
Bialograd Pol 20D2
Bialystok Pol 21E2
Biargtangar C Iceland 12A1
Biarjmand Iran 34D1
Biaro I Indon 45C2
Biarritz France 18B3
Biasca Switz 17C1
Biba Egypt 30B4
Bibai Japan 41E3
Bibala Angola 79B5
Bibbiena Italy 17D3
Biberach W Germ 20B3
Bibiani Ghana 77F4
Bicaz Rom 23F1
Bichi R USSR 41D1
Bicknell USA 65D3
Bida Nig 77H4
Bīdar India 36B1
Bidbid Oman 33G2
Biddeford USA 59E2
Bideford Eng 15C6
Bideford B Eng 15C6
Bidon 5 Alg 76C2
Bié Angola 79B5
Biebrza Pol 21E2
Biel Switz 22B1
Bielawa Pol 20D2
Bielefeld W Germ 20B2
Bieler See L Switz 17B1
Biella Italy 22B1
Bielsk Podlaski Pol 21E2
Bien Hoa Viet 43D3
Biferno R Italy 22C2
Biga Turk 30A1
Bigadiç Turk 23F3
Big Band Nat Pk USA 62B4
Big Belt Mts USA 64D1
Big Black R USA 63E3
Big Blue R USA 63C1
Big Cypress Swamp USA 61E4
Big Delta USA 52D3
Bigent W Germ 18D2
Biggar Kindersley Can 52H4
Biggenden Aust 50D1
Bigger,Mt Can 56L4
Big Hole R USA 64D1
Bighorn R USA 57A2
Bighorn L USA 57A2
Bighorn Mts USA 57A3
Bight of Bangkok B Thai 43C3
Bight of Benin B W Africa 76C4
Bight of Biafra B Cam 76C4
Big I Can 53L3
Big Koniuji I USA 56G4
Big Lake USA 62B3
Bignasco Switz 17C1
Bignona Sen 76A3
Big Pine USA 65C3
Big Rapids USA 58B2
Big River Can 52H4
Big Sandy USA 64D1
Big Sioux R USA 57C3
Big Spring USA 54C3
Big Springs USA 62B1
Big Stone City USA 57C2
Big Stone Gap USA 58C3
Big Timber USA 64E1
Big Trout L Can 53J4
Big Trout Lake Can 53K4
Bihać Yugos 22D2
Bihār India 37C2
Bihar State India 37C3
Biharamulo Tanz 78D4
Bihor Mt Rom 25C6
Bijāpur India 36B1
Bijāpur India 36C1
Bijār Iran 34B1
Bijauri Nepal 37B2
Bijeljina Yugos 23D2
Bijie China 40B4
Bijnor India 35D3
Bijnot Pak 35C3
Bikāner India 35C3
Bikfaya Leb 31C2
Bikin USSR 41C2
Bikin R USSR 41D2
Bikoro Zaïre 78B4
Bila He R China 41A2
Bilara India 35C3
Bilaspur India 35D2
Bilāspur India 37B3
Bilauktaung Range Mts Thai 43B3
Bilbao Spain 19B1
Bilbeis Egypt 31A3
Bilé R Czech 20D3
Bileća Yugos 23D2
Bilecik Turk 30B1
Bili R Zaïre 78C3
Bilibino USSR 27S3
Biliran I Phil 45F8
Billings USA 54C2
Bilma Niger 78B2
Biloxi USA 55E3
Biltine Chad 78C2
Bimbita Ghana 77F4
Bina-Etawa India 35D4
Binalbagan Phil 45F8
Bindura Zim 79D5
Binga Zim 79C5
Binga Mt Zim 79D5
Bingara Aust 50D1
Bingen W Germ 20B3
Bingham USA 59F1
Binghampton USA 55F2
Bingkor Malay 44E1
Bingöl Turk 30D2
Binhai China 40D3
Binjai Indon 44A2
Binjai Indon 44C2
Binongko I Indon 45B4
Bintan I Indon 44B2
Bintuhan Indon 44B3
Bintulu Malay 44D2
Bió Bió R Chile 69B5
Bioko I Atlantic O 74J4
Bīr India 36B1
Bira USSR 41C2
Bīr Abu Husein Well Egypt 75B2
Bi'r al Harash Well Libya 75B2
Birao CAR 78C2
Biratnagar Nepal 37C2
Birch Creek USA 56J2
Birchip Aust 50B3
Birch L USA 57D2
Birch Mts Can 52G4
Bird Can 53J4
Birdsville Aust 48C3
Birdum Aust 48C2
Bīr el 'Agramīya Well Egypt 31A4
Bir el Duweidâr Well Egypt 31B3
Birganj Nepal 37B2
Bîr Gifgâfa Well Egypt 31B3
Bîr Gindali Well Egypt 31A4
Bîr Hasana Well Egypt 31B3
Birigui Brazil 73B3
Bīrīn Syria 31D1
Birjand Iran 34D2
Birkat Qarun L Egypt 30B4
Birkenfeld W Germ 16D2
Birkenhead Eng 15D5
Bîrlad Rom 25D6
Bir Lahfân Well Egypt 31B3
Birmingham Eng 15D5
Birmingham USA 55E3
Bîr Misâha Well Egypt 75B2
Bir Moghrein Maur 76A2
Birnin Gwari Nig 77H3
Birnin Kebbi Nig 77G3
Birni N'Konni Nig 77H3
Birobidzhan USSR 41C2
Birr Irish Rep 15B5
Bir Rabalou Alg 19C2
Birrie R Aust 50C1
Birsay Scot 14D2
Birsk USSR 24K4
Bîr Tarfâwi Well Egypt 75B2
Birtle Can 57B1
Bîr Udelb Well Egypt 31B4
Biryusa USSR 27L4
Birzai USSR 12J7
Bir Zreigat Well Maur 76B2
Bisa I Indon 45C3
Bisbee USA 65E4
Biscay,B of Spain/France 18A2
Biscayne B USA 61E4
Bischofshofen Austria 17E1
Bischwiller France 16D2
Biscotasi L Can 58C1
Bishan China 40B4
Bishop USA 54B3
Bishop Auckland Eng 15E4
Bishop's Stortford Eng 15F6
Bishrāmpur India 37B3
Bishui China 41A1
Biskia Eth 32C3
Biskra Alg 77D2
Bislig Phil 45G9
Bismarck USA 54C2
Bismarck Arch PNG 48D1
Bismarck Range Mts PNG 48D1
Bismarck S PNG 48D1
Bīsotūn Iran 34B2
Bissau Guinea-Bissau 76A3
Bissett Can 55D1
Bistcho L Can 52G4
Bistrita R Rom 23F1
Bitam Gabon 78B3
Bitburg W Germ 20B3
Bitche France 16D2
Bitlis Turk 30D2
Bitola Yugos 23E2
Bitterfeld E Germ 20C2
Bitterfontein S Africa 79B7
Bitter Lakes Egypt 30B3
Bitteroot Range Mts USA 54B2
Bitung Indon 45C2
Biu Nig 77J3
Biwa-ko L Japan 41D4
Biyo Kaboba Eth 78E2
Biysk USSR 26K4
Bizerte Tunisia 77D1
Bj bou Arréridj Alg 19C2
Bjelovar Yugos 22D1
Bj Flye Ste Marie Alg 76B2
Bjørnøya I Barents S 26C2
Black R USA 56K2
Blackall Aust 48D3
Black B Can 58B1
Blackburn Eng 15D5
Blackburn,Mt USA 52D3
Black Canyon City USA 65D4
Blackduck USA 57D2
Black Eagle USA 64D1
Blackfoot USA 64D2
Blackfoot R USA 64D1
Black Hills USA 52H5
Black Isle Pen Scot 14C3
Blackman's Barbados 68Q2
Black Mts USA 65D3
Black Mts Wales 15D6
Blackpool Eng 15D5
Black River Jamaica 68H1
Black River Falls USA 58A2
Black Rock Desert USA 54B2
Black S USSR/Europe 26E5
Blacksburg USA 58C3
Black Sugarloaf Mt Aust 50D2
Black Volta R Ghana 77F4
Blackwater R Irish Rep 13B3
Blackwater L Can 56O3
Blackwell USA 63C2
Blagoevgrad Bulg 23E2
Blagoveshchensk USSR 27O4
Blaikiston,Mt Can 64D1
Blaine USA 64B1
Blair USA 57C3
Blair Atholl Scot 14D3
Blairgowrie Scot 14D3
Blakely USA 61C2
Blanca Peak Mt USA 62A2
Blanche,L Aust 50A1
Blanco R Arg 72A2
Blanco R Arg 72B1
Blanco R Mexico 67C1
Blanco,C USA 54A2
Blanc Sablon Can 53N4
Blandford Forum Eng 15D6
Blanding USA 65E3
Blangy-sur-Bresle France 16A2
Blankenberge Belg 16B1
Blanquillo Urug 72D2
Blantyre Malawi 79D5
Blaye France 18B2
Blayney Aust 50C2
Blenheim NZ 49G5
Bléone R France 17B2
Blida Alg 77C1
Blind River Can 58C1
Blinman Aust 50A2
Blitar Indon 44D4
Blitta Togo 77G4
Block I USA 59E2
Block Island Sd USA 60E2
Bloemfontein S Africa 79C6
Bloemhof Dam S Africa 79C6
Blois France 16A3
Blommesteinmeer L Suriname 71G3
Blonduós Iceland 12A1
Bloomfield Indiana USA 58B3
Bloomfield Iowa USA 63D1
Bloomfield Nebraska USA 57C3
Bloomfield New Mexico USA 62A2
Bloomington Illinois USA 58B2
Bloomington Indiana USA 58B3
Bloomington Minnesota USA 57D3
Bloomsburg USA 60B2
Blora Indon 44D4
Blossburg USA 60B2
Blosseville Kyst Mts Greenland 53Q3
Bludenz Austria 20B3
Bluefield USA 55E3
Bluefields Nic 70B1
Blue Hill USA 62C1
Blue Knob Mt USA 60A2
Blue Mountain Peak Mt Jamaica 68B3
Blue Mt USA 60B2
Blue Mts Aust 50D2
Blue Mts Jamaica 68J1
Blue Mts USA 54A2
Blue Nile = Bahr el Azraq
Blue Nile = Abbai
Blue Nile R Sudan 78D2
Bluenose L Can 52G3
Blue Ridge USA 61C2
Blue Ridge Mts USA 55E3
Blue Stack Mt Irish Rep 14A4
Bluff NZ 51A3
Bluff USA 65E3
Bluff Knoll Mt Aust 48A4
Blumenau Brazil 69G3
Blundez Austria 18D2
Blunt USA 57C3
Bly USA 64B2
Blying Sd USA 56J4
Blyth Eng 14E4
Blythe USA 54B3
Blytheville USA 55E3
Bo Sierra Leone 76A4
Boac Phil 45F8
Boading China 40D2
Boano I Indon 45C3
Boa Nova Brazil 73D1
Boardman USA 58C2
Boatou China 27M5
Boa Vista Brazil 70F3
Boa Vista I Cape Verde 76A4
Bobai China 43E1
Bobbili India 36C1
Bóbbio Italy 17C2
Bobo Dioulasso U Volta 77F3
Bobrovica USSR 21G2
Bobruysk USSR 24D5
Boca Chica Key I USA 61E4
Bôca do Acre Brazil 70E4
Bocaiúva Brazil 73D2
Boca Jesús Maria Mexico 67C1
Bocaranga CAR 78B3
Boca Raton USA 61E4
Bochnia Pol 21E3
Bocholt W Germ 20B2
Bochum W Germ 16D1
Bocoio Angola 79B5
Boda CAR 78B3
Bodaybo USSR 27N4
Bodega Head Pt USA 65B3
Bodélé Desert Region Chad 78B2
Boden Sweden 12J5
Bodensee L Switz/W Germ 17C1
Bodhan India 36B1
Bodināyakkanūr India 36B2
Bodmin Eng 15C6
Bodmin Moor Upland Eng 15C6
Bodø Nor 12G5
Bodorodskoye USSR 27Q4
Bodrum Turk 23F3
Boende Zaïre 78C4
Boffa Guinea 76A3
Bogale Burma 43B2
Bogalusa USA 63E3
Bogan R Aust 50C2
Bogandé U Volta 77F3
Bogarnes Iceland 53Q3
Boğazlıyan Turk 30C2
Bogdanovich USSR 24L4
Bogda Shan Mt China 38B2
Bogenfels Namibia 79B6
Boggabilla Aust 50D1
Boggabri Aust 50C2
Bogo Phil 45F8
Bogong,Mt Aust 50C3
Bogor Indon 44C4
Bogorodskoye USSR 24J4
Bogotá Colombia 70D3
Bogotol USSR 27K4
Bogra Bang 37C3
Bo Hai B China 40D2
Bohain-en-Vermandois France 16B2
Bohai Wan B China 40D2
Boh Bistrica Yugos 17E1
Bohicon Benin 77G4
Bohmer-wald Upland W Germ 20C3
Bohol I Phil 45F9
Bohol S Phil 45F9
Bois R Brazil 73B2
Bois Blanc I USA 58C1
Boise USA 54B2
Boise City USA 62B2
Boissevain Can 57B2
Bojador,C Mor 76A2
Bojeador,C Phil 45F7
Bojnūrd Iran 34D1
Boké Guinea 76A3
Bokhara R Aust 50C1
Boknafjord Inlet Nor 12F7
Boko Congo 78B4
Bokor Camb 43C3
Bokoro Chad 78B2
Bokungu Zaïre 78C4
Bol Chad 78B2
Bolaãnos Mexico 67B1
Bolama Guinea-Bissau 76A3
Bolanos R Mexico 67B1
Bolbec France 18C2
Bole Ghana 77F4
Bolen USSR 41D1
Boleslawiec Pol 20D2
Bolgatanga Ghana 77F3
Bolgrad USSR 25D6
Boli China 41C2
Bolívar Arg 72C3
Bolivar Missouri USA 63D2
Bolivar Tennessee USA 63E2
Bolivia Republic S America 70E7
Bollnas Sweden 12H6
Bollon Aust 50C1
Bolívar Mt Ven 70D2
Bologna Italy 22C2
Bologoye USSR 24E4
Bolon USSR 41D2
Bol'shezemel'skaya Tundra Plain USSR 24J2
Bol'shoy Anyuy R USSR 27S3
Bol'shoy Irgiz R USSR 25H5
Bol'shoy Kamen USSR 41C3
Bolshoykavka Mts USSR 25G7
Bol'shoy Kavkaz Mts USSR 26F5
Bol'shoy Uzen R USSR 25H6
Bolson de Mapimi Desert Mexico 54C4
Bolton Eng 15D5
Bolu Turk 30B1
Bolugarvik Iceland 12A1
Bolvadin Turk 30B2
Bolzano Italy 22C1
Boma Zaïre 78B4
Bombala Aust 48D4
Bombay India 36A1
Bombo Uganda 78D3
Bomdila India 37D2
Bomi China 37E2
Bomi Hills Lib 76A4
Bom Jesus da Lapa Brazil 71K6
Bomnak USSR 27O4
Bomokandi R Zaïre 78C3
Bomu R CAR/Zaïre 78C3
Bon Air USA 59D3
Bonaire I Caribbean 68D4
Bona,Mt USA 56K3
Bonanza Nic 66D3
Bonavista Can 53N5
Bon Bon Aust 50A2
Bon Despacho Brazil 73C2
Bondo Zaïre 78C3
Bondoukou Ivory Coast 77F4
Bône = 'Annaba
Bone Indon 45B4
Bonelipu Indon 45B3
Bonesteel USA 57C3
Bonfim Guyana 71G3
Bongandanga Zaïre 78C3
Bongka R Indon 45B3
Bongor Chad 78B2
Bongouanou Ivory Coast 77F4
Bonham USA 63C3
Bonifacio Corse 22B2
Bonifacio,Str of Chan Medit S 22B2
Bonin Is = Ogasawara Gunto
Bonita Springs USA 61E4
Bonito Brazil 73A3
Bonn W Germ 20B2
Bonners Ferry USA 64C1
Bonnétable France 16A2
Bonnet Plume R Can 56M2
Bonneval France 16A2
Bonthain Indon 48A1
Bonthe Sierra Leone 76A4
Bontosunggu Indon 45A4
Booaaso Somalia 75D3
Booligal Aust 50B2
Boonah Aust 50D1
Boone Colorado USA 62B2
Boone Iowa USA 57D3
Boone North Carolina USA 61C1
Booneville USA 59D2
Boorowa Aust 50C2
Boothia,G of Can 53J2
Boothia Pen Can 53J2
Boué Gabon 78B4
Bopeechee Aust 50A1
Boquillas Mexico 62B4
Bor Sudan 78D3
Bor Turk 30B2
Bor Yugos 23E2
Borah Peak Mt USA 54B2
Borås Sweden 12G7
Borāzjān Iran 34C3
Borda,C Aust 50A3
Bordeaux France 18B3
Borden I Can 52G2
Borden Pen Can 53K2
Bordentown USA 60C2
Borders Region Scot 14D4
Bordertown Aust 50B3
Bordighera Italy 17B3
Bordi Omar Dris Alg 76C2
Bordj bou Arreridj Alg 77C1
Borens River Can 54D1
Borgå Fin 12K6
Borgarnes Iceland 12A2
Borger USA 54C3
Borgholm Sweden 12H7
Borgo San Lorenzo Italy 17D3
Borgosia Italy 17C2
Borgo Val di Taro Italy 17C2
Borgo Valsugana Italy 17D1
Borislav USSR 21E3
Borisoglebsk USSR 25G5
Borisov USSR 24D5
Borisovka USSR 25F5
Borja Par 73A4
Borkou Desert Region Chad 78B2
Borlänge Sweden 12H6
Bormida Italy 17C2
Bormio Italy 17D1
Bornholm I Den 12H7

Borno **Cabo de Salinas**

Borno State Nig 77J3
Bornova Turk 23F3
Boro R Sudan 78C3
Borogontsy USSR 27P3
Boromo U Volta 77F3
Borovichi USSR 24E4
Borroloola Aust 48C2
Borsa Rom 23E1
Borūjed Iran 34B2
Borūjen Iran 34C2
Bory Tucholskie Region Pol 20D2
Borzna USSR 21G2
Borzya USSR 27N4
Bose China 40B5
Boshnyakovo USSR 41E2
Bosna R Yugos 23D2
Bōsō-hantō B Japan 42D3
Bosporus = Karadeniz Boğazi
Bosquet Alg 19C2
Bossangoa CAR 78B3
Bossèmbélé CAR 78B3
Bossier City USA 63D3
Bosten Hu L China 26K5
Boston Eng 15E5
Boston USA 55F2
Boston Mts USA 55D3
Bosumtwi,L Ghana 77F4
Botād India 35C4
Botevgrad Bulg 23E2
Bothnia,G of Sweden/Fin 24B3
Botletli R Botswana 79C6
Botosani Rom 25D6
Botswana Republic Africa 79C6
Botte Donato Mt Italy 22D3
Bottineau USA 57B2
Bottrop W Germ 16D1
Botucatu Brazil 73C3
Botupora Brazil 73D1
Botwood Can 53N5
Bouaflé Ivory Coast 76B4
Bouar CAR 78B3
Bouârfa Mor 77B2
Bouba Ndjia Nat Pk Cam 77J4
Bouca CAR 78B3
Boudnib Mor 77B2
Boufarik Alg 19C2
Bougainville I PNG 49E1
Bougie = Bejaïa
Bougouni Mali 76B3
Bougouriba R U Volta 77F3
Bougtob Alg 77C2
Bouillon France 16C2
Bouira Alg 77C1
Bou Izakarn Mor 76B2
Boulay-Moselle France 16D2
Boulder Colorado USA 54C2
Boulder Montana USA 64D1
Boulder City USA 54B3
Boulogne France 18C1
Boumba R CAR 78B3
Bouna Ivory Coast 77F4
Boundary Peak Mt USA 54B3
Boundiali Ivory Coast 76B4
Bountiful USA 64D2
Bounty Is NZ 49G5
Bourail Nouvelle Calédonie 49F3
Bourbonne-les-Bains France 16C3
Bourem Mali 76B3
Bourg France 18D2
Bourg de Péage France 18D2
Bourg-en-Bresse France 17A1
Bourges France 18C2
Bourg-Madame France 18C3
Bourgogne Region France 18C2
Bourgoin-Jallieu France 17A2
Bourg-St-Maurice France 17B2
Bourke Aust 50C2
Bournemouth Eng 15E6
Bou Saâda Alg 77C1
Bousso Chad 78B2
Boutilmit Maur 76A3
Boutourou,Mt Ivory Coast 77F4
Bouvet I Atlantic O 74J7
Bovril Arg 72D2
Bowbells USA 57B2
Bowen Aust 48D2
Bowie Arizona USA 65E4
Bowie Maryland USA 59D3
Bowie Texas USA 63C3
Bowling Green Kentucky USA 55E3
Bowling Green Missouri USA 63D2
Bowling Green Ohio USA 58C2
Bowling Green Virginia USA 59D3
Bowman USA 57B2
Bowmanville Can 59D2
Bowral Aust 50D2
Bo Xian China 40D3
Boxing China 40D2
Boyabat Turk 30B1
Boyali CAR 78B3
Boyarka USSR 21G2
Boyd Can 52J4
Boyertown USA 60C2
Boyle Irish Rep 13B3
Boyne R Irish Rep 15B5
Boynoton Beach USA 61E4
Boyoma Falls Zaïre 78C3
Boysen Res USA 64E2
Bozcaada I Turk 23F3
Boz Dağlari Mts Turk 23F3
Bozeman USA 54B2
Bozen = Bolzano
Bozene Zaïre 78B3
Bozoum CAR 78B3
Bra Italy 17B2
Brač I Yugos 22D2
Bracebridge Can 59D1
Brach Libya 75A2
Bräcke Sweden 12H6
Brackettville USA 62B4
Bradenton USA 61E4
Bradford Eng 15E5
Bradford USA 60A2
Brady USA 62C3
Brae Scot 14E1
Braemar Scot 14D3
Braga Port 19A1
Bragado Arg 72C3
Bragana Port 19A1
Bragança Brazil 71J4
Bragança Paulista Brazil 73C3
Brahman-Baria Bang 37D3
Brāhmani R India 37C3
Brahmaputra R India 37D2
Braie Verte Can 53N5
Brăila Rom 25D6
Brainerd USA 55D2
Brakna Region Maur 76A3
Bralorne Can 52F4
Brampton Can 59D2
Branco R Brazil 70F3
Brandberg Mt Namibia 79B6
Brandenburg E Germ 20C2
Brandon Can 54D2
Brandon USA 57C3
Brandvlei S Africa 79C7
Brandys nad Lebem Czech 20C2
Braniewo Pol 21D2
Brantford Can 55E2
Branxholme Aust 50B3
Bras D'Or L Can 53M5
Brasília de Minas Brazil 73D2
Brasiléia Brazil 70E6
Brasilia Brazil 71J7
Brasov Rom 23F1
Brassay Range Mts Malay 44E2
Bratislava Czech 20D3
Bratsk USSR 27M4
Bratslav USSR 21F3
Brattleboro USA 59E2
Braunschweig W Germ 20C2
Brava I Cape Verde 76A4
Brawley USA 54B3
Bray Irish Rep 15B5
Bray I Can 53L3
Bray-sur-Seine France 16B2
Brazil Basin Atlantic O 74G5
Brazos R USA 54D3
Brazzaville Congo 78B4
Brdy Upland Czech 20C3
Breaksea Sd NZ 51A3
Bream B NZ 51B1
Brebes Indon 44C4
Brechin Scot 14D3
Brecht Belg 16C1
Breckenridge Minnesota USA 57C2
Breckenridge Texas USA 62C3
Břeclav Czech 20D3
Brecon Wales 15D6
Brecon Beacons Mts Wales 15D6
Brecon Beacons Nat Pk Wales 15C5
Breda Neth 20A2
Bredasdorp S Africa 79C7
Bredby Sweden 12H6
Bredbyn Sweden 24B3
Bredy USSR 24K5
Breezewood USA 59D2
Bregenz Austria 17C1
Bregenzer Ache R Austria 17C1
Breiðafjörður B Iceland 12A1
Breisach W Germ 16D2
Brembo Italy 17C2
Brembo R Italy 17C2
Bremen USA 61B2
Bremen W Germ 20B2
Bremerhaven W Germ 20B2
Bremerton USA 64B1
Brendel USA 65E3
Brenham USA 63C3
Brenner Mt Austria 18E2
Brenner P Austria/Italy 20C3
Breno Italy 17D2
Brenta R Italy 17D2
Brescia Italy 22C1
Breslau = Wrocław
Bressanone Italy 17D1
Bressay I Scot 14E1
Bressuire France 18B2
Brest France 18B2
Brest USSR 21E2
Bretagne Region France 18B2
Breteuil France 16B2
Bretevil France 16A2
Breton Sd USA 61B3
Breton Woods USA 60C2
Brett,C NZ 51B1
Brevard USA 61C1
Brewarrina Aust 50C1
Brewer USA 59F2
Brewster New York USA 60D2
Brewster Washington USA 64C1
Brewton USA 61B2
Brežice Yugos 22D1
Bria CAR 78C3
Briancon France 18D3
Briare France 18C2
Bridgeport California USA 65C3
Bridgeport Connecticut USA 59E2
Bridgeport Nebraska USA 57B3
Bridgeport Texas USA 63C3
Bridger USA 64E1
Bridger Peak USA 62A1
Bridgeton USA 60C3
Bridgetown Barbados 68F4
Bridgewater Can 53M5
Bridgewater USA 60E2
Bridgport USA 61B2
Bridgwater Eng 15D6
Bridgwater B Eng 15D6
Bridlington Eng 15E4
Bridport Aust 50E3
Brienne-le-Château France 16C2
Brienzer See L Switz 17B1
Briey France 16C2
Brig Switz 22B1
Brigham City USA 54B2
Bright Aust 50C3
Brighton Eng 15E6
Brignoles France 17B3
Brilhante R Brazil 73A3
Brilon W Germ 16E1
Brindisi Italy 23D2
Brinkley USA 63D3
Brisbane Aust 49E3
Bristol Connecticut USA 59E2
Bristol Eng 15D6
Bristol Pennsylvania USA 59E2
Bristol Rhode Island USA 60E2
Bristol Tennessee USA 55E3
Bristol B USA 56F4
Bristol Chan Eng/Wales 15C6
British Columbia Province Can 52F4
British Empire Range Mts Can 53K1
British Mts USA/Can 56K2
Britstown S Africa 79C7
Britton USA 57C2
Brive France 18C2
Brno Czech 20D3
Broad R USA 61C2
Broadalbin USA 60C1
Broadback R Can 53L4
Broad Bay Inlet Scot 14B2
Broadford Scot 14C3
Broadus USA 57A2
Broadview Can 57B1
Broadwater USA 57B3
Brochet Can 52H4
Brock I Can 52G2
Brockport USA 59D2
Brockton USA 60E1
Brockville Can 59D2
Brockway USA 60A2
Brodeur Pen Can 53K2
Brodick Scot 14C4
Brodnica Pol 21D2
Brody USSR 25D5
Brokem Haltern W Germ 16D1
Broken Bow Nebraska USA 62C1
Broken Bow Oklahoma USA 63D3
Broken Bow L USA 63D3
Broken Hill Aust 48D4
Broni Italy 17C2
Brønnøysund Nor 12G5
Bronx Borough New York USA 60D2
Brooke's Point Phil 45E9
Brookfield Missouri USA 63D2
Brookfield Wisconsin USA 58B2
Brookhaven USA 55D3
Brookings Oregon USA 64B2
Brookings South Dakota USA 54D2
Brookline USA 60E1
Brooklyn USA 57D3
Brooklyn Borough New York USA 60D2
Brooklyn Center USA 57D2
Brooks Can 52G4
Brooks,L USA 56G4
Brooks Mt USA 56E2
Brooks Range Mts USA 52C3
Brooksville USA 61C3
Brookton USA 59E2
Brooloo Aust 50D1
Broome Aust 48B2
Brora Scot 14D2
Brothers USA 64B2
Brothers,The Is S Yemen 33F4
Brou France 16A2
Broulkou Well Chad 78B2
Brovary USSR 21G2
Browerville USA 57D2
Brownfield USA 62B3
Brownsville USA 54D4
Brownwood USA 54D3
Browse I Aust 39F8
Bruay-en-Artois France 16B1
Bruce,Mt Aust 48A3
Bruce Pen Can 58C1
Bruchsal W Germ 16E2
Bruck Austria 17E1
Bruck an der Mur Austria 20D3
Bruges = Brugge
Brugge Belg 16B1
Brühl W Germ 16D1
Brumado Brazil 73D1
Brumath France 16D2
Bruneau USA 64C2
Bruneau R USA 64C2
Brunei Sultanate S E Asia 44D2
Brunico Italy 22C1
Brunner,L NZ 51B2
Brunswick Georgia USA 55E3
Brunswick Maine USA 59F2
Brunswick Mississippi USA 63D2
Brunswick,Pen de Chile 69B8
Bruny I Aust 50E3
Brusenets USSR 24G3
Brush USA 62B1
Brus Laguna Honduras 68A3
Brüssel = Bruxelles
Bruxelles Belg 20A2
Bruyères France 16D2
Bryan USA 54D3
Bryan,Mt Aust 50A2
Bryansk USSR 24E5
Bryant USA 63D3
Brzeg Pol 20D2
Būbīyan I Kuwait/Iraq 30E4
Bubu R Tanz 78D4
Bucaramanga Colombia 70D2
Buchan Oilfield N Sea 14E3
Buchanan Lib 76A4
Buchanan,L USA 62C3
Buchan Deep N Sea 14E3
Buchan G Can 53L2
Buchan Ness Pen Scot 13C2
Buchans Can 53N5
Buchardo Arg 72C2
Bucharest = Bucureşti
Buchs Switz 17C1
Buckeye USA 65D4
Buckingham Eng 15E5
Buckland USA 56F2
Buckland R USA 56F2
Buckleboo Aust 50A2
Bucksport USA 59F2
Buco Zau Congo 78B4
Bucureşti Rom 23F2
Budapest Hung 21D3
Budaun India 35D3
Bude Eng 15C6
Bude USA 63D3
Budennovsk USSR 25G7
Büdingen W Germ 16E1
Budva Yugos 23D2
Buéa Cam 78A3
Buech R France 17A2
Buena Esperanza Arg 72B2
Buenaventura Colombia 70C3
Buenaventura Mexico 62A4
Buena Vista Colorado USA 62A2
Buenavista Mexico 67B2
Buena Vista Virginia USA 59D3
Bueno R Chile 72A4
Buenos Aires Arg 69E4
Buenos Aires State Arg 69E5
Buffalo Missisipi USA 63D2
Buffalo New York USA 55F2
Buffalo South Dakota USA 57B2
Buffalo Texas USA 63C3
Buffalo Wyoming USA 54C2
Buffalo Hump USA 64C1
Buffalo Narrows Can 52H4
Buford USA 61C2
Buftea Rom 23F2
Bug R USSR/Pol 21E2
Buga Colombia 70C3
Bugdayli USSR 34C1
Bugt China 41A2
Bugulma USSR 24J5
Buguruslan USSR 24J5
Buhayrat al Asad Res Syria 30C2
Buhl Idaho USA 64D2
Buhl Minnesota USA 57D2
Bui Dam Ghana 77F4
Builth Wells Wales 13C3
Buin Chile 72A2
Buis-les-Baronnies France 17A2
Buith Wells Wales 15D5
Buje Yugos 17E2
Bujumbura Burundi 78C4
Buka I PNG 49E1
Bukama Zaïre 79C4
Bukavu Zaïre 78C4
Bukhara USSR 28E2
Bukit Batubrok Mt Indon 44D2
Bukittinggi Indon 44B3
Bukoba Tanz 78D4
Buku Gandadiwata Mt Indon 45B3
Buku Saolat Mt Indon 45C2
Bula Indon 39G7
Bulan Phil 45F8
Bulandshahr India 35D3
Bulawayo Zim 79C6
Buldan Turk 23F3
Buldāna India 35D4
Buldir I USA 56B6
Bulgan Mongolia 38D2
Bulgaria Republic Europe 23E2
Buli Indon 45C2
Bulle Switz 17B1
Buller R NZ 51B2
Buller,Mt Aust 50C3
Bullfinch Aust 48A4
Bulloo R Aust 50B1
Bulloo Downs Aust 50B1
Bulloo L Aust 50B1
Bull Shoals Res USA 63D2
Bulnes Chile 72A3
Bulolo PNG 48D1
Bulukumba Indon 45B4
Bum Bum I Malay 44E2
Bu Menderes R Turk 25D8
Bumpa Zaïre 78C3
Bumphal Dam Thai 43B2
Buna Kenya 78D3
Bunbury Aust 48A4
Buncrana Irish Rep 14B4
Bundaberg Aust 49E3
Bundarra Aust 50D2
Būndi India 35D3
Bungil R Aust 50C1
Bungo Angola 79B4
Bungo-suidō Str Japan 42B4
Bunguran I Indon 44C2
Bunia Zaïre 78D3
Bunker USA 63D2
Bunkie USA 63D3
Bunnell USA 61C3
Bunsuru R Nig 77H3
Buntok Indon 44D3
Buol Indon 45B2
Burāg Syria 31D2
Buram Sudan 78C2
Burang China 37B1
Burauen Phil 45G8
Buraydah S Arabia 32D1
Burbank USA 65C4
Burcher Aust 50C2
Burco Somalia 78E3
Burdalyk USSR 34E1
Burdur Turk 25E8
Bureinskiy Khrebet Mts USSR 41C1
Bureya R USSR 41C1
Bûr Fu'ad Egypt 31B3
Burg E Germ 20C2
Burgas Bulg 23F2
Burgaw USA 61D2
Burgdorf Switz 17B1
Burgersdorp S Africa 79C7
Burgin USSR 26K5
Burgos Mexico 67C1
Burgos Spain 19B1
Burgrino USSR 24H2
Burgsvik Sweden 21D1
Burgut USSR 26J3
Burhaniye Turk 23F3
Burhānpur India 35D4
Burias I Phil 45F8
Buriram Thai 43C2
Buritis Brazil 73C2
Burketown Aust 48C2
Burks Falls Can 59D1
Burley USA 54B2
Burlington Colorado USA 62B2
Burlington Iowa USA 55D2
Burlington New Jersey USA 60C2
Burlington North Carolina USA 61D1
Burlington Vermont USA 55F2
Burlington Washington USA 64B1
Burma Republic Asia 29H3
Burnet USA 62C3
Burney USA 64B2
Burnham USA 60B2
Burnie Aust 48D5
Burnley Eng 15D5
Burns USA 64C2
Burns Lake Can 52F4
Burqin China 29G1
Burra Aust 50A2
Burragorang,L Aust 50D2
Burray I Scot 14D2
Burren Junction Aust 50C2
Burrinjuck Res Aust 50C2
Burrundie Aust 39G8
Bursa Turk 25D7
Bur Safâga Egypt 32B1
Bûr Sa'îd = Port Said
Bûr Taufiq Egypt 31B4
Burton USA 58C2
Burton upon Trent Eng 15E5
Burtrask Sweden 12J6
Burtundy Aust 50B2
Buru Indon 45C3
Burundi Republic Africa 78C4
Burung Indon 44B2
Burwell USA 57C3
Buryatskaya ASSR Republic USSR 27N4
Burye Eth 78D2
Burynshik USSR 25J6
Bury St Edmunds Eng 15F5
Būshehr Iran 34C3
Busira R Zaïre 78B4
Buskozdroj Pol 21E2
Busrā ash Shām Syria 31D2
Bussang France 16D3
Busselton Aust 48A4
Busto Italy 18D2
Busto Arsizio Italy 22B1
Bustol USA 58C3
Busuanga I Phil 45E8
Buta Zaïre 78C3
Buta Ranquil Arg 72B3
Butare Rwanda 78C4
Bute I Scot 14C4
Butha Qi China 41A2
Butler USA 59D2
Butte USA 54B2
Butterworth Malay 43C4
Butt of Lewis C Scot 13B2
Button Is Can 53M3
Butuan Phil 45G9
Butung I Indon 45B4
Butung I Indon 48B1
Buturlinovka USSR 25G5
Butwal Nepal 37B2
Butzbach W Germ 16E1
Buulo Barde Somalia 78E3
Buur Hakaba Somalia 78E3
Buy USSR 24G4
Buyant Ovvo Mongolia 40B1
Buynaksk USSR 25H7
Buyr Nuur L Mongolia 27N5
Büyük Ağri Daği Mt Turk 25G8
Buyukly USSR 41E2
Büyük Menderes R Turk 30A2
Buzău Rom 23F1
Buzau R Rom 23F1
Buzuluk USSR 24J5
Buzzards B USA 60E2
Byala Bulg 23F2
Byala Slatina Bulg 23E2
Byam Martin Chan Can 52H2
Byam Martin I Can 52H2
Byblos
Bydgoszcz Pol 21D2
Byers USA 62B2
Bygland Nor 12F7
Bykov USSR 41E2
Bylot I Can 53L2
Byrhov USSR 21G2
Byrock Aust 50C2
Byron,C Aust 50D1
Bytantay R USSR 27P3
Bytom Pol 21D2

C

Caacupé Par 69E3
Caaguazú Par 73A4
Caála Angola 79B5
Caapucú Par 73A4
Caarapó Brazil 73B3
Caazapá Par 69E3
Caballo Res USA 62A3
Cabanatuan Phil 45F7
Cabano Can 59F1
Cabedelo Brazil 71M5
Cabeza del Buey Spain 19A2
Cabildo Arg 72C3
Cabildo Chile 72A2
Cabimas Ven 70D1
Cabinda Angola 78B4
Cabinda Province Angola 78B4
Cabinet Mts USA 64C1
Cabo Beata Dom Rep 68C3
Cabo Binibeca C Spain 19C2
Cabo Cantin C Mor 77A2
Cabo Carbonara C Sardegna 22B3
Cabo Carranza C Chile 72A3
Cabo Carvoeiro C Port 19A2
Cabo Colnett C Mexico 54B3
Cabo Corrientes C Arg 72D3
Cabo Corrientes C Colombia 70C2
Cabo Corrientes C Mexico 66B2
Cabo Cruz C Cuba 68B3
Cabo de Ajo C Spain 19B1
Cabo de Caballeria C Spain 19C1
Cabo de Creus C Spain 19C1
Cabo de Hornos C Chile 69C9
Cabo de la Nao C Spain 19C2
Cabo de Peñas C Spain 19A1
Cabo de Roca C Port 19A2
Cabo de Salinas C Spain 19C2

Caudebec-en-Caux Chongqing

Caudebec-en-Caux France 16A2
Caudry France 16B1
Caungula Angola 79B4
Cauquenes Chile 69B5
Causapscal Can 59F1
Cauvery R India 36B2
Cavaillon France 18D3
Cavalcanta Brazil 73C1
Cavalese Italy 17D1
Cavalier USA 57C2
Cavally R Lib 76B4
Cavan County Irish Rep 15B5
Cavan Irish Rep 15B5
Cavite Phil 45F8
Caxias Brazil 70D4
Caxias Brazil 71K4
Caxias do Sul Brazil 69F3
Caxito Angola 79B4
Cayce USA 61C2
Çayeli Turk 30D1
Cayenne French Guiana 71H3
Cayeux-sur-Mer France 16A1
Cayman Brac I Caribbean 66E3
Cayman Is Caribbean 68A3
Cayman Trench Caribbean 68A3
Caynabo Somalia 78E3
Cayo Romana I Cuba 66E2
Cayos Mistikos Is Nic 66D3
Cay Sal I Caribbean 68A2
Cayuga L USA 60B1
Cazenova USA 60C1
Cazombo Angola 79C5
Ceará = Fortaleza
Ceara State Brazil 71K5
Cebollar Arg 72B1
Cebollati Urug 72E2
Cebu Phil 45F8
Cebu I Phil 45F8
Cecilton USA 60C3
Cecina Italy 22C2
Cecina R Italy 17D3
Cedar R USA 57D3
Cedar City USA 54B3
Cedar Creek Res USA 63C3
Cedar Falls USA 57D3
Cedar L Can 52J4
Cedar Rapids USA 55D2
Cedartown USA 61B2
Cedral Mexico 67B1
Cedros I Mexico 66A2
Ceduna Aust 48C4
Ceelbuur Somalia 78E3
Ceerigaabo Somalia 75D3
Cefalù Italy 22C3
Cegléd Hung 21D3
Cela Angola 79B5
Celaya Mexico 66B2
Celebes = Sulawesi
Celebes S S E Asia 39F6
Celina USA 58C2
Celje Yugos 22D1
Celle W Germ 20C2
Celtic S UK 15B6
Cendrawasih Pen Indon 39G7
Ceno R Italy 17C2
Center USA 63D3
Center Moriches USA 60D2
Cento Italy 17D2
Central Region Scot 14C3
Central USA 62A3
Central African Republic Africa 78B3
Central City Nebraska USA 63C1
Central City Pennsylvania USA 60A2
Centralia Illinois USA 58B3
Centralia Washington USA 54A2
Central Makran Range Mts Pak 34E3
Central Point USA 64B2
Central Range Mts PNG 39H7
Central Square USA 60B1
Centre Hill L USA 61B1
Centre Point USA 61B2
Centreville Alabama USA 61B2
Centreville Maryland USA 60B3
Cepu Indon 44D4
Ceram = Seram
Ceram Sea Indonesia 39F7
Cereales Arg 72C3
Ceres Arg 72C1
Ceres Brazil 71J7
Ceres S Africa 79B7
Cergy-Pontoise France 18C2
Cerignola Italy 22D2
Cernavodă Rom 25D7
Cernay France 16D3
Cerralvo I Mexico 54C4
Cerritos Mexico 67B1
Cerro Aconcagua Mt Arg 72B2
Cerro Azul Mexico 67C1
Cerro Boneta Mt Arg 72B1
Cerro Campanario Mt Chile 72A3
Cerro Champaqui Mt Arg 72C2
Cerro Chatto Urug 72D2
Cerro Cuachaia Mt Mexico 67B2
Cerro de Astillero Mexico 67C1
Cerro del Potro Mt Chile/Arg 72B1
Cerro del Tigre Mt Mexico 67C1
Cerro del Toro Mt Chile/Arg 72B1
Cerro de Olivares Mt Arg 72B2
Cerro de Pasco Peru 70C6
Cerro de Punta Mt Puerto Rico 68D3
Cerro El Cantado Mt Mexico 67B2
Cerro El Nevado Arg 72B3
Cerro General M Belgrano Mt Arg 72B1
Cerro Grande Mts Mexico 67B2
Cerro Huehueto Mt Mexico 67A1
Cerro Juncal Mt Arg/Chile 72A2
Cerro la Ardilla Mts Mexico 67B1
Cerro las Tortolas Mt Chile 72A1
Cerro Laurel Mt Mexico 67B2
Cerro Mercedario Mt Arg 72A2
Cerro Mora Mt Chile 72A3
Cerron Mt Ven 68C4
Cerro Payún Mt Arg 72B3
Cerro Peña Nevada Mt Mexico 67C1
Cerro Penón del Rosario Mt Mexico 67C2
Cerro Sosneado Mt Arg 72B2
Cerro Teotepec Mt Mexico 67B2
Cerro Tupungato Mt Arg 72B2
Cerro Yucuyacau Mt Mexico 67C2
Cervia Italy 17E2
Cervo R Italy 17C2
Cesena Italy 22C2
Cēsis USSR 24C4
České Budějovice Czech 20C3
České Zemé Region Czech 20C3
Českomoravská Vysočina U Czech 20D3
Çeşme Turk 23F3
Cessnock Aust 48E4
Cetina R Yugos 22D2
Ceuta N W Africa 77A1
Ceyham Turk 30C2
Ceyhan R Turk 30C2
Ceylanpınar Turk 30C2
Ceylon = Sri Lanka
Chaa-Khol USSR 27L4
Chaâteaudun France 18C2
Chablais Region France 17B1
Chablis France 16B3
Chacabuco Arg 72C2
Chachapoyas Peru 70C5
Chacharramendi Arg 72B3
Chachran Pak 35C3
Chaco State Arg 69D3
Chad Republic Africa 78B2
Chad L C Africa 78B2
Chadileuvu R Arg 72B3
Chadron USA 54C2
Chaffee USA 63E2
Chagai Pak 35A3
Chagai Hills Pak 34E3
Chagda USSR 27P4
Chaghcharan Afghan 35B2
Chagos Arch Indian O 46E5
Chaguanas Trinidad 68L1
Chagai Burjak Afghan 34E3
Chāh Bahār Iran 34E3
Ch'aho N Korea 42A2
Chai Badan Thai 43C2
Chaîne de l'Atakor Mts Benin 77G3
Chaine des Cardamomes Mts Camb 43C3
Chaine des Mitumba Mts Zaïre 79C4
Chaiyaphum Thai 43C2
Chajari Arg 72D2
Chakhansur Afghan 34E2
Chakwal Pak 35C2
Chala Peru 70D7
Chalabesa Zambia 79D5
Chalap Dalam Mts Afghan 35A2
Chalindrey France 16C3
Chaling China 40C4
Chālisgaon India 35D4
Chalkyitsik USA 56K2
Challerange France 16C2
Challis USA 64D2
Châlons sur Marne France 16C2
Chalon sur Saône France 18C2
Cham W Germ 20C3
Chama USA 62A2
Chaman Pak 35B2
Chamba India 35D2
Chambal R India 35D3
Chamberlain USA 57C3
Chamberlin,Mt USA 56J2
Chambersburg USA 59D3
Chambéry France 18D2
Chambly France 16B2
Chambord Can 59E1
Chambor Kalat Pak 35A3
Chamela Mexico 67A2
Chamgordān Iran 34C2
Chamical Arg 72B2
Chamonix France 17B2
Champa India 37B3
Champagne Region France 18C2
Champagnole France 17A1
Champaign USA 55E2
Champassak Laos 43D3
Champlain,L USA 55F2
Champlitte France 17A1
Chāmrājnagar India 36B2
Chañaral Chile 69B3
Chanco Chile 72A3
Chandalar USA 52D3
Chandalar R USA 52D3
Chandeleur Is USA 61B3
Chandīgarh India 35D2
Chandler USA 65D4
Chandpur Bang 37D3
Chandrapur India 35D5
Chānf Iran 34E3
Changara Mozam 79D5
Changbai China 41B3
Changchun China 41B3
Changde China 40C4
Changdo N Korea 42A3
Changhang S Korea 42A3
Changhowan S Korea 42A3
Chang-hua Taiwan 38E4
Changhung S Korea 42A4
Changjiang China 43D2
Chang Jiang R China 40D3
Changjin N Korea 41B3
Changjin R N Korea 42A2
Changjin Res N Korea 42A2
Changling China 41A3
Changsha China 40C4
Changshu China 40E3
Changtu China 41A3
Changwu China 40B2
Changyŏn N Korea 41B4
Changzhi China 40C2
Changzhou China 40E3
Channel Is UK 18B2
Channel Is USA 54B3
Channel Port-aux-Basques Can 53N5
Chanthaburi Thai 43C3
Chantilly France 16B2
Chanute USA 63C2
Chaoàn China 40D5
Chao'an China 40D5
Chao Hu L China 40D3
Chao Phraya R Thai 43C3
Chaor He R China 41A2
Chaouen Mor 77A1
Chaoyang China 40E1
Chaozhong China 41A1
Chapada Diamantina Mts Brazil 71K6
Chapadinha Brazil 71K4
Chapala Mexico 67B1
Chapala,Lac de L Mexico 67B1
Chapayevo USSR 25J5
Chapecó Brazil 69F3
Chapel Hill USA 61D1
Chapeltown Jamaica 68H1
Chapleau Can 53K5
Chaplygin USSR 24G5
Chappell USA 62B1
Charada Arg 72D1
Charcot I Ant 80G3
Chardzhou USSR 28E2
Charef Mor 77B2
Charente R France 18C2
Chari R Chad 78B2
Chari Baguirmi Region Chad 78B2
Charikar Afghan 35B1
Chariton R USA 63D1
Charity Guyana 71G2
Charkhāri India 35D3
Charleroi Belg 16C1
Charles,C USA 55F3
Charleston Illinois USA 58B3
Charleston Missouri USA 63E2
Charleston S Carolina USA 55F3
Charleston W Virginia USA 55E3
Charleston Peak Mt USA 65C3
Charles Town USA 60B3
Charlestown USA 60D1
Charlesville Zaïre 78C4
Charleville Aust 48D3
Charleville-Mézières France 18C2
Charlevoix USA 58B1
Charlotte Michigan USA 58C2
Charlotte N Carolina USA 55E3
Charlotte Harbour B USA 61E4
Charlottesville USA 55F3
Charlottetown Can 53M5
Charlotteville Tobago 68K1
Charlton Aust 50B3
Charlton I Can 55F1
Charmes France 16D2
Charsadda Pak 35C2
Charters Towers Aust 48D3
Chartres France 18C2
Chaschuil Arg 72B1
Chascomús Arg 69E5
Chasong N Korea 42A2
Château-Arnoux France 17A2
Châteaubriant France 18B2
Château-du-Loir France 16A3
Châteaudun France 16A2
Châteaulin France 18B2
Châteauneuf-en Thymerais France 16A2
Châteauneuf-sur-Loire France 16B3
Château Renault France 16A3
Châteauroux France 18C2
Château-Salins France 16D2
Château-Thierry France 18C2
Châtelet Belg 16C1
Châtellerault France 18C2
Chatfield USA 57D3
Chatham Eng 15F6
Chatham Massachusets USA 60E2
Chatham New Brunswick Can 53M5
Chatham New York USA 60D1
Chatham Ontario Can 58C2
Chatham Virginia USA 59D3
Chatham Is NZ 49H5
Chatham Str. USA 52E4
Chatham Str USA 56M4
Châtillon France 18C2
Châtillon-Coligny France 16B3
Châtillon-sur-Siene France 16C3
Chatrapur India 37B4
Chatsworth USA 60C3
Chattahoochee USA 61C2
Chattahoochee R USA 61B2
Chattanooga USA 55E3
Châttilon Italy 17B2
Chauk Burma 43A1
Chaumont France 18D2
Chauny France 16B2
Chau Phu Viet 43D3
Chaura I Indian O 36E3
Chaussin France 17A1
Chaves Port 19A1
Chazaouet Alg 19B2
Chazón Arg 72C2
Chcontá Colombia 70D2
Cheb Czech 20C2
Cheboksary USSR 26F4
Cheboygan USA 55E2
Chechersk USSR 21G2
Chech'on S Korea 41B4
Chechro Pak 35C3
Checotah USA 63C2
Cheduba I Burma 43A2
Cheepie Aust 50B1
Chegdomyn USSR 41C1
Chegga Maur 76B2
Chegutu Zim 79D5
Chegytun' USSR 56D2
Chehalis USA 64B1
Cheju S Korea 41B5
Cheju do I S Korea 41B5
Cheju-haehyŏp Str S Korea 41B5
Chekhov USSR 41E2
Chekunda USSR 27P4
Chelan,L USA 64B1
Cheleken USSR 25J8
Chelforo Arg 72B3
Chéliff R Alg 77C1
Chelkar USSR 28D1
Chelm Pol 21E2
Chelmno Pol 21D2
Chelmsford Eng 15F6
Cheltenham Eng 15D6
Chelyabinsk USSR 26H4
Chemba Mozam 79D5
Chemung USA 60B1
Chenab R India/Pak 35D2
Chenachen Alg 76B2
Chenango R USA 60C1
Cheney USA 64C1
Cheney Res USA 63C2
Chengda China 40D1
Chengdu China 40A3
Chengshan Jiao Pt China 40E2
Chenxi China 40C4
Chen Xian China 40C4
Cheo Xian China 40D3
Chepén Peru 70C5
Chepes Arg 72B2
Chequamegon B USA 58A1
Cher R France 18C2
Cheran Mexico 67B2
Cheraw USA 61D2
Cherbourg France 18B2
Chercas Mexico 67B1
Cherchell Alg 77C1
Chercher Eth 32C4
Cherdyn USSR 24K3
Cheremkhovo USSR 27M4
Cherepovets USSR 24F4
Cherkassy USSR 25E6
Cherkessk USSR 25G7
Chernigov USSR 25E5
Chernobyl USSR 21G2
Chernovtsy USSR 25D6
Chernushka USSR 24K4
Chernyakhovsk USSR 24C5
Chernyye Zemli Region USSR 25H6
Cherokee Iowa USA 57C3
Cherokee Oklahoma USA 62C2
Cherokees,L o'the USA 63C2
Cherquenco Chile 72A3
Cherrapunji India 37D2
Cherry I Solomon Is 49F2
Cherskiy USSR 27S3
Cherven' USSR 24D5
Chervonograd USSR 21E2
Chesapeake USA 59D3
Chesapeake B USA 59D3
Cheshire County Eng 15D5
Cheshire USA 60D1
Chëshskaya Guba B USSR 24H2
Chester California USA 65B2
Chester Eng 15D5
Chester Illinois USA 58B3
Chester Massachusets USA 60D1
Chester Montana USA 64D1
Chester Pennsylvania USA 59D3
Chester S Carolina USA 61C2
Chester Vermont USA 60D1
Chester R USA 60B3
Chesterfield Eng 15E5
Chesterfield Inlet Can 53J3
Chestertown USA 60B3
Chesuncook L USA 59F1
Chetumal Mexico 66D3
Chevak USA 56E3
Cheviot NZ 51B2
Cheviots Hills Eng/Scot 13C2
Cheyenne USA 62B1
Cheyenne R USA 57B3
Cheyenne Wells USA 62B2
Chhapra India 37B2
Chhātak Bang 37D2
Chhatarpur India 35D4
Chhindwāra India 35D4
Chhuka Bhutan 37C2
Chia'i Taiwan 40E5
Chiange Angola 79B5
Chiang Kham Thai 43C2
Chiang Mai Thai 43B2
Chiapa R Mexico 67D2
Chiavari Italy 17C2
Chiavenna Italy 17C1
Chiba Japan 41E4
Chībāsa India 37C3
Chibia Angola 79B5
Chibougamou Can 53L4
Chiburi-jima I Japan 42B3
Chibuto Mozam 79D6
Chicago USA 55E2
Chicago Heights USA 58B2
Chichagof I USA 56L4
Chichago I. USA 52E4
Chichester Eng 15E6
Chichibu Japan 42C3
Chichi-jima I Japan 38H4
Chickamauga L USA 55E3
Chickasawhay R USA 63E3
Chickasha USA 54D3
Chicken USA 56K3
Chiclayo Peru 70B5
Chico USA 54A3
Chico R Arg 69C6
Chicoa Mozam 79D5
Chicopee USA 59E2
Chicoutimi Can 53L5
Chicualacuala Mozam 79D6
Chidambaram India 36B2
Chidley,C Can 53M3
Chiefland USA 61C3
Chiehn Lib 76B4
Chiengi Zambia 79C4
Chienti R Italy 17E3
Chieri Italy 17B2
Chiers R France 16C2
Chiesa Italy 17C1
Chiese R Italy 17D2
Chieti Italy 22C2
Chifeng China 40D1
Chiginigak,Mt USA 56G4
Chigmit Mts USA 52C2
Chignahuapán Mexico 67C2
Chignik USA 56G4
Chihuahua Mexico 66B2
Chihuahua State Mexico 62A4
Chik Ballāpur India 36B2
Chikmagalūr India 36B2
Chikuminuk L USA 56G3
Chikwawa Malawi 79D5
Chi-kyaw Burma 43A1
Chilakalūrupet India 36C1
Chilapa Mexico 67C2
Chilaw Sri Lanka 36B3
Childers Aust 50D1
Childress USA 62B3
Chilecito La Rioja Arg 72B1
Chilecito Mendoza Arg 72B2
Chililabombwe Zambia 79C5
Chilka L India 37C3
Chilko L Can 52F4
Chillán Chile 72A3
Chillar Arg 72C3
Chillicothe Missouri USA 63D2
Chillicothe Ohio USA 58C3
Chilmari India 37C2
Chilmborazo Mt Ecuador 70C4
Chilongozi Zambia 79D5
Chiloquin USA 64B2
Chilpancingo Mexico 66C3
Chiltern Hills Upland Eng 15E6
Chilton USA 58B2
Chilumba Malawi 79D5
Chi-lung Taiwan 38F4
Chilwa L Malawi 79D5
Chimay Belg 16C1
Chimbay USSR 26G5
Chimbote Peru 70C5
Chimkent USSR 26H5
Chimoio Mozam 79D5
Chinacates Mexico 67A1
China National Republic = Taiwan
Chinandega Nic 66D3
Chinati Peak Mt USA 62B4
Chincha Alta Peru 70C6
Chinchilla Aust 50D1
Chinde Mozam 79D5
Chindo S Korea 42A4
Chindwin R Burma 37D3
Chingola Zambia 79C5
Chinguar Angola 79B5
Chinguetti Maur 76A2
Chinhae S Korea 41B4
Chinhoyi Zim 79D5
Chiniak,C USA 56H4
Chiniot Pak 35C2
Chinju S Korea 41B4
Chinko R CAR 78C3
Chino Japan 42C3
Chinsali Zambia 79D5
Chioggia Italy 22C1
Chipata Zambia 79D5
Chipinge Zim 79D6
Chiplūn India 36A1
Chippenham Eng 15D6
Chippewa R USA 58A1
Chippewa Falls USA 55D2
Chippewa,L USA 58A1
Chipuriro Zim 79D5
Chira R Peru 70B4
Chīrāla India 36C1
Chiredzi Zim 79D6
Chirfa Niger 78B1
Chiricahua Peak Mt USA 65E4
Chirikof I USA 56G4
Chiriqui Mt Panama 70B2
Chirpan Bulg 23F2
Chirripo Grande Mt Costa Rica 70B2
Chirstchurch NZ 49G5
Chirundu Zim 79C5
Chisamba Zambia 79C5
Chisholm USA 57D2
Chishui He R China 40B4
Chisone Italy 17B2
Chita USSR 38E1
Chitado Angola 79B5
Chitembo Angola 79B5
Chitina USA 56K3
Chitina R USA 56K3
Chitose Japan 42D2
Chitradurga India 36B2
Chitral Pak 35C1
Chitré Panama 70B2
Chittagong Bang 37D3
Chittaurgarh India 35C4
Chittoor India 36B2
Chiume Angola 79C5
Chiusa Italy 17D1
Chiusi Italy 17D3
Chivasso Italy 17B2
Chivilcoy Arg 69D4
Chivu Zim 79D5
Chizu Japan 42B3
Choch'iwŏn S Korea 42A3
Ch'o-do I S Korea 42A4
Choele Choel Arg 69C5
Choique Arg 72C3
Choiseul I Solomon Is 49E1
Choix Mexico 66B2
Chojnice Pol 21D2
Chokai-san Mt Japan 42D3
Choke Mts Eth 78D2
Chokurdakh USSR 27Q2
Cholet France 18B2
Cholula Mexico 67C2
Choluteca Honduras 70A1
Choma Zambia 79C5
Chŏmch'ŏn S Korea 42A3
Chomo Yummo Mt China/India 37C2
Chomutov Czech 20C2
Chona R USSR 27M3
Ch'ŏnan S Korea 41B4
Chon Buri Thai 43C3
Chonchon N Korea 42A2
Chone Ecuador 70C4
Chongdo S Korea 42A3
Ch'ŏngjin N Korea 41B3
Chongju N Korea 41B4
Ch'ŏngju S Korea 41B4
Chongoroi Angola 79B5
Chongpyong N Korea 42A3
Chongqing China 40B4

Chŏngsŏn Çorlu

Chŏngsŏn *S Korea* 42A3
Chŏngŭp *S Korea* 41B4
Chŏnju *S Korea* 41B4
Chooyu Mt *China/Nepal* 37C2
Chopim R *Brazil* 73B4
Chortkov *USSR* 21F3
Ch'ŏrwŏn *N Korea* 41B4
Chorzow *Pol* 21D2
Chosan *N Korea* 42A2
Choshi *Japan* 41E4
Chos-Malal *Arg* 72A3
Choszczno *Pol* 20D2
Chotanāgpur Region *India* 37B3
Choteau *USA* 64D1
Chott ech Chergui *Alg* 77B2
Chott el Hodna *Alg* 77D1
Chott Jerid *Tunisia* 77D2
Chott Melrhir *Alg* 77D2
Choybalsan *Mongolia* 27N5
Chranbrey Inlet B *Can* 53J3
Chraykovskiy *USSR* 24J4
Christchurch *NZ* 51B2
Christiana *S Africa* 79C6
Christian,C *Can* 53M2
Christian Sd *USA* 56M4
Christianshab *Greenland* 53N3
Christmas I *Indian O* 46G5
Christopol *USSR* 24H4
Chu *USSR* 26J5
Chu R *USSR* 26J5
Chubbuck *USA* 64D2
Chubut State *Arg* 69C6
Chubut R *Arg* 69C6
Chudovo *USSR* 24E4
Chudskoye Ozer L *USSR* 26D4
Chugach Mts *USA* 52D3
Chugiak *USA* 56J3
Chugiak Nat Pk *USA* 56J3
Chuginadak I *USA* 56E5
Chūgoku-sanchi Mts *Japan* 42B3
Chugwater *USA* 57B3
Chuí *Brazil* 72E2
Chuillán *Chile* 69B5
Chukai *Malay* 43C5
Chukchi S *USSR/USA* 56E2
Chukotskiy Khrebet Mts *USSR* 27T3
Chukotskiy Poluostrov Pen *USSR* 27U3
Chu Lai *Viet* 43D2
Chula Vista *USA* 65C4
Chulitna *USA* 56J3
Chulman *USSR* 38F1
Chulucanas *Peru* 70B5
Chulumani *Bol* 70E7
Chulym *USSR* 26K4
Chulym R *USSR* 27K4
Chuma R *USSR* 27L4
Chumar *India* 35D2
Chumbicha *Arg* 72B1
Chumikan *USSR* 27P4
Chumphon *Thai* 43B3
Ch'unch'ŏn *S Korea* 41B4
Chunchura *India* 37C3
Ch'ungju *S Korea* 41B4
Chungking = Chongqing
Ch'ungmu *S Korea* 42A4
Chungwa *N Korea* 42A3
Chunya *Tanz* 79D4
Chunya R *USSR* 27M3
Ch'unyang *S Korea* 42A3
Chupara Pt *Trinidad* 68L1
Chuquicamata *Chile* 69C2
Chur *Switz* 22B1
Churāchāndpur *India* 37D3
Churapcha *USSR* 27P3
Churchill *Can* 53J4
Churchill R *Can* 52H4
Churchill R Labrador *Can* 53M4
Churchill R Manitoba *Can* 53J4
Churchill,C *Can* 53J4
Churchill Falls *Can* 53M4
Churchill L *Can* 52H4
Chūru *India* 35C3
Churumuco *Mexico* 67B2
Chusovoy *USSR* 24K4
Chuvashkaya ASSR Republic *USSR* 24H4
Chuxiong *China* 38C4
Chu Yang Sin Mt *Viet* 43D3
Cianjur *Indon* 44C4
Ciano d'Enza *Italy* 17D2
Cianorte *Brazil* 73B3
Ciechanow *Pol* 21E2
Ciedad Altamirano *Mexico* 67B2
Ciedad Ojeda *Ven* 70D1
Ciego de Avila *Cuba* 66E2
Ciénaga *Colombia* 70D1
Cienfuegos *Cuba* 66D2
Cieszyn *Pol* 21D3
Cieza *Spain* 19B2
Cihanbeyli *Turk* 30B2
Cihuatlán *Mexico* 67B2
Cijulang *Indon* 44C4
Cilacap *Indon* 44C4
Cimarron *USA* 62B2
Cimarron R *USA* 62C2
Cime du Cheiron Mt *France* 17B3
Cîmpina *Rom* 23F1
Cinca R *Spain* 19C1
Činčer Mt *Yugos* 22D2
Cincinatti *USA* 55E3
Cindad Obregon *Mexico* 66B2
Cindrelu Mt *Rom* 23E1
Cine R *Turk* 23F3
Ciney *Belg* 16C1
Cintalapa *Mexico* 67D2
Cipolletti *Arg* 72B3
Circle Alaska *USA* 52D3
Circle Montana *USA* 57A2
Circleville *USA* 58C3
Cirebon *Indon* 44C4
Cirencester *Eng* 15E6
Cisco *USA* 62C3
Citadella *Italy* 17D2
Citlaltepetl Mt *Mexico* 66C3
Citrusdal *S Africa* 79B7
Citta del Vaticano *Italy* 22C2
Città di Castello *Italy* 22C2
Ciudad Acuña *Mexico* 66B2
Ciudad Bolivar *Ven* 70F2
Ciudad Camargo *Mexico* 66B2
Ciudad del Carmen *Mexico* 66C3
Ciudadela *Spain* 19C2
Ciudad Guayana *Ven* 70F2
Ciudad Guzman *Mexico* 66B3
Ciudad Hidalgo *Mexico* 67B2
Ciudad Juárez *Mexico* 66B1
Ciudad Lerdo *Mexico* 54C4
Ciudad Madero *Mexico* 66C2
Ciudad Mendoza *Mexico* 67C2
Ciudad Obregon *Mexico* 66B2
Ciudad Ojeda *Ven* 68C4
Ciudad Piar *Ven* 70F2
Ciudad Real *Spain* 19B2
Ciudad Rodrigo *Spain* 19A1
Ciudad Valles *Mexico* 66C2
Ciudad Victoria *Mexico* 66C2
Cividale del Friuli *Italy* 17E1
Civitanova Marche *Italy* 17E3
Civitavecchia *Italy* 22C2
Cizre *Turk* 30D2
Clacton-on-Sea *Eng* 15F6
Claire,L *Can* 52G4
Clairton *USA* 59D2
Clairvaux *France* 17A1
Clanton *USA* 61B2
Clanwilliam *S Africa* 79B7
Clara *Irish Rep* 15B5
Claraz *Arg* 72D3
Clare *USA* 58C2
Claremont *USA* 59E2
Claremore *USA* 63C2
Clarence R *Aust* 50D1
Clarence R *NZ* 51B2
Clarence Str *Aust* 48C2
Clarence Str *USA* 56M4
Clarendon *USA* 63D3
Clarenville *Can* 53N5
Claresholm *Can* 52G4
Clarinda *USA* 63C1
Clarion Iowa *USA* 57D3
Clarion Pennsylvania *USA* 59D2
Clarión I *Mexico* 66A3
Clarion R *USA* 59D2
Clarion Fracture Zone *Pacific O* 47M4
Clark Hill Res *USA* 55E3
Clark,Mt *Can* 56O3
Clark Mt *USA* 65C3
Clark,Pt *Can* 58C2
Clarksburg *USA* 58C3
Clarksdale *USA* 55D3
Clarks Point *USA* 56G4
Clarkston *USA* 64C1
Clarksville Arkansas *USA* 63D2
Clarksville Tennessee *USA* 61B1
Claro R *Brazil* 73B2
Claromecó *Arg* 69E5
Clay Center *USA* 63C2
Claymore Oilfield *N Sea* 14E2
Clayton New Mexico *USA* 54C3
Clayton New York *USA* 59D2
Clear C *Irish Rep* 13B3
Cleare,C *USA* 56J4
Clearfield Pennsylvania *USA* 60A2
Clearfield Utah *USA* 64D2
Clear L *USA* 65B3
Clear Lake *USA* 57D3
Clear Lake Res *USA* 64B2
Clearmont *USA* 57A3
Clearwater *USA* 55E4
Clearwater Mts *USA* 64C1
Cleburne *USA* 54D3
Cleopatra Needle Mt *Phil* 45E8
Clermont *Aust* 48D3
Clermont *France* 16B2
Clermont-en-Argonne *France* 16C2
Clermont-Ferrand *France* 18C2
Clervaux *W Germ* 16D1
Cles *Italy* 17D1
Cleve *Aust* 50A2
Cleveland County *Eng* 15E4
Cleveland Mississippi *USA* 63D3
Cleveland Ohio *USA* 55E2
Cleveland Tennessee *USA* 61C1
Cleveland Texas *USA* 63C3
Cleveland Heights *USA* 58C2
Clevelândia *Brazil* 73B4
Cleveland,Mt *USA* 64D1
Clew B *Irish Rep* 13B3
Clifton Arizona *USA* 65E4
Clifton *Aust* 50D1
Clifton New Jersey *USA* 60C2
Clifton Hills *Aust* 50A1
Clinch R *USA* 61C1
Clinch Mts *USA* 61C1
Clinton Arkansas *USA* 63D2
Clinton *Can* 52F4
Clinton Connecticut *USA* 60D2
Clinton Iowa *USA* 58A2
Clinton Massachusetts *USA* 60E1
Clinton Mississippi *USA* 63D3
Clinton Missouri *USA* 63D2
Clinton N Carolina *USA* 61D2
Clinton New Jersey *USA* 60C2
Clinton Oklahoma *USA* 62C2
Clinton-Colden L *Can* 52H3
Clipperton I *Pacific O* 66B3
Cliza *Bol* 70E7
Clodomira *Arg* 72C1
Cloncurry *Aust* 48D3
Clones *Irish Rep* 15B4
Clonmel *Irish Rep* 15B5
Cloquet *USA* 55D2
Clorinda *Arg* 73A4
Cloud Peak Mt *USA* 57A3
Cloudy Mt *USA* 56G3
Clovis New Mexico *USA* 54C3
Cluj *Rom* 25C6
Cluj-Napoca *Rom* 23E1
Cluses *France* 17B1
Clusone *Italy* 17C2
Clutha R *NZ* 51A3
Clwyd County *Wales* 15D5
Clyde *Can* 53M2
Clyde *NZ* 51A3
Clyde *USA* 60B1
Clyde R *Scot* 14C4
Coachella *USA* 65C4
Coahuayana *Mexico* 67B2
Coahuila State *Mexico* 62B4
Coal R *Can* 56N3
Coalcomán *Mexico* 67B2
Coaldale *USA* 65C3
Coalinga *USA* 65B3
Coalville *USA* 64D2
Coaraci *Brazil* 73E1
Coari R *Brazil* 70F5
Coastal Plain *USA* 61B2
Coast Mts *Can* 52E4
Coast Ranges Mts *USA* 54A2
Coatbridge *Scot* 14C4
Coatepec *Mexico* 67C2
Coatesville *USA* 60C3
Coaticook *Can* 59E1
Coats I *Can* 53K3
Coats Land Region *Ant* 80F1
Coatzacoalcas *Mexico* 66C3
Coatzacoalcos R *Mexico* 67D2
Cobalt *Can* 53L5
Cobán *Guatemala* 66C3
Cobar *Aust* 48D4
Cobargo *Aust* 50C3
Cobija *Bol* 70E6
Cobleskill *USA* 60C1
Cobo de Palos C *Spain* 19B2
Cobourg *Can* 53L5
Cobourg Pen *Aust* 48C2
Coburg *W Germ* 20C2
Coca *Ecuador* 70C4
Coca *USA* 61C3
Cocalinho *Brazil* 73B1
Cochabamba *Bol* 70E7
Cochem *W Germ* 16D1
Cochin *India* 36B3
Cochrane Ontario *Can* 53K5
Cockburn *Aust* 50B2
Cockeysville *USA* 60B3
Cockpit Country,The *Jamaica* 68H1
Coco R *Honduras/Nic* 66D3
Cocobeach *Gabon* 78A3
Coco Channel *Andaman Is* 36E2
Côcos *Brazil* 73D1
Cocos B *Trinidad* 68L1
Cocos Is *Indian O* 46F5
Cocos Ridge *Pacific O* 47P4
Cocula *Mexico* 67B1
Cod Oilfield *N Sea* 14G3
Cod,C *USA* 55F2
Codfish I *NZ* 51A3
Cod I *Can* 53M4
Codigoro *Italy* 17E2
Codó *Brazil* 71K4
Codogno *Italy* 17C2
Cody *USA* 54C2
Coen *Aust* 39H8
Coesfeld *W Germ* 20B2
Coeur d'Alene *USA* 54B2
Coffeyville *USA* 54D3
Coffin B *Aust* 50A2
Coff's Harbour *Aust* 50D2
Cofre de Perote Mt *Mexico* 67C2
Cognac *France* 18B2
Cohocton *USA* 60B1
Cohocton R *USA* 60B1
Cohoes *USA* 59E2
Cohuna *Aust* 50B3
Coihaique *Chile* 69B7
Coimbatore *India* 36B2
Coimbra *Port* 19A1
Cojimies *Ecuador* 70B3
Cokeville *USA* 64D2
Colac *Aust* 48D4
Colatina *Brazil* 71K7
Colbeck,C *Ant* 80F6
Colby *USA* 62B2
Colchester *Eng* 15F6
Colchester *USA* 60D2
Col de la Faucille *France* 17B1
Col du Grand St Bernard P *Switz/Italy* 22B1
Col du Lautaret P *France* 17B2
Col du Mont Cenis P *Italy/France* 22B1
Col du Mt Cenis P *Italy* 18D2
Coldwater *USA* 58C2
Coleen R *USA* 56K2
Coleman *Can* 64D1
Coleman Michigan *USA* 58C2
Coleman Texas *USA* 62C3
Coleraine *N Ire* 14B4
Coleridge,L *NZ* 51B2
Colesberg *S Africa* 79C7
Colfax California *USA* 65B3
Colfax Louisiana *USA* 63D3
Colfax Washington *USA* 64C1
Colima *Mexico* 66B3
Colima State *Mexico* 67B2
Colina *Chile* 72A2
Coll I *Scot* 14B3
Collarenebri *Aust* 50C1
Colle de Tende P *Italy/France* 22B2
Colle di Val d'Elsa *Italy* 17D3
College *USA* 56J3
College Park Georgia *USA* 61C2
College Park Washington *USA* 60B3
College Station *USA* 63C3
Collie *Aust* 48A4
Collier B *Aust* 48B2
Colline Metallifere Mts *Italy* 17D3
Collines de L'Artois Mts *France* 16A1
Collines De Thiérache *France* 16B2
Collines du Perche Mts *France* 16A2
Collingwood *Can* 58C2
Collingwood *NZ* 51B2
Collins Mississippi *USA* 63E3
Collins New York *USA* 60A1
Collinson Pen *Can* 52H2
Collinsville *Aust* 48D3
Collinsville Illinois *USA* 58B3
Collinsville Oklahoma *USA* 63C2
Collipulli *Chile* 72A3
Colmar *France* 18D2
Colmena *Arg* 72C1
Colne R *Eng* 16A1
Cologne = Köln
Colômbia *Brazil* 73C3
Colombia Republic *S America* 70D3
Colombia *USA* 59D3
Colombo *Sri Lanka* 36B3
Colón *Arg* 69E4
Colon *Cuba* 66D2
Colón *Panama* 70C2
Colonia *Urug* 69E4
Colonia del Sacramento *Urug* 72D2
Colonia 25 de Mayo *Arg* 72B3
Colonia Dora *Arg* 72C1
Colonia Josefa *Arg* 72B3
Colonia Las Heras *Arg* 69C7
Colonial Heights *USA* 59D3
Colonsay I *Scot* 14B3
Coloradito *Ven* 68E5
Colorado State *USA* 54C3
Colorado R Arizona *USA* 54B3
Colorado R Buenos Aires *Arg* 69D5
Colorado R La Rioja *Arg* 72B1
Colorado R Texas *USA* 54D3
Colorado City *USA* 62B3
Colorado Plat *USA* 54B3
Colorado Springs *USA* 54C3
Colptlán *Mexico* 67B1
Columbia Maryland *USA* 60B3
Columbia Mississippi *USA* 63E3
Columbia Missouri *USA* 55D3
Columbia Pennsylvania *USA* 59D2
Columbia S Carolina *USA* 55E3
Columbia Tennessee *USA* 55E3
Columbia R *USA* 54A2
Columbia Falls *USA* 64D1
Columbia,Mt *Can* 52G4
Columbia Plat *USA* 64C1
Columbus Georgia *USA* 55E3
Columbus Indiana *USA* 58B3
Columbus Mississippi *USA* 55E3
Columbus Montana *USA* 64E1
Columbus Nebraska *USA* 54D2
Columbus New Mexico *USA* 62A3
Columbus Ohio *USA* 55E2
Columbus Texas *USA* 63C4
Columbus Wisconsin *USA* 58B2
Colville *USA* 64C1
Colville R *USA* 52C3
Colville,C *NZ* 51C1
Colville L *Can* 52F3
Colwyn Bay *Wales* 15D5
Comacchio *Italy* 17E2
Comalcalco *Mexico* 67D2
Comanche *USA* 62C3
Comayagua *Honduras* 66D3
Combarbalá *Chile* 72A2
Comber *N Ire* 15C4
Combermere B *Burma* 37D4
Combeufontaine *France* 16C3
Comeglians *Italy* 17E1
Comeragh Mts *Irish Rep* 15B5
Comfort *USA* 62C3
Comilla *Bang* 37D3
Comitán *Mexico* 66C3
Commercy *France* 16C2
Committees B *Can* 53K3
Como *Italy* 22B1
Comodoro Rivadavia *Arg* 69C7
Comonfort *Mexico* 67B1
Comorin,C *India* 36B3
Comoros Is *Indian O* 79E5
Compiègne *France* 18C2
Compostela *Mexico* 67B1
Comte Salas *Arg* 72B2
Cona *China* 37D2
Conakry *Guinea* 76A4
Conay *Chile* 72A1
Concarán *Arg* 72B2
Concarneau *France* 18B2
Conceiçao da Barra *Brazil* 73E2
Conceição do Araguaia *Brazil* 71J5
Conceiçao do Mato Dentro *Brazil* 73D2
Concepción *Arg* 72B1
Concepción *Brazil/Par* 73A3
Concepción *Chile* 69B5
Concepción *Par* 69E2
Concepción R *Arg* 69E4
Concepcion del Oro *Mexico* 66B2
Concepcion del Uruguay *Arg* 72D2
Conception,Pt *USA* 54A3
Conchas *Brazil* 73C3
Conchas L *USA* 62B2
Conches *France* 16A2
Conchos R *Mexico* 54C4
Concord California *USA* 65B3
Concord New Hampshire *USA* 55F2
Concord North Carolina *USA* 61C1
Concordia *Arg* 69E4
Concordia *Mexico* 67A1
Concordia *USA* 54D3
Concrete *USA* 64B1
Condamine *Aust* 50D1
Condeuba *Brazil* 73D1
Condobolin *Aust* 48D4
Condon *USA* 64B1
Condrina *Brazil* 71H8
Conecuh R *USA* 61B2
Conegliano *Italy* 17E2
Conesus L *USA* 60B1
Confuso R *Par* 73A3
Congo,R = Zaire
Coniston *Can* 58C1
Conneaut *USA* 58C2
Connecticut State *USA* 55F2
Connecticut R *USA* 59E2
Connellsville *USA* 59D2
Connerré *France* 16A2
Connersville *USA* 58B3
Conoble *Aust* 50B2
Conrad *USA* 64D1
Conroe *USA* 63C3
Conselheiro Lafaiete *Brazil* 73D3
Con Son Is *Viet* 43D4
Constance,L = Bodensee
Constanta *Rom* 25D7
Constantine *Alg* 77D1
Constantine,C *USA* 56G4
Constitución *Chile* 69B5
Constitución *Urug* 72D2
Contact *USA* 64D2
Contarina *Italy* 17E2
Contas R *Brazil* 71K6
Contreras *Mexico* 67C2
Contrexéville *France* 16C2
Contuoyto L *Can* 52H3
Conway Arkansas *USA* 55D3
Conway New Hampshire *USA* 59E2
Conway South Carolina *USA* 61D2
Conway,L *Aust* 50A1
Conwy *Wales* 15D5
Coober Pedy *Aust* 48C3
Cookeville *USA* 61B1
Cook Inlet B *USA* 52C3
Cook Is *Pacific O* 47L5
Cook,Mt *NZ* 51B2
Cook Str *NZ* 49G5
Cooktown *Aust* 48D2
Coolabah *Aust* 50C2
Cooladdi *Aust* 50C1
Coolah *Aust* 50C2
Coolamon *Aust* 50C2
Coolgardie *Aust* 48B4
Coolidge *USA* 65D4
Cooma *Aust* 50C3
Coonabarabran *Aust* 50C2
Coonambie *Aust* 50C2
Coonbah *Aust* 50B2
Coondambo *Aust* 50A2
Coondapoor *India* 36A2
Coongoola *Aust* 50C1
Coonoor *India* 36B2
Cooper Basin *Aust* 50B1
Cooper Creek *Aust* 48C3
Cooper Creek R *Aust* 50B1
Cooperstown New York *USA* 60C1
Cooperstown North Dakota *USA* 57C2
Coorong,The *Aust* 50A3
Cooroy *Aust* 50D1
Coos B *USA* 64B2
Coos Bay *USA* 64B2
Cootamundra *Aust* 48D4
Cootehill *Irish Rep* 15B4
Copacabana *Arg* 72B1
Copala *Mexico* 67C2
Copalillo *Mexico* 67C2
Cope *USA* 62B2
Copenhagen = København
Copiapó *Chile* 69B3
Copiapó R *Chile* 72B1
Copparo *Italy* 17D2
Copper R *USA* 56K3
Copper Centre *USA* 52D3
Copper Cliff *Can* 58C1
Copper Harbour *USA* 58B1
Coppermine *Can* 52G3
Coppermine R *Can* 52G3
Coppermine Pt *Can* 58C1
Co Prieto Mt *Mexico* 67A1
Coquilhatville = Mbandaka
Coquimbo *Chile* 69B3
Corabia *Rom* 23E2
Coral Gables *USA* 61E4
Coral Harbour *Can* 53K3
Coral S *Aust/PNG* 48E2
Coral Sea Basin *Pacific O* 46J5
Coral Sea Island Territories *Aust* 48E2
Corangamite,L *Aust* 50B3
Corantijn R *Suriname/Guyana* 71G3
Corbeil-Essonnes *France* 16B2
Corbin *USA* 58C3
Corcubíon *Spain* 19A1
Cord Cantabrica Mts *Spain* 18A3
Cordele *USA* 55E3
Cordillera Cantabrica Mts *Spain* 19A1
Cordillera Central Mts *Dom Rep* 68C3
Cordillera Central Mts *Phil* 45F7
Cordillera de Ansita Mts *Arg* 72B2
Cordillera de Caaguazú *Par* 73A4
Cordillera de la Punilla Mts *Chile* 72A1
Cordillera de los Andes Mts *Peru* 70C5
Cordillera del Toro Mt *Arg* 69C3
Cordillera de Mérida *Ven* 70D2
Cordillera de Viento Mts *Arg* 72A3
Cordillera Isabelia Mts *Nicaragua* 66D3
Cordillera Occidental Mts *Colombia* 70C2
Cordillera Oriental Mts *Colombia* 70C3
Cordillo Downs *Aust* 50B1
Córdoba *Arg* 69D4
Córdoba *Mexico* 66C3
Córdoba *Spain* 19B2
Córdoba State *Arg* 69D4
Cordova *USA* 52D3
Cordova B *USA* 56M5
Corfu = Kérkira
Coribe *Brazil* 73D1
Coricudgy,Mt *Aust* 50D2
Corigliano Calabro *Italy* 22D3
Corinth Mississippi *USA* 55E3
Corinth New York *USA* 60D1
Corinto *Brazil* 71K7
Cork *Irish Rep* 13B3
Çorlu *Turk* 30A1

Cornel Fabriciano **Dehri**

Cornel Fabriciano *Brazil* 71K7
Cornelio Procópio *Brazil* 73B3
Corner Brook *Can* 53N5
Corner Inlet B *Aust* 50C3
Cornimont *France* 16D3
Corning *USA* 59D2
Cornwall *Can* 53L5
Cornwall County *Eng* 15C6
Cornwall,C *Eng* 15C6
Cornwall I *Can* 52H2
Cornwallis I *Can* 53J2
Coro *Ven* 70D1
Coroatá *Brazil* 71K4
Coroico *Bol* 70E7
Coromandel *Brazil* 73C2
Coromandel Coast *India* 36C2
Coromandel Pen *NZ* 51C1
Coromandel Range Mts *NZ* 51C1
Corona New Mexico *USA* 62A3
Coronation G *Can* 52G3
Coronda *Arg* 72C2
Coronel *Chile* 69B5
Coronel Brandsen *Arg* 72D3
Coronel Dorrego *Arg* 72C3
Coronel Fabriciano *Brazil* 73D2
Coronel Oviedo *Par* 69E3
Coronel Pringles *Arg* 69D5
Coronel Suárez *Arg* 72C3
Coronel Vidal *Arg* 72D3
Coropuna Mt *Peru* 70D7
Corowa *Aust* 50C3
Corps *France* 18D3
Corpus Christi *USA* 54D4
Corpus Christi,L *USA* 63F4
Corral *Chile* 72A3
Corregidor I *Phil* 45F8
Corrente R Bahia *Brazil* 73D1
Corrente R Goias *Brazil* 73C1
Corrente R Mato Grosso *Brazil* 73B2
Correntina *Brazil* 73D1
Corrientes *Arg* 69E3
Corrientes State *Arg* 69E3
Corrientes R *Arg* 72D1
Corrigan *USA* 63D3
Corrigin *Aust* 48A4
Corringe Is *Aust* 48E2
Corryong *Aust* 50C3
Corse I *Medit S* 22B2
Corsewall Pt *Scot* 14C4
Corsica = Corse
Corsicana *USA* 54D3
Corte *Corse* 22B2
Cortez *USA* 54C3
Cortina d'Ampezzo *Italy* 22C1
Cortland *USA* 59D2
Cortona *Italy* 17D3
Coruca de Catalan *Mexico* 67B2
Çoruh R *Turk* 25G7
Corum *Turk* 25F7
Corumbá *Brazil* 71G7
Corumba R *Brazil* 73C2
Corumbaiba *Brazil* 73C2
Corvallis *USA* 64B2
Corvo I *Açores* 76A1
Corwen *Wales* 15D5
Corwin,C *USA* 56E4
Cosala *Mexico* 67A1
Coscomatopec *Mexico* 67C2
Cosenza *Italy* 22D3
Cosmoledo Is *Seychelles* 79E5
Cosquín *Arg* 72C2
Costa Blanca Region *Spain* 19B2
Costa Brava Region *Spain* 19C1
Costa de la Luz Region *Spain* 19B2
Costa del Sol Region *Spain* 19B2
Costa Rica Republic *C America* 66D3
Cotabato *Phil* 45F9
Cotagaita *Bol* 70E8
Côte d'Azur Region *France* 18D3
Côte-d'Or Department *France* 16C3
Côtes de Meuse Mts *France* 16C2
Cotonou *Benin* 77G4
Cotopaxi Mt *Ecuador* 70C4
Cotswold Hills Upland *Eng* 15D6
Cottage Grove *USA* 64B2
Cottbus *E Germ* 20C2
Cottonwood *USA* 65D4
Cotulla *USA* 63F4
Coudersport *USA* 60A2
Couedic,C du *Aust* 50A3
Couer d'Alene L *USA* 64C1
Coulommiers *France* 16B2
Coulon R *France* 17A3
Coulonge R *Can* 59D1
Council *USA* 52B3
Council Bluffs *USA* 54D2
Courmayeur *Italy* 17B2
Courtalain *France* 16A2
Courtrai = Kortrijk
Coutances *France* 18B2
Coventry *Eng* 15E5
Covilhã *Spain* 19A1
Covington Georgia *USA* 61C2
Covington Kentucky *USA* 58C3
Covington Louisiana *USA* 63D3
Covington Virginia *USA* 59D3
Cowal,L *Aust* 50C2
Cowangie *Aust* 50B3
Cowansville *Can* 59E1
Coward Springs *Aust* 50A1
Cowell *Aust* 50A2
Cowes *Aust* 50C3
Cowichan L *Can* 64B1
Cowlitz R *USA* 64B1
Cowra *Aust* 50C2
Coxilha de Santana Mts *Brazil/Urug* 72D2
Coxilha Grande Mts *Brazil* 72E1
Coxim *Brazil* 71H7
Coxim R *Brazil* 73B2
Coxsackie *USA* 60D1
Cox's Bazar *Bang* 37D3
Coyobitan *Mexico* 67A1
Coyuca de Benitez *Mexico* 67B2
Cozad *USA* 62C1
Cracow *Aust* 50D1
Cradock *S Africa* 79C7
Craig *USA* 54C2
Crailsheim *W Germ* 20C3
Craiova *Rom* 23E2
Cranberry L *USA* 59E2
Cranbrook *Can* 52G5
Crane Oregon *USA* 64C2
Crane Texas *USA* 62B3
Cranston *USA* 60E2
Crater L *USA* 64B2
Crateus *Brazil* 71K5
Crato *Brazil* 71L5
Crawford *USA* 57B3
Crawfordsville *USA* 58B2
Crawfordville *USA* 61C2
Crawley *Eng* 15E6
Crazy Mts *USA* 64D1
Cree L *Can* 52H4
Creil *France* 16B2
Crema *Italy* 17C2
Crémieu *France* 17A2
Cremona *Italy* 22C1
Crentral Falls *USA* 60E2
Crépy-en-Valois *France* 16B2
Cres I *Yugos* 22C2
Crescent *USA* 64B2
Crescent City *USA* 54A2
Cresco *USA* 57D3
Crespo *Arg* 72C2
Creston *USA* 63D1
Crestview *USA* 61B2
Creswick *Aust* 50B3
Crêt de la Neige Mt *France* 17A1
Crete = Kríti
Crete *USA* 63C1
Crete,S of *Greece* 23E3
Creuse R *France* 18C2
Crewe *Eng* 15D5
Crianlarich *Scot* 14C3
Criciuma *Brazil* 69G3
Crieff *Scot* 14D3
Crillon,Mt *USA* 56L4
Cristalina *Brazil* 73C2
Cristalina R *Brazil* 73B1
Crixás *Brazil* 73C1
Crixás Acu R *Brazil* 73C1
Crixás Mirim R *Brazil* 73B1
Croatia Region *Yugos* 22D1
Crocker Range Mts *Malay* 44E1
Crockett *USA* 63C3
Crofton *USA* 57C3
Croker I *Aust* 48C2
Cromarty *Scot* 14D3
Cromer *Eng* 15F5
Cromwell *NZ* 51A3
Crooked I *Bahamas* 55F4
Crookston *USA* 54D2
Crookwell *Aust* 50C2
Croppa Creek *Aust* 50D1
Crosby *USA* 57D2
Cross R *Nig* 77H4
Crossett *USA* 55D3
Cross River State *Nig* 77H4
Cross Sd *USA* 56L4
Crossville *USA* 61B1
Crotone *Italy* 22D3
Crowley *USA* 63D3
Crown Pt *Tobago* 68K1
Crows Nest *Aust* 50D1
Croydon *Aust* 48D2
Croydon *Eng* 15E6
Crozet Basin *Indian O* 46E6
Crozier Chan *Can* 52F2
Cruillas *Mexico* 67C1
Cruz Alta *Brazil* 69F3
Cruz,C *Cuba* 66E3
Cruz del Eje *Arg* 69D4
Cruzeiro *Brazil* 73D3
Cruzeiro do Sul *Brazil* 70D5
Crystal Brook *Aust* 50A2
Crystal City Missouri *USA* 63D2
Crystal City Texas *USA* 63F4
Crystal Falls *USA* 58B1
Cuamba *Mozam* 79D5
Cuando R *Angola* 79C5
Cuangar *Angola* 79B5
Cuango,R = Kwango,R
Cuarto R *Arg* 72C2
Cuauhtémoc *Mexico* 66B2
Cuautla *Mexico* 67C2
Cuba Republic *Caribbean* 66D2
Cuba *USA* 60A1
Cubango R *Angola* 79B5
Cuchi *Angola* 79B5
Cuchi R *Angola* 79B5
Cuchilla de Haedo Mts *Urug* 72D2
Cuchilla Grande Mts *Urug* 72D2
Cuchillo Có *Arg* 72C3
Cucui *Brazil* 70E3
Cúcuta *Colombia* 70D2
Cuddalore *India* 36B2
Cuddapah *India* 36B2
Cue *Aust* 48A3
Cuenca *Ecuador* 70C4
Cuenca *Spain* 19B1
Cuencame *Mexico* 67B1
Cuernavaca *Mexico* 66C3
Cuero *USA* 63C4
Cuiabá *Brazil* 71G7
Cuiabá R *Brazil* 73A1
Cuicatlan *Mexico* 67C2
Cuieté R *Brazil* 73D2
Cuillin Hills Mts *Scot* 14B3
Cuilo R *Angola* 79B4
Cuiseaux *France* 17A1
Cuito R *Angola* 79B5
Cuito Cunavale *Angola* 79B5
Cuitzeo *Mexico* 67B2
Cu Lao Hon I *Viet* 43D3
Culbertson Montana *USA* 57B2
Culbertson Nebraska *USA* 62B1
Culcairn *Aust* 50C3
Culgoa R *Aust* 50C1
Culiacán *Mexico* 66B2
Culion I *Phil* 45E8
Cullman *USA* 61B2
Culoz *France* 17A2
Culpeper *USA* 59D3
Culter Ridge *USA* 61E4
Culuene R *Brazil* 73B1
Culverden *NZ* 51B2
Cumaná *Ven* 70F1
Cumberland Maryland *USA* 55F3
Cumberland Wisconsin *USA* 58A1
Cumberland R *USA* 55E3
Cumberland,L *USA* 55E3
Cumberland Pen *Can* 53M3
Cumberland Plat *USA* 58C3
Cumbernauld Sd *Can* 53M3
Cumbria *Eng* 15D4
Cummings *USA* 65B3
Cummins *Aust* 50A2
Cumnock *Scot* 14C4
Cunco *Chile* 72A3
Cunene R *Angola/Namibia* 79B5
Cuneo *Italy* 22B2
Cunnamulla *Aust* 48D3
Cupar *Scot* 14D3
Ćuprija *Yugos* 23E2
Curaçao I *Caribbean* 68D4
Curacautin *Chile* 72A3
Curaco R *Arg* 72B3
Curanilahue *Chile* 72A3
Curepto *Chile* 72A3
Curicó *Chile* 69B4
Curisevo R *Brazil* 73B1
Curitiba *Brazil* 69G3
Curnamona *Aust* 50A2
Curoca R *Angola* 79B5
Current R *USA* 63D2
Curuzú Cuatiá *Arg* 72D1
Curvelo *Brazil* 71K7
Curwensville *USA* 60A2
Cushing *USA* 63C2
Custer Montana *USA* 64E1
Custer S Dakota *USA* 57B3
Cut Bank *USA* 64D1
Cuthbert *USA* 61C2
Cutral-Có *Arg* 72B3
Cuttack *India* 37C3
Cuvelai *Angola* 79B5
Cuxhaven *W Germ* 20B2
Cuyahoga Falls *USA* 58C2
Cuyo Is *Phil* 45F8
Cuzco *Peru* 70D6
Cyangugu *Zaïre* 78C4
Cyclades = Kikládhes
Cyprus Republic *Medit S* 30B3
Cyrus Field B *Can* 53M3
Czechoslovakia Republic *Europe* 21D3
Częstochowa *Pol* 21D2

D

Da R *Viet* 43C1
Da'an *China* 41A2
Dab'a *Jordan* 31D3
Dabajuro *Ven* 68C4
Dabaro *Somalia* 75D4
Daba Shan Mts *China* 40B3
Dabat *Eth* 78D2
Dabhoi *India* 35C4
Dabie Shan U *China* 40C3
Dabola *Guinea* 76A3
Dabou *Ivory Coast* 76B4
Daboya *Ghana* 77F4
Dabrowa Gorn *Pol* 21D2
Dacca *Bang* 37D3
Dachau *W Germ* 20C3
Dachstein Mt *Austria* 22C1
Dada He R *China* 40A3
Daddato *Djibouti* 32D4
Dade City *USA* 61C3
Dadhar *Pak* 35B3
Dadu *Pak* 35B3
Dadu He R *China* 38D3
Daet *Phil* 45F8
Dafang *China* 40B4
Daga R *Burma* 43B2
Dagabur *Eth* 78E3
Dagana *Sen* 76A3
Dagestanskaya ASSR Republic *USSR* 26F5
Dagupan *Phil* 45F7
Dagzê *China* 37D2
Dahab *Egypt* 30B4
Da Hinggan Line Mts *China* 27O5
Dahlak Arch *Eth* 32D3
Dahlonega *USA* 61C2
Dāhod *India* 35C4
Dahra *Libya* 75A2
Dahra Region *Alg* 19C2
Dailekh *Nepal* 37B2
Daireaux *Arg* 72C3
Dairen = Lüda
Dairût *Egypt* 32B1
Daitō Is *Pacific Oc* 38G4
Dajarra *Aust* 48C3
Daka R *Ghana* 77F4
Dakar *Sen* 76A3
Dakhla *Mor* 76A2
Dakhla Oasis *Egypt* 75B2
Dakoro *Niger* 76C3
Dakota City *USA* 57C3
Dakovica *Yugos* 23E2
Dakovo *Yugos* 23D1
Dala *Angola* 79C5
Dalaba *Guinea* 76A3
Dalai Nur L *China* 40D1
Dalälven R *Sweden* 24B3
Dalandzadgad *Mongolia* 38D2
Dalanganem Is *Phil* 45F8
Dalanjargalan *Mongolia* 38D2
Da Lat *Viet* 43D3
Dalbandin *Pak* 34E3
Dalby *Aust* 48E3
Dale Hollow L *USA* 61B1
Dalen *Nor* 12F7
Dales,The Upland *Eng* 15D4
Daleville *USA* 61B2
Dalhart *USA* 54C3
Dalhousie *Can* 59F1
Dalhousie,C *Can* 52E2
Dalion Hist Site *Cyprus* 31B1
Dallas *USA* 54D3
Dalles,The *USA* 64B1
Dall I. *USA* 52E4
Dall I *USA* 56M5
Dalli Rajhara *India* 37B3
Dallol R *Niger* 76C3
Dallol Bosso R *Niger* 77G3
Dallol Maouri R *Niger* 77G3
Dalmatia Region *Yugos* 22D2
Dal'negorsk *USSR* 41D3
Dal'nerechensk *USSR* 41C2
Daloa *Ivory Coast* 76B4
Dalou Shan Mts *China* 40B4
Dāltenganj *India* 37B3
Dalton Georgia *USA* 61C2
Dalton Massachusetts *USA* 60D1
Daludalu *Indon* 44B2
Daly R *Aust* 48C2
Daly City *USA* 65B3
Daly Waters *Aust* 48C2
Damaguete *Phil* 45F9
Damān *India* 35C4
Damanhûr *Egypt* 30B3
Damar I *Indon* 48B1
Damara *CAR* 78B3
Damascus *Syria* 30C3
Damascus *USA* 60B3
Damaturu *Nig* 77J3
Damavand *Iran* 34C1
Damba *Angola* 79B4
Dambulla *Sri Lanka* 36C3
Damghan *Iran* 34C1
Damietta *Egypt* 31A3
Damoh *India* 35D4
Damongo *Ghana* 77F4
Damot *Eth* 78E3
Damour *Leb* 31C2
Dampier *Aust* 48A3
Damqawt *S Yemen* 33F3
Danā *Jordan* 31C3
Danakil Region *Eth* 32D4
Danané *Lib* 76B4
Da Nang *Viet* 43D2
Danao *Phil* 45F8
Danau Poso Mt *Indon* 45B3
Danau Tobu L *Indon* 44A2
Danau Tuwuti L *Indon* 45B3
Danbu *China* 40A3
Danbury *USA* 59E2
Danby *USA* 60D1
Dandeldhura *Nepal* 37B2
Dandeli *India* 36A1
Dandenong *Aust* 50C3
Dandong *China* 41A3
Danger Pt *S Africa* 79B7
Dangila *Eth* 78D2
Danguard Jenson Land Region *Can* 53M1
Daniel *USA* 64D2
Daniels Harbour *Can* 53N4
Dannebrogs Øy I *Greenland* 53P3
Dannevirke *NZ* 51C2
Dansville *USA* 60B1
Dantewāra *India* 36C1
Danube = Dunărea
Danube = Donau
Danuk *Iraq* 25G8
Danville Illinois *USA* 55E2
Danville Kentucky *USA* 55E3
Danville Pennsylvania *USA* 60B2
Danville Virginia *USA* 55F3
Danzig = Gdańsk
Dao Xian *China* 40C4
Daozhen *China* 40B4
Dapchi *Nig* 77J3
Dapha Bum Mt *India* 37E2
Daphnae Hist Site *Egypt* 31B3
Dapiak,Mt *Phil* 45F9
Dapitan *Phil* 45F9
Da Qaidam *China* 38C3
Dar'a *Syria* 31D2
Dārāb *Iran* 34C3
Daraj *Libya* 75A1
Dārān *Iran* 34C2
Dar'ā Salkhad *Syria* 30C3
Darbhanga *India* 37C2
Dardanelle,L *USA* 63D2
Dar Es Salaam *Tanz* 79D4
Dargaville *NZ* 51B1
Darien *USA* 61C2
Darjeeling = Dārjiling
Dārjiling *India* 37C2
Darling R *Aust* 48D4
Darling Downs *Aust* 50C1
Darling Pen *Can* 53L1
Darlington *Aust* 50B2
Darlington *Eng* 15E4
Darlington *USA* 61D2
Darmstadt *W Germ* 20B3
Darnah *Libya* 75B1
Darnick *Aust* 50B2
Darnley B *Can* 52F3
Darnley,C *Ant* 80G10
Daroca *Spain* 19B1
Dar Rounga Region *CAR* 78C3
Darsa I *S Yemen* 33F4
Dart R *Eng* 15D6
Dartmoor Moorland *Eng* 13C3
Dartmoor Nat Pk *Eng* 15D6
Dartmouth *Can* 53M5
Dartmouth *Eng* 15D6
Daru *PNG* 48D1
Daruvar *Yugos* 22D1
Darweshan *Afghan* 34E2
Darwin *Aust* 48C2
Daryacheh-ye Bakhtegan L *Iran* 34C3
Daryācheh-ye Mahārlū L *Iran* 34C3
Daryācheh-ye Namak Salt Flat *Iran* 34C2
Daryacheh-ye-Sistan Salt Lake *Iran/Afghan* 34E2
Daryacheh-ye Tashk L *Iran* 34C3
Daryācheh-ye Urumīyeh L *Iran* 25H8
Dārzīn *Iran* 34D3
Das I *UAE* 33F1
Dashennonglia Mt *China* 40C3
Dasht *Iran* 34D1
Dasht R *Pak* 34E3
Dasht-e-Kavir Salt Desert *Iran* 34C2
Dasht-e Lut Salt Desert *Iran* 34D2
Dasht-e Naomid Desert Region *Iran* 34E2
Dasht-i-Margo Desert *Afghan* 34E2
Date *Japan* 42D2
Datia *India* 35D3
Datong *China* 40A2
Datong *China* 40C1
Datong He R *China* 40A2
Datu Piang *Phil* 45F9
Daugava R *USSR* 12K7
Daugavpils *USSR* 24D4
Daughiné Region *France* 18D2
Dauguard Jensen Land *Greenland* 53M1
Daulatabad *Afghan* 35A1
Daulpur *India* 35D3
Daun *W Germ* 16D1
Daund *India* 36A1
Dauphin *Can* 52H4
Dauphin *USA* 60B2
Dauphin I *USA* 61B2
Daura *Nig* 76C3
Dausa *India* 35D3
Dāvah Panāh *Iran* 34E3
Dāvangere *India* 36B2
Davao *Phil* 45G9
Davao G *Phil* 45G9
Davenport Iowa *USA* 55D2
David *Panama* 70B2
Davidson Mts *USA* 52D3
Davis *USA* 65B3
Davis Base *Ant* 80G10
Davis Inlet *Can* 53M4
Davis Str *Greenland/Can* 53N3
Davlekanovo *USSR* 24K5
Davos *Switz* 17C1
Dawa R *Eth* 78E3
Dawan *China* 40A4
Dawat Yar *Afghan* 35B2
Dawḩat Salwah B *Qatar/S Arabia* 33F1
Dawkah *Oman* 33F3
Dawna Range Mts *Burma* 43B2
Dawson *Can* 52E3
Dawson Georgia *USA* 61C2
Dawson N Dakota *USA* 57C2
Dawson R *Aust* 48D3
Dawson Creek *Can* 52F4
Dawson Range Mts *Can* 56L3
Dawu *China* 40A3
Dawu *China* 40C3
Dax *France* 18B3
Daxian *China* 40B3
Daxin *China* 40B5
Daxue Shan Mts *China* 40A3
Dayman R *Urug* 72D2
Dayong *China* 40C4
Dayr'Ali *Syria* 31D2
Dayr'Atīyah *Syria* 31D1
Dayr az Zawr *Syria* 30D2
Dayr Shumayyil *Syria* 31D1
Dayton Ohio *USA* 55E3
Dayton Tennessee *USA* 61B1
Dayton Texas *USA* 63D4
Dayton Washington *USA* 64C1
Daytona Beach *USA* 55E4
Dayu *China* 40C4
Dayu *Indon* 44E3
Da Yunhe *China* 40D2
Da Yunhe R *China* 40D2
Dayville *USA* 64C2
Dazhu *China* 40B3
De Aar *S Africa* 79C7
Deadman's Cay *Bahamas* 68C2
Dead S *Israel/Jordan* 30C3
Deadwood *USA* 57B3
Deal *Eng* 16A1
Deán Funes *Arg* 72C2
Dearborn *USA* 58C2
Dease Arm B *Can* 52F3
Dease Lake *Can* 52E4
Death V *USA* 54B3
Deauville *France* 18C2
Debakala *Ivory Coast* 77F4
Debauch Mt *USA* 56F3
Débé *Trinidad* 68L1
Debica *Pol* 21E2
Deblin *Pol* 21E2
Débo,L *Mali* 76B3
Debra Birhan *Eth* 78D3
Debra Markos *Eth* 78D2
Debra Tabor *Eth* 78D2
Debrecen *Hung* 21E3
Decamere *Eth* 32C3
Decatur Alabama *USA* 55E3
Decatur Georgia *USA* 61C2
Decatur Illinois *USA* 55E3
Decatur Indiana *USA* 58C2
Decazeville *France* 18C3
Dechang *China* 40A4
Decorah *USA* 57D3
Dedougou *U Volta* 77F3
Dedu *China* 41B2
Dedza *Malawi* 79D5
Dee R Dumfries and Galloway *Scot* 14C4
Dee R *Eng/Wales* 15D5
Dee R Grampian *Scot* 14D3
Deep River *Can* 59D1
Deep River *USA* 60D2
Deepwater *Aust* 50D1
Deer I *USA* 56F5
Deer Lake *Can* 53N5
Deer Lodge *USA* 54B2
Deésaguadero R *Bol* 70E7
Deeth *USA* 64C2
Defferrari *Arg* 72D3
De Funiak Springs *USA* 61B2
Dêgê *China* 38C3
De Grey R *Aust* 48A3
Deh Bīd *Iran* 34C2
Dehi *Afghan* 35B1
Dehibat *Tunisia* 76D1
Dehiwala-Mt Lavinia *Sri Lanka* 36B3
Dehlorān *Iran* 34B2
Dehra Dūn *India* 35D2
Dehri *India* 37B3

Dehui **Dunmore**

Dehui *China* 41B3
Deim Zubeir *Sudan* 78C3
Deir Abu Sa'id *Jordan* 31C2
Deir el Ahmar *Leb* 31D1
Dej *Rom* 25C6
De Kalb Illinois *USA* 58B2
De Kalb Texas *USA* 63D3
De Kastri *USSR* 27Q4
Dekese *Zaïre* 78C4
Dekoa *CAR* 78B3
Delano *USA* 54B3
Delano Peal Mt *USA* 65D3
Delarof Is *USA* 56C6
Delaware State *USA* 55F3
Delaware *USA* 58C2
Delaware R *USA* 59D2
Delaware B *USA* 55F3
Delegate *Aust* 50C3
Delemont *Switz* 17B1
Delgado C *Mozam* 79E5
Delgo *Sudan* 32B2
Delhi Colorado *USA* 62B2
Delhi *India* 35D3
Delhi New York *USA* 59E2
Delice *Turk* 30B1
Delicias *Mexico* 66B2
Delījān *Iran* 34C2
Delle *France* 17B1
Dell Rapids *USA* 57C3
Dellys *Alg* 77C1
Delmenhorst *W Germ* 12F8
De Long Mts *USA* 56F2
Deloraine *Aust* 50E3
Deloraine *Can* 52H5
Delray Beach *USA* 61E4
Del Rio *USA* 54C4
Delta *USA* 54B3
Delta R *USA* 56J3
Delta Junction *USA* 54J3
Delta Res *USA* 60C1
Delwein *USA* 57D3
Dembidollo *Eth* 78D3
Demer R *Belg* 16C1
Demidov *USSR* 21G1
Deming *USA* 62A3
Demirköy *Turk* 23F2
Demnate *Mor* 77A2
Demonte *Italy* 17B2
Demopolis *USA* 61B2
Denain *France* 18C1
Denau *USSR* 29E2
Denbigh *Wales* 15D5
Denbigh,C *USA* 56F3
Dendang *Indon* 44C3
Dendermond *Belg* 16C1
Dendi Mt *Eth* 78D3
Dèndre R *Belg* 16B1
Dengkou *China* 40B1
Deng Xian *China* 40C3
Den Haag = 's-Gravenhage
Denham,Mt *Jamaica* 68H1
Den Helder *Neth* 20A2
Denia *Spain* 19C2
Deniliquin *Aust* 48D4
Denio *USA* 64C2
Denison Iowa *USA* 57C3
Denison Texas *USA* 54D3
Denison,Mt *USA* 56H4
Denizli *Turk* 25D8
Denmark Kingdom *Europe* 12F7
Denmark Str *Greenland/Iceland* 80C1
Dennery *St Lucia* 68P2
Denpasar *Indon* 44E4
Denton Maryland *USA* 60C3
Denton Texas *USA* 54D3
D'Entrecasteaux Is *PNG* 48E1
Dents du Midi Mt *Switz* 17B1
Denver *USA* 54C3
Déo R *Cam* 78B3
Deoghar *India* 37C3
Deolāli *India* 35C5
Deosai Plain *India* 35D1
Depew *USA* 60A1
Deposit *USA* 60C1
Dépression du Mourdi Desert Region *Chad* 78C2
Deputatskiy *USSR* 27Q3
De Queen *USA* 63D3
Dera *Pak* 35C3
Dera Bugti *Pak* 35B3
Dera Ismail Khan *Pak* 35B2
Derbent *USSR* 25H7
Derby *Aust* 48B2
Derby Connecticut *USA* 60D2
Derby County *Eng* 15E5
Derby *Eng* 15E5
Derby Kansas *USA* 63C2
Dergachi *USSR* 25F5
De Ridder *USA* 63D3
Derna *Libya* 75B1
Derry *USA* 60E1
Derudeb *Sudan* 78D2
De Ruyter *USA* 60C1
Derwent Bridge *Aust* 50E3
Desaguadero *Arg* 72B2
Desaguadero R *Arg* 72B2
Descanso *Mexico* 65C4
Deschutes R *USA* 64B2
Deseado *Arg* 69C7
Deseado R *Arg* 69C7
Desenzano *Italy* 17D2
Deserta Grande I *Medeira* 76A1
Desert Centre *USA* 65C4
Desert Peak Mt *USA* 65D2
Deshu *Afghan* 34E2
Desierto de Atacama Desert *Chile* 69C2
Desloge *USA* 63D2
Des Moines Iowa *USA* 55D2
Des Moines New Mexico *USA* 62B2
Des Moines R *USA* 57D3
Desna R *USSR* 25E5
Desolación I *Chile* 69B8
Des Plaines *USA* 58B2
Dessau *E Germ* 20C2
Dessye *Eth* 78D2
Destruction Bay *Can* 56L3
Desvres *France* 16A1
Deta *Rom* 23E1
Dete *Zim* 79C5
Detmold *W Germ* 16E1
Detroit *USA* 55E2
Detroit Lakes *USA* 57C2
Det Udom *Thai* 43D3
Deva *Rom* 23E1
Deventer *Neth* 20B2
Deveron R *Scot* 14D3
Devikot *India* 35C3
Devil's Hole Region *N Sea* 14F3
Devil's Island = Isla du Diable
Devils L N Dakota *USA* 57C2
Devils L Texas *USA* 62B4
Devils Lake *USA* 54D2
Devils Paw Mt *Can* 56M4
Devizes *Eng* 15E6
Devli *India* 35D3
Devoll R *Alb* 23E2
Dévoluy Mts *France* 17A2
Devon County *Eng* 15C6
Devon I *Can* 53J2
Devonport *Aust* 48D5
Dewangiri *Bhutan* 37D2
Dewās *India* 35D4
De Witt *USA* 63D3
Dexter Missouri *USA* 63E2
Dexter New Mexico *USA* 62B3
Deyang *China* 40A3
Deyhuk *Iran* 34D2
Dezfūl *Iran* 34B2
Dezhou *China* 40D2
Dezh Shāhpūr *Iran* 34B1
Dhahran *S Arabia* 33F1
Dhali *Cyprus* 31B1
Dhamār *Yemen* 32D4
Dhamavaram *India* 36B2
Dhamtari *India* 37B3
Dhanbād *India* 37C3
Dhangarhi *Nepal* 37B2
Dhankuta *Nepal* 37C2
Dhār *India* 35D4
Dharmapuri *India* 36B2
Dharmsāla *India* 35D2
Dhar Oualata Desert Region *Maur* 76B3
Dhaulagiri Mt *Nepal* 37B2
Dhenkānāl *India* 37C3
Dhibah *Jordan* 31C3
Dhíkti Óri Mt *Greece* 23F3
Dhofar Region *Oman* 33F3
Dhomokós *Greece* 23E3
Dhone *India* 36B1
Dhoraji *India* 35C4
Dhrāngadhra *India* 35C4
Dhuburi *India* 37C2
Dhule *India* 35C4
Diablo Range Mts *USA* 65B3
Diamante *Arg* 72C2
Diamante R *Arg* 72B2
Diamantina *Brazil* 71K7
Diamantina R *Aust* 48D3
Diamantino *Brazil* 73A1
Diamond Harbours *India* 37C3
Diamondville *USA* 64D2
Diapaga *U Volta* 77G3
Dibā *UAE* 33G1
Dibaya *Zaïre* 79C4
Dibrugarh *India* 37D2
Dickens *USA* 62B3
Dickinson *USA* 54C2
Dickson *USA* 61B1
Dickson City *USA* 59D2
Dicle R *Turk* 25G8
Dīdwāna *India* 35C3
Die *France* 17A2
Diebougou *U Volta* 77F3
Dieburg *W Germ* 16E2
Diekirch *Lux* 16D2
Diéma *Mali* 76B3
Dien Bien Phu *Viet* 43C1
Diepholz *W Germ* 20B2
Dieppe *France* 18C2
Dier Songhua Jiang R *China* 41B3
Diest *Belg* 16C1
Dieuze *France* 16D2
Diffa *Niger* 77J3
Digboi *India* 37E2
Digby *Can* 53M5
Digne *France* 18D3
Digoin *France* 18C2
Digos *Phil* 45G9
Digul R *Indon* 48C1
Digya Nat Pk *Ghana* 77F4
Dihang R *India* 37D2
Dijlah = Tigris
Dijon *France* 17A1
Dik *Chad* 78B3
Dikhil *Djibouti* 78E2
Dīkirnis *Egypt* 31A3
Diksmuide *Belg* 16B1
Dikson *USSR* 26K2
Dikwa *Nig* 77J3
Dilaram *Afghan* 34E2
Dili *Indon* 48B1
Di Linh *Viet* 43D3
Dillenburg *W Germ* 16E1
Dilley *USA* 63F4
Dilling *Sudan* 78C2
Dillingham *USA* 56G4
Dillon *USA* 54B2
Dillsburg *USA* 60B2
Dilolo *Zaïre* 79C5
Dimas *Mexico* 67A1
Dimashq = Damascus
Dimbelenge *Zaïre* 78C4
Dimbokro *Ivory Coast* 77F4
Dimitrovgrad *Bulg* 23F2
Dimitrovgrad *USSR* 24H5
Dimona *Israel* 31C3
Dimpāpur *India* 37D2
Dinagat I *Phil* 45G8
Dinajpur *India* 37C2
Dinan *France* 18B2
Dinant *Belg* 16C1
Dinar *Turk* 30B2
Dinder R *Sudan* 78D2
Dindigul *India* 36B2
Dingbian *China* 40B2
Dinggyê *China* 37C2
Dingle *Irish Rep* 13A3
Dingle B *Irish Rep* 13A3
Dinguiraye *Guinea* 76A3
Dingwall *Scot* 14C3
Dingxi *China* 40A2
Ding Xian *China* 40D2
Dinh Lap *Viet* 43D1
Dinorwic L *Can* 57D2
Dinosaur *USA* 62A1
Diomede Is *USSR/USA* 56E2
Diouloulou *Sen* 76A3
Diphu *India* 37D2
Diredawa *Eth* 78E3
Dirk Hartog I *Aust* 48A3
Dirkou *Niger* 78B2
Dirranbandi *Aust* 50C1
Dirri *Somalia* 78E3
Disappointment,C *South Georgia* 69J8
Disappointment,C *USA* 64B1
Disappointment,L *Aust* 48B3
Discovery B *Aust* 50B3
Discovery Tablemount *Atlantic O* 74J6
Disentis Muster *Switz* 17C1
Dishna *Egypt* 32B1
Disko *Greenland* 53N3
Disko Bugt B *Greenland* 53N3
Diskorjord *Greenland* 53N3
Dismal Swamp *USA* 59D3
Disna R *USSR* 21F1
Distrito Federal Federal District *Brazil* 73C2
Diu *India* 35C4
Diuat Mts *Phil* 45G9
Dives R *France* 16A2
Divinópolis *Brazil* 71K8
Divnoye *USSR* 25G6
Divriği *Turk* 30C2
Dixon Illinois *USA* 58B2
Dixon Montana *USA* 64D1
Dixon Entrance Sd *Can/USA* 52E4
Diyālā R *Iraq* 30E3
Diyarbakir *Turk* 25G8
Diz *Pak* 34E3
Diz R *Iran* 34B2
Dja R *Cam* 78B3
Djadi R *Alg* 77C2
Djado,Plat du *Niger* 78B1
Djamaa *Alg* 77D2
Djambala *Congo* 78B4
Djanet *Alg* 76C2
Djebel Amour Mts *Alg* 77C2
Djebel Bouhalla Mt *Mor* 19A2
Djebel Chambi Mt *Tunisia* 77D1
Djebel Chélia Mts *Alg* 77D1
Djebel Zaghouan Mt *Tunisia* 77E1
Djebel Zrega Mt *Tunisia* 77D2
Djebobo Mt *Ghana* 77G4
Djelfa *Alg* 77C2
Djéma *CAR* 78C3
Djenné *Mali* 76B3
Djerem R *Cam* 77J4
Djibasso *U Volta* 77F3
Djibo *Upper Volta* 76B3
Djibouti *Djibouti* 78E2
Djibouti Republic *E Africa* 78E2
Djolu *Zaïre* 78C3
Djougou *Benin* 77G4
Djugu *Zaïre* 78D3
Djúpivogur *Iceland* 12C2
Djurdjura Mts *Alg* 19C2
Dmitrov *USSR* 24F4
Dnepr R *USSR* 25E6
Dneprodzerzhinsk *USSR* 25E6
Dnepropetrovsk *USSR* 25F6
Dneprovskaya Nizmennost' Region *USSR* 24D5
Dnestr R *USSR* 25C6
Dno *USSR* 24E4
Doba *Chad* 78B3
Dobele *USSR* 21E1
Doblas *Arg* 72C3
Dobo *Indon* 48C1
Doboj *Yugos* 23D2
Dobrush *USSR* 25E5
Doce R *Brazil* 71K7
Doctor R P Peña *Arg* 69D2
Dod *India* 36B2
Doda Betta Mt *India* 36B2
Dodecanese = Sporádhes
Dodge City *USA* 54C3
Dodgeville *USA* 58A2
Dodoma *Tanz* 78D4
Dogger Bank Sand-bank *N Sea* 14G4
Dog L *Can* 58B1
Dog L *Can* 58C1
Dōgo I *Japan* 42B3
Dogondoutchi *Niger* 76C3
Doğubayazit *Turk* 30D2
Doha *Qatar* 33F1
Doilungdêqên *China* 37D2
Doka *Sudan* 32C4
Dolak I *Indon* 48C1
Doland *USA* 57C3
Dolbeau *Can* 53L5
Dôle *France* 18D2
Doleib Watercourse *Sudan* 32B4
Dolgellau *Wales* 15D5
Dolgeville *USA* 60C1
Dolinsk *USSR* 41E2
Dolo *Eth* 78E3
Dolomitche Mts *Italy* 17D1
Dolores *Arg* 69E5
Dolores *Urug* 72D2
Dolores R *USA* 62A2
Dolores Hidalgo *Mexico* 67B1
Dolphin and Union Str *Can* 52G3
Dolphin,C *Falkland Is* 69E8
Dom Mt *Indon* 39G7
Dombarovskiy *USSR* 26G4
Dombas *Nor* 12F6
Dombasle-sur-Meurthe *France* 16D2
Dombóvár *Hung* 23D1
Domeyko *Chile* 72A1
Domfront *France* 18B2
Dominica I *Caribbean* 68E3
Dominican Republic *Caribbean* 68C3
Dominion,C *Can* 53L3
Domino *Can* 53N4
Domna *USSR* 38E1
Domodossola *Italy* 22B1
Dom Pedrito *Brazil* 72E2
Dompu *Indon* 44E4
Domuyo Mt *Arg* 69B5
Domville,Mt *Aust* 50D1
Dom-yanskoya *USSR* 26H4
Don R *Scot* 14D3
Don R *USSR* 25G6
Donaghadee *N Ire* 14B4
Donato Guerta *Mexico* 67B1
Donau = Dunav
Donau R *Austria* 20C3
Donau R *W Germ* 20C3
Donaueschingen *W Germ* 16E3
Donauwörth *W Germ* 20C3
Don Benito *Spain* 19A2
Doncaster *Eng* 15E5
Dondo *Angola* 79B4
Dondo *Mozam* 79D5
Dondra Head C *Sri Lanka* 36C3
Donegal County *Irish Rep* 14B4
Donegal *Irish Rep* 13B3
Donegal B *Irish Rep* 13B3
Donegal Mts *Irish Rep* 14A4
Donetsk *USSR* 25F6
Donga R *Nig* 77J4
Dong'an *China* 40C4
Dongara *Aust* 48A3
Dongchuan *China* 40A4
Dongfang *China* 43D2
Dongfeng *China* 41B3
Donggala *Indon* 48A1
Donggi Cona L *China* 38C3
Donggou *China* 41A4
Donghai Dao I *China* 40C5
Dong He R *China* 40A1
Dong Hoi *Viet* 43D2
Dong Jiang R *China* 40C5
Donglanghong *China* 41C2
Dongning *China* 41C3
Dongola *Sudan* 78D2
Dongshan *China* 40D5
Dongsha Qundao I *China* 38E4
Dongsheng *China* 40C2
Dongtai *China* 40E3
Dongting Hu L *China* 40C4
Dongxing *China* 40B5
Dongzhi *China* 40D3
Doniphan *USA* 63D2
Donji Vakuf *Yugos* 22D2
Dönna I *Nor* 12G5
Donner P *USA* 65B3
Donnersberg Mt *W Germ* 16D2
Doonerak,Mt *USA* 56H2
Dopolong *Phil* 45F9
Do Qu R *China* 40A3
Dora Baltea R *Italy* 17B2
Dorbirn *Austria* 18D2
Dorbod *China* 41A2
Dorchester *Eng* 15D6
Dorchester,C *Can* 53L3
Dordogne R *France* 18C2
Dordrecht *Neth* 20A2
Dorest Peak Mt *USA* 60D1
Dori *Upper Volta* 76B3
Dormans *France* 16B2
Dornbirn *Austria* 20B3
Dornoch *Scot* 14C3
Dornoch Firth Estuary *Scot* 14C3
Dorotea *Sweden* 12H6
Dorrigo *Aust* 50D2
Dorris *USA* 64B2
Dorset County *Eng* 15D6
Dorsten *W Germ* 16D1
Dortmund *W Germ* 20B2
Doruma *Zaïre* 78C3
Dosatuy *USSR* 27N4
Doshi *Afghan* 35B1
Dosso *Niger* 77G3
Dossor *USSR* 26G5
Dothan *USA* 55E3
Douai *France* 18C1
Douala *Cam* 78A3
Double Island Pt *Aust* 50D1
Double Mountain Fork R *USA* 62B3
Doubs R *France* 18D2
Doubtful Sd *NZ* 51A3
Douentza *Mali* 76B3
Douglas Arizona *USA* 54C3
Douglas *Eng* 15C4
Douglas Georgia *USA* 61C2
Douglas Wyoming *USA* 54C2
Douglas L *USA* 61C1
Douglas,Mt *USA* 56H4
Doulevant-le-Château *France* 16C2
Doullens *France* 16B1
Doun County *N Ire* 15B4
Dourados *Brazil* 71H8
Dourados R *Brazil* 73B3
Dourdan *France* 16B2
Douro R *Port* 19A1
Dove Creek *USA* 62A2
Dover Delaware *USA* 59D3
Dover *Eng* 15F6
Dover New Hampshire *USA* 59E2
Dover New Jersey *USA* 60C2
Dover Ohio *USA* 58C2
Dover R *Eng* 15E5
Dover,Str of *Eng/France* 15F6
Dovsk *USSR* 21G2
Downington *USA* 60C3
Downpatrick *N Ire* 15C4
Downsville *USA* 60C1
Doylestown *USA* 60C2
Dōzen I *Japan* 42B3
Dr'aa R *Mor* 76A2
Drac R *France* 17A2
Dracena *Brazil* 73B3
Dracut *USA* 60E1
Draguignan *France* 18D3
Drake *USA* 57B2
Drakensberg Mts *S Africa* 79D6
Drake Pass *Pacific/Atlantic O* 74E7
Dráma *Greece* 23E2
Drammen *Nor* 12G6
Drangajökull *Iceland* 12A1
Dr Arroyo *Mexico* 67B1
Drau R *Austria* 17E1
Drava R *Yugos* 22D1
Dreaux *France* 18C2
Dresden *E Germ* 20C2
Dreux *France* 16A2
Drewsey *USA* 64C2
Driftwood *USA* 60A2
Drin R *Alb* 23E2
Drina R *Yugos* 23D2
Drissa R *USSR* 21F1
Drogheda *Irish Rep* 15B5
Drogobych *USSR* 21E3
Drôme R *France* 17A2
Dronera *Italy* 17B2
Dronning Maud Land Region *Ant* 80F12
Dr P.P. Penâ *Par* 70F8
Drumheller *Can* 52G4
Drummond *USA* 64D1
Drummond I *USA* 58C1
Drummondville *Can* 59E1
Druskininksi *USSR* 21E2
Druzhina *USSR* 27Q3
Dry B *USA* 56L4
Dryberry L *Can* 57D2
Dryden *Can* 53J5
Dryden *USA* 60B1
Dry Harbour Mts *Jamaica* 68H1
Dschang *Cam* 77J4
Duang I *Burma* 43B3
Dubā *S Arabia* 32C1
Dubai *UAE* 33G1
Dubawnt R *Can* 52H3
Dubawnt L *Can* 52H3
Dubbo *Aust* 48D4
Dublin County *Irish Rep* 15B5
Dublin *Irish Rep* 15B5
Dublin *USA* 61C2
Dubna *USSR* 24F4
Dubno *USSR* 25D5
Dubois Idaho *USA* 64D2
Du Bois *USA* 59D2
Dubois Wyoming *USA* 64E2
Dubossary *USSR* 21F3
Dubrovica *USSR* 21F2
Dubrovnik *Yugos* 23D2
Dubuque *USA* 55D2
Duchesne *USA* 65D2
Duck R *USA* 61B1
Dudelange *Lux* 16D2
Dudinka *USSR* 26K3
Dudley *Eng* 15D5
Dudypta R *USSR* 27L2
Duekoué *Ivory Coast* 76B4
Duero R *Spain* 19B1
Duff Is *Solomon Is* 49F1
Dufftown *Scot* 14D3
Dugi Otok I *Yugos* 22C2
Duisburg *W Germ* 20B2
Dūkan *Iraq* 30E3
Duke I *USA* 56M5
Duk Faiwil *Sudan* 78D3
Dukhān *Qatar* 33F1
Dukou *China* 40A4
Dulan *China* 38C3
Dulce R *Arg* 72C2
Dulit Range Mts *Malay* 44D2
Dullabchara *India* 37D3
Dülmen *W Germ* 16D1
Duluth *USA* 55D2
Dūmā *Syria* 31D2
Dumai *Indon* 44B2
Dumaran I *Phil* 45E8
Dumas *USA* 54C3
Dumayr *Syria* 31D2
Dumbai *Ghana* 77G4
Dumbarton *Scot* 14C4
Dumfries *Scot* 14D4
Dumfries and Galloway Region *Scot* 14C4
Dumka *India* 37C3
Dumoga Kecil *Indon* 45B2
Dumoine,L *Can* 59D1
Dumont d'Urville Base *Ant* 80G8
Dumyåt = Damietta
Dumyat *Egypt* 75C1
Dunărea R *Rom* 23F2
Dunary Head Pt *Irish Rep* 15B5
Dunav R *Bulg* 23E2
Dunav R *Yugos* 23D1
Dunayevtsy *USSR* 21F3
Duncan *USA* 63C3
Duncannon *USA* 60B2
Duncan Pass *Andaman Is* 36E2
Duncansby Head Pt *Scot* 14D2
Dundalk *Irish Rep* 15B4
Dundalk *USA* 60B3
Dundalk B *Irish Rep* 15B5
Dundas *Greenland* 53M2
Dundas I *Can* 56M5
Dundas Pen *Can* 52G2
Dundas Str *Aust* 39G8
Dundee *S Africa* 79D6
Dundee *Scot* 14D3
Dundee *USA* 60B1
Dundoo *Aust* 50B1
Dundrum B *N Ire* 15C4
Dunedin *NZ* 49G5
Dunedin *USA* 61C3
Dunedoo *Aust* 50C2
Dunfermline *Scot* 14D3
Dungarpur *India* 35C4
Dungarvan *Irish Rep* 15B5
Dungeness *Eng* 15F6
Dungog *Aust* 50D2
Dungu *Zaïre* 78C3
Dungunab *Sudan* 78D1
Dunhua *China* 41B3
Dunhuang *China* 38C2
Dunkerque *France* 16B1
Dunkirk *USA* 55F2
Dunkur *Eth* 78D2
Dunkwa *Ghana* 77F4
Dun Laoghaire *Irish Rep* 13B3
Dunmore *USA* 60C2

Dunmore Town Erechim

Dunmore Town *Bahamas* 68B1
Dunn *USA* 61D1
Dunnet Head Pt *Scot* 14D2
Dunning *USA* 57B3
Duns *Scot* 14D4
Dunseith *USA* 57B2
Dunsmuir *USA* 64B2
Dunstan Mts *NZ* 51A2
Dun-sur-Meuse *France* 16C2
Duolun *China* 40D1
Dupree *USA* 57B2
Duque de Braganca *Angola* 79B4
Du Quoin *USA* 58B3
Dura *Israel* 31C3
Durance R *France* 18D3
Durand *USA* 58A2
Durango *Mexico* 66B2
Durango *Spain* 19B1
Durango State *Mexico* 67A1
Durango *USA* 54C3
Durant *USA* 54D3
Duraykish *Syria* 31D1
Durazho *Urug* 69E4
Durban *S Africa* 79D6
Duren *W Germ* 16D1
Durg *India* 37B3
Durgapur *India* 37C3
Durham County *Eng* 14E4
Durham *Eng* 14E4
Durham N Carolina *USA* 55F3
Durham New Hampshire *USA* 60E1
Durham Downs *Aust* 50B1
Durmitor Mt *Yugos* 23D2
Durness *Scot* 14C2
Durrës *Alb* 23D2
Durrie *Aust* 50B1
Dursunbey *Turk* 23F3
D'Urville I *NZ* 51B2
Dushak *USSR* 34E1
Dushan *China* 40B4
Dushanbe *USSR* 29E2
Dushore *USA* 60B2
Dusky Sd *NZ* 51A3
Düsseldorf *W Germ* 20B2
Dutch Harbour *USA* 56E5
Dutton,Mt *USA* 65D3
Duyun *China* 40B4
Düzce *Turk* 30B1
Dvina R *USSR* 24D4
Dvinskaya Guba B *USSR* 24F2
Dwārka *India* 35B4
Dworshak Res *USA* 64C1
Dyer,C *Can* 53M3
Dyersburg *USA* 55E3
Dyfed County *Wales* 15C5
Dykh Tau Dağlari Mt *USSR* 25G7
Dynevor Downs *Aust* 50B1
Dzag *Mongolia* 38C2
Dzamin Uüd *USSR* 27M5
Dzaoudzi *Mayotte* 79E5
Dzarnïn Uüd *Mongolia* 38D2
Dzavhan Gol R *Mongolia* 38C2
Dzehezkazgan *USSR* 28E1
Dzerzhinsk *USSR* 24G4
Dzhalinda *USSR* 27O4
Dzhambul *USSR* 26J5
Dzhankoy *USSR* 25E6
Dzhezkazgan *USSR* 26H4
Dzhilikul' *USSR* 35B1
Dzhungarskiy Alatau Mts *USSR* 26J5
Dzierzoniow *Pol* 20D2
Dzungaria Basin *China* 29G1

E

Eabamet L *Can* 53K4
Eagle Alaska *USA* 56K3
Eagle Colorado *USA* 62A2
Eagle Butte *USA* 57B2
Eagle L California *USA* 64B2
Eagle L *Can* 57D2
Eagle L Maine *USA* 59F1
Eagle Lake *USA* 59F1
Eagle Mountain L *USA* 63C3
Eagle Pass *USA* 54C4
Eagle Peak Mt *USA* 62A3
Eagle Plain *Can* 52E3
Eagle River *USA* 56J3
Ear Falls *Can* 57D1
Earlimart *USA* 65C3
Earp *USA* 65D4
Earth *USA* 62B3
Easley *USA* 61C2
East Aurora *USA* 59D2
East B *USA* 61B3
Eastbourne *Eng* 15F6
East Branch Delaware R *USA* 60C1
East,C *NZ* 49G4
East C *USA* 56B6
East Chicago *USA* 58B2
East China Sea *China/Japan* 38F3
Eastern Ghats Mts *India* 37B4
East Falkland I *Falkland Is* 69E8
East Fork R *USA* 56J2
Eastgate *USA* 65C3
East Germany Republic *Europe* 20C2
East Grand Forks *USA* 57C2
Easthampton *USA* 60D1
East Hampton *USA* 60D2
East Lake *USA* 58B2
East Liverpool *USA* 58C2
East London *S Africa* 79C7
East Main *Can* 53L4
Eastmain R *Can* 53L4
Eastman *USA* 61C2
East Moline *USA* 58A2
Easton Maryland *USA* 59D3
Easton Pennsylvania *USA* 59D2
East Orange *USA* 60C2
East Pacific Ridge *Pacific O* 47O5
East Pacific Rise *Pacific O* 47O4
East Point *USA* 61C2
Eastport *USA* 59F2
East Retford *Eng* 15E5
East Ridge *USA* 61B1
East St Louis *USA* 55D3
East Siberian S *USSR* 27R2
East Sussex County *Eng* 15F6
Eastville *USA* 59D3
Eatonton *USA* 61C2
Eau Claire *USA* 57D3
Eauripik I *Pacific O* 39H6
Ebano *Mexico* 67C1
Ebebiyin *Eq Guinea* 78B3
Eberbach *W Germ* 16E2
Eberswalde *E Germ* 20C2
Ebetsu *Japan* 42D2
Ebian *China* 40A4
Ebinur L *China* 26K5
Eboli *Italy* 22D2
Ebolowa *Cam* 78B3
Ebro R *Spain* 19B1
Eceabat *Turk* 30A1
Eching *China* 40D2
Echo *USA* 64C1
Echo Bay = Port Radium
Echo Bay *Can* 52G3
Echternach *Lux* 16D2
Echuca *Aust* 50B3
Ecija *Spain* 19A2
Eclipse Sd *Can* 53K2
Ecommoy *France* 16A3
Ecuador Republic *S America* 70C4
Eday I *Scot* 14D2
Edd *Eth* 78E2
Edda Oilfield *N Sea* 14G3
Ed Da'ein *Sudan* 78C2
Ed Damasin *Sudan* 32B4
Ed Damer *Sudan* 78D2
Ed Debba *Sudan* 78D2
Eddrachillis B *Scot* 14C2
Ed Dueim *Sudan* 78D2
Eddystone Pt *Aust* 50E3
Ede *Nig* 77G4
Edea *Cam* 78A3
Eden *Aust* 50C3
Eden Texas *USA* 62C3
Eden Wyoming *USA* 64E2
Eden R *Eng* 14D4
Edenburg *S Africa* 79C6
Edendale *NZ* 51A3
Edenkoben *W Germ* 16D2
Edensburg *USA* 60A2
Eder R *W Germ* 16E1
Edgeley *USA* 57C2
Edgell I *Can* 53M3
Edgemont *USA* 57B3
Edgeøya I *Barents S* 26D2
Edgewood *USA* 60B3
Edh Dhahiriya *Israel* 31C3
Edhessa *Greece* 23E2
Edinburg *USA* 63F4
Edinburgh *Scot* 14D3
Edirne *Turk* 25D7
Edisto R *USA* 61C2
Edmonds *USA* 64B1
Edmonton *Can* 52G4
Edmore *USA* 57C2
Edmundston *Can* 53M5
Edna *USA* 63C4
Edna Bay *USA* 56M4
Edolo *Italy* 22C1
Edom Region *Jordan* 31C3
Edremit *Turk* 25D8
Edremit Körfezi B *Turk* 23F3
Edrengiyn Nuruu Mts *Mongolia* 38C2
Edson *Can* 52G4
Eduardo Castex *Arg* 72C3
Eduni,Mt *Can* 56N3
Edward R *Aust* 50B3
Edward,L *Zaïre/Uganda* 78C4
Edwards Creek *Aust* 50A1
Edwards Plat *USA* 54C3
Edwardsville *USA* 58B3
Eek *USA* 56F3
Eeklo *Belg* 16B1
Efate I *Vanuatu* 49F2
Effingham *USA* 55E3
Egan Range Mts *USA* 65D3
Egedesminde *Greenland* 53N3
Egegik *USA* 56G4
Eger *Hung* 21E3
Egersund *Nor* 12F7
Eggegebirge Region *W Germ* 16E1
Egg Harbour City *USA* 60C3
Eglinton I *Can* 52G2
Egmont,C *NZ* 51B1
Egmont,Mt *NZ* 51B1
Eğridir Gölü L *Turk* 30B2
Eguas R *Brazil* 73C1
Egvekinot *USSR* 27T3
Egypt Republic *Africa* 75B2
Ehsenvaara *Fin* 12K6
Eibar *Spain* 19B1
Eibeuf *France* 18C2
Eidsvolo *Aust* 50D1
Eifel Region *W Germ* 16D1
Eigg I *Scot* 14B3
Eight Degree Chan *Indian O* 29F5
Eighty Mile Beach *Aust* 48B2
Eildon,L *Aust* 50C3
Einbeck *W Germ* 16E1
Eindhoven *Neth* 20B2
Einsiedeln *Switz* 17C1
Ein Yahav *Israel* 31C3
Eisenach *E Germ* 20C2
Eisenerz *Austria* 20C3
Eisenhut Mt *Austria* 17E1
Eitorf *W Germ* 16D1
Ejin qi *China* 40A1
Ejuanema,Mt *Ghana* 77F4
Ejura *Ghana* 77F4
Ejutla *Mexico* 67C2
Ekalaka *USA* 57B2
Eketahuna *NZ* 51C2
Ekibastuz *USSR* 28J4
Ekimchan *USSR* 27P4
Ek Mahalla el Kubra *Egypt* 30B3
Eksjo *Sweden* 12H7
Ekwen R *Can* 55E1
El Abbâsa *Egypt* 31A3
El'Alamein *Egypt* 30A3
El Arenal *Mexico* 67B1
El Aricha *Alg* 77B2
El'Arîsh *Egypt* 30B3
El Asnam *Alg* 77C1
Elat *Israel* 30B4
El' Atrun Oasis *Sudan* 78C2
el Attar R *Alg* 77C2
Elazig *Turk* 25F8
El Azraq *Jordan* 30C3
Elba I *Italy* 22C2
El Balyana *Egypt* 75C2
El'ban *USSR* 41D1
El Banco *Colombia* 70D2
Elbasan *Alb* 23E2
El Bauga *Sudan* 32B3
El Baúl *Ven* 68D5
El Bayadh *Alg* 77C2
Elbe R *E Germ/W Germ* 20C2
El Bega'a R *Leb* 31D1
Elberta *USA* 58B2
Elbert,Mt *USA* 54C3
Elberton *USA* 61C2
Elbeuf *France* 16A2
Elbistan *Turk* 30C2
Elblag *Pol* 21D2
El Bolson *Arg* 69B6
Elbow Lake *USA* 57C2
El Bozal *Mexico* 67B1
Elbrus Mt *USSR* 25G7
Elburz Mts = Reshteh-ye Alborz
El Cajon *USA* 65C4
El Campo *USA* 63C4
El Centro *USA* 65C4
Elche *Spain* 19B2
El Cuy *Arg* 72B3
Elda *Spain* 19B2
El'dikan *USSR* 27P3
El Diviso *Colombia* 70C3
El Djouf Desert Region *Maur* 76B2
Eldon *USA* 63D2
Eldorado *Arg* 73B4
El Dorado Arkansas *USA* 55D3
Eldorado *Brazil* 73C3
El Dorado Kansas *USA* 54D3
El Dorado *Mexico* 66B2
Eldorado Texas *USA* 62B3
El Dorado *Ven* 70F2
Eldoret *Kenya* 78D3
Eldred *USA* 60A2
Elea,C *Cyprus* 31C1
Electric Peak Mt *USA* 64D2
El Eglab Region *Alg* 76B2
Elel Watercourse *Egypt* 32B2
Elephant Butte Res *USA* 62A3
El Escorial *Spain* 19B1
Eleşkirt *Turk* 30D2
El Eulma *Alg* 77D1
Eleuthera I *Bahamas* 55F4
El Fahs *Tunisia* 77D1
El Faiyûm *Egypt* 30B4
El Farsia Well *Mor* 76B2
El Fasher *Sudan* 78C2
El Fashn *Egypt* 30B4
El Ferrol del Caudillo *Spain* 19A1
El Firdân *Egypt* 31B3
El Fula *Sudan* 78C2
El Gassi *Alg* 76C1
El Geteina *Sudan* 78D2
El Gezîra Region *Sudan* 78D2
El Ghor V *Israel/Jordan* 31C3
Elgin Illinois *USA* 55E2
Elgin N Dakota *USA* 57B2
Elgin *Scot* 14D3
El Gîza *Egypt* 30B3
El Golea *Alg* 76C1
El Golfo de Santa Clara *Mexico* 65D4
Elgon,Mt *Uganda/Kenya* 78D3
El Goran *Eth* 78E3
El Grullo *Mexico* 67B2
El Guettara Well *Mali* 76B2
El Hamurre *Somalia* 75D4
El Haricha Desert Region *Mali* 76B2
El Harra *Egypt* 30A4
El Harrach *Alg* 19C2
El Hawata *Sudan* 32B4
El Hig *Mexico* 67C1
El Homra *Sudan* 32B4
El Huecu *Arg* 72A3
El'Igma Desert Region *Egypt* 30B4
Elim *USA* 56F3
Elira,C *Can* 52H2
Elisabethville = Lubumbashi
El Iskandarîya = Alexandria
Elista *USSR* 25G6
Elizabeth *Aust* 48C4
Elizabeth *USA* 59E2
Elizabeth City *USA* 55F3
Elizabeth Is *USA* 60E2
Elizabethton Tennessee *USA* 61C1
Elizabethtown Kentucky *USA* 58B3
Elizabethtown N Carolina *USA* 61D2
Elizabethtown Pennsylvania *USA* 60B2
El Jadida *Mor* 77A2
El Jafr *Jordan* 30C3
El Jafr L *Jordan* 31D3
El Jebelein *Sudan* 78D2
El Jem *Tunisia* 77E1
Elk *Pol* 21E2
Elk R Maryland *USA* 60C3
Elk R W Virginia *USA* 58C3
Elkader *USA* 57D3
El Kala *Alg* 77D1
El Kamlin *Sudan* 78D2
El Kef *Tunisia* 77D1
El Khalil = Hebron
El Khandaq *Sudan* 32B3
El Khânka *Egypt* 31A3
El Khârga *Egypt* 32B1
El-Khârga Oasis *Egypt* 32B1
Elkhart *USA* 58B2
El Khenachich Desert Region *Mali* 76B2
Elkhorn R *USA* 57C3
Elkhovo *Bulg* 23F2
Elkins *USA* 59D3
Elkland *USA* 60B2
Elk Mt *USA* 57A3
Elko *Can* 64C1
Elko *USA* 54B2
el Korima R *Alg* 77B2
Elkton *USA* 60C3
El Ku Watercourse *Egypt* 32B2
El Kûbri *Egypt* 31B3
El Kuntilla *Egypt* 30B3
El Lagowa *Sudan* 78C2
Ellef Ringnes I *Can* 52H2
Ellendale *USA* 57C2
Ellen,Mt *USA* 65D3
Ellensburg *USA* 54A2
Ellenville *USA* 60C2
Ellesmere I *Can* 53K2
Ellesmere,L *NZ* 51B2
Ellicott City *USA* 60B3
Elliot *S Africa* 79C7
Elliot Lake *Can* 53K5
Ellis *USA* 64D2
El Lisan Pen *Jordan* 31C3
Ellsworth *USA* 59F2
Ellsworth Land Region *Ant* 80F3
El Ma'âdi *Egypt* 31A4
El Maghra L *Egypt* 75B1
El Manaqil *Sudan* 32B4
El Mansûra *Egypt* 30B3
El Manzala *Egypt* 31A3
El Matariya *Egypt* 31A3
El Matarîya *Egypt* 31B3
Elmer *USA* 60C3
El Merelé Desert Region *Maur* 76B3
El Milagro *Arg* 72B2
El Milia *Alg* 77D1
El Milk Watercourse *Sudan* 32B3
El Mîna *Leb* 31C1
El Minya *Egypt* 30B4
Elmira New York *USA* 55F2
El Mirage *USA* 65D4
el Mitta R *Alg* 77D2
El Moral *Mexico* 63F4
El Mreitl Well *Maur* 76B2
Elmsborn *W Germ* 20B2
El Muglad *Sudan* 78C2
El Mzereb Well *Mali* 76B2
El Nido *Phil* 45E8
El Obeid *Sudan* 78D2
El Oro *Mexico* 67B2
Elota *Mexico* 67A1
El Oued *Alg* 77D2
Eloy *USA* 65D4
El Paso *USA* 54C3
El Porta *USA* 65B3
El Porvenir *Mexico* 62A3
El Potosí *Mexico* 67B1
El Puerto del Sta Maria *Spain* 19A2
El Qâhira = Cairo
El Qantara *Egypt* 31B3
El Quds = Jerusalem
El Quelite *Mexico* 67A1
El Quseima *Egypt* 31C3
El Quwetra *Jordan* 31C4
El Reno *USA* 54D3
Elsa *Can* 52E3
Elsa R *Italy* 17D3
El Saff *Egypt* 31A4
El Sâlhîya *Egypt* 31B3
El Salto *Mexico* 67A1
El Salvador Republic *C America* 66D3
El Sauzal *Mexico* 65C4
El Shallûfa *Egypt* 31B3
El Shatt *Egypt* 31B4
El Simbillâwein *Egypt* 31A3
El Sosneade *Arg* 72B3
Elsterwerde *E Germ* 20C2
El Sueco *Mexico* 62A4
El Suweis = Suez
El Tabbin *Egypt* 31A4
El Teleno Mt *Spain* 19A1
Eltham *NZ* 51B1
El Thamad *Egypt* 31C4
El Tigre *Ven* 70F2
El Tîh Desert Region *Egypt* 30B4
El Tîna *Egypt* 31B3
El Tio *Arg* 72C2
Eltopia *USA* 64C1
El Toro *Chile* 72A1
El Transito *Chile* 72A1
El Tuito *Mexico* 67A1
El Tûr *Egypt* 30B4
Elûru *India* 36C1
Elvas *Port* 19A2
Elvira *Brazil* 70D5
El Volcán *Chile* 72A2
Elwood *USA* 58B2
Ely *Eng* 15F5
Ely Minnesota *USA* 55D2
Ely Nevada *USA* 54B3
Elyria *USA* 58C2
El Zarqa *Egypt* 31A3
Emāmrūd *Iran* 34D1
Emām Sāheb *Afghan* 35B1
Eman R *Sweden* 20D1
Emba *USSR* 25K6
Emba R *USSR* 25K6
Embalse Cerros Colorados L *Arg* 69C5
Embalse de Alarcón Res *Spain* 19B2
Embalse de Alcántarà Res *Spain* 19A2
Embalse de Almendra Res *Spain* 19A1
Embalse de Garcia de Sola Res *Spain* 19A2
Embalse de Guri L *Ven* 70F2
Embalse de Mequinenza Res *Spain* 19B1
Embalse de Ricobayo Res *Spain* 19A1
Embalse de Rio Negro Res *Urug* 69E4
Embalse El Choc1on Res *Arg* 72B3
Embalse Ezequil Ramos Mexia L *Arg* 69C5
Embalse Florentine Ameghino L *Arg* 69C6
Embalse Gabriel y Galan Res *Spain* 19A1
Embalse Rio Hondo Res *Arg* 72B1
Embarcación *Arg* 69D2
Embarras Portage *Can* 52G4
Embrun *France* 17B2
Embu *Kenya* 78D4
Emden *W Germ* 20B2
Emei *China* 40A4
Emerald *Aust* 48D3
Emeri *Can* 53M4
Emerson *Can* 52J5
Emigrant P *USA* 64C2
Emi Koussi Mt *Chad* 78B1
Emilo Mitre *Arg* 72B3
Emirdağ *Turk* 30B2
Emmaus *USA* 60C2
Emmen *Neth* 20B2
Emmendingen *W Germ* 16D2
Emmerich *W Germ* 16D1
Emmett *USA* 64C2
Emmitsburg *USA* 60B3
Emmonak *USA* 56F3
Emory Peak Mt *USA* 54C4
Empalme *Mexico* 66A2
Empangeni *S Africa* 79D6
Empedrado *Arg* 69E3
Emperor Seamount Chain *Pacific O* 47K2
Empoli *Italy* 17D3
Emporia Kansas *USA* 63C2
Emporia Virginia *USA* 59D3
Emporium *USA* 60A2
Ems R *W Germ* 20B2
Enard B *Scot* 14C2
Encarnacion *Mexico* 67B1
Encarnación *Par* 69E3
Enchi *Ghana* 77F4
Encinal *USA* 63F4
Encruzilhada *Brazil* 73D2
Encruzilhada do Sul *Brazil* 72E2
Enda Salassie *Eth* 32C4
Ende *Indon* 48B1
Enderby Land Region *Ant* 80G11
Enderlin *USA* 57C2
Endicott *USA* 59D2
Endicott Mts *USA* 56H2
Enfield *USA* 61D1
Engadin Mts *Switz* 17D1
Engaño,C *Phil* 45F7
Engaru *Japan* 42D2
En Gedi *Israel* 31C3
Engelberg *Switz* 17C1
Engel's *USSR* 25H5
Enggano I *Indon* 44B4
England Country *UK* 13C3
Englee *Can* 53N4
Englehard *USA* 61D1
Englehart *Can* 59D1
Englewood *USA* 62B2
English R *Can* 57D1
English Channel *Eng/France* 13C3
Enid *USA* 63C2
Eniwa *Japan* 42D2
Enji Well *Maur* 76B3
Enkoping *Sweden* 12H7
Enna *Italy* 22C3
En Nahud *Sudan* 78C2
Ennedi Desert Region *Chad* 78C2
Ennelen *USSR* 56C2
Enngonia *Aust* 50C1
Enning *USA* 57B3
Ennis *Irish Rep* 13B3
Ennis Montana *USA* 64D1
Ennis Texas *USA* 63C3
Enniscorthy *Irish Rep* 15B5
Enniskillen *N Ire* 15B4
Enn Nâqoûra *Leb* 31C2
Enns R *Austria* 20C3
Enrekang *Indon* 45A3
Enschede *Neth* 12F8
Ensenada *Mexico* 66A1
Enshi *China* 40B3
Ensisheim *France* 16D3
Entebbe *Uganda* 78D4
Enterprise Alabama *USA* 61B2
Enterprise Oregon *USA* 64C1
Enugu *Nig* 77H4
Enurmino *USSR* 56D2
Enz R *w Germ* 16E2
Enzan *Japan* 42C3
Epe *Nig* 77G4
Epernay *France* 18C2
Ephraim *USA* 65D3
Ephrata Pennsylvania *USA* 60B2
Ephrata Washington *USA* 64C1
Epi I *Vanuatu* 49F2
Épinal *France* 18D2
Episkopi *Cyprus* 31B1
Episkopi B *Cyprus* 31B1
Eppingen *W Germ* 16E2
Epte R *France* 16A2
Epukiro *Namibia* 79B6
Epu pel *Arg* 72C3
Eqlid *Iran* 34C2
Equatorial Guinea Republic *Africa* 78A3
Equinox Mt *USA* 60D1
Equinunk *USA* 60C2
Erba *Italy* 17C2
Erbach *W Germ* 16E2
Erbeskopf Mt *W Germ* 16D2
Ercilla *Chile* 72A3
Erciş *Turk* 30D2
Erciyas Daglari Mt *Turk* 25F8
Erdaobaihe *China* 41B3
Erdene *Mongolia* 40C1
Erdenet *Mongolia* 38D2
Erdi Desert Region *Chad* 78C2
Erechim *Brazil* 69F3

Ereğlī Fort Rupert

Ereğlī Turk 30B1
Ereğli Turk 30B2
Erenhot China 38E2
Eresma R Spain 19B1
Erft R W Germ 16D1
Erfurt E Germ 20C2
Ergani Turk 30C2
Erg Chech Desert Region Alg 76B2
Erg du Djourab Desert Region Chad 78B2
Erg Du Ténéré Desert Region Niger 76D3
Ergene R Turk 30A1
Erg Iguidi Region Alg 76B2
Ērgli USSR 21F1
Erguig R Chad 78B2
Ergun' USSR 27N4
Ergun R USSR 38E1
Ergun Zuoqi China 27O4
Erguveyem R USSR 56C2
Eriba Sudan 78D2
Erie USA 55F2
Erie,L USA/Can 55E2
Erimo-misaki C Japan 42D2
Erin Port Eng 15C4
Eriskay I Scot 14B3
Eritrea Region Eth 32C3
Erkelenz W Germ 16D1
Erlangen W Germ 20C3
Erling,L USA 63D3
Ermelo S Africa 79C6
Ernākulam India 36B3
Erode India 36B2
Eromanga Aust 50B1
Er Rachidia Mor 77B2
Er Rahad Sudan 78D2
Errego Mozam 79D5
Errigal Mt Irish Rep 13B2
Erris Head Pt Irish Rep 13A3
Erromanga I Vanuatu 49F2
Er Roseires Sudan 78D2
er Rtem R Alg 77C2
Er Rummān Jordan 31C2
Erskine USA 57C2
Erstein France 16D2
Erval Brazil 72E2
Erzgebirge Upland E Germ 20C2
Erzincan Turk 25F8
Erzurum Turk 25G8
Esan-misaki C Japan 42D2
Esara R Spain 18C3
Esashi Japan 42D2
Esbjerg Den 20B1
Escalante USA 65D3
Escalón Mexico 54C4
Escanaba USA 55E2
Escárcega Mexico 66C3
Esch Luxembourg 16C2
Escondido USA 65C4
Escuinapa Mexico 66B2
Escuintla Guatemala 66C3
Eséka Cam 78B3
Esera R Spain 19C1
Eşfahān Iran 34C2
Esh Sharā Upland Jordan 31C3
Esino Italy 17E3
Eskdale NZ 51C1
Eskifjörður Iceland 12C1
Eskilstuna Sweden 12H7
Eskimo L Can 52E3
Eskimo Point Can 53J3
Eskisehir Turk 25E8
Esla R Spain 19A1
Esmeraldas Ecuador 70C3
Esmerelda Cuba 68B2
Esmerelda I Chile 69A7
Espalion France 18C3
Espanola Can 58C1
Espanola USA 62A2
Esperance Aust 48B4
Esperanza Arg 72C2
Esperanza Base Ant 80G2
Espírito Santo State Brazil 73D2
Espiritu Santo I Vanuatu 49F2
Espungabera Mozam 79D6
Esquel Arg 69B6
Esquimalt Can 64B1
Esquina Arg 72D2
Es Samra Jordan 31D2
Essaourira Mor 77A2
Es-Sekhira Tunisia 77E2
Essen W Germ 20B2
Essequibo Guyana 71G3
Essex County Eng 15F6
Essexville USA 58C2
Esslingen W Germ 20B3
Essonne France 16B2
Essoyes France 16C2
Estância Brazil 71L6
Estcourt S Africa 79C6
Este Italy 17D2
Esteli Nic 70A1
Esternay France 16B2
Esteros Mexico 67C1
Esteros Par 69D2
Esteros del Iberá Swamp Arg 72D1
Estes Park USA 62A1
Estevan Can 52H5
Estherville USA 57D3
Estill USA 61C2
Estissac France 16B2
Estonskaya SSR Republic USSR 24C4
Estrecho de Magallanes Str Chile 69B8
Estremoz Port 19A2
Esztergom Hung 21D3
Etadunna Aust 50A1
Etam France 16C2
Etampes France 18C2
Etamunbanie,L Aust 50A1
Etaples France 16A1
Etāwah India 35D3
Ethiopia Republic Africa 78D3
Etla Mexico 67C2
Etna Mt Italy 22C3
Etolin I USA 56M4
Etolin Str USA 56E3
Eton Can 53L2
Etosha Nat Pk Namibia 79B5
Etosha Pan Salt L Namibia 79B5
Etowah R USA 61C2
Etretat France 16A2
Ettelbruck Lux 16C2
Eua I Tonga 49H3
Euabalong Aust 50C2
Euclid USA 58C2
Eucumbene,L Aust 50C3
Eudunda Aust 50A2
Eufala L USA 63C2
Eufaula USA 61B2
Eugene USA 54A2
Eulo Aust 50C1
Eunice Louisiana USA 63D3
Eunice New Mexico USA 62B3
Eupen W Germ 16D1
Euphrates R Iraq 30D3
Eupora USA 63E3
Eure Department France 16A2
Eure R France 18C2
Eure-et-Loir Department France 16A2
Eureka California USA 64B2
Eureka Can 53K1
Eureka Montana USA 64C1
Eureka Nevada USA 54B3
Eureka S Dakota USA 57C2
Eureka Utah USA 65D3
Eureka Sd Can 53K2
Euroa Aust 50C3
Eurombah R Aust 50C1
Europa I Mozam Chan 79E6
Europoort Neth 16C1
Euskirchen W Germ 20B2
Eutaw USA 61B2
Evans,C Can 53K1
Evans,L Can 53L4
Evans,Mt Colorado USA 62A2
Evans,Mt Montana USA 64D1
Evans Str Can 53K3
Evanston Illinois USA 58B2
Evanston Wyoming USA 54B2
Evansville Indiana USA 55E3
Evansville Wyoming USA 57A3
Everard,L Aust 48C4
Everest,Mt Nepal/China 29G3
Everett Can 52F4
Everett Pennsylvania USA 60A2
Everett Washington USA 54A2
Everett,Mt USA 60D1
Everglades,The Swamp USA 55E4
Evergreen USA 61B2
Evesham Eng 15E5
Evinayong Eq Guinea 78B3
Evje Nor 12F7
Evolène Switz 17B1
Évora Port 19A2
Evreux France 18C2
Évvoia I Greece 23E3
Ewo Congo 78B4
Excelsior Springs USA 63D2
Exeter California USA 65C3
Exeter Eng 15D6
Exeter New Hampshire USA 59E2
Exmoor Nat Pk Eng 15D6
Exmouth Eng 15D6
Extremadura Region Spain 19A2
Exuma Sd Bahamas 66E2
Eyasi L Tanz 78D4
Eyemouth Scot 14D4
Eyl Somalia 75D4
Eyre Aust 48B4
Eyre Creek R Aust 48C3
Eyre,L Aust 48C3
Eyre Pen Aust 48C4
Eyte I Phil 45F8
Ezatlan Mexico 67B1
Ezine Turk 23F3
Ez Zeidab Sudan 32B3

F

Faber L Can 52G3
Fåborg Den 12F7
Fabriano Italy 22C2
Fabrosa Italy 17B2
Fachi Niger 78B2
Fada Chad 78C2
Fada N'Gourma U Volta 77G3
Faenza Italy 22C2
Faeringehavn Greenland 53N3
Fafa R CAR 78B3
Fafan R Eth 78E3
Faga R U Volta 77G3
Făgăras Rom 23E1
Fagnes Region Belg 16C1
Faguibine,L L Mali 76B3
Fahud Oman 33G2
Faiol I Açores 76A1
Fairacres USA 62A3
Fairbanks USA 52D3
Fairbault USA 53J5
Fairborn USA 58C3
Fairbury USA 54D2
Fairfax USA 60B3
Fairfield California USA 65B3
Fairfield Connecticut USA 60D2
Fairfield Idaho USA 64D2
Fairfield Montana USA 64D1
Fairfield Ohio USA 58C3
Fair Head Pt N Ire 14B4
Fair Isle I Scot 13C2
Fairlie NZ 51B2
Fairmont Minnesota USA 57D3
Fairmont W Virginia USA 58C3
Fairport USA 60B1
Fairview USA 62C2
Fairweather,Mt USA 52E4
Fais I Pacific O 39H6
Faisalabad Pak 35C2
Faith USA 57B2
Faither,The Pen Scot 14E1
Faizabad Afghan 35C1
Faizābād India 37B2
Fakaofo I Tokeau Is 49H1
Fakenham Eng 15F5
Fakfak Indon 48C1
Fakōping Sweden 12G7
Falaise de Banfora U Volta 77F3
Falam Burma 37D3
Falckner Arg 72B4
Falcon Res USA/Mexico 66C2
Falémé R Mali/Sen 76A3
Falfurrias USA 63F4
Falkenberg Sweden 12G7
Falkirk Scot 14D4
Falkland Is Dependency S Atlantic 69D8
Falkland Sd Falkland Is 69E8
Fallon USA 54B3
Fall River USA 59E2
Fall River P USA 62A1
Falls City USA 63C1
Falmouth Eng 15C6
Falmouth Jamaica 68H1
Falmouth Maine USA 59E2
Falmouth Massachusetts USA 60E2
False B S Africa 79B7
Falso,C Mexico 66A2
Falster I Den 20C2
Fălticeni Rom 23F1
Falun Sweden 12H6
Famagusta Cyprus 30B2
Famagusta B Cyprus 31B1
Famatina Arg 72B1
Famenne Region Belg 16C1
Fang Thai 43B2
Fangak Sudan 78D3
Fang liao Taiwan 40E5
Fangzheng China 41B2
Fano Italy 22C2
Fâqûs Egypt 31A3
Faraday Base Ant 80G3
Faradje Zaïre 78C3
Farafangana Madag 79E6
Farafra Oasis Egypt 75B2
Farah Afghan 34E2
Farah R Afghan 34E2
Farallon de Medinilla I Pacific O 39H5
Faranah Guinea 76A3
Faraulep I Pacific O 39H6
Fareham Eng 15E6
Farewell,C = Kap Farvel
Farewell,C NZ 49G5
Farewell Spit Pt NZ 51B2
Fargo USA 54D2
Fari'a R Israel 31C2
Faribault USA 55D2
Faridpur Bang 37C3
Farīmān Iran 34D1
Fâriskûr Egypt 31A3
Farmington Maine USA 59E2
Farmington Missouri USA 63D2
Farmington New Hampshire USA 60E1
Farmington New Mexico USA 54C3
Farmington Utah USA 64D2
Farne Deep N Sea 14E4
Faro Can 56M3
Faro Port 19A2
Fårö I Sweden 12H7
Faro R Cam 77J4
Farrar R Scot 14C3
Farrell USA 58C2
Fársala Greece 23E3
Farsi Afghan 34E2
Farwell USA 62B3
Fasā Iran 34C3
Fastov USSR 25D5
Fatehpur India 37B2
Fatima du Sul Brazil 71H7
Fauquier Can 64C1
Faverges France 17B2
Fawn R Can 53K4
Fax R Sweden 12H6
Faxaflóri B Iceland 12A2
Faya Chad 78B2
Fayette USA 61B2
Fayetteville Arkansas USA 55D3
Fayetteville N Carolina USA 55F3
Fayetteville Tennessee USA 61B1
Fâyid Egypt 31B3
Faylakah I Kuwait 30E4
Fāzilka India 35C2
Fdérik Maur 76A2
Fear,C USA 55F3
Feather USA 65B3
Fécamp France 16A2
Federación Arg 72D2
Federal Arg 72D2
Federal Capital Territory Nig 77H4
Federated States of Micronesia Is Pacific O 39H6
Fehmarn I W Germ 20C2
Feijó Brazil 70D5
Feilai Xai Bei Jiang R China 40C5
Feilding NZ 51C2
Feira Zambia 79D5
Feira de Santan Brazil 71L6
Feke Turk 30C2
Feldberg Mt W Germ 16D3
Feldkirch Austria 20B3
Feliciano R Arg 72D2
Felixstowe Eng 13D3
Feltre Italy 17D1
Femund L Nor 12G6
Fengcheng China 41A3
Fengdu China 40B4
Fenging China 40D1
Fengjie China 40B3
Fengshui Shan Mt China 41A1
Feng Xian China 40B3
Fengzhen China 40C1
Fen He R China 40C2
Fenimore Pass USA 56C6
Fenoarivo Atsinanana Madag 79E5
Feodosiya USSR 25E7
Ferdow Iran 34D2
Fère France 16B2
Fère-Champenoise France 16B2
Fergana USSR 29F2
Fermanagh County N Ire 15B4
Fermo Italy 17E3
Fern Mt Austria 17D1
Fernandez Arg 72C1
Fernandina Beach USA 61C2
Fernando de Noronha I Atlantic O 74G5
Fernandópolis Brazil 73B3
Fernando Poo I Eq Guinea 78C4
Ferndale USA 64B1
Fernie Can 64C1
Fernley USA 65C3
Ferrara Italy 22C2
Ferreñafe Peru 70C5
Ferriday USA 63D3
Ferriéres France 16B2
Fès Mor 77A2
Festus USA 63D2
Feteşti Rom 23F2
Fethiye Turk 30A2
Fetisovo USSR 25J7
Fetlar I Scot 14E1
Fevral'skoye USSR 41C1
Feyzabad Afghan 26J6
Fiambalá Arg 72B1
Fianarantsoa Madag 79E6
Fiche Eth 78D3
Ficksburg S Africa 79C6
Fidenza Italy 17D2
Fier Alb 23D2
Fiera Di Primeiro Italy 17D1
Fife Region Scot 14D3
Fife Ness Pen Scot 14D3
Figeac France 18C3
Figueira da Foz Port 19A1
Figueras Spain 19C1
Figuig Mor 77B2
Fiji Is Pacific O 49G2
Filadelpia Par 71G8
Filiaşi Rom 23E2
Filiatrá Greece 23E3
Filicudi I Italy 22C3
Fillmore California USA 65C4
Fillmore Utah USA 65D3
Finale Ligure Italy 17C2
Findhorn R Scot 14C3
Findlay USA 55E2
Finger Lakes USA 59D2
Fingoè Mozam 79D5
Finike Turk 25E8
Finke R Aust 48C3
Finke Flood Flats Aust 50A1
Finland Republic N Europe 24C3
Finland,G of N Europe 12J7
Finlay R Can 52F4
Finlay Forks Can 52F4
Finley Aust 50C3
Finnsnes Nor 12H5
Finschhafen PNG 39H7
Finsteraarhorn Mt Switz 17C1
Finsterwalde E Germ 20C2
Fintona N Ire 15B4
Fiordland Nat Pk NZ 51A3
Fiq Syria 31C2
Firat R Turk 25F8
Firenze Italy 22C2
Firenzuola Italy 17D2
Firmat Arg 72C2
Firozābād India 35D3
Firozpur India 35C2
Firspång Sweden 12H7
Firth of Clyde Estuary Scot 14C4
Firth of Forth Estuary Scot 14D3
Firth of Lorn Estuary Scot 14B3
Firth of Tay Estuary Scot 13C2
Firūzābād Iran 34C3
Fishers I USA 60D2
Fisher Str Can 53K3
Fishguard Wales 15C6
Fish L Can 56O3
Fiskenaesset Greenland 53N3
Fismes France 16B2
Fitchburg USA 59E2
Fitful Head Pt Scot 14E2
Fitzgerald USA 61C2
Fitzroy R Aust 48B2
Fitzroy Crossing Aust 48B2
Fitzwilliam I Can 58C1
Fiume = Rijeka
Fizi Zaïre 78C4
Flagstaff USA 54B3
Flagstaff L USA 59F1
Flamborough Head C Eng 15E4
Flaming Gorge Res USA 54C2
Flannan Isles Is Scot 14B2
Flat R Can 56N3
Flathead L USA 54B2
Flat River USA 63D2
Flattery,C Aust 39H8
Flattery,C Can 52F5
Flattery,C USA 54A2
Fleetwood Eng 15D5
Flekkefjord Inlet Nor 12F7
Fleming Deep Pacific Oc 38H4
Flemington USA 60C2
Flensburg W Germ 20B2
Fleurier Switz 17B1
Fleury-sur-Andelle France 16A2
Flinders I Aust 48C4
Flinders I Aust 48D5
Flinders R Aust 48B2
Flinders Range Mts Aust 48C4
Flin Flon Can 52H4
Flint USA 55E2
Flint Wales 15D5
Flint R USA 55E3
Flixecourt France 16B1
Floodwood USA 58A1
Florala USA 61B2
Florence = Firenze
Florence Alabama USA 55E3
Florence Arizona USA 65D4
Florence Colorado USA 62A2
Florence Kansas USA 63C2
Florence Oregon USA 64B2
Florence S Carolina USA 55F3
Florencia Colombia 70C3
Florenville Belg 16C2
Flores Guatemala 66D3
Flores I Açores 76A1
Flores I Indon 48B1
Flores R Arg 72D3
Flores S Indon 39E7
Floriano Brazil 71K5
Florianópolis Brazil 69G3
Florida Urug 69E4
Florida B USA 61E4
Florida City USA 61E4
Florida Is Solomon Is 49E1
Florida Keys Is USA 55E4
Florida State USA 66D2
Florida,Strs of USA 55E4
Flórina Greece 23E2
Florø Nor 12F6
Floydada USA 62B3
Fluchthorn Mt Austria 17D1
Fluk Indon 45C3
Fly R PNG 48D1
Foci del Po Delta Italy 17E2
Focsani Rom 23F1
Foggia Italy 22D2
Foglia R Italy 17E3
Fogo I Cape Verde 76A4
Foix France 18C3
Foleyet Can 58C1
Foley I Can 53L3
Foligno Italy 22C2
Folkestone Eng 15F6
Folkston USA 61C2
Follonica Italy 22C2
Fonda USA 60C1
Fond-du-Lac Can 52H4
Fond du Lac USA 55E2
Fontainbleau France 18C2
Fontenac USA 63D2
Fontenay-le-Comte France 18B2
Fonyód Hung 23D1
Foochow = Fuzhou
Foraker,Mt USA 56H3
Forbach France 16D2
Forbes Aust 50C2
Forcados Nig 77H4
Forcalquier France 17A3
Forde Nor 12F6
Fords Bridge Aust 50C1
Fordyce USA 63D3
Forécarian Guinea 76A4
Forel,Mt Greenland 53P3
Foremost Can 64D1
Forest Can 58C2
Forest USA 61B2
Forest City Iowa USA 57D3
Forest City Pennsylvania USA 60C2
Forest Park USA 61C2
Forêt d'Othe France 16B2
Forfar Scot 14D3
Forgan USA 62B2
Forges-les-Eaux France 16A2
Forks USA 64B1
Forlì Italy 22C2
Formentera I Spain 19C2
Formia Italy 22C2
Formigas I Açores 76A1
Formosa = Taiwan
Formosa Arg 69E3
Formosa Brazil 71J7
Formosa State Arg 69D2
Formosa Str Taiwan/China 40D5
Formoso Brazil 73C1
Formoso R Brazil 73C1
Fornovo di Taro Italy 17D2
Forres Scot 14D3
Forrest Aust 48B4
Forrest City USA 55D3
Forsayth Aust 48D2
Forssa Fin 12J6
Forster Aust 50D2
Forsyth Missouri USA 63D2
Forsyth Montana USA 57A2
Fort Abbas Pak 35C3
Fort Albany Can 53K4
Fortaleza Brazil 71L4
Fort Augustus Scot 14C3
Fort Beaufort S Africa 79C7
Fort Benton USA 64D1
Fort Bragg USA 65B3
Fort Chimo Can 53M4
Fort Cobb Res USA 62C2
Fort Collins USA 54C2
Fort Coulogne Can 59D1
Fort Davis USA 62B3
Fort de France Martinique 68E4
Fort Deposit USA 61B2
Fort Dodge USA 55D2
Fortescue R Aust 48A3
Fort Frances Can 53J5
Fort Franklin Can 52F3
Fort George Can 53L4
Fort Good Hope Can 52F3
Fort Grey Aust 50B1
Forth R Scot 14C3
Fort Hancock USA 62A3
Fort Hope Can 53K4
Forties Oilfield N Sea 14F3
Fortin Uno Arg 72B3
Fort Kent USA 59F1
Fort Laird Can 52F3
Fort Lallemand Alg 76C1
Fort Lamy = N'Djamena
Fort Laramie USA 57B3
Fort Lauderdale USA 55E4
Fort Mackay Can 52G4
Fort McLeod Can 52G5
Fort McMurray Can 52G4
Fort McPherson Can 52E3
Fort Madison USA 58A2
Fort Morgan USA 54C2
Fort Myers USA 55E4
Fort Nelson Can 52F4
Fort Norman Can 52F3
Fort Payne USA 61B2
Fort Peck USA 57A2
Fort Peck Res USA 54C2
Fort Pierce USA 55E4
Fort Pierre USA 57B3
Fort Plain USA 60C1
Fort Providence Can 52G3
Fort Randall USA 56F4
Fort Resolution Can 52G3
Fort Rousset Congo 78B4
Fort Rupert Can 53L4

Fort St James Gilgandra

Fort St James *Can* 52F4
Fort St. John *Can* 52F4
Fort Scott *USA* 63D2
Fort Selkirk *Can* 52E3
Fort Severn *Can* 53K4
Fort Shevchenko *USSR* 25J7
Fort Simpson *Can* 52F3
Fort Smith *Can* 52G3
Fort Smith *USA* 55D3
Fort Stockton *USA* 54C3
Fort Sumner *USA* 62B3
Fort Supply *USA* 62C2
Fortuna California *USA* 64B2
Fortuna N Dakota *USA* 57B2
Fort Vermillion *Can* 52G4
Fort Walton Beach *USA* 61B2
Fort Wayne *USA* 55E2
Fort William *Scot* 14C3
Fort Wingate *USA* 62A2
Fort Worth *USA* 54D3
Fortymile R *USA* 56K3
Fort Yukon *USA* 56J2
Foshan *China* 40C5
Fossano *Italy* 17B2
Fossombrone *Italy* 17E3
Fosston *USA* 57C2
Foster,Mt *USA* 56L4
Fougamou *Gabon* 78B4
Fougères *France* 18B2
Foula I *Scot* 14D1
Foulness I *Eng* 15F6
Foulwind,C *NZ* 51B2
Foumban *Cam* 78B3
Fourmies *France* 18C1
Four Mountains,Is of the *USA* 56E5
Foúrnoi I *Greece* 23F3
Fouta Djallon Mts *Guinea* 76A3
Foveaux Str *NZ* 49F5
Fowey *Eng* 15C6
Fowler *USA* 62B2
Fox R *USA* 58B2
Foxe Basin G *Can* 53K3
Foxe Chan *Can* 53K3
Foxe Pen *Can* 53L3
Fox Is *USA* 56E5
Foxpark *USA* 62A1
Foxton *NZ* 51C2
Foz do Cuene *Angola* 79B5
Foz do Iquaçu *Brazil* 69F3
Fracisco I Madero *Mexico* 67B1
Frackville *USA* 60B2
Fraga *Arg* 72B2
Framingham *USA* 60E1
Franca *Brazil* 71J8
France Republic *Europe* 18C2
Frances *Can* 55D2
Frances R *Can* 56N3
France Ville *Gabon* 78B4
Franche Comté Region *France* 18D2
Francis Peak Mt *USA* 64E2
Francistown *Botswana* 79C6
Frankenberg *W Germ* 16E1
Frankfort Indiana *USA* 58B2
Frankfort Kentucky *USA* 55E3
Frankfort New York *USA* 60C1
Frankfurt *W Germ* 20B2
Frankfurt am Main *W Germ* 16E1
Frankfurt-an-der-Oder *E Germ* 20C2
Fränkischer Alb Upland *W Germ* 20C3
Franklin Idaho *USA* 64D2
Franklin Indiana *USA* 58B3
Franklin Louisiana *USA* 63D4
Franklin Massachusetts *USA* 60E1
Franklin N Carolina *USA* 61C1
Franklin New Hampshire *USA* 60E1
Franklin New Jersey *USA* 60C2
Franklin Pennsylvania *USA* 59D2
Franklin Tennessee *USA* 61B1
Franklin Virginia *USA* 59D3
Franklin Region *Can* 52G2
Franklin B *Can* 52F2
Franklin D Roosevelt L *USA* 64C1
Franklin Mts *Can* 52F3
Franklin,Pt *USA* 56G1
Franklin Str *Can* 52J2
Franklinville *USA* 60A1
Frankovsk *USSR* 26D5
Franz Josef Glacier *NZ* 51B2
Franz-Joseph-Land = Zemlya Franza Josifa
Fraser R *Can* 52F4
Fraser R *Can* 52F5
Fraserburgh *Scot* 14D3
Fraser I *Aust* 50D1
Frasne *France* 17B1
Frauenfield *Switz* 17C1
Fray Bentos *Urug* 72D2
Frazerburgh *Scot* 13C2
Frederica *USA* 60C3
Fredericia *Den* 20B1
Frederick Maryland *USA* 59D3
Frederick Oklahoma *USA* 62C3
Fredericksburg Texas *USA* 62C3
Fredericksburg Virginia *USA* 59D3
Frederick Sd *USA* 56M4
Frederickstown *USA* 58A3
Fredericktown *USA* 63D2
Fredericton *Can* 53M5
Frederikshap *Greenland* 53N3
Frederikshavn *Den* 12G7
Fredonia *USA* 59D2
Fredrikstad *Nor* 12G7
Freehold *USA* 60C2
Freeman *USA* 57C3
Freeport *Bahamas* 68B1
Freeport Illinois *USA* 58B2
Freeport Texas *USA* 63C4
Freer *USA* 63F4
Freetown *Sierra Leone* 76A4
Freiburg *W Germ* 20B3
Freiburg im Breisgau *W Germ* 16D2
Freirina *Chile* 72A1
Freistadt *Austria* 20C3
Fréjus *France* 17B3
Fremantle *Aust* 48A4
Fremont Nebraska *USA* 63C1
Fremont Ohio *USA* 58C2
French Guiana Dependency *S America* 71H3
Frenchman R *USA* 57A2
Frenchmans Cap Mt *Aust* 50E3
French Polynesia Is *Pacific O* 47M5
Frenda *Alg* 77C1
Fresnillo *Mexico* 66B2
Fresno *USA* 54B3
Fresno Res *USA* 64D1
Fretigney *France* 17A1
Freudenstadt *W Germ* 16E2
Frévent *France* 16B1
Freycinet Pen *Aust* 50E3
Fria *Guinea* 76A3
Frías *Arg* 72B1
Fribourg *Switz* 22B1
Friedberg *W Germ* 16E1
Friedrichshafen *W Germ* 20B3
Frio R *USA* 62C4
Friona *USA* 62B3
Friuli Region *Italy* 17E1
Frobisher B *Can* 53M3
Frobisher Bay *Can* 53M3
Frobisher L *Can* 52H4
Frolovo *USSR* 25G6
Frome *Eng* 15D6
Frome R *Aust* 50A1
Frome R *Eng* 15D6
Frome,L *Aust* 48C4
Frontera *Mexico* 66C3
Front Royal *USA* 59D3
Frosinone *Italy* 22C2
Frostburg *USA* 60A3
Fruita *USA* 62A2
Frunze *USSR* 29F1
Fuchuan *China* 40C5
Fuding *China* 40E4
Fuerte R *Mexico* 66B2
Fuerte Olimpo *Brazil* 73A3
Fuerte Olimpo *Par* 69E2
Fuerteventura I *Canary Is* 76A2
Fugu *China* 40C2
Fuhai *China* 38B2
Fujairah *UAE* 33G1
Fuji *Japan* 42C3
Fujian Province *China* 40D4
Fujin *China* 41C2
Fujinomiya *Japan* 42C3
Fuji-san Mt *Japan* 41D4
Fujisawa *Japan* 42C3
Fuji-Yoshida *Japan* 42C3
Fukagawa *Japan* 42D2
Fukang *China* 26K5
Fukuchiyima *Japan* 41C4
Fukue *Japan* 42A4
Fukue I *Japan* 42A4
Fukui *Japan* 41D4
Fukuoka *Japan* 41C5
Fukushima *Japan* 41E4
Fukuyama *Japan* 41C5
Fulda *USA* 57C3
Fulda *W Germ* 20B2
Fulda R *W Germ* 20B2
Fuling *China* 40B4
Fullarton *Trinidad* 68L1
Fulton Illinois *USA* 58A2
Fulton Kentucky *USA* 58B3
Fulton New York *USA* 59D2
Fumay *France* 16C1
Funabashi *Japan* 42D3
Funafuti I *Tuvalu* 49G1
Funchal *Madeira* 76A1
Fundão *Brazil* 73D2
Fundy,B of *Can* 53M5
Funhalouro *Mozam* 79D6
Funing *China* 40B5
Funing *China* 40D3
Funtua *Nig* 77H3
Fuqing *China* 40D4
Furancungo *Mozam* 79D5
Furano *Japan* 42D2
Fürg *Iran* 34D3
Furka P *Switz* 17C1
Furneaux Group Is *Aust* 48D5
Fürstenwalde *E Germ* 20C2
Fürth *W Germ* 20C3
Furubira *Japan* 42D2
Furukawa *Japan* 41D4
Fury and Hecla St *Can* 53K3
Fushun Liaoning *China* 41A3
Fushun Sichuan *China* 40A4
Fusong *China* 41B3
Füssen *W Germ* 20C3
Fu Xian *China* 40E2
Fuxin *China* 40E1
Fuyang *China* 40D3
Fuyu *China* 41A2
Fuyuan Heilongjiang *China* 41C2
Fuyuan Liaoning *China* 40E1
Fuyuan Yunnan *China* 40A4
Fuyun *China* 38B2
Fuzhou *China* 40D4
Fyn I *Den* 20C1

G

Gaalkacyo *Somalia* 78E3
Gabbs *USA* 65C3
Gabela *Angola* 79B5
Gabgaba Watercourse *Egypt* 32B2
Gabon Republic *Africa* 78B4
Gaborone *Botswana* 79C6
Gabrovo *Bulg* 23F2
Gach Sārān *Iran* 34C2
Gadsden Alabama *USA* 61B2
Gadsden Arizona *USA* 65D4
Gads L *Can* 55D1
Gaeta *Italy* 22C2
Gaferut I *Pacific O* 39H6
Gaffney *USA* 61C1
Gafsa *Tunisia* 77D2
Gagarin *USSR* 24E4
Gagere R *Nig* 77H3
Gagnon *Can* 53M4
Gagra *USSR* 25G7
Gaibanda *India* 37C2
Gailtaler Alpen Mts *Austria* 17E1
Gaimán *Arg* 69C6
Gainesville Florida *USA* 61C3
Gainesville Georgia *USA* 61C2
Gainesville Texas *USA* 63C3
Gainsborough *Eng* 15E5
Gairdner,L *Aust* 50A2
Gairloch *Scot* 14C3
Gaithersburg *USA* 60B3
Gajendragarh *India* 36B1
Ga Jiang R *China* 40D4
Galadi *Eth* 78E3
Galana R *Kenya* 78D4
Galapagos Is *Pacific O* 74D4
Galashiels *Scot* 14D4
Galaţi *Rom* 23F1
Galax *USA* 58C3
Galeana *Mexico* 62A3
Galela *Indon* 45C2
Galena Alaska *USA* 52C3
Galena Illinois *USA* 58A2
Galena Kansas *USA* 63D2
Galeota Pt *Trinidad* 68L1
Galera Pt *Trinidad* 68L1
Galesburg *USA* 58A2
Galeton *USA* 60B2
Galich *USSR* 24G4
Galicia Region *Spain* 19A1
Galilee,S of = Tiberias,L
Galina Pt *Jamaica* 68J1
Gallabat *Sudan* 32C4
Gallarate *Italy* 17C2
Gallatin *USA* 61B1
Gallatin R *USA* 64D1
Galle *Sri Lanka* 36C3
Gallego *Mexico* 62A4
Gállego R *Spain* 19B1
Gallipoli = Gelibolu
Gallipoli *Italy* 23D2
Gällivare *Sweden* 24C2
Galloway District 14C4
Galloway,Mull of C *Scot* 15C4
Gallup *USA* 62A2
Galma R *Nig* 77H3
Galt *USA* 65B3
Galveston *USA* 66C2
Galveston B *USA* 55D4
Galvez *Arg* 72C2
Galvi *Corse* 18D3
Galway *Irish Rep* 13B3
Galway B *Irish Rep* 13B3
Gam I *Indon* 45D3
Gamba *China* 37C2
Gambaga *Ghana* 77F3
Gambell *USA* 56D3
Gambia R *The Gambia/Sen* 76A3
Gambia,The Republic *Africa* 76A3
Gamboma *Congo* 78B4
Gambos *Angola* 79B5
Gampola *Sri Lanka* 36C3
Ganado *USA* 65E3
Ganale Dorya R *Eth* 78E3
Gananoque *Can* 59D2
Gand = Gent
Ganda *Angola* 79B5
Gandajika *Zaïre* 79C4
Gandava *Pak* 35B3
Gander *Can* 53N5
Gāndhīdhām *India* 35B4
Gāndhīnagar *India* 35C4
Gāndhi Sāgar L *India* 35D4
Gandia *Spain* 19B2
Gandu *Brazil* 73E1
Ganga R *India* 37C3
Ganganar *India* 35C3
Gangaw *Burma* 37D3
Gangaw Range Mts *Burma* 37E3
Gangca *China* 40A2
Gangdise Shan Mts *China* 29G2
Ganges = Ganga
Gangtok *India* 37C2
Gangu *China* 40B3
Gan He R *China* 41A1
Gani *Indon* 45C3
Gannan *China* 41A2
Gannett Peak Mt *USA* 64E2
Ganquan *China* 40B2
Gantheaume C *Aust* 50A3
Gantseviohi *USSR* 12K8
Ganye *Nig* 77J4
Ganzhou *China* 40D4
Gao *Mali* 76C3
Gaolan *China* 40A2
Gaoping *China* 40C2
Gaoua *U Volta* 77F3
Gaoual *Guinea* 76A3
Gaoyou Hu L *China* 40D3
Gaozhou *China* 40C5
Gap *France* 18D3
Gapan *Phil* 45F7
Gar *China* 35D2
Garah *Aust* 50C1
Garanhuns *Brazil* 71L5
Garberville *USA* 65B2
Garça *Brazil* 73C3
Garcias *Brazil* 73B3
Garda *Italy* 17D2
Gardanne *France* 17A3
Garden City *USA* 62B2
Garden Pen *USA* 58B1
Gardey *Arg* 72D3
Gardez *Afghan* 35B2
Gardiner *USA* 64D1
Gardiners I *USA* 60D2
Gardner *USA* 60E1
Gardner I *Phoenix Is* 49H1
Gardone *Italy* 17D2
Gardula *Eth* 78D3
Gareloi I *USA* 56C6
Gargano *Italy* 17D2
Garhākota *India* 35D4
Gari *USSR* 24L4
Garies *S Africa* 79B7
Garissa *Kenya* 78D4
Garland *USA* 63C3
Garmisch-Partenkirchen *W Germ* 20C3
Garmsar *Iran* 34C1
Garnett *USA* 63C2
Garnett Peak Mt *USA* 54B2
Garonne R *France* 18C3
Garoua *Cam* 77J4
Garoua Boulai *Cam* 77J4
Garrison *USA* 57B2
Garry R *Scot* 14C3
Garut *Indon* 44C4
Garwa *India* 37B3
Gary *USA* 58B2
Garyarsa *China* 29G2
Gary L *Can* 52H3
Garza *Arg* 72C1
Garza-Little Elm L *USA* 63C3
Gasan Kuli *USSR* 34C1
Gascogne Region *France* 18B3
Gasconade R *USA* 63D2
Gascoyne R *Aust* 48A3
Gashaka *Nig* 78B3
Gasht *Iran* 34E3
Gashua *Nig* 77J3
Gaspé *Can* 55G2
Gaspé,C *Can* 55G2
Gaspé Pen *Can* 55G2
Gastonia *USA* 61C1
Gaston,L *USA* 61D1
Gata,C *Cyprus* 31B1
Gatchina *USSR* 24D4
Gateshead *Eng* 14D4
Gatesville *USA* 63C3
Gâtinais Region *France* 16B2
Gatineau *Can* 59D1
Gatineau R *Can* 59D1
Gatlinburg *USA* 61C1
Gatton *Aust* 50D1
Gaua I *Vanuatu* 49F2
Gaud-i-Zirreh Salt Desert *Afghan* 34E2
Gauhāti *India* 37D2
Gauja R *USSR* 21E1
Gaurdak *USSR* 34F1
Gauri Phanta *India* 37B2
Gavdhos I *Greece* 23E4
Gavião R *Brazil* 73D1
Gävle *Sweden* 12H6
Gawler Ranges Mts *Aust* 50A2
Gaxun Nur L *China* 40A1
Gaya *India* 37B3
Gaya *Niger* 77G3
Gaya R *China* 41B3
Gaylord *USA* 58C1
Gayndah *Aust* 50D1
Gayny *USSR* 24J3
Gaysin *USSR* 21F3
Gaza *Israel* 30B3
Gaziantep *Turk* 30C2
Gbaringa *Lib* 76B4
Gdańsk *Pol* 21D2
Gdańsk,G of *Pol* 21D2
Gdov *USSR* 12K7
Gdynia *Pol* 21D2
Gebe I *Indon* 45C3
Gebel Abu Rûtha Mt *Egypt* 31C4
Gebel Araif el Naqa Mt *Egypt* 31C3
Gebel Ataqa Mt *Egypt* 31B4
Gebel Budhiya *Egypt* 31B4
Gebel el Galâla Baharîya Desert *Egypt* 31A4
Gebel El Giddi Mt *Egypt* 31B3
Gebel El Tîh Upland *Egypt* 31B4
Gebel Halâl Mt *Egypt* 31B3
Gebel Hamata Mt *Egypt* 32C2
Gebel Katherina Mt *Egypt* 30B4
Gebel Kharim Mt *Egypt* 31B4
Gebel Libni Mt *Egypt* 31B3
Gebel Maghâra Mt *Egypt* 31B3
Gebel Sha'îra Mt *Egypt* 31C4
Gebel Sinn Bishr Mt *Egypt* 31B4
Gebel Yi'allaq Mt *Egypt* 31B3
Gebés *Tunisia* 77E2
Gedad del Maiz *Mexico* 67C1
Gedaref *Sudan* 32C4
Gediz R *Turk* 23F3
Gedser *Den* 20C2
Geel *Belg* 16C1
Geelong *Aust* 50B3
Geeveston *Aust* 50E3
Geidam *Nig* 77J3
Geilenkirchen *W Germ* 16D1
Geita *Tanz* 78D4
Gejiu *China* 40A5
Gela *Italy* 22C3
Geldern *W Germ* 16D1
Gelibolu *Turk* 23F2
Gelidonya Burun *Turk* 30B2
Gelleana *Mexico* 67B1
Gelnhausen *W Germ* 16E1
Gelsenkirchen *W Germ* 16D1
Gelting *W Germ* 12F8
Gemas *Malay* 43C5
Gembloux *Belg* 16C1
Gembut *Nig* 77J4
Gemena *Zaïre* 78B3
Gemerek *Turk* 30C2
Gemlik *Turk* 30A1
Gemona *Italy* 22C1
Gemona del Friuli *Italy* 17E1
Gemsbok Nat Pk *Botswana* 79C6
Geneina *Sudan* 78C2
General Acha *Arg* 72C3
General Alvear Buenos Aires *Arg* 72C3
General Alvear Mendoza *Arg* 72B2
General Arenales *Arg* 72C2
General Belgrano *Arg* 72D3
General Belgrano Base *Ant* 80F2
General Bernardo O'Higgins Base *Ant* 80G2
General Capdevia *Arg* 72C1
General Conesa Buenos Aires *Arg* 72D3
General Conesa Rio Negro *Arg* 72C4
General Eugenio A Garay *Arg* 69D2
General Eugenio A Garay *Par* 70F8
General Guido *Arg* 72D3
General La Madrid *Arg* 72C3
General Lavalle *Arg* 72D3
General Levalle *Arg* 72C2
General Madariaga *Arg* 72D3
General Manuel Belgrano Mt *Arg* 69C3
General Paz Buenos Aires *Arg* 72D3
General Paz Corrientes *Arg* 72D1
General Pico *Arg* 72C3
General Pinto *Arg* 72C2
General Pirán *Arg* 72D3
General Roca *Arg* 69C5
General San Bolivar *Mexico* 67B1
General Santos *Phil* 45G9
General Viamonte *Arg* 72C3
General Villegas *Arg* 72C3
Genesee R *USA* 59D2
Geneseo *USA* 59D2
Geneva = Genève
Geneva Nebraska *USA* 63C1
Geneva New York *USA* 60B1
Geneva,L of = LacLéman
Genève *Switz* 22B1
Genil R *Spain* 19B2
Genoa = Genova
Genoa *Aust* 50C3
Genova *Italy* 22B2
Gent *Belg* 16B1
Genteng *Indon* 44C4
Genthin *E Germ* 20C2
Geokchay *USSR* 25H7
George *S Africa* 79C7
George R *Can* 53M4
George,L *Aust* 50C2
George,L Florida *USA* 61C3
George,L New York *USA* 59E2
George Sd *NZ* 51A2
George Town *Aust* 50E3
Georgetown Delaware *USA* 59D3
Georgetown *Guyana* 71G2
Georgetown Kentucky *USA* 58C3
George Town *Malay* 43C4
Georgetown *St Vincent* 68N2
Georgetown S Carolina *USA* 61D2
Georgetown Texas *USA* 63C3
Georgetown *The Gambia* 76A3
George V Land Region *Ant* 80G8
George West *USA* 63F4
Georgia State *USA* 61C2
Georgian B *Can* 58C1
Georgina R *Aust* 48C3
Georgiu-Dezh *USSR* 25F5
Georgiyevsk *USSR* 25G7
Gera *E Germ* 20C2
Geraldine *NZ* 51B2
Geraldton *Aust* 48A3
Geraldton *Can* 55E2
Gerar R *Israel* 31C3
Gérardmer *France* 16D2
Gerardsbergen *Belg* 16B1
Gerdine,Mt *USA* 52C3
Gerdova Peak Mt *USA* 56J3
Gerik *Malay* 43C4
Gering *USA* 57B3
Gerlachovsky Mt *Pol* 25C6
Gerolstein *W Germ* 16D1
Gerona *Spain* 19C1
Geseke *W Germ* 16E1
Gestro R *Eth* 78E3
Getafe *Spain* 19B1
Gettysburg Pennsylvania *USA* 60B3
Gettysburg S Dakota *USA* 57C2
Getúlio Vargas *Brazil* 72E1
Geumpang *Indon* 44A2
Gevaş *Turk* 30D2
Gevgeliija *Yugos* 23E2
Gex *France* 17B1
Ghabāghib *Syria* 31D2
Ghadamis *Libya* 76C1
Ghaem Shahr *Iran* 34C1
Ghāghara R *India* 37B2
Ghana Republic *Africa* 76B4
Ghanzi *Botswana* 79C6
Ghardaïa *Alg* 77C2
Gharyan *Libya* 75A1
Ghāt *Libya* 75A2
Ghazaouet *Alg* 77B1
Ghāziābād *India* 35D3
Ghazi Khan *Pak* 35C3
Ghazni *Afghan* 35B2
Gheorgheni *Rom* 23F1
Gheorghiu G Dei *Rom* 23F1
Ghubbat al Qamar B *S Yemen* 33F3
Ghubbat Sawqirah B *Oman* 33G3
Ghurian *Afghan* 34E2
Gialo *Libya* 75B2
Giamame *Somalia* 78E3
Giarre *Italy* 22D3
Gibbon *USA* 62C1
Gibeon *Namibia* 79B6
Gibraltar Colony *SW Europe* 19A2
Gibraltar,Str of *Spain/Africa* 19A2
Gibson Desert *Aust* 48B3
Gibsons *Can* 64B1
Giddalūr *India* 36B1
Giddi P *Egypt* 31B3
Gien *France* 16B3
Giessen *W Germ* 20B2
Gifford *USA* 61C3
Gifu *Japan* 41D4
Gigha I *Scot* 14C4
Giglio I *Italy* 22C2
Gijon *Spain* 19A1
Gila R *USA* 65D4
Gila Bend *USA* 65D4
Gila Bend Mts *USA* 65D4
Gilbert R *Aust* 48D2
Gilbert Is *Pacific O* 49G1
Gildford *USA* 64D1
Gilé *Mozam* 79D5
Gilead Region *Jordan* 31C2
Gilf Kebir Plat *Egypt* 75B2
Gilgandra *Aust* 50C2

Gilgit Gros Ventre Range

Gilgit Pak 35C1
Gilgit R Pak 35C1
Gilgunnia Aust 50C2
Gillam Can 53J4
Gilles L Aust 50A2
Gillette USA 57A3
Gills Rock USA 58B1
Gilman USA 58B2
Gilroy USA 65B3
Gimli Can 57C1
Gineifa Egypt 31B3
Gingoog Phil 45G9
Ginir Eth 78E3
Gióna Mt Greece 23E3
Gippsland Mts Aust 50C3
Girard USA 58C2
Girardot Colombia 70D3
Girdle Ness Pen Scot 14D3
Giresun Turk 30C1
Girga Egypt 32B1
Gir Hills India 35C4
Giri R Zaïre 78B3
Girīdīh India 37C3
Girishk Afghan 35A2
Giromagny France 16D3
Gironde R France 18B2
Girvan Scot 14C4
Gisborne NZ 51C2
Gisors France 16A2
Gitega Burundi 78C4
Giuba,R = Juba,R
Giulia Region Italy 17E2
Giurgiu Rom 23F2
Givet Belg 16C1
Gizhiga USSR 27S3
Gizycko Pol 21E2
Gjirokastër Alb 23E2
Gjoatlaven Can 52J3
Gjøvik Nor 12G6
Glace Bay Can 53M5
Glacier Bay Nat Mon USA 56L4
Glacier Peak Mt USA 64B1
Glacier Str Can 53K2
Gladstone Queensland Aust 48E3
Gladstone S Aust Aust 50A2
Gladstone Tasmania Aust 50E3
Gladstone USA 58B1
Glama Mt Iceland 12A1
Glåma R Nor 12G6
Glan R W Germ 16D2
Glarner Mts Switz 17C1
Glarus Switz 17C1
Glasco USA 63C2
Glasgow Kentucky USA 58B3
Glasgow Montana USA 57A2
Glasgow Scot 14C4
Glassboro USA 60C3
Glastenbury Mt USA 60D1
Glastonbury Eng 15D6
Glazov USSR 24J4
Gleisdorf Austria 20D3
Glen Afton NZ 51C1
Glen Burnie USA 60B3
Glendale Arizona USA 65D4
Glendale USA 65C4
Glendive USA 57B2
Glendo Res USA 57B3
Glenhallen USA 56J3
Glen Innes Aust 50D1
Glenmorgan Aust 50C1
Glenreagh Aust 50D2
Glen Rock USA 60B3
Glen Rose USA 63C3
Glens Falls USA 60D1
Glenwood Arkansas USA 63D3
Glenwood Minnesota USA 57C2
Glenwood New Mexico USA 62A3
Glenwood Springs USA 62A2
Glidden USA 58A1
Glittertind Mt Nor 12F6
Gliwice Pol 21D2
Globe USA 65D4
Glogów Pol 20D2
Glomfjord Nor 12G5
Gloucester Aust 50D2
Gloucester Eng 15D6
Gloucester USA 60E1
Gloversville USA 60C1
Glubokoye USSR 21F1
Glukhov USSR 25E5
Gmünd Austria 20D3
Gmunden Austria 20C3
Gniezno Pol 21D2
Goa, Daman and Diu Union Territory India 36A1
Goālpāra India 37D2
Goaso Ghana 77F4
Goba Eth 78D3
Gobabis Namibia 79B6
Gobernador Crespo Arg 72C2
Gobernador Duval Arg 72B3
Gobi Desert China/Mongolia 40B1
Gobo Japan 42C4
Gobza R USSR 21G1
Godag India 36B1
Godāvari R India 36C1
Goderich Can 58C2
Godhavn Greenland 53N3
Godhra India 35C4
Godoy Cruz Arg 72B2
Gods L Can 53J4
Godthab Greenland 53N3
Godwin Austen = K2
Goffstown USA 60E1
Gogama Can 58C1
Gogora Eth 32C4
Goiandira Brazil 73C2
Goianésia Brazil 73C2
Goiânia Brazil 73C2
Goiás Brazil 73B2
Goiás State Brazil 71J6
Goio-Erê Brazil 73B3
Gojab R Eth 78D3
Gökçeada I Turk 23F2
Göksu R Turk 25F8
Göksun Turk 30C2
Gol R USSR 27M5
Golāghāt India 37D2
Gölbaşi Turk 30C2
Gol'chikha USSR 26K2
Golconda USA 64C2
Gold USA 60B2
Gold Beach USA 64B2
Gold Coast Aust 50D1
Golden B NZ 51B2
Goldendale USA 64B1
Golden Meadow USA 63D4
Goldfield USA 65C3
Goldthwaite USA 62C3
Goleniów Pol 20C2
Golfe d'Ajaccio G Corse 22B2
Golfe de Gabes G Tunisia 77E2
Golfe de Gascogne = Biscay,Bay of
Golfe de Hammamet G Tunisia 77E1
Golfe de la Napoule G France 17B3
Golfe de St Florent G Corse 22B2
Golfe de St-Malo B France 18B2
Golfe du Lion G France 18C3
Golfo Corcovado G Chile 69B6
Golfo de Almeira G Spain 19B2
Golfo de Ancud G Chile 69B6
Golfo de Batabano G Cuba 66D2
Golfo de Batano G Cuba 68A2
Golfo de Cadiz G Spain 19A2
Golfo de Cagliari G Sardegna 22B3
Golfo de California G Mexico 66A1
Golfo de Chiriqui G Panama 66D4
Golfo de Fonseca Honduras 66D3
Golfo de Guacanayabo G Cuba 68B2
Golfo de Guayaquil G Ecuador 70B4
Golfo del Darien G Colombia/Panama 68B5
Golfo de los Mosquitos G Panama 70B2
Golfo del Papagaya G Nic 70A1
Golfo de Mazarrón G Spain 19B2
Golfo de Nicoya G Costa Rica 70A2
Golfo de Oristano G Sardegna 22B3
Golfo de Panamá G Panama 66E4
Golfo de Papagayo G Costa Rica 66D3
Golfo de Paria G Ven 68E4
Golfo de Paris G Ven 70F1
Golfo de Penas G Chile 69B7
Golfo de St Florent Corse 18D3
Golfo de San Jorge G Spain 19C1
Golfo de Tehuantepec G Mexico 66C3
Golfo de Torugas G Colombia 70C3
Golfo de Uraba G Colombia 70C2
Golfo de Valencia G Spain 19C2
Golfo de Venezia G Italy 17E2
Golfo de Venezuela G Ven 68C4
Golfo di Genova G Italy 22B2
Golfo di Policastro G Italy 22D3
Golfo di Squillace G Italy 22D3
Golfo di Taranto G Italy 22D2
Golfo di Trieste G Italy 17E2
Golfo di Venezia G Italy 22C1
Golfo Dulce G Costa Rica 66D4
Golfo San Jorge G Arg 69C7
Golfo San Matías G Arg 69D6
Golmud China 38C3
Golocha Eth 78E3
Golovin B USA 56F3
Golovnino USSR 41F3
Goma Zaïre 78C4
Gombe Nig 77J3
Gombi Nig 77J3
Gomel USSR 21G2
Gomera I Canary Is 76A2
Gómez Palacio Mexico 66B2
Gonam R USSR 27O4
Gonbad-e Kāvūs Iran 34D1
Gonda India 37B2
Gondal India 35C4
Gondar Eth 78D2
Gondia India 37B3
Gönen Turk 30A1
Gonen R Turk 23F3
Goney Irish Rep 15B5
Gongbo'gyamba China 37D1
Gongga Shan Mt China 40A4
Gonghe China 40A2
Gongogi R Brazil 73D1
Gongola State Nig 77J4
Gongola R Nig 77J3
Gonzales Texas USA 63C4
Gonzales USA 65B3
Gonzalez Mexico 67C1
Gonzalez Chaves Arg 72C3
Goodhope B USA 56F2
Good Hope,C of S Africa 79B7
Gooding USA 64D2
Goodland USA 62B2
Goodnews Bay USA 56F4
Goodooga R Aust 50C1
Goole Eng 15E5
Goolgowi Aust 50C2
Goolwa Aust 50A3
Goomalling Aust 48A4
Goombalie Aust 50C2
Goomer Aust 50D1
Goomeri Aust 50D1
Goondiwindi Aust 50D1
Goose Bay Can 53N4
Goose Creek USA 61D2
Goose L USA 64B2
Gooty India 36B1
Goraka PNG 48D1
Gora Koyp Mt USSR 24K3
Gora Munku Sardyk Mt USSR 27L4
Gora Narodnaya Mt USSR 24K3
Gora Pay-Yer Mt USSR 24L2
Gora Telpos-Iz Mt 24K3
Goražde Yugos 23D2
Gordon USA 56K2
Gordonsville USA 59D3
Goré Chad 78B3
Gore Eth 78D3
Gore NZ 51A3
Gore Pt USA 56H4
Gore Topko Mt USSR 27P4
Gorgān Iran 34C1
Gorgona I Italy 17C3
Gorinchem Neth 16C1
Goris USSR 30E2
Gorizia Italy 22C1
Gorki Belorusskaya S.S.R. USSR 21G2
Gorki Rossiyskaya S.F.S.R. USSR 24M2
Gor'kiy USSR 26F4
Gor'kovskoye Vodokhranilishche Res USSR 24G4
Gorlitz E Germ 20C2
Gorlovka USSR 25F6
Gorna Orjahovica Bulg 23F2
Gorno-Altaysk USSR 38B1
Gorno Lopatina Mt USSR 41E1
Gorno Medvezh'ya Mt USSR 41D2
Gorno Oblachnaya Mt USSR 41C3
Gorno Tardoki Yani Mt USSR 41D2
Gornozavodsk USSR 41E2
Gornyy USSR 41D1
Goro Denezhkin Kamen' Mt USSR 24K3
Gorodets USSR 24G4
Gorodnya USSR 21G2
Gorodok Belorusskaya S.S. R. USSR 21G1
Gorodok Ukrainskaya S.S. R. USSR 21E3
Gorodok Ukrainskaya S.S. R. USSR 21F3
Goroka PNG 39H7
Gorokhpur India 37B2
Gorong I Indon 45D3
Gorongosa Mozam 79D5
Gorontalo Indon 45B2
Goroubi R U Volta 77G3
Goro Yurma Mt USSR 24L4
Gorutuba R Brazil 73D2
Goryachinsk USSR 27M4
Gory Akkyr Upland USSR 25J7
Gory Byrranga Mts USSR 27L2
Goryn' R USSR 21F3
Gory Putorana Mts USSR 27L1
Góry Świetokrzyskie Upland Pol 21E2
Gory Tel'pos-iz' Mt USSR 26G3
Gorzow Wielkopolski Pol 12H8
Goshogawara Japan 41E3
Gosku R Turk 25F8
Gospić Yugos 22D2
Gostivar Yugos 23E2
Gostynin Pol 21D2
Göteborg Sweden 12G7
Gotel Mts Nig 78B3
Gothenburg USA 62B1
Gotland I Sweden 12H7
Gotō-retto I Japan 41B5
Gotska Sandön I Sweden 12H7
Gōtsu Japan 41C4
Gottwaldov Czech 21D3
Gouda Neth 16C1
Goudoumaria Niger 78B2
Gough I Atlantic O 74H7
Goulburn Aust 50C2
Goumbou Mali 76B3
Goundam Mali 76B3
Gouré Niger 78B2
Gourma Rharous Mali 76B3
Gournay-en-Bray France 16A2
Gouro Chad 78B2
Govenlock Can 64E1
Gove Pen Aust 39G8
Goverla Mt USSR 25C6
Governador Valadares Brazil 73D2
Governador Virasoro Arg 72D1
Govind Ballabh Paht Sāgar L India 37B3
Gowanda USA 60A1
Gowārān Afghan 35B3
Goya Arg 72D1
Goz-Beïda Chad 78C2
Gozo I Medit S 22C3
Goz Regeb Sudan 32C3
Graaff Reiner S Africa 79C7
Gracefield Can 59D1
Grado Italy 17E2
Grafton Aust 49E3
Grafton Aust 50D1
Grafton N Dakota USA 57C2
Grafton W Virginia USA 58C3
Graham I Can 52E4
Graham,Mt USA 65E4
Grahamstown S Africa 79C7
Grajaú Brazil 71J5
Grajewo Pol 21E2
Grámmos Mt Greece/Alb 23E2
Grampian Region Scot 14D3
Grampian Mts Scot 14C3
Granada Colombia 70D3
Granada Nic 70A1
Granada Spain 19B2
Granby Can 59E1
Granby USA 62A1
Gran Canaria I Canary Is 76A2
Gran Chaco Region Arg 69D3
Grand R Michigan USA 58B2
Grand R Missouri USA 63D1
Grand B Dominica 68Q2
Grand Bahama I Bahamas 55F4
Grand Ballon Mt France 16D3
Grand Bank Can 53N5
Grand Banks Atlantic O 74F1
Grand Bassam Ivory Coast 77F4
Grand Bérard Mt France 17B2
Grand Canyon USA 65D3
Grand Canyon Nat Pk USA 65D3
Grand Cayman I Caribbean 68A3
Grand Coulee USA 64C1
Grande R Arg 72B3
Grande R Bahia Brazil 71K6
Grande R Minas Gerais/São Paulo Brazil 73C2
Grande Chartreuse Region France 17A2
Grande Comore I Comoros 79E5
Grand Erg de Bilma Desert Region Niger 78B2
Grand erg Occidental Mts Alg 76C1
Grand erg Oriental Mts Alg 76C1
Grande Rivière de la Baleine R Can 53L4
Grande Ronde R USA 64C1
Gran Desierto USA 65D4
Grand Falls New Brunswick Can 53M5
Grand Falls Newfoundland Can 53N5
Grand Forks Can 64C1
Grand Forks USA 57C2
Grand Gorge USA 60C1
Grand Haven USA 58B2
Grand Island USA 62C1
Grand Isle USA 63E3
Grand Junction USA 62A2
Grand L USA 63D4
Grand Marais USA 58A1
Grand Mère Can 59E1
Grãndola Port 19A2
Grand Rapids Can 52J4
Grand Rapids Michigan USA 58B2
Grand Rapids Minnesota USA 58A1
Grand St Bernard P Italy/Switz 17B2
Grand Teton Mt USA 54B2
Grand Teton Nat Pk USA 64D2
Grand Valley USA 62A2
Grandvilliers France 16A2
Grangeburg USA 66D1
Grangeville USA 64C1
Granite Peak Mt Montana USA 64E1
Granite Peak Mt Utah USA 65D2
Granollérs Spain 19C1
Gran Paradiso Mt Italy 22B1
Gran Pilastro Mt Austria/Italy 17D1
Grantham Eng 15E5
Grant,Mt USA 65C3
Grantown-on-Spey Scot 14D3
Grants USA 62A2
Grants Pass USA 64B2
Granville France 18B2
Granville USA 60D1
Granville L Can 52H4
Grão Mogol Brazil 73D2
Grasse France 18D3
Grassrange USA 64E1
Grass Valley USA 65B3
Gravelbourg Can 52H5
Gravelines France 16B1
Gravelotte S Africa 79D6
Gravenhurst Can 59D2
Grave Peak Mt USA 64D1
Gravesend Aust 50D1
Gravina I USA 56M4
Gray France 17A1
Grayling USA 56F3
Grays Harbour B USA 64B1
Grays L USA 64D2
Grayson USA 58C3
Grayville USA 58B3
Graz Austria 20D3
Great R Jamaica 68H1
Great Abaco I Bahamas 55F4
Great Australian Bight G Aust 48B4
Great B New Hampshire USA 60E1
Great B New Jersey USA 60C3
Great Bahama Bank Bahamas 66E2
Great Barrier I NZ 51C1
Great Barrier Reef Is Aust 48D2
Great Barrington USA 60D1
Great Basin USA 65C2
Great Bear R Can 56O2
Great Bear L Can 52F3
Great Bend USA 62C2
Great Bitter L Egypt 31B3
Great Cacapon USA 60A3
Great Coco I Burma 36E2
Great Dividing Range Mts Aust 48D3
Great Driffield Eng 15E4
Great Egg Harbour B USA 60C3
Greater Antarctic Region Ant 80F10
Greater Antilles Is Caribbean 68B2
Greater London Metropolitan County Eng 15E6
Greater Manchester Metropolitan County Eng 15D5
Great Exuma I Bahamas 66E2
Great Falls USA 64D1
Great Glen V Scot 14C3
Great Himalayan Range Mts Asia 37C2
Great Inagua I Bahamas 55F4
Great Karroo Reg. S Africa 79C7
Great L Aust 50E3
Great Namaland Region Namibia 79B6
Great Nicobar I Indian O 36E3
Great Ormes Head C Wales 15D5
Great Pt USA 60E2
Great Ragged I Bahamas 55F4
Great Ruaha R Tanz 79D4
Great Sacandaga L USA 59E2
Great Salt L USA 64D2
Great Salt Lake Desert USA 64D2
Great Sand Sea Libya/Egypt 75B2
Great Sandy Desert Aust 48B3
Great Sandy Desert USA 54A2
Great Sandy I = Fraser I
Great Sitkin I USA 56C6
Great Slave L Can 52G3
Great Smoky Mts USA 61C1
Great Smoky Mts Nat Pk USA 61C1
Great South B USA 60D2
Great Victoria Desert Aust 48B3
Great Wall China 40B2
Great Yarmouth Eng 15F5
Greco,C Cyprus 31C1
Greece Republic Europe 23E3
Greece USA 59D2
Greeley USA 62B1
Greely Fjord Can 53K1
Green R Kentucky USA 58B3
Green R Utah USA 65D3
Green B USA 58B1
Green Bay USA 58B2
Greencastle Indiana USA 58B3
Greencastle Pennsylvania USA 60B3
Greene USA 60C1
Greeneville USA 61C1
Greenfield Massachusetts USA 60D1
Greenfield Wisconsin USA 58B2
Greenland Dependency N Atlantic 53O2
Greenland Basin Greenland S 74H1
Greenland S Greenland 80B1
Greenock Scot 14C4
Greenport USA 60D2
Green River Utah USA 65D3
Green River Wyoming USA 64E2
Greensboro Maryland USA 60C3
Greensboro N Carolina USA 61D1
Greensburg Kansas USA 62C2
Greensburg Kentucky USA 58B3
Greensburg Pennsylvania USA 59D2
Greenstone Pt Scot 14C3
Greenup USA 58B3
Green Valley USA 65D4
Greenville Alabama USA 61B2
Greenville Lib 76B4
Greenville Mississippi USA 63D3
Greenville N Carolina USA 61D1
Greenville N Hampshire USA 60E1
Greenville Ohio USA 58C2
Greenville S Carolina USA 61C2
Greenville Texas USA 63C3
Greenville,C Aust 39H8
Greenwich Eng 15F6
Greenwich USA 60D2
Greenwood Delaware USA 60C3
Greenwood Mississippi USA 63D3
Greenwood S Carolina USA 61C2
Greers Ferry L USA 63D2
Gregory USA 57C3
Gregory,L Aust 50A1
Gregory Range Mts Aust 48D2
Greifswald E Germ 20C2
Gremikha USSR 24F2
Grenå Den 20C1
Grenada USA 63E3
Grenada I Caribbean 68E4
Grenadines,The Is Caribbean 68E4
Grenfell Aust 50C2
Grenoble France 18D2
Grenville Grenada 68M2
Grenville,C Aust 48D2
Gresham USA 64B1
Gresik Jawa Indon 44D4
Gresik Sumatera Indon 44B3
Gretna USA 63D4
Grey R NZ 51B2
Greybull USA 64E2
Grey Hunter Pk Mt Can 56L3
Grey Is Can 53N4
Greylock,Mt USA 60D1
Greymouth NZ 51B2
Grey Range Mts Aust 48D3
Greystones Irish Rep 15B5
Greytown S Africa 79D6
Griffin USA 61C2
Griffith Aust 50C2
Grim,C Aust 48D5
Grimsby Can 59D2
Grimsby Eng 15E5
Grimsey I Iceland 12B1
Grimstad Nor 12F7
Grindelwald Switz 17C1
Grinnell USA 57D3
Grinnell Pen Can 53J2
Grise Fjord Can 53K2
Griva USSR 24J3
Grizzly Bear Mt Can 56O2
Grobina USSR 12J7
Gröbming Austria 17E1
Grodno USSR 21E2
Gromati R India 37B2
Groningen Neth 20B2
Groom USA 62B2
Groote Eylandt I Aust 48C2
Grootfontein Namibia 79B5
Gros Islet St Lucia 68P2
Grosser Feldberg Mt W Germ 16E1
Grosseto Italy 22C2
Gross-Gerau W Germ 16E2
Grossglockner Mt Austria 20C3
Gross Venediger Mt Austria 17E1
Grosvenor,L USA 56G4
Gros Ventre Range Mts USA 64D2

Groton Hayden

Groton USA 57C2
Groundhog R Can 58C1
Grove Hill USA 61B2
Grover City USA 65B3
Groveton USA 59E2
Groznyy USSR 25H7
Grudziadz Pol 21D2
Grunau Namibia 79B6
Grutness Scot 14E2
Gruzinskaya SSR Republic USSR 25G7
Gryazi USSR 25G5
Gryazovets USSR 24F4
Grytviken South Georgia 69J8
Guaçuí Brazil 73D3
Guadalajara Mexico 67B1
Guadalajara Spain 19B1
Guadalcanal I Solomon Is 49E1
Guadalimar R Spain 19B2
Guadalope R Spain 19B1
Guadalqivir R Spain 19B2
Guadalupe Mexico 66B2
Guadalupe R USA 62C4
Guadalupe Peak Mt USA 62B3
Guadalupe Victoria Mexico 67B1
Guadalupe Mexico 67B1
Guadeloupe I Caribbean 68E3
Guadian R Spain 19B2
Gûadiana R Port 19A2
Guadiana R Spain 19B2
Guadix Spain 19B2
Guaira Brazil 73B3
Guajará Mirim Brazil 70E6
Guajira,Pen de Colombia 70D1
Gualaceo Ecuador 70C4
Gualdo Tadino Italy 17E3
Gualeguay Arg 72D2
Gualeguaychú Arg 72D2
Guam I Pacific O 39H5
Guamini Arg 72C3
Gua Musang Malay 43C5
Guanajuato Mexico 67B1
Guanajuato State Mexico 67B1
Guanambi Brazil 73D1
Guanare Ven 70E2
Guandacol Arg 72B1
Guane Cuba 66D2
Guangdong Province China 40C5
Guanghan China 40A3
Guanghua China 40C3
Guangmao Shan Mt China 40A4
Guangnan China 40A5
Guangyuan China 40B3
Guangze China 40D4
Guangzhon China 40C5
Guanhães Brazil 73D2
Guania R Colombia 70E3
Guanipa R Ven 68E5
Guantánamo Cuba 68B2
Guanting Shuiku Res China 40D1
Guanxi Province China 40B5
Guan Xian China 40A3
Guapa Colombia 70C2
Guaporé Brazil 72E1
Guaporé R Brazil 72E1
Guaporé R Brazil/Bol 70F6
Guaquí Bol 70E7
Guará R Brazil 73D1
Guarapuava Brazil 73B4
Guaraqueçaba Brazil 73C4
Guaratinguetá Brazil 73C3
Guarda Port 19A1
Guardafui,C Somalia 75E3
Guarda Mor Brazil 73C2
Guardia Chile 72B1
Guardia Mitre Arg 72C4
Guarita R Brazil 72E1
Guasave Mexico 54C4
Guastalla Italy 17D2
Guatemala Guatemala 66C3
Guatemala Republic C America 66C3
Guatraché Arg 72C3
Guavrare R Colombia 70D3
Guaxupé Brazil 73C3
Guayaguayare Trinidad 68L1
Guayaquil Ecuador 70B4
Guaymas Mexico 66A2
Guayquiraro R Arg 72D2
Guba Eth 78D3
Guba Zaïre 79C5
Guba Buorkhaya B USSR 27P2
Guban Region Somalia 78E3
Gubat Phil 45F8
Gubbio Italy 17E3
Gubin Pol 20C2
Gubio Nig 77J3
Güdür India 36B2
Guebwiller France 16D3
Guelma Alg 77D1
Guelpho Can 58C2
Guelta Zemmur Mor 76A2
Güemez Mexico 67C1
Guenabacoa Cuba 68A2
Guerara Alg 77C2
Guéréda Chad 78C2
Guéret France 18C2
Guernsey USA 57B3
Guernsey I UK 18B2
Guerrero State Mexico 67B2
Gughe Mt Eth 78D3
Gugigu China 27O4
Guguan I Pacific O 39H5
Guiargambone Aust 50C2
Guichón Urug 72D2
Guider Cam 77J4
Guidong China 40C4
Guiglo Ivory Coast 76B4
Gui Jiang R China 40C5
Guildford Eng 15E6
Guilin China 40C4
Guillestre France 17B2
Guinan China 40A2
Guinea Republic Africa 76A3
Guinea Basin Atlantic O 74H4
Guinea-Bissau Republic Africa 76A3
Guinea,G of W Africa 76C4
Güines Cuba 68A2
Guir Well Mali 76B3
Guiranwala Pak 35C2
Guiratinga Brazil 73B2
Güiria Ven 70F1
Guise France 16B2
Guiuan Phil 45G8
Gui Xian China 40B5
Guiyang China 40B4
Guizhou Province China 40B4
Gujarāt State India 35C4
Gujrat Pak 35C2
Gulbarga India 36B1
Gulbene USSR 21F1
Guledagudda India 36B1
Gulfport USA 61B2
Gulf,The S W Asia 28D3
Gulgong Aust 50C2
Gulian China 41A1
Gulin China 40B4
Gulkana USA 56J3
Gulkana R USA 56J3
Gulu Uganda 78D3
Guluguba Aust 50C1
Gulung Chamah Mt Malay 44F6
Gumel Nig 77H3
Gummersbach W Germ 16D1
Gummi Nig 77H3
Gumpla India 37B3
Gümüşhane Turk 30C1
Gümüşhane Turk 30C2
Guna India 35D4
Guna Mt Eth 78D2
Gundagai Aust 50C3
Gungu Zaïre 78B4
Gunnedah Aust 50D2
Gunnison USA 62A2
Gunnison R USA 62A2
Guntakal India 36B1
Guntersville USA 61B2
Guntersville L USA 61B2
Guntūr India 36C1
Gunung Batu Putch Mt Malay 43C5
Gunung Benom Mt Malay 44G7
Gunung Besar Mt Indon 44E3
Gunung Besar Mt Malay 44F6
Gunung Besar Mt Malay 44G7
Gunung Bulu Mt Indon 44E2
Gunung Gedang Mt Indon 44B3
Gunung Geureudong Mt Indon 44A2
Gunung Kulabu Mt Indon 44A2
Gunung Lawit Mt Malay 44D2
Gunung Lawu Mt Indon 44D4
Gunung Leuser Mt Indon 44A2
Gunung Lokilalaka Mt Indon 45B3
Gunung Mekongga Mt Indon 45B3
Gunung Menyapa Mt Indon 44E2
Gunung Niapa Mt Indon 44E2
Gunung Ogoamas Mt Indon 45B2
Gunung Patah Mt Indon 44B3
Gunung Raung Mt Indon 44D4
Gunung Resag Mt Indon 44B3
Gunung Sarempaka Mt Indon 44E3
Gunungsitoli Indon 44A2
Gunung Sumbing Mt Indon 44D4
Gunung Tahan Mt Malay 43C5
Gunung Talakmau Mt Indon 44B2
Gunung Tapis Mt Malay 44G7
Gunung Tokala Mt Indon 45B3
Gunza Angola 79B5
Guoyang China 40D3
Guranda Ecuador 70C4
Gurara Nig 77H4
Gurdāspur India 35D2
Gurgaon India 35D3
Gurkha Nepal 37B2
Gurktaler Alpen Mts Austria 17E1
Gurskoye USSR 41D1
Gürün Turk 30C2
Gurupi R Brazil 71J4
Gurvan Sayhan Uul Upland Mongolia 40A1
Gur'yev USSR 25J6
Gurzinskaya Republic USSR 26F5
Gusau Nig 77H3
Gusev USSR 21E2
Gushan China 41A4
Gus'khrustalnyy USSR 24G4
Gustavas USA 52E4
Gustavus USA 56L4
Gustine USA 65B3
Guston USA 55E3
Gütersloh W Germ 20B2
Guthrie Kentucky USA 58B3
Guthrie Oklahoma USA 63C2
Guthrie Texas USA 62B3
Gutiérrez Zamora Mexico 67C1
Guttenberg USA 57D3
Guyana Republic S America 71G3
Guyana Basin Atlantic O 74F4
Guyang China 40C1
Guyenne Region France 18B3
Guymon USA 62B2
Guyra Aust 50D2
Guyuan China 40B2
Guzar USSR 34F1
Gwa Burma 37D4
Gwabegar Aust 50C2
Gwadabawa Nig 77H3
Gwalior India 35D3
Gwane Zaïre 78C3
Gwardar Pak 34E3
Gwent County Wales 15D6
Gweru Zim 79C5
Gwydir R Aust 50C1
Gwynedd Wales 15D4
Gyangzê China 37C2
Gyaring Hu L China 38C3
Gydanskiy Poluostrov Pen USSR 26J2
Gyirong China 37C2
Gyldenløues Greenland 53O3
Gympie Aust 50D1
Gyöngyös Hung 21D3
Györ Hung 21D3

H

Ha'apai Group Is Tonga 49H2
Haapajärvi Fin 12K6
Haapsalu USSR 24C4
Haarlem Neth 20A2
Haarstrang Region W Germ 16D1
Habana Cuba 66D2
Habarūt Oman 33F3
Habbān S Yemen 33E4
Habiganj Bang 37D3
Habomai Shoto I USSR 41F3
Hachijō-jima I Japan 41D5
Hachiman Japan 42C3
Hachinohe Japan 41E3
Hachioji Japan 42C3
Hackettstown USA 60C2
Hack,Mt Mt Aust 50A2
Hadbaram Oman 33G3
Haddington Scot 14D4
Haddon Corner Aust 50B1
Haddon Downs Aust 50B1
Hadejia Nig 77J3
Hadejia R Nig 77H3
Hadera Israel 31C2
Haderslev Den 20B1
Hadiboh Socotra 33F4
Hadley B Can 52H2
Hadong S Korea 42A3
Hadong Vietnam 40B5
Hadramawt Region S Yemen 33E3
Hadsund Den 20C1
Haeju N Korea 41B4
Haeju-man B N Korea 42A3
Haenam S Korea 42A4
Hafar al Bātin S Arabia 33E1
Haffners Bjerg Mt Greenland 53M2
Hafir Sudan 32B3
Hafizabad Pak 35C2
Hāflong India 37D2
Hafnafjörður Iceland 12A2
Hag'Abdullah Sudan 32B4
Hagemeister I USA 56F4
Hagen W Germ 20B2
Hagerstown USA 60B3
Hagi Japan 42B4
Ha Giang Vietnam 40A5
Hagondange France 16D2
Haguenan France 16D2
Hagunia Well Mor 76A2
Haha-jima I Japan 38H4
Hah Xil Hu L China 38C3
Haicheng China 41A3
Hai Duong Viet 43D1
Haifa Israel 31C2
Haifa,B of Israel 31C2
Hai He R China 40D2
Haikang China 40C5
Haikou China 43E1
Ha'il S Arabia 32D1
Hailākāndi India 37D3
Hailar China 27N5
Hailong China 41B3
Hailun China 41B2
Hailuoto I Fin 12J5
Hainan I China 43D2
Haines USA 52E4
Haines USA 56L4
Haines Junction Can 56L3
Hainfeld Austria 20D3
Haiphong Vietnam 40B5
Haiti Republic Caribbean 68C3
Haiya Sudan 78D2
Haiyan China 40A2
Haiyuan China 40B2
Haizhou Wan B China 40D3
Hajdúböszörmény Hung 21E3
Hajfah Yemen 32D3
Hajiki-saki Pt Japan 42C3
Haka Burma 37D3
Hakkâri Turk 30D2
Hakodate Japan 41E3
Hakui Japan 42C3
Haku-san Mt Japan 42C3
Halab Syria 25F8
Halabja Iraq 30E3
Halaib Sudan 78D1
Halba Leb 31D1
Halberstadt E Germ 20C2
Halcon,Mt Phil 45F8
Halden Nor 12G7
Haldia India 37C3
Haldwāni India 35D3
Halifax Can 53M5
Halifax Eng 15E5
Halifax USA 59D3
Halkett,C USA 56H1
Halla-San Mt S Korea 42A4
Hall Basin Sd Can 53M1
Hall Beach Can 53K3
Halle Belg 16C1
Halle E Germ 20C2
Halley Base Ant 80F1
Halleybury Can 59D1
Hall I USA 56D3
Halliday USA 57B2
Hallingdal R Nor 12F6
Hallock USA 57C2
Hall Pen Can 53M3
Hall's Creek Aust 48B2
Hallstead USA 60C2
Halmahera I Indon 45C2
Halmahera S Indon 45C3
Halmstad Sweden 12G7
Haltern W Germ 20B2
Haltia Mt Nor 12J5
Haltwhistle Eng 14D4
Halul I Qatar 33F1
Haluza Hist Site Israel 31C3
Hamada Japan 42B4
Hamada de Tinrhert Desert Region Alg 76C2
Hamada du Dra Upland Alg 76B2
Hamadān Iran 34B2
Hamada Tounassine Region Alg 76B2
Hamāh Syria 25F8
Hamamatsu Japan 42C4
Hamar Nor 12G6
Hama-Tombetsu Japan 42D1
Hambantota Sri Lanka 36C3
Hamburg Arkansas USA 63D3
Hamburg Iowa USA 63C1
Hamburg New York USA 60A1
Hamburg Pennsylvania USA 60C2
Hamburg W Germ 20B2
Hamden USA 60D2
Hämeeninna Fin 12J6
Hamersley Range Mts Aust 48A3
Hamgyong Sanmaek Mts N Korea 41B3
Hamhŭng N Korea 41B3
Hami China 38C2
Hamīdīyah Syria 31C1
Hamilton Alabama USA 61B2
Hamilton Aust 50B3
Hamilton Can 59D2
Hamilton Montana USA 64D1
Hamilton New York USA 60C1
Hamilton NZ 51C1
Hamilton Ohio USA 58C3
Hamilton Scot 14C4
Hamilton Inlet B Can 53N4
Hamina Fin 12K6
Hamirpur India 37B2
Hamju N Korea 42A3
Hamm W Germ 20B2
Hammādāh al Hamra Upland Libya 75A2
Hammerdal Sweden 12H6
Hammerfest Nor 12J4
Hammond Illinois USA 58B2
Hammond Louisiana USA 63D3
Hammond Montana USA 57B2
Hammonton USA 60C3
Hampden NZ 51B3
Hampshire County Eng 15E6
Hampton Arkansas USA 63D3
Hampton Iowa USA 57D3
Hampton New Hampshire USA 60E1
Hampton Virginia USA 59D3
Hāmūn-e Jaz Mūrīan L Iran 34D3
Hamun-i-Lora Salt L Pak 35B3
Hamun-i Mashkel Salt Plain Pak 34E3
Han R S Korea 42A3
Hanamaki Japan 41E4
Hanau W Germ 16E1
Hancheng China 40C2
Hanchuan China 40C3
Hancock Maryland USA 59D3
Hancock Michigan USA 58B1
Hancock New York USA 60C2
Handa Japan 42C4
Handan China 40C2
Handeni Tanz 78D4
Hanford USA 65C3
Hanggin Qi China 40B2
Hangö Fin 12J7
Hangzhou China 40E3
Hangzhou Wan B China 40E3
Hanīsh I Yemen 32D4
Hankinson USA 57C2
Hanksville USA 65D3
Hanmer Springs NZ 51B2
Hanna Can 52G4
Hannibal USA 63D2
Hannover W Germ 20B2
Hanöbukten B Sweden 12G7
Hanoi Viet 43D1
Hanover USA 60B3
Hanover I Chile 69B8
Han Shui China 40B3
Han Shui R China 40C3
Hānsi India 35D3
Hantay Mongolia 38D2
Hanzhong China 40B3
Hāora India 37C3
Haparanda Sweden 12J5
Hapch'on S Korea 42A3
Hapevi Brazil 72D1
Hāpoli India 37D2
Haql S Arabia 30C4
Harad Yemen 32D3
Haradh S Arabia 33E2
Hara Fanna Eth 78E3
Haraja S Arabia 32D3
Haramachi Japan 42D3
Harar Eth 78E3
Harare Zim 79D5
Harazé Chad 78C2
Harbin China 41B2
Harbor Beach USA 58C2
Harda India 35D4
Hardangerfjord Inlet Nor 12F6
Hardin USA 57A2
Harding S Africa 79D7
Hardt Region W Germ 16D2
Hardwicke B Aust 50A2
Hardy USA 63D2
Hargeysa Somalia 78E3
Har Hakippa Mt Israel 31C3
Harhu L China 38C3
Hari R Indon 44B3
Harīb Yemen 33E4
Harima-nada B Japan 42B4
Harlan USA 58C3
Harlem USA 64E1
Harlingen Neth 20B2
Harlingen USA 63F4
Harlow Eng 15F6
Harlowtown USA 64E1
Har Meron Mt Israel 31C2
Harney Basin USA 64C2
Harney L USA 64C2
Härnösand Sweden 12H6
Har Nuur L Mongolia 27L5
Harper Lib 76B4
Harper,Mt USA 56K3
Harpers Ferry USA 59D3
Har Ramon Mt Israel 31C3
Harrāt al 'Uwayrid U Region S Arabia 32C1
Harrât Kishb Region S Arabia 32D2
Harrat Nawaāsīf Region S Arabia 32D2
Harrat Rahat Region S Arabia 32D2
Harricanaw R Can 53L4
Harriman USA 61C1
Harriman Res USA 60D1
Harrington USA 60C3
Harrington Harbour Can 53N4
Harris District Scot 14B3
Harrisburg Illinois USA 58B3
Harrisburg Pennsylvania USA 60B2
Harrismith S Africa 79C6
Harrison USA 63D2
Harrison B USA 56H1
Harrisonburg USA 59D3
Harrison,C Can 53N4
Harrisonville USA 63D2
Harris,Sound of Chan Scot 14B3
Harrisville USA 58C2
Harrogate Eng 15E4
Har Saggi Mt Israel 31C3
Harstad Nor 12H5
Hart R Can 56L3
Hårteigen Mt Nor 12F6
Hartford Connecticut USA 60D2
Hartford Michigan USA 58B2
Hartford S Dakota USA 57C3
Hartkjølen Mt Nor 12G6
Hart,L Aust 50A2
Hartland Can 59F1
Hartland Pt Eng 15C6
Hartlepool Eng 14E4
Hartley USA 62B2
Hartselle USA 61B2
Hartshorne USA 63C3
Hartwell Res USA 61C2
Har Us Nuur L Mongolia 38C2
Harut R Afghan 34E2
Harvard,Mt USA 62A2
Harvey USA 57B2
Harwich Eng 15F6
Haryāna State India 35D3
Hāsā Jordan 31C3
Hasaheisa Sudan 32B4
Hāsbaiya Leb 31C2
Haselmere Eng 15E6
Hashimoto Japan 42C4
Hashtpar Iran 34B1
Hashtrūd Iran 34B1
Hāsik Oman 33G3
Haskell USA 62C3
Hassan India 36B2
Hasselt Belg 20B2
Hassi Inifel Alg 76C2
Hassi Mdakane Well Alg 76B2
Hassi Messaoud Alg 76C1
Hassi R'mel Alg 77C2
Hassleholm Sweden 12G4
Hastings Aust 50C3
Hastings Eng 15F6
Hastings Minnesota USA 57D3
Hastings Nebraska USA 54D2
Hastings NZ 51C1
Hatchie R USA 61B1
Hatfield Aust 50B2
Hatham Inlet USA 56F2
Hāthras India 35D3
Ha Tinh Viet 43D2
Hattah Aust 50B2
Hatteras,C USA 55F3
Hattiesburg USA 63E3
Hatvan Hung 21D3
Hau Bon Viet 43D3
Haud Region Eth 78E3
Haugesund Nor 12F7
Hauhungaroa Range Mts NZ 51C1
Hauraki G NZ 51B1
Hauroko,L NZ 51A3
Hausstock Mt Switz 17C1
Haut Atlas Mts Mor 77A2
Haute Kotto Region CAR 78C3
Haute-Marne Department France 16C2
Haute-Saône Department France 16C3
Hautes Fagnes Mts Belg 16C1
Hauteville-Lompnès France 17A2
Hautmont Belg 16C1
Haut-Rhin Department France 16D3
Hauts Plateaux Mts Alg 77B2
Hauzdar Iran 34E2
Hauz Qala Afghan 35A2
Havana USA 58A2
Havana = Habana
Havankulam Sri Lanka 36B3
Havasu L USA 65D4
Havelock USA 61D2
Havelock North NZ 51C1
Haverfordwest West 15C6
Haverhill USA 60E1
Hāveri India 36B2
Haverstraw USA 60D2
Havlíčkův Brod Czech 20D3
Havre USA 64E1
Havre de Grace USA 60B3
Havre-St-Pierre Can 53M4
Havsa Turk 23F2
Hawal R Nig 77J3
Hawea,L NZ 51A2
Hawera NZ 51B1
Hawick Scot 14D4
Hawkdun Range Mts NZ 51A2
Hawke B NZ 51C1
Hawke,C Aust 50D2
Hawker Aust 50A2
Hawley USA 60C2
Hawng Luk Burma 43B1
Hawr al Habbaniyah L Iraq 30D3
Hawr al Hammār L Iraq 30E3
Hawthorne USA 65C3
Hay Aust 50B2
Hay R Can 52G3
Hayange France 16C2
Haycock USA 52B3
Hayden Arizona USA 65D4

Hayden Huron

Hayden Colorado *USA* 62A1
Hayes R *Can* 53J4
Hayes Halvø Region *Greenland* 53M2
Hayes,Mt *USA* 56J3
Haymarket *USA* 60B3
Haynin *S Yemen* 33E3
Hay River *Can* 52G3
Hays *USA* 62C2
Hays *Yemen* 32D4
Haysville *USA* 63C2
Hayward *USA* 65B3
Hayward Wisconsin *USA* 58A1
Hazard *USA* 58C3
Hazārībāg *India* 37C3
Hazebrouck *France* 16B1
Hazelhurst *USA* 63D3
Hazel Str *Can* 52G2
Hazelton *Can* 52F4
Hazen B *USA* 56E3
Hazen L *Can* 53L1
Hazeva *Israel* 31C3
Hazleton *USA* 60C2
Healdsburg *USA* 65B3
Healesville *Aust* 50C3
Healy *USA* 56J3
Heard I *Indian O* 46E7
Hearne *USA* 63C3
Hearst *Can* 55E2
Heart R *USA* 57B2
Hebbronville *USA* 63F4
Hebei Province *China* 40D2
Hebel *Aust* 50C1
Heber City *USA* 64D2
Hebger L *USA* 64D2
Hebi *China* 40C2
Hebian *China* 40C2
Hebron *Can* 53M4
Hebron *Israel* 31C3
Hebron N. Dakota *USA* 57B2
Hebron Nebraska *USA* 63C1
Hecate Str. *Can* 52E4
Heceta I *USA* 56M4
Hechi *China* 40B5
Hechingen *W Germ* 16E2
Hecla and Griper B *Can* 52G2
Hector,Mt *NZ* 51C2
Hede *Sweden* 12G6
Hedemora *Sweden* 12H6
He Devil Mt *USA* 64C1
Heerenveen *Neth* 20B2
Heerlen *Neth* 16C1
Hefa = Haifa
Hefei *China* 40D3
Hefeng *China* 40B4
Hegang *China* 41C2
Hegura-jima I *Japan* 42C3
Heho *Burma* 37E3
Heiburg I *Can* 53J2
Heidan R *Jordan* 31C3
Heide *W Germ* 20B2
Heidelberg *W Germ* 20B3
Heihe *China* 27O4
Heilbron *S Africa* 79C6
Heilbronn *W Germ* 20B3
Heiligenstadt *E Germ* 20C2
Heilongjiang Province *China* 41B2
Heilong Jiang R *China* 41A1
Heinola *Fin* 12K6
Hejiang *China* 40B4
Hekla Mt *Iceland* 53R3
Hekou *Viet* 43C1
Hekou Yaozou Zizhixian *China* 40A5
Helan *China* 40B2
Helan Shan Mt *China* 40B2
Helena Arkansas *USA* 63D3
Helena Montana *USA* 64D1
Helen Reef I *Pacific O* 45D2
Helensburgh *Scot* 14C3
Heliopolis *Egypt* 31A3
Helleh R *Iran* 34C3
Hellin *Spain* 19B2
Hells Canyon R *USA* 64C1
Hellweg Region *W Germ* 16D1
Helmand R *Afghan* 34E2
Helmeringhausen *Namibia* 79B6
Helmond *Neth* 16C1
Helmsdale *Scot* 14D2
Helong *China* 41B3
Helsingborg *Sweden* 12G7
Helsingfors = Helsinki
Helsingør *Den* 20C1
Helsinki *Fin* 12J6
Helston *Eng* 15C6
Helwân *Egypt* 30B4
Hempstead *USA* 63C3
Hemse *Sweden* 12H7
Henan *China* 40A3
Henan Province *China* 40C3
Hen and Chicken Is *NZ* 51B1
Henashi-zaki C *Japan* 42C2
Henderson Kentucky *USA* 58B3
Henderson N. Carolina *USA* 61D1
Henderson Nevada *USA* 65D3
Henderson Texas *USA* 63D3
Hendersonville N. Carolina *USA* 61C1
Hendersonville Tennessee *USA* 61B1
Heng-ch'un *Taiwan* 40E5
Henguduan Shan Mts *China* 38C4
Hengelo *Neth* 20B2
Hengshan *China* 40B2
Hengshui *China* 40D2
Heng Xian *China* 43D1
Hengyang *China* 40C4
Henhoaha *Nicobar Is* 43A4
Henley-on-Thames *Eng* 15E6
Henlopen,C *USA* 60C3
Henniker *USA* 60E1
Henrietta *USA* 62C3
Henrietta Maria,C *Can* 53K4
Henrieville *USA* 65D3
Henryetta *USA* 63C2
Henry Kater Pen *Can* 53M3
Hentiyn Nuruu Mts *Mongolia* 38D2
Henzada *Burma* 43B2
Hepu *China* 40B5
Herat *Afghan* 34E2
Herbert *Can* 52H4
Herbert I *USA* 56D5
Herbertville *NZ* 51C2
Herborn *W Germ* 16E1
Heredia *Costa Rica* 68A4
Hereford *Eng* 15D5
Hereford *USA* 62B3
Hereford & Worcester County *Eng* 15D5
Herentals *Belg* 16C1
Héricourt *France* 17B1
Herington *USA* 63C2
Heriot *NZ* 51A3
Herisau *Switz* 17C1
Herkimer *USA* 60C1
Hermagor *Austria* 17E1
Herma Ness Pen *Scot* 14E1
Hermidale *Aust* 50C2
Hermitage *NZ* 51B2
Hermit Is *PNG* 48D1
Hermon,Mt = Jebel ash Shaykh
Hermosillo *Mexico* 66A2
Hernandarias *Par* 73B4
Herndon *USA* 60B2
Herne *W Germ* 16D1
Herning *Den* 20B1
Herowābad *Iran* 34B1
Herradura *Arg* 73A4
Herrera *Arg* 72C1
Herrera del Duque *Spain* 19B2
Herschel I *Can* 56L2
Hershey *USA* 60B2
Hertford County *Eng* 15E6
Herzliyya *Israel* 31C2
Hesbaye Region *Belg* 16C1
Hesdin *France* 16A1
Heshui *China* 40B2
Hess R *Can* 56M3
Hessen State *W Germ* 20B2
Hettinger *USA* 57B2
Heweth Oilfield *N Sea* 15F5
Hexham *Eng* 14D4
He Xian *China* 40C5
Heyuan *China* 40C5
Heywood *Aust* 50B3
Heze *China* 40D2
Hialeah *USA* 61E4
Hibbing *USA* 57D2
Hickory *USA* 61C1
Hicks Bay *NZ* 51C1
Hicks,Pt *Aust* 50C3
Hico *USA* 63C3
Hidaka-sammyaku Mts *Japan* 42D2
Hidalgo *Mexico* 67C1
Hidalgo State *Mexico* 67C1
Hidalgo del Parral *Mexico* 66B2
Hidrolândia *Brazil* 73C2
Hierro I *Canary Is* 76A2
Higashine *Japan* 42D3
Higashi-suidō Str *Japan* 41B5
High Desert *USA* 64B2
High Island *USA* 63D4
Highland Region *Scot* 14C2
Highlands Falls *USA* 60C2
High Point *USA* 61C1
High Prairie *Can* 52G4
High River *Can* 52G4
High Springs *USA* 61C3
Hightstown *USA* 60C2
High Wycombe *Eng* 15E6
Hiiumaa I *USSR* 12J7
Hiiumaa I *USSR* 24C4
Hijaz Region *S Arabia* 32C1
Hikigawa *Japan* 42C4
Hiko *USA* 65C3
Hikone *Japan* 42C3
Hikurangi *NZ* 51B1
Hildago *Mexico* 54C4
Hildago del Parral *Mexico* 54C4
Hildesheim *W Germ* 20B2
Hillaby,Mt *Barbados* 68Q2
Hill City *USA* 62C2
Hillerød *Den* 20C1
Hillsboro N. Dakota *USA* 57C2
Hillsboro New Hampshire *USA* 60E1
Hillsboro New Mexico *USA* 62A3
Hillsboro Ohio *USA* 58C3
Hillsboro Oregon *USA* 64B1
Hillsboro Texas *USA* 63C3
Hillston *Aust* 50C2
Hillsville *USA* 58C3
Hillswick *Scot* 14E1
Hilton *USA* 60B1
Hilton Head Island *USA* 61C2
Hilvan *Turk* 30C2
Hilversum *Neth* 20B2
Himachal Pradesh State *India* 35D2
Himalaya = Great Himalayan Range
Himalaya Mts *Asia* 29G3
Himatnagar *India* 35C4
Himeji *Japan* 41C5
Himi *Japan* 41D4
Himş *Syria* 25F9
Hinchinbrook Entrance *USA* 56J3
Hinchinbrook I *USA* 56J3
Hindaun *India* 35D3
Hindu Kush Mts *Afghan* 35B1
Hindupur *India* 36B2
Hines Creek *Can* 52G4
Hinganghāt *India* 35D4
Hinggan Ling Upland *China* 41B2
Hingol R *Pak* 35B3
Hingoli *India* 35D5
Hinkley Minnesota *USA* 57D2
Hinnøya I *Nor* 12H5
Hinsdale *USA* 60D1
Hinton *USA* 62C2
Hipolito Itrogoyen *Arg* 72B2
Hirado *Japan* 42A4
Hirado-shima I *Japan* 42A4
Hirakud Res *India* 37B3
Hirfanli Baraji Res *Turk* 30B2
Hirihar *India* 36B2
Hiroo *Japan* 42D2
Hirosaki *Japan* 41E3
Hiroshima *Japan* 41C5
Hirson *France* 16C2
Hirşova *Rom* 23F2
Hirtshals *Den* 20B1
Hisār *India* 35D3
Hisn al 'Abr *S Yemen* 33E3
Hispaniola I *Caribbean* 68C3
Hisyah *Syria* 31D1
Hīt *Iraq* 30D3
Hitachi *Japan* 41E4
Hitachi-Ota *Japan* 42D3
Hitchin *Eng* 15E6
Hitra I *Nor* 12F6
Hiuchi-nada B *Japan* 42B4
Hiwasa *Japan* 42B4
Hiyon R *Israel* 31C3
Hjørring *Den* 20B1
Hka R *Burma* 43B1
Ho *Ghana* 77G4
Hoa Binh *Viet* 43D1
Hoa Da *Viet* 43D3
Hobart *Aust* 50E3
Hobart *USA* 62C3
Hobbs *USA* 62B3
Hobro *Den* 20B1
Hobyo *Somalia* 75D4
Hochalm Spitze Mt *Austria* 17E1
Hochgolling Mt *Austria* 17E1
Ho Chi Minh = Saigon
Hochkonig Mt *Austria* 20C3
Hochon *N Korea* 42A2
Hockenheim *W Germ* 16E2
Hockönig Mt *Austria* 17E1
Hódmezö'hely *Hung* 23E1
Hodonin *Czech* 20D3
Hoek van Holland *Neth* 16C1
Hoengsŏng *S Korea* 42A3
Hoeryong *N Korea* 41B3
Hoeyang *N Korea* 42A3
Hof *W Germ* 20C2
Hofsjökull Mts *Iceland* 12B2
Hōfu *Japan* 41C5
Hoggar Upland *Alg* 76C2
Hohe Acht Mt *W Germ* 16D1
Hohes Gras Mts *W Germ* 16E1
Hohe Tauern Mts *Austria* 17E1
Hohhot *China* 40C1
Höhn *Iceland* 53R3
Hoh Sai Hu L *China* 38C3
Hoh Xil Shan Mts *China* 29G2
Hoima *Uganda* 78D3
Hojāi *India* 37D2
Hojo *Japan* 42B4
Hokianga Harbour B *NZ* 51B1
Hokitika *NZ* 51B2
Hokkaidō *Japan* 41E3
Hokmābād *Iran* 34D1
Hokota *Japan* 42D3
Holbrook *Aust* 50C3
Holbrook *USA* 65D4
Holden *USA* 65D3
Holdenville *USA* 63C2
Holdrege *USA* 62C1
Hole Narsipur *India* 36B2
Holetown *Barbados* 68Q2
Holguín *Cuba* 68B2
Holitika *NZ* 51B2
Holitna R *USA* 56G3
Hollabrunn *Austria* 20D3
Holland *USA* 58B2
Hollidaysburg *USA* 60A2
Hollis *USA* 62C3
Holly Springs *USA* 63E3
Hollywood Florida *USA* 61E4
Holman Island *Can* 52G2
Holmsund *Sweden* 12J6
Holon *Israel* 31C2
Holstebro *Den* 20B1
Holstein *USA* 57C3
Holsteinborg *Greenland* 53N3
Holston R *USA* 61C1
Holt *USA* 58C2
Holton *USA* 63C2
Holy Cross *USA* 56G3
Holyhead *Wales* 15C5
Holy I *Eng* 14E4
Holy I *Wales* 15C5
Holyoke Colorado *USA* 62B1
Holyoke Massachusetts *USA* 60D1
Holzminden *W Germ* 16E1
Homalin *Burma* 37D3
Homburg *W Germ* 16E1
Home B *Can* 53M3
Homer Alaska *USA* 56H4
Homer Louisiana *USA* 63D3
Homer Tunnel *NZ* 51A2
Homerville *USA* 61C2
Homestead *USA* 61E4
Homewood *USA* 61B2
Homnābād *India* 36B1
Homoine *Mozam* 79D6
Hondo New Mexico *USA* 62A3
Hondo Texas *USA* 62C4
Hondo R *Mexico* 66C3
Honduras Republic *C America* 66D3
Honduras,G of *Honduras* 66D3
Hønefoss *Nor* 12G6
Honesdale *USA* 60C2
Honey L *USA* 65B2
Honfleur *France* 16A2
Hong = Nui Con Voi
Hong R *Viet* 43C1
Hon Gai *Viet* 43D1
Hongchŏn *S Korea* 42A3
Hongguo *China* 40A4
Hong Hu L *China* 40C4
Honghui *China* 40B2
Hongjiang *China* 40C4
Hong Kong Colony *S E Asia* 40C5
Hongor *Mongolia* 38E2
Hongshui He R *China* 40B5
Hongsong *S Korea* 42A3
Hongwon *N Korea* 42A3
Hongyuan *China* 40A3
Hongze Hu L *China* 40D3
Honiara *Solomon Is* 49E1
Honjō *Japan* 42D3
Hon Khoai I *Camb* 43C4
Hon Lan I *Viet* 43D3
Honnigsvåg *Nor* 12K4
Honningsvåg *Nor* 24D1
Hon Panjang I *Viet* 43C4
Honshu I *Japan* 41D4
Hood,Mt *USA* 64B1
Hood River *USA* 64B1
Hooker *USA* 62B2
Hook Head C *Irish Rep* 15B5
Hoonah *USA* 52E4
Hoonah *USA* 56L4
Hooper Bay *USA* 56E3
Hoorn *Neth* 20A2
Hoosick Falls *USA* 60D1
Hoover Dam *USA* 54B3
Hope Alaska *USA* 56J3
Hope Arkansas *USA* 63D3
Hopedale *Can* 53M4
Hopen I *Barents S* 26D2
Hopes Advance,C *Can* 53M3
Hopetoun *Aust* 50B3
Hopetown *S Africa* 79C6
Hopewell Pennsylvania *USA* 60A2
Hopewell Virginia *USA* 59D3
Hopkinsville *USA* 58B3
Hoquiam *USA* 64B1
Horasan *Turk* 30D2
Horb *W Germ* 16E2
Hordiyo *Somalia* 75E3
Horgen *Switz* 17C1
Horizon Depth *Pacific O* 47L6
Hormuz,Str of *Oman/Iran* 33G1
Horn *Austria* 20D3
Horn C *Iceland* 53Q3
Hornaday R *Can* 56O2
Hornavan L *Sweden* 12H5
Hornbeck *USA* 63D3
Hornbrook *USA* 64B2
Hornby *NZ* 51B2
Hornell *USA* 60B1
Hornepayne *Can* 53K5
Horn I *USA* 61B2
Horn Mts *Can* 52F3
Hornsea *Eng* 15E5
Horn Uul Mt *Mongolia* 40B1
Horqin-Youyi Qianqi *China* 41A2
Horqin Zuoyi *China* 41A3
Horqueta *Par* 69E2
Horseheads *USA* 60B1
Horsens *Den* 20C1
Horseshoe Bay *Can* 64B1
Horseshoe Bend *USA* 64C2
Horsham *Aust* 50B3
Horsham *Eng* 15E6
Horten *Nor* 12G7
Horton R *Can* 56O2
Hose Mts *Malay* 44D2
Hoshab *Pak* 34E3
Hoshangābād *India* 35D4
Hoshiārpur *India* 35D2
Hospet *India* 36B1
Hoste I *Chile* 69C9
Hotan *China* 29F2
Hot Springs Arkansas *USA* 63D3
Hot Springs S. Dakota *USA* 57B3
Hottah *Can* 52G3
Houdan *France* 16A2
Houghton *USA* 58B1
Houlton *USA* 59F1
Houma *China* 40C2
Houma *USA* 63D4
Houmet Essouq *Tunisia* 77E2
Houndé *U Volta* 77F3
Houqi *China* 41A3
Housatonic R *USA* 60D2
Houston Mississippi *USA* 63E3
Houston Texas *USA* 63C4
Houtman Is *Aust* 48A3
Houtzdale *USA* 60A2
Hovd *Mongolia* 38C2
Hövsgol Nuur L *Mongolia* 38D1
Howard *Aust* 50D1
Howard City *USA* 58B2
Howard P *USA* 56G2
Howe,C *Aust* 50C3
Howe Sd *Can* 64B1
Howland *USA* 59F1
Höxter *W Germ* 16E1
Hoy I *Scot* 14D2
Høyanger *Nor* 12F6
Hoyt Lakes *USA* 57D2
Hradeç-Krâlové *Czech* 20D2
Hranice *Czech* 21D3
Hron R *Czech* 21D3
Hsin-chu *Taiwan* 40E5
Hsipaw *Burma* 37E3
Hsüeh Shan Mt *Taiwan* 40E5
Hsuyong *S Korea* 42A4
Huachi *China* 40B2
Huacho *Peru* 70C6
Huade *China* 40C1
Huaibei *China* 40D3
Huaibin *China* 40D3
Huaide *China* 41A3
Huai He R *China* 40D3
Huaihua *China* 40C4
Huaiji *China* 40C5
Huainan *China* 40D3
Hualapai Peak Mt *USA* 65D3
Hualfin *Arg* 72B1
Hua-lien *Taiwan* 38F4
Huallaga R *Peru* 70C5
Huallanca *Peru* 70C5
Huamachuco *Peru* 70C5
Huambo *Angola* 79B5
Huanan *China* 41C2
Huanay *Bol* 70E7
Huancabamba *Peru* 70C5
Huancavelica *Peru* 70C6
Huancayo *Peru* 70C6
Huangchuan *China* 40D3
Huange He R *China* 40A3
Huang Hai = Yellow S
Huang He R *China* 40D2
Huangling *China* 40B2
Huangliu *China* 43D2
Huangnihe *China* 41B3
Huangpi *China* 40C3
Huangshi *China* 40D3
Huanguelén *Arg* 72C3
Huangyan *China* 40E4
Huanren *China* 41B3
Huānuco *Peru* 70C5
Huanuni *Bol* 69C1
Huan Xian *China* 40B2
Huaráz *Peru* 70C5
Huarmey *Peru* 70C6
Huascarán Mt *Peru* 70C5
Huasco *Chile* 72A1
Huasco R *Chile* 72A1
Huatusco *Mexico* 67C2
Huauchinango *Mexico* 67C1
Huaunamota R *Mexico* 67B1
Huautla *Mexico* 67C2
Hua Xian *China* 40C2
Huayapan R *Mexico* 66B2
Hubei Province *China* 40C3
Huben *Austria* 17E1
Hubli *India* 36B1
Hucal *Arg* 72C3
Huch'ang *N Korea* 41B3
Huddersfield *Eng* 15E5
Hudiksvall *Sweden* 12H6
Hudson Florida *USA* 61C3
Hudson Michigan *USA* 58C2
Hudson New York *USA* 60D1
Hudson R *USA* 60D1
Hudson B *Can* 53K4
Hudson Bay *Can* 52H4
Hudson Falls *USA* 60D1
Hudson Str *Can* 53L3
Hue *Viet* 43D2
Huejuqvilla *Mexico* 67B1
Huejutla *Mexico* 67C1
Huelva *Spain* 19A2
Hueramo *Mexico* 67B2
Húercal Overa *Spain* 19B2
Huertecillas *Mexico* 67B1
Huesca *Spain* 19B1
Huexotla Hist Site *Mexico* 67C2
Hughenden *Aust* 48D3
Hughes *USA* 56H2
Hugli R *India* 37C3
Hugo *USA* 63C3
Hugoton *USA* 62B2
Hui'an *China* 40D4
Huiarau Range Mts *NZ* 51C1
Hüich'ŏn *N Korea* 41B3
Huifa He R *China* 41B3
Huilai *China* 40D5
Huili *China* 40A4
Huillapima *Arg* 72B1
Huimanguillo *Mexico* 67D2
Huinan *China* 41B3
Huinca Renancó *Arg* 72C2
Huisne R *France* 16A2
Huixtla *Mexico* 66C3
Huizache *Mexico* 67B1
Huize *China* 40A4
Huizhou *China* 40C5
Hujuápan de Léon *Mexico* 67C2
Hukawng Valley *Burma* 37E2
Hulan *China* 41B2
Hulayfah *S Arabia* 32D1
Hulin *China* 41C2
Hull *Can* 59D1
Hull *Eng* 15E5
Hull I *Phoenix Is* 49H1
Hulla Mt *Colombia* 70C3
Hultsfred *Sweden* 20D1
Hulun Nur L *China* 27N5
Huma *China* 41B1
Huma He R *China* 41A1
Humaita *Brazil* 70F5
Humansdorp *S Africa* 79C7
Humber R *Eng* 15E5
Humberside County *Eng* 15E5
Humboldt *Can* 52H4
Humboldt Iowa *USA* 57D3
Humboldt Tennessee *USA* 61B1
Humboldt R *USA* 64C2
Humboldt B *USA* 64B2
Humboldt Gletscher Gl *Greenland* 53M2
Humeburn *Aust* 50C1
Hume,L *Aust* 50C3
Humpata *Angola* 79B5
Humphreys Peak Mt Arizona *USA* 65D3
Húnaflóri B *Iceland* 12A1
Hunan Province *China* 40C4
Hunchun *China* 41C3
Hunedoara *Rom* 23E1
Hünfeld *W Germ* 16E1
Hungary Republic *Europe* 21D3
Hungerford *Aust* 50B1
Hŭngnam *N Korea* 41B4
Hungry Horse Res *USA* 64D1
Hunjiang *China* 41B3
Hunsrück Mts *W Germ* 16D2
Hunter R *Aust* 50D2
Hunter Is *Aust* 50E3
Hunter,Mt *USA* 56H3
Huntingburg *USA* 58B3
Huntingdon *Eng* 15E5
Huntingdon Indiana *USA* 58B2
Huntingdon New York *USA* 60D2
Huntingdon Pennsylvania *USA* 60A2
Huntingdon Beach *USA* 65C4
Huntington *USA* 58C3
Huntly *NZ* 51C1
Huntly *Scot* 14D3
Hunt,Mt *Can* 56N3
Hunt Pen *Aust* 50A1
Huntsville Alabama *USA* 61B2
Huntsville *Can* 59D1
Huntsville Texas *USA* 63C3
Huolongmen *China* 41B2
Huong Khe *Viet* 43D2
Huon Peninsula Pen *PNG* 39H7
Huonville *Anst* 50E3
Hurd,C *Can* 58C1
Hurghada *Egypt* 32B1
Hurley *USA* 58A1
Huron S. Dakota *USA* 57C3

Huron,L Ixmiquilpa

Huron,L USA/Can 58C1
Hurtado Chile 72A2
Hurunui R NZ 51B2
Husavik Iceland 12B1
Huşi Rom 23F1
Huskvarna Sweden 12G7
Huslia USA 56G2
Husn Jordan 31C2
Husum W Germ 20B2
Hutchinson USA 63C2
Hutton,Mt Aust 50C1
Hutuo He R China 40D2
Huy Belg 16C1
Huzhu China 40A2
Hvar I Yugos 22D2
Hwadae N Korea 42A2
Hwange Zim 79C5
Hwange Nat Pk Zim 79C5
Hwapyong N Korea 42A2
Hyannis Massachusetts USA 60E2
Hyannis Nebraska USA 57B3
Hyaryas Nuur L Mongolia 38C2
Hydaburg USA 52E4
Hyde Park USA 60D2
Hyderābād India 36B1
Hyderabad Pak 35B3
Hyères France 17B3
Hyland R Can 56N3
Hyndman USA 60A3
Hyndman Peak Mt USA 54B2
Hyrynsalmi Fin 24D3
Hyūga Japan 41C5
Hyvikää Fin 12J6

I

Iaçu Brazil 71K6
Ialomiţa R Rom 23F2
Iärpen Sweden 12G6
Iaşi Rom 23F1
Ibadan Nig 77G4
Ibagué Colombia 70C3
Ibar R Yugos 23E2
Ibarra Ecuador 70C3
Ibb Yemen 32D4
Ibi Nig 77H4
Ibiá Brazil 73C2
Ibicaraí Brazil 73E1
Ibicui R Brazil 72D1
Ibicuy Arg 72D2
Ibirubá Brazil 72E1
Ibiza Spain 19C2
Ibiza I Spain 19C2
Ibo Mozam 79E5
Ibotirama Brazil 71K6
'Ibrī Oman 33G2
Ica Peru 70C6
Icá R Brazil 70E4
Icana Brazil 70E3
Ice B USA 56K4
Iceland Republic N Atlantic O 12A1
Icha USSR 27R4
Ichalkaranji India 36A1
Ichihara Japan 41E4
Ichinomiya Japan 42C3
Ichinoseki Japan 41E4
Icy C USA 56F1
Ida R USSR 27L4
Idabell USA 63D3
Ida Grove USA 57C3
Idah Nig 77H4
Idaho State USA 64D2
Idaho City USA 64C2
Idaho Falls USA 64D2
Idaho Springs USA 62A2
Idanha USA 64B2
Idar Oberstein W Germ 16D2
Idehan Marzūg Desert Libya 75A2
Idehan Ubari Desert Libya 75A2
Idelés Alg 76C2
Iderlym Gol R Mongolia 38C2
Idfu Egypt 32B2
Ídhi Óros Mt Greece 23E3
Ídhra I Greece 23E3
Idiofa Zaïre 78B4
Iditarod R USA 56G3
Idlib Syria 30C2
Idrija Yugos 17E2
Idritsa USSR 12K7
Idutywa S Africa 79C7
Ierápetra Greece 23F3
Iesi Italy 17E3
Ifakara Tanz 79D4
Ifalik I Pacific 39H6
Ifanadiana Madag 79E6
Ife Nig 77G4
Iférouane Niger 76C3
Igan Malay 44D2
Igaranava Brazil 73C3
Igarka USSR 26K3
Igatimi Par 73A3
Igbetti Nig 77G4
Igdir Iran 30E2
Iggesund Sweden 12H6
Iglesias Sardegna 22B3
Igloolik Can 53K3
Ignace Can 55D2
Iğneada Burun Pt Turk 30A1
Ignoitijala Andaman Is 36E2
Igoumenítsa Greece 23E3
Igra USSR 24J4
Igrim USSR 24L3
Iguala Mexico 67C2
Iguape Brazil 69G2
Iguatama Brazil 73C3
Iguatemi Brazil 73B3
Iguatemi R Brazil 73A3
Iguatu Brazil 71L5
Iguéla Gabon 78A4
Igumale Nig 77H4
Ihiala Nig 77H4
Ihosy Madag 79E6
Iida Japan 41D4
Iide-san Mt Japan 42C3
Iisalmi Fin 12K6
Iizuka Japan 42B4
Ijebulgbo Nig 77G4
Ijebu Ode Nig 77G4
Ijsselmeer S Neth 20B2
Ijuí Brazil 72E1
Ijui R Brazil 72D1
Ikaría I Greece 23F3
Ikeda Japan 41E3
Ikela Zaïre 78C4
Ikerre Nig 77H4
Ikhtiman Bulg 23E2
Iki I Japan 42A4
Ikire Nig 77G4
Ikolik,C USA 56H4
Ikopa R Madag 79E5
Ila Nig 77G4
Ilagan Phil 45F7
Ilām Iran 34B2
Ilanskiy USSR 38C1
Ilanz Switz 17C1
Ilaro Nig 77G4
Île De France Region France 16B2
Île de Jerba I Tunisia 77E2
Ile de Noirmoutier I France 18B2
Ile de Ré I France 18B2
Île des Pins I Nouvelle Calédonie 49F3
Ile d'Orleans Can 59E1
Ile d'Ouessant I France 18A2
Ile d'Yeu I France 18B2
Ilek R USSR 25K5
Ile María Cleofas I Mexico 67A1
Ile María Madre I Mexico 67A1
Ile María Magdalena Mexico 67A1
Ile San Juanico I Mexico 67A1
Îles Bélèp Nouvelle Calédonie 49F2
Îles Chesterfield Nouvelle Calédonie 49E2
Îles de Horn Is Pacific O 49H2
Iles d'Hyleres Is France 18D3
Ilesha Nig 77G4
Iles Kerkenna Is Tunisia 77E2
Ilfracombe Eng 15C6
Ilgaz Dağları Mts Turk 30B1
Ilha Bazaruto I Mozam 79D6
Ilha Comprida I Brazil 73C3
Ilha de Boipeba I Brazil 73E1
Ilha De Maracá I Brazil 71H3
Ilha de Marajó I Brazil 71H4
Ilha de São Francisco I Brazil 73C4
Ilha de São Sebastião I Brazil 73C3
Ilha de Tinharé I Brazil 73E1
Ilha do Bananal Region Brazil 71H6
Ilha do Cardoso I Brazil 73C4
Ilha Grande I Brazil 73D3
Ilha Grande ou Sete Quedas I Brazil 73B3
Ilha Santo Amaro I Brazil 73C3
Ilhas Selvegens I Atlantic O 76A2
Ilhéus Brazil 71L6
Iliamna L USA 56G4
Iliamna V USA 56H3
Iliers France 16A2
Iligan Phil 45F9
Ilim R USSR 38D1
Il'inskiy USSR 41E2
Iliodhrómia I Greece 23E3
Ilion USA 60C1
Illana B Phil 45F9
Illapel Chile 72A2
Illapel R Chile 72A2
Illéla Niger 76C3
Iller R W Germ 17D1
Illescas Mexico 67B1
Îlles Wallis Is Pacific O 49H2
Illiamna L USA 52C4
Illinois State USA 58B2
Illinois R USA 58A3
Illizi Alg 76C2
Ilo Peru 70D7
Iloilo Phil 45F8
Ilomantsi Fin 12L6
Ilorin Nig 77G4
Ilwaki Indon 45C4
Il'yino USSR 21G1
Imabari Japan 42B4
Imalchi Japan 42C3
Imari Japan 42A4
Imatra Fin 24D3
Imbituba Brazil 69G3
Imbitura Brazil 73B4
Imi Eth 78E3
Imjin R N Korea 42A3
Imlay USA 64C2
Immenstadt W Germ 17D1
Imo State Nig 77H4
Imola Italy 22C2
Imperatriz Brazil 71J5
Imperia Italy 22B2
Imperial USA 62B1
Imperial V USA 65C4
Impfondo Congo 78B3
Imphāl India 37D3
Imst Austria 17D1
Imuruk L USA 56F2
Ina Japan 42C3
In Afahleleh Well Alg 76C2
In Amenas Alg 76C2
Inamba-jima I Japan 42C4
Inari Fin 12K5
Inarijärvi L Fin 12K5
Inawashiro-ko L Japan 42D3
In Belbel Alg 76C2
Ince Burun Pt Turk 25F7
Incekum Burun Pt Turk 30B2
Inch'ŏn S Korea 41B4
In Dagouber Well Mali 76B2
Indais R Brazil 73C2
Indals R Sweden 12H6
Indefatigable Gasfield N Sea 15G5
Independence Iowa USA 57D3
Independence Kansas USA 63C2
Independence Missouri USA 63D2
Independence USA 65C3
Independence Mts USA 64C2
Inderagiri R Indon 44B3
Inderborskly USSR 25J6
India Federal Republic Asia 29F4
Indiana State USA 58B2
Indiana USA 59D2
Indian-Antarctic Basin Indian O 46F7
Indian-Antarctic Ridge Indian O 46F7
Indianapolis USA 58B3
Indian Desert = Thar Desert
Indian Harbour Can 53N4
Indian O 46E5
Indianola Iowa USA 63D1
Indianola Mississippi USA 63D3
Indianópolis Brazil 73C2
Indian Springs USA 65C3
Indiga USSR 24H2
Indigirka R USSR 27Q3
Indo China Region S E Asia 43D2
Indonesia Republic S E Asia 39F7
Indore India 35D4
Indramayu Indon 44C4
Indre R France 18C2
Indus R Pak 35B3
Inebdu Turk 25E7
In Ebeggi Well Alg 76C2
Inebolu Turk 30B1
In Ecker Alg 76C2
Inegöl Turk 30A1
In Ezzane Alg 76D2
Ingal Niger 76C3
Ingersoll Can 58C2
Ingham Aust 48D2
Inglefield Land Region Can 53M2
Inglewood NZ 51B1
Inglewood Queensland Aust 50D1
Inglewood Victoria Aust 50B3
Ingólfshöfði I Iceland 12B2
Ingolstadt W Germ 20C3
Ingrāj Bāzār India 37C3
In-Guezzam Well Alg 76C3
Inhambane Mozam 79D6
Inharrime Mozam 79D6
Inhumas Brazil 73C2
Inirida R Colombia 70E3
Inishowen District Irish Rep 14B4
Injune Aust 50C1
Inklin R Can 56M4
Inland L USA 56G2
Inn R Austria 17D1
Innamincka Aust 50B1
Inner Mongolia Autonomous Region China 38D2
Innisfail Aust 48D2
Innokent'yevskiy USSR 41E2
Innoko R USA 56G3
Innsbruck Austria 20C3
Inongo Zaïre 78B4
Inoucdjouac Can 53L4
Inowrocław Pol 21D2
In Salah Alg 76C2
Insil S Korea 42A3
Inta USSR 24K2
Interlaken Switz 17B1
International Date Line 49H3
International Falls USA 57D2
Intiyaco Arg 72C1
Intra Italy 17C2
Intu Indon 44E3
Inubo-saki C Japan 42D3
Inuvik Can 52E3
Inveraray Scot 14C3
Invercargill NZ 51A3
Inverell Aust 50D1
Inverness Scot 14C2
Inverurie Scot 14D3
Investigator Str Aust 50A3
Inya USSR 38B1
Inya R USSR 27Q3
Inyanga Zim 79D5
Inyokern USA 65C3
Inzia R Zaïre 78B4
Ioánnina Greece 23E3
Iola USA 63C2
Iolotan USSR 34E1
Iona I Scot 14B3
Iôna Nat Pk Angola 79B5
Ione USA 64C1
Ionian Is = Iónioi Nísoi
Ionian S Italy/Greece 23D3
Iónioi Nísoi Is Greece 23E3
Ioniveyem R USSR 56D2
Íos I Greece 23F3
Iowa State USA 57D3
Iowa R USA 57D3
Iowa City USA 58A2
Iowa Falls USA 57D3
Ipameri Brazil 73C2
Ipanema Brazil 73D2
Ipatovo USSR 25G6
Ipiales Colombia 70C3
Ipiaú Brazil 73E1
Ipiranga Brazil 73B4
Ipoh Malay 43C5
Iporá Brazil 71H7
Ipsala Turk 23F2
Ipswich Aust 50D1
Ipswich Eng 15F5
Ipswich USA 60E1
Iput R USSR 21G2
Iquape Brazil 73C3
Iquique Chile 69B2
Iquitos Peru 70D4
Irai Brazil 72E1
Iráklion Greece 23F3
Iran Republic S W Asia 28D2
Irānshahr Iran 34E3
Irapuato Mexico 67B1
Iraq Republic S W Asia 30D3
Irati Brazil 73B4
Irā Wan Watercourse Libya 75A2
Irbid Jordan 31C2
Irbit USSR 24L4
Irbit USSR 26H4
Ireng R Guyana 71G3
Iri S Korea 41B4
Irian Jaya Province Indon 39G7
Iriba Chad 78C2
Iriga Phil 45F8
Iringa Tanz 79D4
Iriomote I Japan 38F4
Iriona Honduras 68A3
Iriri R Brazil 71H5
Irish S Eng/Irish Rep 15C5
Irkillik R USA 56H2
Irkutsk USSR 27M4
Irlysh USSR 26J4
Iron Knob Aust 50A2
Iron Mountain USA 58B1
Iron Range Aust 48D2
Iron River USA 58B1
Irontown USA 58C3
Ironwood USA 58A1
Iroquois Falls Can 55E2
Iro-zaki C Japan 42C4
Irrawaddy R Burma 37E4
Irrawaddy,Mouths of the Burma 43A2
Irtysh R USSR 26H4
Irun Spain 19B1
Irvine Scot 14C4
Irving USA 63C3
Isa Nig 77H3
Isabela Phil 45F9
Isachsen Can 52H2
Isachsen,C Can 52H2
Isafjörður Iceland 53Q3
Isahaya Japan 41C5
Isangi Zaïre 78C3
Isar R W Germ 17D1
Isarco R Italy 17D1
Isbister Scot 14E1
Ischgl Austria 17D1
Ischia I Italy 22C2
Ise Japan 42C4
Iseo Italy 17D2
Isère R France 17A2
Iserlohn W Germ 16D1
Isernia Italy 22C2
Ise-wan B Japan 42C4
Iseyin Nig 77G4
Ishigaki I Japan 38F4
Ishikari R Japan 41E3
Ishikari-wan B Japan 41E3
Ishim USSR 26H4
Ishim R USSR 26H4
Ishinomaki Japan 41E4
Ishioka Japan 42D3
Ishkashim Afghan 35C1
Ishpeming USA 58B1
Isil'kul USSR 26J4
Isimu Indon 45B2
Isiolo Kenya 78D3
Isiro Zaïre 78C3
Iskenderun Turk 30C2
Iskenferun Körfezi B Turk 30C2
Iskilip Turk 30B1
Iskitim USSR 26K4
Iskur R Bulg 23E2
Iskut R Can/USA 56M4
Isla Mexico 67C2
Isla Apipe Grande Arg 72D1
Isla Beata Dom Rep 68C3
Isla Bermejo I Arg 72C3
Isla Blanquilla Ven 68E4
Isla Coiba I Panama 70B2
Isla de Cedros I Mexico 54B4
Isla de Chiloé I Chile 69B6
Isla de Cozumel I Mexico 66D2
Isla de la Gonâve Cuba 68C3
Isla de la Juventud I Cuba 68A2
Isla de las Lechiguanas I Arg 72D2
Isla del Maiz I Caribbean 66D3
Isla de Lobos I Mexico 67C1
Isla de los Estados I Arg 69D8
Isla de Pascua I Pacific O 47O6
Isla de Providencia I Caribbean 68A4
Isla de San Andres I Caribbean 68A4
Isla de Santa Catarina I Brazil 69G3
Isla du Diable I French Guiana 71H2
Isla Fernando de Noronha I Brazil 71M4
Isla Grande de Tierra del Fuego I Arg/Chile 69C8
Isla la Tortuga I Ven 68D4
Islamabad Pak 35C2
Isla Magdalena I Mexico 66A2
Isla Margarita Ven 68E4
Isla Mocha Chile 72A3
Islamorada USA 61E4
Island L Can 55D1
Island Lg Aust 50A2
Island Park USA 64D2
Islands,B of NZ 51B1
Isla Providencia I Colombia 70B1
Isla Puná I Ecuador 70B4
Isla San Ambrosia I Pacific O 74D6
Isla San Felix I Pacific O 74D6
Isla Santa Margarita I Mexico 66A2
Isla Santa Maria I Chile 72A3
Islas Baleares Is Spain 19C2
Islas Canarias Is Atlantic O 76A2
Islas Columbretes Is Spain 19C2
Islas de la Bahia Is Honduras 66D3
Islas del Maíz Is Caribbean 68A4
Islas de Margarita Is Ven 70F1
Islas Diego Ramírez Is Chile 69C9
Islas Galapagos Is Pacific O 70N
Islas Juan Fernandez Is Pacific O 70Q
Islas los Roques Is Ven 70E1
Islas Malvinas = Falkland Is
Islas Revilla Gigedo Is Pacific O 47O4
Islas Wollaston Is Chile 69C9
Isla Tidra I Maur 76A3
Isla Wellington I Chile 69B7
Islay I Scot 14B4
Isle R France 18C2
Isle Amsterdam I Indian O 46E6
Isle au Haut I USA 59F2
Isle of Wight I Eng 15E6
Isle Royale I USA 58B1
Isle St Paul I Indian O 46E6
Îsles Crozet I Indian O 46D7
Îsles de la Société Pacific O 47M5
Îsles Gambier Is Pacific O 47N6
Isles Glorieuses Is Madag 79E5
Îsles Kerguelen Is Indian O 46E7
Îsles Loyauté Is Nouvelle Calédonie 49F3
Îsles Marquises Is Pacific O 47N5
Îsles Tuamotu Is Pacific O 47M6
Îsles Tubai Is Pacific O 47M6
Ismâ'ilîya Egypt 30B3
Isna Egypt 32B1
Isoanala Madag 79E6
Isoka Zambia 79D5
Isola di Capraia I Italy 17C3
Isola Egadi I Italy 22C3
Isola Ponziane I Italy 22C2
Isole Lipari Is Italy 22C3
Isoles Tremiti Is Italy 22D2
Isosaki Japan 42C3
Isparta Turk 30B2
Israel Republic S W Asia 31C2
Isser R Alg 19C2
Issoire France 18C2
Issoudun France 18C2
Is-sur-Tille France 17A1
Istanbul Turk 30A1
Istiáia Greece 23E3
Istmo de Tehuantepec Isthmus Mexico 67D2
Istokpoga,L USA 61E4
Istra Pen Yugos 22C1
Istranca Dağlari Upland Turk 23F2
Itaberai Brazil 73C2
Itabira Brazil 73D2
Itabirito Brazil 73D3
Itabuna Brazil 73E1
Itacaré Brazil 73E1
Itacoatiara Brazil 71G4
Itacurubi del Rosario Par 73A3
Itagui Colombia 70C2
Itaituba Brazil 71G4
Itajaí Brazil 69G3
Itajuba Brazil 73C3
Italy Repubic Europe 22C2
Itamaraju Brazil 73E2
Itamarandiba Brazil 73D2
Itambacuri Brazil 73D2
Itambe Brazil 73D2
Itambé Mt Brazil 73D2
Itānagar India 37D2
Itanhaém Brazil 73C3
Itanhém Brazil 73D2
Itanhém R Brazil 73D2
Itaobím Brazil 73D2
Itapaci Brazil 73C1
Itapecerica Brazil 73C3
Itaperuna Brazil 73D3
Itapetinga Brazil 71K7
Itapetininga Brazil 73C3
Itapeva Brazil 73C3
Itapipoca Brazil 71L4
Itapuranga Brazil 73C2
Itaquari R Brazil 73C1
Itaqui Brazil 72D1
Itarantim Brazil 73D2
Itararé Brazil 73C3
Itararé R Brazil 73C3
Itaúna Brazil 73D3
Iténez R Brazil/Bol 70F6
Ithaca USA 59D2
Ith Hills Mts W Germ 16E1
Itimbiri R Zaïre 78C3
Itinga Brazil 73D2
Itiquira R Brazil 73A2
Itivdleg Greenland 53N3
Itjørdal Nor 12G6
Ito Japan 42C4
Itoigawa Japan 41D4
Iton R France 16A2
Itonomas R Bol 70F6
Itu Brazil 73C3
Itu Nig 77H4
Ituberá Brazil 73E1
Itumbiara Brazil 73C2
Iturama Brazil 73B2
Iturbe Arg 69C2
Iturbide Mexico 67C1
Iturutaba Brazil 73C2
Ituzzaingó Arg 72D1
Itzehoe W Germ 20B2
Iul'tin USSR 27T3
Iurga USSR 26K4
Ivacevichi USSR 21F2
Ivai R Brazil 73B3
Ivalo Fin 12K5
Ivangrad Yugos 23D2
Ivanhoe Aust 50B2
Ivano USSR 26D5
Ivano-Frankovsk USSR 21E3
Ivanovo USSR 24G4
Ivdel' USSR 24L3
Ivindo R Gabon 78B3
Ivinhema Brazil 73B3
Ivinhema R Brazil 73B3
Ivohibe Madag 79E6
Ivongo Soanierana Madag 79E5
Ivory Coast Republic Africa 76B4
Ivrea Italy 22B1
Ivugivie Can 53L3
Iwaki Japan 41E4
Iwaki R Japan 42D2
Iwaki-san Mt Japan 42D2
Iwakuni Japan 41C5
Iwamizawa Japan 42D2
Iwanai Japan 41E3
Iwo Nig 77G4
Iwo Jima I Japan 38H4
Ixcuintla Mexico 67B1
Ixmiquilpa Mexico 67C1

Ixtapa Kākināda

Ixtapa *Mexico* 67B2
Ixtepec *Mexico* 67C2
Ixtlán *Mexico* 67B1
Iyo *Japan* 42B4
Iyo-nada B *Japan* 42B4
Izhevsk *USSR* 26G4
Izhma *USSR* 24J2
Izhma R *USSR* 24J2
Izigan,C *USA* 56E5
Izkī *Oman* 33G2
Izmail *USSR* 21F3
Izmir *Turk* 30A2
Izmir Körfezi B *Turk* 23F3
Izmit *Turk* 30A1
Iznik *Turk* 30A1
Iznik Golü L *Turk* 23F2
Izra' *Syria* 31D2
Izúcar de Matamoros *Mexico* 67C2
Izuhara *Japan* 42A4
Izumi-sano *Japan* 42C4
Izumo *Japan* 42B3
Izu-shotō Is *Japan* 41D5
Izvestkovyy *USSR* 41C2

J

Jabal al Akhdar Mts *Libya* 75B1
Jabal al 'Arab *Syria* 31D2
Jabal al Qara' Mts *Oman* 33F3
Jabal an Nuşayrīyah Mts *Syria* 31D1
Jabal as Sawdā Mts *Libya* 75A2
Jabal az Zannah *UAE* 33F2
Jabal Halīmah Mt *Syria/Leb* 31D1
Jabal Mahrāt Mts *S Yemen* 33F3
Jabalpur *India* 37B3
Jabal Shammar Region *S Arabia* 32D1
Jabal Tuwayq Mts *S Arabia* 33E2
Jablah *Syria* 31C1
Jablonec nad Nisou *Czech* 20D2
Jaboatão *Brazil* 71L5
Jaca *Spain* 19B1
Jacala *Mexico* 67C1
Jacareacanga *Brazil* 71G5
Jacarezinho *Brazil* 71H8
Jacarie *Brazil* 73C3
Jáchal *Arg* 69C4
Jaciara *Brazil* 73B2
Jacinto *Brazil* 73D2
Jackman *USA* 59E1
Jacksboro *USA* 62C3
Jacks Mt *USA* 60B2
Jackson Alabama *USA* 61B2
Jackson *Aust* 50C1
Jackson Michigan *USA* 58C2
Jackson Minnesota *USA* 57D3
Jackson Mississippi *USA* 63D3
Jackson Missouri *USA* 58B3
Jackson Ohio *USA* 58C3
Jackson Tennessee *USA* 61B1
Jackson Wyoming *USA* 64D2
Jackson,C *NZ* 51B2
Jackson Head Pt *NZ* 51A2
Jackson L *USA* 64D2
Jacksonville Arkansas *USA* 63D3
Jacksonville Florida *USA* 61C2
Jacksonville Illinois *USA* 58A3
Jacksonville N Carolina *USA* 61D2
Jacksonville Texas *USA* 63C3
Jacksonville Beach *USA* 61C2
Jacmel *Haiti* 68C3
Jacobabad *Pak* 35B3
Jacobina *Brazil* 71K6
Jacona *Mexico* 67B2
Jacui R *Brazil* 72E1
Jādib *S Yemen* 33F3
Jadotville = Likasi
Jaén *Peru* 70C5
Jaén *Spain* 19B2
Jaffa = Tel Aviv Yafo
Jaffa,C *Aust* 50A3
Jaffna *Sri Lanka* 36B3
Jaffrey *USA* 60D1
Jagannathganj Ghat *Bang* 37C3
Jagdalpur *India* 36C1
Jagdaqi *China* 41A1
Jagin R *Iran* 34D3
Jagtial *India* 36B1
Jaguaquara *Brazil* 73E1
Jaguarão *Brazil* 72E2
Jaguarão R *Brazil* 72E2
Jaguariaíva *Brazil* 73C3
Jagüé *Arg* 72B1
Jagüé R *Arg* 72B1
Jahan Dāgh Mt *Iran* 25H8
Jahrom *Iran* 34C3
Jailolo *Indon* 45C2
Jāina *India* 35D5
Jainca *China* 40A2
Jaipur *India* 35D3
Jaisalmer *India* 35C3
Jajarm *Iran* 34D1
Jajce *Yugos* 22D2
Jakarta *Indon* 44C4
Jakobshavn *Greenland* 53N3
Jakobstad *Fin* 12J6
Jal *USA* 62B3
Jalaca *Mexico* 67C2
Jalaid Qi *China* 41A2
Jalai-Kut *Afghan* 35B2
Jalapa *Mexico* 67C2
Jales *Brazil* 73B3
Jaleswar *Nepal* 37C2
Jalgaon *India* 35D4
Jalingo *Nig* 77J4
Jalisco State *Mexico* 67A2
Jalón R *Spain* 19B1
Jalo Oasis *Libya* 75B2
Jālor *India* 35C3
Jalostotitlan *Mexico* 67B1
Jalpāiguri *India* 37C2
Jalpan *Mexico* 67C1
Jama *Ecuador* 70B4
Jamaaré R *Nig* 77H3
Jamaica I *Caribbean* 68B3
Jamaica Chan *Caribbean* 68B3
Jamalpur *Bang* 37C3
Jambi *Indon* 44B3
Jambussar *India* 35C4
James R N. Dakota *USA* 57C2
James R Virginia *USA* 59D3
James B *Can* 53K4
Jameston *USA* 52J5
Jamestown *Aust* 50A2
Jamestown N. Dakota *USA* 57C2
Jamestown New York *USA* 59D2
Jamestown Rhode Island *USA* 60E2
Jamiltepec *Mexico* 67C2
Jamkhandi *India* 36B1
Jammu *India* 35C2
Jammu and Kashmir State *India* 35D2
Jamnagar *India* 35B4
Jampur *Pak* 35C3
Jämsä *Fin* 24C3
Jamshedpur *India* 37C3
Janakpur *Nepal* 37C2
Janaúba *Brazil* 73D2
Jandaq *Iran* 34C2
Jandowae *Aust* 50D1
Janesville *USA* 58B2
Jan Mayen I *Norwegian S* 80B1
Januária *Brazil* 73D2
Jaora *India* 35D4
Japan Empire *E Asia* 41
Japan,S of *S E Asia* 41C4
Japan Trench *Pacific O* 46J3
Japurá R *Brazil* 70E4
Jarābulus *Syria* 30C2
Jaraguá *Brazil* 73C2
Jaraguari *Brazil* 73B3
Jarama R *Spain* 19B1
Jarash *Jordan* 31C2
Jardim *Brazil* 73A3
Jardin R *Spain* 19B2
Jardines de la Reina Is *Cuba* 68B2
Jargalant = Hovd
Jari R *Brazil* 71H3
Jaria Jhānjail *Bang* 37D2
Jarny *France* 16C2
Jarocin *Pol* 20D2
Jaroslaw *Pol* 21E2
Järpen *Sweden* 24A3
Jartai *China* 40B2
Jasdan *India* 35C4
Jasikan *Ghana* 77G4
Jāsk *Iran* 34D3
Jaslo *Pol* 21E3
Jason Is *Falkland Is* 69D8
Jasper Alabama *USA* 61B2
Jasper Arkansas *USA* 63D2
Jasper Florida *USA* 61C2
Jasper Indiana *USA* 58B3
Jasper Texas *USA* 63D3
Jasper Park *Can* 52G4
Jastrowie *Pol* 20D2
Jataí *Brazil* 73B2
Játiva *Spain* 19B2
Jatobá *Brazil* 71J4
Jau *Brazil* 73C3
Jauja *Peru* 70C6
Jaumave *Mexico* 67C1
Jaunpur *India* 37B2
Java = Jawa
Javadi Hills *India* 36B2
Javand *Afghan* 34E1
Javari = Yavari
Java S *Indon* 39D7
Java Trench *Indon* 48A2
Jawa I *Indon* 44C4
Jayapura *Indon* 39H7
Jayrūd *Syria* 31D2
Jazā'ir Farasān Is *S Arabia* 32D3
Jazīrat Maşīrah I *Oman* 33G2
Jazminal *Mexico* 67B1
Jbel Ayachi Mt *Mor* 77B2
Jbel Ouarkziz Mts *Mor* 76B2
Jbel Sarhro Mt *Mor* 76B1
Jeanerette *USA* 63D4
Jebba *Nig* 77G4
Jebel 'Abd al 'Azīz Mt *Syria* 30D2
Jebel Abyad Desert Region *Sudan* 78C2
Jebel Akhdar Mt *Oman* 33G2
Jebel al Lawz Mt *S Arabia* 30C4
Jebel ash Shaykh Mt *Syria* 31C2
Jebel Asoteriba Mt *Sudan* 78D1
Jebel az Zāwīyah Upland *Syria* 31D1
Jebel Bāqir Mt *Jordan* 31C4
Jebel Belaia Mt *Eth* 32C4
Jebel Ed Dabab Mt *Jordan* 31C3
Jebel el Ata'ita Mt *Jordan* 31C3
Jebel el Harad Mt *Jordan* 31C4
Jebel esh Sharqi Mts *Leb/Syria* 30C3
Jebel Hamoyet Mt *Sudan* 32C3
Jebel Hārūn Mt *Jordan* 31C3
Jebel Ithrīyat Mt *Jordan* 31D3
Jebel Ja'lan Mt *Oman* 33G2
Jebel Liban Mts *Leb* 31C2
Jebel Ma'lūlā Mt *Syria* 31D2
Jebel Marra Mt *Sudan* 78C2
Jebel Mubrak Mt *Jordan* 31C3
Jebel Mudeisisat Mt *Jordan* 31D3
Jebel Oda Mt *Sudan* 32C2
Jebel Qasr ed Deir Mt *Jordan* 31C3
Jebel Qatim Mt *Jordan* 31C4
Jebel Ram *Jordan* 31C4
Jebel Um ed Daraj Mt *Jordan* 31C2
Jebel Um el Hashim Mt *Jordan* 31C4
Jebel Um Ishrīn Mt *Jordan* 31C4
Jebel Uweinat Mt *Sudan* 78C1
Jedburgh *Scot* 14D4
Jedda = Jiddah
Jedrzejów *Pol* 21E2
Jefferson Iowa *USA* 57D3
Jefferson Texas *USA* 63D3
Jefferson R *USA* 64D1
Jefferson City *USA* 55D3
Jefferson,Mt *USA* 54B3
Jeffersonville *USA* 58B3
Jega *Nig* 77G3
Jejui-Guazú R *Par* 73A3
Jekabpils *USSR* 24D4
Jelena Gora *Pol* 20D2
Jelgava *USSR* 24C4
Jember *Indon* 44D4
Jemez Pueblo *USA* 62A2
Jena *E Germ* 20C2
Jenaja I *Indon* 44C2
Jenbach *Austria* 17D1
Jendouba *Tunisia* 77D1
Jenin *Israel* 31C2
Jennings *USA* 63D3
Jenseniky Upland *Czech* 20D2
Jensen Nunatakker Mt *Greenland* 53O3
Jens Munk I *Can* 53K3
Jeparit *Aust* 50B3
Jequié *Brazil* 71L6
Jequital R *Brazil* 73D2
Jequitinhonha *Brazil* 73D2
Jequitinhonha R *Brazil* 71K7
Jerada *Mor* 77B2
Jerantut *Malay* 44G7
Jerez *Mexico* 67B1
Jerez de la Frontera *Spain* 19A2
Jerez de los Caballeros *Spain* 19A2
Jericho *Israel* 31C3
Jerilderie *Aust* 50C3
Jerome *USA* 64D2
Jersey I *UK* 18B2
Jersey City *USA* 55F2
Jersey Shore *USA* 59D2
Jerseyville *USA* 58A3
Jerusalem *Israel* 30C3
Jervis B *Aust* 50D3
Jesenice *Yugos* 22C1
Jessore *Bang* 37C3
Jesup *USA* 55E3
Jesus Carranza *Mexico* 67D2
Jesus Maria *Arg* 72C2
Jetmore *USA* 62C2
Jewett City *USA* 60E2
Jeypore *India* 36C1
Jezerce Mt *Alb* 23D2
Jezioro Mamry L *Pol* 21E2
Jezioro Śniardwy L *Pol* 21E2
Jezzine *Leb* 31C2
Jhābua *India* 35C4
Jhālāwār *India* 35D4
Jhang Maghiana *Pak* 35C2
Jhānsi *India* 35D3
Jhārsuguda *India* 37B3
Jhelum *Pak* 35C2
Jhelum R *Pak* 35C2
J H Kerr L *USA* 55F3
Jhunjhunūn *India* 35D3
Jiamusi *China* 41C2
Ji'an Jiangxi *China* 40C4
Ji'an Jilin *China* 41B3
Jiande *China* 40D4
Jiang'an *China* 40B4
Jiangbiancun *China* 40D4
Jiangcheng *China* 40A5
Jiang Jiang R *China* 40B3
Jiangjin *China* 53B4
Jiangmen *China* 40C5
Jiangsu Province *China* 40D3
Jiangxi Province *China* 40C4
Jiangyou *China* 40A3
Jianping *China* 40D1
Jianshui *China* 40A5
Jian Xi R *China* 40D4
Jianyang *China* 40D4
Jiaohe *China* 41B3
Jiaonan *China* 40E2
Jiao Xian *China* 40E2
Jiaozhou Wan B *China* 40E2
Jiaozuo *China* 40C2
Jiaxiang *China* 40E3
Jiayin *China* 41C2
Jiayuguan *China* 38C3
Jiddah *S Arabia* 32C2
Jiddat Al Harāsīs Region *Oman* 33G3
Jiddat az Zawlīyah Region *Oman* 33G2
Jieshou *China* 40D3
Jiexiu *China* 40C2
Jigzhi *China* 40A3
Jihlava *Czech* 20D3
Jijel *Alg* 77D1
Jilib *Somalia* 78E3
Jilin *China* 41B3
Jilin Province *China* 41B3
Jiliu He R *China* 41A1
Jiloca R *Spain* 19B1
Jiménez Coahuila *Mexico* 62B4
Jiménez Tamaulipas *Mexico* 67C1
Jimma *Eth* 78D3
Jinan *China* 40D2
Jind *India* 35D3
Jingbian *China* 40B2
Jingdezhen *China* 40D4
Jinghong *China* 43C1
Jingmen *China* 40C3
Jingning *China* 40B2
Jing Xiang *China* 40B4
Jinhua *China* 40D4
Jining Nei Monggol *China* 40C1
Jining Shandong *China* 40D2
Jinja *Uganda* 78D3
Jinping *China* 43C1
Jinsha Jiang R *China* 40A4
Jinshi *China* 40C4
Jinxi *China* 40E1
Jin Xian *China* 40E2
Jinzhou *China* 40E1
Jiparaná R *Brazil* 70F5
Jipijapa *Ecuador* 70B4
Jiquilpan *Mexico* 67B2
Jīroft *Iran* 34D3
Jishou *China* 40B4
Jisr ash Shughūr *Syria* 30C2
Jiu R *Rom* 23E2
Jiujiang *China* 40D4
Jiulong *China* 40A4
Jiulong Jiang R *China* 40D4
Jiutai *China* 41B3
Jiwani *Pak* 34E3
Jixi *China* 41C2
Jiza *Jordan* 31C3
Jīzan *S Arabia* 32D3
Joal *Sen* 76A3
João Monlevade *Brazil* 73D2
João Pessoa *Brazil* 71M5
João Pinheiro *Brazil* 71J7
João Pirheiro *Brazil* 73C2
Joboticabal *Brazil* 73C3
Jocoli *Arg* 72B2
Jodhpur *India* 35C3
Joensuu *Fin* 12K6
Joeuf *France* 16C2
Jogbani *India* 37C2
Jog Falls *India* 36A2
Johannesburg *S Africa* 79C6
Johannesburg *USA* 65C3
Johan Pen *Can* 53L2
John R *USA* 56H2
John Day *USA* 64C2
John Day R *USA* 64B1
John Martin Res *USA* 62B2
John O'Groats *Scot* 14D2
John Redmond Res *USA* 63C2
Johnsonburg *USA* 60A2
Johnson City New York *USA* 60C1
Johnson City Tennessee *USA* 61C1
Johnston *USA* 61C2
Johnston Pt *St Vincent* 68N2
Johnstown New York *USA* 60C1
Johnstown Pennsylvania *USA* 59D2
Johor Bharu *Malay* 43C5
Joigny *France* 18C2
Joinville *Brazil* 69G3
Joinville *France* 16C2
Jok R *USSR* 24J5
Jokkmokk *Sweden* 12H5
Jōl Mts *S Yemen* 33E4
Jolfa *Iran* 25H8
Joliet *USA* 55E2
Joliette *Can* 53L5
Jolo *Phil* 45F9
Jolo I *Phil* 45F9
Joma Mt *China* 29H2
Jonava *USSR* 21E1
Jonê *China* 40A3
Jonesboro Arkansas *USA* 55D3
Jonesboro Arkansas *USA* 58A3
Jonesboro Louisiana *USA* 63D3
Jones Sd *Can* 53K2
Joniśkis *USSR* 21E1
Jönköping *Sweden* 12G7
Jonquière *Can* 59E1
Joplin *USA* 55D3
Jordan Kingdom *S W Asia* 30C3
Jordan Montana *USA* 57A2
Jordan New York *USA* 60B1
Jordan R *Israel* 31C2
Jordan Valley *USA* 64C2
Jordão R *Brazil* 73B4
Jorhāt *India* 37D2
Jörn *Sweden* 24C2
Jorong *Indon* 44D3
Jørpeland *Nor* 12F7
Jos *Nig* 77H4
José Batlle y Ordoñez *Urug* 72E2
Jose Pañganiban *Phil* 45F8
José Pedro Varela *Urug* 72E2
Joseph Bonaparte G *Aust* 48B2
Joseph City *USA* 65D3
Josephine Oilfield *N Sea* 14G3
Jos Plat *Nig* 77H4
Jotunheimen Mt *Nor* 26B3
Jouai'ya *Leb* 31C2
Jounié *Leb* 31C2
Jowal *India* 37D2
Jowhar *Somalia* 78E3
Joy,Mt *Can* 56M3
Juàjeiro *Brazil* 71K5
Juan Aldama *Mexico* 67B1
Juan de Fuca,Str of *USA/Can* 52F5
Juan de Nova I *Mozam Chan* 79E5
Juárez *Arg* 72D3
Juazeiro do Norte *Brazil* 71L5
Juba *Sudan* 78D3
Juba R *Somalia* 78E3
Jubail *Leb* 31C1
Jubbah *S Arabia* 30D3
Jucar R *Spain* 19B2
Juchatengo *Mexico* 67C2
Juchipila R *Mexico* 67B1
Juchitán *Mexico* 67C2
Juchitlan *Mexico* 67B1
Judenburg *Austria* 20C3
Juilaca *Peru* 70D7
Juiling Shan Hills *China* 40C4
Juiz de Fora *Brazil* 71K8
Jujuy State *Arg* 69C2
Julesburg *USA* 62B1
Juli *Peru* 70E7
Julianatop Mt *Suriname* 71G3
Julianehab *Greenland* 53O3
Jülich *W Germ* 16D1
Julijske Alpen Mts *Yugos* 17E1
Júlio de Castilhos *Brazil* 72E1
Jullundur *India* 35D2
Jumla *Nepal* 37B2
Jum Suwwāna Mt *Jordan* 31C3
Jūnāgadh *India* 35C4
Junan *China* 40D2
Junction Texas *USA* 62C3
Junction Utah *USA* 65D3
Junction City *USA* 54D3
Jundiaí *Brazil* 69G2
Juneau *USA* 52E4
Junee *Aust* 48D4
Jungfrau Mt *Switz* 22B1
Juniata R *USA* 60B2
Junín *Arg* 69D4
Junin de los Andes *Arg* 72A3
Junlian *China* 40A4
Juquiá *Brazil* 69G2
Jur R *Sudan* 78C3
Jura I *Scot* 14C4
Jura Mts *France* 18D2
Jura,Sound of Chan *Scot* 14C3
Jurf ed Darāwīsh *Jordan* 31C3
Jūrmala *USSR* 24C4
Juruá R *Brazil* 70E4
Juruena R *Brazil* 71G6
Jusheng *China* 41B2
Jūsīyah *Syria* 31D1
Justo Daract *Arg* 72B2
Jutai R *Brazil* 70E4
Juticalpa *Honduras* 66D3
Jutland = Jylland
Jüymand *Iran* 34D2
Jylland Pen *Den* 20B1
Jyväskyla *Fin* 12K6

K

K2 Mt *China/India* 29F2
Ka R *Nig* 77H3
Kaakhka *USSR* 34D1
Kabaena I *Indon* 48B1
Kabala *Sierra Leone* 76A4
Kabale *Rwanda* 78D4
Kabalo *Zaïre* 78C4
Kabambare *Zaïre* 78C4
Kabarole *Uganda* 78D3
Kabba *Nig* 77H4
Kabia I *Indon* 48B1
Kabinakagami L *Can* 58C1
Kabinda *Zaïre* 78C4
Kabīr R *Syria* 31C1
Kabir Kuh Mts *Iran* 34B2
Kabompo *Zambia* 79C5
Kabompo R *Zambia* 79C5
Kabongo *Zaïre* 79C4
Kabul *Afghan* 35B2
Kaburuang I *Indon* 45C2
Kabushiya *Sudan* 32B3
Kachchh,G of *India* 35B4
Kachkanar *USSR* 24K4
Kachug *USSR* 27M4
Kadan *Burma* 43B3
Kadapongan I *Indon* 44E3
Kadavu I *Fiji* 55G2
Kadi *India* 35C4
Kadina *Aust* 50A2
Kadınhanı *Turk* 30B2
Kadiri *India* 36B2
Kadiyevka *USSR* 25F6
Kadoka *USA* 57B3
Kadoma *Zim* 79C5
Kadugli *Sudan* 78C2
Kaduna *Nig* 77H3
Kaduna State *Nig* 77H3
Kaduna R *Nig* 77H3
Kadūr *India* 36B2
Kadusam Mt *China* 37E2
Kadzherom *USSR* 24K3
Kaechon *N Korea* 42A3
Kaédi *Maur* 76A3
Kaesŏng *N Korea* 41B4
Kafanchan *Nig* 77H4
Kaffrine *Sen* 76A3
Kafr Behum *Syria* 31D1
Kafr Sa'd *Egypt* 31A3
Kafr Saqv *Egypt* 31A3
Kafrūn Bashūr *Syria* 31D1
Kafue *Zambia* 79C5
Kafue R *Zambia* 79C5
Kafue Nat Pk *Zambia* 79C5
Kaga *Japan* 41D4
Kagalaska I *USA* 56C6
Kagamil I *USA* 56D5
Kagan *USSR* 26H6
Kağizman *Turk* 25G7
Kagmar *Sudan* 32B4
Kagoshima *Japan* 41C5
Kagul *USSR* 21F3
Kāhak *Iran* 34D1
Kahama *Tanz* 78D4
Kahan *Pak* 35B3
Kahayan R *Indon* 44D3
Kahemba *Zaïre* 79B4
Kahler Asten Mt *W Germ* 16E1
Kahnūj *Iran* 34D3
Kahoka *USA* 58A2
Kahramanmaraş *Turk* 30C2
Kaiapoi *NZ* 51B2
Kaibab Plat *USA* 65D3
Kaieteur Fall *Guyana* 71G2
Kaifeng *China* 40C3
Kaikohe *NZ* 51B1
Kaikoura *NZ* 49G5
Kaikoura Pen *NZ* 51B2
Kaikoura Range Mts *NZ* 51B2
Kaili *China* 40B4
Kaimana *Indon* 39G7
Kainan *Japan* 42C4
Kainji Res *Nig* 77G3
Kaipara Harbour B *NZ* 51B1
Kaiping *China* 40C5
Kairouan *Tunisia* 77E1
Kaiserslautern *W Germ* 18D2
Kaiserslautern *W Germ* 20B3
Kaishantun *China* 41B3
Kaisiadorys *USSR* 21F2
Kaitaia *NZ* 51B1
Kaitangata *NZ* 51A3
Kaithal *India* 35D3
Kai Xian *China* 40B3
Kaiyuan Liaoning *China* 40A5
Kaiyuan Yunnan *China* 41A3
Kaiyuh Mts *USA* 56G3
Kajaani *Fin* 12K6
Kajaki *Afghan* 35B2
Kajang *Malay* 44F7
Kajiado *Kenya* 78D4
Kajrān *Afghan* 35B2
Kaka *Sudan* 78D2
Kakabeka Falls *Can* 58B1
Kakamega *Kenya* 78D3
Kake *Japan* 42B4
Kake *USA* 56M4
Kakhonak Bay *USA* 56H4
Kakhovskoye Vodokhranilishche Res *USSR* 26E5
Kākī *Iran* 34C3
Kākināda *India* 36C1

Kakogawa Ketia

Kakogawa Japan 42B4
Kaktovik USA 56K1
Kakuda Japan 42D3
Kalaa El Khasba Tunisia 77D1
Kalabahi Indon 45B4
Kalabáka Greece 23E3
Kalabakan Malay 44E2
Kalabo Zambia 79C5
Kalach USSR 25G5
Kalach-na-Donu USSR 25G6
Kaladan R Burma 37D3
Kalahari Desert Botswana 79C6
Kalai-Mor USSR 34E1
Kalajoki Fin 24C3
Kalakan USSR 27N4
Kalakepen Indon 44A2
Kalam Pak 35C1
Kalámai Greece 23E3
Kalamazoo USA 55E2
Kalao I Indon 45B4
Kalaotoa I Indon 45B4
Kalarsh USSR 21F3
Kalat Pak 35B3
Kalban OMan 33G2
Kalecik Turk 30B1
Kaledupa I Indon 45B4
Kalembau I Indon 44E3
Kalémié Zaïre 78C4
Kalevala USSR 24E2
Kalewa Burma 37D3
Kalgin I USA 56H3
Kalgoorlie Aust 48B4
Kali R India 37B2
Kalianda Indon 44C4
Kalibo Phil 45F8
Kalima Zaïre 78C4
Kalimantan Province Indon 44D3
Kálimnos I Greece 23F3
Kālimpang India 37C2
Kalinigrad USSR 12J8
Kalinin USSR 24F4
Kaliningrad USSR 24B5
Kalinkovichi USSR 25D5
Kalinovka USSR 21F3
Kalispell USA 54B2
Kalisz Pol 21D2
Kaliua Tanz 78D4
Kalix R Sweden 12J5
Kalkfeld Namibia 79B6
Kalkrand Namibia 79B6
Kallakoopah R Aust 50A1
Kallávesi L Fin 12K6
Kallonis Kólpos B Greece 23F3
Kalluk USA 52C4
Kalmar Sweden 12H7
Kalmytskaya ASSR Republic USSR 25H6
Kalolio Indon 45B3
Kalomo Zambia 79C5
Kalona USA 58A2
Kalpeni I India 36A2
Kālpi India 35D3
Kalskag USA 56F3
Kaltag USA 56G3
Kaluga USSR 24F5
Kalundborg Den 12G7
Kalush USSR 21E3
Kalyān India 36A1
Kalyandurg India 36B2
Kalyazin USSR 24F4
Kam R Nig 77J4
Kama R USSR 24J3
Kamaishi Japan 41E4
Kamalia Pak 35C2
Kamanawa Mts NZ 51C1
Kamanjab Namibia 79B5
Kamara China 27O4
Kamarān I Yemen 32D3
Kamat Mt India 35D2
Kamban India 36B3
Kambarka USSR 24J4
Kambia Sierra Leone 76A4
Kamchatka Pen USSR 27S4
Kamenets Podolskiy USSR 21F3
Kamenka USSR 24G5
Kamen-na-Obi USSR 26K4
Kamen' Rybolov USSR 41C3
Kamenskoya USSR 27S3
Kamensk-Ural'skiy USSR 24L4
Kamilukuak L Can 52H3
Kamina Zaïre 79C4
Kaminak L Can 53J3
Kaminoyama Japan 42D3
Kamloops Can 52F4
Kamo USSR 30E1
Kamogawa Japan 42D3
Kampala Uganda 78D3
Kampar Malay 43C5
Kampar R Indon 44B2
Kampen Neth 20B2
Kamphaeng Phet Thai 43B2
Kampot Camb 43C3
Kampuchea = Cambodia
Kamsaptar Iran 34E3
Kamskoye Vodokhranilishche Res USSR 24K4
Kāmthi India 35D4
Kamyshin USSR 25H5
Kamyshlov USSR 24L4
Kanaaupscow R Can 53L4
Kanab USA 65D3
Kanaga I USA 56C6
Kanal Yugos 17E1
Kananga Zaïre 78C4
Kanash USSR 24H4
Kanayama Japan 42C3
Kanazawa Japan 41D4
Kanbisha USA 52C3
Kānchipuram India 36B2
Kandahar Afghan 35B2
Kandalaksha USSR 26E3
Kandalakshskaya Guba B USSR 12L5
Kandé Togo 77G4
Kandel Mt W Germ 16D2
Kandi Benin 77G3
Kandos Aust 50C2
Kandy Sri Lanka 36C3
Kane USA 59D2
Kane Basin B Can 53L1
Kanem Desert Region Chad 78B2
Kanevka USSR 24F2
Kanfanar Yugos 17E2
Kangaba Mali 76B3
Kangal Turk 30C2
Kangâmiut Greenland 53N3
Kangān Iran 34C3
Kangar Malay 43C4
Kangaroo I Aust 48C4
Kanga'tsiaq Greenland 53N3
Kangavar Iran 34B2
Kangbao China 40C1
Kangchenjunga Mt Nepal 29G3
Kangding China 40A4
Kangerdlugssuaq B Greenland 53P3
Kangerdlugssvatsaiq B Greenland 53P3
Kangetet Kenya 78D3
Kanggye N Korea 41B3
Kangnŭng S Korea 41B4
Kango Gabon 78B3
Kangto Mt China 38C4
Kang Xian China 40B3
Kanh Hung Viet 43D4
Kaniama Zaïre 79C4
Kani Giri India 36B1
Kanin Nos Pt USSR 26F3
Kankaanpää Fin 12J6
Kankakee USA 58B2
Kankakee R USA 58B2
Kankan Guinea 76B3
Kānker India 37B3
Kannapolis USA 61C1
Kanniyākuman India 36B3
Kano Nig 77H3
Kano State Nig 77H3
Kano R Nig 77H3
Kanorado USA 62B2
Kanoya Japan 41C5
Kānpur India 37B2
Kansas State USA 54D3
Kansas R USA 63C2
Kansas City USA 55D3
Kanshi China 40D5
Kansk USSR 38C1
Kansŏng S Korea 42A3
Kantchari U Volta 77G3
Kanthi India 37C3
Kantishna USA 56H3
Kantishna R USA 56H3
Kanye Botswana 79C6
Kao-hsiung Taiwan 38E4
Kaoka Veld Plain Namibia 79B5
Kaolack Sen 76A3
Kaoma Zambia 79C5
Kapanga Zaïre 79C4
Kap Cort Adelaer C Greenland 53O3
Kap Dalton C Greenland 53Q3
Kapellskär Sweden 12H7
Kap Farvel C Greenland 53O3
Kap Gustav Holm C Greenland 53P3
Kapiri Zambia 79C5
Kapit Malay 44D2
Kaplan USA 63D3
Kaplice Czech 20C3
Kapoe Thai 43B4
Kapona Zaïre 79C4
Kaposvár Hung 23D1
Kap Parry C Can 53L2
Kap Ravn C Greenland 53Q3
Kapsan N Korea 42A2
Kapsukas USSR 24C5
Kapuas R Indon 44C3
Kapunda Aust 50A2
Kapurthala India 35D2
Kapuskasing Can 53K5
Kapuskasing R Can 58C1
Kaputar Mt Aust 50D2
Kapydzhik Mt USSR 25H8
Kapyŏng S Korea 42A3
Kap York C Greenland 53M2
Kara R Togo 77G4
Karabük Turk 30B1
Karacabey Turk 23F2
Karachi Pak 35B4
Karād India 36A1
Kara Daglari Mt Turk 25F7
Karadeniz Boğazi Sd Turk 25D7
Karaftit USSR 38E1
Karaganda USSR 26J5
Karagayly USSR 26J5
Kāraikāl India 36B2
Karaj Iran 34C1
Karak Jordan 30C3
Karak Malay 44F7
Kara Kalpakskaya Republic USSR 26G5
Karakax He R China 35D1
Karakelong I Indon 45C2
Karakoram Mts India 35D1
Karakoram P India/China 35D1
Karakoro R Maur/Sen 76A3
Karakumskiy Kanal USSR 34E1
Karakumy Desert USSR 26G6
Karama Jordan 31C3
Karama R Indon 45A3
Karaman Turk 25E8
Karamay China 26K5
Karamea NZ 51B2
Karamea Bight B NZ 51B2
Karanhk R Turk 25E8
Kāranja India 35D4
Karapınar Turk 30B2
Kara S USSR 26J2
Karasburg Namibia 79B6
Karasjok Nor 12K5
Karasuk USSR 26J4
Karataş Turk 30C2
Kara Tau Mts USSR 26H5
Karathuri Burma 43B3
Karatsu Japan 41B5
Karaul USSR 26K3
Karavostasi Cyprus 31B1
Karawanken Mts Austria 17E1
Karāz Iran 34C3
Karbalā' Iraq 30D3
Karcag Hung 21E3
Kardhítsa Greece 23E3
Karel'skaya ASSR Republic USSR 24E3
Karen Andaman Is 36E2
Karepino USSR 24K3
Karesvando Sweden 12J5
Karet Desert Region Maur 76B2
Kargasok USSR 26K4
Kargopol' USSR 24F3
Karh R Turk 25G8
Kari Nig 77J3
Kariba Zim 79C5
Kariba L Zim/Zambia 79C5
Kariba Dam Zim/Zambia 79C5
Karima Sudan 78D2
Karimata I Indon 44C3
Karimganj Bang 37D3
Karīmnagar India 36B1
Karin Somalia 78E2
Karis Fin 12J6
Karishimbe Mt Zaïre 78C4
Káristos Greece 23E3
Kārkal India 36A2
Karkar I PNG 39H7
Karkheh R Iran 34B2
Karkinitskiy Zaliv B USSR 25E6
Karlik Shan Mt China 27L5
Karlino Pol 20D2
Karl Marx Stadt E Germ 20C2
Karlobag Yugos 22D2
Karlovac Yugos 22D1
Karlovo Bulg 23E2
Karlovy Vary Czech 20C2
Karlshamn Sweden 12G7
Karlskoga Sweden 12G7
Karlskrona Sweden 12H7
Karlsruhe W Germ 20B3
Karlstad Sweden 12G7
Karlstad USA 57C2
Karluk USA 56H4
Karnafuli Res Bang 37D3
Karnal India 35D3
Karnataka State India 36A1
Karnobat Bulg 23F2
Kärnten Province Austria 17E1
Karoi Zim 79C5
Karonga Malawi 79D4
Karora Sudan 78D2
Karossa Indon 45A3
Kárpathos I Greece 23F3
Karrats Fjord Greenland 53N2
Kars Turk 25G7
Karsakpay USSR 26H4
Kārsava USSR 21F1
Karshi USSR 28E2
Karstula Fin 12J6
Kartaba Leb 31C1
Kartal Turk 23F2
Kartaly USSR 24L5
Karthaus USA 60A2
Kārūn R Iran 34B2
Karwa India 37B2
Kārwār India 36A2
Karymskoye USSR 38E1
Kasai R Zaïre 78B4
Kasaji Zaïre 79C5
Kasama Zambia 79D5
Kasanga Tanz 79D4
Kāsaragod India 36A2
Kasba L Can 52H3
Kasba Tadla Mor 77A2
Kasegaluk Lg USA 56F1
Kasempa Zambia 79C5
Kasenga Zaïre 79C5
Kasese Uganda 78D3
Kāshān Iran 34C2
Kashegelok USA 56G3
Kashi China 29F2
Kashima Japan 42B4
Kāshipur India 35D3
Kashiwazaki Japan 41D4
Kashmar Iran 34D1
Kasimov USSR 24G5
Kasiruta I Indon 45C3
Kaskaskia USA 58B3
Kasko Fin 12J6
Kasli USSR 24L4
Kaslo Can 52G5
Kasonga Zaïre 78C4
Kasongo-Lunda Zaïre 79B4
Kásos I Greece 23F3
Kaspiyskiy USSR 25H6
Kassala Sudan 78D2
Kassel W Germ 20B2
Kasserine Tunisia 77D1
Kassinga Angola 79B5
Kastamonou Turk 30B1
Kastélli Greece 23E3
Kastellorizon I Greece 30A2
Kastoría Greece 23E2
Kástron Greece 23F3
Kasugai Japan 41D4
Kasumi Japan 42B3
Kasungu Malawi 79D5
Kasur Pak 35C2
Kataba Zambia 79C5
Katahdin,Mt USA 59F1
Katako-kombe Zaïre 78C4
Katalla USA 52D3
Katangli USSR 27Q4
Katanning Aust 48A4
Katchall I Indian O 36E3
Katerîni Greece 23E2
Kates Needle Mt Can/USA 52E4
Katha Burma 37E3
Katherine Aust 48C2
Kāthiāwār Pen India 35C4
Kathib El Henu Egypt 31B3
Kathmandu Nepal 37C2
Kathua India 35D2
Katihār India 37C2
Katima Mulilo Namibia 79C5
Katmai,Mt USA 52C4
Katmai Nat Mon USA 56H4
Katni India 37B3
Katoomba Aust 50D2
Katowice Pol 21D2
Katrineholm Sweden 12H7
Katsina Nig 77H3
Katsina Ala Nig 77H4
Katsina Ala R Nig 77H4
Katsuta Japan 42D3
Katsuura Japan 42D3
Katsuy Japan 42C3
Kattakurgan USSR 26H5
Kattegat Str Denmark/Sweden 12G7
Katzenbuckel Mt W Germ 16E2
Kau Indon 45C2
Kaunas USSR 24C5
Kaura Namoda Nig 77H3
Kautokeino Nor 12J5
Kavadarci Yugos 23E2
Kavajë Alb 23D2
Kavalerovo USSR 41D3
Kavali India 36B2
Kavála Greece 23E2
Kāvda India 35B4
Kavieng PNG 48E1
Kawagoe Japan 42C3
Kawaguchi Japan 42C3
Kawakawa NZ 51B1
Kawambwa Zambia 79C4
Kawardha India 37B3
Kawartha Lakes Can 59D2
Kawasaki Japan 41D4
Kawerau NZ 51C1
Kawhia NZ 51B1
Kaya U Volta 77F3
Kayak I USA 56K4
Kayan R Indon 44E2
Kāyankulam India 36B3
Kaycee USA 57A3
Kayeli Indon 45C3
Kayenta USA 65D3
Kayes Mali 76A3
Kayseri Turk 25F8
Kazach'ye USSR 27P2
Kazakh USSR 30E1
Kazakhskaya SSR Republic USSR 26G5
Kazan' USSR 24H4
Kazanlük Bulg 23F2
Kazan Retto Is Japan 38H4
Kazatin USSR 21F3
Kazbek Mt USSR 25G7
Kāzerūn Iran 34C3
Kazhim USSR 24J3
Kazi Magomed USSR 30E1
Kazincbarcika Hung 21E3
Kazym R USSR 24M3
Kazymskaya USSR 24M3
Kéa I Greece 23E3
Kearney Arizona USA 65D4
Kearney Nebraska USA 54D2
Keban Baraji Res Turk 30C2
Kébémer Sen 76A3
Kebi R Chad 77J4
Kebili Tunisia 77D2
Kebīr R Syria/Leb 31D1
Kebrekaise Mt Sweden 12H5
Kecskemet Hung 21D3
Kedainiai USSR 21E1
Kedgwick Can 59F1
Kedong China 41B2
Kédougou Sen 76A3
Kedva USSR 24J3
Keechiga R Can 56N4
Keele R Can 56N3
Keele Pk Mt Can 56M3
Keeler USA 65C3
Keene New Hampshire USA 59E2
Keewanee USA 58B2
Keewatin Can 57D2
Keewatin USA 58A1
Keewatin Region Can 53J3
Kefallinía I Greece 23E3
Kefamenanu Indon 45B4
Kefar Sava Israel 31C2
Keffi Nig 77H4
Keflavik Iceland 12A2
Keg River Can 52G4
Keheili Sudan 32B3
Kehsi Mansam Burma 43B1
Keith Aust 50B3
Keith Scot 14D3
Keith Arm B Can 52F3
Kekertuk Can 53M3
Kekri India 35D3
Kelang Malay 43C5
Kelang I Indon 45C3
Kelantan R Malay 43C4
Kelibia Tunisia 77E1
Kelif USSR 35B1
Kelkit R Turk 30C1
Kellé Congo 78B4
Keller L Can 56O3
Kellet,C Can 52F2
Kellogg USA 64C1
Kelloselka Fin 26D3
Kells Irish Rep 15B5
Kells Range Hills Scot 14C4
Kelme USSR 21E1
Kelowna Can 52G5
Kelsey Bay Can 52F4
Kelso Scot 14D4
Kelso USA 64B1
Kem' USSR 26E3
Kem' R USSR 24E3
Ke Macina Mali 76B3
Kemerovo USSR 26K4
Kemi Fin 12J5
Kemi R Fin 12K5
Kemijärvi Fin 12K5
Kemmerer USA 64D2
Kempen Region Belg 16C1
Kemp,L USA 62C3
Kemps Bay Bahamas 68B2
Kempsey Aust 50D2
Kempten W Germ 20C3
Kempt,L Can 59E1
Kenai USA 56H3
Kenai Mts USA 56H4
Kenai Pen USA 56H3
Kenamuke Swamp Sudan 78D3
Kendal Eng 15D4
Kendall Aust 50D2
Kendari Indon 48B1
Kendawangan Indon 44D3
Kendrāpāra India 37C3
Kendrick USA 64C1
Kenedy USA 63F4
Kenema Sierra Leone 76A4
Kenge Zaïre 78B4
Kengtung Burma 43B1
Kenhardt S Africa 79C6
Kéniéba Mali 76A3
Kenitra Mor 77A2
Kenka L USA 60B1
Kenmare USA 57B2
Kenna USA 62B3
Kennebec R USA 59F1
Kennebunk USA 60E1
Kennedy USA 60A1
Kenner USA 63D4
Kennett USA 63E2
Kennett Square USA 60C3
Kennewick USA 64C1
Kenny Dam Can 52F4
Kenora Can 53J5
Kenosha USA 55E2
Kent County Eng 15F6
Kent Texas USA 62B3
Kent Washington USA 64B1
Kentland USA 58B2
Kenton USA 58C2
Kent Pen Can 52H3
Kentucky State USA 55E3
Kentucky R USA 58C3
Kentucky L USA 55E3
Kentwood Louisiana USA 63D3
Kentwood Michigan USA 58B2
Kenya Republic Africa 78D3
Kenya,Mt Kenya 78D4
Keokuk USA 58A2
Keonchi India 37B3
Keonjhargarh India 37C3
Kepaluan Tanimbar Arch Indon 39G7
Keplavik Iceland 53Q3
Kepno Pol 21D2
Kepuluan Widi Arch Indon 45C3
Kepulauan Alor Arch Indon 45B4
Kepulauan Anambas Arch Indon 44C2
Kepulauan Aru Arch Indon 39G7
Kepulauan Babar I Indon 48B1
Kepulauan Badas Is Indon 44C2
Kepulauan Banda Arch Indon 39G7
Kepulauan Banggai I Indon 48B1
Kepulauan Barat Daya Is Indon 48B1
Kepulauan Bunguran Seletan Arch Indon 44C2
Kepulauan Gorong Arch Indon 45D3
Kepulauan Kai Arch Indon 39G7
Kepulauan Kawio Arch Indon 45C2
Kepulauan Leti I Indon 48B1
Kepulauan Lingga Is Indon 44B3
Kepulauan Loloda Arch Indon 45C2
Kepulauan Mentawi Arch Indon 44A3
Kepulauan Nenusa Arch Indon 45C2
Kepulauan Obi Arch Indon 45C3
Kepulauan Riau Arch Indon 44B2
Kepulauan Sabalana Arch Indon 44E4
Kepulauan Sangihe Arch Indon 45C2
Kepulauan Sermata I Indon 48B1
Kepulauan Sula I Indon 48B1
Kepulauan Talaud Arch Indon 45C2
Kepulauan Tambelan Is Indon 44C2
Kepulauan Tanimbar I Indon 48C1
Kepulauan Togian I Indon 48B1
Kepulauan Tukangbesi Is Indon 48B1
Kepulauan Watubela Arch Indon 45D3
Kepulauan Yef Fam Arch Indon 45C3
Kepulaun Solor Arch Indon 45B4
Kerala State India 36B2
Kerang Aust 50B3
Kerava Fin 12J6
Kerbi R USSR 41D1
Kerch' USSR 25F6
Kerchem'ya USSR 24J3
Kerema PNG 48D1
Keremeps Can 64C1
Keren Eth 78D2
Kerguelen Ridge Indian O 46E7
Kericho Kenya 78D4
Kerinci Mt Indon 44B3
Kerio R Kenya 78D3
Kerki USSR 28E2
Kérkira Greece 23D3
Kérkira I Greece 23D3
Kermadec Is NZ 49H3
Kermadec Trench Pacific O 49H4
Kerman Iran 34D2
Kermānshāh Iran 34B2
Kerme Körfezi B Turk 23F3
Kermit USA 62B3
Kern R USA 65C3
Keros USSR 24J3
Kerr Res USA 59D3
Kerrville USA 62C3
Kershaw USA 61C2
Kertamulia Indon 44C3
Kerulen R Mongolia 27N5
Kerzaz Alg 76B2
Keşan Turk 23F2
Kesennuma Japan 41E4
Keshan China 41B2
Kesir Daglari Mt Turk 25G7
Kestenga USSR 12L5
Keswick Eng 15D4
Kéta Ghana 77G4
Ketapang Indon 44D3
Ketchikan USA 52E4
Ketia Niger 76C3

Ko Samui **La Huerta**

Ko Samui I *Thai* 43C4
Kosan *N Korea* 42A3
Koscierzyna *Pol* 21D2
Kosciusko *USA* 61B2
Kosciusko Mt *Aust* 48D4
Kosciusko I *USA* 56M4
Koshikijima-retto I *Japan* 41B5
Košice *Czech* 21E3
Kosma R *USSR* 24J2
Kosong *N Korea* 41B4
Kosovska Mitrovica *Yugos* 23E2
Kossou L *Ivory Coast* 76B4
Kosti *Sudan* 78D2
Kostopol' *USSR* 21F2
Kostroma *USSR* 24G4
Kostrzyn *Pol* 20C2
Kos'yu *USSR* 24K2
Koszalin *Pol* 12H8
Kota *India* 35D3
Kotaagung *Indon* 44B4
Kotabaharu *Indon* 44D3
Kotabaru *Indon* 44E3
Kota Bharu *Malay* 43C4
Kotabum *Indon* 44C3
Kot Addu *Pak* 35C2
Kota Kinabulu *Malay* 44E1
Kotamobagu *Indon* 45B2
Kotapad *India* 36C1
Kotapinang I *Indon* 44F7
Kota Tinggi *Malay* 44G8
Kotel'nich *USSR* 24H4
Kotel'nikovo *USSR* 25G6
Kotka *Fin* 12K6
Kotlas *USSR* 24H3
Kotlik *USA* 56F3
Koton Karifi *Nig* 77H4
Kotor *Yugos* 23D2
Kotovsk *USSR* 25D6
Kotri *Pak* 35B3
Kötschach *Austria* 17E1
Kottagüdem *India* 36C1
Kottayam *India* 36B3
Kotto R *CAR* 78C3
Kottūru *India* 36B2
Kotuy R *USSR* 27L3
Kotzebue *USA* 56F2
Kotzebue Sd *USA* 52B3
Kouande *Benin* 77G3
Kouango *CAR* 78C3
Koudougou *U Volta* 77F3
Koulamoutou *Gabon* 78B4
Koulikoro *Mali* 76B3
Koupéla *U Volta* 77F3
Kouri *Mali* 77F3
Kourou *French Guiana* 71H2
Kouroussa *Guinea* 76B3
Kousséri *Cam* 78B2
Kouvola *Fin* 12K6
Kovdor *USSR* 24D2
Kovel *USSR* 25C5
Kovno = Kaunas
Kovrov *USSR* 24G4
Kovylkino *USSR* 24G5
Kovzha R *USSR* 24F3
Ko Way I *Thai* 43C4
Kowloon *Hong Kong* 40C5
Kowŏn *N Korea* 42A3
Kowt-e-Ashrow *Afghan* 35B2
Köyceğğiz *Turk* 30A2
Koyda *USSR* 24G2
Koydor *USSR* 12L5
Koyna Res *India* 36A1
Koynas *USSR* 24H3
Koyoa I *Indon* 45C2
Koyuk *USA* 56F3
Koyuk R *USA* 56F2
Koyukuk *USA* 56G3
Koyukuk R *USA* 56G2
Kozan *Turk* 30C2
Kozańi *Greece* 23E2
Kozhikode = Calicut
Kozhim *USSR* 24K2
Koz'modemyansk *USSR* 24H4
Koztroma *USSR* 24G4
Kōzu-shima I *Japan* 42C4
Kpandu *Ghana* 77G4
Kragerø *Nor* 12F7
Kragujevac *Yugos* 23E2
Kra,Isthmus of *Burma/ Malay* 43B3
Krakatau = Rakata
Krak des Chevaliers Hist Site *Syria* 31D1
Kraków *Pol* 21D2
Kraljevo *Yugos* 23E2
Kramatorsk *USSR* 25F6
Kramfors *Sweden* 12H6
Kranj *Yugos* 22C1
Krapotkin *USSR* 25G6
Krasavino *USSR* 24H3
Krashnokamsk *USSR* 24K4
Krasino *USSR* 26G2
Kraśnik *Pol* 21E2
Krasnoarmeysk *USSR* 25H5
Krasnodar *USSR* 25F7
Krasnogorsk *USSR* 41E2
Krasnotur'insk *USSR* 24L4
Krasnoufimsk *USSR* 24K4
Krasnousol'-skiy *USSR* 24K5
Krasnovishersk *USSR* 24K3
Krasnovodsk *USSR* 25J7
Krasnoyarsk *USSR* 27K4
Krasnystaw *Pol* 21E2
Krasnyy Kut *USSR* 25H5
Krasnyy Luch *USSR* 25F6
Krasnyy Yar *USSR* 25H6
Kratie *Camb* 43D3
Kraulshavn *Greenland* 53N2
Krefeld *W Germ* 20B2
Kremenchug *USSR* 25E6
Kremenchugskoye Vodokhranilische Res *USSR* 25E6
Kremenets *USSR* 21F2
Kremming *USA* 62A1
Krenitzin Is *USA* 56E5
Kribi *Cam* 78A3
Krichev *USSR* 24E5
Krimml *Austria* 17E1
Krinstinestad *Fin* 12J6
Krishna R *India* 36B1
Krishnagiri *India* 36B2
Krishnangar *India* 37C3
Kristiansand *Nor* 12F7
Kristianstad *Sweden* 12G7
Kristiansund *Nor* 26B3
Kristineham *Sweden* 12G7
Kriti I *Greece* 23E3
Krivoy Rog *USSR* 25E6
Krk I *Yugos* 22C1
Kronotskaya Sopka Mt *USSR* 27S4
Kronprins Frederik Bjerge Mts *Greenland* 53P3
Kronshtadt *USSR* 12K7
Kroonstad *S Africa* 79C6
Kropotkin *USSR* 26F5
Kruger Nat Pk *S Africa* 79D6
Krugersdorp *S Africa* 79C6
Krui *Indon* 44B4
Kruje *Alb* 23D2
Krupki *USSR* 21F2
Krusenstern,C *USA* 56F2
Kruševac *Yugos* 23E2
Krustpils *USSR* 12K7
Kruzof I *USA* 56L4
Krym Pen *USSR* 26E5
Krym R *USSR* 25E7
Krymsk *USSR* 25F7
Krzyz *Pol* 20D2
Ksar El Boukhari *Alg* 77C1
Ksar el Kebir *Mor* 77A2
Kuala *Indon* 44A2
Kuala Dungun *Malay* 43C5
Kuala Kangsar *Malay* 44F6
Kuala Kelawang *Malay* 44G7
Kuala Kerai *Malay* 43C4
Kuala Kubu Baharu *Malay* 43C5
Kuala Lipis *Malay* 43C5
Kuala Lumpur *Malay* 43C5
Kuala Pilah *Malay* 44G7
Kuala Selangor *Malay* 44F7
Kualasimpang *Indon* 44A2
Kuala Trengganu *Malay* 43C4
Kuamut *Malay* 44E1
Kuandian *China* 41A3
Kuantan *Malay* 43C5
Kuba *USSR* 25H7
Kubar *PNG* 39H7
Kuching *Malay* 44D2
Kudat *Malay* 44E1
Kudus *Indon* 44D4
Kudymkar *USSR* 24J4
Kufstein *Austria* 20C3
Kugaluk R *Can* 56M2
Kugmallit B *Can* 56M2
Kuhak *Iran* 34E3
Kuh Duren Upland *Iran* 34D2
Kūh-e Bazmān Mt *Iran* 34D3
Kūh-e Dinar Mt *Iran* 34C2
Kūh-e-Hazār Masjed Mts *Iran* 34D1
Kūh-e Jebāl Barez Mts *Iran* 34D3
Kūh-e Karkas Mts *Iran* 34C2
Kūh-e Laleh Zar Mt *Iran* 34D3
Kūh-e Sahand Mt *Iran* 34B1
Kuh e Taftān Mt *Iran* 34E3
Kūhhaye Alvand Mts *Iran* 25H9
Kūhhaye Sabalan Mts *Iran* 25H8
Kūhjā-ye Zāgros Mts *Iran* 34B2
Kuhmo *Fin* 12K6
Kūhpāyeh *Iran* 34C2
Kūhpāyeh Mt *Iran* 34D2
Kūh ye Bashākerd Mts *Iran* 34D3
Kūh ye Sabalan Mt *Iran* 34B1
Kuibis *Namibia* 79B6
Kuigillingok *USA* 52B4
Kuiu I *USA* 56M4
Kujang *N Korea* 42A3
Kuji *Japan* 41E3
Kuju-san Mt *Japan* 42B4
Kukaklek L *USA* 56G4
Kukës *Alb* 23E2
Kukpowruk R *USA* 56F2
Kukup *Malay* 43C5
Kūl R *Iran* 34D3
Kula *Turk* 23F3
Kulai *Malay* 44G8
Kulakshi *USSR* 25K6
Kulal,Mt *Kenya* 78D3
Kulata *Bulg* 23E2
Kuldīga *USSR* 24C4
Kulim *Malay* 44F6
Kulov R *USSR* 24G2
Kulpawn R *Ghana* 77F3
Kul'sary *USSR* 25J6
Kulu *India* 35D2
Kulu *Turk* 30B2
Kululli *Eth* 32D4
Kulunda *USSR* 26J4
Kulwin *Aust* 50B2
Kuma R *USSR* 25H7
Kumagaya *Japan* 42C3
Kumai *Indon* 44D3
Kumak *USSR* 25L5
Kumamoto *Japan* 41C5
Kumano *Japan* 42C4
Kumanovo *Yugos* 23E2
Kumara *China* 41B1
Kumasi *Ghana* 77F4
Kumba *Cam* 78A3
Kumbakonam *India* 36B2
Kumbo *Cam* 77J4
Kümch'ŏn *N Korea* 42A3
Kumdah *S Arabia* 33E2
Kumertau *USSR* 24K5
Kumgang *N Korea* 42A3
Kŭmhwa *S Korea* 41B4
Kumla *Sweden* 12H7
Kŭmnyŏng *S Korea* 42A4
Kŭmo-do I *S Korea* 42A4
Kumon Range Mts *Burma* 37E2
Kumta *India* 36A2
Kümüx *China* 29G1
Kunar R *Afghan* 35C2
Kunda *USSR* 12K7
Kundla *India* 35C4
Kunduz *Afghan* 35B1
Kunghit I *Can* 56M5
Kungsbacka *Sweden* 12G7
Kungur *USSR* 24K4
Kunhing *Burma* 43B1
Kunlun Shan Mts *China* 29G2
Kunming *China* 40A4
Kunovat R *USSR* 24M3
Kunsan *S Korea* 41B4
Kuopio *Fin* 12K6
Kupa R *Yugos* 22D1
Kupang *Indon* 48B2
Kupiano *PNG* 48D2
Kupreanof I. *USA* 52E4
Kupreanof I *USA* 56M4
Kupreanof Pt *USA* 56G4
Kupyansk *USSR* 25F6
Kuqa *China* 29G1
Kur R *USSR* 41C2
Kura R *USSR* 25H8
Kurabe *Japan* 42C3
Kurashiki *Japan* 41C5
Kurayoshi *Japan* 42B3
Kurdistan Region *Iran* 34B1
Kŭrdzhali *Bulg* 23F2
Kure *Japan* 41C5
Kureyka R *USSR* 27L3
Kurgan *USSR* 26H4
Kuria Muria Is = Khūryan Mūryān
Kurikka *Fin* 12J6
Kuril Is = Kuril'skoye Osrova
Kuril'sk *USSR* 41F2
Kuril'skiye Ostrova Is *USSR* 27Q5
Kuril Trench *Pacific O* 46J2
Kurinskaya Kosa Sand Spit *USSR* 25H8
Kurnool *India* 36B1
Kuroishi *Japan* 42D2
Kuroiso *Japan* 42D3
Kurow *NZ* 51B2
Kurri Kurri *Aust* 50D2
Kursk *USSR* 25F5
Kurskiy Zaliv Lg *USSR* 21E1
Kuruktag R *China* 38B2
Kuruman *S Africa* 79C6
Kurume *Japan* 41C5
Kurunegala *Sri Lanka* 36C3
Kurunktag R *China* 26K5
Kur'ya *USSR* 24K3
Kusa *USSR* 24K4
Kuşadasi Körfezi B *Turk* 23F3
Kus Golü L *Turk* 23F2
Kushimoto *Japan* 41D5
Kushiro *Japan* 41E3
Kushka *Afghan* 34E1
Kushtia *Bang* 37C3
Kushum R *USSR* 25J5
Kushva *USSR* 26H4
Kuskokwim R *USA* 56F3
Kuskokwim B *USA* 56F4
Kuskokwim Mts *USA* 52C3
Kuskowim Mts *USA* 56G3
Kusma *Nepal* 37B2
Kussharo-ko L *Japan* 41E3
Kustanay *USSR* 26H4
Kütahya *Turk* 25D8
Kutai R *Indon* 44E3
Kutaisi *USSR* 25G7
Kutchan *Japan* 42D2
Kutná Hora *Czech* 20D3
Kutno *Pol* 21D2
Kutu *Zaïre* 78B4
Kutubdia I *Bang* 37D3
Kutum *Sudan* 78C2
Kuusamo *Fin* 12K5
Kuvandyk *USSR* 25K5
Kuwait *Kuwait* 30E4
Kuwait Sheikdom *S W Asia* 28C3
Kuwana *Japan* 42C3
Kuyahoora,L *USA* 60C1
Kuybyshev *USSR* 26G4
Kuybyshev *USSR* 26J4
Kuybyshevskoye Vodokhranilishche Res *USSR* 24H5
Kuytun *USSR* 27M4
Kuzey Anadolu Daglari Mts *Turk* 25F7
Kuznetsk *USSR* 25H5
Kuzomen *USSR* 24F2
Kvaenangen Sd *Nor* 24C2
Kvichak R *USA* 56G4
Kvichak B *USA* 56G4
Kvigtind Mt *Nor* 12G5
Kvikkjokk *Sweden* 24B2
Kwale *Kenya* 78D4
Kwale *Nig* 77H4
Kwangju *S Korea* 41B4
Kwango R *Zaïre* 78B4
Kwangyang *S Korea* 42A3
Kwanmo-bong Mt *N Korea* 42A2
Kwara State *Nig* 77H4
Kwekwe *Zim* 79C5
Kwethluk *USA* 56F3
Kwethluk R *USA* 56F3
Kwidzyn *Pol* 21D2
Kwoka Mt *Indon* 39G7
Kyabram *Aust* 50C3
Kyaikkami *Burma* 43B2
Kyaikto *Burma* 43B2
Kyakhta *USSR* 38D1
Kyancutta *Aust* 50A2
Kyaukme *Burma* 43B1
Kyauk-padaung *Burma* 43B1
Kyaukpyu *Burma* 43A2
Kyaukse *Burma* 37E3
Kychema *USSR* 24G2
Kyle of Lochalsh *Scot* 13B2
Kyll R *W Germ* 16D1
Kyneton *Aust* 50B3
Kyoga L *Uganda* 78D3
Kyogle *Aust* 50D1
Kyŏngju *S Korea* 41B4
Kyongsang Sanmaek Mts *S Korea* 42A3
Kyŏngsŏng *N Korea* 42A2
Kyonpyaw *Burma* 37E4
Kyoto *Japan* 41D4
Kyrenia *Cyprus* 31B1
Kyrta *USSR* 24K3
Kyshtym *USSR* 26H4
Kythrea *Cyprus* 31B1
Kyūshū I *Japan* 41C5
Kyushu-Palau Ridge *Pacific O* 46H4
Kyustendil *Bulg* 23E2
Kyusyur *USSR* 27O2
Kyzyl *USSR* 38C1
Kyzylkum Desert *USSR* 26H5
Kzyl Orda *USSR* 26H5

L

Laas Caanood *Somalia* 78E3
La Ascensíon *Mexico* 67C1
Laasphe *W Germ* 16E1
Laas Qoray *Somalia* 75D3
La Asunción *Ven* 70F1
La Banda *Arg* 72C1
La Barca *Mexico* 67B1
La Barge *USA* 64D2
Labasa *Fiji* 55G2
Labé *Guinea* 76A3
Labe R *Czech* 20D2
Labelle *Can* 59E1
La Belle *USA* 61E4
Laberge,L *Can* 56L3
Labi *Brunei* 44D2
Labinsk *USSR* 25G7
Labis *Malay* 44G7
Laboué *Leb* 31D1
Laboulaye *Arg* 72C2
Labrador Region *Can* 53M4
Labrador City *Can* 53M4
Labrador S *Greenland/Can* 53N4
Lábrea *Brazil* 70F5
Labuan I *Malay* 44E1
Labuha *Indon* 45C3
Labuhan *Indon* 44C4
Labuhanbajo *Indon* 45B4
Labuhanbatu *Indon* 44F7
Labuhanbilik *Indon* 44B2
Labutta *Burma* 43A2
Labytnangi *USSR* 24M2
La Capelle *France* 16B1
La Carlota *Arg* 72C2
La Carlota *Phil* 45F8
Lac Belot L *Can* 56N2
Lac Bienville L *Can* 53L4
Laccadive Is = Lakshadweep
Laccadive Is *India* 29F4
Lac d'Annecy L *France* 17B2
Lac de Gras L *Can* 52G3
Lac de Joux L *Switz* 17B1
Lac de Neuchâtel L *Switz* 17B1
Lac de Patzcuaro L *Mexico* 67B2
Lac de Sayula L *Mexico* 67B2
Lac des Bois L *Can* 52F3
Lac des Milles Lacs L *Can* 57D2
Lac du Bonnet *Can* 57C1
Lac du Bourget L *France* 17A2
La Ceiba *Honduras* 66D3
Lacepede B *Aust* 50A3
La Châtre *France* 18C2
La Châtre-sur-le-Loir *France* 16A3
La-Chaux-de-Fonds *Switz* 17B1
Lachish Hist Site *Israel* 31C3
Lachlan R *Aust* 48D4
La Chorrera *Panama* 70C2
Lachute *Can* 59E1
La Ciotat *France* 17A3
La Ciudad *Mexico* 67A1
Lac Joseph L *Can* 53M4
Lackawanna *USA* 59D2
Lac la Biche *Can* 52G4
Lac la Martre L *Can* 52G3
Lac la Ronge L *Can* 52H4
Lac L'eau Claire *Can* 53L4
Lac Léman L *Switz/France* 22B1
Lac Manouane *Can* 53L4
Lac Manouane L *Can* 55F1
Lac Maunoir L *Can* 56N2
Lac Megantic *Can* 59E1
Lac Mistassini L *Can* 53L4
La Cocha *Arg* 72B1
Lacombe *Can* 52G4
Laconia *USA* 59E2
La Coruña *Spain* 19A1
La Côte-St-André *France* 17A2
La Crosse *USA* 55D2
La Cruces *USA* 54C3
La Cruz *Arg* 72D1
La Cruz *Mexico* 67A1
Lac Seul L *Can* 53J4
La Cygne *USA* 63D2
Ladākh Range *India* 35D2
Ladismith *S Africa* 79C7
Lādīz *Iran* 34E3
Lādnūn *India* 35C3
Ladong *China* 40B5
Ladozhskoye Ozero L *USSR* 24E3
Lady Ann Str *Can* 53K2
Lady Barron *Aust* 50E3
Ladysmith *S Africa* 79D6
Ladysmith *USA* 58A1
Lae *PNG* 48D1
Laem Ngop *Thai* 43C3
Laesø I *Den* 20C1
Lafayette Colorado *USA* 62A2
Lafayette Indiana *USA* 55E2
Lafayette Louisiana *USA* 55D3
La Fène *France* 16B2
La-Ferté-Barnard *France* 16A2
La Ferté-St-Aubin *France* 16B2
La-Ferté-sous-Jouarre *France* 16B2
Lafia *Nig* 77H4
Lafiagi *Nig* 77H4
La Flèche *France* 18B2
La Galite I *Tunisia* 77D1
Lagan R *Sweden* 20C1
Lagarto *Brazil* 71L6
Laghouat *Alg* 77C2
Lagoa de Araruama *Brazil* 73D3
Lagoa de Castillos L *Urug* 72E2
Lagoa de Rocha *Urug* 72E2
Lagoa dos Patos Lg *Brazil* 69F4
Lagoa Feia *Brazil* 73D3
Lago Agrio *Ecuador* 70C4
Lagoa Juparanã L *Brazil* 73D2
Lagoa Mandiore L *Brazil* 73A2
Lagoa Mangueira L *Brazil* 72E2
Lagoa mar Chiguita L *Arg* 69D4
Lagoa Mirim L *Urug/Brazil* 69F4
Lagoa Negra L *Urug* 72E2
Lago Argentino L *Arg* 69B8
Lagoa Uberaba L *Brazil* 73A2
Lagoa Vermelha *Brazil* 72E1
Lago Buenos Aries L *Arg* 69B7
Lago Cochrane L *Chile/ Arg* 69B7
Lago Colhué Huapi L *Arg* 69C7
Lago de Chapala L *Mexico* 66B2
Lago de Chiriqui L *Panama* 70B2
Lago de Cuitzeo L *Mexico* 67B2
Lago de la Laja L *Chile* 69B5
Lago del Coghinas L *Sardegna* 22B2
Lago de Maracaibo L *Ven* 70D2
Lago de Nicaragua L *Nic* 70A1
Lago de Perlas L *Nic* 70B1
Lago de Santiaguillo L *Mexico* 67B1
Lago di Bolsena L *Italy* 22C2
Lago di Bracciano L *Italy* 22C2
Lago di Como L *Italy* 22B1
Lago d'Idro L *Italy* 17D2
Lago di Garda L *Italy* 22C1
Lago di Lecco L *Italy* 17C2
Lago di Lugano L *Italy* 17C2
Lago d'Iseo L *Italy* 17D2
Lago d'Orta L *Italy* 17C2
Lago General Carrera L *Chile* 69B7
Lago Maggiore L *Italy* 22B1
Lago Musters L *Arg* 69C7
Lagon *France* 18B3
Lago Nahuel Haupi L *Arg* 69B6
Lago O'Higgins L *Chile* 69B7
Lago Omodeo L *Sardegna* 22B2
Lago Poopó L *Bol* 70E7
Lago Ranco L *Chile* 69B6
Lago Rogaguado L *Bol* 70E6
Lagos *Nig* 77G4
Lagos *Port* 19A2
Lagos State *Nig* 77G4
Lago San Martin L *Chile/ Arg* 69B7
Lagos de Moreno *Mexico* 66B2
Lago Titicaca *Bol/Peru* 70E7
Lago Trasimeno L *Italy* 17E3
La Goulette *Tunisia* 77E1
Lago Viedma L *Arg* 69B7
La Grande *USA* 54B2
La Grande Rivière R *Can* 53L4
Lagrange *Aust* 48B2
La Grange Georgia *USA* 55E3
La Grange Kentucky *USA* 58B3
La Grange N Carolina *USA* 61D1
La Grange Texas *USA* 63C4
La Gran Sabana Mts *Ven* 70F2
La Grave *France* 17B2
Lagronño *Spain* 18B3
Laguna *USA* 62A3
Laguna Agua Brava *Mexico* 67A1
Laguna Aluminé L *Arg* 72A3
Laguna Beach *USA* 65C4
Laguna Colorada Grande L *Arg* 72C3
Laguna de Bay Lg *Phil* 45F8
Laguna de Caratasca Lg *Honduras* 66D3
Laguna de Chiriqui L *Panama* 66D4
Laguna de Guzmán L *Mexico* 62A3
Laguna del Abra L *Arg* 72C4
Laguna del Caimanero L *Mexico* 67A1
Laguna de Managua L *Nicaragua* 66D3
Laguna de Nicaragua L *Nicaragua* 66D3
Laguna de Perlas Lg *Nic* 68A4
Laguna de Pueblo Viejo L *Mexico* 67C1
Laguna de Santa Maria L *Mexico* 62A3
Laguna de Tamiahua Lg *Mexico* 66C2
Laguna de Términos Lg *Mexico* 66C3
Laguna de Yuriria L *Mexico* 67B1
Laguna Iberá *Arg* 72D1
Laguna Itati L *Arg* 72D1
Laguna le Altamira *Mexico* 67C1
Laguna Madre Lg *Mexico* 66C2
Laguna Madre Lg *USA* 63F4
Laguna Mar Chiquita L *Arg* 72C2
Laguna Nahuel Huapi L *Arg* 72A4
Laguna Nutauge Lg *USSR* 56C2
Laguna Paiva *Arg* 72C2
Laguna Panguipulli L *Chile* 72A3
Laguna Puyehue L *Chile* 72A4
Laguna Ranco *Chile* 72A4
Laguna Repanco L *Chile* 72A4
Laguna Salada L *Mexico* 65C4
Laguna Seca *Mexico* 54C4
Laguna Superior L *Mexico* 67C2
Laguna Tenkergynpil'gyn Lg *USSR* 56C2
Laguna Tortugas L *Mexico* 67C1
Laguna Traful L *Arg* 72A4
Laguna Trin L *Arg* 72D1
Laguna Vankarem Lg *USSR* 56C2
Laguna Veneta Lg *Italy* 17E2
Laguna Villarrica L *Chile* 72A3
Lagund Seca *Mexico* 67B1
Lahat *Indon* 44B3
Lahewa *Indon* 44A2
Lahia *Fin* 12J6
Lahij *S Yemen* 32D4
Lāhījān *Iran* 34C1
Lahn R *W Germ* 16D1
Lahnstein *W Germ* 16D1
Lahore *Pak* 35C2
Lahr *France* 16D2
Lahti *Fin* 12K6
lahud Datu *Malay* 44E1
La Huerta *Mexico* 67B2

Lai Ligonha

Lai *Chad* 78B3
Laibin *China* 40B5
Lai Chau *Viet* 43C1
L'Aigle *France* 16A2
Laingsburg *S Africa* 79C7
Lairg *Scot* 14C2
Lais *Indon* 44B3
Lais *Phil* 45G9
Laiwui *Indon* 45C3
Laiyang *China* 40E2
Laizhou Wan B *China* 40D2
Laja R *Chile* 72A3
Lajeado *Brazil* 72E1
Lajes *Brazil* 69F3
La Junta *USA* 54C3
Lake Andes *USA* 57C3
Lake Cargelligo *Aust* 50C2
Lake Charles *USA* 55D3
Lake City Florida *USA* 61C2
Lake City Minnesota *USA* 57D3
Lake City S Carolina *USA* 61D2
Lake District Region *Eng* 15D4
Lake Eyre Basin *Aust* 48C3
Lakefield *Can* 59D2
Lake Geneva *USA* 58B2
Lake George *USA* 60D1
Lake Harbour *Can* 53M3
Lake Havasu City *USA* 65D4
Lakehurst *USA* 60C2
Lake Jackson *USA* 63C4
Lakeland *USA* 61C3
Lake of the Woods *Can* 53J5
Lake Oswego *USA* 64B1
Lakeport *USA* 65B3
Lake Providence *USA* 63D3
Lake Pukaki *NZ* 51B2
Lakes Entrance *Aust* 50C3
Lake Stewart *Aust* 50B1
Lake Traverse *Can* 59D1
Lakeview *USA* 54A2
Lakeview Mt *Can* 64B1
Lake Village *USA* 63D3
Lake Wales *USA* 61C3
Lakewood Colorado *USA* 62A2
Lakewood New Jersey *USA* 60C2
Lakewood Ohio *USA* 58C2
Lake Worth *USA* 61E4
Lakhimpur *India* 37B2
Lakhpat *India* 35B4
Lakin *USA* 62B2
Lakki *Pak* 35C2
Lakonikós Kólpos G *Greece* 23E3
Lakor I *Indon* 45C4
Lakota *Ivory Coast* 76B4
Laksefjord Inlet *Nor* 12K4
Lakselv *Nor* 12K4
Lakshadweep Is *India* 36A2
La Laguna *Arg* 72C2
Lalibela *Eth* 32C4
La Libertad *Ecuador* 70B4
La Ligua *Chile* 72A2
Lalindi *Indon* 45B5
Lalindu R *Indon* 45B3
La Linea *Spain* 19A2
Lalitpur *India* 35D4
Laloa *Indon* 45B3
La Loche *Can* 52H4
La Loupe *France* 16A2
La Louvière *Belg* 16C1
La Luz *Nic* 68A4
La Madrid *Arg* 72B1
Lama Kara *Togo* 77G4
La Malbaie *Can* 53L5
La Malinche Mt *Mexico* 67C2
La Mancha *Mexico* 67B1
La Mancha Region *Spain* 19B2
Lamar Colorado *USA* 54C3
Lamar Missouri *USA* 63D2
Lamarque *Arg* 72B3
La Marque *USA* 63C4
Lambaréné *Gabon* 78B4
Lambayeque *Peru* 70B5
Lambert Gl *Ant* 80F10
Lambertville *USA* 60C2
Lamblon,C *Can* 52F2
Lambro R *Italy* 17C2
Lam Chi R *Thai* 43C2
Lamego *Port* 19A1
La Meije Mt *France* 17B2
La Merced *Arg* 72B1
La Merced *Peru* 70C6
Lamesa *USA* 62B3
La Mesa *USA* 65C4
Lamía *Greece* 23E3
Lammermuir Hills *Scot* 14D4
Lammhult *Sweden* 12G7
Lamon B *Phil* 45F8
Lamone R *Italy* 17D2
Lamoni *USA* 63D1
Lamont Wyoming *USA* 57A3
Lamotrek I *Pacific O* 39H6
Lamotte Beuvron *France* 16B3
La Moure *USA* 57C2
Lampasas *USA* 62C3
Lampeter *Wales* 15C5
Lamu *Kenya* 78E4
La Mure *France* 17A2
Lana *Italy* 17D1
Lanark *Scot* 14D4
Lanbi I *Burma* 43B3
Lancang R *China* 43C1
Lancashire County *Eng* 15D5
Lancaster California *USA* 65C4
Lancaster *Eng* 15D4
Lancaster Mississippi *USA* 63D1
Lancaster New Hampshire *USA* 59E2
Lancaster New York *USA* 60A1
Lancaster Ohio *USA* 58C3
Lancaster Pennsylvania *USA* 55F3
Lancaster S Carolina *USA* 61C2
Lancaster Sd *Can* 53K2
Landak R *Indon* 44C3
Landan *W Germ* 16E2
Landeck *Austria* 20C3
Lander *USA* 54C2
Landeta *Arg* 72C2
Landrum *USA* 61C1
Landsberg *W Germ* 20C3
Lands End C *Can* 52F2
Land's End Pt *Eng* 15C6
Landshut *W Germ* 20C3
Làndskrona *Sweden* 12G7
Lanett *USA* 61B2
La'nga Co L *China* 37B1
Langdon *USA* 57C2
Langeb Watercourse *Sudan* 32C3
Langenhagen *W Germ* 20B2
Langenthal *Switz* 17B1
Langholm *Scot* 14D4
Langjökull Mts *Iceland* 12A2
Langkawi I *Malay* 43B4
Langlo R *Aust* 50C1
Langnau *Switz* 17B1
Langres *France* 18D2
langsa *Indon* 44A2
Lang Shan Mts *China* 38D2
Lang Son *Viet* 43D1
Langtry *USA* 62B4
Languedoc Region *France* 18C3
Lanin Mt *Arg* 69B5
Lanoa,L L *Phil* 45F9
Lansdale *USA* 60C2
Lansdowne House *Can* 53K4
Lansford *USA* 60C2
Lansing *USA* 55E2
Lanslebourg *France* 17B2
Lanzarote I *Canary Is* 76A2
Lanzhou *China* 40A2
Lanzo Torinese *Italy* 17B2
Laoag *Phil* 45F7
Lao Cai *Viet* 43C1
Laoha He R *China* 40D1
Laois County *Irish Rep* 15B5
Laoise Port *Irish Rep* 15B5
Laoling *China* 42A2
Laon *France* 16B2
La Orova *Peru* 70C6
Laos Republic *S E Asia* 43C2
Lapa *Brazil* 73C4
Lapalisse *France* 18C2
La Palma I *Canary Is* 76A2
La Palmas *Panama* 70C2
La Paloma *Urug* 72E2
La Pampa State *Arg* 72B3
La Paragua *Ven* 70F2
La Paz *Arg* 69E4
La Paz *Arg* 72B2
La Paz *Bol* 70E7
La Paz *Mexico* 66A2
La Perouse Str *USSR/Japan* 41E2
La Pesca *Mexico* 67C1
La Piedad *Mexico* 67B1
La Pine *USA* 64B2
Lapithos *Cyprus* 31B1
Laplace *USA* 63D3
la Placita *Mexico* 67B2
La Plant *USA* 57B2
La Plata *Arg* 69E4
La Porte *USA* 58B2
Laporte *USA* 60B2
Lappeenranta *Fin* 12K6
Lappland Region *Sweden/Fin* 12H5
Laprida *Arg* 72C3
La Pryor *USA* 63F4
Laptev S *USSR* 27O2
Lapua *Fin* 12J6
La Puerta *Arg* 72B1
Lapu-Lapu *Phil* 45F8
La Punta *Arg* 72C1
La Purisma *Mexico* 54B4
Laqiya Arba'in Well *Sudan* 78C1
La Quiaca *Arg* 69C2
L'Aquila *Italy* 22C2
Lār *Iran* 34C3
Larache *Mor* 77A1
Laragne *France* 17A2
Laramie *USA* 54C2
Laramie Mts *USA* 57A3
Laramie Range Mts *USA* 54C2
Laranjeiras do Sul *Brazil* 73B4
Larantuka *Indon* 45B4
Larat I *Indon* 45D4
Larca *Spain* 19B2
Laredo *USA* 54D4
Larestan Region *Iran* 34C3
Largeau = Faya
L'Argentière *France* 17B2
Largo *USA* 61C3
Largs *Scot* 14C4
Lāri *Iran* 34B1
Lariang R *Indon* 45A3
La Rioja *Arg* 69C3
La Rioja State *Arg* 69C3
Lárisa *Greece* 23E3
Larkana *Pak* 35B3
Larnaca *Cyprus* 30B3
Larnaca B *Cyprus* 31B1
Larne *N Ire* 14B4
Larned *USA* 62C2
La Robla *Spain* 19A1
La Roche-en-Ardenne *Belg* 16C1
La Rochelle *France* 18B2
La Roche-sur-Foron *France* 17B1
La Roche-sur-Yon *France* 18B2
La Roda *Spain* 19B2
La Romana *Dom Rep* 68D3
La Ronge *Can* 52H4
Larvik *Nor* 12F7
Lar'yak *USSR* 26J3
La Sabana *Arg* 72D1
La Sagra Mt *Spain* 19B2
La Salle *Can* 59E1
La Salle *USA* 58B2
Las Animas *USA* 62B2
La Sarre *Can* 53L5
Las Avispas *Arg* 72C1
Las Cabras *Chile* 72A2
Lascano *Urug* 72E2
Lascombe *Can* 52G4
Las Cruces *USA* 62A3
La Selle Mt *Haiti* 68C3
Lasengmia *China* 40B2
La Serena *Chile* 69B3
La Seyne *France* 17A3
Las Flores *Arg* 69E5
Lash-e-Joveyn *Afghan* 34E2
Lashio *Burma* 43B1
La Sila Mts *Italy* 22D3
Läsjerd *Iran* 34C1
Laskar Grah *Afghan* 35A2
Las Lajas *Chile* 72A3
Las Marismas Marshland *Spain* 19A2
la Soledad *Mexico* 67B1
Lasolo *Indon* 45B3
Lasolo R *Indon* 45B3
Las Palmas de Gran Canaria *Canary Is* 76A2
La Spezia *Italy* 22B2
Las Piedras *Urug* 72D2
Las Plumas *Arg* 69C6
Las Rosas *Arg* 72C2
Lassen Peak Mt *USA* 64B2
Las Termas *Arg* 72C1
las Tinai *Mexico* 67C2
Las Tinajos *Arg* 72C1
Las Toscas *Arg* 72D1
Lastoursville *Gabon* 78B4
Lastovo I *Yugos* 22D2
Las Tres Marias Is *Mexico* 66B2
Las Varas *Mexico* 67A1
Las Varillas *Arg* 72C2
Las Vegas *USA* 54C3
Latakia = Al Lādhiqīyah
Latina *Italy* 22C2
La Toma *Arg* 72B2
La Tortuga I *Ven* 70E1
La Trinidad *Phil* 45F7
Latrobe *Aust* 50E3
La Troya R *Arg* 72B1
Latrun *Israel* 31C3
La Tuque *Can* 53L5
Lātūr *India* 36B1
Latviyskaya SSR Republic *USSR* 24C4
Laugh Allen L *Irish Rep* 15B4
Laugh Boderg L *Irish Rep* 15B5
Laugh Bouna L *Irish Rep* 15B5
Laugh Carlingford L *N Ire* 15B4
Laugh Derravaragh L *Irish Rep* 15B5
Laugh Erne L *N Ire* 15B4
Laugh Oughter L *Irish Rep* 15B4
Laugh Ree L *Irish Rep* 15B5
Laugh Sheelin L *Irish Rep* 15B5
Lau Group Is *Fiji* 49H2
Launceston *Aust* 48D5
Launceston *Eng* 15C6
La Unión *Chile* 69B6
La Union *El Salvador* 66D3
La Union *Mexico* 67B2
La Unión *Peru* 70C5
Laura *Aust* 48D2
Laurel Delaware *USA* 59D3
Laurel Maryland *USA* 60B3
Laurel Mississippi *USA* 55E3
Laurel Montana *USA* 64E1
Laurens *USA* 61C2
Laurinburg *USA* 61D2
Lausanne *Switz* 22B1
Laut I *Indon* 44E3
Lautaro *Chile* 69B7
Lauterbach *W Germ* 16E1
Lauterecken *W Germ* 16D2
Lautoka I *Fiji* 55G2
Lavaca B *USA* 63F4
Laval *Can* 59E1
Laval *France* 18B2
Laveno *Italy* 17C2
La Ventura *Mexico* 67B1
La Verá *Par* 73A4
Lavina *USA* 64E1
La Vôge Region *France* 16C2
Lavras *Brazil* 71K8
Lavras do Sul *Brazil* 72E2
Lavrentiya *USSR* 56D2
Lawas *Malay* 44E2
Lawdar *S Yemen* 33E4
Lawele *Indon* 45B4
Lawksawk *Burma* 43B1
Lawra *Ghana* 77F3
Lawrence Kansas *USA* 63C2
Lawrence Massachusetts *USA* 59E2
Lawrence *NZ* 51A3
Lawrenceburg *USA* 61B1
Lawrenceville Illinois *USA* 58B3
Lawrenceville Pennsylvania *USA* 60B2
Lawton *USA* 54D3
Layla *S Arabia* 33E2
Laylo *Sudan* 78D3
La'youn *Mor* 76A2
Lazarev *USSR* 41E1
Lázaro Cárdenas *Mexico* 67B2
Laz Daua *Somalia* 75D3
Lazi *Phil* 45F9
Lazo *USSR* 41C3
Lead *USA* 54C2
Leadville *USA* 62A2
Leaf R *USA* 61B2
Leakey *USA* 62C4
Leandro N Alem *Arg* 72D1
Leavenworth *USA* 63C2
Leba *Pol* 21D2
Lebanon Kansas *USA* 62C2
Lebanon Missouri *USA* 63D2
Lebanon Oregon *USA* 64B2
Lebanon Pennsylvania *USA* 59D2
Lebanon Republic *S W Asia* 30C3
Lebanon Tennessee *USA* 58B3
Lebombo Mts *Mozam/S Africa/Swaziland* 79D6
Lebork *Pol* 21D2
Le Bourg-d'Oisans *France* 17B2
Le Brassus *Switz* 17B1
Lebu *Chile* 69B5
Le Buet Mt *France* 17B1
Le Cateau *France* 16B1
Lecce *Italy* 23D2
Lecco *Italy* 22B1
Lech R *Austria* 17D1
Le Champ de Feu Mt *France* 16D2
Lechtaler Alpen Mts *Austria* 17D1
Le Creusot *France* 18C2
Ledbury *Eng* 15D5
Ledo *India* 37E2
Lee *USA* 60D1
Leech L *USA* 57D2
Leeds *Eng* 13C3
Leek *Eng* 15D5
Leer *W Germ* 20B2
Leesburg Florida *USA* 61C3
Leesburg Virginia *USA* 60B3
Leesville *USA* 63D3
Leeton *Aust* 50C2
Leeuwarden *Neth* 20B2
Leeuwin,C *Aust* 48A4
Leeward Is *Caribbean* 68E3
Lefka *Cyprus* 31B1
Lefkara *Cyprus* 31B1
Lefkoniko *Cyprus* 31B1
Legazpi *Phil* 45F8
Legnago *Italy* 17D2
Legnica *Pol* 20D2
Le Grand-Luce *France* 16A3
Le Grand Veymont Mt *France* 17A2
Legulzamo *Colombia* 70D4
Legvan Inlet *Guyana* 71G2
Leh *India* 35D2
Le Harve *France* 18C2
Lehi *USA* 65D2
Lehigh R *USA* 60C2
Lehighton *USA* 60C2
Le Hohneck Mt *France* 16D2
Leiah *Pak* 35C2
Leibnitz *Austria* 20D3
Leicester County *Eng* 15E5
Leicester *Eng* 15E5
Leichhardt R *Aust* 48C2
Leiden *Neth* 20A2
Leie R *Belg* 16B1
Leigh Creek *Aust* 48C4
Leighton Buzzard *Eng* 15E6
Leine R *W Germ* 20B2
Leinster Region *Irish Rep* 15B5
Leipzig *E Germ* 20C2
Leiria *Port* 19A2
Leirvik *Nor* 12F7
Leiyang *China* 40C4
Leizhou Bandao Pen *China* 40B5
Leizhou Wan B *China* 40C5
Lek R *Neth* 20A2
Lekemti *Eth* 78D3
Lekitobi *Indon* 45B3
Leksula *Indon* 45C3
Leland *USA* 63D3
Le Lavendou *France* 17B3
Lelija Mt *Yugos* 23D2
Le Locle *France* 17B1
Le Lude *France* 16A3
Lema R *Mexico* 67B1
Le Mans *France* 18C2
Le Mars *USA* 57C3
Lemhi Range Mts *USA* 64D2
Lemicux Is *Can* 53M3
Lemmon *USA* 54C2
Lemmon,Mt *USA* 65D4
Lemon Bank Oilfield *N Sea* 15G5
Lemoore *USA* 65C3
Lempdes *France* 18C2
Lemro R *Burma* 37D3
Le Murge Region *Italy* 22D2
Lena *USSR* 38D1
Lena R *USSR* 27O3
Lend *Austria* 17E1
Lendery *USSR* 24E3
Lengshujiang *China* 40C4
Leninabad *USSR* 29E1
Leninakan *USSR* 26F5
Leningrad *USSR* 24E4
Leningradskaya Base *Ant* 80F7
Leninogorsk Tatar ASSR *USSR* 24J5
Leninogorsk *USSR* 38B1
Leninsk-Kuznetskiy *USSR* 26K4
Leninskoye *USSR* 41C2
Lenkoran' *USSR* 25H8
Lenne R *W Germ* 16E1
Lenoir *USA* 61C1
Lenox *USA* 60D1
Lens *France* 16B1
Lensk *USSR* 27N3
Lentini *Italy* 22C3
Lenya R *Burma* 43B3
Léo *U Volta* 77F3
Leoben *Austria* 22C1
Leominster *Eng* 15D5
Leominster *USA* 60E1
Leon *Mexico* 66B2
León *Nic* 70A1
Leon Region *Spain* 19A1
León *Spain* 19A1
León State *Mexico* 67C1
Leonardville *Namibia* 79B6
Leonarisso *Cyprus* 31C1
Leonidovo *USSR* 41E2
Leonora *Aust* 48B3
Leopoldina *Brazil* 73D3
Léopoldville = Kinshasa
Lepel *USSR* 24D5
Leper *Belg* 16B1
Leping *China* 40D4
Le Puy *France* 18C2
Léraba R *Ivory Coast* 77F4
Léré *Chad* 78B3
Lerici *Italy* 17C2
Lérida *Spain* 19C1
Lermoos *Austria* 17D1
Léros I *Greece* 23F3
Le Roy *USA* 60B1
Lerwick *Scot* 13C1
Les Andelys *France* 16A2
Les Arcs *France* 17B3
Les Cayes *Haiti* 68C3
Les Echelles *France* 17A2
Les Ecrins Mt *France* 17B2
Les Escoumins *Can* 59F1
Leshan *China* 40A4
Les Iles Belcher Is *Can* 53L4
Leskovac *Yugos* 23E2
Les Landes Region *France* 18B3
Lesnoy *USSR* 24J4
Lesogorsk *USSR* 41E2
Lesosibirsk *USSR* 27L4
Lesozavodsk *USSR* 41C2
Les Sables-d'Olonne *France* 18B2
Lesser Antarctica Region *Ant* 80E
Lesser Antilles Is *Caribbean* 68D4
Les Trois Evêchés Mt *France* 17B2
Lésvos I *Greece* 23F3
Leszno *Pol* 20D2
Letha Range Mts *Burma* 37D3
Lethbridge *Can* 52G5
Lethbridge *Can* 52G5
Lethem *Guyana* 71G3
Leti I *Indon* 45C4
Letichev *USSR* 21F3
Let Oktyobr'ya *USSR* 27N4
Letong *Indon* 44C2
le Touquet-Paris-Plage *France* 15F6
Letpadan *Burma* 43B2
Le Tréport *France* 18C1
Leuk *Switz* 17B1
Leuven *Belg* 20A2
Levádhia *Greece* 23E3
Levanger *Nor* 12G6
Levanna Mt *Italy* 17B2
Levanto *Italy* 17C2
Levelland *USA* 62B3
Levens *France* 17B3
Lévêque,C *Aust* 39F8
Leverkusen *W Germ* 16D1
Levice *Czech* 21D3
Levico *Italy* 17D2
Levin *NZ* 51C2
Lévis *Can* 53L5
Levittown *USA* 59E2
Lévka Óri Mt *Greece* 23E3
Levkás *Greece* 23E3
Levkás I *Greece* 23E3
Lévque,C *Aust* 48B2
Levski *Bulg* 23F2
Lewes *Eng* 15F6
Lewis *USA* 62C2
Lewis I *Scot* 13B2
Lewisburg *USA* 60B2
Lewis P *NZ* 51B2
Lewis Range Mts *USA* 54B2
Lewis Smith,L *USA* 61B2
Lewiston Idaho *USA* 54B2
Lewiston Maine *USA* 55F2
Lewistown Montana *USA* 54C2
Lewistown Pennsylvania *USA* 59D2
Lewisville *USA* 63D3
Lexington Kentucky *USA* 55E3
Lexington Missouri *USA* 63D2
Lexington N Carolina *USA* 61C1
Lexington Nebraska *USA* 62C1
Lexington Virginia *USA* 59D3
Lexington Park *USA* 59D3
Leyte G *Phil* 45G8
Lezhe *Alb* 23D2
Iglesia *Arg* 72B2
Lhasa *China* 29H2
Lhazê *China* 37C2
Lhokseumawe *Indon* 44A1
Lhozhag *China* 37D2
Lhunze *China* 38C4
Liancourt Rocks = Tok-do
Lianga *Phil* 45G9
Liangdang *China* 40B3
Lianjiang *China* 40C5
Lianping *China* 40C5
Lian Xian *China* 40C5
Lianyungang *China* 40D3
Liaoding Bandao Pen *China* 40E1
Liaodong Wan B *China* 40E1
Liao He R *China* 40E1
Liaoning Province *China* 40E1
Liaoyang *China* 40E1
Liaoyuan *China* 40E1
Liaoyuang *China* 41B3
Liard R *Can* 52F3
Liard River *Can* 52F4
Liart *France* 16C2
Libby *USA* 64C1
Libenge *Zaïre* 78B3
Liberal *USA* 54C3
Liberec *Czech* 20C2
Liberia Republic *Africa* 76A4
Liberty Missouri *USA* 63D2
Liberty New York *USA* 59E2
Liberty Pennsylvania *USA* 60B2
Liberty Texas *USA* 63D3
Libourne *France* 18B3
libres *Mexico* 67C2
Libreville *Gabon* 78A3
Libya Republic *Africa* 75A2
Libyan Desert *Libya* 75B2
Libyan Plat *Egypt* 75B1
Licata *Italy* 22C3
Lichfield *Eng* 15E5
Lichinga *Mozam* 79D5
Lichtenburg *S Africa* 79C6
Licking R *USA* 58C3
Lida *USSR* 24D5
LidKöping *Sweden* 12G7
Lido di Ostia *Italy* 22C2
Liechtenstein Principality *Europe* 22B1
Liège *Belg* 20B2
Lielupe R *USSR* 21E1
Lienart *Zaïre* 78C3
Lienz *Austria* 20C3
Liepāja *USSR* 12J7
Liepāja *USSR* 24C4
Lier *Belg* 16C1
Liestal *Switz* 17B1
Liévre R *Can* 59E1
Liezen *Austria* 20C3
Liffey R *Irish Rep* 15B5
Lifford *Irish Rep* 14B4
Lifu I *Nouvelle Calédonie* 49F3
Lightning Ridge *Aust* 50C1
Ligny-en-Barrois *France* 16C2
Ligonha R *Mozam* 79D5

Liguria **Luverne**

Liguria Region *Italy* 17C2
Ligurian S *Italy* 22B2
Lihir Group Is *PNG* 49E1
Likasi *Zaïre* 79C5
Likupang *Indon* 45C2
Lille *France* 18C1
Lillebonne *France* 16A2
Lillehammer *Nor* 12G6
Lillers *France* 16B1
Lillestøm *Nor* 12G6
Lilongwe *Malawi* 79D5
Liloy *Phil* 45F9
Lim R *Yugos* 23D2
Lima *Peru* 70C6
Lima *Spain* 19A1
Lima *USA* 55E2
Lima Res *USA* 64D2
Limassol *Cyprus* 30B3
Limavady *N Ire* 14B4
Limay R *Arg* 72B3
Limay Mahuida *Arg* 72B3
Limbe *Malawi* 79D5
Limbotto *Indon* 45B2
Limburg *W Gem* 20B2
Limeira *Brazil* 71J8
Limerick *Irish Rep* 13B3
Limfjorden L *Den* 20B1
Limmen Bight B *Aust* 48C2
Límnos I *Greece* 23F3
Limoeiro *Brazil* 71L5
Limoges *France* 18C2
Limón *Costa Rica* 66D4
Limon *USA* 54C3
Limone *Italy* 17B2
Limousin Region *France* 18C2
Limpopo R *Mozam/S Africa* 79D6
Linanes *Mexico* 67C1
Linapacan Str *Phil* 45E8
Linares *Chile* 69B5
Linares *Mexico* 54D4
Linares *Spain* 19B2
Lincang *China* 38C4
Lincoln *Arg* 69D4
Lincoln California *USA* 63C1
Lincoln County *Eng* 15E5
Lincoln *Eng* 15E5
Lincoln Illinois *USA* 58B2
Lincoln Maine *USA* 59F1
Lincoln Nebraska *USA* 54D2
Lincoln New Hampshire *USA* 59E2
Lincoln *NZ* 51B2
Lincoln S *Greenland* 80A
Lincoln City *USA* 64B2
Lincoln Park *USA* 58C2
L'Incudina Mt *Corse* 22B2
Lindau *W Germ* 20B3
Linden *Guyana* 71G2
Lindesnes C *Nor* 12F7
Lindi *Tanz* 79D4
Lindi R *Zaïre* 78C3
Lindley *S Africa* 79C6
Lindos *Greece* 23F3
Lindsay *Can* 59D2
Lindsay Montana *USA* 57A2
Line Is *Pacific O* 47M4
Linfen *China* 40C2
Lingao *China* 43D2
Lingayen *Phil* 45F7
Lingen *W Germ* 20B2
Lingle *USA* 57B3
Lingling *China* 40C4
Lingshan *China* 40B5
Lingshi *China* 40C2
Linguère *Sen* 76A3
Linhai Heilongjiang *China* 41A1
Linhai Rhejiang *China* 40E4
Linhares *Brazil* 71L7
Linhe *China* 40B1
Linjiang *China* 41B3
Linköping *Sweden* 12H7
Linkou *China* 41C2
Linqing *China* 40D2
Lins *Brazil* 73C3
Lintao *China* 40A2
Linthal *Switz* 17C1
Linton *USA* 57B2
Linxi *China* 38E2
Linxia *China* 40A2
Linz *Austria* 20C3
Lipa *Phil* 45F8
Lipari I *Italy* 22C3
Lipetsk *USSR* 25F5
Lipova *Rom* 23E1
Lippe R *W Germ* 20B2
Lippstadt *W Germ* 16E1
Lira *Uganda* 78D3
Liranga *Congo* 78B4
Lisala *Zaïre* 78C3
Lisboa *Port* 19A2
Lisbon = Lisboa
Lisbon *USA* 57C2
Lisburn *N Ire* 15B4
Lisburne,C *USA* 56E2
Lishui *China* 40D4
Li Shui R *China* 40C4
Lisichansk *USSR* 25F6
Lisieux *France* 18C2
L'Isle-Adam *France* 16B2
L'Isle-sur-le-Doubs *France* 17B1
Lismore *Aust* 49E3
Litang *China* 40B5
Lītanī R *Leb* 31C2
Litani R *Suriname* 71H3
Litchfield Illinois *USA* 58B3
Litchfield Minnesota *USA* 57D2
Lithgow *Aust* 48E4
Lititz *USA* 60B2
Litke *USSR* 41E1
Litovko *USSR* 41D2
Litovskaya SSR Republic *USSR* 24C4
Little R *USA* 63C3
Little Abaco I *Bahamas* 55F4
Little Aden *S Yemen* 32D4
Little Andaman I *Andaman Is* 36E2
Little Barrier I *NZ* 51C1
Little Belt Mts *USA* 64D1
Little Bitter L *Egypt* 31B3
Little Cayman I *Caribbean* 66D3
Little Egg Harbour B *USA* 60C3
Little Falls Minnesota *USA* 57D2
Little Falls New York *USA* 60C1
Littlefield *USA* 62B3
Littlefork *USA* 57D2
Little Fork R *USA* 57D2
Little Halibut Bank Sandbank *Scot* 14E2
Little Inagua I *Caribbean* 68C2
Little Koniuji I *USA* 56G4
Little Missouri R *USA* 57B2
Little Nicobar I *Nicobar Is* 43A4
Little Rock *USA* 55D3
Little Sitkin I *USA* 56B6
Littlestown *USA* 60B3
Little Tanaga I *USA* 56C6
Littleton Colorado *USA* 62A2
Littleton New Hampshire *USA* 59E2
Liuhe *China* 41B3
Liuzhou *China* 40B5
Livanátais *Greece* 23E3
Līvāni *USSR* 21F1
Livarot *France* 16A2
Livengood *USA* 56J2
Livenza R *Italy* 17E2
Live Oak *USA* 61C2
Livermore *USA* 65B3
Livermore,Mt *USA* 62B3
Liverpool *Can* 53M5
Liverpool *Eng* 15D5
Liverpool B *Can* 52E2
Liverpool B *Eng* 15D5
Liverpool,C *Can* 53L2
Liverpool Range Mts *Aust* 50D2
Livingston Montana *USA* 54B2
Livingston Tennessee *USA* 61B1
Livingston Texas *USA* 63D3
Livingstone = Maramba
Livingston,L *USA* 63C3
Livno *Yugos* 22D2
Livny *USSR* 25F5
Livonia *USA* 58C2
Livorno *Italy* 22C2
Livramento do Brumado *Brazil* 73D1
Liwale *Tanz* 79D4
Lizard Pt *Eng* 15C7
Ljubljana *Yugos* 22C1
Ljungan R *Sweden* 12G6
Ljungby *Sweden* 12G7
Ljusdal *Sweden* 12H6
Ljusnan R *Sweden* 24B3
Llandeilo *Wales* 15D6
Llandovery *Wales* 15D6
Llandrindod Wells *Wales* 15D5
Llandudno *Wales* 15D5
Llanelli *Wales* 15C6
Llangollen *Wales* 15D5
Llano *USA* 62C3
Llano R *USA* 62C3
Llano Estacado Plat *USA* 54C3
Llanos Region *Colombia/Ven* Z4D2
Llanos de Chiquitos Region *Bol* 70F7
Llera *Mexico* 67C1
Llerena *Spain* 19A2
Lleyn Pen *Wales* 15C5
Llimsk *USSR* 27M4
Llin *USSR* 27M4
Lloydminster *Can* 52H4
Llullaillaco Mt *Chile/Arg* 69C2
Loa R *Chile* 69C2
Loan *France* 18C2
Loange R *Zaïre* 78B4
Lobatse *Botswana* 79C6
Lobaye R *CAR* 78B3
Loberia *Arg* 72D3
Lobito *Angola* 79B5
Lobos *Arg* 72D3
Locano *Italy* 17B2
Locarno *Switz* 17C1
Loch Awe L *Scot* 14C3
Lochboisdale *Scot* 14B3
Loch Bracadale Inlet *Scot* 14B3
Loch Broom Estuary *Scot* 14C3
Loch Doon L *Scot* 14C4
Loch Earn L *Scot* 14C3
Loch Eriboll Inlet *Scot* 14C2
Loch Ericht L *Scot* 14C3
Loches *France* 18C2
Loch Etive Inlet *Scot* 14C3
Loch Ewe Inlet *Scot* 14C3
Loch Fyne Inlet *Scot* 14C3
Loch Hourn Inlet *Scot* 14C3
Loch Indaal Inlet *Scot* 14B4
Lochinver *Scot* 14C2
Loch Katrine L *Scot* 14C3
Loch Leven L *Scot* 14D3
Loch Linnhe Inlet *Scot* 14C3
Loch Lochy L *Scot* 14C3
Loch Lomond L *Scot* 14C3
Loch Long Inlet *Scot* 14C3
Lochmaddy *Scot* 14B3
Loch Maree L *Scot* 14C3
Loch Morar L *Scot* 14C3
Lochnagar Mt *Scot* 14D3
Loch Ness L *Scot* 14C3
Loch Rannoch L *Scot* 14C3
Loch Roag Inlet *Scot* 14B2
Lochsa R *USA* 64C1
Loch Sheil L *Scot* 14C3
Loch Shin L *Scot* 14C2
Loch Snizort Inlet *Scot* 14B3
Loch Sunart Inlet *Scot* 14C3
Loch Tay L *Scot* 14C3
Loch Torridon Inlet *Scot* 14C3
Lock *Aust* 50A2
Lockerbie *Scot* 14D4
Lock Haven *USA* 59D2
Lockport *USA* 59D2
Loc Ninh *Viet* 43D3
Locri *Italy* 22D3
Lod *Israel* 31C3
Loddon R *Aust* 50B3
Lodeynoye Pole *USSR* 24E3
Lodge Grass *USA* 64E1
Lodhran *Pak* 35C3
Lodi *Italy* 22B1
Lodi *USA* 65B3
Lodja *Zaïre* 78C4
Lods *France* 17B1
Lodwar *Kenya* 78D3
Łódź *Pol* 21D2
Lofer *Austria* 17E1
Lofoten Is *Nor* 12G5
Logan New Mexico *USA* 62B2
Logan Utah *USA* 54B2
Logan,Mt *Can* 52D3
Logan Mts *Can* 56N3
Logansport Indiana *USA* 58B2
Logansport Louisiana *USA* 63D3
Loganton *USA* 60B2
Logroño *Spain* 19B1
Lohārdaga *India* 37B3
Lohja *Fin* 12J6
Lohr *W Germ* 16E2
Loikaw *Burma* 43B2
Loimaa *Fin* 12J6
Loing R *France* 16B2
Loir R *France* 18C2
Loire R *France* 18C2
Loire et Cher Department *France* 16A3
Loiret Department *France* 16B3
Loja *Ecuador* 70C4
Loja *Spain* 19B2
Loji *Indon* 45C3
Lokan Tekojärvi Res *Fin* 12K5
Lokeren *Belg* 16B1
Lokitaung *Kenya* 78D3
Loknya *USSR* 21F1
Lokoja *Nig* 77H4
Lokolo R *Zaïre* 78C4
Lokoro R *Zaïre* 78C4
Loks Land I *Can* 53M3
Lolland I *Den* 20C2
Loloda *Indon* 45C2
Lolo P *USA* 64D1
Lom *Bulg* 23E2
Lom R *Cam* 77J4
Lomami R *Zaïre* 79C4
Loma Mts *Sierra Leone/Guinea* 76A4
Lombagin *Indon* 45B2
Lombardia Region *Italy* 17C2
Lomblen I *Indon* 45B4
Lombok I *Indon* 44E4
Lomé *Togo* 77G4
Lomela *Zaïre* 78C4
Lomela R *Zaïre* 78C4
Lomond Oilfield *N Sea* 14G3
Lomonosov *USSR* 24D4
Lomont Region *France* 17B1
Lompoc *USA* 65B4
Łomza *Pol* 21E2
Lonāvale *India* 36A1
Loncoche *Chile* 69B5
London *Can* 53K5
London *Eng* 15E6
London *USA* 58C3
Londonderry County *N Ire* 14B4
Londonderry *N Ire* 14B4
Londonderry I *Chile* 69B9
Londonderry,C *Aust* 48B2
Londres *Arg* 69C3
Londrina *Brazil* 69F2
Long I *Bahamas* 55F4
Long I *PNG* 39H7
Long Akah *Malay* 44D2
Longarone *Italy* 17E1
Longavi Mt *Chile* 72A3
Long B *Jamaica* 68H2
Long B *USA* 61D2
Long Beach California *USA* 54B3
Long Beach New York *USA* 59E2
Long Branch *USA* 59E2
Longchuan *China* 40D5
Long Creek *USA* 64C2
Longford *Aust* 50E3
Longford County *Irish Rep* 15B5
Longford *Irish Rep* 15B5
Long Forties Region *N Sea* 14E3
Longhua *China* 40D1
Long I *Can* 53L4
Long I *PNG* 48D1
Long I *USA* 55F2
Long Island Sd *USA* 60D2
Longjiang *China* 41A2
Long L *Can* 58B1
Long L *USA* 57B2
Longlac *Can* 53K4
Longlin *China* 40B5
Longmont *USA* 54C2
Longnawan *Indon* 44E2
Longny *France* 16C2
Long Prairie *USA* 57D2
Longquimay *Chile* 69B5
Longreach *Aust* 48D3
Longshou Shan Upland *China* 40A2
Longs Peak Mt *USA* 62A1
Longtown *Eng* 14D4
Longueuil *Can* 59E1
Longuimay *Chile* 72A3
Longuyon *France* 16C2
Longview Texas *USA* 55D3
Longview Washington *USA* 54A2
Longwy *France* 18D2
Longxi *China* 40A3
Long Xuyen *Viet* 43D3
Longyan *China* 40D4
Longzhou *China* 40B5
Lonigo *Italy* 17D2
Lons-le-Saunier *France* 18D2
Lookout,C *USA* 55F3
Loolmalasin Mt *Tanz* 78D4
Lop Buri *Thai* 43C3
Lopez C *Gabon* 78A4
Lop Nur L *China* 38C2
Lora del Rio *Spain* 19A2
Lorain *USA* 55E2
Loralai *Pak* 35B2
Lordegān *Iran* 34C2
Lord Howe I *Aust* 49E4
Lord Howe Rise *Pacific O* 47K5
Lord Mayor B *Can* 53J3
Lordsburg *USA* 54C3
Lorena *Brazil* 73C3
Loreo *Italy* 17E2
Loreto *Mexico* 67B1
Lorient *France* 18B2
Lorne *Aust* 50B3
Lörrach *W Germ* 20B3
Lorraine Region *France* 18D2
Los Alamos *USA* 54C3
Los Andes *Chile* 72A2
Los Angeles *Chile* 69B5
Los Angeles *USA* 54B3
Los Banos *USA* 65B3
Los Cerrillos *Arg* 72B2
Los Corchos *Mexico* 67A1
Los Gatos *USA* 65B3
Lošinj I *Yugos* 22C2
Los Juries *Arg* 72C1
Los Lagos *Chile* 72A3
Los Laiaderoz *Mexico* 67C1
Los Loros *Chile* 72A1
Los Luncas *USA* 62A3
Los Menucos *Arg* 72B4
Los Mochis *Mexico* 66B2
Los Sauces *Chile* 72A3
Losser *USSR* 24J3
Lossiemouth *Scot* 14D3
Los Telares *Arg* 72C1
Los Testigos Is *Ven* 68E4
Lost Trail P *USA* 64D1
Los Vilos *Chile* 69B4
Lot R *France* 18C3
Lota *Chile* 72A3
Lothian Region *Scot* 14D4
Lotikipi Plain *Sudan/Kenya* 78D3
Loto *Zaïre* 78C4
Lötschberg Tunnel *Switz* 17B1
Lotta R *Fin USSR* 12K5
Loudéac *France* 18B2
Louga *Sen* 76A3
Lough Allen L *Irish Rep* 13B3
Loughborough *Eng* 15E5
Lough Conn L *Irish Rep* 13B3
Lough Corrib L *Irish Rep* 13B3
Lough Derg L *Irish Rep* 13B3
Loughead I *Can* 52H2
Lough Ennell L *Irish Rep* 15B5
Lough Erne L *N Ire* 13B3
Lough Foyle Estuary *N Ire/Irish Rep* 13B2
Lough Neagh L *N Ire* 13B3
Lough Ree L *Irish Rep* 13B3
Lough Strangford L *Irish Rep* 15C4
Lough Swilly Estuary *Irish Rep* 14B4
Louhans *France* 17A1
Louisa *USA* 58C3
Louisa Reef I *S E Asia* 44D1
Louise I *Can* 56M5
Louise,L *USA* 56J3
Louisiade Arch *Solomon Is* 49E2
Louisiana State *USA* 55D3
Louis Trichardt *S Africa* 79D6
Louisville Georgia *USA* 61C2
Louisville Kentucky *USA* 55E3
Louisville Mississippi *USA* 61B2
Loukhi *USSR* 24E2
Lount L *Can* 57D1
Loup R *France* 17B3
Loup R *USA* 62C1
Lourdes *France* 18B3
Lourenço Marques = Maputo
Louth *Aust* 50C2
Louth County *Irish Rep* 15B5
Louth *Eng* 15E5
Louvain = Leuven
Louviers *France* 18C2
Lovat R *USSR* 24E4
Lovech *Bulg* 23E2
Loveland *USA* 62A1
Loveland P *USA* 62A2
Lovell *USA* 64E2
Lovelock *USA* 65C2
Lóvere *Italy* 22C1
Lovington *USA* 62B3
Lovozero *USSR* 24F2
Low,C *Can* 53K3
Lowell Massachusetts *USA* 55F2
Lowell Oregon *USA* 64B2
Lowell *USA* 60E1
Lower Arrow L *Can* 64C1
Lower Hutt *NZ* 51B2
Lower Post *Can* 56N4
Lower Seal,L *Can* 53L4
Lowestoft *Eng* 15F5
Łowicz *Pol* 21D2
Loxton *Aust* 50B2
Loyalstock Creek R *USA* 60B2
Loyd George,Mt *Can* 52F4
Loznica *Yugos* 23D2
loz Reyes *Mexico* 67B2
Lozva R *USSR* 26H3
Luacano *Angola* 79C5
Luachimo *Angola* 79C4
Lualaba R *Zaïre* 78C4
Luampa *Zambia* 79C5
Luân *Angola* 79C5
Lu'an *China* 40D3
Luanda *Angola* 79B4
Luando R *Angola* 79B5
Luanginga R *Angola* 79C5
Luang Namtha *Laos* 43C1
Luang Prabang *Laos* 43C2
Luangue R *Angola* 79B4
Luangwa R *Zambia* 79D5
Luan He R *China* 40D1
Luanping *China* 40D1
Luanshya *Zambia* 79C5
Luapula R *Zaïre* 79C5
Luarca *Spain* 19A1
Lubalo *Angola* 79B4
L'uban *USSR* 21F2
Lubang Is *Phil* 45F8
Lubango *Angola* 79B5
Lubbock *USA* 54C3
Lübeck *W Germ* 20C2
Lubefu *Zaïre* 78C4
Lubefu R *Zaïre* 78C4
Lubero *Zaïre* 78C3
Lubéron R *France* 17A3
Lubilash R *Zaïre* 79C4
Lublin *Pol* 21E2
Lubny *USSR* 25E5
Lubok Antu *Malay* 44D2
Lubudi *Zaïre* 79C4
Lubudi R *Zaïre* 79C4
Lubuklinggau *Indon* 44B3
Lubumbashi *Zaïre* 79C5
Lubutu *Zaïre* 78C4
Lucas *Brazil* 73A1
Lucban *Phil* 45F8
Lucca *Italy* 22C2
Luce B *Scot* 14C4
Lucedale *USA* 63E3
Lucena *Phil* 45F8
Lucenec *Czech* 21D3
Lucerne = Luzern
Lucero *Mexico* 62A3
Luchegorsk *USSR* 41C2
Luchuan *China* 40C5
Luckenwalde *E Germ* 20C2
Lucknow *India* 37B2
Lucusse *Angola* 79C5
Lüda *China* 40E2
Lüdenscheid *W Germ* 16D1
Lüderitz *Namibie* 79B6
Ludhiana *India* 35D2
Ludington *USA* 58B2
Ludlow California *USA* 65C4
Ludlow *Eng* 15D5
Ludlow Vermont *USA* 60D1
Ludogorie Upland *Bulg* 23F2
Ludowici *USA* 61C2
Luduş *Rom* 23E1
Ludvika *Sweden* 12H6
Ludwigsburg *W Germ* 20B3
Ludwigshafen *W Germ* 20B3
Ludwigslust *E Germ* 20C2
Luebo *Zaïre* 78C4
Luema R *Zaïre* 78C4
Luembe R *Angola* 79C4
Luena *Angola* 79B5
Luene R *Angola* 79C5
Lüeyang *China* 40B3
Lufeng *China* 40D5
Lufkin *USA* 55D3
Luga *USSR* 24D4
Luga R *USSR* 24D4
Lugano *Switz* 22B1
Lugela *Mozam* 79D5
Lugenda R *Mozam* 79D5
Lugo *Italy* 17D2
Lugo *Spain* 19A1
Lugoj *Rom* 23E1
Luhuo *China* 40A3
Lui R *Angola* 79B4
Luiana *Angola* 79C5
Luiana R *Angola* 79C5
Luichow Peninsula = Leizhou Bandao
Luino *Italy* 17C2
Luionga R *Zaïre* 78B3
Luipan Shan Upland *China* 40B2
Luiro R *Fin* 24D2
Luishia *Zaïre* 79C5
Luixi *China* 38C4
Luiza *Zaïre* 79C4
Luján *Arg* 72B2
Luján *Arg* 72D2
Lujiang *China* 40D3
Lukenie R *Zaïre* 78B4
Lukeville *USA* 65D4
Luki *USSR* 26E4
Lukolela *Zaïre* 78B4
Łuków *Pol* 21E2
Lukuga R *Zaïre* 78C4
Lukulu *Zambia* 79C5
Lule R *Sweden* 24C2
Luleå *Sweden* 12J5
Lüleburgaz *Turk* 23F2
Lüliang Shan Mts *China* 40C2
Luling *USA* 63C4
Lullaillaco Mt *Chile* 70E8
Lulonga R *Zaïre* 78C3
Luluabourg = Kananga
Lumbala *Angola* 79C5
Lumberton *USA* 55F3
Lumbis *Indon* 44E2
Lumbovka *USSR* 24G2
Lumding *India* 37D2
Lumeje *Angola* 79C5
Lumsden *NZ* 51A3
Lund *Sweden* 12G7
Lundar *Can* 57C1
Lundazi *Zambia* 79D5
Lundi R *Zim* 79D6
Lundy I *Eng* 15C6
Lüneburg *W Germ* 20C2
Lunéville *France* 16D2
Lunga R *Zambia* 79C5
Lunglei *India* 37D3
Lungue Bungo R *Angola* 79B5
Luninec *USSR* 21F2
Luobei *China* 41C2
Luobomo *Congo* 78B4
Luocheng *China* 40B5
Luoding *China* 40C5
Luohe *China* 40C3
Luo He R Henan *China* 40C3
Luo He R Shaanxi *China* 40B2
Luoxiao Shan Hills *China* 40C4
Luoyang *China* 40C3
Luozi *Zaïre* 78B4
Lupane *Zim* 79C5
Lupilichi *Mozam* 79D5
Lu Qu = Tao He
Luque *Par* 69E3
Lure *France* 16D3
Lurgan *N Ire* 15B4
Lurio R *Mozam* 79D5
Luristan Region *Iran* 34B2
Lusaka *Zambia* 79C5
Lusambo *Zaïre* 78C4
Lushnjë *Alb* 23D2
Lushoto *Tanz* 78D4
Lushui *China* 38C4
Lüshun *China* 40E2
Lusk *USA* 57B3
Luton *Eng* 15E6
Lutsk *USSR* 25D5
Luuq *Somalia* 78E3
Luverne *USA* 57C3

Luvua Ma Qu

Luvua R Zaïre 79C4
Luwegu R Tanz 79D4
Luwingu Zambia 79D5
Luwuk Indon 45B3
Luxembourg Grand Duchy N W Europe 16D2
Luxembourg Lux 18D2
Luxeuil-les-Bains France 16D3
Luxi China 40A5
Luxor Egypt 75C2
Luza USSR 24H3
Luza R USSR 24H3
Luzern Switz 22B1
Luzerne USA 60D1
Luzhai China 40B5
Luzhi China 40B4
Luzhou China 40B4
Luziânia Brazil 73C2
Luzon I Phil 45F7
Luzon Str Phil 45F6
L'vov USSR 21E3
Lybster Scot 14D2
Lycksele Sweden 12H6
Lydenburg S Africa 79C6
Lyell,Mt USA 54B3
Lykens USA 60B2
Lyman USA 64D2
Lyme B Eng 15D6
Lyme Regis Eng 15D6
Lynchburg USA 55F3
Lyndhurst Aust 50A2
Lynn USA 59E2
Lynn Haven USA 61B2
Lynn Lake Can 52H4
Lynx L Can 52H3
Lyon France 18C2
Lyon Canal Sd USA 56L4
Lyons Georgia USA 61C2
Lyons New York USA 60B1
Lyons R Aust 48A3
Lys R Italy 17B2
Lys'va USSR 24K4
Lyttelton NZ 51B2
Lyubeshov USSR 21F2
Lyublino USSR 24F4

M

Ma R Viet 43C1
Ma'agan Jordan 31C2
Ma'alot Tarshīha Israel 31C2
Ma'an Jordan 30C3
Ma'anshan China 40D3
Ma'arrat an Nu'mān Syria 31D1
Maas R Neth 16C1
Maaseik Belg 16C1
Maasin Phil 45F8
Maastricht Belg 20B2
Mabaruma Guyana 71G2
Mablethorpe Eng 15F5
Mabote Mozam 79D6
Mabrita USSR 21E2
M'adel USSR 21F2
Macaé Brazil 73D3
McAlester USA 54D3
McAllen USA 54D4
Macaloge Mozam 79D5
Macao Dependency China 40C5
Macapá Brazil 71H3
Macarani Brazil 73D2
Macas Ecuador 70C4
Macaú Brazil 71L5
Macaúbas Brazil 73D1
M'Bari R CAR 78C3
McCall USA 64C2
McCamey USA 62B3
McCammon USA 64D2
McCarthy USA 56K3
Macclesfield Eng 15D5
McClintock B Can 53K1
McClintock Chan Can 52H2
McClure USA 60B2
McClure Str Can 52G2
McComb USA 63D3
McConaughy,L USA 62B1
McCook USA 54C2
Macculloch,C Can 53L2
McDame Can 52F4
McDermitt USA 64C2
Mcdonald Peak Mt USA 64D1
Macdonnell Ranges Mts Aust 48C3
Macedo de Cavaleiros Port 19A1
Maceió Brazil 71L5
Macenta Guinea 76B4
Macerata Italy 22C2
Macfarlane,L Aust 50A2
McGehee USA 63D3
McGill USA 65D3
McGrath USA 52C3
McGuire,Mt USA 64D1
Machado Brazil 73C3
Machaila Mozam 79D6
Machakos Kenya 78D4
Machala Ecuador 70C4
Machaze Mozam 79D6
Mācherla India 36B1
Machgharab Leb 31C2
Machias USA 59F2
Machilipatnam India 36C1
Machiques Ven 70D1
Machu-Picchu Hist Site Peru 70D6
Macia Mozam 79D6
Macias Nguema = Fernando Poo
McIntosh USA 57B2
MacIntyre R Aust 50C1
Mack USA 62A2
Mackay Aust 48D3
Mackay USA 64D2
Mackay,L Aust 48B3
McKean I Phoenix Is 49H1
McKeesport USA 59D2
Mackenzie R Can 52F3
Mackenzie Region Can 52F3
Mackenzie B Can 52E3
Mackenzie King I Can 52G2
Mackenzie Mts Can 52E3
Mackinac,Str of USA 58C1
Mackinaw City USA 58C1
McKinley,Mt USA 56H3
McKinney USA 63C3
Mackinson Inlet B Can 53L2
Macksville Aust 50D2
Mclaoughlin,Mt USA 64B2
McLaughlin USA 57B2
Maclean Aust 50D1
Maclear S Africa 79C7
McLennan Can 52G4
McLeod B Can 52G3
McLeod,L Aust 48A3
Macmillan R Can 52E3
McMillan,L USA 62B3
Macmillan P Can 56M3
McMinnville Oregon USA 64B1
McMinnville Tennessee USA 61B1
McMurdo Base Ant 80F7
McNary USA 65E4
Macomb USA 58A2
Macomer Sardegna 22B2
Macomia Mozam 79D5
Mâcon France 18C2
Macon Georgia USA 55E3
Macon Missouri USA 63D2
Macondo Angola 79C5
McPherson USA 63C2
Macquarie Is Aust 46J7
Macquarie R Aust 50C2
Macquarie Harbour B Aust 50E3
Macquarie,L Aust 50D2
McRae USA 61C2
MacRobertsn Land Region Ant 80F11
M'saken Tunisia 77E1
M'Sila Alg 77C1
McTavish Arm B Can 52G3
Macumba R Aust 50A1
Macunaga Italy 17C2
McVicar Arm B Can 52F3
M'yaróvár Hung 20D3
Mada R Nig 77H4
Mādabā Jordan 31C3
Madadi Well Chad 78C2
Madagascar Basin Indian O 46D6
Madama Niger 78B1
Madang PNG 48D1
Madaoua Niger 76C3
Madaripur Bang 37D3
Madau USSR 34C1
Madawaska R Can 59D1
Madaya Burma 37E3
Madeira I Atlantic O 76A1
Madeira R Brazil 70F5
Madelia USA 57D3
Madera Mexico 66B2
Madera USA 65B3
Madgaon India 36A1
Madhubani India 37C2
Madhya Pradesh State India 37B3
Madicine Bow Mts USA 62A1
Madikeri India 36B2
Madimba Zaïre 78B4
Madingo Kayes Congo 78B4
Madingou Congo 78B4
Madison Indiana USA 55E3
Madison Minnesota USA 57C2
Madison Nebraska USA 57C3
Madison S Dakota USA 57C3
Madison Wisconsin USA 55E2
Madison R USA 64D1
Madisonville Kentucky USA 58B3
Madisonville Texas USA 63C3
Madiun Indon 44D4
Mado Gashi Kenya 78D3
Madonna Di Campiglio Italy 17D1
Madras India 36C2
Madras USA 64B2
Madre de Dios I Chile 69A8
Madre de Dios R Bol 70E6
Madrid Spain 19B1
Madridejos Spain 19B2
Madura I Indon 44D4
Madurai India 36B3
Maebashi Japan 42C3
Mae Khlong R Thai 43B3
Mae Nam Lunang R Thai 43B4
Mae Nam Mun R Thai 43C2
Mae Nam Ping R Thai 43B2
Maengsan N Korea 42A3
Maevatanana Madag 79E5
Maewo I Vanuatu 49F2
Mafeking S Africa 79C6
Maffra Aust 50C3
Mafia I Tanz 79D4
Mafra Brazil 69G3
Mafraq Jordan 30C3
Magadan USSR 27O4
Magargué Colombia 70D2
Magaria Niger 77H3
Magdagachi USSR 41B1
Magdalena Arg 72D3
Magdalena Mexico 54B3
Magdalena USA 62A3
Magdalena R Colombia 68C4
Magdalena,Mt Malay 44E2
Magdalene Mexico 66A1
Magdalen Is Can 53M5
Magdeburg E Germ 20C2
Magdelena R Colombia 70D2
Magé Brazil 71K8
Magelang Indon 44D4
Maggia R Switz 17C1
Maghâgha Egypt 30B4
Magherafelt N Ire 14B4
Maglie Italy 23D2
Magnitogorsk USSR 24K5
Magnolia USA 63D3
Mago USSR 41E1
Magoé Mozam 79D5
Magog Can 59E1
Magosal Mexico 67C1
Magra R Italy 17C2
Maguse River Can 53J3
Magwe Burma 43B1
Mahābād Iran 25H8
Mahabharat Range Mts Nepal 37C2
Mahād India 36A1
Mahadeo Hills India 35D4
Mahaffey USA 60A2
Mahajanga Madag 79E5
Mahalapye Botswana 79C6
Mahānadi R India 37B3
Mahanoro Madag 79E5
Mahanoy City USA 60B2
Maharashtra State India 36A1
Māhāsamund India 37B3
Maha Sarakham Thai 43C2
Mahavavy R Madag 79E5
Mahbūbnagar India 36B1
Mahdia Tunisia 77E1
Mahe India 36B2
Mahekar India 35D4
Mahéli I Comoros 79E5
Mahendragarh India 37B3
Mahenge Tanz 79D4
Mahesāna India 35C4
Mahia Pen NZ 51C1
Mahnomen USA 57C2
Mahoba India 35D3
Mahón Spain 19C2
Mahony L Can 56N2
Mahrés Tunisia 77E2
Mahuva India 35C4
Maicao Colombia 70D1
Maîche France 17B1
Maichew Eth 32C4
Maidstone Eng 15F6
Maiduguri Nig 78B2
Maigomaj R Sweden 24B3
Maihar India 37B3
Maijdi Bang 37D3
Mail Kyun I Burma 43B3
Maimana Afghan 35A1
Main R W Germ 16E2
Main Chan Can 58C1
Mai-Ndombe L Zaïre 78B4
Maine State USA 55G2
Maine Region France 16A3
Mainé-Soroa Niger 77J3
Mainland I Scot 14D2
Mainpuri India 35D3
Maintenon France 16A2
Maintirano Madag 79E5
Mainz W Germ 20B2
Maio I Cape Verde 76A4
Maipó Mt Arg/Chile 69C4
Maipú Arg 72D3
Maiquetía Ven 70E1
Maira R Italy 17B2
Mairābāri India 37D2
Maiskhal I Bang 37D3
Maitland New South Wales Aust 48E4
Maitland S Australia Aust 50A2
Maiz W Germ 18D1
Maizuru Japan 41D4
Majene Indon 48A1
Majes R Peru 70D7
Maji Eth 78D3
Majia He R China 40D2
Majunga = Mahajanga
Makale Eth 78D2
Makale Indon 45A3
Makalo Indon 44B3
Makalu Mt China/Nepal 37C2
Makarikha USSR 24K2
Makarov USSR 41E2
Makarska Yugos 22D2
Makaryev USSR 24G4
Makassar = Ujung Pandang
Makassar Str Indon 44E3
Makat USSR 25J6
Makeni Sierra Leone 76A4
Makeyevka USSR 25F6
Makgadikgadi Salt Pan Botswana 79C6
Makhachkala USSR 25H7
Makharadze USSR 30D1
Makian I Indon 45C2
Makindu Kenya 78D4
Makkah = Mecca
Makkovik Can 53N4
Makó Hung 21E3
Makokou Gabon 78B3
Makorako,Mt NZ 51C1
Makoua Congo 78B3
Makrāna India 35C3
Makran Coast Range Mts Pak 35A3
Maksimovka USSR 41D2
Maksotag Iran 34E3
Maktar Tunisia 77D1
Mākū Iran 25G8
Makumbi Zaïre 78C4
Makurazaki Japan 41C5
Makurdi Nig 77H4
Makushin V USA 56E5
Malabang Phil 45F9
Malabar Coast India 36B2
Malabrigo Arg 72D1
Malacca,Str of S E Asia 43C5
Malad City USA 64D2
Málaga Colombia 70D2
Malaga Spain 19B2
Malaga USA 62B3
Malaimbandy Madag 79E6
Malaita I Solomon Is 49F1
Malakal Sudan 78D3
Malakand Pak 35C2
Malamala Indon 45B3
Malang Indon 44D4
Malange Angola 79B4
Malanville Benin 77G3
Mal Anyuy R USSR 27S3
Mälaren L Sweden 12H7
Malargüe Arg 72B3
Malartic Can 59D1
Malaspina Gl USA 56K4
Malatya Turk 25F8
Malawi Republic Africa 79D5
Malawi,L = Nyasa,L
Malaya Sidima USSR 41D2
Malaybalay Phil 45G9
Malāyer Iran 34B2
Malaysia Federation S E Asia 39D6
Malazgirt Turk 30D2
Malbork Pol 21D2
Malbrán Arg 72C1
Malchin E Germ 20C2
Malden USA 63E2
Maldives Is Indian O 29F5
Maldives Ridge Indian O 46E4
Maldon Eng 16A1
Maldonado Urug 69F4
Male Italy 17D1
Malegaon India 35C4
Malé Karpaty Upland Czech 20D3
Malekula I Vanuatu 49F2
Malema Mozam 79D5
Malen'ga USSR 24F2
Malesherbes France 16B2
Mālestān Afghan 35B2
Maleuz USSR 24K5
Malgomaj L Sweden 12H5
Malha Well Sudan 78C2
Malheur L USA 64C2
Mali Republic Africa 76B3
Mali Hka R Burma 37E2
Malili Indon 45B3
Malin USSR 21F2
Malinau Indon 44E2
Malindi Kenya 78E4
Malines = Mechelen
Malin Head Pt Irish Rep 13B2
Malkala Range Mts India 37B3
Malkāpur India 35D4
Malkara Turk 23F2
Malko Tŭrnovo Bulg 23F2
Mallaig Scot 14C3
Mallawi Egypt 75C2
Málles Venosta Italy 17D1
Mallorca I Spain 19C2
Malm Nor 12G6
Malmberget Sweden 12J5
Malmédy W Germ 16D1
Malmesbury Eng 15D6
Malmesbury S Africa 79B7
Malmö Sweden 12G7
Malmyzh USSR 24H4
Malolos Phil 45F8
Malone USA 59E2
Måloy Nor 12F6
Malozemel'skaya Tundra Plain USSR 24J2
Mal Paso Mexico 67B1
Malpaso Mexico 67D2
Malpo R Chile 72A2
Mālpura India 35D3
Malta Idaho USA 64D2
Malta Montana USA 54C2
Malta Chan Malta/Italy 22C3
Malta I Medit S 22C3
Malta Höhe Namibia 79B6
Malton Eng 15E4
Malung Sweden 12G6
Mālvan India 36A1
Malvern USA 63D3
Malwa Plat India 35D4
Malyy Kavkaz Mts USSR 26F5
Malyy Uzen' R USSR H6
Mama USSR 27N4
Mamadysh USSR 24J4
Mambasa Zaïre 78C3
Mamberamo R Aust 48C1
Mamberamo R Indon 39G7
Mambéré R CAR 78B3
Mamciju Indon 45A3
Mamers France 16A2
Mamfé Cam 78A3
Mammoth USA 65D4
Mamoré R Bol 70E6
Mamou Guinea 76A3
Mampikony Madag 79E5
Mampong Ghana 77F4
Mamshit Hist Site Israel 31C3
Ma'mūl Oman 33G3
Mamuno Botswana 79C6
Man Ivory Coast 76B4
Manabo Madag 79E6
Manacapuru Brazil 70F4
Manacor Spain 19C2
Manado Indon 45B2
Managua Nic 70A1
Manakara Madag 79E6
Manam I PNG 48D1
Mananara Madag 79E5
Mananjary Madag 79E6
Manapouri NZ 51A3
Manapouri,L NZ 51A3
Manas Bhutan 37D2
Manas China 29G1
Manas Hu L China 26K5
Manaslu Mt Nepal 37B2
Manasquan USA 60C2
Manaus Brazil 71G4
Manavgat Turk 25E8
Manbij Syria 30C2
Manbilla Plat Nig 77J4
Man,Calf of I Eng 15C4
Mancheral India 36B1
Manchester Connecticut USA 59E2
Manchester Eng 15D5
Manchester Kentucky USA 58C3
Manchester New Hampshire USA 55F2
Manchester Pennsylvania USA 60B2
Manchester Tennessee USA 61B1
Manchester Vermont USA 60D1
Manchuria Hist Region China 41B2
Mand R Iran 34C3
Manda Tanz 79D5
Mandaguari Brazil 73B3
Mandal Nor 12F7
Mandalay Burma 43B1
Mandalgovĭ Mongolia 38D2
Mandal Ovoo Mongolia 40A1
Mandalya Körfezi B Turk 23F3
Mandan USA 54C2
Mandelona USA 58B2
Mandera Eth 78E3
Mandeville Jamaica 68B3
Mandidzudzure Zim 79D5
Mandimba Mozam 79D5
Mandioli I Indon 45C3
Mandla India 37B3
Mandritsara Madag 79E5
Mandsaur India 35D4
Manduria Italy 23D2
Māndvi India 35B4
Mandya India 36B2
Manevichi USSR 21F2
Manfalût Egypt 32B1
Manfield Eng 15E5
Manfredonia Italy 22D2
Manga Brazil 73D1
Manga U Volta 77F3
Manga Desert Region Niger 78B2
Mangakino NZ 51C1
Mangalia Rom 23F2
Mangalmé Chad 78C2
Mangalore India 36A2
Manggar Indon 44C3
Mangin Range Mts Burma 37E3
Mangnia China 38C3
Mangoche Malawi 79D5
Mangoky R Madag 79E6
Mangole I Indon 45C3
Māngral India 35B4
Manguerinha Brazil 73B4
Mangui China 27O4
Mangum USA 62C3
Manhattan USA 54D3
Manhica Mozam 79D6
Manhuacu Brazil 71K8
Mania R Madag 79E5
Maniago Italy 17E1
Manica Mozam 79D5
Manicouagan R Can 53M5
Manicouagan Res Can 53M4
Manifah S Arabia 33E1
Manila Phil 45F8
Manila USA 64E2
Manilla Aust 50D2
Maninian Ivory Coast 76B3
Manipa I Indon 45C3
Manipur State India 37D3
Manipur R Burma 37D3
Manisa Turk 25D8
Man,Isle of Irish Sea 13C3
Manistee USA 58B2
Manistee R USA 58B2
Manistique USA 58B1
Manitoba Province Can 52J4
Manitoba,L Can 52J4
Manitou Can 57C2
Manitou Falls Can 57D1
Manitou Is USA 58B1
Manitoulin I Can 53K5
Manitou Springs USA 62B2
Manitowik L Can 58C1
Manitowoc USA 58B2
Maniwaki Can 59D1
Manizales Colombia 70C2
Manja Madag 79E6
Manjimup Aust 48A4
Mānjra R India 36B1
Mankato USA 55D2
Mankono Ivory Coast 76B4
Manley Hot Springs USA 56H3
Manly NZ 51B1
Manmād India 35C4
Manna Indon 44B3
Mannahill Aust 50A2
Mannar Sri Lanka 36B3
Mannār,G of India 36B3
Mannārgudi India 36B2
Mannheim W Germ 20B3
Manning USA 61C2
Mannum Aust 50A2
Mano Sierra Leone 76A4
Manokwari Indon 48C1
Manono Zaïre 79C4
Manoron Burma 43B3
Manosque France 17A3
Mano-wan B Japan 42C3
Manp'o N Korea 41B3
Mānsa India 35D2
Mansa Zambia 79C5
Mansel I Can 53K3
Mansfield Arkansas USA 63D2
Mansfield Aust 50C3
Mansfield Louisiana USA 63D3
Mansfield Massachusetts USA 60E1
Mansfield Ohio USA 55E2
Mansfield Pennsylvania USA 59D2
Manso R Brazil 73B2
Manston USA 58A2
Mansyu Deep Pacific O 39G5
Mantalingajan,Mt Phil 45E9
Mantap-san Mt N Korea 42A2
Mantaro R Peru 70C6
Manteo USA 61D1
Mantes France 18C2
Manti USA 65D3
Mantova Italy 22C1
Mantta Fin 12J6
Manturovo USSR 24G4
Manuel Mexico 67C1
Manuel Benavides Mexico 62B4
Manuel Ribas Brazil 73B3
Manui I Indon 45B3
Manukan Phil 45F9
Manukau NZ 49G4
Manus I Pacific O 39H7
Manzanares Spain 19B2
Manzanillo Cuba 66E2
Manzanillo Mexico 66B3
Manzhouli USSR 27N5
Manzil Jordan 31D3
Manzini Swaziland 79D6
Mao Chad 78B2
Maomao Shan Mt China 40A2
Maoming China 40C5
Mapai Mozam 79D6
Mapam Yumco L China 37B1
Mapia Is Pacific O 39G6
Maple Creek Can 52H5
Maputo Mozam 79D6
Ma Qu = Huange He

Maqu Meshik

Maqu China 40A3
Maquan He R China 37C2
Maquela do Zombo Angola 78B4
Maquinchao Arg 69C6
Marabá Brazil 71J5
Maracaibo Ven 70D1
Maracaju Brazil 73A3
Máracás Brazil 73D1
Maracay Ven 70E1
Marādah Libya 75A2
Maradi Niger 76C3
Marāgheh Iran 25H8
Maralal Kenya 78D3
Maramasike I Solomon Is 49F1
Maramba Zambia 79C5
Maran Malay 44G7
Marana USA 65D4
Marand Iran 25H8
Maranhão R Brazil 73C1
Maranhõa State Brazil 71J4
Maranoa R Aust 50C1
Marañón R Peru 70C4
Maras Turk 25F8
Marathon Can 53K5
Marathon Florida USA 61E4
Marathon New York USA 60B1
Marathon Texas USA 62B3
Maratua I Indon 44E2
Maraú Brazil 73E1
Maravatio Mexico 67B2
Marawi Phil 45F9
Marayes Arg 72B2
Mar'ayt S Yemen 33F3
Marbella Spain 19B2
Marble Bar Aust 48C3
Marble Canyon USA 65D3
Marblehall 79C6
Marblehead USA 60E1
Marburg W Germ 20B2
Marcelino Ramos Brazil 72E1
Marche Belg 20B2
Marche Region Italy 17E3
Marchean Spain 19A2
Marche-en-Famenne Belg 16C1
Marco Island USA 61E4
Marcos Juárez Arg 72C2
Marcus Baker,Mt USA 56J3
Marcy,Mt USA 59E2
Mar Dağlari Mt Turk 25G8
Mardan Pak 35C2
Mar del Plata Arg 69E5
Mardin Turk 25G8
Maré I Nouvelle Calédonie 49F3
Mareb R Eth 78D2
Mareeba Aust 39H8
Marfa USA 62B3
Margaretville USA 60C1
Margarita Arg 72C1
Margate Eng 15F6
Marghita Rom 23E1
Maria I Aust 50E3
Mariana Is Pacific O 46J3
Marianas Trench Pacific O 46J4
Mariāni India 37D2
Marianna Arkansas USA 63D3
Marianna Florida USA 61B2
Marias R USA 64D1
Maria Van Diemen,C NZ 55G4
Mariazell Austria 20D3
Ma'rib Yemen 33E3
Maribor Yugos 22D1
Maricourt Can 53L3
Maridi Sudan 78C3
Marie Byrd Land Region Ant 80F5
Marie Galante I Caribbean 68E3
Mariehamn Fin 12H6
Mariembourg Belg 16C1
Marienburg Suriname 71H2
Mariental Namibia 79B6
Mariestad Sweden 12G7
Marietta Georgia USA 61C2
Marietta Ohio USA 58C3
Marietta Oklahoma USA 63C3
Mariga R Nig 77H3
Marigot Dominica 68Q2
Marilia Brazil 69G2
Marimba Angola 79B4
Marinduque I Phil 45F8
Marinette USA 55E2
Maringá Brazil 69F2
Maringa R Zaïre 78C3
Marion Arkansas USA 63D2
Marion Illinois USA 58B3
Marion Indiana USA 55E2
Marion Ohio USA 55E2
Marion S Carolina USA 61D2
Marion,L USA 55E3
Marion Reef Aust 49E2
Mariposa USA 65C3
Marisa Indon 45B2
Marista R Bulg 25D7
Mariyskaya ASSR Republic USSR 24H4
Marjayoun Leb 31C2
Marjina Gorki USSR 21F2
Marka Jordan 31C3
Marka Somalia 78E3
Markaryd Sweden 20C1
Market Drayton Eng 15D5
Market Harborough Eng 15E5
Markham,Mt Ant 80E
Markovo USSR 27S3
Marlboro Massachusetts USA 60E1
Marlboro New Hampshire USA 60D1
Marlborough Aust 48D3
Marle France 16B2
Marlin USA 63C3
Marlow USA 60D1
Marmande France 18C3
Marmara Adi I Turk 23F2
Marmara,S of Turk 30A1
Marmaris Turk 23F3
Marmath USA 57B2
Marmet USA 58C3
Marmion L Can 57D2
Marmolada Mt Italy 22C1
Marmot B USA 56H4
Mar Muerto Lg Mexico 67D2
Marnay France 17A1
Marne Department France 16C2
Marne R France 16B2
Maro Chad 78B3
Maroantsetra Madag 79E5
Marondera Zim 79D5
Maroni R French Guiana 71H3
Maroochydore Aust 50D1
Maros Indon 45A3
Maroua Cam 78B2
Marovoay Madag 79E5
Marquesas Keys Is USA 55E4
Marquette USA 55E2
Marquise France 16A1
Marra R Aust 50C2
Marrakech Mor 76B1
Marree Aust 48C3
Marrero USA 63D4
Marromeu Mozam 79D5
Marrupa Mozam 79D5
Marsa Alam Egypt 32B1
Marsabit Kenya 78D3
Marsala Italy 22C3
Marsberg W Germ 16E1
Marseille France 18D3
Marshal USA 56F3
Marshall Illinois USA 58B3
Marshall Michigan USA 58C2
Marshall Minnesota USA 57C3
Marshall Missouri USA 63D2
Marshall Texas USA 55D3
Marshall Virginia USA 60B3
Marshall Is Pacific O 47K4
Marshalltown USA 57D3
Marshfield Missouri USA 63D2
Marshfield Wisconsin USA 58A2
Marsh Harbour Bahamas 68B1
Marsh I USA 63D4
Marsh L Can 56M3
Marta Ecuador 70B4
Martaban,G of Burma 43B2
Martapura Indon 44B3
Martapura Indon 44D3
Martha's Vineyard I USA 59E2
Martigny Switz 18D2
Martin Czech 21D3
Martin S Dakota USA 57B3
Martin Tennessee USA 61B1
Martinborough NZ 51C2
Martín de Loyola Arg 72B3
Martínez de la Torre Mexico 67C1
Martinique I Caribbean 68E4
Martin,L USA 61B2
Martin Pt USA 56K1
Martinsburg USA 59D3
Martins Ferry USA 58C2
Martinsville USA 59D3
Martin Vaz I Atlantic O 74G5
Martiques France 18D3
Marton NZ 51C2
Martos Spain 19B2
Marudi Malay 44D2
Maruf Afghan 35B2
Marugame Japan 42B4
Marvine,Mt Mt USA 65D3
Mārwār India 35C3
Mary USSR 26H6
Maryborough Queensland Aust 49E3
Maryborough Victoria Aust 50B3
Mary Henry,Mt Can 52F4
Maryland State USA 55F3
Maryport Eng 14D4
Marysville California USA 65B3
Marysville Kansas USA 63C2
Marysville Washington USA 64B1
Maryville Iowa USA 55D2
Maryville Missouri USA 63D1
Maryville Tennessee USA 61C1
Marzuq Libya 75A2
Masabb Dumyât C Egypt 31A3
Masada = Mezada
Mas'adah Syria 31C2
Masai Steppe Upland Tanz 78D4
Masaka Uganda 78D4
Masally USSR 30E2
Masamba Indon 45B3
Masan S Korea 41B4
Masasi Tanz 79D5
Masaya Nic 66D3
Masbate Phil 45F8
Masbate I Phil 45F8
Mascara Alg 77C1
Mascarene Ridge Indian O 46D5
Mascota Mexico 67B1
Mascote Brazil 73E2
Masela I Indon 45C4
Maseru S Africa 79C6
Mashaki Afghan 35B2
Mashhad Iran 34D1
Mashkel R Pak 34E3
Masi-Manimba Zaïre 78B4
Masindi Uganda 78D3
Masisi Zaïre 78C4
Masjed Soleyman Iran 34B2
Masoala C Madag 79F5
Mason Texas USA 62C3
Mason City USA 55D2
Masqat Oman 33G2
Mass R Neth 20B2
Massa Italy 22C2
Massachusetts State USA 55F2
Massachusetts B USA 59E2
Massachusetts Bay USA 59E2
Massakori Chad 78B2
Massa Marittima Italy 17D3
Massangena Mozam 79D6
Massawa Eth 78D2
Massawa Chan Eth 32C3
Massena USA 59E2
Massénya Chad 78B2
Massey Can 58C1
Massif Central Mts France 18C2
Massif de l'Ouarsenis Mts Alg 77C1
Massif de l'Adamaoua Mts Cam 78B3
Massif de la Hotte Mts Haiti 68C3
Massif de l'Isalo Upland Madag 79E6
Massif des Bongo Upland CAR 78C3
Massif du Pelvoux Mts France 18D2
Massif du Tsaratanana Mt Madag 79E5
Massillon USA 58C2
Massina Region Mali 76B3
Massinga Mozam 79D6
Masteksay USSR 25J6
Masterton NZ 49G5
Masuda Japan 41C5
Maşyāf Syria 30C2
Matachewan Can 58C1
Matachie Mexico 62A4
Matadi Zaïre 78B4
Matagalpa Nic 70A1
Matagami Can 53L4
Matagorda B USA 54D4
Matagorda I USA 63F4
Matakana I NZ 51C1
Matala Angola 79B5
Matale Sri Lanka 36C3
Matam Sen 76A3
Matameye Niger 76C3
Matamoros Mexico 66C2
Ma'tan as Sarra Well Libya 75B2
Matane Can 53M5
Matanó Spain 19C1
Matanzas Cuba 66D2
Matapédia R Can 59F1
Mataquito R Chile 72A2
Matara Sri Lanka 36C3
Mataram Indon 48A1
Matarani Peru 70D7
Mataripe Brazil 73E1
Mataura NZ 51A3
Matehuala Mexico 66B2
Matelica Italy 17E3
Matelot Trinidad 68L1
Matera Italy 22D2
Mátészalka Hung 21E3
Mateur Tunisia 77D1
Matheson Can 58C1
Mathis USA 63F4
Mathura India 35D3
Mati Phil 45G9
Matías Romero Mexico 67C2
Matisiri I Indon 44E3
Matlock Eng 15E5
Matmatma Tunisia 77D2
Mato Grosso Brazil 71G6
Mato Grosso State Brazil 71G6
Mato Grosso do Sul State Brazil 71G7
Matrah Oman 33G2
Matrel im Osttirol Austria 17E1
Matrûh Egypt 30A3
Matruh Egypt 75B1
Matsue Japan 41C4
Matsumae Japan 41E3
Matsumoto Japan 41D4
Matsusaka Japan 41D5
Matsuyama Japan 41C5
Mattagami R Can 53K5
Mattawa Can 59D1
Matterhorn Mt Switz/Italy 22B1
Matterhorn Mt USA 64C2
Matthew Town Bahamas 68C2
Mattituck USA 60D2
Mattoon USA 58B3
Matun Afghan 35B2
Matura B Trinidad 68L1
Maturin Ven 70F2
Mau India 37B2
Maúa Mozam 79D5
Maubeuge France 18C1
Maude Aust 50B2
Maud Seamount Atlantic O 74J8
Maule R Chile 72A3
Maumee USA 58C2
Maumee R USA 58C2
Maumere Indon 45B4
Maun Botswana 79C5
Maunoir,L Can 52F3
Maures Mts France 17B3
Mauriac France 18C2
Mauritania Republic Africa 76A2
Mauterndorf Austria 17E1
Mavinga Angola 79C5
Mawlaik Burma 37E3
Mawson Base Ant 80G10
Max USA 57B2
Maxcaltzin Mexico 67C1
Maya I Indon 44C3
Maya R USSR 27P4
Mayādīn Syria 30D2
Mayaguana I Bahamas 55F4
Mayagüez Puerto Rico 68D3
Mayahi Niger 76C3
Mayama Congo 78B4
Mayamey Iran 34D1
Mayanobab Indon 45D4
Maybole Scot 14C4
May,C USA 55F3
Maydena Aust 50E3
Mayen W Germ 16D1
Mayenne France 18B2
Mayer USA 65D4
Mayfa'ah S Yemen 33E4
Mayfield USA 58B3
Mayhill USA 62A3
Maykop USSR 25F7
Maymaneh Afghan 26H6
Maymyo Burma 43B1
Mayo Can 52E3
Mayo USA 60B3
Mayo Deo R Cam 77J4
Mayon Mt Phil 45F8
Mayor Mt Spain 19C2
Mayor Buratovich Arg 72C3
Mayor I NZ 51C1
Mayor P Lagerenza Par 69D1
Mayotte I Indian O 79E5
May Pen Jamaica 68H2
May Point,C USA 60C3
Mayrhofen Austria 17D1
Mayskiy USSR 41B1
Mays Landing USA 60C3
Maysville USA 58C3
Mayumba Gabon 78B4
Mayville USA 57C2
Maywood USA 62B1
Mazabuka Zambia 79C5
Mazaffarnagar India 35D3
Mazapil Mexico 67B1
Mazar China 35D1
Mazār Jordan 31C3
Mazara del Vallo Italy 22C3
Mazar-i-Sharif Afghan 35B1
Mazatlán Mexico 66B2
Mazeikiai USSR 24C4
Mazra Jordan 31C3
Mbabane Swaziland 79D6
Mbabo,Mt Cam 77J4
Mbaïki CAR 78B3
Mbala Zambia 79D4
Mbalabala Zim 79C6
Mbale Uganda 78D3
Mbalmayo Cam 78B3
Mbam R Cam 78B3
Mbamba Bay Tanz 79D5
Mbandaka Zaïre 78B3
Mbanza Congo Angola 78B4
Mbanza-Ngungu Zaïre 78B4
Mbarara Uganda 78D4
Mbé Cam 77J4
Mbengwi Cam 77J4
Mbènza Congo 78B3
Mbére R Cam 78B3
Mbeya Tanz 79D4
Mbinda Congo 78B4
Mbouda Cam 77J4
Mbout Maur 76A3
Mbuji-Mayi Zaïre 78C4
Mbuli R Nig 77J3
Mbulu Tanz 78D4
Mburucuyá Arg 72D1
Mcherrah Region Alg 76B2
Mchinji Malawi 79D5
Mdrak Viet 43D3
Meade USA 62B2
Meade R USA 56G1
Mead,L USA 54B3
Meadow Lake Can 52H4
Meadville USA 58C2
Me-akan dake Mt Japan 42D2
Mealy Mts Can 53N4
Meandarra Aust 50C1
Meander River Can 52G4
Meath Irish Rep 15B5
Meaux France 18C2
Mecca S Arabia 32C2
Mecca USA 65C4
Mechanicville USA 60D1
Mechelen Belg 20A2
Mecheria Alg 77B2
Mecklenburger Bucht B E Germ 20C2
Meconta Mozam 79D5
Mecuburi Mozam 79D5
Mecufi Mozam 79E5
Mecula Mozam 79D5
Medan Indon 44A2
Medanos Arg 72C3
Médanos Arg 72D2
Médéa Alg 77C1
Medecine Bow Peak Mt USA 62A1
Medellin Colombia 70C2
Medenine Tunisia 77E2
Medford USA 54A2
Medgidia Rom 23F2
Media Agua Arg 72B2
Mediaş Rom 23E1
Medical Lake USA 64C1
Medicine Bow USA 57A3
Medicine Bow Mt USA 57A3
Medicine Hat Can 52G5
Medicine Lodge USA 62C2
Medina Brazil 73D2
Medina N Dakota USA 57C2
Medina New York USA 60A1
Medina S Arabia 32C2
Medinaceli Spain 19B1
Medina del Campo Spain 19A1
Medina de Rio Seco Spain 19A1
Medina L USA 62C4
Medinīpur India 37C3
Mednogorsk USSR 25K5
Mêdog China 37E2
Medouneu Gabon 78B3
Medvedista R USSR 25G5
Medvezh'i Ova I USSR 27S2
Medvezh'yegorsk USSR 26E3
Meekatharra Aust 48A3
Meeker USA 62A1
Meerut India 35D3
Meeteetse USA 64E2
Mega Eth 78D3
Megalópolis Greece 23E3
Mégara Greece 23E3
Meghālaya State India 37D2
Meghna R Bang 37D3
Megido Hist Site Israel 31C2
Mehaïguene R Alg 77C2
Mehoryuk USA 56E3
Mehran R Iran 34C3
Mehriz Iran 34C2
Meia Ponte R Brazil 73C2
Meiganga Cam 78B3
Meiktila Burma 43B1
Meiringen Switz 17C1
Meishan China 40A4
Meissen E Germ 20C2
Mei Xian China 40D5
Meizhou China 40D5
Mejillones Chile 70D8
Mekambo Gabon 78B3
Meknès Mor 77A2
Mekong = Lancang
Mekong R Camb 43D3
Mekrou R Benin 77G3
Melaka Malay 43C5
Melanesia Region Pacific O 46J5
Melawi R Indon 44D3
Melbourne Aust 48D4
Melbourne USA 55E4
Melchor Múzguiz Mexico 54C4
Melfi Chad 78B2
Melfort Can 52H4
Melilla N W Africa 77B1
Melimoyu Mt Chile 69B6
Melincué Arg 72C2
Melipilla Chile 72A2
Melita Can 57B2
Melitopol' USSR 25F6
Meliville Bugt B Greenland 53M2
Mellègue R Tunisia 77D1
Melli R Eth 32D4
Melo Arg 72C2
Melo Urug 69F4
Melo R Brazil 73A3
Melozitna R USA 56H2
Melrose USA 57D2
Mels Switz 17C1
Melsungen W Germ 16E1
Melta,Mt Malay 44E1
Melton Mowbry Eng 15E5
Melun France 18C2
Melville Can 52H4
Melville,C Dominica 68Q2
Melville Hills Mts Can 52F3
Melville I Aust 48C2
Melville I Can 52G2
Melville,L Can 53N4
Melville Pen Can 53K3
Memba Mozam 79E5
Memboro Indon 48A1
Memmingen W Germ 20C3
Mempawan Indon 44C2
Memphis Tennessee USA 55E3
Memphis Texas USA 62B3
Mena USA 63D3
Mena USSR 21G2
Menai Str Wales 15C5
Ménaka Mali 76C3
Menasha USA 58B2
Mencué Arg 72B4
Mendawai R Indon 44D3
Mende France 18C3
Mendebo Mts Eth 78D3
Mendenhall,C USA 56E4
Mendi PNG 48D1
Mendip Hills Upland Eng 15D6
Mendocino,C USA 64B2
Mendocino Seascarp Pacific O 47M3
Mendota Illinois USA 58B2
Mendoza Arg 69C4
Mendoza State Arg 69C5
Menemen Turk 23F3
Menen Belg 16B1
Mengcheng China 40D3
Menggala Indon 44C3
Menghai China 43B1
Mengla China 40A5
Menglian China 43B1
Mengzi China 40A5
Menindee Aust 48D4
Menindee L Aust 50B2
Meningie Aust 50A3
Menominee USA 58B1
Menomonee Falls USA 58B2
Menomonie USA 58A2
Menongue Angola 79B5
Menorca I Spain 19C1
Mentasta Mts USA 56K3
Mentmore USA 62A2
Mentok Indon 44C3
Menton France 17B3
Mentor USA 58C2
Ménu France 16B2
Menyuan China 40A2
Menzelinsk USSR 24J4
Meppen W Germ 20B2
Mer France 16A3
Merah Indon 44E2
Meramec R USA 63D2
Merano Italy 22C1
Merauke Indon 48D1
Merced USA 54A3
Mercedario Mt Chile 69B4
Mercedes Arg 69C4
Mercedes Buenos Aires Arg 69E4
Mercedes Corrientes Arg 69E3
Mercedes Urug 69E4
Mercury B NZ 51C1
Mercury Is NZ 51C1
Mercy B Can 52F2
Mercy,C Can 53M3
Meredith,L L USA 62B2
Meregh Somalia 78E3
Mergui Burma 43B3
Mergui Arch Burma 43B3
Mérida Mexico 66D2
Mérida Spain 19A2
Mérida Ven 70D2
Meridan USA 55E3
Meridian USA 63E3
Merimbula Aust 50C3
Meringur Aust 50B2
Merkel USA 62B3
Merowe Sudan 78D2
Merredin Aust 48A4
Merrick Mt Scot 14C4
Merrill USA 58B1
Merrillville USA 58B2
Merrimack R USA 60E1
Merriman USA 57B3
Merritt Island USA 61C3
Merriwa Aust 50D2
Mersa Fatma Eth 32D4
Mers el Kebir Alg 19B2
Mersey R Eng 15D5
Merseyside Metropolitan County Eng 15D5
Mersin Turk 25E8
Mersing Malay 43C5
Merta India 35C3
Merthyr Tydfil Wales 15D6
Mertola Port 19A2
Meru Mt Tanz 78D4
Merzifon Turk 25F7
Merzig W Germ 16D2
Mesa USA 54B3
Meschede W Germ 16E1
Mescit Dağ Mt Turk 30D1
Meshik USA 56G4

Meshra Er Req **Montmirail**

Meshra Er Req *Sudan* 78C3
Mesocco *Switz* 17C1
Mesolóngion *Greece* 23E3
Mesquite Nevada *USA* 65D3
Mesquite Texas *USA* 63C3
Messaad *Alg* 77C2
Messalo R *Mozam* 79D5
Messina *Italy* 22D3
Messina *S Africa* 79C6
Messíni *Greece* 23E3
Messiniakós Kólpos G *Greece* 23E3
Mesta = Néstos
Mesta R *Bulg* 23E2
Mestre *Italy* 22C1
Meta R *Colombia* 70D3
Meta R *USSR* 24E4
Meta R *Ven* 70E2
Meta Incognito Pen *Can* 53L3
Metairie *USA* 63D4
Metaline Falls *USA* 64C1
Metán *Arg* 69D3
Metangula *Mozam* 79D5
Metaponto *Italy* 22D2
Metauro R *Italy* 17E3
Metemma *Eth* 32C4
Methil *Scot* 14D3
Methuen *USA* 60E1
Methven *NZ* 51B2
Metlakatla *USA* 52E4
Metlakatla *USA* 56M4
Metlaoui *Tunisia* 77D2
Metropolis *USA* 58B3
Mettūr *India* 36B2
Metz *France* 18D2
Metzingen *W Germ* 16E2
Meulaboh *Indon* 44A2
Meulan *France* 16A2
Meung-sur-Loire *France* 16A3
Meurthe R *France* 16D2
Meurthe-et-Moselle Department *France* 16D2
Meuse Department *France* 16C2
Meuse R *Belg* 16C1
Meuse R *France* 18D2
Mexia *USA* 63C3
Mexicali *Mexico* 66A1
Mexican Hat *USA* 65E3
Mexico Federal Republic *Central America* 66B2
México *Mexico* 66C3
México State *Mexico* 67B2
Mexico *USA* 63D2
Mexico,G of *C America* 66C2
Meximieux *France* 17A2
Mezada Hist Site *Israel* 31C3
Mezcala *Mexico* 67C2
Mezcalapa R *Mexico* 67D2
Mezen' *USSR* 26F3
Mezen R *USSR* 24H3
Mezha R *USSR* 21G1
Mezhdusharskiy I *USSR* 24J1
Mezquital *Mexico* 67B1
Mezquital R *Mexico* 67B1
Mgachi *USSR* 41E1
Mhow *India* 35D4
Miahuatlán *Mexico* 67C2
Miami Arizona *USA* 65D4
Miami Florida *USA* 55E4
Miami Oklahoma *USA* 63D2
Miami Beach *USA* 55E4
Miandowāb *Iran* 25H8
Miandrivazo *Madag* 79E5
Mīāneh *Iran* 25H8
Mianwali *Pak* 35C2
Mianyang *China* 40A3
Mianyang *China* 40C3
Mianzhu *China* 40A3
Miaodao Qundao Arch *China* 40E2
Miao Ling Upland *China* 40B4
Miass *USSR* 24L5
Michalovce *Czech* 21E3
Michel *Can* 64D1
Miches *Dom Rep* 68D3
Michigan State *USA* 55E2
Michigan City *USA* 58B2
Michigan,L *USA* 55E2
Michipicoten *Can* 58C1
Michipicoten I *Can* 53K5
Michoacan State *Mexico* 67B2
Michunnsk *USSR* 26F4
Michurin *Bulg* 23F2
Michurinsk *USSR* 25G5
Micronesia Region *Pacific O* 46J4
Midai I *Indon* 44C2
Mid Atlantic Ridge *Atlantic O* 74F4
Middelburg *Neth* 16B1
Middelburg *S Africa* 79C6
Middelburg *S Africa* 79C7
Middle Alkali L *USA* 64B2
Middle America Trench *Pacific O* 47O4
Middle Andaman I *Indian O* 36E2
Middleboro *USA* 60E2
Middleburg Pennsylvania *USA* 60B2
Middleburg Virginia *USA* 60B3
Middleburgh *USA* 60C1
Middlebury *USA* 59E2
Middlesboro *USA* 55E3
Middlesbrough *Eng* 15E4
Middletown Connecticut *USA* 60D2
Middletown Delaware *USA* 60C3
Middletown New York *USA* 59E2
Middletown Ohio *USA* 58C3
Middletown Pennsylvania *USA* 60B2
Middleville *USA* 60C1
Midelt *Mor* 77B2
Mid Glamorgan County *Wales* 15D6
Mīdī *Yemen* 32D3
Mid Indian Basin *Indian O* 46E5
Mid Indian Ridge *Indian O* 46E5
Midland *Can* 53L5
Midland Michigan *USA* 58C2
Midland Texas *USA* 54C3
Midongy Atsimo *Madag* 79E6
Mid Pacific Mts *Pacific O* 47K4
Midvale *USA* 64C2
Midway Is *Pacific O* 47L3
Midwest *USA* 57A3
Midwest City *USA* 63C2
Midyat *Turk* 30D2
Midžor Mt *Yugos* 23E2
Mielec *Pol* 21E2
Miercurea-Ciuc *Rom* 23F1
Mieres *Spain* 19A1
Mifflintown *USA* 60B2
Miguel Auza *Mexico* 67B1
Miguihuana *Mexico* 67C1
Mihara *Japan* 42B4
Mijun Shuiku Res *China* 40D1
Mikhayiovka *USSR* 26F4
Mikhaylovgrad *Bulg* 23E2
Mikhaylovka *USSR* 25G5
Mikhaylovskiy *USSR* 26J4
Mikhrot Timna *Israel* 31C4
Mikkeli *Fin* 12K6
Míkonos I *Greece* 23F3
Mikulov *Czech* 20D3
Mikumi *Tanz* 79D4
Mikun *USSR* 24J3
Mikuni-sammyaku Mts *Japan* 41D4
Mikura-jima I *Japan* 42C4
Milaca *USA* 57D2
Milagro *Ecuador* 70C4
Milan = Milano
Milan *USA* 61B1
Milana *Alg* 19C2
Milange *Mozam* 79D5
Milango R *Indon* 45B2
Milano *Italy* 22B1
Milas *Turk* 25D8
Milbank *USA* 57C2
Mildura *Aust* 48D4
Mile *China* 40A5
Mileh Tharthār L *Iraq* 30D3
Miles *Aust* 48E3
Miles City *USA* 54C2
Milford Connecticut *USA* 60D2
Milford Delaware *USA* 59D3
Milford Massachusetts *USA* 59E2
Milford Nebraska *USA* 63C1
Milford New Hampshire *USA* 60E1
Milford Pennsylvania *USA* 60C2
Milford Utah *USA* 65D3
Milford Haven *Wales* 15C6
Milford Haven Sd *Wales* 15C6
Milford L *USA* 63C2
Milford Sd *NZ* 51A2
Miliana *Alg* 77C1
Milk R *Can* 52G5
Milk R *USA* 57A2
Mil'Kovo *USSR* 27R4
Millau *France* 18C3
Millbrook *USA* 60D2
Milledgeville *USA* 61C2
Mille Lacs L *USA* 57D2
Miller *USA* 57C3
Miller,Mt *USA* 56K3
Millerovo *USSR* 25G6
Millersburg *USA* 60B2
Millers Creek *Aust* 50A1
Millers Falls *USA* 60D1
Millerton *USA* 60D2
Millicent *Aust* 50B3
Millington *USA* 61B1
Millinocket *USA* 59F1
Millmerran *Aust* 50D1
Millstätter See L *Austria* 17E1
Milltown *Can* 59F1
Milltown *USA* 64D1
Millville *USA* 59E3
Milne Land I *Greenland* 53Q2
Mílos I *Greece* 23E3
Milparinka *Aust* 48D3
Milroy *USA* 60B2
Milton Florida *USA* 61B2
Milton *NZ* 51A3
Milton Pennsylvania *USA* 60B2
Milwaukee *USA* 55E2
Mimmaya *Japan* 42D2
Mina R *Alg* 19C2
Mīnā' al Ahmadī *Kuwait* 30E4
Mīnāb *Iran* 34D3
Minahassa Pen *Indon* 45B2
Minaki *Can* 57D1
Minamata *Japan* 41C5
Minas *Indon* 44B2
Minas *Urug* 69E4
Minas Gerais State *Brazil* 71J7
Minas Novas *Brazil* 73D2
Minatitlan *Mexico* 66C3
Minbu *Burma* 43A1
Minbya *Burma* 43A1
Mincha *Chile* 72A2
Minch,Little Sd *Scot* 14B3
Minch,North Sd *Scot* 14B2
Minch,The Sd *Scot* 13B2
Minchumina,L *USA* 56H3
Mincio R *Italy* 17D2
Mindanao I *Phil* 45F9
Minden Louisiana *USA* 63D3
Minden *W Germ* 20B2
Mindona L *Aust* 50B2
Mindoro I *Phil* 45F8
Mindoro Str *Phil* 45F8
Minehead *Eng* 15D6
Mineiros *Brazil* 71H7
Mineola *USA* 63C3
Mineral de Monte *Mexico* 67C1
Mineral Wells *USA* 62C3
Minersville *USA* 60B2
Mingary *Aust* 50B2
Mingechaurskoye Vodokhranilische Res *USSR* 25H7
Mingshui *China* 41B2
Minhe *China* 40A2
Minialo *Italy* 17D3
Minicoy I *India* 36A3
Min Jiang R Fujian *China* 40D4
Min Jiang R Sichuan *China* 40A4
Minlaton *Aust* 50A2
Minle *China* 40A2
Minna *Nig* 77H4
Minneapolis *USA* 55D2
Minnedosa *Can* 52H4
Minnedosa *Can* 52J4
Minnesota State *USA* 55D2
Minnesota R *USA* 57C3
Minnitaki L *Can* 57D2
Miño R *Spain* 19A1
Minot *USA* 54C2
Minqin *China* 40A2
Min Shan Upland *China* 40A3
Minsk *USSR* 24D5
Minsk Mazowiecki *Pol* 21E2
Minto *USA* 56J3
Minto Inlet B *Can* 52G2
Minto,L *Can* 53L4
Minturn *USA* 62A2
Minusinsk *USSR* 38C1
Min Xian *China* 40A3
Minyael Qamn *Egypt* 31A3
Miquelon *Can* 53N5
Miraj *India* 36A1
Miramar *Arg* 69E5
Miram Shah *Pak* 35B2
Miranda R *Brazil* 73A2
Miranda de Ebro *Spain* 19B1
Mirandia *Brazil* 73A3
Mirandola *Italy* 17D2
Mir Bachchen Kūt *Afghan* 35B2
Mirbāt *Oman* 33F3
Mirebeau *France* 17A1
Mirecourt *France* 16C2
Miri *Malay* 44D2
Miri Mt *Pak* 34E3
Mirik,C *Maur* 76A3
Mirinay R *Arg* 72D1
Mīrjāveh *Iran* 34E3
Mirna R *Yugos* 17E2
Mirnoye *USSR* 27K3
Mirnyy *USSR* 27N3
Mirnyy Base *Ant* 80G9
Mironovka *USSR* 21G3
Mirpur *Pak* 35C2
Mirpur Khas *Pak* 35B3
Mirtoan S *Greece* 23E3
Miryang *S Korea* 41B4
Mirzāpur *India* 37B2
Misantla *Mexico* 67C2
Misgar *Pak* 35C1
Mishan *China* 41C2
Mishawaka *USA* 58B2
Misheguk Mt *USA* 56F2
Mi-shima I *Japan* 42B4
Mishmi Hills *India* 37E2
Misima I *Solomon Is* 49E2
Misiones State *Arg* 69F3
Miskolc *Hung* 21E3
Mismīyah *Syria* 31D2
Misoöl I *Indon* 39G7
Misrātah *Libya* 75A1
Missinaibi R *Can* 53K5
Missinaibi L *Can* 58C1
Mission S Dakota *USA* 57B3
Mission Texas *USA* 63F4
Mission City *Can* 64B1
Mississauga *Can* 59D2
Mississippi State *USA* 55D3
Mississippi R *USA* 55D3
Mississippi Delta *USA* 63E3
Missoula *USA* 54B2
Missour *Mor* 77B2
Missouri State *USA* 55D3
Missouri R *USA* 55D2
Missouri Valley *USA* 57C3
Mistassini,L *Can* 55F1
Misti Mt *Peru* 70D7
Mitchell *Aust* 50C1
Mitchell *USA* 54D2
Mitchell R *Aust* 48D2
Mitchell,Mt *USA* 55E3
Mitchell River *Aust* 39H8
Mit el Nasâra *Egypt* 31A3
Mît Ghamr *Egypt* 31A3
Mithankot *Pak* 35B3
Mitilíni *Greece* 23F3
Mitla *Mexico* 67C2
Mitla P *Egypt* 31B3
Mitre I *Solomon Is* 49G2
Mitrofania I *USA* 56G4
Mittersill *Austria* 17E1
Mitu *Colombia* 70D3
Mitumbar Mts *Zaïre* 78C4
Mitwaba *Zaïre* 79C4
Mitzic *Gabon* 78B3
Miura *Japan* 42C3
Mi Xian *China* 40C3
Miyake I *Japan* 38G3
Miyake-jima I *Japan* 42C4
Miyako I *Japan* 38F4
Miyakonojō *Japan* 41C5
Miyazaki *Japan* 41C5
Miyazu *Japan* 42C3
Miyoshi *Japan* 41C5
Miyun *China* 40D1
Mi-zaki Pt *Japan* 42D2
Mizan Teferi *Eth* 78D3
Mizdah *Libya* 75A1
Mizil *Rom* 23F1
Mizo Hills *India* 37D3
Mizoram Union Territory *India* 37D3
Mizpe Ramon *Israel* 31C3
Mizuho Base *Ant* 80F11
Mizusawa *Japan* 41E4
Mjolby *Sweden* 12H7
Mkushi *Zambia* 79C5
Mladá Boleslav *Czech* 20C2
Mława *Pol* 21E2
Mljet I *Yugos* 23D2
Mmabatho *Botswana* 79C6
Mnadi *India* 35D2
Moa I *Indon* 45C4
Moa R *Sierra Leone* 76A4
Moab Region *Jordan* 31C3
Moab *USA* 54C3
Moamba *Mozam* 79D6
Moanda *Congo* 78B4
Moanda *Gabon* 78B4
Moba *Zaïre* 79C4
Mobara *Japan* 42D3
Mobaye *CAR* 78C3
Mobayi *Zaire* 78C3
Moberly *USA* 55D3
Mobile *USA* 55E3
Mobile B *USA* 55E3
Mobile Pt *USA* 61B2
Mobridge *USA* 54C2
Moçambique *Mozam* 79E5
Moçâmedes *Angola* 79B5
Moc Chau *Viet* 43C1
Mocimboa da Praia *Mozam* 79E5
Mocoa *Colombia* 70C3
Mococa *Brazil* 73C3
Mocoreta R *Arg* 72D2
Moctezulma R *Mexico* 67C1
Moctezuma *Mexico* 67B1
Mocuba *Mozam* 79D5
Modane *France* 17B2
Modena *Italy* 22C2
Moder R *France* 16D2
Modesto *USA* 54A3
Modica *Italy* 22C3
Mödling *Austria* 20D3
Moe *Aust* 48D4
Moesa R *Switz* 17C1
Moffat *Scot* 14D4
Moga *India* 35D2
Mogaung *Burma* 37E2
Mogi das Cruzes *Brazil* 73C3
Mogilev *USSR* 24D5
Mogilev Podolskiy *USSR* 25D6
Mogi-Mirim *Brazil* 73C3
Mogincual *Mozam* 79E5
Moglev *USSR* 21G2
Mogliano *Italy* 17E2
Mogna *Arg* 72B2
Mogocha *USSR* 38E1
Mogochin *USSR* 26K4
Mogok *Burma* 37E3
Moguer *Spain* 19A2
Mohaka R *NZ* 51C1
Mohall *USA* 57B2
Mohammadia *Alg* 77C1
Mohammedia *Mor* 77A2
Mohanganj *Bang* 37D3
Mohave,L *USA* 65D3
Mohawk *USA* 60C1
Mohawk R *USA* 59E2
Mohican,C *USA* 56E3
Mohoro *Tanz* 79D4
Mointy *USSR* 26J5
Mo i Rana *Nor* 12G5
Moissac *France* 18C3
Mojave *USA* 65C3
Mojave *USA* 65C3
Mojave Desert *USA* 54B3
Mojokerto *Indon* 44D4
Mokada Mt *Eth* 32C4
Mokama *India* 37C2
Mokau R *NZ* 51B1
Moknine *Tunisia* 77E1
Mokokchūng *India* 37D2
Mokolo *Cam* 78B2
Mokp'o *S Korea* 41B5
Moksha R *USSR* 24G5
Molango *Mexico* 67C1
Moláoi *Greece* 23E3
Moldavskaya SSR Republic *USSR* 25D6
Molde *Nor* 12F6
Moldoveanu Mt *Rom* 23E1
Mole Nat Pk *Ghana* 77F4
Molesheim *France* 16D2
Molfetta *Italy* 22D2
Molina *Chile* 72A3
Möll R *Austria* 17E1
Mollendo *Peru* 70D7
Molodechno *USSR* 24D5
Molodezhnaya Base *Ant* 80G11
Moloma R *USSR* 24H4
Molong *Aust* 50C2
Molopo R *Botswana/S Africa* 79C6
Molounddu *Cam* 78B3
Molson L *Can* 54D1
Molucca S *Indon* 48B1
Moluccas Is *Indon* 39F7
Moma *Mozam* 79D5
Mombaca *Brazil* 71K5
Mombasa *Kenya* 78D4
Mombetsu *Japan* 42D2
Mompono *Zaïre* 78C3
Mon I *Den* 20C2
Monach Is *Scot* 14B3
Monaco Principality *Europe* 18D3
Monadhliath Mts *Scot* 14C3
Monaghan County *Irish Rep* 15B4
Monaghan *Irish Rep* 15B4
Monahans *USA* 62B3
Mona Pass *Caribbean* 68D3
Monarch P *USA* 62A2
Monashee Mts *Can* 52G4
Monastereven *Irish Rep* 13B3
Monbetsu *Japan* 42D2
Moncalieri *Italy* 17B2
Monção *Brazil* 71J4
Monchegorsk *USSR* 12L5
Mönchen-gladbach *W Germ* 20B2
Monclova *Mexico* 66B2
Moncton *Can* 53M5
Monctova *Mexico* 54C4
Mondego R *Port* 19A1
Mondovi *Italy* 22B2
Moneague *Jamaica* 68H1
Monessen *USA* 59D2
Monett *USA* 63D2
Monfalcone *Italy* 22C1
Monforte de Lemos *Spain* 19A1
Monga *Zaïre* 78C3
Mongala R *Zaïre* 78C3
Mongalla *Sudan* 78D3
Mong Cai *Viet* 43D1
Mongo *Chad* 78B2
Mongolia Republic *Asia* 38C2
Mongu *Zambia* 79C5
Mönhhaan *Mongolia* 27N5
Monitor Range Mts *USA* 65C3
Monkoto *Zaïre* 78C4
Monmouth *Eng* 15D6
Monmouth *USA* 58A2
Mono R *Togo* 77G4
Mono L *USA* 65C3
Monopoli *Italy* 23D2
Monreal del Campo *Spain* 19B1
Monroe Louisiana *USA* 63D3
Monroe Michigan *USA* 58C2
Monroe N Carolina *USA* 61C2
Monroe Washington *USA* 64B1
Monroe Wisconsin *USA* 58B2
Monroe City *USA* 63D2
Monrovia *Lib* 76A4
Mons *Belg* 20A2
Monselice *Italy* 17D2
Monson *USA* 60D1
Mönsterås *Sweden* 20D1
Montagne d'Ambre Mt *Madag* 79E5
Montagnes des Ouled Naïl Mts *Alg* 77C2
Montague I *USA* 56J4
Montaigu *France* 18B2
Montallo Mt *Italy* 22D3
Montana State *USA* 54B2
Montañas de León Mts *Spain* 19A1
Montargis *France* 18C2
Montauban *France* 18C3
Montauk *USA* 59E2
Montauk Pt *USA* 59E2
Montbard *France* 16C3
Montbéliard *France* 18D2
Mont Blanc Mt *France/Italy* 22B1
Montceau les Mines *France* 18C2
Montceny Mt *Spain* 19C1
Mont Cinto Mt *Corse* 18D3
Montcornet *France* 16C2
Mont d'Amain Mt *France* 16A2
Mont-de-Marsin *France* 18B3
Montdidier *France* 18C2
Monteagudo *Bol* 70F7
Monte Alegre *Brazil* 71H4
Monte Amiata Mt *Italy* 22C2
Monte Azul *Brazil* 73D2
Monte Baldo Mt *Italy* 17D2
Montebello *Can* 59D1
Monte Bello Is *Aust* 48A3
Montebelluna *Italy* 17E2
Monte Carlo *France* 17B3
Monte Carmelo *Brazil* 73C2
Monte Caseros *Arg* 72D2
Montecatini *Italy* 17D3
Monte Catria Mt *Italy* 17E3
Monte Cimone Mt *Italy* 22C2
Monte Cinto Mt *Corse* 22B2
Monte Coman *Arg* 72B2
Monte Corno Mt *Italy* 22C2
Montecristi *Dom Rep* 68C3
Montecristo I *Italy* 22C2
Monte Escobedo *Mexico* 67B1
Monte Falterona Mt *Italy* 17D3
Monte Gargano Mt *Italy* 22D2
Montego Bay *Jamaica* 68B3
Monte Grappa Mt *Italy* 17D2
Monte Lesima Mt *Italy* 17C2
Montélimar *France* 18C3
Montelindo R *Par* 73A3
Monte Miletto Mt *Italy* 22C2
Montemo-o-Novo *Port* 19A2
Montemorelos *Mexico* 66C2
Montená *Colombia* 68B5
Montenegro Region *Yugos* 23D2
Montengero *Brazil* 72E1
Monte Orsaro Mt *Italy* 17C3
Monte Pascoal Mt *Brazil* 73E2
Monte Patria *Chile* 72A2
Monte Pennino Mt *Italy* 17E3
Monte Pississ Mt *Arg* 72B1
Monte Pollino Mt *Italy* 22D3
Monte Pramaggiore Mt *Italy* 17E2
Montepuez *Mozam* 79D5
Montepulciano *Italy* 17D3
Montereau-Faut-Yonne *France* 16B2
Monterey California *USA* 54A3
Monterey Virginia *USA* 59D3
Monterey B *USA* 54A3
Monterey B *USA* 65B3
Montería *Colombia* 70C2
Montero *Bol* 70F7
Monte Rosa Mt *Italy/Switz* 17B2
Monterrey *Mexico* 66B2
Montes Claros *Brazil* 71K7
Montes de Toledo Mts *Spain* 19B2
Montevarchi *Italy* 17D3
Montevideo *Urug* 69E4
Montevideo *USA* 57C3
Montevil *France* 15F6
Monte Viso Mt *Italy* 22B2
Monte Vista *USA* 62A2
Montezuma *USA* 62B2
Mont Gimie Mt *St Lucia* 68P2
Montgomery Alabama *USA* 55E3
Montgomery Pennsylvania *USA* 60B2
Mont Gréboun *Niger* 76C2
Montherme *France* 16C2
Monthey *Switz* 17B1
Monticello Arkansas *USA* 63D3
Monticello Iowa *USA* 58A2
Monticello Minnesota *USA* 57D2
Monticello New York *USA* 60C2
Monticello Utah *USA* 54C3
Monti del Gennargentu Mt *Sardegna* 22B2
Montier-en-Der *France* 16C2
Monti Lessini Mts *Italy* 17D2
Monti Nebrodi Mts *Italy* 22C3
Montivilliers *France* 16A2
Mont-Laurier *Can* 53L5
Montluçon *France* 18C2
Montmagny *Can* 53L5
Montmédy *France* 16C2
Montmirail *France* 16B2

Montmorency Nagha Kalat

Montmorency *Can* 59E1
Mont Mounier Mt *France* 17B2
Montoro *Spain* 19B2
Montoursville *USA* 60B2
Mont Pelat Mt *France* 18D3
Montpelier Idaho *USA* 64D2
Montpelier Ohio *USA* 58C2
Montpelier Vermont *USA* 55F2
Montpellier *France* 18C3
Montréal *Can* 53L5
Montreuil *France* 18C1
Montreux *Switz* 22B1
Montrevel *France* 17A1
Mont Risoux Mt *France* 17B1
Montrose Colorado *USA* 54C3
Montrose Pennsylvania *USA* 60C2
Montrose *Scot* 13C2
Montrose Oilfield *N Sea* 14F3
Mont-St-Michel *France* 18B2
Monts des Ksour Mts *Alg* 77B2
Monts des Ouled Neil Mts *Alg* 19C3
Monts du Hodna Mts *Alg* 19C2
Montserrat I *Caribbean* 68E3
Mont Ventoux Mt *France* 17A2
Monument Mt *USA* 56F2
Monument V *USA* 54B3
Monveda *Zaïre* 78C3
Monywa *Burma* 43B1
Monza *Italy* 22B1
Monze *Zambia* 79C5
Moomba *Aust* 50B1
Moonbi Range Mts *Aust* 50D2
Moonda L *Aust* 50B1
Moonie *Aust* 50D1
Moonie R *Aust* 50C1
Moonta *Aust* 50A2
Moora *Aust* 48A4
Mooraberree *Aust* 50B1
Moorcroft *USA* 57B3
Moore,L *Aust* 48A3
Moorfoot Hills *Scot* 14D4
Moorhead *USA* 54D2
Moose R *Can* 53K4
Moosehead L *USA* 59F1
Moose Jaw *Can* 52H4
Moose Lake *USA* 57D2
Moosomin *Can* 52H4
Moosonee *Can* 53K4
Moosup *USA* 60E2
Mopeia *Mozam* 79D5
Mopti *Mali* 76B3
Moquegua *Peru* 70D7
Mora *Cam* 77J3
Mora *Sweden* 12G6
Mora *USA* 57D2
Morada *Brazil* 71L5
Morādābād *India* 35D3
Morada Nova de Minas L *Brazil* 73C2
Morafenobe *Madag* 79E5
Moramanga *Madag* 79E5
Moran *USA* 64D2
Morant Bay *Jamaica* 68J2
Morant Pt *Jamaica* 68J2
Moratuwa *Sri Lanka* 36B3
Morava R *Austria/Czech* 20D3
Morava R *Yugos* 23E2
Moraveh Tappeh *Iran* 34D1
Moray Firth Estuary *Scot* 13C2
Morbegno *Italy* 17C1
Morbi *India* 35C4
Morcillo *Mexico* 67B1
Mor Dağ Mt *Turk* 30D2
Morden *Can* 52J5
Mordovskaya ASSR Republic *USSR* 24G5
Moreau R *USA* 57B2
Morecambe *Eng* 15D4
Morecambe B *Eng* 15D4
Moree *Aust* 48D3
Morée *France* 16A3
Morehead *USA* 58C3
Morehead City *USA* 61D2
Mörel *Switz* 17C1
Morelia *Mexico* 66B3
Morelos *Mexico* 67B1
Morelos *Mexico* 67C1
Morelos State *Mexico* 67C2
Morena *India* 35D3
Moresby I *Can* 52E4
Moreton I *Aust* 50D1
Moreuil *France* 16B2
Morez *France* 17B1
Morgan City *USA* 63D4
Morganton *USA* 61C1
Morgantown *USA* 59D3
Morges *Switz* 17B1
Morhange *France* 16D2
Mori *Japan* 41E3
Moriarty *USA* 62A3
Moriatio *Tobago* 68K1
Morin Dawa *China* 41A2
Morioka *Japan* 41E4
Morisset *Aust* 50D2
Morkoka R *USSR* 27N3
Morlaix *France* 18B2
Morne Diablotin Mt *Dominica* 68Q2
Morney *Aust* 50B1
Mornington I *Aust* 48C2
Moro *Pak* 35B3
Morobe *PNG* 48D1
Morocco Kingdom *Africa* 76B1
Moro G *Phil* 45F9
Morogoro *Tanz* 79D4
Moroleon *Mexico* 67B1
Morombe *Madag* 79E6
Morón *Cuba* 68B2
Morondava *Madag* 79E6
Moron de la Frontera *Spain* 19A2
Moroni *Comoros* 79E5
Morotai I *Indon* 45C2
Moroto *Uganda* 78D3
Morozovsk *USSR* 25G6
Morpeth *Eng* 14E4
Morphou *Cyprus* 31B1
Morphou B *Cyprus* 31B1
Morrill *USA* 57B3
Morrilton *USA* 63D2
Morrinhos *Brazil* 73C2
Morrinsville *NZ* 51C1
Morris *Can* 57C2
Morris *USA* 57C2
Morristown New Jersey *USA* 60C2
Morristown New York *USA* 59D2
Morristown Tennessee *USA* 61C1
Morrisville New York *USA* 60C1
Morrisville Pennsylvania *USA* 60C2
Morro Bay *USA* 65B3
Morro de Papanoa *Mexico* 67B2
Morro de Petatlán *Mexico* 67B2
Morrumbala *Mozam* 79D5
Morrumbene *Mozam* 79D6
Morshansk *USSR* 24G5
Mortagne-au-Perche *France* 16A2
Mortara *Italy* 17C2
Morteros *Arg* 72C2
Mortes = Manso
Mortes R Malo Grosso *Brazil* 71H6
Mortes R Minas Gerais *Brazil* 73D3
Mortlake *Aust* 50B3
Morton *USA* 62B3
Moruga *Trinidad* 68L1
Moruya *Aust* 50D3
Morven *Aust* 50C1
Morvern Pen *Scot* 14C3
Morwell *Aust* 50C3
Morzhovoi B *USA* 56F4
Mosbach *W Germ* 16E2
Moscos Is *Burma* 43B3
Moscow = Moskva
Moscow Idaho *USA* 64C1
Moscow Pennsylvania *USA* 60C2
Mosel R *W Germ* 20B2
Moselle Department *France* 16D2
Moselle R *France* 16D2
Moses Lake *USA* 64C1
Mosgiel *NZ* 51B3
Moshi *Tanz* 78D4
Mosinee *USA* 58B2
Mosjøen *Nor* 12G5
Moskal'vo *USSR* 27Q4
Moskva *USSR* 26E4
Mosquero *USA* 62B2
Mosquito R *Brazil* 73D2
Moss *Nor* 12G7
Mossaka *Congo* 78B4
Mossâmedes = Moçâmedes
Mossel Bay *S Africa* 79C7
Mossendjo *Congo* 78B4
Mossgiel *Aust* 50B2
Mossoró *Brazil* 71L5
Most *Czech* 20C2
Mostaganem *Alg* 77C1
Mostar *Yugos* 23D2
Mostardos *Brazil* 72E2
Mosty *USSR* 21E2
Mosul *Iraq* 30D2
Motala *Sweden* 12G7
Motherwell *Scot* 14D4
Motihāri *India* 37B2
Motilla del Palancar *Spain* 19B2
Motovun *Yugos* 17E2
Motril *Spain* 19B2
Mott *USA* 57B2
Motueka *NZ* 51B2
Motueka R *NZ* 51B2
Moudon *Switz* 17B1
Mouila *Gabon* 78B4
Moulamein *Aust* 50B2
Mould Bay *Can* 52G2
Moulins *France* 18C2
Moulmein *Burma* 43B2
Moulouya R *Mor* 77B2
Moultrie *USA* 61C2
Moultrie,L *USA* 61D2
Mound City Illinois *USA* 58B3
Mound City Missouri *USA* 63C1
Moundou *Chad* 78B3
Moundsville *USA* 58C3
Mount Aigoual Mt *France* 18C3
Mountain R *Can* 56N2
Mountain Brook *USA* 61B2
Mountain Grove *USA* 63D2
Mountain Home Arkansas *USA* 63D2
Mountain Home Idaho *USA* 64C2
Mountain Village *USA* 56F3
Mount Airy Maryland *USA* 60B3
Mount Airy N Carolina *USA* 61C1
Mount Carmel *USA* 60B2
Mount Conellsburg *USA* 60B3
Mount Desert I *USA* 59F2
Mount Dutton *Aust* 50A1
Mount Eba *Aust* 50A2
Mount Gambier *Aust* 50B3
Mount Hagen *PNG* 48D1
Mount Holly *USA* 60C3
Mount Holly Springs *USA* 60B2
Mount Hope *Aust* 50A2
Mount Isa *Aust* 48C3
Mount Jackson *USA* 60A3
Mount Jewett *USA* 60A2
Mount Lofty Range Mts *Aust* 50A2
Mount McKinley Nat Pk *USA* 56H3
Mount Magnet *Aust* 48A3
Mount Manara *Aust* 50B2
Mount Mézenc Mt *France* 18C3
Mount Morgan *Aust* 48E3
Mount Morris *USA* 60B1
Mount Perry *Aust* 50D1
Mount Pleasant Texas *USA* 63D3
Mount Pleasant Utah *USA* 65D3
Mount Pocono *USA* 60C2
Mount Rainier Nat Pk *USA* 64B1
Mounts B *Eng* 15C6
Mount Shasta *USA* 64B2
Mount Union *USA* 60B2
Mount Vernon Alabama *USA* 61B2
Mount Vernon Illinois *USA* 58B3
Mount Vernon Kentucky *USA* 63C3
Mount Vernon Washington *USA* 64B1
Mourne Mts *N Ire* 15B4
Moussa Ali Mt *Djibouti* 32D4
Moussoro *Chad* 78B2
Moustiers Ste Marie *France* 17B3
Mouth of the Indus *Pak* 35B4
Mouths of the Ganga *India/Bang* 37C3
Mouths of the Mekong *Viet* 43D4
Mouths of the Niger *Nigeria* 76C4
Moutier *Switz* 17B1
Moûtiers *France* 17B2
Moutong *Indon* 45B2
Mouydir Mts *Alg* 76C2
Mouyondzi *Congo* 78B4
Mouzon *France* 16C2
Moyahua *Mexico* 67B1
Moyale *Kenya* 78D3
Moyamba *Sierra Leone* 76A4
Moyen Atlas Mts *Mor* 77A2
Moyeni *Lesotho* 79C7
Moyero R *USSR* 27M3
Moyo *Uganda* 78D3
Moyobamba *Peru* 70C5
Moyu *China* 35D1
Mozambique Republic *Africa* 79D6
Mozambique Chan *Mozam/Madag* 79D6
Mozhga *USSR* 24J4
Mozyr *USSR* 25D5
Mozyr R *USSR* 12K8
Mpanda *Tanz* 78D4
Mpika *Zambia* 79D5
Mporokosa *Zambia* 79D4
Mposhi *Zambia* 79C5
Mpulungu *Zambia* 79D4
Mpwapwa *Tanz* 78D4
Mstislavl' *USSR* 21G2
Mtsensk *USSR* 24F5
Mtubatuba *S Africa* 79D6
Mtwara *Tanz* 79E5
Muang Chainat *Thai* 43C2
Muang Chiang Rai *Thai* 43C2
Muang Kalasin *Thai* 43C2
Muang Khon Kaen *Thai* 43C2
Muang Lampang *Thai* 43B2
Muang Lamphun *Thai* 43B2
Muang Loei *Thai* 43C2
Muang Lom Sak *Thai* 43C2
Muang Nakhon Phanom *Thai* 43C2
Muang Nakhon Sawan *Thai* 43B2
Muang Nan *Thai* 43C2
Muang Phayao *Thai* 43C2
Muang Phetchabun *Thai* 43C2
Muang Phichit *Thai* 43C2
Muang Phitsanulok *Thai* 43C2
Muang Phrae *Thai* 43C2
Muang Roi Et *Thai* 43C2
Muang Sakon Nakhon *Thai* 43C2
Muang Samut Prakan *Thai* 43C3
Muang Uthai Thani *Thai* 43C2
Muang Yasothon *Thai* 43C2
Muar *Malay* 43C5
Muara *Brunei* 44D2
Muara *Indon* 44B3
Muaralakitan *Indon* 44B3
Muaratebo *Indon* 44B3
Muaratewah *Indon* 44E3
Muarenim *Indon* 44B3
Muaungmaya *Burma* 43A2
Mubende *Uganda* 78D3
Mubi *Nig* 77J3
Muchinga Mts *Zambia* 79D5
Muck I *Scot* 14B3
Muckadilla *Aust* 50C1
Mucuri *Brazil* 73E2
Mucuri R *Brazil* 73D2
Mucusso *Angola* 79C5
Mudanjiang *China* 41B3
Mudayy *Oman* 33F3
Muddy Gap P *USA* 57A3
Mudgee *Aust* 50C2
Mudon *Burma* 43B2
Mud'vuga *USSR* 24F3
Mue *Nouvelle Calédonie* 49F3
Mueda *Mozam* 79D5
Mufreesboro *USA* 61D1
Mufulira *Zambia* 79C5
Mufu Shan Hills *China* 40C4
Mugadishu = Muqdisho
Mugadzhary Mts *USSR* 25K6
Mughayra *S Arabia* 30C4
Mugla *Turk* 30A2
Mugodzhary Mts *USSR* 26G5
Mugu *Nepal* 37B2
Muguaping *China* 40A3
Muhammad Qol *Sudan* 32C2
Muhaywir *Iraq* 30D3
Mühlacker *W Germ* 16E2
Mühldorf *W Germ* 20C3
Muhlhausen *E Germ* 20C2
Muhos *Fin* 12K6
Mui Bai Bung C *Camb* 43C4
Muine Bheag *Irish Rep* 15B5
Mujimbeji *Zambia* 79C5
Mukachevo *USSR* 21E3
Mukah *Malay* 44D2
Mukawa *Japan* 42D2
Muko-jima I *Japan* 38H4
Muktinath *Nepal* 37B2
Mukur *Afghan* 35B2
Mulan *China* 41B2
Mulberry *USA* 63D2
Mulchatna R *USA* 56G3
Mulchén *Chile* 72B3
Mulde R *E Germ* 20C2
Mule Creek Junction *USA* 57B3
Muleshoe *USA* 62B3
Mulgrave I *Aust* 39H8
Mulhacén Mt *Spain* 19B2
Mülheim *W Germ* 16D1
Mulhouse *France* 16D3
Muli *China* 40A4
Muling *China* 41C3
Muling He R *China* 41C2
Mull I *Scot* 14C3
Mullaitvu *Sri Lanka* 36C3
Mullaley *Aust* 50C2
Mullewa *Aust* 48A3
Müllheim *W Germ* 16D3
Mullica R *USA* 60C3
Mullingar *Irish Rep* 15B5
Mull of Kintyre Pt *Scot* 14C4
Mull of Oa C *Scot* 14B4
Mullumbimby *Aust* 50D1
Mulobezi *Zambia* 79C5
Multan *Pak* 35C2
Muluku Is *Indon* 45C3
Mumbwa *Zambia* 79C5
Mumra *USSR* 25H6
Muna I *Indon* 45B4
München *W Germ* 20C3
Munchŏn *N Korea* 42A3
Muncie *USA* 58B2
Munconnie,L *Aust* 50A1
Muncy *USA* 60B2
Münden *W Germ* 20B2
Mundubbera *Aust* 50D1
Mungallala *Aust* 50C1
Mungallala R *Aust* 50C1
Mungbere *Zaïre* 78C3
Mungeli *India* 37B3
Munger *India* 37C2
Mungindi *Aust* 50C1
Munich = München
Munising *USA* 58B1
Muñoz Gomero,Pen *Chile* 69B8
Munsan *S Korea* 42A3
Münsingen *W Germ* 16E2
Munster *France* 16D2
Münster *Switz* 17C1
Münster *W Germ* 20B2
Münsterland Region *W Germ* 16D1
Muntii Apuseni Mts *Rom* 23E1
Muntii Călimanilor Mts *Rom* 23E1
Muntii Carpaţii Meridionali Mts *Rom* 23E1
Muntii Rodnei Mts *Rom* 23E1
Muntii Zarandului Mts *Rom* 23E1
Munzur Silsilesi Mts *Turk* 30C2
Muomio *Fin* 26D3
Muong Khoua *Laos* 43C1
Muong Man *Viet* 43D3
Muong Nong *Laos* 43D2
Muong Ou Neua *Laos* 43C1
Muong Sai *Laos* 43C1
Muong Sen *Viet* 43C2
Muong Sing *Laos* 43C1
Muong Son *Laos* 43C1
Muonio *Fin* 12J5
Muonio R *Sweden/Fin* 12J5
Muqaddam Watercourse *Sudan* 32B3
Muqdisho *Somalia* 78E3
Mur R *Austria* 22C1
Murakami *Japan* 41D4
Murallón Mt *Chile/Arg* 69B7
Murashi *USSR* 24H4
Murat R *Turk* 30D2
Muravera *Sardegna* 22B3
Murayama *Japan* 42D3
Murcanyo *Somalia* 33F4
Murcheh Khvort *Iran* 34C2
Murchison *NZ* 51B2
Murchison R *Aust* 48A3
Murcia Region *Spain* 19B2
Murcia *Spain* 19B2
Murdo *USA* 57B3
Mureş R *Rom* 23E1
Muresui R *Rom* 23E1
Murfreesboro *USA* 61B1
Murg R *W Germ* 16E2
Murgab R *USSR* 26H6
Murgha Kibzai *Pak* 35B2
Murgon *Aust* 50D1
Muri *India* 37C3
Muriaé *Brazil* 73D3
Muriege *Angola* 79C4
Murmansk *USSR* 24E2
Murom *USSR* 24G4
Muroran *Japan* 41E3
Muros *Spain* 19A1
Muroto *Japan* 41C5
Muroto-zaki C *Japan* 42B4
Murphy Idaho *USA* 64C2
Murphy N Carolina *USA* 61C1
Murray Kentucky *USA* 58B3
Murray Utah *USA* 64D2
Murray R *Aust* 50B2
Murray Bridge *Aust* 50A3
Murray,L *PNG* 39H7
Murray,L *USA* 61C2
Murray Seacarp *Pacific O* 47M3
Murrhardt *W Germ* 16E2
Murrumbidgee R *Aust* 50B2
Murrumburrah *Aust* 50C2
Murrurundi *Aust* 50D2
Murten *Switz* 17B1
Murtoa *Aust* 50B3
Murupara *NZ* 51C1
Murwāra *India* 37B3
Murwillimbah *Aust* 50D1
Muş *Turk* 30D2
Musala Mt *Bulg* 23E2
Musan *N Korea* 41B3
Musandam Pen *Oman* 33G1
Muscat = Masqat
Muscat Region *Oman* 33G2
Muscatine *USA* 57D3
Musgrave Range Mts *Aust* 48C3
Mushie *Zaïre* 78B4
Muskeget Chan *USA* 60E2
Muskegon *USA* 58B2
Muskegon R *USA* 58B2
Muskogee *USA* 63C2
Muskoka,L *Can* 59D2
Musmar *Sudan* 32C3
Musoma *Tanz* 78D4
Mussau I *PNG* 48D1
Musselshell R *USA* 64E1
Mussende *Angola* 79B5
Mussidan *France* 18C2
Mustafa-Kemalpasa *Turk* 23F2
Mustang *Nepal* 37B2
Musu-dan C *N Korea* 42A2
Muswelibrook *Aust* 50D2
Mut *Egypt* 75B2
Mutarara *Mozam* 79D5
Mutare *Zim* 79D5
Mutis Mt *Indon* 45B4
Mutnyy Materik *USSR* 24K2
Mutoko *Zim* 79D5
Mutsamudu *Comoros* 79E5
Mutshatsha *Zaïre* 79C5
Mutsu *Japan* 41E3
Mutsu-wan B *Japan* 41E3
Mutunópolis *Brazil* 73C1
Mu Us Shamo Desert *China* 40B2
Muxima *Angola* 79B4
Muya *USSR* 27N4
Muyezerskiy *USSR* 24E3
Muyinga *Burundi* 78D4
Muyumba *Zaïre* 79C4
Muyun Kum Desert *USSR* 29E1
Muzaffarābad *Pak* 35C2
Muzaffargarh *Pak* 35C2
Muzaffarpur *India* 37C2
Muzhi *USSR* 26H3
Muzlag Mt *China* 29G2
Muztagala Mt *China* 29F2
Mvuma *Zim* 79D5
Mwanza *Tanz* 78D4
Mwanza *Zaïre* 79C4
Mweka *Zaïre* 78C4
Mwene Ditu *Zaïre* 79C4
Mwenezi *Zim* 79D6
Mwenga *Zaïre* 78C4
Mwenzi *Mozam* 79D6
Mweru L *Zambia* 79C4
Mwinilunga *Zambia* 79C5
Myanaung *Burma* 37E4
Myingyao *Burma* 43B1
Myinmoletkat Mt *Burma* 43B3
Myinmu *Burma* 37E3
Myitkyina *Burma* 37E2
Myitta *Burma* 43B3
Myittha *Burma* 37E3
Mymensingh *Bang* 37D3
Myojin I *Japan* 38G3
Myongchon *N Korea* 42A2
Myonggan *N Korea* 42A2
Myrdal *Nor* 12F6
Myrdalsjökur Mts *Iceland* 12B2
Myrtle Beach *USA* 61D2
Myrtle Creek *USA* 64B2
Mys Chaplino C *USSR* 27U3
Mys Chelyuskin C *USSR* 27M2
Mys Chukotskiy Pt *USSR* 56D3
Mys Dezhneva Pt *USSR* 56E2
Mysen *Nor* 12G7
Mysiloborz *Pol* 20C2
Mys Kanin Nos C *USSR* 24G2
Mys Kronotskiy C *USSR* 27S4
Myślenice *Pol* 21D3
Mys Lopatka C *USSR* 27R4
Mys Navarin C *USSR* 27T3
Mys Nygchigen Pt *USSR* 56D2
Mys Olyutorskiy C *USSR* 27T3
Mysore *India* 36B2
Mys Sarych C *USSR* 25E7
Mys Serdtse Kamen Pt *USSR* 56D2
Mys Shelagskiy C *USSR* 27T2
Mys Shmidta *USSR* 27T3
Mys Sivuchiy C *USSR* 27S4
Mys Svyatoy Nos C *USSR* 24F2
Mystic *USA* 60E2
Mys Tyub-Karagan Pt *USSR* 25J7
Mys Yelizavety C *USSR* 27Q4
Mys Zhelaniya C *USSR* 26H2
My Tho *Viet* 43D3
Mytle Point *USA* 64B2
Mzimba *Malawi* 79D5
Mzuzú *Malawi* 79D5

N

Naantali *Fin* 12J6
Naas *Irish Rep* 15B5
Nabari *Japan* 42C4
Naberezhnyye Chelny *USSR* 24J4
Nabesna R *USA* 56K3
Nabeul *Tunisia* 77E1
Nabileque R *Brazil* 73A3
Nablus *Israel* 31C2
Nacala *Mozam* 79E5
Naches *USA* 64B1
Nachingwea *Tanz* 79D5
Nacogdoches *USA* 63D3
Nacondam I *Indian O* 43A3
Nacozari *Mexico* 66B1
Nadel Mt *W Germ* 16E1
Nadi *Fiji* 55G2
Nadiād *India* 35C4
Nador *Mor* 19B2
Nadūshan *Iran* 34C2
Nadvoitsy *USSR* 24E3
Nadvornaya *USSR* 21E3
Naestved *Den* 20C1
Nafoora *Libya* 75B2
Nagahama *Japan* 42B4
Naga Hills *Burma* 37E2
Nagai *Japan* 42C3
Nagai I *USA* 56G5
Nāgāland State *India* 37D2
Nagano *Japan* 41D4
Nagaoka *Japan* 41D4
Nāgappattinam *India* 36B2
Nagar Parkar *Pak* 35C4
Nagasaki *Japan* 41B5
Nagashima *Japan* 42C4
Nagato *Japan* 42B4
Nāgaur *India* 35C3
Nāgercoil *India* 36B3
Nagha Kalat *Pak* 35B3

Nagīna **Niltepec**

Nagīna *India* 35D3
Nagold *W Germ* 16E2
Nagoya *Japan* 41D4
Nāgpur *India* 35D4
Nagqu *China* 29H2
Nagykanizsa *Hung* 20D3
Nagykörös *Hung* 21D3
Naha *Japan* 38F4
Nahaimo *Can* 54A2
Nāhan *India* 35D2
Nahang R *Iran* 34E3
Nahanni Butte *Can* 52F3
Nahanni Nat Pk *Can* 56N3
Nahanni Range Mts *Can* 56O3
Nahariya *Israel* 31C2
Nahar Ouassel R *Alg* 77C1
Nahāvand *Iran* 34B2
Nahe R *W Germ* 16D2
Nahpu *China* 40D2
Nahuel Niyeu *Arg* 72B4
Naikliu *Indon* 45B4
Naimen Qi *China* 40E1
Nain *Can* 53M4
Nā'īn *Iran* 34C2
Naini Tai *India* 35D3
Nainpur *India* 37B3
Nairn *Scot* 14D3
Nairobi *Kenya* 78D4
Najafābād *Iran* 34C2
Najd Region *S Arabia* 32D1
Najin *N Korea* 41C3
Najrān *S Arabia* 32D3
Naju *S Korea* 42A3
Nakadori-jima *Japan* 42A4
Nakama *Japan* 42B4
Nakaminato *Japan* 41E4
Nakamura *Japan* 42B4
Nakano *Japan* 42C3
Nakano-shima I *Japan* 42B3
Nakatsu *Japan* 41C5
Nakatsu-gawa *Japan* 42C3
Nakfa *Eth* 32C3
Nakhichevan *USSR* 25H8
Nakhl *Egypt* 31B4
Nakhodka *USSR* 41C3
Nakhon Pathom *Thai* 43C3
Nakhon Ratchasima *Thai* 43C3
Nakhon Si Thammarat *Thai* 43C4
Nakina Ontario *Can* 53K4
Naknek *USA* 56G4
Naknek L *USA* 56G4
Nakrek *USA* 52C4
Nakskov *Den* 12G7
Naktong R *S Korea* 42A3
Nakuru *Kenya* 78D4
Nal'chik *USSR* 25G7
Nalgonda *India* 36B1
Nallamala Range Mts *India* 36B1
Naltia Mt *Nor/Fin* 24C2
Nālūt *Libya* 75A1
Namak L *Iran* 26G6
Namakzar-e Shadad Salt Flat *Iran* 34D2
Namangan *USSR* 26J5
Namapa *Mozam* 79D5
Namaqualand Region *S Africa* 79B7
Nambour *Aust* 50D1
Nambucca Heads *Aust* 50D2
Nam Can *Viet* 43D4
Namcha Barwa Mt *China* 29H2
Nam Co L *China* 29H2
Nam Dinh *Viet* 43D1
Nametil *Mozam* 79D5
Namhae-do I *S Korea* 41B5
Namib Desert *Namibia* 79B6
Namibia Dependency *Africa* 79B6
Namlea *Indon* 45C3
Namling *China* 37C2
Namo *Indon* 45B3
Namoi R *Aust* 50C2
Nampa *USA* 64C2
Nampala *Mali* 76B3
Nam Phong *Thai* 43C2
Namp'o *N Korea* 41B4
Nampula *Mozam* 79D5
Namsos *Nor* 12G6
Namton *Burma* 43B1
Namtsy *USSR* 27O3
Namtu *Burma* 37E3
Namuno *Mozam* 79D5
Namur *Belg* 16C1
Namutoni *Namibia* 79B5
Namwŏn *S Korea* 41B4
Nanam *N Korea* 41B3
Nanango *Aust* 50D1
Nanao *Japan* 41D4
Nanatsu-jima I *Japan* 42C3
Nanbu *China* 40B3
Nancha *China* 41B2
Nanchang *China* 40D4
Nanchong *China* 40B3
Nancowry I *Indian O* 36E3
Nancy *France* 18D2
Nanda Devi Mt *India* 37B1
Nānded *India* 36B1
Nandewar Range Mts *Aust* 50D2
Nandurbar *India* 35C4
Nandyāl *India* 36B1
Nanga Eboko *Cam* 78B3
Nangahale *Indon* 45B4
Nanga Parbat Mt *Pak* 35C1
Nangapinoh *Indon* 44D3
Nangatayap *Indon* 44D3
Nangis *France* 16B2
Nangnim *N Korea* 42A2
Nangnim Sanmaek Mts *N Korea* 41B3
Nang Xian *China* 37D2
Nanjangūd *India* 36B2
Nanjing *China* 40D3
Nanking = Nanjing
Nankoku *Japan* 42B4
Nan Ling Region *China* 40C4
Nanliu R *China* 43D1
Nanning *China* 40B5
Nanortalik *Greenland* 53O3
Nanpan Jiang R *China* 40A5
Nānpāra *India* 37B2
Nanping *China* 40D4
Nansen Sd *Can* 53J1
Nansio *Tanz* 78D4
Nantes *France* 18B2
Nanticoke *USA* 60C2
Nantong *China* 40E3
Nantua *France* 17A1
Nantucket *USA* 60E2
Nantucket I *USA* 60E2
Nantucket Sd *USA* 60E2
Nanty Glo *USA* 60A2
Nanumanga I *Tuvalu* 49G1
Nanumea I *Tuvalu* 49G1
Nanuque *Brazil* 73D2
Nanyang *China* 40C3
Nanyang Hu L *China* 40D2
Nanyuki *Kenya* 78D3
Naoetsu *Japan* 41D4
Naokot *Pak* 35B4
Napa *USA* 65B3
Napaiskak *USA* 56F3
Napanee *Can* 59D2
Napas *USSR* 26K4
Napassoq *Greenland* 53N3
Nape *Laos* 43D2
Napier *NZ* 51C1
Naples = Napoli
Naples Florida *USA* 61E4
Naples New York *USA* 60B1
Naples Texas *USA* 63D3
Napo *China* 40B5
Napo R *Peru/Ecuador* 70D4
Napoleon *USA* 57C2
Napoli *Italy* 22C2
Naqadeh *Iran* 34B1
Naqb Ishtar *Jordan* 31C3
Nara *Japan* 42C4
Nara *Mali* 76B3
Naracoorte *Aust* 48D4
Naranjos *Mexico* 67C1
Narasarāopet *India* 36B1
Narathiwat *Thai* 43C4
Narayanganj *Bang* 37D3
Nārāyenpet *India* 36B1
Narbonne *France* 18C3
Narendranagar *India* 35D2
Nares Str *Can* 53L2
Narew R *Pol* 21E2
Narita *Japan* 42D3
Narmada R *India* 35C4
Nārnaul *India* 35D3
Naro Fominsk *USSR* 24F4
Narok *Kenya* 78D4
Narowal *Pak* 35C2
Narrabri *Aust* 48D4
Narran L *Aust* 50C1
Narran R *Aust* 50C1
Narrandera *Aust* 50C2
Narrogin *Aust* 48A4
Narromine *Aust* 50C2
Narrows *USA* 58C3
Narrowsburg *USA* 60C2
Narsimhapur *India* 35D4
Narsīpatnam *India* 36C1
Narssalik *Greenland* 53O3
Narssaq *Greenland* 53O3
Narssarssuaq *Greenland* 53O3
Narugo *Japan* 42D3
Naruto *Japan* 42B4
Narva *USSR* 24D4
Narvik *Nor* 12H5
Narwāna *India* 35D3
Nar'yan Mar *USSR* 24J2
Narylico *Aust* 50B1
Naryn *USSR* 26J5
Nasarawa *Nig* 77H4
Nasca Ridge *Pacific O* 74D5
Nashua *USA* 60E1
Nashville Arkansas *USA* 63D3
Nashville Tennessee *USA* 61B1
Našice *Yugos* 23D1
Nāsik *India* 35C4
Nasir *Sudan* 78D3
Nassau *Bahamas* 68B1
Nassau *USA* 60D1
Nasser,L *Egypt* 75C2
Nassian *Ivory Coast* 77F4
Nässjö *Sweden* 12G7
Nastapoka Is *Can* 53L4
Nata *Botswana* 79C6
Natal *Brazil* 71L5
Natal *Indon* 44A2
Natal Province *S Africa* 79D6
Natal Basin *Indian O* 46C6
Natanz *Iran* 34C2
Natashquan *Can* 53M4
Natashquan R *Can* 53M4
Natchez *USA* 63D3
Natchitoches *USA* 63D3
Nathalia *Aust* 50C3
Nathorsts Land Region *Greenland* 53Q2
National City *USA* 65C4
National Republic of China = Taiwan
Natitingou *Benin* 77G3
Natori *Japan* 42D3
Natovi'a *USSR* 21F2
Natron L *Tanz* 78D4
Naturaliste,C *Aust* 48A4
Nauders *Austria* 17D1
Nauen *E Germ* 20C2
Naugatuck *USA* 60D2
Naumburg *E Germ* 20C2
Naur *Jordan* 31C3
Nauru I *Pacific O* 49F1
Naushki *USSR* 27M4
Nautla *Mexico* 67C1
Nauzad *Afghan* 34E2
Navajo Res *USA* 54C3
Navalmoral de la Mata *Spain* 19A2
Navarino I *Chile* 69C9
Navarra Province *Spain* 19B1
Navarro *Arg* 72D3
Navasota *USA* 63C3
Navasota R *USA* 63C3
Navia R *Spain* 19A1
Navidad *Chile* 72A2
Naviraí *Brazil* 73B3
Navlakhi *India* 35C4
Navlya *USSR* 25E5
Navojoa *Mexico* 66B2
Návpaktos *Greece* 23E3
Návplion *Greece* 23E3
Navrongo *Ghana* 77F3
Navsāri *India* 35C4
Nawá *Syria* 31D2
Nawāda *India* 37C3
Nawah *Afghan* 35B2
Nawrabshah *Pak* 35B3
Naxi *China* 40B4
Náxos I *Greece* 23F3
Nayar *Mexico* 67B1
Nayarit State *Mexico* 67A1
Nāy Band *Iran* 34C3
Nay Band *Iran* 34D2
Nayoro *Japan* 41E3
Nazaré *Brazil* 73E1
Nazareth *Israel* 31C2
Nazay *France* 18B2
Nazca *Peru* 70D6
Nazilli *Turk* 30A2
Nazimovo *USSR* 27L4
Nazwa *Oman* 33G2
Nazyvayevsk *USSR* 26J4
Ndalatando *Angola* 79B4
Ndélé *CAR* 78C3
Ndendé *Gabon* 78B4
Ndende I *Solomon Is* 49F2
N'Djamena *Chad* 78B2
Ndjolé *Gabon* 78B4
Ndola *Zambia* 79C5
Ndouci *Ivory Coast* 77F4
Neabul *Aust* 50C1
Neales R *Aust* 50A1
Neápolis *Greece* 23E3
Near Is *USA* 56A6
Neath *Wales* 15D6
Nebine R *Aust* 50C1
Nebit Dag *USSR* 26G6
Nebraska State *USA* 54C2
Nebraska City *USA* 63C1
Neches R *USA* 63C3
Neckar R *W Germ* 16E2
Necochea *Arg* 72D3
Nêdong *China* 37D2
Needles *USA* 65D4
Neenah *USA* 58B2
Neepawra *Can* 52J4
Neerpelt *Belg* 16C1
Nefta *Tunisia* 77D2
Neftegorsk *USSR* 41E1
Neftelensk *USSR* 27M4
Negelli *Eth* 78D3
Negev Desert *Israel* 31C3
Negla R *Par* 73A3
Negolu Mt *Rom* 25C6
Negombo *Sri Lanka* 36B3
Negrais,C *Burma* 43A2
Negritos *Peru* 70B4
Negro R Amazonas *Brazil* 70F4
Negro R *Arg* 72C4
Negro R Mato Grosso de Sul *Brazil* 73A2
Negro R *Par* 73A3
Negro R *Urug* 72D2
Negros I *Phil* 45F8
Negru Voda *Rom* 23F2
Nehbāndan *Iran* 34E2
Nehe *China* 41A2
Neijiang *China* 40B4
Neillsville *USA* 58A2
Nei Monggol Autonomous Region *China* 40B1
Neira *Colombia* 70C3
Nejo *Eth* 78D3
Nelidovo *USSR* 24E4
Neligh *USA* 57C3
Nellore *India* 36B2
Nel'ma *USSR* 41D2
Nelson *Can* 52G5
Nelson *NZ* 51B2
Nelson R *Can* 53J4
Nelson,C *Aust* 50B3
Nelson I *USA* 56F3
Nelspruit *S Africa* 79D6
Néma *Maur* 76B3
Nemagt Uul Mt *Mongolia* 40A1
Neman R *USSR* 21E1
Neman R *USSR* 21F2
Nemilen R *USSR* 41D1
Nemira Mt *Rom* 23F1
Nemor He R *China* 41B2
Nemours *France* 16B2
Nemuro *Japan* 41F3
Nen R *China* 27O5
Nenagh *Irish Rep* 13B3
Nenana *USA* 56J3
Nenana R *USA* 56J3
Nene R *Eng* 15E5
Nenggiri R *Malay* 44F6
Nenjiang *China* 41B2
Neodesha *USA* 63C2
Neosho *USA* 63D2
Nepa *USSR* 27M4
Nepal Kingdom *Asia* 29G3
Nepalganj *Nepal* 37B2
Nephi *USA* 65D3
Neqarot R *Israel* 31C3
Nequén State *Arg* 72A3
Nerchinsk *USSR* 38E1
Neretva R *Yugos* 23D2
Nero Deep *Pacific O* 39H5
Nes' *USSR* 24G2
Neskaupstaður *Iceland* 12C1
Nesle *France* 16B2
Nesleyville *Can* 53N5
Ness City *USA* 62C2
Néstos R *Greece* 23E2
Netanya *Israel* 31C2
Netcong *USA* 60C2
Netherlands Kingdom *Europe* 20B2
Netrakona *Bang* 37D3
Nettling L *Can* 53L3
Neubrandenburg *E Germ* 20C2
Neuchâtel *Switz* 17B1
Neufchâteau *Belg* 16C2
Neufchâteau *France* 16C2
Neufchâtel *France* 18C2
Neufchâtel-en-Bray *France* 16A2
Neumünster *W Germ* 20B2
Neunkirchen *Austria* 22D1
Neunkirchen *W Germ* 16D2
Neuquén *Arg* 72B3
Neuquén State *Arg* 69B6
Neuquén R *Arg* 72B3
Neuruppin *E Germ* 20C2
Neuse R *USA* 61D1
Neuss *W Germ* 16D1
Neustadt *W Germ* 20C2
Neustadt an der Weinstrasse *W Germ* 16E2
Neustadt im Schwarzwakl *W Germ* 16E3
Neustrelitz *E Germ* 20C2
Neuwied *W Germ* 16D1
Nevada State *USA* 54B3
Nevada *USA* 63D2
Nevada de Chillán Mts *Chile/Arg* 72A3
Nevada de Collima *Mexico* 67B2
Nevada de Toluca Mt *Mexico* 67C2
Nevatim *Israel* 31C3
Nevel *USSR* 24D4
Nevel'sk *USSR* 41E2
Never *USSR* 41A1
Nevers *France* 18C2
Nevertire *Aust* 50C2
Nevis I *Caribbean* 68E3
Nevis R *USSR* 21F2
Nevşehir *Turk* 30B2
Nev'yansk *USSR* 24L4
New R *USA* 58C3
Newala *Tanz* 79D5
New Albany Indiana *USA* 58B3
New Albany Mississippi *USA* 63E3
New Amsterdam *Guyana* 71G2
New Angledool *Aust* 50C1
Newark Delaware *USA* 59D3
Newark New Jersey *USA* 55F2
Newark New York *USA* 60B1
Newark Ohio *USA* 58C2
Newark-upon-Trent *Eng* 15E5
New Bedford *USA* 59E2
Newberg *USA* 64B1
New Bern *USA* 61D1
Newberry *USA* 61C2
New Bight *Bahamas* 68B2
New Boston *USA* 58C3
New Braunfels *USA* 62C4
New Britain *USA* 60D2
New Britain I *PNG* 48E1
New Britain Trench *PNG* 48E1
New Brunswick Province *Can* 53M5
New Brunswick *USA* 60C2
Newburgh *USA* 60C2
Newbury *Eng* 15E6
Newburyport *USA* 60E1
New Canaan *USA* 60D2
Newcastle *Aust* 50D2
New Castle Indiana *USA* 58B3
Newcastle *N Ire* 15C4
New Castle Pennsylvania *USA* 58C2
Newcastle *S Africa* 79C6
Newcastle Wyoming *USA* 57B3
Newcastle upon Tyne *Eng* 14E4
Newcastle Waters *Aust* 48C2
New Delhi *India* 35D3
New England Range Mts *Aust* 50D2
Newenham,C *USA* 56F4
Newfane *USA* 60A1
New Forest,The *Eng* 15E6
Newfoundland Province *Can* 53M4
Newfoundland I *Can* 53N5
Newfoundland Basin *Atlantic O* 74F2
New Franklin *USA* 63D2
New Galloway *Scot* 14C4
New Georgia I *Solomon Is* 49E1
New Glasgow *Can* 53M5
New Guinea I *S E Asia* 48D1
New Haifa *Sudan* 32C3
Newhalen *USA* 56H4
New Hampshire State *USA* 55F2
New Hampton *USA* 57D3
New Hanover I *PNG* 48E1
Newhaven *Eng* 15F6
New Haven *USA* 59E2
New Hebrides Trench *Pacific O* 49F3
New Iberia *USA* 63D3
New Ireland I *PNG* 48E1
New Jersey State *USA* 55F2
Newkirk *USA* 62B3
New Liskeard *Can* 53L5
New London *USA* 60D2
Newman *Aust* 48A3
Newmarket *Eng* 15F5
New Market *USA* 59D3
New Meadows *USA* 64C2
New Mexico State *USA* 54C3
New Milford Connecticut *USA* 60D2
New Milford New York *USA* 60C2
Newnan *USA* 61C2
New Norfolk *Aust* 50E3
New Orleans *USA* 55D3
New Paltz *USA* 60C2
New Philadelphia *USA* 58C2
New Plymouth *NZ* 51B1
Newport Arkansas *USA* 63D2
Newport *Eng* 15E6
Newport Kentucky *USA* 58C3
Newport New Hampshire *USA* 60D1
Newport Oregon *USA* 64B2
Newport Pennsylvania *USA* 60B2
Newport Rhode Island *USA* 59E2
Newport Vermont *USA* 59E2
Newport *Wales* 15D6
Newport Washington *USA* 64C1
Newport News *USA* 55F3
New Providence I *Caribbean* 68B1
Newquay *Eng* 15C6
New Quebe Crater *Can* 53L3
New Ross *Irish Rep* 15B5
Newry *N Ire* 15B4
New Siberian Is = Novosibirskye Ostrova
New Smyrna Beach *USA* 61C3
New South Wales State *Aust* 48D4
New Stuyahok *USA* 56G4
Newton Iowa *USA* 57D3
Newton Kansas *USA* 63C2
Newton Massachusetts *USA* 60E1
Newton Mississippi *USA* 63E3
Newton New York *USA* 60C2
Newton Abbot *Eng* 15D6
Newton Stewart *N Ire* 14B4
Newton Stewart *Scot* 14C4
New Town *USA* 57B2
Newtown *Wales* 15D5
Newtownards *N Ire* 15C4
New Ulm *USA* 57D3
Newville *USA* 60B2
New Westminster *Can* 52F5
New York State *USA* 55F2
New York *USA* 55F2
New Zealand Dominion *SW Pacifico* 49G5
New Zealand Plat *Pacific O* 47K7
Neya *USSR* 24G4
Neyrīz *Iran* 34C3
Neyshābūr *Iran* 34D1
Nezeto *Angola* 79B4
Nezhin *USSR* 25E5
Ngabé *Congo* 78B4
Ngadda *Nig* 77J3
Ngami L *Botswana* 79C6
N'Gaoundéré *Cam* 77J4
Ngaruawahia *NZ* 51C1
Ngaruroro R *NZ* 51C1
Ngauruhoe,Mt *NZ* 51C1
Ngo *Congo* 78B4
Ngoc Linh Mt *Viet* 43D2
Ngoko R *Cam* 78B3
Ngoring Hu L *China* 38C3
Ngorongoro Crater *Tanz* 78D4
N'Gounié R *Gabon* 78B4
Nguigmi *Niger* 78B2
Ngulu I *Pacific O* 39G6
Nguru *Nig* 77J3
Nha Trang *Viet* 43D3
Nhecolandia *Brazil* 73A2
Nhill *Aust* 50B3
Nhommarath *Laos* 43D2
Nhulunbuy *Aust* 48C2
Niafounké *Mali* 76B3
Niagara *USA* 58B1
Niagara Falls *Can* 59D2
Niagara Falls *USA* 59D2
Niah *Malay* 44D2
Niakaramandougou *Ivory Coast* 76B4
Niamey *Niger* 76C3
Niangara *Zaïre* 78C3
Niangoloko *U Volta* 77F3
Nia Nia *Zaïre* 78C3
Nianzishan *China* 41A2
Nias I *Indon* 44A2
Nicaragua Republic *C America* 66D3
Nicastro *Italy* 22D3
Nice *France* 18D3
Nicholl's Town *Bahamas* 68B1
Nicholson *USA* 60C2
Nicobar Is *Indian O* 29H5
Nicosia *Cyprus* 31B1
Nicoya,Pen de *Costa Rica* 66D3
Nidda R *W Germ* 16E1
Nidzica *Pol* 21E2
Niederbronn *France* 16D2
Niedere Tauern Mts *Austria* 17E1
Niedersachsen State *W Germ* 20B2
Niemba *Zaïre* 78C4
Nienburg *W Germ* 20B2
Niers R *W Germ* 16D1
Niete,Mt *Lib* 76B4
Nieuw Amsterdam *Suriname* 71G2
Nieuw Nickeire *Suriname* 71G2
Nieuwpoort *Belg* 16B1
Nieves *Mexico* 67B1
Niğde *Turk* 30B2
Niger Republic *Africa* 76C3
Niger State *Nig* 77H4
Niger R *Nig* 77H4
Nigeria Federal Republic *Africa* 76C4
Nighthawk L *Can* 58C1
Nigrīta *Greece* 23E2
Nihommatsu *Japan* 42D3
Niigata *Japan* 41D4
Niihama *Japan* 41C5
Nii-jima I *Japan* 42C4
Niimi *Japan* 42B4
Niitsu *Japan* 41D4
Nijil *Jordan* 31C3
Nijmegen *Neth* 20B2
Nikel' *USSR* 24E2
Nikki *Benin* 77G3
Nikko *Japan* 41D4
Nikolayev *USSR* 25E6
Nikolayevsk *USSR* 25H6
Nikolayevsk-na-Amure *USSR* 27Q4
Nikol'sk Penza *USSR* 24H5
Nikol'sk RSFSR *USSR* 24H4
Nikolski *USA* 56E5
Nikopol *USSR* 25E6
Niksar *Turk* 30C1
Nīkshahr *Iran* 34E3
Nikšić *Yugos* 23D2
Nikunau I *Kiribati* 49G1
Nila I *Indon* 45C4
Nile R *N E Africa* 28B3
Niles *USA* 58B2
Nilgiri Hills *India* 36B2
Niltepec *Mexico* 67D2

Nimach Okanagan Falls

Nimach *India* 35C4
Nîmes *France* 18C3
Nimmitabel *Aust* 50C3
Nimule *Sudan* 78D3
Nine Degree Chan *Indian O* 29F5
Ninety-East Ridge *Indian O* 46F5
Ninety Mile Beach *Aust* 50C3
Ning'an *China* 41B3
Ningde *China* 40D4
Ningdu *China* 40D4
Ningjing Shan Mts *China* 38C3
Ningming *China* 43D1
Ningnan *China* 40A4
Ningxia Province *China* 40B2
Ning Xian *China* 40B2
Ninh Binh *Vietnam* 40B5
Ninigo Is *PNG* 48D1
Ninilchik *USA* 56H3
Nioaque *Brazil* 73A3
Niobrara *USA* 57B3
Niobrara R *USA* 54D2
Nioki *Zaïre* 78B4
Nioro du Sahel *Mali* 76B3
Niort *France* 18B2
Nipawin *Can* 52H4
Nipigon *Can* 53K5
Nipigon B *Can* 58B1
Nipigon,L *Can* 53K5
Nipissing R *Can* 53K5
Nipissing,L *Can* 58C1
Nipton *USA* 65C3
Niquelândia *Brazil* 73C1
Nirmal *India* 36B1
Nirmāli *India* 37C2
Niš *Yugos* 23E2
Nisāb *S Yemen* 33E4
Nishinoomote *Japan* 41C5
Nishino-shima I *Japan* 38G4
Nishino-shima I *Japan* 42B3
Nishi-suidō Str *S Korea* 42A4
Nishiwaki *Japan* 42B4
Nisling R *Can* 56L3
Nissan Is *PNG* 49E1
Nisutlin R *Can* 56M3
Nitchequon *Can* 53L4
Niterói *Brazil* 71K8
Nith R *Scot* 14D4
Nitibe *Indon* 45B4
Nitra *Czech* 21D3
Nitro *USA* 58C3
Niue I *Pacific O* 49J2
Niulakita I *Tuvalu* 49G2
Niut Mt *Malay* 44D2
Niutao I *Tuvalu* 49G1
Nivelles *Belg* 16C1
Nivernais Region *France* 18C2
Nivskiy *USSR* 12L5
Nizāmābād *India* 36B1
Nizana Hist Site *Israel* 31C3
Nizhneudinsk *USSR* 38C1
Nizhniye Sergi *USSR* 24K4
Nizhniy Lomov *USSR* 24G5
Nizhniy Odes *USSR* 24J3
Nizhniy Tagil *USSR* 26G4
Nizhnyaya R *USSR* 27L3
Nizhnyaya Zolotitsa *USSR* 24G2
Nizip *Turk* 30C2
Nizmennost *USSR* 25E6
Njoko R *Zambia* 79C5
Njombe *Tanz* 79D4
Nkambé *Cam* 78B3
Nkawkaw *Ghana* 77F4
Nkhata Bay *Malawi* 79D5
Nkongsamba *Cam* 78B3
N'Konni *Niger* 76C3
Noakhali *Bang* 37D3
Noatak *USA* 56F2
Noatak R *USA* 56G2
Nobeoka *Japan* 41C5
Noboribetsu *Japan* 42D2
Nobres *Brazil* 73A1
Noce R *Italy* 17D1
Nochistlán *Mexico* 67B1
Nochixtlán *Mexico* 67C2
Nocona *USA* 63C3
Nogales Sonora *Mexico* 66A1
Nogales *USA* 65D4
Nogales Veracruz *Mexico* 67C2
Nogara *Italy* 17D2
Nogata *Japan* 42B4
Nogent-en-Bassigny *France* 16C2
Nogent-le-Rotrou *France* 16A2
Nogent-sur-Seine *France* 16B2
Noginsk *USSR* 24F4
Nogliki *USSR* 41E1
Nogoyá *Arg* 72D2
Nogoyá R *Arg* 72D2
Nohar *India* 35C3
Noheji *Japan* 42D2
Nojima-zaki C *Japan* 42C4
Nok Kundi *Pak* 34E3
Nola *CAR* 78B3
Nolinsk *USSR* 24H4
Nomans Land I *USA* 60E2
Nombre de Dioz *Mexico* 67B1
Nome *USA* 56E3
Nomeny *France* 16D2
Nomgon *Mongolia* 40B1
Nomo-saki Pt *Japan* 42A4
Nonachol L *Can* 52H3
Nong'an *China* 41B3
Nong Khai *Thai* 43C2
Nongoma *S Africa* 79D6
Nonouti I *Kiribati* 49G1
Nonsan *S Korea* 42A3
Noorvik *USA* 56F2
Nopala *Mexico* 67C2
Noqui *Angola* 78B4
Noranda *Can* 53L5
Nord Department *France* 16B1
Nordaustlandet I *Barents S* 26D2
Nordfjord Inlet *Nor* 12F6
Nordfriesische Is *W Germ* 12F8
Nordhausen *E Germ* 20C2
Nordrhein Westfalen State *W Germ* 20B2
Nordkapp C *Nor* 12J4
Nordre *Greenland* 53N3
Nord Stronfjället Mt *Sweden* 12G5
Nordvik *USSR* 27N2
Nore R *Irish Rep* 15B5
Norfolk County *Eng* 15F5
Norfolk Nebraska *USA* 57C3
Norfolk Virginia *USA* 59D3
Norfolk I *Aust* 49F3
Norfolk L *USA* 63D2
Norfolk Ridge *Pacific O* 47K5
Noril'sk *USSR* 27K3
Normal *USA* 58B2
Norman *USA* 63C2
Normandie Region *France* 18B2
Norman,L *USA* 61C1
Normanton *Aust* 48D2
Norman Wells *Can* 56N2
Norne *USA* 52B3
Norra Storfjället Mt *Sweden* 24B2
Norris L *USA* 61C1
Norristown *USA* 59D2
Norrköping *Sweden* 12H7
Norrsundet *Sweden* 12H6
Norrtälje *Sweden* 12H7
Norseman *Aust* 48B4
Norsk *USSR* 41C1
Nortelândia *Brazil* 73A1
North S *N W Europe* 74J2
North Adam *USA* 60D1
Northallerton *Eng* 15E4
Northam *Aust* 48A4
North American Basin *Atlantic O* 74E3
Northampton *Aust* 48A3
Northampton County *Eng* 15E5
Northampton *Eng* 15E5
Northampton *USA* 59E2
North Andaman I *Indian O* 36E2
North Arm B *Can* 52G3
North Augusta *USA* 61C2
North Aulatsvik I *Can* 53M4
North Bay *Can* 53L5
North Bend *USA* 64B2
North Berwick *Scot* 14D3
North Berwick *USA* 60E1
North,C *Can* 53M5
North C *NZ* 55G4
North C *USA* 56D5
North Canadian R *USA* 62B2
North Carolina State *USA* 55E3
North Cascade Nat Pk *USA* 64B1
North Chan *Can* 58C1
North Chan *Ire/Scot* 14C4
North Collins *USA* 60A1
North Dakota State *USA* 54C2
North Downs *Eng* 15F6
North Downs Upland *Eng* 16A1
North East *USA* 59D2
North East Atlantic Basin *Atlantic O* 74H1
Northeast C *USA* 56E3
Northern Ireland *UK* 13B3
Northern Light L *Can* 57D2
Northern Range Mts *Trinidad* 68L1
Northern Territory *Aust* 48C2
North Esk R *Scot* 14D3
Northfield Massachusetts *USA* 60D1
Northfield Minnesota *USA* 57D3
North Foreland *Eng* 15F6
North Foreland Pt *Eng* 16A1
North Fork R *USA* 56H2
North Fork R *USA* 56H3
North I *NZ* 51B1
North Korea Republic *S E Asia* 41B4
North Land = Severnaya Zemlya
North Little Rock *USA* 63D3
North Loup R *USA* 57B3
North Magnetic Pole *Can* 80B4
North Miami *USA* 61E4
North Miami Beach *USA* 61E4
North Nahanni R *Can* 56O3
North Platte *USA* 62B1
North Platte R *USA* 54C2
North Pole *Arctic* 80A
North Pt *Barbados* 68Q2
North Pt *USA* 58C1
North Raccoon R *USA* 57D3
North Rona I *Scot* 13B2
North Ronaldsay I *Scot* 14D2
North Sea *N W Europe* 13D2
North Sentinel *Andaman Is* 36E2
North Slope *USA* 56J2
North Slope Region *USA* 52D3
North Stradbroke I *Aust* 50D1
North Syracuse *USA* 60B1
North Taranaki Bight B *NZ* 51B1
North Tonawanda *USA* 60A1
North Truchas Peak Mt *USA* 54C3
North Uist I *Scot* 14B3
Northumberland County *Eng* 14D4
Northumberland Is *Aust* 48E3
Northumberland Str *Can* 53M5
North Vancouver *Can* 64B1
Northville *USA* 60C1
North Walsham *Eng* 15F5
Northway *USA* 56K3
North West C *Aust* 48A3
North West Frontier Province *Pak* 35C2
North West River *Can* 53M4
North West Territories *Can* 52G3
Northwood *USA* 57C2
North York Moors Nat Pk *Eng* 15E4
Norton R *USA* 62C2
Norton B *USA* 56F3
Norton Sd *USA* 56F3
Norvegia,C *Ant* 80F1
Norwalk Connecticut *USA* 60D2
Norwalk Ohio *USA* 58C2
Norway Kingdom *Europe* 12F6
Norway House *Can* 52J4
Norwegian B *Can* 53J2
Norwegian Basin *Norewegian S* 74H1
Norwegian S *N W Europe* 26B3
Norwich Connecticut *USA* 60D2
Norwich *Eng* 15F5
Norwich New York *USA* 60C1
Norwood Massachusetts *USA* 60E1
Norwood Ohio *USA* 58C3
Nos Emine C *Bulg* 23F2
Noshiro *Japan* 41D3
Nos Kaliakra C *Bulg* 23F2
Nosovaya *USSR* 24J2
Nosovka *USSR* 21G2
Noss I *Scot* 14E1
Nossob R *Botswana/S Africa* 79C6
Nostrābād *Iran* 34E3
Nosy Barren I *Madag* 79E5
Nosy Bé I *Madag* 79E5
Nosy Boraha I *Madag* 79F5
Nosy Varika *Madag* 79E6
Notéc R *Pol* 20D2
Notikeuin *Can* 52G4
Noto *Italy* 22D3
Notodden *Nor* 12F7
Noto-hantō Pen *Japan* 42C3
Notre Dams B *Can* 53N5
Nottingham County *Eng* 15E5
Nottingham *Eng* 15E5
Nottingham I *Can* 53L3
Nottingham Island *Can* 53L3
Notukeu Creek R *Can* 57A2
Nouadhibou *Maur* 76A2
Nouakchott *Maur* 76A3
Nouméa *Nouvelle Calédonie* 49F3
Nouna *U Volta* 77F3
Noupoort *S Africa* 79C7
Nouveau Comptoir *Can* 53L4
Nouvelle Anvers *Zaïre* 78B3
Nouvelle Calédonie I *S W Pacific O* 49F3
Nova América *Brazil* 73C2
Nova Caipemba *Angola* 79B4
Nova Chaves *Angola* 79C5
Nova Esperança *Brazil* 73B3
Nova Friburgo *Brazil* 73D3
Nova Gaia *Angola* 79B5
Nova Granada *Brazil* 73C3
Nova Herizonte *Brazil* 73C3
Nova Lima *Brazil* 73D3
Nova Lisboa = Huambo
Nova Londrina *Brazil* 73B3
Nova Mambone *Mozam* 79D6
Novara *Italy* 17C2
Nova Roma *Brazil* 73C1
Nova Sagres *Indon* 45C4
Nova Scotia Province *Can* 53M5
Nova Venécia *Brazil* 73D2
Novaya Kakhovka *USSR* 25E6
Novaya Zemlya I *Barents S* 26G2
Nova Zagora *Bulg* 23F2
Nove Russas *Brazil* 71K4
Nové Zámky *Czech* 23D1
Novgorod *USSR* 24E4
Novigrad *Yugos* 17E2
Novikovo *USSR* 41E2
Novi Ligure *Italy* 17C2
Novillero *Mexico* 67A1
Novi Pazar *Bulg* 23F2
Novi Pazar *Yugos* 23E2
Novi Sad *Yugos* 23D1
Novoalekseyevka *USSR* 25K5
Novoanninskiy *USSR* 25G5
Novobureyskiy *USSR* 41C2
Novocherkassk *USSR* 25F6
Novodvinsk *USSR* 24G3
Novograd Volynskiy *USSR* 25D5
Novogrudok *USSR* 21F2
Novo Hamburgo *Brazil* 72E1
Novokazalinsk *USSR* 26H5
Novokuznetsk *USSR* 26K4
Novolazarevskaya Base *Ant* 80F12
Novo Mesto *Yugos* 22D1
Novomirgorod *USSR* 21G3
Novomoskovsk *USSR* 24F5
Novo Redondo *Angola* 79B5
Novorossiysk *USSR* 25F7
Novorybnoye *USSR* 27M2
Novosibirsk *USSR* 26K4
Novosibirskye Ostrova I *USSR* 27P2
Novotroitsk *USSR* 25K5
Novo Uzensk *USSR* 25H5
Novovolynsk *USSR* 21E2
Novo Vyatsk *USSR* 24H4
Novozybkov *USSR* 25E5
Novvy Port *USSR* 26J3
Novy Dwór Mazowiecki *Pol* 21E2
Novyy Lyalya *USSR* 24L4
Novyy Port *USSR* 24N2
Novyy Uzem *USSR* 25J7
Nowa Sól *Pol* 20D2
Nowata *USA* 63C2
Nowgong *India* 37D2
Nowra *Aust* 50D2
Now Shahr *Iran* 34C1
Nowshera *Pak* 35C2
Nowy Sącz *Pol* 21E3
Noyes I *USA* 56M4
Noyon *France* 16B2
Nsawam *Ghana* 77F4
Nsukka *Nig* 77H4
Nuatja *Togo* 77G4
Nuba Mts *Sudan* 78D2
Nubian Desert *Sudan* 32B2
Nuble R *Chile* 72A3
Nueces R *USA* 54D4
Nueltin L *Can* 52J3
Nueva Casas Grandes *Mexico* 66B1
Nueva Germania *Par* 73A3
Nueva Gerona *Cuba* 68A2
Nueva Imperial *Chile* 72A3
Nueva Laredo *Mexico* 54C4
Nueva Palmira *Urug* 72D2
Nueva Rosita *Mexico* 66B2
Nuevitas *Cuba* 68B2
Nuevo State *Mexico* 67B1
Nuevo Casas Grandes *Mexico* 66B1
Nuevo Ideal *Mexico* 67A1
Nuevo Laredo *Mexico* 66C2
Nugaal Region *Somalia* 75D4
Nûgâtsiaq *Greenland* 53N2
Nugssuag Pen *Greenland* 53N2
Nûgussuag I *Greenland* 53N2
Nui I *Tuvalu* 49G1
Nui Con Voi R *Vietnam* 40A5
Nuits *France* 16C3
Nu Jiang R *China* 37E2
Nukey Bluff Mt *Aust* 50A2
Nukhayb *Iraq* 30D3
Nukufetau I *Tuvalu* 49G1
Nukulaelae I *Tuvalu* 49G1
Nukunon I *Tokelau Is* 49H1
Nukus *USSR* 26G5
Nulato *USA* 56G3
Nullarbor Plain *Aust* 48B4
Numan *Nig* 77J4
Numata *Japan* 42C3
Numatinna R *Sudan* 78C3
Numazu *Japan* 41D4
Numfoor I *Indon* 39G7
Numurkah *Aust* 50C3
Nunapitchuk *USA* 56F3
Nunda *USA* 60A1
Nunivak I *USA* 56E3
Nunkun Mt *India* 35D2
Nunligran *USSR* 56C3
Nuomin He R *China* 41A1
Nuoro *Sardegna* 22B2
Nurābād *Iran* 34C2
Nure R *Italy* 17C2
Nuriootpa *Aust* 50A2
Nuristan Upland *Afghan* 35C1
Nurlat *USSR* 24J5
Nurmes *Fin* 12K6
Nürnberg *W Germ* 20C3
Nurri,Mt *Aust* 50C2
Nusa Tenggara Is *Indon* 44E4
Nusa Tenggara Timor Province *Indon* 45B4
Nusaybin *Turk* 30D2
Nushagak R *USA* 56G4
Nushagak B *USA* 56G4
Nushagak Pen *USA* 56G4
Nushki *Pak* 35B3
Nutak *Can* 53M4
Nutzotin Mts *USA* 56K3
Nuwakot *Nepal* 37B2
Nuwara-Eliya *Sri Lanka* 36C3
Nuyukjuak *Can* 53L3
Nyack *USA* 60D2
Nyahururu Falls *Kenya* 78D3
Nyah West *Aust* 50B3
Nyai *USA* 52C3
Nyaingentanglha Shan Mts *China* 38C3
Nyakabindi *Tanz* 78D4
Nyaksimvol' *USSR* 24L3
Nyala *Sudan* 78C2
Nyalam *China* 37C2
Nyamlell *Sudan* 78C3
Nyanda *Zim* 79D6
Nyandoma *USSR* 24G3
Nyanga R *Gabon* 78B4
Nyang Qu *China* 37D2
Nyasa L *Malawi/Mozam* 79D5
Nyaunglebin *Burma* 43B2
Nyazepetrovsk *USSR* 24K4
Nyborg *Den* 12G7
Nybro *Sweden* 12H7
Nyda *USSR* 26J3
Nyeboes Land Region *Can* 53M1
Nyenchentanglha Range Mts *China* 37D1
Nyeri *Kenya* 78D4
Nyimba *Zambia* 79D5
Nyingchi *China* 29H2
Nyíregyháza *Hung* 21E3
Nyiru,Mt *Kenya* 78D3
Nyistroom *S Africa* 79C6
Nykarleby *Fin* 12J6
Nykøbing *Den* 12F7
Nykøbing *Den* 12G8
Nyköping *Sweden* 12H7
Nymagee *Aust* 50C2
Nynäshamn *Sweden* 12H7
Nyngan *Aust* 50C2
Nyon *Switz* 17B1
Nyong R *Cam* 78B3
Nyongwol *S Korea* 42A3
Nyongwon *N Korea* 42A3
Nyons *France* 18D3
Nysa *Pol* 20D2
Nysh *USSR* 41E1
Nyssa *USA* 64C2
Nyukhcha *USSR* 24H3
Nyukzha R *USSR* 38F1
Nyurba *USSR* 27N3
Nzega *Tanz* 78D4
Nzérékore *Guinea* 76B4
Nzi R *Ivory Coast* 77F4

O

Oacoma *USA* 57C3
Oaggsimiut *Greenland* 53O3
Oahe,L *USA* 57B3
Oahe Res *USA* 54C2
Oakbank *Aust* 50B2
Oakdale *USA* 65B3
Oakes *USA* 57C2
Oakey *Aust* 50D1
Oakland California *USA* 65B3
Oakland Nebraska *USA* 57C3
Oakland Oregon *USA* 64B2
Oakland City *USA* 58B3
Oak Lawn *USA* 58B2
Oakley Kansas *USA* 62B2
Oak Ridge *USA* 61C1
Oakridge *USA* 64B2
Oakville *Can* 59D2
Oamaru *NZ* 51B3
Oasis Nevada *USA* 64D2
Oates Land Region *Ant* 80F7
Oatlands *Aust* 50E3
Oaxaca *Mexico* 67C2
Oaxaca State *Mexico* 67C2
Ob' R *USSR* 26J3
Obama *Japan* 42C3
Oban *NZ* 51A3
Oban *Scot* 14C3
Obanazawa *Japan* 42D3
Oban Hills *Nig* 77H4
Obeh *Afghan* 34E2
Oberammergau *W Germ* 17D1
Oberdrauburg *Austria* 17E1
Oberhausen *W Germ* 16D1
Oberlin *USA* 62B2
Obernburg *W Germ* 16E2
Oberstdorf *W Germ* 17D1
Obervellach *Austria* 17E1
Obi I *Indon* 45C3
Obidos *Brazil* 71G4
Obihiro *Japan* 41E3
Obluch'ye *USSR* 41C2
Obo *CAR* 78C3
Obock *Djibouti* 78E2
Oborniki *Pol* 20D2
Oboyan *USSR* 25F5
O'Brien *USA* 64B2
Obshchiy Syrt Mts *USSR* 25J5
Obskava Guba B *USSR* 26J2
Obuasi *Ghana* 77F4
Ocala *USA* 61C3
Ocampo *Mexico* 67C1
Ocana *Colombia* 70D2
Ocaño *Spain* 19B2
Ocean C *USA* 56L4
Ocean City Maryland *USA* 59D3
Ocean City New Jersey *USA* 60C3
Ocean Falls *Can* 52F4
Ocean I = Banaba
Oceanside *USA* 65C4
Ocean Springs *USA* 63E3
Ocher *USSR* 24J4
Ochil Hills *Scot* 14D3
Ochlockonee R *USA* 61C2
Ocho Rios *Jamaica* 68H1
Ocmulgee R *USA* 61C2
Oconee R *USA* 61C2
Oconto *USA* 58B2
Ocotlán Jalisco *Mexico* 67B1
Ocotlán Oaxaca *Mexico* 67C2
Ocozocoautla *Mexico* 67D2
Oda *Ghana* 77F4
Oda *Japan* 42B3
Ŏdaejin *N Korea* 42A2
Ódáðahraun Region *Iceland* 12B2
Odate *Japan* 41E3
Odawara *Japan* 41D4
Odda *Nor* 12F6
Odem *USA* 63F4
Odemira *Port* 19A2
Ödemiş *Turk* 23F3
Odense *Den* 12G7
Odenwald Region *W Germ* 16E2
Oder R *Pol/E Germ* 20C2
Oderzo *Italy* 17E2
Odessa Texas *USA* 62B3
Odessa *USSR* 25E6
Odessa Washington *USA* 64C1
Odienné *Ivory Coast* 76B4
Odra = Oder
Odra R *Pol* 21D2
Oeiras *Brazil* 71K5
Oelrichs *USA* 57B3
Ofanto R *Italy* 22D2
Ofaqim *Israel* 31C3
Offa *Nig* 77G4
Offaly County *Irish Rep* 15B5
Offenbach *W Germ* 16E1
Offenburg *W Germ* 16D2
Ofunato *Japan* 42D3
Oga *Japan* 41D4
Ogaden Region *Eth* 78E3
Ogaki *Japan* 41D4
Ogallala *USA* 62B1
Ogasawara Gunto Is *Japan* 38H4
Ogbomosho *Nig* 77G4
Ogden Iowa *USA* 57D3
Ogden Utah *USA* 64D2
Ogdensburg *USA* 59D2
Ogeechee R *USA* 61C2
Ogilvie *Can* 56L2
Ogilvie Mts *Can* 52E3
Oglethorpe,Mt *USA* 61C2
Oglio R *Italy* 17D2
Ognon R *France* 17B1
Ogoja *Nig* 77H4
Ogooué R *Gabon* 78A4
Ogou R *Togo* 77G4
Ogre *USSR* 21E1
Oguilet Khenachich Well *Mali* 76B2
Ogulin *Yugos* 22D1
Ogun State *Nig* 77G4
Ogunquit *USA* 60E1
Ohai *NZ* 51A3
Ohakune *NZ* 51C1
Ohanet *Alg* 76C2
Ōhata *Japan* 42D2
Ohau,L *NZ* 51A2
Ohio State *USA* 55E2
Ohio R *USA* 58B3
Ohm R *W Germ* 16E1
Ohopoho *Namibia* 79B5
Ohre R *Czech* 20C2
Ohrid *Yugos* 23E2
Ohridsko Jezero L *Yugos/Alb* 23E2
Ohura *NZ* 51B1
Oiapoque *French Guiana* 71H3
Oijiaojing *China* 38C2
Oil City *USA* 59D2
Oildale *USA* 65C3
Oilian Shan Mts *China* 27L6
Oise Department *France* 16B2
Oise R *France* 18C2
Ōita *Japan* 41C5
Ojinaga *Mexico* 66B2
Ojitlán *Mexico* 67C2
Ojiya *Japan* 42C3
Ojocaliente *Mexico* 67B1
Ojos del Salado Mt *Arg* 69C3
Ojueloz *Mexico* 67B1
Oka R *USSR* 24F5
Okahandja *Namibia* 79B6
Okanagan Falls *Can* 64C1

Pakrac Petrolina

Pakrac *Yugos* 22D1
Paks *Hung* 23D1
Pak Sane *Laos* 43C2
Pakse *Laos* 43D2
Pakwach *Uganda* 78D3
Pala *Chad* 78B3
Palagruža I *Yugos* 22D2
Palaiseau *France* 16B2
Palalankwe *Andaman Is* 36E2
Palana *USSR* 27R4
Palangkaraya *Indon* 44D3
Palani *India* 36B2
Palanpur *India* 35C4
Palapye *Botswana* 79C6
Palatka *USA* 61C3
Palau Is *Pacific O* 39G6
Palaw *Burma* 43B3
Palawan I *Phil* 45E9
Palawan Pass *Phil* 45E9
Palayankottai *India* 36B3
Paldiski *USSR* 12J7
Paleleh *Indon* 45B2
Palembang *Indon* 44B3
Palencia *Spain* 19B1
Paleokhorio *Cyprus* 31B1
Palermo *Italy* 22C3
Palestine Region *Israel* 31C3
Palestine *USA* 63C3
Paletwa *Burma* 37D3
Pālghāt *India* 36B2
Pāli *India* 35C3
Palimé *Togo* 77G4
Palin,Mt *Malay* 44E1
Palisade *USA* 62A2
Pālitāna *India* 35C4
Palk Str *India/Sri Lanka* 36B3
Pallasovka *USSR* 25H5
Pallastunturi Mt *Fin* 12J5
Palliser B *NZ* 51B2
Palliser,C *NZ* 51C2
Palma *Mozam* 79E5
Palma de Mallorca *Spain* 19C2
Palmares *Brazil* 71L5
Palmares do Sul *Brazil* 72E2
Palmar Sur *Costa Rica* 68A5
Palmas *Brazil* 73B4
Palmas,C *Lib* 76B4
Palmas de Monte Alto *Brazil* 73D1
Palma Soriano *Cuba* 68B2
Palm Bay *USA* 61C3
Palm Beach *USA* 61E4
Palmeira *Brazil* 73C4
Palmeira dos Indos *Brazil* 71L5
Palmer *USA* 56J3
Palmer Base *Ant* 80G3
Palmer Arch *Ant* 80G3
Palmer Land Region *Ant* 80F3
Palmerston *NZ* 51B3
Palmerston North *NZ* 51C2
Palmerton *USA* 60C2
Palmetto *USA* 61E4
Palmi *Italy* 22D3
Palmiera das Missões *Brazil* 72E1
Palmillas *Mexico* 67C1
Palmira *Colombia* 70C3
Palm Is *Aust* 48D2
Palm Springs *USA* 65C4
Palmyra Missouri *USA* 58A3
Palmyra New York *USA* 60B1
Palmyra Pennsylvania *USA* 60B2
Palmyras Pt *India* 37C3
Paloh *Indon* 44C2
Paloích *Sudan* 78D2
Palomares *Mexico* 67C2
Palomar Mt *USA* 65C4
Palopo *Indon* 45B3
Palu *Indon* 45A3
Palu *Turk* 30C2
Palwal *India* 35D3
Palyavaam R *USSR* 56B2
Pama *U Volta* 77G3
Pamekasan *Indon* 44D4
Pameungpeuk *Indon* 44C4
Pamiers *France* 18C3
Pamir Mts *China* 29F2
Pamir R *USSR* 26J6
Pamlico R *USA* 61D1
Pamlico Sd *USA* 61D1
Pampa *USA* 62B2
Pampa de la Salinas Salt pan *Arg* 72B2
Pampa de la Varita Plain *Arg* 72B3
Pampanua *Indon* 45B3
Pampeiro *Brazil* 72D2
Pamplona *Colombia* 70D2
Pamplona *Spain* 19B1
Pampton Lake *USA* 60C2
Pana *USA* 58B3
Panaca *USA* 65D3
Panagyurishte *Bulg* 23E2
Panaji *India* 36A1
Panamá *Panama* 70C2
Panama Republic *C America* 70B2
Panama Canal *Panama* 68B5
Panama City *USA* 61B2
Panamint Range Mts *USA* 65C3
Panaro R *Italy* 17D2
Panay I *Phil* 45F8
Pancevo *Yugos* 23E2
Pandan *Phil* 45F8
Pandharpur *India* 36B1
Pandie Pandie *Aust* 50A1
Panevežys *USSR* 21E1
Panfilov *USSR* 26K5
Pang R *Burma* 43B1
Pangani *Tanz* 78D4
Pangani R *Tanz* 78D4
Pangi *Zaïre* 78C4
Pangkajene *Indon* 45A3
Pangkalpinang *Indon* 44C3
Pangnirtung *Can* 53M3
Pangtara *Burma* 43B1
Panguitch *USA* 65D3
Pangutaran Group Is *Phil* 45F9
Panhandle *USA* 62B2
Pānīpat *India* 35D3
Panjao *Afghan* 35B2
Panjgur *Pak* 34E3
Pankof,C *USA* 56F5
Pankshin *Nig* 77H4
P'anmunjŏm *N Korea* 41B4
Panna *India* 37B3
Panorama *Brazil* 73B3
Pantanal de São Lourenço Swamp *Brazil* 73A2
Pantanal do Rio Negro Swamp *Brazil* 73A2
Pantanal do Taquari Swamp *Brazil* 73A2
Pantar I *Indon* 45B4
Pantelleria I *Medit S* 22C3
Pantepec *Mexico* 67C1
Panuco *Mexico* 67C1
Pánuco R *Mexico* 67C1
Pan Xian *China* 40A4
Paola *Italy* 22D3
Paola *USA* 63D2
Paoli *USA* 58B3
Papa *Hung* 20D3
Papakura *NZ* 51B1
Papaloapan R *Mexico* 67C2
Papantla *Mexico* 67C1
Papa Stour I *Scot* 14E1
Papatoetoe *NZ* 51B1
Papa Westray I *Scot* 14D2
Paphos *Cyprus* 31B1
Papua,G of *PNG* 48D1
Papua New Guinea Republic *S E Asia* 48D1
Papudo *Chile* 72A2
Papun *Burma* 43B2
Pará State *Brazil* 71H4
Pará R *Brazil* 71J4
Paraburdoo *Aust* 48A3
Paracas,Pen de *Peru* 70C6
Paracatu *Brazil* 73C2
Paracatu R *Brazil* 73C2
Paracel Is *S E Asia* 43E2
Parachilna *Aust* 50A2
Parachinar *Pak* 35C2
Paracin *Yugos* 23E2
Pará de Minas *Brazil* 73D2
Paradise California *USA* 65B3
Paradise Nevada *USA* 65D3
Paragould *USA* 63D2
Paraguá R *Bol* 70F6
Paragua R *Ven* 70F2
Paraguaçu R *Brazil* 73D1
Paraguai R *Brazil* 71G7
Paraguari *Par* 73A4
Paraguay Republic *S America* 69E2
Paraguay R *Par* 69E2
Paraiba State *Brazil* 71L5
Paraíba do Sul R *Brazil* 73D3
Paraiso *Mexico* 67D2
Parakou *Benin* 77G4
Parakylia *Aust* 50A2
Paramakkudi *India* 36B3
Paramaribo *Suriname* 71G2
Paramirim *Brazil* 73D1
Paramushir I *USSR* 38J1
Paraná *Brazil* 73B3
Paraná State *Brazil* 69F2
Paraná *Urug* 72C2
Paraná R *Arg* 69E4
Paranã R *Brazil* 71J6
Paranaguá *Brazil* 73C4
Paranaiba *Brazil* 73B2
Paranaiba R *Brazil* 73B2
Paranapanema R *Brazil* 73B3
Paranavai *Brazil* 73B3
Parang *Phil* 45F9
Paraope R *Brazil* 73D2
Paraparaumu *NZ* 51B2
Paratinga *Brazil* 73D1
Parbhani *India* 36B1
Parc National d'Arly *U Volta* 77G3
Parc National de la Komoé *Ivory Coast* 77F4
Parc National de la Pendjari *Benin* 77G3
Parcs Nationaux du W *Benin* 77G3
Pardes Hanna *Israel* 31C2
Pardo *Arg* 72D3
Pardo R Bahia *Brazil* 73E2
Pardo R Mato Grosso do Sul *Brazil* 73B3
Pardo R Minas Gerais *Brazil* 73C2
Pardo R Sao Paulo *Brazil* 73C3
Pardubice *Czech* 20D2
Parece Vela Reef *Pacific O* 38G4
Parecis *Brazil* 73A1
Parent *Can* 55F2
Parent,L *Can* 59D1
Parepare *Indon* 45A3
Parepare *Indon* 48A1
Parera *Arg* 72C3
Pariaman *Indon* 44B3
Paria,Pen de *Ven* 70F1
Parigi *Indon* 45B3
Paris *France* 18C2
Paris Kentucky *USA* 58C3
Paris Tennessee *USA* 61B1
Paris Texas *USA* 63C3
Parker *USA* 65D4
Parkersburg *USA* 58C3
Parkes *Aust* 50C2
Parkesburg *USA* 60C3
Park Falls *USA* 58A1
Park Forest *USA* 58B2
Park Rapids *USA* 57C2
Parkston *USA* 57C3
Parksville *Can* 64B1
Park Valley *USA* 64D2
Parlākimidi *India* 36C1
Parli *India* 36B1
Parma *Italy* 17D2
Parma *USA* 58C2
Parnaiba *Brazil* 71K4
Parnaiba R *Brazil* 71K4
Párnon Óros Mts *Greece* 23E3
Pärnu *USSR* 24C4
Paro *Bhutan* 37C2
Paroo R *Aust* 50B1
Paroo Channel R *Aust* 50B2
Paropamisus Mts *Afghan* 34E2
Páros I *Greece* 23F3
Parowan *USA* 65D3
Parpaillon Mts *France* 17B2
Parral *Chile* 72A3
Parramatta *Aust* 50D2
Parras *Mexico* 54C4
Parry B *Can* 53K3
Parry,C *Can* 56O1
Parry Is *Can* 52G2
Parry Pen *Can* 56O2
Parry Sd *Can* 53L5
Parry Sound *Can* 58C1
Parsberg *W Germ* 20C3
Parsnip R *Can* 52F4
Parsons Kansas *USA* 63C2
Parsons West Virginia *USA* 59D3
Parthenay *France* 18B2
Partinico *Italy* 22C3
Partizansk *USSR* 41C3
Paru R *Brazil* 71H4
Páruco *Mexico* 67A1
Parvatipuram *India* 36C1
Parys *S Africa* 79C6
Pasadena Texas *USA* 63C4
Pasadena *USA* 65C4
Pasangkayu *Indon* 45A3
Pasarwajo *Indon* 45B4
Pasawing *Burma* 43B2
Pascagoula *USA* 63E3
Paşcani *Rom* 23F1
Pasco *USA* 64C1
Pas-de-Calais Department *France* 16B1
Pasewalk *W Germ* 12G8
Pashū'īyeh *Iran* 34D3
Pasley,C *Aust* 48B4
Pasni *Pak* 34E3
Paso de los Libres *Arg* 72D1
Paso de los Toros *Urug* 69E4
Paso Limay *Arg* 69B6
Paso Robles *USA* 65B3
Passaic *USA* 60C2
Passau *W Germ* 20C3
Passo de los Libres *Arg* 69E3
Passo del Toro Mt *Mexico* 67B1
Passo di Stelvio Mt *Italy* 17D1
Passo di Tonale *Italy* 17D1
Passo Fundo *Brazil* 72E1
Passos *Brazil* 73C3
Passy *France* 17B2
Pastaza R *Peru* 70C4
Pasteur *Arg* 72C3
Pas,The *Can* 52H4
Pasto *Colombia* 70C3
Pastol B *USA* 56F3
Pasubio Mt *Italy* 17D2
Pasuruan *Indon* 44D4
Pasvalys *USSR* 21E1
Pātan *India* 35C4
Pātan *Nepal* 37C2
Patchewollock *Aust* 50B3
Patea *NZ* 51B1
Patea R *NZ* 51B2
Paterno *Italy* 22C3
Paterson *USA* 60C2
Paterson Inlet B *NZ* 51A3
Pathankot *India* 35D2
Pathfinder Res *USA* 57A3
Patiāla *India* 35D2
Pativilca *Peru* 70C6
Pátmos I *Greece* 23F3
Patna *India* 37C2
Patnos *Turk* 30D2
Patos *Brazil* 71L5
Patos de Minas *Brazil* 73C2
Patquia *Arg* 72B2
Pátrai *Greece* 23E3
Patrasuy *USSR* 24L3
Patrocinio *Brazil* 73C2
Patta I *Kenya* 78E4
Pattallasang *Indon* 45A4
Pattani *Thai* 43C4
Patterson Louisiana *USA* 63D4
Patterson,Mt *Can* 56M3
Patton *USA* 60A2
Patu *Brazil* 71L5
Patuakhali *Bang* 37D3
Patuca R *Honduras* 66D3
Patzcuaro *Mexico* 67B2
Pau *France* 18B3
Paulatuk *Can* 56O2
Paulistana *Brazil* 71K5
Pauls Valley *USA* 63C3
Paungde *Burma* 43B2
Pauri *India* 35D2
Pauskie *Nor* 12H5
Pavão *Brazil* 73D2
Pavia *Italy* 17C2
Pavlodar *USSR* 26J4
Pavlof V *USA* 56F4
Pavlov B *USA* 56F4
Pavlovich *USSR* 27O4
Pavlovka *USSR* 24K4
Pavlovo *USSR* 24G4
Pavlovsk *USSR* 25G5
Pavullo nel Frigano *Italy* 17D2
Pawan R *Indon* 44D3
Pawhuska *USA* 63C2
Paw Paw *USA* 60A3
Pawtucket *USA* 60E2
Paxton *USA* 62B1
Payakumbuh *Indon* 44B3
Payerne *Switz* 17B1
Payette *USA* 64C2
Payne,L *Can* 53L4
Paynesville *USA* 57D2
Paysandu *Urug* 72D2
Pays d'Auge Region *France* 16A2
Pays-de-Bray Region *France* 16A2
Pays de Caux Region *France* 16A2
Pays d'Ouche Region *France* 16A2
Pazardzhik *Bulg* 23E2
Pazin *Yugos* 17E2
Peace R *Can* 52F4
Peace R *Can* 52G4
Peace R *USA* 61E4
Peace River *Can* 52G4
Peach Springs *USA* 65D3
Peak District Nat Pk *Eng* 15E5
Peake R *Aust* 50A1
Peaked Mt *USA* 59F1
Peak Hill *Aust* 50C2
Peak Mandala Mt *Indon* 39G7
Peak,The Mt *Eng* 15E5
Peale,Mt *USA* 65E3
Pearl R *USA* 63D3
Pearsall *USA* 63F4
Peary Chan *Can* 52H2
Pebane *Mozam* 79D5
Peć *Yugos* 23E2
Peçanha *Brazil* 73D2
Pecan Island *USA* 63D4
Pechenga *USSR* 12L5
Pechora *USSR* 24K2
Pechora R *USSR* 24J2
Pechorskaya Guba G *USSR* 24J2
Pechorskoye More S *USSR* 24J2
Pecoraro Mt *Italy* 22D3
Pecos *USA* 62B3
Pecos R *USA* 62B3
Pécs *Hung* 21D3
Pedang Endau *Malay* 44G7
Pedhoulas *Cyprus* 31B1
Pedirka *Aust* 50A1
Pedra Azul *Brazil* 73D2
Pedregulho *Brazil* 73C3
Pedro Cays Is *Caribbean* 68B3
Pedro de Valdivia *Chile* 69C2
Pedro Gomes *Brazil* 73B2
Pedro Juan Caballero *Par* 73A3
Pedro Luro *Arg* 72C3
Pedro Mentova *Mexico* 67C1
Pedro,Pt *Sri Lanka* 36C3
Pedro R Fernandez *Arg* 72D1
Peebinga *Aust* 50B2
Peebles *Scot* 14D4
Pee Dee R *USA* 61D2
Peekskill *USA* 60D2
Peel *Eng* 15C4
Peel R *Can* 56M2
Peel Sd *Can* 52J2
Peensylvania State *USA* 55F2
Peera Peera Poolanna L *Aust* 50A1
Peg Arfak Mt *Indon* 39G7
Pegasus B *NZ* 51B2
Pegtmel' R *USSR* 56B2
Pegu *Burma* 37E4
Pegunungan Barisan Mts *Indon* 44B3
Pegunungan Iran Mts *Malay Indon* 44D2
Pegunungan Maoke Mts *Indon* 48C1
Pegunungan Meratus Mts *Indon* 44E3
Pegunungan Muller Mts *Indon* 44D2
Pegunungan Schwanet Mts *Indon* 44D3
Pegunungan Tigapuluh Mts *Indon* 44B3
Pegu Yoma Mts *Burma* 43B2
Pehuajó *Arg* 72C3
Peixe R Mato Grosso *Brazil* 73B1
Peixe R Sao Paulo *Brazil* 73B3
Pei Xian *China* 40D3
Pekalongan *Indon* 44C4
Pekan *Malay* 43C5
Pekanbaru *Indon* 44B2
Pekin *USA* 58B2
Peking = Beijing
Pelabohan Kelang *Malay* 43C5
Pelagie Is *Mediterranean S* 77E1
Pelau Pelau Boö Is *Indon* 45C3
Pelau Pelau Kangean Is *Indon* 44E4
Pelau Pelau Karimunjawa Arch *Indon* 44D4
Pelau Pelau Maisel Is *Indon* 45C4
Pelau Pelau Penyu Is *Indon* 45C4
Pelau Pelau Postilyon Is *Indon* 44E4
Pelau Pelau Salabangka Is *Indon* 45B3
Peleaga Mt *Rom* 23E1
Peleduy *USSR* 27N4
Pelee I *Can* 58C2
Peleng I *Indon* 48B1
Pelican *USA* 56L4
Pelican L *USA* 57D2
Pellegrini *Arg* 72C3
Pello *Fin* 12J5
Pelly R *Can* 56M3
Pelly Bay *Can* 53J3
Pelly Crossing *Can* 56L3
Pelly Mts *Can* 56M3
Pelotas *Brazil* 72E2
Pelotas R *Brazil* 69F3
Pelusium Hist Site *Egypt* 31B3
Pelvoux Region *France* 17B2
Pelym R *USSR* 24L3
Pemalang *Indon* 44C4
Pematang *Indon* 44B3
Pematangsiantar *Indon* 44A2
Pemba *Mozam* 79E5
Pemba I *Tanz* 78D4
Pembina *USA* 57C2
Pembroke *Can* 59D1
Pembroke *USA* 61C2
Pembroke *Wales* 15C6
Pemuco *Chile* 72A3
Penacook *USA* 60E1
Penambo Range Mts *Malay* 44E2
Penápolis *Brazil* 73B3
Peñarroya *Spain* 19A2
Penarroya Mt *Spain* 19B1
Peña Trevina Mt *Spain* 19A1
Pende R *Chad* 78B3
Pendelton,Mt *Can* 56N4
Pendjari R *Benin* 77G3
Pendleton *USA* 64C1
Pend Oreille R *USA* 64C1
Penedo *Brazil* 71L6
Penganga R *India* 35D5
P'eng hu Lieh tao Is *Taiwan* 40D5
Penglai *China* 40E2
Pengshui *China* 40B4
Pengunungan Maoke Mts *Indon* 39G7
Península de la Guajiri Pen *Colombia* 68C4
Península de Paria Pen *Ven* 68E4
Peninsular Malaysia *Malay* 43C5
Penjamo *Mexico* 67B1
Pennabilli *Italy* 17E3
Penner R *India* 36B2
Pennine Chain Mts *Eng* 14D4
Penns Grove *USA* 60C3
Pennsylvania State *USA* 55F2
Penn Yan *USA* 60B1
Penny Highlands Mts *Can* 53M3
Penobscot R *USA* 59F1
Penobscot B *USA* 59F2
Penola *Aust* 50B3
Penong *Aust* 48C4
Penonomé *Panama* 68A5
Penrith *Eng* 15D4
Pensacola *USA* 61B2
Pensacola Mts *Ant* 80E
Pensiangan *Malay* 44E2
Pentecost I *Vanuatu* 49F2
Penticton *Can* 52G5
Pentland Firth Chan *Scot* 14D2
Pentland Hills *Scot* 14D4
Penza *USSR* 24H5
Penzance *Eng* 15C6
Penzhina R *USSR* 27S3
Penzhinskaya Guba B *USSR* 27S3
Peoria *USA* 58B2
Perabumulih *Indon* 44B3
Perak R *Malay* 43C5
Perawang *Indon* 44B2
Perdido R *Brazil* 73A3
Pereira *Colombia* 70C3
Pereira Barreto *Brazil* 73B3
Perelazovskiy *USSR* 25G6
Perenosa B *USA* 56H4
Pereyaslav *USSR* 21G2
Pereyaslavka *USSR* 41D2
Pergamino *Arg* 72C2
Pergola *Italy* 17E3
Peribonca R *Can* 53L4
Perim I *S Yemen* 32D4
Périqueux *France* 18C2
Perlas Arch de Is *Panama* 66E4
Perm' *USSR* 24K4
Pernambuco = Recife
Pernambuco State *Brazil* 71L5
Pernatty Lg *Aust* 50A2
Pernik *Bulg* 23E2
Péronne *France* 16B2
Perote *Mexico* 67C2
Perpignan *France* 18C3
Perry Florida *USA* 61C2
Perry Georgia *USA* 61C2
Perry New York *USA* 60A1
Perry Oklahoma *USA* 63C2
Perry River *Can* 52H3
Perrysburg *USA* 58C2
Perryton *USA* 62B2
Perryville Alaska *USA* 56G4
Perryville Missouri *USA* 63E2
Perth *Aust* 48A4
Perth *Can* 59D2
Perth *Scot* 14D3
Perth Amboy *USA* 60C2
Pertuis *France* 17A3
Peru Republic *S America* 70D6
Peru *USA* 58B2
Peru Basin *Pacific O* 47P5
Peru-Chile Trench *Pacific O* 74E6
Perugia *Italy* 22C2
Perugorria *Arg* 72D1
Perušic *Yugos* 22D2
Pervari *Turk* 30D2
Pervomaysk RSFSR *USSR* 24G5
Pervomaysk Ukraine SSR *USSR* 25E6
Pervoural'sk *USSR* 24K4
Pesaro *Italy* 17E3
Pescadores = P'eng-hu Lieh-tao
Pescara *Italy* 22C2
Peschiera *Italy* 17D2
Pescia *Italy* 17D3
Peshawar *Pak* 35C2
Peshkopi *Alb* 23E2
Peshtigo *USA* 58B1
Pestovo *USSR* 24F4
Petah Tiqwa *Israel* 31C2
Petaluma *USA* 65B3
Pétange *Lux* 16C2
Petatlán *Mexico* 67B2
Petauke *Zambia* 79D5
Petenwell L *USA* 58B2
Peterborough *Aust* 50A2
Peterborough *Can* 59D2
Peterborough *Eng* 15E5
Peterborough *USA* 60E1
Peterhead *Scot* 14E3
Petermann Gletscher Gl *Greenland* 53M1
Petermann Range Mts *Aust* 48B3
Peteroa Mt *Chile/Arg* 69B5
Petersburg Alaska *USA* 56M4
Petersburg *USA* 52E4
Petersburg Virginia *USA* 59D3
Petlād *India* 35C4
Petlalcingo *Mexico* 67C2
Peto *Mexico* 66D2
Petomskoye Nagor'ye Upland *USSR* 27N4
Petorca *Chile* 72A2
Petoskey *USA* 58C1
Petra Hist Site *Jordan* 31C3
Petral Base *Ant* 80G2
Petrified Forest Nat Pk *USA* 65E3
Petrolina *Brazil* 71K5

Petropavlovsk Porttipahdan Tekojärvi

Petropavlovsk *USSR* 26H4
Petropavlovsk-Kamchatskiy *USSR* 38J1
Petrópolis *Brazil* 73D3
Petrovadovsk *USSR* 26E3
Petrovsk *USSR* 25H5
Petrovsk Zabaykal'skiy *USSR* 38D1
Petrozavodsk *USSR* 24E3
Pevek *USSR* 27T3
Peza *R USSR* 24H2
Pfälzer Wald Region *W Germ* 16D2
Pforzheim *W Germ* 20B3
Phagwara *India* 35D2
Phalodi *India* 35C3
Phalsbourg *France* 16D2
Phaltan *India* 36A1
Phangnga *Thai* 43B4
Phanom Dang Mts *Camb* 43C3
Phan Rang *Viet* 43D3
Phan Thiet *Viet* 43D3
Pharr *USA* 63F4
Phelps L *USA* 61D1
Phenix City *USA* 61B2
Phet Buri *Thai* 43B3
Phiafay *Laos* 43D3
Philadelphia Mississippi *USA* 63E3
Philadelphia Pennsylvania *USA* 60C2
Philip *USA* 57B3
Philippeville = Skikda
Philippeville *Belg* 16C1
Philippine S *Pacific O* 39F5
Philippines Republic *S E Asia* 39F5
Philippine Trench *Pacific O* 46H4
Philipsburg Montana *USA* 64D1
Philipsburg Pennsylvania *USA* 59D2
Philip Smith Mts *USA* 56J2
Phillipine S *Phil* 45F7
Phillips B *Can* 53K1
Phillipsburg Kansas *USA* 62C2
Phillipsburg New Jersey *USA* 60C2
Philpots Pen *Can* 53K2
Phnom Penh *Camb* 43C3
Phoenix Arizona *USA* 65D4
Phoenix New York *USA* 60B1
Phoenix Is *Pacific O* 49H1
Phoenixville *USA* 60C2
Phong Saly *Laos* 43C1
Phu Bia Mt *Laos* 43C2
Phu Cuong *Viet* 43D3
Phuket *Thai* 43B4
Phulbāni *India* 37B3
Phu Miang Mt *Thai* 43C2
Phu Set Mt *Laos* 43D2
Phu Tho *Viet* 43D1
Phu Vinh *Viet* 43D4
Phyäselkä L *Fin* 12K6
Piacenza *Italy* 17C2
Pialba *Aust* 50D1
Pian R *Aust* 50C2
Pianoro *Italy* 17D2
Pianosa I *Italy* 22C2
Pianosa I *Italy* 22D2
Piaseczno *Pol* 21E2
Piata *Brazil* 73D1
Piatra-Neamţ *Rom* 23F1
Piaui State *Brazil* 71K5
Piave *Italy* 17E2
Piave R *Italy* 17E1
Pibor R *Sudan* 78D3
Pibor Post *Sudan* 78D3
Picardie Region *France* 16B2
Picayune *USA* 63E3
Pic de Rochebrune Mt *France* 17B2
Pichilemu *Chile* 72A2
Pichi Mahuida *Arg* 72C3
Pichucalco *Mexico* 67D2
Pickering *Eng* 15E4
Pickle Lake *Can* 53J4
Pico I *Açores* 76A1
Pico Bernina Mt *Switz* 17C1
Pico Bolivar Mt *Ven* 68C5
Pico de Anito Mt *Spain* 19C1
Pico del Infiernillo Mt *Mexico* 66B3
Pico Duarte Mt *Dom Rep* 68C3
Picos *Brazil* 71K5
Picos de Europa Mt *Spain* 19B1
Picton *Aust* 50D2
Picton *NZ* 51B2
Pic Toussidé Mt *Chad* 78B1
Picún Leufú R *Arg* 72A3
Piedade *Brazil* 73C3
Piedra de Aguila *Arg* 72B4
Piedras Negras *Mexico* 66B2
Pie I *Can* 58B1
Pieksämäki *Fin* 12K6
Pielinen L *Fin* 12K6
Piemonte Region *Italy* 17B2
Pierre *USA* 57B3
Pieštany *Czech* 21D3
Pietermaritzburg *S Africa* 79D6
Pietersburg *S Africa* 79C6
Pietrasanta *Italy* 17D3
Piet Retief *S Africa* 79D6
Pietrosu Mt *Rom* 25C6
Pietrosul Mt *Rom* 23F1
Pieve di Cadore *Italy* 17E1
Pigailoe I *Pacific O* 39H6
Piggott *USA* 63D2
Pigüé *Arg* 72C3
Pijijapan *Mexico* 67D2
Pikangikum L *Can* 53J4
Pikes Peak *USA* 62A2
Piketberg *S Africa* 79B7
Pikeville *USA* 58C3
Pikintaleq *Greenland* 53O3
Pik Kommunizma Mt *USSR* 29F2
Pikounda *Congo* 78B3
Pik Pobedy Mt *China/USSR* 29G1
Pila *Arg* 72D3
Pila *Pol* 20D2
Pilar *Par* 69E3
Pilcomayo R *Arg/Par* 69D2
Pīlībhīt *India* 35D3
Pilica R *Pol* 21D2
Pillar,C *Aust* 50E3
Pílos *Greece* 23E3
Pilot Knob Mt *USA* 64C1
Pilot Point *USA* 56G4
Pilot Station *USA* 56F3
Pilottown *USA* 63E3
Pimenta *Brazil* 71G4
Pinang I *Malay* 43C4
Pinar del Rio *Cuba* 68A2
Pinas *Arg* 72B2
Pinche *Belg* 16C1
Pindaré R *Brazil* 71J4
Píndhos Mts *Greece* 23E3
Pine Bluff *USA* 63D3
Pine Bluffs *USA* 62B1
Pine City *USA* 57D2
Pine Creek *Aust* 48C2
Pine Creek R *USA* 60B2
Pinedale *USA* 65C3
Pinedale Wyoming *USA* 64E2
Pine Falls *Can* 57C1
Pine Flat Res. *USA* 65C3
Pinega *USSR* 24G3
Pinega R *USSR* 24H3
Pine Grove *USA* 60B2
Pine Hills *USA* 61C3
Pinehurst *USA* 61D1
Pine I *USA* 61E4
Pineland *USA* 63D3
Pinellas Park *USA* 61C3
Pine Ridge *USA* 57B3
Pinerolo *Italy* 17B2
Pines,Lo'the *USA* 63D3
Pineville *USA* 63D3
Pingdingshan *China* 40C3
Pingguo *China* 40B5
Pingliang *China* 40B2
Pingluo *China* 40B2
Pingtan Dao I *China* 40D4
P'ing tung *Taiwan* 40E5
Pingwu *China* 40A3
Pingxiang Guangxi *China* 40B5
Pingxiang Jiangxi *China* 40C4
Pinheiro *Brazil* 71J4
Pinheiro Machado *Brazil* 72E2
Pini I *Indon* 44A2
Piniós R *Greece* 23E3
Pinjang *Indon* 45B2
Pinjarra *Aust* 48A4
Pinnaroo *Aust* 50B3
Pinos,I de I = Islas de la Juventud
Pinos,Pt *USA* 65B3
Pinotepa Nacional *Mexico* 67C2
Pinrang *Indon* 45A3
Pinsk *USSR* 25D5
Pinto *Arg* 72C1
Pinyug *USSR* 24H3
Pioche *USA* 65D3
Piombino *Italy* 22C2
Pioneer Mts *USA* 64D1
Pionerskiy *USSR* 24L3
Piórsá *Iceland* 53Q3
Piotrków Trybunalski *Pol* 21D2
Piper Oilfield *N Sea* 14F2
Piper Pk *USA* 65C3
Pipestone *USA* 57C3
Pipinas *Arg* 72D3
Pipmuacan Res *Can* 55F2
Pipmudcan Res *Can* 53M4
Piqua *USA* 58C2
Piquiri R *Brazil* 73B4
Piracanjuba *Brazil* 73C2
Piracicaba *Brazil* 73C3
Piraçununga *Brazil* 73C3
Pirai do Sul *Brazil* 73C3
Piraiévs *Greece* 23E3
Pirajui *Brazil* 73C3
Piran *Yugos* 17E2
Piranhas *Brazil* 73B2
Pirapora *Brazil* 73D2
Piratina R *Brazil* 72D1
Piratini R *Brazil* 72E2
Pirdop *Bulg* 23E2
Pirenópolis *Brazil* 73C2
Pires do Rio *Brazil* 73C2
Pírgos *Greece* 23E3
Pirineos = Pyrénées
Pirineos Mts *Spain* 18B3
Piripiri *Brazil* 71K4
Pirmasens *W Germ* 16D2
Pirot *Yugos* 23E2
Pir Panjāl Range Mts *Pak* 35C2
Piru *Indon* 45C3
Pisa *Italy* 17D3
Pisco *Peru* 70C6
Piseco *USA* 60C1
Písek *Czech* 20C3
Pishin *Pak* 35B2
Pissis Mt *Arg* 69C3
Pistoia *Italy* 17D3
Pisuerga R *Spain* 19B1
Pit R *USA* 64B2
Pitalito *Colombia* 70C3
Pitanga *Brazil* 73B3
Pitcairn I *Pacific O* 47N6
Pite R *Sweden* 12H5
Piteå *Sweden* 12J5
Piteşti *Rom* 23E2
Pit Gorodok *USSR* 27L4
Pithiviers *France* 16B2
Pitkyaranta *USSR* 24E3
Pitlochry *Scot* 14D3
Pitlyar *USSR* 24M2
Pitrutquén *Chile* 72A3
Pitt I *NZ* 49H5
Pitt I. *Can* 52F4
Pittsburg Kansas *USA* 63D2
Pittsburgh *USA* 59D2
Pittsfield Illinois *USA* 58A3
Pittsfield Massachusetts *USA* 60D1
Pittston *USA* 60C2
Pittsworth *Aust* 50D1
Piuthan *Nepal* 37B2
Pivan' *USSR* 41D1
Pizzo Redorta Mt *Italy* 17D1
Pjórsá *Iceland* 12B2
Pjura *Peru* 70B5
Placentia B *Can* 53N5
Placerville *USA* 65B3
Plaine d'Alsace Plain *France* 16D2
Plaine des Flandres Plain *France/Belg* 16B1
Plaine du Tidikelt Desert Region 76C2
Plaine Lorraine Region *France* 16C2
Plains *USA* 62B2
Plainview Nebraska *USA* 57C3
Plainview Texas *USA* 62B3
Planalto de Mato Grosso Plat *Brazil* 71H7
Planalto do Borborema Plat *Brazil* 71L5
Planalto do Mato Grosso Mts *Brazil* 70B1
Planet Deep *PNG* 49E1
Plankinton *USA* 57C3
Plano *USA* 63C3
Plantation *USA* 61E4
Plant City *USA* 61C3
Plasencia *Spain* 19A1
Plast *USSR* 24L5
Plastun *USSR* 41D3
Plateau State *Nig* 77H4
Plateau de Dadango *Togo* 77G3
Plateau de Langres Plat *France* 16C3
Plateau De St Christol Region *France* 17A2
Plateau du Tademait *Alg* 76C2
Plateau Lorrain Plat *France* 16D2
Plateaux de Limousin Plat *France* 18C2
Plateaux du Sersou Plat *Alg* 19C2
Plato *Colombia* 68C5
Plato Ustyurt Plat *USSR* 26G5
Platres *Cyprus* 31B1
Platte *USA* 57C3
Platte R *USA* 62B1
Platteville *USA* 58A2
Plattsburgh *USA* 59E2
Plattsmouth *USA* 63C1
Plauen *E Germ* 20C2
Plavsk *USSR* 24F5
Playa Azul *Mexico* 67B2
Playas *Ecuador* 70B4
Playa Vincente *Mexico* 67C2
Plaza de Moro Almanzor Mt *Spain* 19A1
Pleasanton Texas *USA* 63F4
Pleasantville *USA* 60C3
Pleasure Ridge Park *USA* 58B3
Pleiku *Viet* 43D3
Plenty,B of *NZ* 51C1
Plentywood *USA* 57B2
Pleszew *Pol* 21D2
Pletipi,L *Can* 53L4
Pleven *Bulg* 23E2
Plevlja *Yugos* 23D2
Plezetsk *USSR* 24F3
Ploče *Yugos* 23D2
Płock *Pol* 21D2
Ploërmel *France* 18B2
Ploieşti *Rom* 23F2
Plombières-les-Bains *France* 16D3
Płońsk *Pol* 24C5
Plovdiv *Bulg* 23E2
Plummer *USA* 64C1
Plummer,Mt *USA* 56G3
Plumtree *Zim* 79C6
Plymouth *Eng* 15C6
Plymouth Indiana *USA* 58B2
Plymouth Massachusetts *USA* 60E2
Plymouth Pennsylvania *USA* 60C2
Plymouth B *USA* 60E2
Plymouth Sd *Eng* 15C6
Plynlimon Mt *Wales* 15D5
Plzeň *Czech* 20C3
Pniewy *Pol* 20D2
Pô *U Volta* 77F3
Po R *Italy* 17E2
Pobé *Benin* 77G4
Pobedino *USSR* 41E2
Pocatello *USA* 64D2
Pochutla *Mexico* 67C2
Poções *Brazil* 73D1
Pocomoke City *USA* 59D3
Poconé *Brazil* 73A2
Pocos de Caldas *Brazil* 73C3
Po di Volano R *Italy* 17D2
Podkamennaya Tunguska R *USSR* 27L3
Podolsk *USSR* 24F4
Podol'skaya Vozvyshennost' Upland *USSR* 21F3
Podporozh'ye *USSR* 24E3
Podyuga *USSR* 24G3
Pofadder *S Africa* 79B6
Poggibonsi *Italy* 17D3
Poghdar *Afghan* 35A2
Pogranichnyy *USSR* 41C3
Poh *Indon* 45B3
P'ohang *S Korea* 41B4
Poinsett,C *Ant* 80G9
Point *Aust* 50C2
Pointe-à-Pitre *Guadeloupe* 68E3
Pointe de Barfleur Pt *France* 18B2
Pointe Noire *Congo* 78B4
Pointe Pongara Pt *Gabon* 78A3
Point Fairy *Aust* 50B3
Point Fortin *Trinidad* 68L1
Point Hope *USA* 56E2
Point L *Can* 52G3
Point Lay *USA* 56F2
Point Pleasant New Jersey *USA* 60C2
Point Pleasant W Virginia *USA* 58C3
Point St Bernard Mt *France* 17B2
Poitiers *France* 18C2
Poitou Region *France* 18B2
Poix *France* 16A2
Pokaran *India* 35C3
Pokataroo *Aust* 50C1
Pokhara *Nepal* 37B2
Pokrovsk *USSR* 27O3
Polacca *USA* 65D3
Poland Republic *Europe* 21D2
Poland *USA* 60C1
Polath *Turk* 25E8
Polatli *Turk* 30B2
Poleang *Indon* 45B3
Polewali *Indon* 45A3
Poli *Cam* 77J4
Poligny *France* 17A1
Poliny Osipenko *USSR* 27P4
Polis *Cyprus* 31B1
Políyiros *Greece* 23E2
Pollāchi *India* 36B2
Polollo Is *Phil* 45F8
Polonnye *USSR* 21F2
Polotsk *USSR* 21F1
Polson *USA* 64D1
Poltava *USSR* 25E6
Pölten *Austria* 22D1
Polunochoye *USSR* 24K3
Poluostrov Kanin Pen *USSR* 24G2
Poluostrov Mangyshiak Pen *USSR* 25J7
Poluostrov Rybachiy Pen *USSR* 12L5
Poluostrov Taymyr Pen *USSR* 27L2
Poluostrov Yamal Pen *USSR* 26J2
Polvadera *USA* 62A3
Polyarnyy Murmansk *USSR* 24E2
Polyarnyy Yakutskaya *USSR* 27Q2
Polyarnyy Ural Mts *USSR* 24L2
Polynesia Region *Pacific O* 47L4
Pomabamba *Peru* 70C5
Pomba R *Brazil* 73D3
Pomona *USA* 65C4
Pomona Res *USA* 63C2
Pompano Beach *USA* 61E4
Ponca City *USA* 63C2
Ponce *Puerto Rico* 68D3
Ponce de Leon B *USA* 61E4
Pondicherry *India* 36B2
Pond Inlet *Can* 53L2
Ponferrade *Spain* 19A1
Pongo R *Sudan* 78C3
Ponnāni *India* 36B2
Ponnyadoung Range Mts *Burma* 37D3
Ponoy *USSR* 26F3
Ponoy R *USSR* 24G2
Pons *France* 18B2
Ponta da Baleia Pt *Brazil* 73E2
Ponta Delgada *Açores* 76A1
Ponta do Mutá Pt *Brazil* 73E1
Ponta do Padrão Pt *Angola* 78B4
Ponta dos Búzios Pt *Brazil* 73D3
Ponta Grossa *Brazil* 73B4
Pontailler-sur-Saône *France* 17A1
Pontal *Brazil* 73C3
Pont-à-Mousson *France* 16C2
Ponta Pora *Brazil* 73A3
Pontarlier *France* 18D2
Pontassieve *Italy* 17D3
Pontchartrain,L *USA* 63D3
Pont d'Ain *France* 17A1
Ponte de Pedra *Brazil* 73A1
Pontedera *Italy* 22C2
Ponte Lecca *Corse* 22B2
Pontevedra *Spain* 19A1
Pontiac Illinois *USA* 58B2
Pontiac Michigan *USA* 58C2
Pontianak *Indon* 44C3
Pontivy *France* 18B2
Pontoise *France* 16B2
Pontotoc *USA* 63E3
Pontremoli *Italy* 17C2
Pont-sur-Yonne *France* 16B2
Pontypool *Wales* 15D6
Pontypridd *Wales* 15D6
Poole *Eng* 15E6
Poona = Pune
Pooncarie *Aust* 50B2
Poopelloe,L L *Aust* 50B2
Poorman *USA* 56G3
Popayán *Colombia* 70C3
Poperinge *Belg* 16B1
Popilta L *Aust* 50B2
Poplar *USA* 57A2
Poplar Bluff *USA* 63D2
Poplarville *USA* 63E3
Popndetta *PNG* 48D1
Popocatepetl Mt *Mexico* 67C2
Popof I *USA* 56F4
Popokabaka *Zaïre* 78B4
Popondetta *PNG* 39H7
Popovo *Bulg* 23F2
Poraiba R *Brazil* 73C3
Porangatu *Brazil* 73C1
Porbandar *India* 35B4
Porcos R *Brazil* 73C1
Porcupine R *USA/Can* 56K2
Pordenone *Italy* 17E2
Poreč *Yugos* 22C1
Porecatu *Brazil* 73B3
Pori *Fin* 12J6
Porirua *NZ* 51B2
Porjus *Sweden* 12H5
Poronay R *USSR* 41E1
Poronaysk *USSR* 41E2
Porosozero *USSR* 24E3
Porrentruy *Switz* 17B1
Porretta *Italy* 17D3
Porsangen Inlet *Nor* 12K4
Porsgrunn *Nor* 12F7
Portadown *N Ire* 15B4
Portage *USA* 58B2
Portage La Prairie *Can* 57C2
Portal *USA* 57B2
Port Alberni *Can* 52F5
Portalegre *Port* 19A2
Portales *USA* 62B3
Port Alfred *Can* 53L5
Port Alfred *S Africa* 79C7
Port Alice *Can* 52F4
Port Allegany *USA* 60A2
Port Allen *USA* 63D3
Port Angeles *USA* 64B1
Port Antonio *Jamaica* 68B3
Portarlington *Irish Rep* 15B5
Port Arthur *USA* 63D4
Port Askaig *Scot* 14B4
Port-Audemer *France* 16A2
Port Augusta *Aust* 50A2
Port-au-Prince *Haiti* 68C3
Port Austin *USA* 58C2
Port Blair *Andaman Is* 36E2
Port Campbell *Aust* 50B3
Port Canning *India* 37C3
Port Cartier *Can* 53M5
Port Chalmers *NZ* 51B3
Port Charlotte *USA* 61E4
Port Chester *USA* 60D2
Port Colborne *Can* 59D2
Port Credit *Can* 59D2
Port Davey *Aust* 50E3
Port-de-Paix *Haiti* 68C3
Port Dickson *Malay* 43C5
Port Edward *S Africa* 79C7
Porteirinha *Brazil* 73D2
Port Elgin *Can* 58C2
Port Elizabeth *S Africa* 79C7
Port Ellen *Scot* 14B4
Porter Pt *St Vincent* 68N2
Porterville *USA* 65C3
Port Fairy *Aust* 48D4
Port Gentil *Gabon* 78A4
Port Gibson *USA* 63D3
Port Graham *USA* 56H4
Port Hammond *Can* 64B1
Port Hardy *Can* 52F4
Port Hawkesbury *Can* 53M5
Port Hedland *Aust* 48A3
Port Heiden = Meshik
Porthmadog *Wales* 15C5
Port Hope Simpson *Can* 53N4
Port Huron *USA* 58C2
Portimão *Port* 19A2
Port Jackson B *Aust* 50D2
Port Jefferson *USA* 60D2
Port Jervis *USA* 60C2
Port Kembla *Aust* 50D2
Portland Indiana *USA* 58C2
Portland Maine *USA* 59E2
Portland New South Wales *Aust* 50C2
Portland Oregon *USA* 64B1
Portland Victoria *Aust* 50B3
Portland Bight B *Jamaica* 68H2
Portland Bill Pt *Eng* 15D6
Portland,C *Aust* 50E3
Portland Canal Sd *USA/Can* 56M4
Portland I *NZ* 51C1
Portland Pt *Jamaica* 68H2
Port Laoise *Irish Rep* 13B3
Port Lavaca *USA* 63F4
Port-l'Evêque *France* 16A2
Port Lincoln *Aust* 50A2
Port Loko *Sierra Leone* 76A4
Port Louis *Mauritius* 79F6
Port MacDonnell *Aust* 50B3
Port Macquarie *Aust* 50D2
Port Matilda *USA* 60A2
Port Moller *USA* 56F4
Port Moresby *PNG* 48D1
Port Nolloth *S Africa* 79B6
Port Norris *USA* 60C3
Port-Nouveau-Québec *Can* 53M4
Porto *Port* 19A1
Pôrto Alegre *Brazil* 69F4
Porto Alexandre *Angola* 79B5
Porto Armuelles *Panama* 68A5
Pôrto Artur *Brazil* 73A1
Pôrto 15 de Novembro *Brazil* 73B3
Pôrto dos Meinacos *Brazil* 73B1
Pôrto E Cunha *Brazil* 69F2
Pôrto Esperança *Brazil* 73A2
Portoferraio *Italy* 22C2
Port of Spain *Trinidad* 68E4
Portogruaro *Italy* 17E2
Porto Jofre *Brazil* 73A2
Porto Lucena *Brazil* 72D1
Portomaggiore *Italy* 17D2
Porto Mendez *Brazil* 73B3
Porto Murtinho *Brazil* 73A3
Porto Novo *Benin* 77G4
Port Orchard *USA* 64B1
Porto Recanati *Italy* 17E3
Port Orford *USA* 64B2
Porto Santo I *Medeira* 76A1
Porto São José *Brazil* 73B3
Pôrto Seguro *Brazil* 71L7
Porto Torres *Sardegna* 22B2
Porto União *Brazil* 73B4
Porto Vecchio *Corse* 22B2
Pôrto Velho *Brazil* 70F5
Port Pegasus B *NZ* 51A3
Port Phillip B *Aust* 50B3
Port Pirie *Aust* 50A2
Port Radium *Can* 56P2
Portree *Scot* 14B3
Port Renfrew *Can* 64B1
Port Royal *Jamaica* 68J2
Port Royal Sd *USA* 61C2
Portrush *N Ire* 14B4
Port Said *Egypt* 31B3
Port St Joe *USA* 61B3
Port St. John's *S Africa* 79C7
Port Saunders *Can* 53N4
Port Shepstone *S Africa* 79D7
Portsmouth *Dominica* 68Q2
Portsmouth *Eng* 15E6
Portsmouth New Hampshire *USA* 60E1
Portsmouth Ohio *USA* 58C3
Portsmouth Virginia *USA* 59D3
Port Stephens B *Aust* 50D2
Port Sudan *Sudan* 78D2
Port Sulphur *USA* 63E3
Porttipahdan Tekojärvi Res *Fin* 12K5

Portugal

Quimili

Portugal Republic Europe 19A2
Portville USA 60A1
Port Washington USA 58B2
Port Weld Malay 43C5
Porvenir Bol 70E6
Posadas Arg 69E3
Posadas Spain 19A2
Poschiavo Switz 17D1
Posheim Pen Can 53K2
Poshinok USSR 21G2
Posht-e Badam Iran 34D2
Poso Indon 45B3
Posŏng S Korea 42A4
Posse Brazil 73C1
Post USA 62B3
Postavy USSR 21F1
Post Clinton USA 58C2
Poste-de-la-Baleine Can 53L4
Poste-de-Mistassini Can 53L4
Postmasburg S Africa 79C6
Postojna Yugos 22C1
Pos'yet USSR 41C3
Pota Indon 45B4
Potchefstroom S Africa 79C6
Poteau USA 63D2
Potenza Italy 22D2
Potgietersrus S Africa 79C6
Poth USA 62C4
Poti USSR 25G7
Potiskum Nig 77J3
Potlatch USA 64C1
Pot Mt USA 64C1
Potomac R USA 59D3
Potomac South Branch R USA 60A3
Potosi Bol 70E7
Potrerillos Chile 69C3
Potsdam E Germ 20C2
Potter USA 62B1
Pottstown USA 60C2
Pottsville USA 60B2
Poughkeepsie USA 60D2
Pouso Alegre Brazil 73C3
Poverty B NZ 51C1
Povonets USSR 24F3
Povorino USSR 25G5
Povungnituk Can 53L4
Powder R USA 57A2
Powder River USA 57A3
Powell USA 64E2
Powell Creek Aust 48C2
Powell,L USA 65D3
Powell River Can 52F5
Power R USA 54C2
Powys County Wales 15D5
Poxoréo Brazil 73B2
Poyang Hu L China 40D4
Poyarkovo USSR 41B2
Pozantı Turk 30C2
Poza Rica Mexico 67C1
Poznań Pol 20D2
Pozo Colorado Par 69E2
Poz Poluy USSR 24M2
Pozzuoli Italy 22C2
Pra R Ghana 77F4
Prachin Buri Thai 43C3
Prachuap Khiri Khan Thai 43B3
Pradĕd Mt Czech 20D2
Pradelles France 18C3
Prado Brazil 73E2
Prague = Praha
Praha Czech 20C2
Praia Cape Verde 76A4
Praia Rica Brazil 73A1
Prainha Brazil 70F5
Prairie Dog Town Fork R USA 62B3
Prairie du Chien USA 58A2
Prairie Village USA 63D2
Prakhon Chai Thai 43C3
Prata Brazil 73C2
Prata R Brazil 73C2
Prates = Dongsha Qundao
Prato Italy 17D3
Pratomagno Mt Italy 17D3
Pratt USA 62C2
Prattsville USA 60C1
Prattville USA 61B2
Prawle Pt Eng 18B1
Praya Indon 44E4
Predazzo Italy 17D1
Predivinsk USSR 27L4
Predporozhnyy USSR 27O3
Pregolyu R USSR 21E2
Prek Kak Camb 43D3
Prentice USA 58A1
Prenzlau E Germ 20C2
Preparis I Burma 36E2
Preparis North Chan Burma 43A2
Preparis South Chan Burma 43A3
Přerov Czech 20D3
Presa de les Adjuntas Mexico 67C1
Presa del Infiernillo Mexico 67B2
Presa de Salto Grande Urug 72D2
Presa Netzahualcóyotl Mexico 67D2
Prescott Arizona USA 65D4
Prescott Arkansas USA 63D3
Prescott Can 59D2
Presho USA 57B3
Presidencia Roque Sáenz Peña Arg 69D3
Presidente Epitácio Brazil 73B3
Presidente Frei Base Ant 80G2
Presidente Migúel Aleman L Mexico 67C2
Presidente Murtinho Brazil 73B2
Presidente Prudente Brazil 73B3
Presidenté Vargas Brazil 71H8
Presidente Venceslau Brazil 73B3
Presidio USA 62B4
Presidio R Mexico 67A1
Prešov Czech 21E3
Prespansko Jezero L Yugos 23E2
Presque Isle USA 59F1
Prestea Ghana 77F4
Preston Eng 15D5
Preston Idaho USA 54B2
Preston Minnesota USA 57D3
Preston Missouri USA 63D2
Prestwick Scot 14C4
Prêto Brazil 71J8
Prêto R Brazil 73C2
Pretoria S Africa 79C6
Préveza Greece 23E3
Prey Veng Camb 43D3
Pribilof Is USA 56E4
Price USA 65D3
Prichard USA 61B2
Prichernomorskaya Nizmennost' Lowland USSR 25E6
Prickly Pt Grenada 68M2
Pridneprovskaya Vozvyshennost' Upland USSR 21F3
Priekule USSR 21E1
Prieska S Africa 79C6
Priest L USA 64C1
Priest River USA 64C1
Prikaspiyskaya Nizmennost' Region USSR 25H6
Prilep Yugos 23E2
Priluki USSR 25E5
Primero R Arg 72C2
Primorsk USSR 12K6
Primorsko-Akhtarsk USSR 25F6
Prince Albert,C Can 52F2
Prince Albert Pen Can 52G2
Prince Albert Sd Can 52G2
Prince Charles I Can 53L3
Prince Charles Mts Ant 80G10
Prince Edward I Indian O 46C7
Prince Edward I Can 53M5
Prince George Can 52F4
Prince Gustaf Adolp S Can 52H2
Prince of Wales,C USA 56E2
Prince of Wales I Aust 39H8
Prince of Wales I Can 52H2
Prince of Wales I. USA 52E4
Prince of Wales Str Can 52G2
Prince Patrick I Can 52F2
Prince Regent Inlet Str Can 53J2
Prince Rupert Can 52E4
Princess Charlotte B Aust 48D2
Princes Town Trinidad 68L1
Princeton Can 52F5
Princeton Illinois USA 58B2
Princeton Kentucky USA 58B3
Princeton Missouri USA 63D1
Princeton New Jersey USA 60C2
Princeton W Virginia USA 58C3
Prince William USA 52D3
Prince William Sd USA 56J3
Principe I W Africa 76C4
Prineville USA 64B2
Pringle,Mt USA 56J2
Prins Christian Sund Sd Greenland 53O3
Prinsesse Astrid Kyst Region Ant 80F12
Prinsesse Ragnhild Kyst Region Ant 80F12
Prins Karls Forland I Barents S 26C2
Prinzapolca Nic 66D3
Priozerzk USSR 24E3
Pripyat R USSR 12K8
Pripyat' R USSR 21F2
Priština Yugos 23E2
Pritzwalk E Germ 20C2
Privolzhskaya Vozvyshennost' Upland USSR 24G5
Prizren Yugos 23E2
Probolinggo Indon 44D4
Procatello USA 52G5
Proctor USA 57D2
Proddatūr India 36B2
Progreso Mexico 66D2
Progress USSR 41B2
Project City USA 64B2
Prokhladnyy USSR 25G7
Prokop'yevsk USSR 26K4
Proletarskaya USSR 25G6
Proliv Dmitriya Lapteva Str USSR 27P2
Proliv Karskiye Vorota Str USSR 26G2
Proliv Longa Str USSR 27T2
Proliv Vilritskago Str USSR 27L2
Prome Burma 37E4
Promissão Brazil 73A2
Pronya R USSR 21G2
Propriá Brazil 71L6
Prospect New York USA 60C1
Prospect Oregon USA 64B2
Prosperine Aust 48D3
Prostějov Czech 20D3
Prøven Greenland 53N2
Provence Region France 18D3
Providence USA 60E2
Provideniya USSR 27U3
Provincetown USA 60E1
Provins France 16B2
Provo USA 65D2
Provost Can 52G4
Prudentópolis Brazil 73B4
Prudhoe B USA 56J1
Prudhoe Bay USA 56J1
Prudhoe Land Greenland 53M2
Pruszkow Pol 21E2
Prut R Rom/USSR 21F3
Prutul R USSR 25D6
Pruzhany USSR 21E2
Pryor USA 63C2
Przemys'l Pol 21E3
Psará I Greece 23F3
Pskov USSR 24D4
Ptich R USSR 21F2
Ptolemaïs Greece 23E2
Puan S Korea 42A3
Pucallpa Peru 70D5
Pucheng China 40D4
Pucón Chile 72A3
Pudasjärvi Fin 12K5
Pudozh USSR 24F3
Pudukkottai India 36B2
Puebai de Trives Spain 19A1
Puebla Mexico 67C2
Puebla State Mexico 67C2
Puebla de Sanabria Spain 19A1
Pueblo USA 62B2
Puelches Arg 72B3
Puelén Arg 72B3
Puenta Ixbapa Mexico 67B2
Puente del Inca Arg 72B2
Puerta Aguja Peru 70B5
Puerta Coles Peru 70D7
Puerta de los Llanos Arg 72B2
Puerta de Mita Mexico 67A1
Puerta do Calcanhar Pt Brazil 71L5
Puerta Galera Mexico 67C2
Puerta Gallinas Colombia 70D1
Puerta Maldonado Pt Mexico 67C2
Puerta Mariato Panama 70B2
Puerta Médanosa Pt Arg 69C7
Puerta Mongrove Mexico 67B2
Puerta Roca Partida Mexico 67C2
Puerta San Blas Pt Panama 66E4
Puerta San Telmo Mexico 67B2
Puerto Adela Brazil 73B3
Puerto Aisén Chile 69B7
Puerto Angel Mexico 67C2
Puerto Armuelles Panama 66D4
Puerto Artur Brazil 71G6
Puerto Asis Colombia 70C3
Puerto Ayacucho Ven 70E2
Puerto Barrios Guatemala 66D3
Puerto Berrio Colombia 70D2
Puerto Cabello Ven 70E1
Puerto Cabezas Nic 66D3
Puerto Carreño Ven 70E2
Puerto Casado Brazil 73A3
Puerto Cavezas Nic 70B1
Puerto Cooper Brazil 73A3
Puerto Cortes Costa Rica 66D4
Puerto Cortés Honduras 66D3
Puerto del Rosario Canary Is 76A2
Puerto E Cunha Brazil 71H8
Puerto Escondido Mexico 67C2
Puerto Fijo Ven 70D1
Puerto Franco Brazil 71J5
Puerto Guarani Brazil 73A3
Puerto Heath Bol 70E6
Puerto Juarez Mexico 66D2
Puerto la Cruz Ven 70F1
Puertollano Spain 19B2
Puerto Lopez Colombia 68C4
Puerto Madryn Arg 69D6
Puerto Maldonado Peru 70E6
Puerto Marquéz Mexico 67C2
Puerto Montt Chile 69B6
Puerto Murtinho Brazil 71G8
Puerto Natales Chile 69B8
Puerto Peñasco Mexico 66A1
Puerto Pinasco Brazil 73A3
Puerto Pirámides Arg 69D6
Puerto Plata Dom Rep 68C3
Puerto Princesa Phil 45E9
Puerto Rico Colombia 70C3
Puerto Rico I Caribbean 68D3
Puerto Rico Trench Caribbean 68D3
Puerto San Juan de Lima Mexico 67B2
Puerto Santanga Brazil 71H4
Puerto Sastre Brazil 73A3
Puerto Suárez Bol 69E1
Puerto Vallarta Mexico 67A1
Puerto Varas Chile 69B6
Puerto Villarroel Bol 70F7
Pugachev USSR 25H5
Pugal India 35C3
Puigcerdá Spain 19C1
Pujŏn N Korea 42A2
Pujŏn Res N Korea 42A2
Pukaki,L L NZ 51B2
Pukchin N Korea 42A2
Pukch'ŏng N Korea 41B3
Pukekobe NZ 51B1
Puketeraki Range Mts NZ 51B2
Puksoozero USSR 24G3
Pula Yugos 22C2
Pulaski New York USA 59D2
Pulaski Tennessee USA 61B1
Pulaski Virginia USA 58C3
Pulau Kolepom I Indon 39G7
Pulau Pulau Asia Is Indon 45D2
Pulau Pulau Ayu Is Indon 45D2
Pulau Pulau Banyak Arch Indon 44A2
Pulau Pulau Batu Is Indon 44A3
Pulau Pulau Kangean Is Indon 48A1
Pulau Pulau Macan Is Indon 48B1
Pulau Pulau Pisang Is Indon 45D3
Pulautelo Indon 44A3
Pulawy Pol 21E2
Pulicat,L India 36C2
Pul-i-Khumri Afghan 35B1
Puliyangudi India 36B3
Pullendorf W Germ 16E3
Pullman USA 64C1
Pulo Anna Merir I Pacific I 39G6
Pulog,Mt Phil 45F7
Pulozero USSR 12L5
Pultusk Pol 21E2
Puna de Atacama Arg 69C3
Punakha Bhutan 37C2
Punch Pak 35C2
Pune India 36A1
Punéper Mexico 67B2
Pungsan N Korea 42A2
Pungso N Korea 42A2
Punia Zaïre 78C4
Punitaqui Chile 72A2
Punjab Province Pak 35C2
Punjab State India 35D2
Puno Peru 70D7
Punta Abreojos Pt Mexico 66A2
Punta Alice Pt Italy 22D3
Punta Alta Arg 72C3
Punta Arenas Chile 69B8
Punta Baja Pt Mexico 66A2
Punta Bermeja Pt Arg 72C4
Punta Curaumilla Pt Chile 72A2
Punta da Marca Pt Angola 79B5
Punta de Barra Falsa Pt Mozam 79D6
Punta del Este Urug 72E2
Punta di Portofino Pt Italy 17C2
Punta Eugenia Pt Mexico 66A2
Punta Galera Chile 72A3
Punta Gorda Belize 66D3
Punta Gorda USA 61E4
Punta Lavapié Pt Chile 72A3
Punta Lengua de Vaca Pt Chile 72A2
Punta Licosa Pt Italy 22C2
Punta Norte Pt Arg 72D3
Punta Piedras Pt Arg 72D3
Punta Poroto Pt Chile 72A1
Punta Rasa Pt Arg 72C4
Puntarenas Costa Rica 70B1
Punta Rubia Pt Arg 72C4
Punta San Antonia Pt Mexico 54B4
Punta Sur Arg 72D3
Punta Topocalma Chile 72A2
Puntjak Ranakah Mt Indon 45B4
Punxsutawney USA 60A2
Puper Indon 45D3
Puqi China 40C4
Purcell USA 63C2
Purcell Mt USA 56G2
Purén Chile 72A3
Purgatoire R USA 62B2
Puri India 37C3
Pūrna India 36B1
Pūrnia India 37C2
Pursat Camb 43C3
Puruandro Mexico 67B1
Purus R Brazil 70F4
Purvis USA 63E3
Purwokerto Indon 44C4
Purworejo Indon 44D4
Pusad India 35D5
Pusan S Korea 41B4
Pushakhta USSR 24F3
Pushkin USSR 24E4
Pustochka USSR 21F1
Putaendo Chilè 72A2
Putao Burma 37E2
Putaruru NZ 51C1
Putian China 40D4
Putnam USA 60E2
Putney USA 60D1
Puttalam Sri Lanka 36B3
Puttgarden W Germ 20C2
Putumayo R Ecuador 70C4
Putussibau Indon 44D2
Puulavesl L Fin 12K6
Puyallup USA 64B1
Puy de Sancy Mt France 18C2
Puyehue Chile 72A4
Puysegur Pt NZ 51A3
Pweto Zaïre 79C4
Pwllheli Wales 15C5
Pyalma USSR 24F3
Pyapon Burma 43B2
Pyasina R USSR 27K2
Pyatigorsk USSR 25G7
Pyinmana Burma 37E4
Pyŏktong N Korea 42A2
Pyonggang N Korea 42A3
Pyŏnggok-dong S Korea 42A3
P'Yŏngsann N Korea 42A3
P'yongt'aek S Korea 42A3
P'yŏngyang N Korea 41B4
Pyramid Hill Aust 50B3
Pyramid L USA 65C2
Pyramid,Mt NZ 51A2
Pyrénées Mts France 18B3
Pytalovo USSR 21F1
Pyu Burma 43B2

Q

Qabatiya Israel 31C2
Qabr Hūd S Yemen 33E3
Qa'el Hafīra Mud Flats Jordan 31D3
Qa'el Jinz Mud Flats Jordan 31D3
Qaidam Pendi Salt Flat China 38C3
Qaisar Afghan 34E1
Qa Khanna Salt Marsh Jordan 31D2
Qala Adras Kand Afghan 34E2
Qala'en Nahl Sudan 78D2
Qala Nau Afghan 34E2
Qalat Afghan 35B2
Qal'at al Hisn Syria 31D1
Qal'at al Marqab Hist Site 31C1
Qal'at Bīshah S Arabia 32D2
Qal'at Sālih Iraq 30E3
Qamdo China 38C3
Qara Egypt 75B2
Qareh Dāgh Mts Iran 25H8
Qaṭe Shīrīn Iran 34B2
Qaryat al Ulyā S Arabia 33E1
Qasr el Kharana Jordan 31D3
Qasr-e-Qand Iran 34E3
Qasr Farafra Egypt 75B2
Qaṭana Syria 31D2
Qatar Emirate Arabian Pen 33F1
Qatrāna Jordan 31D3
Qattâra Depression Egypt 75B2
Qāyen Iran 34D2
Qazvīn Iran 34C1
Qena Egypt 32B1
Qeydār Iran 34B1
Qeys I Iran 34C3
Qezel Owzan R Iran 25H8
Qian'an China 41A3
Qian Gorlos China 41A2
Qian Jiang R China 40B5
Qian Shan Upland China 40E1
Qidong China 40E3
Qijiang China 40B4
Qila Ladgasht Pak 34E3
Qila Saifullah Pak 35B2
Qilian China 40A2
Qilian Shan China 38C3
Qin'an China 40B3
Qingdao China 40E2
Qinggang China 41B2
Qinghai Province China 40A2
Qinghai Hu L China 38C3
Qinghai Hu L China 40A2
Qinghai Hu L China 40A2
Qingjiang Jiangsu China 40D3
Qingjiang Jiangxi China 40D4
Qing Jiang R China 40B3
Qingshuihe China 40C2
Qingshui He R China 40B2
Qingtonxia China 40B2
Qingyang China 40B2
Qingyuan Liaoning China 41B3
Qingyuan Zhejiang China 40D4
Qing Zang Upland China 29G2
Qingzhou China 40B5
Qingzhou China 43D1
Qinhuangdao China 40D2
Qin Ling Mts China 40B3
Qionghai China 43E2
Qionglai Shan Upland China 40A3
Qiongzhou Haixia Str China 43D1
Qiqihar China 41A2
Qiryat Ata Israel 31C2
Qiryat Gat Israel 31C3
Qiryat Shemona Israel 31C2
Qiryat Yam Israel 31C2
Qishn S Yemen 33F3
Qishon R Israel 31C2
Qishran I S Arabia 32C2
Qitai China 27K5
Qitaihe China 41C2
Qixing He R China 41C2
Qiyang China 40C4
Qog Qi China 40B1
Qolleh-ye-Damavand Mt Iran 25J8
Qolleh-ye Damavand Mt Iran 34C1
Qom Iran 34C2
Qomisheh Iran 34C2
Qomolangma Feng Mt = Everest,Mt
Qornet es Saouda Mt Leb 31D1
Qôrnoq Greenland 53N3
Qorveh Iran 34B1
Qotābad Iran 34D3
Qotūr R Iran 25H8
Quabbin Res USA 60D1
Quakertown USA 60C2
Quam Phu Quoc I Viet 43C3
Quanah USA 62C3
Quang Ngai Viet 43D2
Quang Tri Viet 43D2
Quan Long Viet 43D4
Quanzhou Fujian China 40D5
Quanzhou Guangxi China 40C4
Qu'Appelle Can 57B1
Qu' Appelle R Can 52H4
Quarai R Urug 72D2
Quaral Brazil 72D2
Quarayyāt Oman 33G2
Quardho Somalia 75D4
Quarkoye U Volta 77F3
Quartzsite USA 65D4
Quchan Iran 34D1
Queanbeyan Aust 50C3
Québec Can 59E1
Quebec Province Can 53L4
Quebra-Anzol R Brazil 73C2
Quebracho Urug 72D2
Quedas do Iguaçu Brazil/Arg 69F3
Queen Anne USA 60B3
Queen Charlotte Is. Can 52E4
Queen Charlotte Sd. Can 52E4
Queen Charlotte Str. Can 52F4
Queen Elizabeth Is Can 52H1
Queen Mary Land Region Ant 80G9
Queen Maud G Can 52H3
Queen Maud Mts Ant 80E
Queens Borough New York USA 60D2
Queens Chan Can 52J2
Queens Ch Aust 39F8
Queenscliff Aust 50B3
Queensland State Aust 48D3
Queenstown Aust 50E3
Queenstown NZ 51A3
Queenstown S Africa 79C7
Queenstown USA 60B3
Quela Angola 79B4
Quelimane Mozam 79D5
Quemado USA 62A3
Quémé R Benin 77G4
Quemuquemú Arg 72C3
Quequén Arg 72D3
Quequén R Arg 72D3
Querétaro Mexico 67B1
Queretaro State Mexico 67B1
Quesnel Can 52F4
Quetta Pak 35B2
Quezaltenango Guatemala 66C3
Queziot Israel 31C3
Quezon City Phil 45F8
Quibala Angola 79B5
Quibaxe Angola 79B4
Quibdó Colombia 70C2
Quiberon France 18B2
Quicama Nat Pk Angola 79B4
Quiindy Par 73A4
Quijing China 40A4
Quilima Chile 72A2
Quilino Arg 72C2
Quillabamba Peru 70D6
Quillacollo Bol 70E7
Quillan France 18C3
Quill L Can 52H4
Quillota Chile 72A2
Quilon India 36B3
Quilpie Aust 50B1
Quilpué Chile 72A2
Quimbele Angola 79B4
Quimili Arg 72C1

Quimper Roanoke

Quimper France 18B2
Quimperlé France 18B2
Quincy California USA 65B3
Quincy Illinois USA 58A3
Quincy Massachusetts USA 60E1
Quines Arg 72B2
Quinhagak USA 56F4
Qui Nhon Viet 43D3
Quintanar de la Orden Spain 19B2
Quintero Chile 72A2
Quinto R Arg 72C2
Quirihue Chile 72A3
Quirima Angola 79B5
Quirindi Aust 50D2
Quissanga Mozam 79E5
Quissico Mozam 79D6
Quito Ecuador 70C4
Quixadá Brazil 71L4
Quorn Aust 50A2
Qus Egypt 32B1
Quşayir Oman 33F4
Quseir Egypt 32B1
Qutdligssat Greenland 53N3
Quthing = Moyeni
Qu Xian Sichuan China 40B3
Qu Xian Zhejiang China 40D4
Quynh Luu Viet 43D2
Quzhou China 40C2
Qūzū China 37D2

R

Raahe Fin 12J6
Raasay I Scot 14B3
Raasay,Sound of Chan Scot 14B3
Raas Caseyr C Somalia 33F4
Rab I Yugos 22C2
Raba Indon 44E4
Rába R Hung 20D3
Rabak Sudan 32B4
Rabat Mor 77A2
Rabaul PNG 48E1
Rabba Jordan 31C3
Rabigh S Arabia 32C2
Racconigi Italy 17B2
Race,C Can 53N5
Race Pt USA 60E1
Rachaya Leb 31C2
Rachel Mt W Germ 20C3
Rach Gia Viet 43D3
Racine USA 58B2
Radā' Yemen 32D4
Rădăuţi Rom 21F3
Radcliff USA 58B3
Radford USA 58C3
Radhanpur India 35C4
Radix,Pt Trinidad 68L1
Radom Pol 21E2
Radomsko Pol 21D2
Radomyshl' USSR 21F2
Radstadt Austria 17E1
Radviliškis USSR 21E1
Rae Can 52G3
Rāe Bareli India 37B2
Rae Isthmus Can 53K3
Rae L Can 52G3
Raetihi NZ 51C1
Rafaela Arg 72C2
Rafah Egypt 31C3
Rafai CAR 78C3
Rafhā Al Jumaymah S Arabia 30D3
Rafsanjān Iran 34D2
Raga Sudan 78C3
Ragged Pt Barbados 69Q2
Raguba Libya 75A2
Ragusa Italy 22C3
Raha Indon 45B3
Rahad R Sudan 32C4
Raheita Eth 32D4
Rahimyar Khan Pak 35C3
Rāhjerd Iran 34C2
Raices Arg 72D2
Rāichur India 36B1
Raigarh India 37B3
Rainbow Aust 50B3
Rainbow City USA 61B2
Rainier USA 64B1
Rainier,Mt USA 64B1
Rainy R USA 57D2
Rainy L Can 57D2
Rainy P USA 56H3
Rainy River Can 57D2
Raipur India 37B3
Rājahmundry India 36C1
Rajang R Malay 44D2
Rajanpur Pak 35C3
Rājapālaiyam India 36B3
Rājasthan State India 35C3
Rājgarh India 35D3
Rājgarh State India 35D4
Rājkot India 35C4
Rājmahāl Hills India 37C3
Raj Nāndgaon India 37B3
Rājpīpla India 35C4
Rajshahi Bang 37C3
Rajur India 35D4
Rakaia R NZ 51B2
Rakata I Indon 44C4
Raka Zangbo R China 29G3
Rakhov USSR 21E3
Rakhshan R Pak 34E3
Rakhyūt Oman 33F3
Rakops Botswana 79C6
Rakov USSR 21F2
Raleigh USA 61D1
Ralny L Can 53J5
Ram Jordan 31C4
Rama Israel 31C2
Ramallah Israel 31C3
Rāmanāthapuram India 36B3
Ramapo Deep Pacific Oc 38H3
Ramat Gan Israel 31C2
Rambervillers France 16D2
Rambouillet France 16A2
Rāmgarh Bihar India 37C3
Rāmgarh Rajosthan India 35C3
Rāmhormoz Iran 34B2
Ramla Israel 31C3
Ramlat Al Wahibah Region Oman 33G2
Ramlat as Sab'atayn Region S Yemen 33E3
Ramona USA 65C4
Rāmpur India 35D3
Rāmpura India 35D4
Ramree I Burma 37D4
Rāmsar Iran 25J8
Ramsey Eng 15C4
Ramsey USA 60C2
Ramsey I Wales 15C6
Ramsgate Eng 15F6
Ramtha Jordan 31D2
Ramu R PNG 48D1
Ranau Malay 44E1
Rancagua Chile 72A2
Ranchester USA 57A3
Rānchi India 37C3
Rānchi Plat India 37B3
Randers Den 12F7
Randolph New York USA 60A1
Randolph Vermont USA 59E2
Ranfurly NZ 51B3
Rangamati Bang 37D3
Rangely USA 62A1
Rangiora NZ 51B2
Rangitaiki R NZ 51C1
Rangitate R NZ 51B2
Rangitikei R NZ 51C1
Rangoon Burma 43B2
Rangpur India 37C2
Rānībennur India 36B2
Ranier,Mt Mt USA 54A2
Rānīganj India 37C3
Rankins Springs Aust 50C2
Ranklin Inlet Can 53J3
Rann of Kachchh Flood Area India 35B4
Ranong Thai 43B4
Rantauparapat Indon 44A2
Rantepao Indon 45A3
Rantoul USA 58B2
Ranuro R Brazil 73B1
Raohe China 41C2
Raon-l'Etape France 16D2
Raoul I NZ 49H3
Rapallo Italy 17C2
Rapel R Chile 72A2
Raper,C Can 53M3
Rapid City USA 57B3
Rapid River USA 58B1
Rappahannock R USA 59D3
Rappang Indon 45A3
Rapperswil Switz 17C1
Raritan B USA 60C2
Ras Abū Dâra C Egypt 32C2
Ra's Abu Madd C S Arabia 32C2
Ras Abu Shagara C Sudan 32C2
Ra's al 'Ayn Syria 30D2
Ra's al Hadd C Oman 33G2
Ras al Kaimah UAE 33G1
Ra's al Kalb C S Yemen 33E4
Ras-al-Kuh C Iran 33G1
Ra's al Madrakah C Oman 33G3
Ras Andadda C Eth 32D3
Ra's ash Sharbatāt C Oman 33G3
Ra's Asis C Sudan 32C3
Ra's at Tarfā C S Arabia 32D3
Ra's az Zawr C S Arabia 33E1
Rās Bânas C Egypt 32C2
Ras Burûn C Egypt 31B3
Ras Dashan Mt Eth 32C4
Ra's Duqm Oman 33G3
Ra's-e-Barkan Pt Iran 34B2
Ra's-e-Fasteh C Iran 34E3
Rās el Barr C Egypt 31A3
Rās el Kenāyis Pt Egypt 30A3
Ras el Nafas Mt Egypt 31C4
Rās El Sudr C Egypt 31B4
Ras en Naqb Upland Jordan 31C4
Ra's Fartak C S Yemen 33F3
Rås Ghârib Egypt 32B1
Rashad Sudan 78D2
Ras Hadarba C Egypt 32C2
Rashādīya Jordan 31C3
Rashîd Egypt 30B3
Rasht Iran 34B1
Ra's ibn Hāni C Syria 31C1
Ra's Jaddi C Pak 34E3
Ra's Jibish C Oman 33G2
Rāsk Iran 34E3
Ra's Kasar C Sudan 32C3
Ras Khanzira C Somalia 78E2
Ras Koh Mt Pak 35B3
Râs Matarma C Egypt 31B4
Ra's Momi C Socotra 33F4
Râs Muhammad C Egypt 32B1
Ras Nouadhibou C Maur 76A2
Ra's Nuh C Pak 34E3
Ra's Ormara C Pak 34E3
Ra's Sharwayn C S Yemen 33F3
Rasshua I USSR 38J2
Ra's Shu'ab C Socotra 33F4
Rass Kaboudia Pt Tunisia 77E1
Rasskazovo USSR 25G5
Ra's Tanāqib C S Arabia 33E1
Ra's Tannūrah S Arabia 33F1
Rastatt W Germ 20B3
Ra's 'Tsa C Yemen 32D3
Ras Uarc = Cabo Tres Foreas
Ras Um Seisaban Mt Jordan 31C4
Ras Xaafuun C Somalia 75E3
Ratangarh India 35C3
Rat Buri Thai 43B3
Rath India 35D3
Ratherow E Germ 20C2
Rathlin I N Ire 14B4
Rat I USA 56B6
Rat Is USA 56B6
Ratlām India 35C4
Ratnāgiri India 36A1
Ratnapura Sri Lanka 36C3
Ratno USSR 21E2
Raton USA 62B2
Rattenberg Austria 17D1
Rättvik Sweden 12H6
Rau I Indon 45C2
Raub Malay 44F7
Rauch Arg 72D3
Raukumara Range Mts NZ 51C1
Raul Soares Brazil 73D3
Rauma Fin 12J6
Raurkela India 37B3
Ravānsar Iran 34B2
Rāvar Iran 34D2
Rava Russkaya USSR 21E2
Ravena USA 60D1
Ravenna Italy 17E2
Ravensburg W Germ 20B3
Ravenshoe Aust 48D2
Ravi R Pak 35C2
Ravno USSR 21F2
Rawalpindi Pak 35C2
Rawāndiz Iraq 25G3
Rawicz Pol 20D2
Rawlinna Aust 48B4
Rawlins USA 54C2
Rawñdiz Iraq 30D2
Rawson Arg 69D6
Rawu China 37E2
Raya Mt Indon 44D3
Rāyadurg India 36B2
Rāyagada India 36C1
Rayak Leb 31D2
Ray,C Can 53N5
Raychikhinsk USSR 41B2
Raydah Yemen 32D3
Rāyen Iran 34D3
Raymond Can 64D1
Raymond New Hampshire USA 60E1
Raymond Washington USA 64B1
Raymond Terrace Aust 50D2
Raymondville USA 63F4
Ray Mts USA 56H2
Rayon Mexico 67C1
Raysūt Oman 33F3
Razan Iran 34B1
Razdel'naya USSR 21G3
Razdol'noye USSR 41C3
Razgrad Bulg 23F2
Razim L Rom 23F2
Rdbyhavn Den 12G8
Reading Eng 15E6
Reading USA 60C2
Read Island Can 52G3
Readsboro USA 60D1
Real de Padre Arg 72B2
Realicó Arg 72C3
Rebiana Well Libya 75B2
Rebiana Sand Sea Libya 75B2
Reboly USSR 12L6
Rebun-tō I Japan 41E2
Recherche,Arch of the Is Aust 48B4
Rechitsa USSR 21G2
Recife Brazil 71M5
Recifes da Pedra Grande Arch Brazil 73E2
Récifs D'Entrecasteaux Nouvelle Calédonie 49F2
Recklinghausen W Germ 16D1
Reconquista Arg 72D1
Recreo Arg 72C1
Red R Can/USA 57C2
Red R USA 63D3
Redang I Malay 43C4
Red Bank New Jersey USA 60C2
Red Bank Tennessee USA 61B1
Red Bluff USA 65B2
Red Bluff L USA 62B3
Redcar Eng 15E4
Redcliffe Aust 50D1
Red Cliffs Aust 50B2
Red Cloud USA 62C1
Red Deer Can 52G4
Redding USA 64B2
Redfield USA 57C3
Red Hills USA 62C2
Red L USA 55D2
Red Lake Can 53J4
Red Lake R USA 57C2
Redlands USA 65C4
Red Lion USA 60B3
Red Lodge USA 64E1
Redmond USA 64B2
Red Oak USA 63C1
Redon France 18B2
Redoubt V USA 56H3
Red River Delta Vietnam 40B5
Red Sea Africa/Arabian Pen 28B3
Redstone R Can 56N3
Redwater Can 52G4
Red Wing USA 57D3
Redwood City USA 65B3
Redwood Falls USA 57C3
Reed City USA 58B2
Reedsport USA 64B2
Reedville USA 59D3
Reefton NZ 51B2
Refahiye Turk 30C2
Refugio USA 63F4
Regência Brazil 73E2
Regensburg W Germ 20C3
Reggane Alg 76C2
Reggio di Calabria Italy 22D3
Reggio Nell'Emilia Italy 17D2
Reghin Rom 23E1
Regina Can 52H4
Registan Region Afghan 34E2
Regocijo Mexico 67A1
Rehoboth Beach USA 59D3
Rehovot Israel 31C3
Reicito Ven 70E1
Reidsville USA 61D1
Reigate Eng 15E6
Reims France 16B2
Reinbeck USA 57D3
Reindeer L. Can 52H4
Reinosa Spain 19B1
Reisterstown USA 60B3
Reliance Can 52H3
Reliance USA 64E2
Relizane Alg 77C1
Remarkable,Mt Aust 50A2
Rembang Indon 44D4
Remeshk Iran 34D3
Remiremont France 16D2
Remscheid W Germ 16D1
Remsen USA 60C1
Rémuzat France 17A2
Rend L USA 58B3
Rendsburg W Germ 20B2
Renfrew Can 59D1
Rengat Indon 44B3
Rengo Chile 72A2
Reni USSR 21F3
Renk Sudan 78D2
Renland Pen Greenland 53Q2
Renmark Aust 50B2
Rennell I Solomon Is 49F2
Rennes France 18B2
Reno USA 65C3
Reno R Italy 17D2
Renovo USA 60B2
Rensselaer USA 60D1
Renton USA 64B1
Reo Indon 45B4
Réo Upper Volta 77F3
Repetek USSR 34E1
Repki USSR 21G2
Reprêsa de Furnas Dam Brazil 73C3
Reprêsa Três Marias Dam Brazil 73C2
Republic USA 64C1
Republican R USA 62C1
Republic of Ireland NW Europe 13B3
Repulse Bay Can 53K3
Rergus Falls USA 57C2
Réservoir Baskatong Res Can 59D1
Réservoir Cabonga Res Can 59D1
Réservoir Decelles Res Can 59D1
Réservoir Dozois Res Can 59D1
Réservoire Cabonga Res Can 53L5
Réservoire Gouin Res Can 53L5
Réservoire Manicouagan Res Can 55G1
Reshteh-ye Alborz Mts Iran 34C1
Reshui China 40A2
Resistencia Arg 69E3
Resita Rom 23E1
Resolute Can 53J2
Resolution I NZ 51A3
Resolution Island Can 53M3
Restinga Seca Brazil 72E1
Retamito Arg 72B2
Rethel France 16C2
Réthimnon Greece 23E3
Reunion I Indian O 46D6
Reus Spain 19C1
Reuss R Switz 17C1
Reutlingen W Germ 16E2
Reutte Austria 17D1
Revda USSR 24L5
Revelstoke Can 52G4
Revillagigedo Is Mexico 66A3
Revillagigedo I USA 56M4
Revin France 16C2
Revivim Israel 31C3
Rewa India 37B3
Rewari India 35D3
Rexburg USA 64D2
Reykjavik Iceland 12A2
Reynoldsville USA 60A2
Reynosa Mexico 66C2
Rezé France 18B2
Rezekne USSR 21F1
Rezh USSR 24L4
Rhātikon Mts Austria/Switz 17C1
Rhazīr Republic Leb 31C1
Rheda Wiedenbrück W Germ 16E1
Rhein R W Europe 20B2
Rheine W Germ 20B2
Rheinfielden Switz 17B1
Rheinland Pfalz Region W Germ 18D2
Rheinwaldhorn Mt Switz 17C1
Rhine = Rhein
Rhinebeck USA 60D2
Rhinelander USA 58B1
Rho Italy 17C2
Rhode Island State USA 59E2
Rhode Island Sd USA 60E2
Rhodes = Ródhos
Rhodes Peak Mt USA 64D1
Rhône R France 18C3
Rhyl Wales 15D5
Riachão do Jacuipe Brazil 71L6
Ria de Arosa B Spain 19A1
Ria de Betanzos B Spain 19A1
Ria de Corcubion B Spain 19A1
Ria de Lage B Spain 19A1
Ria de Sta Marta B Spain 19A1
Ria de Vigo B Spain 19A1
Riāsi Pak 35C2
Ribadeo Spain 19A1
Ribas do Rio Pardo Brazil 73B3
Ribauè Mozam 79D5
Ribble R Eng 15D5
Ribeira Brazil 73C3
Ribeirão Prêto Brazil 73C3
Riberala Bol 70E6
Riccione Italy 17E3
Rice L Can 59D2
Rice Lake USA 58A1
Richao de Santana Brazil 73D1
Richards I Can 56L2
Richardson USA 63C3
Richardson Mts Can 56L2
Richfield USA 65D3
Richfield Springs USA 60C1
Richland USA 64C1
Richlands USA 58C3
Richmond Kentucky USA 58C3
Richmond New South Wales Aust 50D2
Richmond NZ 51B2
Richmond Queensland Aust 48D3
Richmond Virginia USA 59D3
Richmond Range Mts NZ 51B2
Richmondville USA 60C1
Rideau,L Can 59D2
Ridgeland USA 61C2
Ridgway USA 60A2
Riding Mountain Nat Pk Can 57B1
Riecito Ven 68D4
Rienza R Italy 17D1
Riesa E Germ 20C2
Riesco I Chile 69B8
Rieti Italy 22C2
Riez France 17B3
Rif Mts Mor 19B2
Rifle USA 62A2
Riga USSR 21E1
Riga,G of USSR 24C4
Rīgān Iran 34D3
Rigby USA 64D2
Riggins USA 64C1
Rigolet Can 53N4
Riihimaki Fin 12J6
Rijeka Yugos 22C1
Rikuzen-Tanaka Japan 42D3
Rima R Nig 77H3
Rimbo Sweden 12H7
Rimini Italy 17E2
Rîmnicu Sărat Rom 23F1
Rîmnicu Vîlcea Rom 23E1
Rimouski Can 55G2
Rincón de Romos Mexico 67B1
Ringkøbing Den 12F7
Riñihue Chile 72A3
Rinja I Indon 45A4
Rio Benito Eq Guinea 78A3
Rio Branco Brazil 70E5
Rio Branco Urug 72E2
Rio Branco do Sul Brazil 73C4
Rio Bravo Mexico 63F4
Rio Bravo del Norte R USA/Mexico 66B1
Rio Brilhante Brazil 73B3
Rio Bueno Chile 72A4
Riochacha Colombia 70D1
Rio Claro Brazil 73C3
Rio Claro Trinidad 68L1
Rio Colorado Arg 72C3
Rio Cuarto Arg 72C2
Rio de Jacuipe Brazil 71L6
Rio de Janeiro Brazil 73D3
Rio de Janeiro State Brazil 73D3
Rio de la Plata Estuary Arg/Urug 72D2
Rio Gallegos Arg 69C8
Rio Grande Arg 69C8
Rio Grande Brazil 72E2
Rio Grande Mexico 67B1
Rio Grande Nic 68A4
Rio Grande R Nicaragua 66D3
Rio Grande R USA/Mexico 66B2
Rio Grande City USA 63F4
Rio Grande de Santiago Mexico 67B1
Rio Grande do Norte State Brazil 71L5
Rio Grande do Sul State Brazil 72E1
Rio Grande Rise Atlantic O 74G6
Riohacha Colombia 68C4
Riom France 18C2
Riombamba Ecuador 70C4
Rio Mulatos Bol 70E7
Rio Negro Brazil 73C4
Río Negro State Arg 72B4
Rio Pardo Brazil 69F3
Rio Tercero Arg 72C2
Rio Theodore Roosevelt R Brazil 70F6
Rio Turbio Arg 69B8
Rio Verde Brazil 73B2
Rio Verde Mexico 67B1
Rio Verde de Mato Grosso Brazil 73B2
Ripley Ohio USA 58C3
Ripley Tennessee USA 61B1
Ripley West Virginia USA 58C3
Ripon Eng 15E4
Rishiri-tō I Japan 41E2
Rishon le Zion Israel 31C3
Rising Sun USA 60B3
Risle R France 16A2
Risør Nor 12F7
Ritchie's Arch Andaman Is 36E2
Ritenberk Greenland 53N2
Ritzville USA 64C1
Rivadavia Arg 72B2
Rivadavia Chile 72A1
Rivadavia Gonzalez Moreno Arg 72C3
Riva de Garda Italy 17D2
Rivas Nic 70A1
Rivera Arg 72C3
Rivera Urug 72D2
River Cess Lib 76B4
Riverhead USA 60D2
Riverina Aust 50B3
River Junction USA 59E2
Rivers State Nig 77H4
Riversdale NZ 51A3
Riverside USA 65C4
Riverton NZ 51A3
Riverton USA 64E2
Rives France 17A2
Riviera Beach USA 61E4
Rivière aux Feuilles R Can 53L4
Rivière de la Baleine R Can 53M4
Rivière-du-Loup Can 59F1
Rivière du Petit Mècatina R Can 53M4
Rivigny-sur-Ornain France 16C2
Riwon N Korea 42A2
Riyadh S Arabia 33E2
Rize Turk 30D1
Rizhao China 40D2
Rizhskiy Zaliv = Riga,G of
Rizokaipaso Cyprus 31C1
Rjukan Nor 12F7
Roanes Pen Can 53K2
Roanne France 18C2
Roanoke Alabama USA 61B2
Roanoke Virginia USA 59D3
Roanoke R USA 59D3

Roanoke Rapids St. Paul

Roanoke Rapids USA 61D1
Roan Plat USA 65D3
Roberts USA 64D2
Roberts Creek Mt USA 65C3
Robertsforz Sweden 12J6
Robert S Kerr Res USA 63D2
Robertsport Lib 76A4
Roberval Can 53L5
Robinvale Aust 50B2
Robstown USA 63F4
Roca Partida I Mexico 66A3
Rocas I Atlantic O 74G5
Rocas I Brazil 71M4
Rocca San Casciano Italy 17D2
Rocha Urug 72E2
Rochdale Eng 15D5
Rochedo Brazil 73B2
Rochefort France 18B2
Rochelle USA 58B2
Rocher River Can 52G3
Rochester Aust 50B3
Rochester Can 53L5
Rochester Eng 15F6
Rochester Minnesota USA 57D3
Rochester New Hampshire USA 60E1
Rochester New York USA 60B1
Rock R USA 58B2
Rockford USA 58B2
Rock Hill USA 61C2
Rockingham USA 61D2
Rock Island USA 58A2
Rockland USA 58B1
Rocklands Res Aust 50B3
Rockledge USA 61C3
Rockport USA 63F4
Rock Rapids USA 57C3
Rock River USA 57A3
Rock Springs Montana USA 57A2
Rocksprings Texas USA 62B3
Rock Springs Wyoming USA 64E2
Rocks Pt NZ 51B2
Rock,The Aust 50C3
Rockville Connecticut USA 60D2
Rockville Indiana USA 58B3
Rockville Maryland USA 60B3
Rockwood USA 59F1
Rocky Ford USA 62B2
Rocky Island L Can 58C1
Rocky Mount USA 61D1
Rocky Mountain Nat Pk USA 62A1
Rocky Mts Can/USA 54B1
Rocky Pt USA 56F3
Rødbyhavn Den 20C2
Rodeo Arg 72B2
Rodez France 18C3
Ródhos Greece 23F3
Ródhos I Greece 23F3
Rodi Garganico Italy 22D2
Rodopi Planina Mts Bulg 23E2
Roebourne Aust 48A3
Roer R Neth 16D1
Roermond Neth 16C1
Roeselare Belg 16B1
Roes Welcome Sd Can 53K3
Rogachev USSR 21F2
Rogers USA 63D2
Rogers City USA 58C1
Rogers,Mt USA 58C3
Rogerson USA 64D2
Rogue R USA 64B2
Rohn Pak 35B3
Rohtak India 35D3
Roja USSR 21E1
Rolândia Brazil 73B3
Rolla USA 63D2
Rollins USA 64D1
Roma Aust 50C1
Roma Italy 22C2
Romagna Region Italy 17D2
Romagnano Italy 17C2
Romain,C USA 61D2
Roman Rom 23F1
Romanche Gap Atlantic O 74H4
Romang I Indon 45C4
Romania Republic E Europe 25C6
Romano,C USA 61E4
Romans sur Isère France 18D2
Romanzof,C USA 56E3
Romanzof Mts USA 56K2
Romblon Phil 45F8
Rome = Roma
Rome Georgia USA 61B2
Rome New York USA 60C1
Rome USA 59D2
Romilly-sur-Seine France 18C2
Rommani Mor 77A2
Romney USA 59D3
Romny USSR 25E5
Rømø I Den 20B1
Romont Switz 17B1
Romoratin France 18C2
Rompin Malay 44G7
Rompin R Malay 44G7
Ronco Italy 17D2
Ronda Spain 19A2
Rondônia Brazil 70F6
Rondônia State Brazil 70F6
Rondonópolis Brazil 73B2
Rong'an China 40B4
Rongchang China 40B4
Rongcheng China 40E2
Rongjiang China 40B4
Rong Jiang R China 40B4
Rongklang Range Mts Burma 43A1
Rønne Denmark 12G7
Ronneby Sweden 12H7
Ronne Ice Shelf Ant 80F2
Ronse Belg 16B1
Ronthieu Region France 16A1
Roof Butte Mt USA 54C3
Roorkee India 35D3
Roosendaal Neth 16C1
Roosevelt USA 65D2
Roosevelt I Ant 80E
Root R Can 56Q3
Root R USA 57D3
Roper R Aust 48C2
Roquevaire France 17A3
Roraima State Brazil 70F3
Roraime Mt Ven 70F2
Røros Nor 24A3
Rorschach Switz 17C1
Rørvik Nor 12G6
Ros' R USSR 21G3
Rosalie Dominica 69Q2
Rosamorada Mexico 67A1
Rosario Arg 72C2
Rosário Brazil 71K4
Rosario Mexico 67A1
Rosario Par 73A3
Rosario Urug 72D2
Rosario del Tala Arg 72D2
Rosário do Sul Brazil 72E2
Rosário Oeste Brazil 73A1
Roscoe USA 60C2
Roscoff France 18B2
Roscommon Irish Rep 13B3
Roscrea Irish Rep 15B5
Roseau Dominica 69Q2
Rosebery Aust 50E3
Rosebud USA 57A2
Roseburg USA 64B2
Rosenberg USA 63C4
Rosenheim W Germ 20C3
Rosetown Can 52H4
Roseville USA 65B3
Rosiorii de Verde Rom 23E2
Roskilde Den 12G7
Roslavl' USSR 24E5
Roslyatino USSR 24G4
Ross NZ 51B2
Ross R Can 56M3
Rossan Pt Irish Rep 13B3
Rossano Italy 22D3
Ross Barnet Res USA 63E3
Rosseau L L Can 59D1
Rossel I Solomon Is 49E2
Ross Ice Shelf Ant 80E
Rossiyskaya S.F.S.R. Republic USSR 24E4
Ross L USA 64B1
Rosslare Irish Rep 15B5
Ross,Mt NZ 51C2
Rosso Maur 76A3
Ross-on-Wye Eng 15D6
Rossosh USSR 25F6
Ross River Can 52E3
Ross S Ant 80F6
Rostāq Iran 34C3
Rostock E Germ 20C2
Rostov USSR 24F4
Rostov-na-Donu USSR 25F6
Roswell Georgia USA 61C2
Roswell New Mexico USA 62B3
Rota Pacific O 39H5
Rotenburg Hessen W Germ 16E1
Rotenburg Niedersachsen W Germ 20B2
Rothaar-Geb Region W Germ 16E1
Rothera Base Ant 80G3
Rotherham Eng 15E5
Rothesay Scot 14C4
Roti I Indon 45B5
Roto Aust 50C2
Rotoiti,L NZ 51B2
Rotoroa,L NZ 51B2
Rotorua NZ 51C1
Rotorua,L NZ 51C1
Rottenburg W Germ 16E2
Rotterdam Neth 20A2
Rottweil W Germ 16E2
Rotuma I Fiji 49G2
Roubaix France 16B1
Rouen France 18C2
Rough Oilfield N Sea 15F5
Roulers = Roeselare
Round I Mauritius 79F6
Round Mt Aust 50D2
Roundup USA 64E1
Rousay I Scot 14D2
Roussillon Region France 18C3
Rouyn Can 59D1
Rovaniemi Fin 12K5
Rovereto Italy 17D2
Rovigo Italy 17D2
Rovinj Yugos 22C1
Rovno USSR 25D5
Row'ān Iran 34B1
Rowena Aust 50C1
Rowley I Can 53L3
Rowley Shoals Aust 48A2
Roxas Palawan Phil 45E8
Roxas Panay Phil 45F8
Roxboro USA 61D1
Roxburgh NZ 51A3
Roy USA 64E1
Royal Canal Irish Rep 15B5
Royal Leamington Spa Eng 15E5
Royal Oak USA 58C2
Royal Tunbridge Wells Eng 15F6
Royan France 18B2
Roye France 16B2
Royston Eng 15E5
Rožňava Czech 21E3
Rozoy France 16B2
Rros Nor 12G6
Rtishchevo USSR 25G5
Rt Kamenjak C Yugos 17E2
Ruaha Nat Pk Tanz 79D4
Ruahine Range Mts NZ 51C1
Ruapehu,Mt NZ 51C1
Rub al Khālī Desert S Arabia 33D3
Rubha Hunish Scot 14B3
Rubinéia Brazil 73B3
Rubtsoysk USSR 26K4
Ruby USA 56G3
Ruby Mts USA 65C2
Rudan Iran 34D3
Rudbar Afghan 34E2
Rūdbār Iran 34B1
Rudnaya Pristan' USSR 41D3
Rudnya USSR 21G2
Rudnyy USSR 41C3
Rudoka Planina Mt Yugos 23E2
Rudolf,L Kenya/Eth 78D3
Rudong China 40E3
Rudyard USA 58C1
Rue France 16A1
Rufa'a Sudan 32B4
Ruffec France 18C2
Rufiji R Tanz 79D4
Rufino Arg 72C2
Rufisque Sen 76A3
Rufunsa Zambia 79C5
Rugby Eng 15E5
Rugby USA 57B2
Rügen I E Germ 12G8
Ruhr R W Germ 16D1
Ruhr R W Germ 20B2
Ruijin China 40D4
Rujen Mt Bulg/Yugos 23E2
Rukwa L Tanz 79D4
Rum I Scot 14B3
Ruma Yugos 23D1
Rumāh S Arabia 33E1
Rumbek Sudan 78C3
Rum Cay I Caribbean 68C2
Rumford USA 59E2
Rumilly France 17A2
Rum Jungle Aust 48C2
Rumoi Japan 42D2
Rumphi Malawi 79D5
Runanga NZ 51B2
Runaway,C NZ 51C1
Rundu Namibia 79B5
Rungwa Tanz 79D4
Rungwa R Tanz 79D4
Rungwe Mt Tanz 79D4
Ruoqiang China 29G2
Ruo Shui R China 38D2
Rupat I Indon 44F7
Rupea Rom 23F1
Rupert USA 64D2
Rupert R Can 53L4
Rur R W Germ 16D1
Rurrenabaque Bol 70E6
Rusape Zim 79D5
Ruse Bulg 23F2
Rushville Illinois USA 58A2
Rushville Nebraska USA 57B3
Rushworth Aust 50B3
Rusk USA 63C3
Ruskin USA 61E4
Russell NZ 51B1
Russell USA 62C2
Russellville Alabama USA 61B2
Russellville Arkansas USA 63D2
Russellville Kentucky USA 58B3
Russian R USA 65B3
Russian Socialist Federated Soviet Rep USSR 24C5
Rustavi USSR 30E1
Rustenburg S Africa 79C6
Ruston USA 63D3
Rutana Burundi 78C4
Ruteng Indon 45B4
Ruth USA 65C3
Rüthen W Germ 16E1
Rutla Mexico 67C2
Rutland USA 59E2
Rutland I Andaman Is 36E2
Rutog China 35D2
Ruvu = Pangani
Ruvuma R Tanz/Mozam 79E5
Ruwenzori Range Mts Uganda/Zaïre 78D3
Ruya R Zim 79D5
Ružomberok Czech 21D3
Rwanda Republic Africa 78C4
Ryazan' USSR 24F5
Ryazhsk USSR 24G5
Rybinsk USSR 24F4
Rybinskoye Vodokhranilishche Res USSR 24F4
Rybnitsa USSR 21F3
Ryde Eng 15E6
Rye Eng 15F6
Rye Patch Res USA 64C2
Ryl'sk USSR 25E5
Ryn Peskt Desert USSR 25H6
Ryoju S Korea 42A3
Ryōtsu Japan 41D4
Ryskany USSR 21F3
Ryūkyū Retto Arch Japan 38F4
Rzeszów Pol 21E2
Rzhev USSR 24E4

S

Sa'ādatābād Iran 34C2
Saad el Aali Dam Egypt 32B2
Saale R E Germ 20C2
Saanen Switz 17B1
Saar R W Germ 16D2
Saarbrücken W Germ 16D2
Saarburg W Germ 16D2
Saaremaa I USSR 12J7
Saarland State W Germ 16D2
Saarlouis W Germ 16D2
Saavedra Arg 72C3
Saba'a Egypt 31B3
Šabac Yugos 23D2
Sabadell Spain 19C1
Sabae Japan 42C3
Sabah State Malay 44E1
Sabak,C USA 56A6
Sabal Indon 45B3
Sabanalarga Colombia 68C4
Sabang Indon 44A1
Sabang Indon 45A2
Sabari R India 36C1
Sabastiya Israel 31C2
Sabaya Bol 70E7
Sab'Bi'ār Syria 30C3
Sabderat Eth 32C3
Sabhā Jordan 31D2
Sabhā Libya 75A2
Sabi R Zim 79D6
Sabinas Mexico 66B2
Sabinas Hidalgo Mexico 66B2
Sabine R USA 63C3
Sabine L USA 63D4
Sabkhat Maṭṭi Salt Marsh UAE 33F2
Sabkhet El Bardawîl Lg Egypt 31B3
Sablayan Phil 45F8
Sable,C Can 53M5
Sable,C USA 61E4
Sable I Can 53M5
Sabzevār Iran 34D1
Sacajawea Peak USA 64C1
Sacandaga Res USA 60C1
Sac City USA 57D3
Sachigo R Can 55D1
Sach'on S Korea 42A3
Sachs Harbour Can 52F2
Sacile Italy 17E2
Säckingen W Germ 17B1
Saco Maine USA 59E2
Saco Montana USA 57A2
Sacramento USA 54A3
Sacramento Mts USA 54C3
Sacramento V USA 65B2
Sacramento Mts USA 62A3
Sa'dah Yemen 32D3
Sadanski Bulg 23E2
Sadh Oman 33G3
Sadiya India 37E2
Sado R Port 19A2
Sado-shima I Japan 41D4
Sādri India 35C3
Safad = Zefat
Safed Koh Mts Afghan 35A2
Safer Afghan 34E2
Saffle Sweden 12G7
Safford USA 65E4
Safi Jordan 30C3
Safi Mor 77A2
Safidabeh Iran 34E2
Şāfītā Syria 31D1
Safonovo USSR 21G1
Safwān Iraq 30E3
Saga China 37C2
Saga Japan 42B4
Sagaing Burma 43B1
Sagami-nada B Japan 42C4
Sāgar India 35D4
Sagavan Ktok R USA 56J2
Sag Harbour USA 60D2
Saginaw USA 58C2
Saginaw B USA 58C2
Saglek B Can 53M4
Saglouc Can 53L3
Sagŏ-ri S Korea 42A3
Saguache USA 62A2
Sagua de Tánamo Cuba 68B2
Sagua la Grande Cuba 68B2
Saguenay R Can 53L5
Sagunto Spain 19B2
Sahāb Jordan 31D3
Sahagún Spain 19A1
Sahara Desert N Africa 76C2
Saharanpur India 35D3
Sahiwal Pak 35C2
Şahrā al Hijārah Desert Region Iraq 30D3
Sahra esh Sharqiya Desert Region Egypt 32B1
Sahuayo Mexico 67B1
Sahyun Hist Site Syria 31D1
Saibai I Aust 48D1
Saïda Alg 77C2
Saïda Leb 31C2
Sa'īdabad Iran 34D3
Saidia Mor 19B2
Saidpur India 37C2
Saidu Pak 35C2
Saigō Japan 42B3
Saigon Viet 43D3
Saiha India 37D3
Saihan Tal China 38E2
Saijo Japan 42B4
Saiki Japan 41C5
Saimaa L Fin 24D3
Sain Alto Mexico 67B1
Saindak Pak 34E3
St Abb's Head Pt Scot 14D4
St Albans Eng 15E6
St Albans Vermont USA 59E2
St Albans West Virginia USA 58C3
St Albans Head C Eng 15D6
St Amand-les-Eaux France 16B1
St Amand-Mont Rond France 18C2
St-Amour France 17A1
St André C Madag 79E5
St-André-de-l'Eure France 16A2
St Andrew B USA 61B3
St Andrews Scot 14D3
St Andrew Sd USA 61C2
Ste Anne Can 57C2
Ste Anne de Beaupré Can 59E1
St Ann's Bay Jamaica 68H1
St Anthony Can 53N4
St Anthony USA 64D2
St Arnaud Aust 50B3
St Augustine USA 61C3
St Austell Eng 15C6
St-Avold France 16D2
St Bees Head Pt Eng 15D4
St Boniface Can 57C2
St-Bonnet France 17B2
St Brides B Wales 15C6
St-Brieuc France 18B2
St-Calais France 16A3
St Catharines Can 59D2
St Catherine,Mt Grenada 68M2
St Catherines I USA 61C2
St Catherines Pt Eng 15E6
St Chamond France 18C2
St Charles Idaho USA 64D2
St Charles Missouri USA 63D2
St Clair USA 58C2
St Clair,L USA/Can 58C2
St Clair Shores USA 58C2
St Claud France 18D2
St Cloud USA 57D2
Ste Croix Switz 17B1
St Croix I Caribbean 68E3
St Croix R USA 58A1
St Croix R USA/Can 59F1
St Croix Falls USA 58A1
St Davids Head Pt Wales 15C6
St Denis France 16B2
St Denis Réunion 79F6
St-Dié France 16D2
St Dizier France 16C2
St Elena B S Africa 79B7
St Elias,Mt USA 56K3
St Elias Mts Can 56L3
Saintes France 18B2
St Étienne France 18C2
St Étienne-de-Tinée France 17B2
St-Félicien Can 59E1
St-Florentin France 16B2
St Francis USA 62B2
St Francis R USA 63D2
St. Francis,C S Africa 79C7
St Gallen Switz 17C1
St-Gaudens France 18C3
St George Aust 50C1
St George South Carolina USA 61C2
St George Utah USA 65D3
St George I Alaska USA 56E4
St George I Florida USA 61C3
St Georgen im Schwarzwald W Germ 16E2
St George,Pt USA 64B2
St-Georges Can 59E1
St George's Grenada 68E4
St Georges Chan Irish Rep/Wales 15B5
St Georges Chan PNG 49E1
St Germain-du-Bois France 17A1
St German-en-laye France 16A2
St-Gervais France 17B2
St Gotthard P Switz 17C1
St Govans Head Pt Wales 15C6
St Helena I Atlantic O 74H5
St Helena Sd USA 61C2
St Helens Aust 50E3
St Helens Eng 15D5
St Helens USA 64B1
St Helens,Mt USA 64B1
St Helier Jersey 18B2
St Hippolyte France 17B1
St-Hubert Belg 16C1
St-Hyacinthe Can 53L5
St Ignace USA 58C1
St Ignace I Can 58B1
St Ives Eng 15C6
St James Minnesota USA 57D3
St James Missouri USA 63D2
St. James,C Can 52E4
St Jean Can 59E1
St Jean-d'Angely France 18B2
St-Jean-de-Losne France 17A1
St-Jean-de-Maurienne France 17B2
St-Jean,L Can 59E1
St-Jérôme Can 59E1
St Joe USA 64C1
St Johann im Pongau Austria 17E1
Saint John Can 53M5
St John R USA Can 59F1
St Johns Arizona USA 65E4
St John's Can 53N5
St Johns Michigan USA 58C2
St Johns R USA 61C3
St Johnsbury USA 59E2
St Johnsville USA 60C1
St-Joseph Can 59E1
St Joseph Louisiana USA 63D3
St Joseph Michigan USA 58B2
St Joseph Missouri USA 63D2
St Joseph Trinidad 68L1
St Joseph R USA 58C2
St Joseph I Can 58C1
St Joseph I USA 63F4
St Joseph,L Can 53J4
St Julien France 17B1
St-Junien France 18C2
St-Just-en-Chaussée France 16B2
St Kilda I Scot 14A3
St Kitts I Caribbean 68E3
St-Laurent France 17A1
St Lawrence R Can 53M5
Saint Lawrence,G of Can 53M5
St Lawrence I USA 56D3
St Lawrence Seaway Can/USA 59D2
St Leonard Can 59F1
St Lô France 18B2
St Louis Sen 76A3
St Louis USA 58A3
St-Loup-sur-Semou France 16D3
St Lucia I Caribbean 68E4
St Lucia,C S Africa 79D6
St Lucia,L S Africa 79D6
St Magnus B Scot 14E1
St Malo France 18B2
St Marcellin France 17A2
Ste Marie C Madag 79E6
Ste-Marie-aux-Mines France 16D2
St Maries USA 64C1
St Martin I Caribbean 68E3
St-Martin-Vésubie France 17B2
St Mary,Mt PNG 48D1
St Mary Peak Mt Aust 50A2
St Marys Aust 50E3
St Marys USA 59D2
St Marys I UK 15B7
St Marys R USA 61C2
Saint Mathias Group Is PNG 48E1
St Matthew I USA 56D3
St Maurice R Can 59E1
St-Maximin France 17A3
Ste-Menehould France 16C2
St Michael USA 56F3
St Michaels USA 60B3
St-Michel France 17B2
St-Mihiel France 16C2
St Moritz Switz 17C1
St-Nazaire France 18B2
St-Niklaas Belg 16C1
St-Omer France 16B1
St Pascal Can 59F1
St. Paul Can 52G4

Santos Shahdol

Santos Brazil 73C3
Santos Dumont Brazil 73D3
Santo Tomas Mexico 65C4
Santo Tomé Arg 72D1
San Valentin Mt Chile 69B7
San Vicente Chile 72A2
San Vicente Mexico 67B1
San Vito al Tagliamento Italy 17E2
Sanza Pomba Angola 79B4
São Borja Brazil 72D1
São Carlos Brazil 73C3
São Domingos Brazil 73C1
São Félix Mato Grosso Brazil 71H5
São Fidélis Brazil 73D3
São Francisco Brazil 73D2
São Francisco R Brazil 71L5
São Francisco de Assis Brazil 72D1
São Francisco do Sul Brazil 69G3
São Gabriel Brazil 72E2
São Gotardo Brazil 73C2
Sao Hill Tanz 79D4
São João da Barra Brazil 73D3
São João da Boa Vista Brazil 73C3
São João d'Aliança Brazil 73C1
São João da Ponte Brazil 73D2
São João del Rei Brazil 73D3
São João do Paraíso Brazil 73D2
São Joaquim da Barra Brazil 73C3
São Jorge I Açores 76A1
São José do Norte Brazil 72E2
São José do Rio Prêto Brazil 73C3
São José dos Campos Brazil 73C3
São José dos Pinhais Brazil 73C4
São Lourenço R Brazil 73A2
São Lourenço do Sul Brazil 72E2
São Luis Brazil 71K4
Sao Luis Gonzaga Brazil 72E1
Sao Marcos R Brazil 73C2
São Maria do Suaçui Brazil 73D2
São Mateus Brazil 73E2
São Mateus R Brazil 73D2
São Miguel I Açores 76A1
São Miguel de Araguaia Brazil 73B1
Saône R France 18C2
São Nicolau I Cape Verde 76A4
São Onofre R Brazil 73D1
São Paulo Brazil 73C3
São Paulo State Brazil 73B3
São Pedro do Sul Brazil 72E1
São Raimundo Nonato Brazil 71K5
São Romão Brazil 73C2
São Sebastia do Paraiso Brazil 73C3
São Sepé Brazil 72E2
São Simão Goias Brazil 73B2
São Simão Sao Paulo Brazil 73C3
São Tiago I Cape Verde 76A4
São Tomé I W Africa 76C4
São Tomé and Principe Republic W Africa 76C4
Saoura Watercourse Alg 76B2
Saouriuiná R Brazil 73A1
São Vicente Brazil 73C3
São Vincente I Cape Verde 76A4
Sápai Greece 23F2
Saparua Indon 45C3
Sape Indon 44E4
Sapele Nig 77H4
Sapporo Japan 41E3
Sapri Italy 22D2
Saprsborg Nor 12G7
Sapulpa USA 63C2
Saqqez Iran 34B1
Saquenay R Can 55F2
Sarāb Iran 25H8
Sarafa USSR 23F1
Sarajevo Yugos 23D2
Sarakhs Iran 34E1
Saraktash USSR 25K5
Sarala USSR 27K4
Saranac L USA 59E2
Saranac Lake USA 59E2
Sarandë Alb 23E3
Sarandi Brazil 72E1
Sarandi del Yi Urug 72D2
Sarandi Grande Urug 72D2
Sarangani Is Phil 45G9
Saranpaul' USSR 24L3
Saransk USSR 24H5
Saranza Italy 17C2
Sara Peak Mt Nig 77H4
Sarapul USSR 24J4
Sarasota USA 61E4
Saratoga USA 57A3
Saratoga Springs USA 60D1
Saratok Malay 44D2
Saratov USSR 25H5
Saratovskoye Vodokhranilishche Res USSR 25H5
Saraykoy Turk 30A2
Sarbāz Iran 34E3
Sarbisheh Iran 34D2
Sarca R Italy 17D1
Sardalais Libya 75A2
Sar Dasht Iran 34B1
Sardegna I Medit S 22B2
Sardinia = Sardegna
Sardis L USA 63E3
Sarektjåkkå Mt Sweden 12H5
Sarenga Eth 32C4
Sargodha Pak 35C2
Sarh Chad 78B3
Sārī Iran 34C1
Sarida R Isreal 31C2
Sarikamiş Turk 30D1
Sarina Aust 48D3
Sarine R Switz 17B1
Sar-i-Pul Afghan 35B1
Sarir Libya 75B2
Sarir Tibesti Desert Libya 75A2
Sariwŏn N Korea 41B4
Sark I UK 18B2
Şarkişla Turk 30C2
Sarmi Indon 39G7
Sarmiento Arg 69C7
Särna Sweden 12G6
Sarnen Switz 17C1
Sarnia Can 58C2
Sarny USSR 21F2
Saroaq Greenland 53N2
Sarobi Afghan 35B2
Sarolangun Indon 44B3
Saronikós Kólpos G Greece 23E3
Saronno Italy 17C2
Saros Körfezi B Turk 23F2
Saroto USSR 24M2
Sarralbe France 16D2
Sarrebourg France 16D2
Sarreguemines France 16D2
Sarre-Union France 16D2
Sarrion Spain 19B1
Sartanahu Pak 35B3
Sartène Corse 22B2
Sarthe Department France 16A3
Sarthe R France 18B2
Sārūt Syria 31D1
Sarvan Iran 34E3
Sarykamys USSR 25J6
Sarysu R USSR 26H5
Sasarām India 37B3
Sasebo Japan 41B5
Sashi R Botswana 79C6
Saskatchewan Province Can 52H4
Saskatchewan R Can 52H4
Saskatoon Can 52H4
Saskylakh USSR 27N2
Sasovo USSR 24G5
Sassandra Ivory Coast 76B4
Sassandra R Ivory Coast 76B4
Sassari Sardegna 22B2
Sassnitz E Germ 20C2
Sassuolo Italy 17D2
Sastre Arg 72C2
Sasuna Japan 42A4
Sātāra India 36A1
Satellite B Can 52G2
Satengar Is Indon 44E4
Säter Sweden 12H6
Satilla R USA 61C2
Satka USSR 24K4
Satluj R India 35D2
Satna India 37B3
Sātpura Range Mts India 35C4
Satu Mare Rom 23E1
Satu Mare Rom 25C6
Sauce Arg 72D2
Sauda Nor 12F7
Saudi Arabia Kingdom Arabian Pen 28C3
Sauer R W Germ/Lux 16D2
Sauerland Region W Germ 16D1
Sauðárkrókur Iceland 12B1
Saugatuck USA 58B2
Saugerties USA 60D1
Sauk Centre USA 57D2
Sauk City USA 58B2
Sault Sainte Marie Can 53K5
Sault Ste Marie Can 58C1
Sault Ste Marie USA 58C1
Saumlaki Indon 39G7
Saumur France 18B2
Saurimo Angola 79C4
Sauteurs Grenada 68M2
Sava R Yugos 23D2
Savai'i I Western Samoa 49H2
Savalou Benin 77G4
Savan R Iran 25H9
Savannah Georgia USA 61C2
Savannah Tennessee USA 61B1
Savannah R USA 61C2
Savannakhet Laos 43C2
Savanna la Mar Jamaica 68B3
Savant Lake Can 53J4
Savarane Laos 43D2
Savé Benin 77G4
Save R Mozam 79D6
Sāveh Iran 34C2
Saverne France 16D2
Savigliano Italy 17B2
Savigny France 16B2
Savinskiy USSR 24F3
Savio R Italy 17E3
Savoie Region France 18D2
Savona Italy 17C2
Savonlinna Fin 12K6
Savoonga USA 56D3
Savudrija Rtič Pt Yugos 17E2
Savukoski Fin 12K5
Savu S Indon 45B4
Saw Burma 43A1
Sawai Indon 45C3
Sawai Mādhopur India 35D3
Sawang Indon 44B2
Sawankhalok Thai 43C2
Sawara Japan 42D3
Sawatch Mts USA 62A2
Sawknah Libya 75A2
Sawtooth Mt USA 56J2
Sawtooth Range Mts USA 64C2
Sawu I Indon 48B2
Saxton USA 60A2
Say Niger 77G3
Sayghan Afghan 35B1
Sayhandulaan Mongolia 40B1
Sayh Hajmah Oman 33G3
Sayhūt S Yemen 33F2
Saykhin USSR 25H6
Saynshand Mongolia 38D2
Sayre Oklahoma USA 62C2
Sayre Pennsylvania USA 60B2
Sayula Mexico 67C2
Sayulita Mexico 67A1
Say-Utes USSR 25J7
Sayville USA 60D2
Sázava R Czech 20C3
Sbisseb R Alg 19C2
Scafell Pike Mt Eng 15D4
Scalloway Scot 14E1
Scapa Flow Sd Scot 14D2
Scarborough Can 59D2
Scarborough Eng 15E4
Scarborough Tobago 68E4
Scarp I Scot 14B2
Schaffhausen Switz 22B1
Scharding Austria 20C3
Scharteberg Mt W Germ 16D1
Schefferville Can 53M4
Schelde R Belg 16B1
Schell Creek Range Mts USA 65D3
Schenectady USA 60D1
Schertz USA 62C4
Schiedam Neth 16C1
Schio Italy 17D2
Schleiden W Germ 16D1
Schleswig W Germ 20B2
Schleswig Holstein State W Germ 20B2
Schoharie USA 60C1
Schouten Is PNG 48D1
Schramberg W Germ 16E2
Schreiber Can 53K5
Schurz USA 65C3
Schuykill Haven USA 60B2
Schuylkill R USA 60C2
Schwabische Alb Upland W Germ 20B3
Schwarzwald Mts W Germ 16E2
Schwarzwald Upland W Germ 20B3
Schwatka Mts USA 56G2
Schwaz Austria 17D1
Schweinfurt W Germ 20C2
Schwerin E Germ 20C2
Schwyz Switz 17C1
Sciacca Italy 22C3
Scilly Isles Is UK 15B7
Scioto R USA 58C3
Scobey USA 57A2
Scone Aust 50D2
Scoresby Sd Greenland 53Q2
Scotia Ridge Atlantic O 74F7
Scotia S Atlantic O 74F7
Scotland Country U K 14C3
Scott Base Ant 80F7
Scott City USA 62B2
Scott I Ant 80G6
Scott Inlet B Can 53L2
Scott,Mt USA 64B2
Scott Reef Timor S 48B2
Scottsbluff USA 57B3
Scottsboro USA 61B2
Scottsdale Aust 50E3
Scottsdale USA 65D4
Scranton USA 60C2
Scribner USA 57C3
Scuol Switz 17D1
Scutari = Shkodër
Seal R Can 52J4
Sea Lake Aust 50B3
Searchlight USA 65D3
Searcy USA 63D2
Seaside Oregon USA 64B1
Seaside Park USA 60C3
Seattle USA 64B1
Seba Indon 45B5
Sebago L L USA 59E2
Sebanga Indon 44B2
Sebez USSR 21F1
Sebring USA 61E4
Secchia R Italy 17D2
Secretary I NZ 51A3
Sedalia USA 63D2
Sedan France 16C2
Sedanka I USA 56E5
Seddonville NZ 51B2
Sede Boqer Israel 31C3
Sederot Israel 31C3
Sédhiou Sen 76A3
Sedom Israel 31C3
Sedona USA 65D4
Seeheim Namibia 79B6
Seelig,Mt Ant 80E
Sées France 16A2
Sefrou Mor 77B2
Sefton,Mt NZ 51B2
Segamat Malay 43C5
Segezha USSR 24E3
Segorbe Spain 19B2
Ségou Mali 76B3
Segovia = Coco
Segovia Spain 19B1
Segre R Spain 19C1
Seguam I USA 56D6
Seguam Pass USA 56D6
Séguéla Ivory Coast 76B4
Seguia el Hamra Watercourse Mor 76A2
Seguin USA 63C4
Segundo R Arg 72C2
Seguntur Indon 44E2
Segura R Spain 19B2
Sehwan Pak 35B3
Seiling USA 62C2
Seille R France 16D2
Seinäjoki Fin 12J6
Seine R Can 57D2
Seine R France 18C2
Seine-et-Marne Department France 16B2
Seine-Maritime Department France 16A2
Sekenke Tanz 78D4
Selah USA 64B1
Selaru I Indon 39G7
Selat Alas Str Indon 44E4
Selat Bangka Str Indon 44C3
Selat Berhala B Indon 44B3
Selat Dampier Str Indon 39G7
Selat Gaspar Str Indon 44C3
Selat Lombok Str Indon 44E4
Selat Mentawi Str Indon 44A3
Selat Sape Str Indon 44E4
Selat Sumba Str Indon 45B4
Selat Sunda Str Indon 44C4
Selat Wetar Chan Indon 45C4
Selawati I Indon 45D3
Selawik USA 56F2
Selawik R USA 56G2
Selawik L USA 56F2
Selby Eng 15E5
Selby USA 57C2
Selçuk Turk 23F3
Seldovia USA 56H4
Selebi-Pikwe Botswana 79C6
Selemdzha R USSR 41C1
Selemdzhinsk USSR 41C1
Selennyakh R USSR 27Q3
Selestat France 16D2
Selfoss Iceland 53Q3
Selfridge USA 57B2
Selima Oasis Sudan 78C1
Selizharovo USSR 21G1
Selkirk Can 52J4
Selkirk Scot 14D4
Selma Alabama USA 61B2
Selmer USA 61B1
Selongey France 17A1
Selouane Mor 19B2
Selous,Mt Can 56M3
Selta Karimata Str Indon 44C3
Selva Arg 72C1
Selvas Region Brazil 70D5
Selway USA 64C1
Selwyn Aust 48D3
Selwyn Mts Can 52E3
Semarang Indon 44D4
Semenov USSR 24G4
Semichi Is USA 56A5
Semidi I USA 56G4
Semiluki USSR 25F5
Seminoe Res USA 57A3
Seminole Oklahoma USA 63C2
Seminole Texas USA 62B3
Seminole,L USA 61C2
Semipalatinsk USSR 26K4
Semirara Is Phil 45F8
Semirom Iran 34C2
Semisopochnoi I USA 56B6
Semitau Indon 44D2
Semnān Iran 34C1
Semois R Belg 16C2
Sempoala Hist Site Mexico 67C2
Semporna Malay 44E2
Sena Madureira Brazil 70E5
Senanga Zambia 79C5
Senatobia USA 63E3
Sendai Honshū Japan 41E4
Sendai Kyūshū Japan 41C5
Sendwha India 35D4
Seneca Falls USA 60B1
Seneca L USA 60B1
Senecu Mexico 62A3
Senegal Republic Africa 76A3
Sénégal R Maur Sen 76A3
Sengkang Indon 45B3
Senhor do Bonfim Brazil 71L6
Senigallia Italy 22C2
Senj Yugos 22D2
Senkaku Gunto Is Japan 38F4
Senlin Shan Mt China 41C3
Senlis France 16B2
Sennar Sudan 78D2
Senneterre Can 53L5
Senones France 16D2
Sens France 16B2
Senta Yugos 23D1
Sentery Zaïre 78C4
Seoni India 35D4
Seoul = Soul
Separation Pt NZ 51B2
Sep'o N Korea 42A3
Sepone Laos 43D2
Sepotuba R Brazil 73A2
Sept-Iles Can 53M4
Séquédine Niger 78B1
Sequora Nat. Pk. USA 65C4
Serai Syria 31C1
Seram I Indon 45C3
Serang Indon 44C4
Serasan I Indon 44C2
Serbia Region Yugos 23D2
Serchio R Italy 17D2
Serdobsk USSR 25G5
Serein R France 16B3
Seremban Malay 43C5
Serengeti Nat Pk Tanz 78D4
Serenje Zambia 79D5
Seret R USSR 21F3
Sergach USSR 24H4
Sergeyevka USSR 41C3
Sergino USSR 26H3
Sergipe State Brazil 71L6
Seria Brunei 44D2
Serian Malay 44D2
Sérifos I Greece 23E3
Serio R Italy 17C2
Serir Calanscio Desert Libya 75B2
Sermaize-les-Bains France 16C2
Sernovodsk USSR 24J5
Serov USSR 26H4
Serowe Botswana 79C6
Serpa Port 19A2
Serpukhov USSR 24F5
Serra Amamba Par 73A3
Serra Azul Brazil 73B1
Serra da Canastra Mts Brazil 73C3
Serra da Estrela Mts Port 19A1
Serra da Mantiqueira Mts Brazil 73C3
Serra da Mombuca Brazil 73B2
Serra das Furnas Mts Brazil 73B2
Serra de Arrajas Mts Brazil 73C1
Serra de Fartura Mts Brazil 73B4
Serra de Maracaju Mts Brazil 73A3
Serra de São Jeronimo Brazil 73A2
Serra do Boquairao Mts Brazil 72D1
Serra do Cabral Mt Brazil 73D2
Serra do Cachimbo Mts Brazil 71G5
Serra do Caiapó Mts Brazil 73B2
Serra do Canguču Mts Brazil 72E2
Serra do Cantu Mts Brazil 73B3
Serra do Caparaó Mts Brazil 73D3
Serra do Chifre Brazil 71K7
Serra do Espinhaço Mts Brazil 73D2
Serra do Espinilho Mts Brazil 72D1
Serra do Jibão Mts Brazil 73C2
Serra do Mar Mts Brazil 73C3
Serra do Mirante Mts Brazil 73B3
Serra do Navio Brazil 71H3
Serra do Paranapiacaba Mts Brazil 73C3
Serra do Ramalho Mts Brazil 73D1
Serra do Roncador Mts Brazil 73B1
Serra dos Caiabis Mts Brazil 71G6
Serra dos Dourados Mts Brazil 73B3
Serra do Sincora Mts Brazil 73D1
Serra dos Parecis Mts Brazil 70F6
Serra dos Pilões Mts Brazil 73C2
Serra do Taquaral Mts Brazil 73B2
Serra Dourada Mts Brazil 73B2
Serra Dourada Mts Brazil 73C1
Serra Encantadas Mts Brazil 72E2
Serra Formosa Mts Brazil 71G6
Serra Geral Mts Bahia Brazil 73D2
Serra Geral Mts Parona Brazil 73B4
Serra Geral de Goiás Mts Brazil 73C1
Serra Geral do Parana Mts Brazil 73C2
Sérrai Greece 23E2
Serrana Bank Is Caribbean 66D3
Serrana de Cuenca Mts Spain 19B1
Serranias del Burro Mts Mexico 62B4
Serranópolis Brazil 73B2
Serra Pacaraima Mts Brazil/Ven 70F3
Serra Parima Mts Brazil 70F3
Serra Tumucumaque Brazil 71H3
Serre R France 16B2
Serres France 17A2
Serrezuela Arg 72B2
Serrinha Brazil 71L6
Serrmilik Greenland 53P3
Serro Brazil 73D2
Sertanópolis Brazil 73B3
Sêrtar China 40A3
Serua I Indon 45D4
Seruwai Indon 44A2
Seruyan R Indon 44D3
Seryshevo USSR 41B1
Seseganaga L Can 57D1
Sesfontein Namibia 79B5
Sesheke Zambia 79C5
Sestriere Italy 17B2
Sestri Levante Italy 17C2
Setana Japan 41D3
Sète France 18C3
Sete Lagoas Brazil 73D2
Sétif Alg 77D1
Setit R Sudan 32C4
Seto Japan 42C3
Seto Naikai S Japan 42B4
Settat Mor 77A2
Settle Eng 15D4
Settler Can 52G4
Sētūbal Port 19A2
Seurre France 17A1
Sevastopol' USSR 25E7
Severn R Can 53K4
Severn R Eng 15D5
Severnaya Dvina R USSR 24G3
Severnaya Zemlya I USSR 27M1
Severnyy Sos'va R USSR 24L3
Severnyy Ural Mts USSR 24K3
Severo-Baykalskoye Nagorye Mts USSR 27M4
Severo Donets USSR 25F6
Severodvinsk USSR 24F3
Severo Sos'va R USSR 26H3
Severoural'sk USSR 24L3
Sevier R USA 65D3
Sevier Desert USA 65D3
Sevier L USA 65D3
Sevilla Spain 19A2
Seville = Sevilla
Sevlievo Bulg 23F2
Sewa R Sierra Leone 76A4
Seward Alaska USA 56J3
Seward Nebraska USA 63C1
Seward Pen USA 56E2
Seyðdisfjörðdor Iceland 12C1
Seyðisfjörður Iceland 12C1
Seyhan Turk 30C2
Seym R USSR 25F5
Seymohan USSR 27R3
Seymour Aust 50C3
Seymour Connecticut USA 60D2
Seymour Indiana USA 58B3
Seymour Texas USA 62C3
Seyne France 17B2
Sežana Yugos 17E2
Sézanne France 16B2
Sfax Tunisia 77E2
Sfîntu Gheorghe Rom 23F1
's-Gravenhage Neth 20A2
Shaanxi Province China 40B3
Shabunda Zaïre 78C4
Shache China 29F2
Shackleton Ice Shelf Ant 80G9
Shadadkot Pak 35B3
Shādhām R Iran 34C2
Shaftesbury Eng 15D6
Shagamu Nig 77G4
Shag Rocks Is South Georgia 69J8
Shāhabād Iran 34B2
Shah Alam Malay 44F7
Shahbā Syria 31D2
Shahdap Iran 34D2
Shahdol India 37B3

Shāhīn Dezh
Smith Arm

Shāhīn Dezh Iran 34B1
Shāh Kūh Iran 34D2
Shahrak Afghan 34E2
Shahr-e Bābak Iran 34D2
Shahresa = Qomisheh
Shahr Kord Iran 34C2
Shahsavār Iran 25J8
Shaim USSR 24L3
Shājābād India 36B1
Shājahānpur India 35D3
Shājāpur India 35D4
Shakhtersk USSR 41E2
Shakhty USSR 25G6
Shakhun'ya USSR 24H4
Shaki Nig 77G4
Shakopee USA 57D3
Shakotan-misaki C Japan 42D2
Shaktoolik USA 56F3
Shamary USSR 24K4
Shambe Sudan 78D3
Shamokin USA 60B2
Shamrock USA 62B2
Shandaken USA 60C1
Shandong Province China 40D2
Shangchuan Dao I China 40C5
Shangdu China 40C1
Shanghai China 40E3
Shangnan China 40C3
Shangombo Zambia 79C5
Shangra China 40D4
Shangsi China 40B5
Shang Xian China 40C3
Shangzhi China 41B2
Shannon R Irish Rep 13B3
Shanqiu China 40D3
Shansonggang China 41B3
Shantarskiye Ostrova I USSR 38G1
Shantou China 40D5
Shanxi Province China 40C2
Shan Xian China 40D3
Shaoguan China 40C5
Shaoxing China 40E4
Shaoyang China 40C4
Shapinsay I Scot 14D2
Shaqqā Syria 31D2
Shaqqat aj Kharitah Region S Arabia 33E3
Shaqra' S Arabia 33E1
Shaqrā' S Yemen 33E4
Sharawrah S Arabia 33E3
Shari Japan 42D2
Sharifābād Iran 34D1
Sharjah UAE 33G1
Shark B Aust 48A3
Sharlauk USSR 34D1
Sharon,Plain of Israel 31C2
Sharpsburg USA 60B3
Sharya USSR 24H4
Shashamanna Eth 78D3
Shashi China 40C3
Shashone Mts USA 54B3
Shasta L USA 64B2
Shasta,Mt USA 64B2
Shathah at Tahtā Syria 31D1
Shaṭṭ al Gharrat R Iraq 30E3
Shaubak Jordan 31C3
Shawangunk Mt USA 60C2
Shawano USA 58B2
Shawinigan Can 59E1
Shawnee Oklahoma USA 63C2
Shawnee Wyoming USA 57A3
Sha Xian China 40D4
Shay Gap Aust 48B3
Shaykh Miskīn Syria 31D2
Shaykh 'Uthmān S Yemen 32D4
Shchigry USSR 25F5
Shchors USSR 25E5
Shchuchinsk USSR 26J4
Sheboygan USA 58B2
Shebshi Mts Nig 78B3
Shebunino USSR 41E2
Sheenjek R USA 56K2
Sheep Haven Estuary Irish Rep 14B4
Sheerness Eng 15F6
Shefar'am Israel 31C2
Sheffield Alabama USA 61B2
Sheffield Eng 15E5
Sheffield Pennsylvania USA 60A2
Sheffield Texas USA 62B3
Shekhupura Pak 35C2
Shelburne Falls USA 60D1
Shelby Michigan USA 58B2
Shelby Montana USA 64D1
Shelby N Carolina USA 61C1
Shelbyville Indiana USA 58B3
Shelbyville Tennessee USA 61B1
Sheldon USA 57C3
Sheldon,Mt Can 56M3
Shelikof Str USA 56H4
Shelley USA 64D2
Shellharbour Aust 50D2
Shelter Pt NZ 51A3
Shelton USA 64B1
Shemakha USSR 30E1
Shenandoah Iowa USA 63C1
Shenandoah Virginia USA 59D3
Shenandoah R USA 59D3
Shenandoah Mt USA 60A3
Shenandoah Nat Pk USA 59D3
Shendam Nig 77H4
Shendi Sudan 32B3
Shenkursk USSR 24G3
Shenmu China 40C2
Shenyang China 40E1
Shenzhen China 40C5
Sheopur India 35D3
Sheperdstown USA 60B3
Shepetovka USSR 21F2
Shepparton Aust 50C3
Sheppey,I of Eng 16A1
Sherard,C Can 53K2
Sherborne Eng 15D6
Sherbro I Sierra Leone 76A4
Sherbrooke Can 59E1
Sherburne USA 60C1
Shereik Sudan 32B3
Shergarh India 35C3
Sheridan Arkansas USA 63D3
Sheridan Wyoming USA 57A3
Sherman USA 63C3
s-Hertogenbosh Neth 20B2
Sheslay Can 56M4
Shetland Is Scot 13C1
Shevchenko USSR 25J7
Shevli R USSR 41C1
Sheyenne USA 57C2
Sheyenne R USA 57C2
Sheyk Sho'eyb I Iran 34C3
Shiashkotan I USSR 38J2
Shibarghan Afghan 35B1
Shibata Japan 41D4
Shibeli R Eth 78E3
Shibetsu Japan 42D2
Shibin el Kom Egypt 75C1
Shibîn el Qanâtir Egypt 31A3
Shibukawa Japan 42C3
Shickshinny USA 60B2
Shijiazhuang China 40C2
Shika R USSR 41A1
Shikarpur Pak 35B3
Shikoku-sanchi Mts Japan 42B4
Shikotsu-ko L Japan 42D2
Shilega USSR 24G3
Shiliguri India 37C2
Shilka USSR 38E1
Shilka R USSR 38E1
Shillington USA 60C2
Shillong India 37D2
Shilovo USSR 24G5
Shimabara Japan 42B4
Shimada Japan 42C4
Shimanovsk USSR 41B1
Shimizu Japan 41D4
Shimoda Japan 42C4
Shimoga India 36B2
Shimonoseki Japan 41C5
Shinano R Japan 42C3
Shināş Oman 33G2
Shinglehouse USA 60A2
Shingū Japan 41D5
Shinjō Japan 42D3
Shinminato Japan 41D4
Shinshār Syria 31D1
Shinyanga Tanz 78D4
Shiogama Japan 41E4
Shiono-misaki C Japan 42C4
Shiping China 40A5
Shippensburg USA 60B2
Shiprock USA 62A2
Shiqāq al Ma'ātif Region S Yemen 33E3
Shiquan China 40B3
Shirakawa Japan 42D3
Shirane-san Mt Japan 42C3
Shirani-san Mt Japan 42C3
Shīrāz Iran 34C3
Shirbīn Egypt 31A3
Shiriya-saki C Japan 42D2
Shīr Kūh Iran 34C2
Shirotori Japan 42C3
Shirvān Iran 34D1
Shishaldin V USA 56F5
Shishmaref USA 56E2
Shishmaref Inlet USA 56E2
Shishmaret USA 52B3
Shitanjing China 40B2
Shively USA 58B3
Shivpuri India 35D3
Shivta Hist Site Israel 31C3
Shivwits Plat USA 65D3
Shiwa Ngandu Zambia 79D5
Shiyan China 40C3
Shizuishan China 40B2
Shizuoka Japan 42C3
Shkodër Alb 23D2
Shkov USSR 21G2
Shoalhaven R Aust 50D2
Shobara Japan 42B4
Shoranūr India 36B2
Shorāpur India 36B1
Shoshon USA 64E2
Shoshone California USA 65C3
Shoshone Idaho USA 64D2
Shoshone R USA 64E2
Shoshone L USA 64D2
Shoshone Mts USA 65C3
Shostka USSR 25E5
Showak Sudan 32C4
Show Low USA 65D4
Shreveport USA 63D3
Shrewsbury Eng 15D5
Shropshire County Eng 15D5
Shuangcheng China 41B2
Shuanglia China 40E1
Shuangyashan China 41C2
Shubar kuduk USSR 25K6
Shublik Mts USA 56J2
Shuga USSR 24N2
Shu He R China 40D2
Shuicheng China 40A4
Shujaabad Pak 35C3
Shujālpur India 35D4
Shulan China 41B3
Shule He China 38C2
Shumagin Is USA 56G5
Shumen Bulg 23F2
Shumerlya USSR 24H4
Shuncheng China 40D4
Shungnak USA 56G2
Shuo Xian China 40C2
Shūr Gaz Iran 34D3
Shurugwi Zim 79C5
Shuya USSR 24G4
Shuyak I USA 56H4
Shwebo Burma 37E3
Shwegyin Burma 43B2
Shweli R Burma 37E3
Siahan Range Mts Pak 34E3
Siah Koh Mts Afghan 35A2
Sialkot Pak 35C2
Sian = Xi'an
Siarao I Phil 45G9
Siaton Phil 45F9
Siau I Indon 45C2
Šiauliai USSR 21E1
Sibay USSR 26G4
Šibenik Yugos 22D2
Siberut I Indon 44A3
Sibi Pak 35B3
Sibirskoye USSR 38D1
Sibirtsevo USSR 41C3
Sibiti Congo 78B4
Sibiti R Tanz 78D4
Sibiu Rom 23E1
Sibley USA 57C3
Siboa Indon 45A2
Sibolga Indon 44A2
Sibsāgār India 37D2
Sibu Malay 44D2
Sibuguay B Phil 45F9
Sibut CAR 78B3
Sibutu Pass Malay/Phil 44E1
Sibuyan I Phil 45F8
Sibuyan S Phil 45F8
Sichuan Province China 40A3
Sicilia I Medit S 22C3
Sicilian Chan Italy/Tunisia 22C3
Sicily = Sicilia
Sicuari Peru 70D6
Siddhapur India 35C4
Siddipet India 36B1
Sidhi India 37B3
Sidi Barrani Egypt 75B1
Sidi bel Abbès Alg 77B1
Sidi Kacem Mor 77A2
Sidlaw Hills Scot 14D3
Sidley,Mt Ant 80F5
Sidney Can 64B1
Sidney Montana USA 57B2
Sidney Nebraska USA 62B1
Sidney New York USA 60C1
Sidney Ohio USA 58C2
Sidney Lanier,L USA 61C2
Sidon = Säida
Sidrolândia Brazil 73B3
Siedlce Pol 21E2
Sieg R W Germ 16D1
Siegburg W Germ 16D1
Siegen W Germ 16D1
Sielle R France 17A1
Siem Reap Camb 43C3
Siena Italy 22C2
Siene R France 16C3
Sierpc Pol 21D2
Sierra Andrés Tuxtla Mexico 67C2
Sierra Auca Mahuida Mts Arg 72B3
Sierra Blanca USA 62A3
Sierra Blanca Mts Arg 72B4
Sierra Colorada Arg 72B4
Sierra de Albarracin Mts Spain 19B1
Sierra de Alcaraz Mts Spain 19B2
Sierra de Ancasti Mts Arg 72B1
Sierra de Cordoba Mts Arg 72B2
Sierra de Famantina Mts Arg 72B1
Sierra de Gredos Mts Spain 19A1
Sierra de Guadalupe Mts Spain 19A2
Sierra de Guadarrama Mts Spain 19B1
Sierra de Guara Mts Spain 19B1
Sierra de Gudar Mts Spain 19B1
Sierra de Juárez Mexico 67C2
Sierra de la Ventana Mts Arg 72C3
Sierra del Codi Mts Spain 19C1
Sierra del Imán Mts Arg 72D1
Sierra del Morro Mt Arg 72B2
Sierra del Nevado Mts Arg 72B3
Sierra de los Alamitos Mts Mexico 66B2
Sierra de los Filabres Spain 19B2
Sierra de los Huicholes Mexico 67B1
Sierra de Miahuatlán Mexico 67C2
Sierra de Morones Mts Mexico 67B1
Sierra de Ronda Mts Spain 19A2
Sierra de San Luis Mts Arg 72B2
Sierra de Segura Mts Spain 19B2
Sierra de Tamaulipas Mexico 67C1
Sierra de Urbion Mts Spain 19B1
Sierra de Uspallata Mts Arg 72B2
Sierra de Valasco Mts Arg 72B1
Sierra de Valle Fértil Mts Arg 72B2
Sierra de Zacatécas Mts Mexico 67B1
Sierra de Zongolica Mexico 67C2
Sierra Grande Mts Arg 72C2
Sierra Leone Republic Africa 76A4
Sierra Leone,C Sierra Leone 76A4
Sierra Madre Mts Phil 45F7
Sierra Madre del Sur Mts Mexico 67B2
Sierra Madre Occidental Mts Mexico 66B2
Sierra Madre Oriental Mts Mexico 67B1
Sierra Malanzan Mts Arg 72B2
Sierra Mojada Mexico 54C4
Sierra Morena Mts Spain 19A2
Sierra Nevada Mts Spain 19B2
Sierra Nevada Mts. USA 54A3
Sierra Nevada Mts USA 65B3
Sierra Nevada de santa Marta Mts Colombia 70D1
Sierra Pié de Palo Mts Arg 72B2
Sierra Vista USA 65D4
Sierre Switz 17B1
Siete Puntas R Par 73A3
Sífnos I Greece 23E3
Sig Alg 77B1
Sig USSR 24E2
Sigep Indon 44A3
Sighet Rom 21E3
Sighisoara Rom 23E1
Sigli Indon 44A1
Siglufjörður Iceland 12B1
Sigmaringen W Germ 16E2
Siguatepeque Honduras 70A1
Sigüenza Spain 19B1
Siguiri Guinea 76B3
Sihora India 35D4
Siirt Turk 30D2
Sikai Hu L China 38C3
Sikar India 35D3
Sikaram Mt Afghan 35B2
Sikasso Mali 76B3
Sikeli Indon 45B4
Sikeston USA 63E2
Síkinos I Greece 23F3
Sikionía Greece 23E3
Sikkim State India 37C2
Siktyakh USSR 27O2
Sil R Spain 19A1
Silandro Italy 17D1
Silao Mexico 67B1
Silay Phil 45F8
Silchar India 37D3
Silet Alg 76C2
Silgarhi Nepal 37B2
Silifke Turk 30B2
Silinfah Syria 31D1
Siling Co L China 29G2
Silistra Bulg 23F2
Siljan L Sweden 24A3
Silkeborg Den 12F7
Sillian Austria 17E1
Siloam Springs USA 63D2
Silsbee USA 63D3
Siltou Well Chad 78B2
Šilute USSR 21E1
Silvan Turk 30D2
Silvania Brazil 73C2
Silvassa India 35C4
Silver Bay USA 57D2
Silver City Nevada USA 65C3
Silver City New Mexico USA 62A3
Silver Lake USA 64B2
Silver Spring USA 60B3
Silverton Aust 50B2
Silverton USA 62A2
Silvretta Mts Austria/Switz 17D1
Simanggang Malay 44D2
Simao China 43C1
Simard,L Can 59D1
Simareh R Iran 34B2
Simav Turk 23F3
Simav R Turk 23F3
Simcoe,L Can 59D2
Simeohof I USA 56G5
Simeulue I Indon 44A2
Simferopol' USSR 25E7
Sími I Greece 23F3
Simikot Nepal 37B2
Simla India 35D2
Simla USA 62B2
Simmern W Germ 16D1
Simplon Mt Switz 18D2
Simplon P Switz 17C1
Simpson,C USA 52C2
Simpson Desert Aust 48C3
Simpson L Can 56N2
Simpson Pen Can 53K3
Simrishamn Sweden 12G7
Simushir I USSR 38J2
Sinabang Indon 44A2
Sinadogo Somalia 78E3
Sinai Pen Egypt 30B4
Sinaloa State Mexico 67A1
Sinalunga Italy 17D3
Sincelejo Colombia 70C2
Sinclair,L USA 61C2
Sind Pak 35B3
Sind R India 35D3
Sindirği Turk 23F3
Sindri India 37C3
Sinegorsk USSR 41E2
Sines Port 19A2
Singa Sudan 78D2
Singapore Republic S E Asia 43C5
Singapore,Str of S E Asia 43C5
Singaraja Indon 44E4
Singen W Germ 16E3
Singida Tanz 78D4
Singkaling Hkamti Burma 37E2
Singkawang Indon 44C2
Singleton Aust 50D2
Singtep I Indon 44B3
Singu Burma 43B1
Sin'gye N Korea 42A3
Sinhŭng N Korea 42A2
Siniscola Sardgena 22B2
Sinjai Indon 45B4
Sinjár Iraq 30D2
Sinkai Hills Mts Afghan 35B2
Sinkat Sudan 32C3
Sinkiang Autonomous Region 29G1
Sinn R W Germ 16E1
Sinnamary French Guiana 71H2
Sinnyong S Korea 42A3
Sinop Turk 30C1
Sinpa N Korea 42A2
Sinp'o N Korea 42A2
Sinp'yong N Korea 42A3
Sintana Rom 23E1
Sintang Indon 44D2
Sinton USA 63F4
Sintra Port 19A2
Sinú R Colombia 70C2
Sinŭiju N Korea 41A3
Siofok Hung 21D3
Sion Switz 17B1
Sioux City USA 57C3
Sioux Falls USA 57C3
Sioux Lookout Can 57D1
Sipalay Phil 45F9
Siparia Trinidad 68L1
Siping China 41A3
Siple Base Ant 80F3
Siple I Ant 80F5
Sipocot Phil 45F8
Sipora Indon 44A3
Sipsey R USA 61B2
Siqueros Mexico 67A1
Siquijor I Phil 45F9
Sira India 36B2
Siracusa Italy 22D3
Sirajganj Bang 37C3
Sirba R U Volta 77G3
Sīr Banī Yās I UAE 33F2
Sir Edward Pellew Group Is Aust 48C2
Siret R Rom 23F1
Sir James McBrien,Mt Can 56N3
Sir Kālahasti India 36B2
Şirnak Turk 30D2
Sirohi India 35C4
Sironcha India 36C1
Sironj India 35D4
Síros I Greece 23E3
Sirri I Iran 34C3
Sirsa India 35C3
Sirsi India 36A2
Sirt Libya 75A1
Sirte Desert Libya 75A1
Sirte,G of Libya 75A1
Sisak Yugos 22D1
Sisaket Thai 43C2
Sishen S Africa 79C6
Sisophon Camb 43C3
Sisseton USA 57C2
Sissili R U Volta 77F3
Sissonne France 16B2
Sistan Region Iran/Afghan 34E2
Sisteron France 18D3
Sistig Khem USSR 27L4
Sītāpur India 37B2
Sitía Greece 23F3
Sitio d'Abadia Brazil 73C1
Sitka USA 52E4
Sitkalidak I USA 56H4
Sitkinak I USA 56H4
Sittang R Burma 43B2
Sittard Neth 16C1
Sittwe Burma 37D3
Situbondo Indon 44D4
Sivaki USSR 41B1
Sivas Turk 30C2
Siverek Turk 30C2
Sivrihisar Turk 30B2
Siwa Egypt 75B2
Siwalik Range Mts India 35D2
Siwalik Range Mts Nepal 37B2
Siya USSR 24G3
Siyang China 40D3
Sjaelland I Den 20C1
Skagen Den 12G7
Skagerrak Str Nor/Den 12F7
Skagit R USA 64B1
Skagit Mt Can 64B1
Skagway USA 52E4
Skaneateles USA 60B1
Skaneateles L USA 60B1
Skara Sweden 12G7
Skarzysko-Kamienna Pol 21E2
Skeena R Can 52F4
Skeene Mts. Can 52F4
Skeenjek R USA 52D3
Skegness Eng 15F5
Skellefte R Sweden 24B2
Skellefteå Sweden 12J6
Skíathos I Greece 23E3
Skidegate Can 52E4
Skiemiewice Pol 21E2
Skien Nor 12F7
Skikda Alg 77D1
Skikoku I Japan 41C5
Skipton Eng 15E5
Skíros I Greece 23E3
Skive Den 12F7
Skjern Den 20B1
Skjoldungen Greenland 53O3
Skokie USA 58B2
Skópelos I Greece 23E3
Skopje Yugos 23E2
Skövde Sweden 12G7
Skovorodino USSR 27O4
Skowhegan USA 59F2
Skwentna USA 52C3
Skwierzyna Pol 20D2
Skye I Scot 13B2
Slagelse Den 12G7
Slaney R Irish Rep 15B5
Slatina Rom 23E2
Slaung Indon 44D4
Slav Brod Yugos 23D1
Slave R Can 52G3
Slavgorod Belorusskoya USSR 21G2
Slavgorod Rossiyskaya USSR 26J4
Slavuta USSR 21F2
Slavyansk USSR 25F6
Sleat,Sound of Chan Scot 14C3
Sleetmute USA 56G3
Sleeve Bloom Mts Irish Rep 15B5
Slidell USA 63E3
Slide Mt USA 60C2
Sligo Irish Rep 13B3
Sligo B Irish Rep 13B3
Sliven Bulg 23F2
Sloan USA 65C3
Slobozia Rom 23F2
Slonim USSR 21F2
Slough Eng 15E6
Slovensko Region Czech 21D3
Slubice Pol 20C2
Sluch' R USSR 21F2
Sludyanka USSR 38D1
Słupsk Pol 20D2
Slutsk USSR 21F2
Slutsk R USSR 21F2
Slyne Head Pt Irish Rep 13A3
Slyudvanka USSR 27M4
Smallwood Res Can 53M4
Smara Mor 76A2
Smederevo Yugos 23E2
Smederevska Palanka, Yugos 23E2
Smela USSR 25E6
Smethport USA 60A2
Smidovich USSR 41C2
Smirnykh USSR 41E2
Smith Arm B Can 56O2

Sühbaatar Tashtyp

Sühbaatar *Mongolia* 38D1
Sui *Pak* 35B3
Suibin *China* 41C2
Suide *China* 40C2
Suifenhe *China* 41C3
Suihua *China* 41B2
Suileng *China* 41B2
Suining *China* 40B3
Suippes *France* 16C2
Suir R *Irish Rep* 13B3
Sui Xian *China* 40C3
Suizhong *China* 40E1
Sujāngarh *India* 35C3
Sukabumi *Indon* 44C4
Sukadana Borneo *Indon* 44D3
Sukadana Sumatra *Indon* 44C4
Sukagawa *Japan* 41E4
Sukaraya *Indon* 44D3
Sukhinichi Shchekino *USSR* 24F5
Sukhona R *USSR* 24G4
Sukhumi *USSR* 25G7
Sukkertoppen *Greenland* 53N3
Sukkertoppen L *Greenland* 53N3
Sukkozero *USSR* 12L6
Sukkur *Pak* 35B3
Sukma *India* 36C1
Sukpay R *USSR* 41D2
Sukses *Namibia* 79B6
Sukumo *Japan* 42B4
Sula R *USSR* 25F5
Sulaiman Range Mts *Pak* 35B3
Sula Sgeir I *Scot* 14B2
Sulawesi I *Indon* 45B3
Sulawesi Sulatan Prov *Indon* 45B3
Sulawesi Tengah Prov *Indon* 45B3
Sulawesi Tenggara Prov *Indon* 45B3
Sulawesi Utara Prov *Indon* 45B3
Sulaymānīyah *Iraq* 30E3
Suleja *Nig* 77H4
Sule Skerry I *Scot* 14C2
Sulina *Rom* 23F1
Sulitjelma *Nor* 12H5
Sullana *Peru* 70B4
Sullivan *USA* 63D2
Sully-sur-Loire *France* 16B3
Sulmona *Italy* 22C2
Sulphur Louisiana *USA* 63D3
Sulphur Oklahoma *USA* 63C3
Sulphur Springs *USA* 63C3
Sultan Dağlari Mts *Turk* 25E8
Sultānpur *India* 37B2
Sulu Arch *Phil* 45F9
Sulu S *Philip* 39E6
Sulz *W Germ* 16E2
Sumampa *Arg* 69D3
Sumatera I *Indon* 44A2
Sumba I *Indon* 45B4
Sumbawa I *Indon* 44E4
Sumbawa Besar *Indon* 44E4
Sumbawanga *Tanz* 79D4
Sumburgh Head Pt *Scot* 14E2
Sumenep *Indon* 44D4
Sumgait *USSR* 25H7
sumi-kaikyō Str *Japan* 41C5
sumi-shotō Is *Japan* 41C5
Sumisu I *Japan* 38H3
Summerland Key *USA* 61E4
Summit Lake *Can* 52F4
Summits Mt *USA* 65C3
Sumner,L *NZ* 51B2
Sumoto *Japan* 42B4
Sumter *USA* 61C2
Sumy *USSR* 25E5
Sun R *USA* 64D1
Sunagawa *Japan* 42D2
Sunan *N Korea* 42A3
Sunbury *USA* 60B2
Sunchales *Arg* 72C2
Suncho Corral *Arg* 72C1
Sunch'ŏn *N Korea* 41B4
Sunch'ŏn *S Korea* 41B5
Sundance *USA* 57B3
Sundargarh *India* 37B3
Sunderbans Swamp *India* 37C3
Sunderland *Eng* 14E4
Sundridge *Can* 59D1
Sundsvaall *Sweden* 12H6
Sungaianyar *Indon* 44E3
Sungaisalak *Indon* 44B3
Sungai Siput *Malay* 44F6
Sungei Petani *Malay* 44F6
Sungguminasa *Indon* 45A4
Sunnyside *USA* 64C1
Sunnyvale *USA* 65B3
Sun Prairie *USA* 58B2
Suntar *USSR* 27N3
Suntsar *Pak* 34E3
Sun Valley *USA* 64D2
Sunwu *China* 41B2
Sunyani *Ghana* 77F4
Suojarvi *USSR* 24E3
Suō-nada B *Japan* 42B4
Suonejoki *Fin* 12K6
Supaul *India* 37C2
Superior Arizona *USA* 65D4
Superior Nebraska *USA* 63C1
Superior Wisconsin *USA* 58A1
Superior,L *USA/Can* 58B1
Suphan Buri *Thai* 43C3
Süphan Dağ *Turk* 30D2
Supiori I *Indon* 39G7
Supu *Indon* 45C2
Sūq 'Abs *Yemen* 32D3
Suq ash Suyukh *Iraq* 30E3
Suqaylibīyah *Syria* 31D1
Suqian *China* 40D3
Suqutra = Socotra
Sūr *Oman* 33G2
Surabaya *Indon* 44D4
Suraga-wan B *Japan* 42C4
Surakarta *Indon* 44D4
Sūrān *Syria* 31D1
Surar R *USSR* 24H5
Surat *Aust* 50C1
Sūrat *India* 35C4
Sūratgarh *India* 35C3
Surat Thani *Thai* 43B4
Surendranagar *India* 35C4
Surf City *USA* 60C3
Suriāpet *India* 36B1
Sürich *Switz* 18D2
Surigao *Phil* 45G9
Surin *Thai* 43C3
Surinam Republic 71G3
Surrey County *Eng* 15E6
Sursee *Switz* 17C1
Surtsey I *Iceland* 12A2
Surulangan *Indon* 44B3
Susa *Italy* 17B2
Susa *Japan* 42B4
Susaki *Japan* 42B4
Susanville *USA* 65B2
Süsch *Switz* 17D1
Susitna R *USA* 56J3
Susquehanna *USA* 60C2
Susquehanna R *USA* 60B3
Sussex *USA* 60C2
Sussex West *Eng* 15E6
Susulatna R *USA* 56H3
Sutherland *S Africa* 79C7
Sutherland *USA* 62B1
Sutlej R *Pak* 35C2
Sutter Creek *USA* 65B3
Sutton *USA* 58C3
Suttsu *Japan* 42D2
Sutwik I *USA* 56G4
Suva *Fiji* 55G2
Suwa *Japan* 41D4
Suwałki *Pol* 21E2
Suwannee R *USA* 61C3
Suweilih *Jordan* 31C2
Suwŏn *S Korea* 41B4
Su Xian *China* 40D3
Suzaka *Japan* 42C3
Suzhou *China* 40E3
Suzu *Japan* 41D4
Suzuka *Japan* 42C4
Suzu-misaki C *Japan* 42C3
Svalbard Is *Barents S* 26C2
Svalyava *USSR* 21E3
Svartenhuk Halvø Region *Greenland* 52N2
Svartisen Mt *Nor* 12G5
Svay Rieng *Camb* 43D3
Sveg *Sweden* 12G6
Svendborg *Den* 12G7
Sverdlovsk *USSR* 26H4
Sverdrup Chan *Can* 53J1
Svetlaya *USSR* 41D2
Svetlogorsk *USSR* 21E2
Svetogorsk *Fin* 12K6
Svetozarevo *Yugos* 23E2
Svilengrad *Bulg* 23F2
Svir' *USSR* 21F2
Svit R *USSR* 24E3
Švitavy *Czech* 20D3
Svobodnyy *USSR* 41B1
Svolvaer *Nor* 12G5
Swain Reefs *Aust* 49E3
Swains I *American Samoa* 49H2
Swainsboro *USA* 61C2
Swakopomund *Namibia* 79B6
Swale R *Eng* 15E4
Swallow Reef I *S E Asia* 44D1
Swāmihalli *India* 36B2
Swan I *Honduras* 66D3
Swanage *Eng* 15E6
Swan Hill *Aust* 50B3
Swan I *Caribbean* 68A3
Swan River *Can* 52H4
Swansea *Wales* 15D6
Swansea B *Wales* 15D6
Swatow
Swaziland Kingdom *Africa* 79D6
Swaziland Kingdom *S Africa* 79D6
Sweden Kingdom *N Europe* 12G7
Swedru *Ghana* 77F4
Sweet Home *USA* 64B2
Sweetwater *USA* 62B3
Sweetwater R *USA* 57A3
Swellendam *S Africa* 79C7
Świdnica *Pol* 20D2
Świdwin *Pol* 20D2
Świebodzin *Pol* 20D2
Świecie *Pol* 21D2
Swift Current *Can* 52H4
Swift Current Creek R *Can* 57A1
Swindon *Eng* 15E6
Świnoujście *Pol* 20C2
Switzerland Federal Republic *Europe* 18D2
Swords *Irish Rep* 15B5
Syderø *Faroes* 12D3
Sydney *Aust* 50D2
Sydney *Can* 53M5
Sydney L *Can* 57D1
Syktyvakar *USSR* 24H3
Sylacauga *USA* 61B2
Sylarna Mt *Sweden* 12G6
Sylhet *Bang* 37D3
Sylt I *W Germ* 20B1
Sylvania *USA* 58C2
Symon *Mexico* 67B1
Syowa Base *Ant* 80G11
Syracuse = Siracusa
Syracuse Kansas *USA* 62B2
Syracuse New York *USA* 60B1
Syracuse *USA* 59D2
Syrdal'ya R *USSR* 26H5
Syria Republic *S W Asia* 30C2
Sysert' *USSR* 24K4
Syzran' *USSR* 24H5
Szczecin *Pol* 20C2
Szczecinek *Pol* 20D2
Szczytno *Pol* 21E2
Szeged *Hung* 21E3
Székesfehérvar *Hung* 21D3
Szekszard *Hung* 21D3
Szolnok *Hung* 21D3
Szombathely *Hung* 20D3
Szprotawa *Pol* 20D2

T

Tabar Is *PNG* 48E1
Tabas *Iran* 34D2
Tabasco *Mexico* 67B1
Tabasco State *Mexico* 67D2
Tabatinga *Brazil* 70E4
Tabelbala *Alg* 76B2
Tabeng *Camb* 43C3
Taber *Can* 52G5
Tablas I *Phil* 45F8
Table Mt *S Africa* 79B7
Table Mt *USA* 56K2
Table Rock Res *USA* 63D2
Taboali *Indon* 44C3
Tábor *Czech* 20C3
Tabora *Tanz* 78D4
Tabory *USSR* 24L4
Tabou *Ivory Coast* 76B4
Tabouresouk *Tunisia* 77D1
Tabrīz *Iran* 34B1
Tabūk *S Arabia* 30C4
Tacámbaro *Mexico* 67B2
Tacheng *China* 29G1
Tacloban *Phil* 45G8
Tacna *Peru* 70D7
Tacna *USA* 65D4
Tacoma *USA* 54A2
Taconic Range *USA* 60D1
Tacuan R *Urug* 72E2
Tacuarembó *Urug* 72D2
Tacuati *Par* 73A3
Tadjoura *Djibouti* 78E2
Tadjoura,G of *Djibouti* 32D4
Tadoussac *Can* 59F1
Tādpatri *India* 36B2
Tadzhen *USSR* 26H6
Tadzhikskaya SSR Republic *USSR* 29E2
Taebaek Sanmaek Mts *S Korea* 41B4
Taech'on *S Korea* 42A3
Taedong R *N Korea* 42A3
Taegang-got Pen *N Korea* 42A3
Taegu *S Korea* 41B4
Taehŭksan I *S Korea* 41B5
Taehung *N Korea* 42A2
Taejŏn *S Korea* 41B4
Taesek Dampar L *Malay* 44G7
Tafalla *Spain* 19B1
Tafasaset Watercourse *Alg* 76C2
Taff R *Wales* 15D6
Tafila *Jordan* 31C3
Tagant Region *Maur* 76A3
Tagaung *Burma* 37E3
Tagbilaran *Phil* 45F9
Tagliamento R *Italy* 17E1
Taguenout Hagguerete Well *Maur* 76B2
Tagula I *Solomon Is* 49E2
Tagum *Phil* 45G9
Tagus = Tejo
Tahat Mt *Alg* 76C2
Tahiti I *Pacific O* 47M5
Tahlab R *Iran* 34E3
Tahlequah *USA* 63C2
Tahoe City *USA* 65B3
Tahoe,L *USA* 65B3
Tahoka *USA* 62B3
Tahoua *Niger* 76C3
Tahta *Egypt* 32B1
Tahulandang I *Indon* 45C2
Tahuna *Indon* 45C2
Tai'an *China* 40D2
Taiani *Can* 53J3
Taibai Shan Mt *China* 40B3
Taibus Qi *China* 40D1
T'ai-chung *Taiwan* 40E5
Taieri R *NZ* 51B3
Taihang Shan *China* 40C2
Taihape *NZ* 51C1
Tai Hu L *China* 40E3
Taiki *Japan* 42D2
Tailai *China* 41A2
Taileleo *Indon* 44A3
Tailem Bend *Aust* 50A3
Tain *Scot* 14C3
T'ai-nan *Taiwan* 40E5
Taiobeiras *Brazil* 73D2
T'ai pei *Taiwan* 40E5
Taiping *Malay* 43C5
Taira *Japan* 42D3
Tais *Indon* 44B3
Taisha *Japan* 42B3
Taitao,Pen de *Chile* 69B7
T'ai-tung *Taiwan* 40E5
Taivelkoski *Fin* 12K5
Taiwan Republic *China* 38F4
Taiwan Haixia = Formosa Str
Taiyiba *Jordan* 31C3
Taiyuan *China* 40C2
Taizhou *China* 40D3
Ta 'izz *Yemen* 32D4
Tajo R *Spain* 19B1
Tak *Thai* 43B2
Takada *Japan* 41D4
Takahashi *Japan* 42B4
Takaka *NZ* 51B2
Takamatsu *Japan* 41C5
Takaoka *Japan* 41D4
Takapuna *NZ* 51B1
Takasaki *Japan* 41D4
Takayama *Japan* 42C3
Takazie R *Eth* 32C4
Takefu *Japan* 41D4
Takeo *Camb* 43C3
Takeo *Japan* 42B4
Take-shima = Tok-do
Takestān *Iran* 34B1
Taketa *Japan* 42B4
Takikawa *Japan* 42D2
Takingeun *Indon* 44A2
Takinoue *Japan* 42D2
Takjvak L *Can* 52G3
Takkaze R *Eth* 78D2
Takslesluk L *USA* 56F3
Taku Arm R *Can* 56M3
Takum *Nig* 77J4
Tala *Mexico* 67B1
Talabanya *Hung* 21D3
Talaga *Indon* 45C3
Talagang *Pak* 35C2
Talagante *Chile* 72A2
Talaimannar *Sri Lanka* 36B3
Talak Desert Region *Niger* 76C3
Talangbetutu *Indon* 44B3
Talara *Peru* 70B4
Talasea *PNG* 48E1
Talata *Egypt* 31B3
Talavera de la Reina *Spain* 19A1
Talca *Chile* 72A3
Talcahuano *Chile* 72A3
Tālcher *India* 37C3
Talden *USSR* 41A1
Taldy Kurgan *USSR* 29F1
Taliabu *Indon* 45B3
Taligan *Afghan* 35B1
Tali Post *Sudan* 78D3
Taliwang *Indon* 44E4
Talkeetna *USA* 56H3
Talkeetna Mts *USA* 56J3
Talkha *Egypt* 31A3
Talladega *USA* 61B2
Tall 'Afar *Iraq* 30D2
Tallahassee *USA* 61C2
Tallard *France* 17B2
Tall Bīsah *Syria* 31D1
Tallinn *USSR* 24C4
Tall Kalakh *Syria* 30C3
Tallulah *USA* 63D3
Tal'menka *USSR* 38B1
Tal'noye *USSR* 25E6
Talpaki *USSR* 21E2
Taltal *Chile* 69B3
Talwood *Aust* 50C1
Tama *USA* 57D3
Tamabo Range Mts *Malay* 44E2
Tamale *Ghana* 77F4
Tamanrasset *Alg* 76C2
Tamanrasset Watercourse *Alg* 76C2
Tamaqua *USA* 60C2
Tamatave = Toamasina
Tamazula Durango *Mexico* 67A1
Tamazula Jalisco *Mexico* 67B2
Tamazulapán *Mexico* 67C2
Tamazunchale *Mexico* 67C1
Tambacounda *Sen* 76A3
Tambores *Urug* 72D2
Tambov *USSR* 25G5
Tambre R *Spain* 19A1
Tambu *Indon* 45B3
Tambura *Sudan* 78C3
Tamchaket *Maur* 76A3
Tamega R *Port* 19A1
Tamiahua *Mexico* 67C1
Tamil Nādu State *India* 36B2
Tamis R *Rom* 23E1
Tam Ky *Viet* 43D2
Tampa *USA* 61C3
Tampa B *USA* 61E4
Tampere *Fin* 12J6
Tampico *Mexico* 67C1
Tampin *Malay* 44G7
Tamsagbulag *Mongolia* 38E2
Tamsweg *Austria* 17E1
Tamu *Burma* 37D3
Tamuis *Mexico* 67C1
Tamworth *Aust* 50D2
Tamworth *Eng* 15E5
Tana *Nor* 12K4
Tana *Nor* 24D1
Tana L *Eth* 78D2
Tana R *Kenya* 78E4
Tana R *Nor/Fin* 12K5
Tanabe *Japan* 42C4
Tanafjord Inlet *Nor* 12K4
Tanaga I *USA* 56C6
Tanahgrogot *Indon* 44E3
Tanahjampea I *Indon* 45B4
Tanahmerah *Indon* 39G7
Tanakeke I *Indon* 45A4
Tanana *USA* 56H2
Tanana R *USA* 56J3
Tananarive = Antananarivo
Tananga Pass *USA* 56C6
Tanaro R *Italy* 17C2
Tanch'ŏn *N Korea* 41B3
Tandaho *Eth* 78E2
Tandil *Arg* 72D3
Tandjong Datu Pt *Indon* 44C2
Tandjung d'Urville C *Indon* 39G7
Tandjung Jambuair C *Indon* 44A1
Tandjung Layar C *Indon* 44E3
Tandjung Lumut C *Indon* 44C3
Tandjung Mangkalihet C *Indon* 44E2
Tandjung Sambar C *Indon* 44D3
Tandjung Sirik C *Malay* 44D2
Tandjung Vals C *Indon* 39G7
Tando Adam *Pak* 35B3
Tando Muhammad Khan *Pak* 35B3
Tandou L *Aust* 50B2
Tāndūr *India* 36B1
Taneatua *NZ* 51C1
Tanega-shima I *Japan* 41C5
Tanen Range Mts *Burma/Thai* 43B2
Tanezrouft Desert Region *Alg* 76B2
Tang *Iran* 34D3
Tanga *Tanz* 78D4
Tanga Is *PNG* 49E1
Tanganrog *USSR* 25F6
Tanganyika,L *Tanz/Zaïre* 78C4
Tanger *Mor* 77A1
Tanggula Shan Mts *China* 29H2
Tangier = Tanger
Tangjin *S Korea* 42A3
Tangjungpinang *Indon* 44B2
Tangkak *Malay* 44G7
Tangra Yumco L *China* 29G2
Tangshan *China* 40D2
Tangub *Phil* 45F9
Tanguy *USSR* 38D1
Tangwang He R *China* 41B2
Tangyuan *China* 41B2
Tanjay *Phil* 45F9
Tanjong Bugel C *Indon* 44D4
Tanjong Cangkuang C *Indon* 44C4
Tanjong Malim *Malay* 44F7
Tanjong Puting C *Indon* 44D3
Tanjong Selatan C *Indon* 44D3
Tanjung *Indon* 44E3
Tanjungbalai *Indon* 44A2
Tanjungbaliha *Indon* 45C3
Tanjung Jabung Pt *Indon* 44B3
Tanjung Karossa *Indon* 45A4
Tanjung Manimbaya Pt *Indon* 45A2
Tanjungpandan *Indon* 44C3
Tanjung Priok *Indon* 44C4
Tanjungredeb *Indon* 44E2
Tanjung Selatan Pt *Indon* 48A1
Tanjungselor *Indon* 44E2
Tanjung Torawitan C *Indon* 45B2
Tanjung Vals Pt *Indon* 48C1
Tank *Pak* 35C2
Tanna I *Vanuatu* 49F2
Tannu Ola Mts *USSR* 38C1
Tano R *Ghana* 77F4
Tanout *Niger* 76C3
Tanquián *Mexico* 67C1
Tan-shui *Taiwan* 40E4
Tansing *Nepal* 37B2
Tanta *Egypt* 75C1
Tan-Tan *Mor* 76A2
Tanunak *USA* 52B3
Tanyang *S Korea* 42A3
Tanzania Republic *Africa* 78D4
Tao'an *China* 41A2
Tao'er He R *China* 41A2
Tao He R *China* 40A3
Taolañaro *Madag* 79E6
Taole *China* 40B2
Taos *USA* 62A2
Taounate *Mor* 77B2
Taourirt *Mor* 77B2
Tapa *USSR* 24D4
Tapachula *Mexico* 66C3
Tapah *Malay* 44F6
Tapajós R *Brazil* 71G4
Tapaktuan *Indon* 44A2
Tapalquén *Arg* 72C3
Tapan *Indon* 44B3
Tapanatepec *Mexico* 67D2
Tapanui *NZ* 51A3
Tapauá R *Brazil* 70E5
Tapes *Brazil* 72E2
Tapi R *India* 35D4
Taplejung *Nepal* 37C2
Tapoa R *U Volta* 77G3
Tappahannock *USA* 59D3
Tapuaeniku Mt *NZ* 51B2
Tapuaritinga *Brazil* 73C3
Tapul Group Is *Phil* 45F9
Tapurucuara *Brazil* 70F4
Taquari R *Brazil* 73B2
Tara *Aust* 50D1
Tara *USSR* 26J4
Tara R *USSR* 26J4
Tara R *Yugos* 23D2
Taraba R *Nig* 77J4
Tarabuco *Bol* 70F7
Tarābulus = Tripoli
Taracón *Spain* 19B1
Taradale *NZ* 51C1
Tarakan *Indon* 44E2
Taramana *Indon* 45B4
Taransay I *Scot* 14B3
Taranto *Italy* 22D2
Tarapoto *Peru* 70C5
Tarare *France* 18C2
Tararua Range Mts *NZ* 51C2
Tarasovo *USSR* 24H2
Tarat *Alg* 76C2
Tarawera *NZ* 51C1
Tarazona *Spain* 19B1
Tarbat Ness Pen *Scot* 14D3
Tarbela Res *Pak* 35C2
Tarbert Strathclyde *Scot* 14C4
Tarbert Western Isles *Scot* 14B3
Tarbes *France* 18B3
Tarboro *USA* 61D1
Tarcoola *Aust* 48C4
Tarcoon *Aust* 50C2
Taree *Aust* 50D2
Tarfaya *Mor* 76A2
Targhee P *USA* 64D2
Tarhūnah *Libya* 75A1
Tarīf *UAE* 33F2
Tarija *Bol* 70F8
Tarikere *India* 36B2
Tarīm *S Yemen* 33E3
Tarime *Tanz* 78D4
Tarim He R *China* 29G1
Tarim Pendi Basin *China* 29G2
Tarin Kut *Afghan* 35B2
Tarkio *USA* 63C1
Tarkwa *Ghana* 77F4
Tarlac *Phil* 45F7
Tarma *Peru* 70C6
Tarn R *France* 18C3
Tarnobrzeg *Pol* 21E2
Tarnów *Pol* 21E3
Taro R *Italy* 17C2
Taroom *Aust* 48D3
Tarragona *Spain* 19C1
Tarraleah *Aust* 50E3
Tarrasa *Spain* 19C1
Tarrytown *USA* 60D2
Tarsus *Turk* 30B2
Tartan Oilfield *N Sea* 14E2
Tartaro R *Italy* 17D2
Tartarskaya ASSR Republic *USSR* 24H4
Tartu *USSR* 24D4
Tartūs *Syria* 30C3
Tarumirim *Brazil* 73D2
Tarutung *Indon* 44A2
Tarvisio *Italy* 17E1
Taschereau *Can* 59D1
Tashauz *USSR* 28D1
Tashigang *Bhutan* 37D2
Tashkent *USSR* 29E1
Tashkepri *USSR* 34E1
Tashtagol *USSR* 26K4
Tashtyp *USSR* 27L4

Tasikmalaya Tokuyama

Tasikmalaya *Indon* 44C4
Tasīl *Syria* 31C2
Tasiussaq *Greenland* 53N2
Tasker Well *Niger* 78B2
Tasman B *NZ* 51B2
Tasmania I *Aust* 48D5
Tasman Mts *NZ* 51B2
Tasman Pen *Aust* 50E3
Tasman S *NZ Aust* 49E4
Taşova *Turk* 30C1
Tassili du Hoggar Desert Region *Alg* 76C2
Tassili N'jjer Desert Region *Alg* 76C2
Tata *Mor* 76B2
Tataouine *Tunisia* 77E2
Tatarsk *USSR* 26J4
Tatarskiy Proliv Str *USSR* 41E2
Tateyama *Japan* 42C3
Tathlith *S Arabia* 32D3
Tatitlek *USA* 56J3
Tatry Mts *Pol/Czech* 21D3
Tatsuno *Japan* 42B4
Tatta *Pak* 35B4
Tatuí *Brazil* 73C3
Tatum *USA* 62B3
Tatvan *Turk* 30D2
Ta'u I *American Samoa* 49H2
Tauá *Brazil* 71K5
Taubaté *Brazil* 73C3
Taufstein Mt *W Germ* 16E1
Taumarunui *NZ* 51C1
Taungdwingyi *Burma* 43B2
Taung-gyi *Burma* 43B1
Taungup *Burma* 43A2
Taunsa *Pak* 35C2
Taunton *Eng* 15D6
Taunton *USA* 60E2
Taunus Region *W Germ* 16E1
Taupo *NZ* 51C1
Taupo,L *NZ* 51C1
Taurage *USSR* 21E1
Tauranga *NZ* 51C1
Tauranga Harbour B *NZ* 51C1
Tauroa Pt *NZ* 51B1
Taveuni I *Fiji* 49H2
Tavira *Port* 19A2
Tavistock *Eng* 15C6
Tavoy *Burma* 43B3
Tavoy Pt *Burma* 43B3
Tavsanli *Turk* 30A2
Tawa *NZ* 51B2
Tawakoni,L *USA* 63C3
Tawas City *USA* 58C2
Tawau *Malay* 44E2
Taweisha *Sudan* 78C2
Tawitawi I *Phil* 45F9
Tawitawi Group Is *Phil* 45F9
Taxco *Mexico* 67C2
Taxcoco *Mexico* 67C2
Tay R *Scot* 14D3
Tayan *Indon* 44D3
Taylor Alaska *USA* 56F2
Taylor Michigan *USA* 58C2
Taylor Texas *USA* 63C3
Taylor,Mt *USA* 62A2
Taylorville *USA* 58B3
Taymā' *S Arabia* 32C1
Taymura R *USSR* 27L3
Tay Ninh *Viet* 43D3
Tayoltita *Mexico* 67A1
Tayshet *USSR* 27L4
Tayshir *Mongolia* 38C2
Tayside Region *Scot* 14D3
Taytay *Phil* 45E8
Tayyebāt *Iran* 34E2
Taza *Mor* 77C2
Tazawako *Japan* 42D3
Tazawa-ko L *Japan* 42D3
Tazerbo Region *Libya* 75B2
Tazlina L *USA* 56J3
Tazovskiy *USSR* 26J3
Tbilisi *USSR* 25G7
Tchaourou *Benin* 77G4
Tchibanga *Gabon* 78B4
Tchigai,Plat du *Niger* 78B1
Tchin Tabaradene *Niger* 76C3
Tcholliré *Cam* 78B3
Tczew *Pol* 21D2
Teacapán *Mexico* 67A1
Te Anau *NZ* 51A3
Te Anua,L *NZ* 51A3
Te Aroha *NZ* 51C1
Te Awamutu *NZ* 51C1
Tébessa *Alg* 77D1
Tebingtinggi *Indon* 44A2
Teboman *Mexico* 67B2
Tecailtlān *Mexico* 67B2
Tecate *Mexico* 65C4
Tecclotlán *Mexico* 67B1
Techa R *USSR* 24L4
Tečpan *Mexico* 67B2
Tecuala *Mexico* 67A1
Tecuci *Rom* 23F1
Tecumseh *USA* 63C1
Tedzhen *USSR* 28E2
Tedzhen R *USSR* 26H6
Tees R *Eng* 15E4
Tefé *Brazil* 70F4
Tegal *Indon* 44C4
Tegineneng *Indon* 44C4
Tegucigalpa *Honduras* 66D3
Tehachapi Mts. *USA* 65C4
Tehachapi P *USA* 65C3
Tehek L *Can* 52J3
Tehoru *Indon* 45C3
Tehrān *Iran* 34C1
Tehuacán *Mexico* 67C2
Tehuantepec *Mexico* 67C2
Tehuitzingo *Mexico* 67C2
Teifi R *Wales* 15C5
Tejo R *Port* 19A2
Tejupilco *Mexico* 67B2
Tekamah *USA* 57C3
Tekapo,L *NZ* 51B2
Tekeli *USSR* 29F1
Tekirdağ *Turk* 30A1
Tekir Dağlari Mts *Turk* 23F2
Teknaf *Bang* 37D3
Teku *Indon* 45B3
Te Kuiti *NZ* 51C1
Tela *Honduras* 66D3
Telavi *USSR* 25H7
Tel Aviv Yafo *Israel* 31C2
Telegraph Creek *Can* 52E4
Telén *Arg* 72B3
Telescope Peak Mt *USA* 65C3
Teles Pires R *Brazil* 71G5
Telfs *Austria* 17D1
Teli *USSR* 27K4
Telkalakh *Syria* 25F9
Tell el Meise Mt *Jordan* 31C3
Teller *USA* 56E2
Tellicherry *India* 36B2
Telok Anson *Malay* 43C5
Tělok Buli B *Indon* 45C2
Tělok Darvel *Malay* 44E2
Tělok Dondo B *Indon* 45B2
Tělok Flamingo B *Indon* 39G7
Tělok Kau B *Indon* 45C2
Tělok Kumai B *Indon* 44D3
Tělok Labuk B *Malay* 44E1
T14elok Pelabuanratu B *Indon* 44C4
Tělok Saleh B *Indon* 44E4
Tělok Sampit B *Indon* 44D3
Tělok Sukadona B *Indon* 44C3
Teloloapán *Mexico* 67C2
Telšiai *USSR* 21E1
Telukbatang *Indon* 44D3
Teluk Berau B *Indon* 39G7
Telukbetung *Indom* 44C4
Teluk Bone B *Indon* 45B3
Teluk Cendrawasih B *Indon* 39G7
Telukdalam *Indon* 44A2
Teluk Mandar B *Indon* 45A3
Teluk Tolo B *Indon* 45B3
Teluk Tomini B *Indon* 45B3
Těluk Weda B *Indon* 45C2
Tema *Ghana* 77F4
Temagami,L *Can* 58C1
Temascal *Mexico* 67C2
Tembesi R *Indon* 44B3
Tembilahan *Indon* 44B3
Temblador *Ven* 68E5
Temerloh *Malay* 43C5
Temir *USSR* 26G5
Temirtau *USSR* 26J4
Temiscaming *Can* 59D1
Témiscouata,L *Can* 59F1
Temora *Aust* 50C2
Tempe *USA* 54B3
Temple Arizona *USA* 65D4
Temple Texas *USA* 63C3
Templemore *Irish Rep* 15B5
Tempoal *Mexico* 67C1
Temuco *Chile* 72A3
Temuka *NZ* 51B2
Tena *Ecuador* 70C4
Tenāli *India* 36C1
Tenancingo *Mexico* 67C2
Tenasserim *Burma* 43B3
Tenby *Wales* 15C6
Tenco R *Par* 69D2
Tendaho *Eth* 32D4
Tende *France* 17B2
Tende P *Italy* 17B2
Ten Degree Chan *Indian O* 36E3
Tendrara *Mor* 77B2
Ténéré Desert Region *Niger* 78B2
Tenerife I *Canary Is* 76A2
Ténès *Alg* 77C1
Tenessee P *USA* 62A2
Teng R *Burma* 43B1
Tenggarong *Indon* 44E3
Tengger Shamo Desert *China* 40A2
Tenkāsi *India* 36B3
Tenke *Zaïre* 79C5
Tenkodogo *U Volta* 77F3
Tenna R *Italy* 17E3
Tennant Creek *Aust* 48C2
Tennessee State *USA* 55E3
Tennessee R *USA* 63E2
Teno *Chile* 72A2
Tenom *Malay* 44E1
Tenosique *Mexico* 66C3
Tensift R *Mor* 77A2
Tentena *Indon* 45B3
Tenterfield *Aust* 50D1
Ten Thousand Is *USA* 61E4
Teocaltiche *Mexico* 67B1
Teófilo Otôni *Brazil* 73D2
Teotihiucan Hist Site *Mexico* 67C2
Teotitlan *Mexico* 67C2
Tepa *Indon* 45C4
Tepatitlan *Mexico* 67B1
Tepehuanes *Mexico* 66B2
Tepeji *Mexico* 67C2
Tepic *Mexico* 67B1
Teplice *Czech* 20C2
Te Puke *NZ* 51C1
Tequila *Mexico* 67B1
Tequistepec *Mexico* 67C2
Ter R *Spain* 19C1
Téra *Niger* 76C3
Teradomari *Japan* 42C3
Teramo *Italy* 22C2
Terceira I *Açores* 76A1
Tereboviya *USSR* 21F3
Terenoz *Brazil* 73B2
Teresina *Brazil* 71K5
Teresópolis *Brazil* 73D3
Teressa I *Indian O* 36E3
Teriang *Malay* 44G7
Terme *Turk* 30C1
Termez *USSR* 28E2
Termoli *Italy* 22C2
Ternate *Indon* 45C2
Terney *USSR* 41D3
Terni *Italy* 22C2
Ternopol *USSR* 21F3
Terrace *Can* 52F4
Terrace Bay *Can* 58B1
Terracina *Italy* 22C2
Terrafirma *S Africa* 79C6
Terre Adélie Region *Ant* 80G8
Terre Haute *USA* 58B3
Terrell *USA* 63C3
Terry *USA* 57A2
Terschelling I *Neth* 20B2
Teruel *Spain* 19B1
Teshekpuk *USA* 52C2
Teshekpuk L *USA* 56H1
Teshi R *Nig* 77G4
Teshikaga *Japan* 42D2
Teshio R *Japan* 41E3
Teshio dake Mt *Japan* 42D2
Tesiyn Gol Mts *Mongolia* 38C2
Teslin *Can* 56M3
Teslin R *Can* 56M4
Teslin L *Can* 56M3
Teslyn Gol R *Mongolia* 27L5
Tessalit *Mali* 76C2
Tessaoua *Niger* 76C3
Tessaout R *Mor* 77A2
Tessenei *Eth* 32C3
Tete *Mozam* 79D5
Tetela *Mexico* 67B2
Teterev R *USSR* 21F2
Teton R *USA* 64D1
Teton Range Mts *USA* 64D2
Tetouan *Mor* 77A1
Tetyushi *USSR* 24H4
Teuco R *Arg* 70F8
Teúl de Gonzalez Ortega *Mexico* 67B1
Teun I *Indon* 45C4
Teuri-tō I *Japan* 42D2
Tevere R *Italy* 22C2
Teviot R *Scot* 14D4
Tevriz *USSR* 26J4
Te Waewae B *NZ* 51A3
Tewah *Indon* 44D3
Tewantin *Aust* 50D1
Têwo *China* 40A3
Texarkana *USA* 63D3
Texarkana,L *USA* 63D3
Texas *Aust* 50D1
Texas State *USA* 54C3
Texas City *USA* 63D4
Texel I *Neth* 20A2
Texhoma *USA* 62B2
Texoma,L *USA* 63C3
Teyuarah *Afghan* 35A2
Teziutlán *Mexico* 67C2
Tezouro *Brazil* 73B2
Tezpur *India* 37D2
Tha *Laos* 43C1
Thabana Ntlenyana Mt *Lesotho* 79C6
Thagyettaw *Burma* 43B3
Thai Binh *Viet* 43D1
Thailand Kingdom *S E Asia* 43C2
Thailand,G of *Thai* 43C3
Thai Nguyen *Viet* 43D1
Thakhek *Laos* 43D2
Thal *Pak* 35C2
Thale Luang L *Thai* 43C4
Thallon *Aust* 50C1
Thamarit *Oman* 33F3
Thames *NZ* 51C1
Thames R *Eng* 15F6
Thamūd *S Yemen* 33E3
Thāne *India* 36A1
Thanh Hoah *Viet* 43D2
Thanjavur *India* 36B2
Thann *France* 16D3
Thar Desert *India* 35C3
Thargomindah *Aust* 50B1
Tharrawaddy *Burma* 37E4
Thásos I *Greece* 23E2
Thaton *Burma* 43B2
Thayetmyo *Burma* 43A2
Thazi *Burma* 37E3
The Dalles *USA* 52F5
Thedford *USA* 57B3
The Gulf *S W Asia* 33F1
Thelon R *Can* 52H3
The Naze *Eng* 16A1
Theodore *Aust* 48E3
Theodore Roosevelt L *USA* 65D4
Thermaïkós Kólpos G *Greece* 23E2
Thermopolis *USA* 64E2
Thesiger B *Can* 52F2
Thessalon *Can* 58C1
Thessaloníki *Greece* 23E2
Thetford *Eng* 15F5
Thetford Mines *Can* 59E1
Thibodaux *USA* 63D4
Thicket Portage *Can* 52J4
Thief River Falls *USA* 57C2
Thielsen,Mt *USA* 64B2
Thiers *France* 18C2
Thiès *Sen* 76A3
Thika *Kenya* 78D4
Thimphu *Bhutan* 37C2
Thionville *France* 18D2
Thíra I *Greece* 23F3
Thirsk *Eng* 15E4
Thisted *Den* 12F7
Thívai *Greece* 23E3
Thiviers *France* 18C2
Thomaston Georgia *USA* 61C2
Thomaston Maine *USA* 59F2
Thomastown *Irish Rep* 15B5
Thomasville Alabama *USA* 61B2
Thomasville Georgia *USA* 61C2
Thomasville N Carolina *USA* 61D1
Thom Bay *Can* 53J2
Thompson *Can* 52J4
Thompson *USA* 63D1
Thompson Falls *USA* 64C1
Thompson Landing *Can* 52G3
Thompsonville *USA* 60D2
Thomson *USA* 61C2
Thomson R *Aust* 48D3
Thon Buri *Thai* 43C3
Thongwa *Burma* 43B2
Thonon-les-Bains *France* 17B1
Thoreau *USA* 62A1
Thornhill *Scot* 14D4
Thouars *France* 18B2
Thousand Is *Can/USA* 59D2
Three Forks *USA* 64D1
Three Kings Is *NZ* 55G4
Three Lakes *USA* 58B1
Three Pagodas P *Thai* 43B2
Three Rivers Michigan *USA* 58B2
Three Rivers Texas *USA* 63F4
Three Sisters Mt *USA* 64B2
Thule *Greenland* 53M2
Thun *Switz* 17B1
Thunder Bay *Can* 58B1
Thunder Mt *USA* 56F2
Thuner See L *Switz* 17B1
Thung Song *Thai* 43B4
Thur R *Switz* 17C1
Thüringen Wald Upland *E Germ* 20C2
Thurles *Irish Rep* 15B5
Thursday I *Aust* 39H8
Thurso *Scot* 14D2
Thurston I *Ant* 80F4
Thusis *Switz* 17C1
Thylungra *Aust* 50B1
Tiandong *China* 40B5
Tian'e *China* 40B5
Tianjin *China* 40D2
Tianlin *China* 40B5
Tianqiaoling *China* 41B3
Tiān Shan Mts *C Asia* 29G1
Tianshui *China* 40B3
Tianzhu *China* 40A2
Tiaret *Alg* 77C1
Tibagi R *Brazil* 73B3
Tibati *Cam* 77J4
Tiberias *Israel* 31C2
Tiberias,L *Israel* 31C2
Tiber,R = Tevere,R
Tiber Res *USA* 64D1
Tibesti Mountain Region *Chad* 78B1
Tibet Autonomous Region *China* 29G2
Tibooburra *Aust* 50B1
Tibrikot *Nepal* 37B2
Tiburón I *Mexico* 66A2
Tichitt *Maur* 76B3
Tichla *Mor* 76A2
Ticino R *Italy/Switz* 17C2
Ticonderoga *USA* 59E2
Ticul *Mexico* 66D2
Tidjikja *Maur* 76A3
Tiefencastel *Switz* 17C1
Tiel *Neth* 16C1
Tieli *China* 41B2
Tieling *China* 41A3
Tielt *Belg* 16B1
Tienen *Belg* 16C1
Tiengen *W Germ* 16E3
Tien Shan Mts *USSR/China* 26J5
Tientsin *China* 40D2
Tierp *Sweden* 12H6
Tierra Amarilla *Chile* 72A1
Tierra Amarilla *USA* 62A2
Tierra Blanca *Mexico* 67C2
Tierra Colorada *Mexico* 67C2
Tierra del Fuego Territory *Arg* 69C8
Tietê *Brazil* 73C3
Tiete R *Brazil* 73B3
Tiffin *USA* 58C2
Tifton *USA* 61C2
Tifu *Indon* 45C3
Tigalda I *USA* 56F5
Tigil *USSR* 27R4
Tignere *Cam* 77J4
Tigre R *Peru* 70C4
Tigre R *Ven* 70F2
Tigris R *Iraq* 30E3
Tihuatlán *Mexico* 67C1
Tijuana *Mexico* 65C4
Tikamgarh *India* 35D4
Tikchik L *USA* 56G3
Tikhin *USSR* 24E4
Tikhoretsk *USSR* 25G6
Tikopia I *Solomon Is* 49F2
Tikrīt *Iraq* 30D3
Tiksi *USSR* 27O2
Tilamuta *Indon* 45B2
Tilburg *Neth* 16C1
Tilbury *Eng* 15F6
Tilcara *Arg* 69C2
Tilcha *Aust* 50B1
Tilin *Burma* 43A1
Tillabéri *Niger* 76C3
Tillamook *USA* 64B1
Tillanchong I *Indian O* 36E3
Tillia *Niger* 76C3
Tílos I *Greece* 23F3
Tilpa *Aust* 50B2
Tiluá *Colombia* 70C3
Timanskiy Kryazh Mts *USSR* 24H2
Timaru *NZ* 51B2
Timashevsk *USSR* 25F6
Timbákion *Greece* 23E3
Timbalier B *USA* 63D4
Timbédra *Maur* 76B3
Timbuktu = Tombouctou
Timétrine Monts Mts *Mali* 76B3
Timia *Niger* 76C3
Timimoun *Alg* 76C2
Timişoara *Rom* 23E1
Timmins *Can* 58C1
Timor I *Indon* 48B1
Timor S *Aust/Indon* 48B2
Timote *Arg* 72C3
Timsâh,L *Egypt* 31B3
Tims Ford L *USA* 61B1
Tinaca Pt *Phil* 45G9
Tinaco *Ven* 68D5
Tindivanam *India* 36B2
Tindouf *Alg* 76B2
Tinée R *France* 17B2
Tinfouchy *Alg* 76B2
Tin Fouye *Alg* 76C2
Tingmerkpuk Mt *USA* 56F2
Tingmiarmiut *Greenland* 53O3
Tingo Maria *Peru* 70C5
Tingrela *Ivory Coast* 76B3
Tingri *China* 37C2
Tinian *Pacific O* 39H5
Tinogasta *Arg* 72B1
Tínos I *Greece* 23F3
Tinsukia *India* 37E2
Tintagel Head Pt *Eng* 15C6
Tin Tarabine Watercourse *Alg* 76C2
Tintinara *Aust* 50B3
Tin Zaouaten *Alg* 76C2
Tioga *USA* 57B2
Tioga R *USA* 60B2
Tioman I *Malay* 43C5
Tione *Italy* 17D1
Tioughnioga R *USA* 60B1
Tipperary County *Irish Rep* 15B5
Tipperary *Irish Rep* 13B3
Tipton Missouri *USA* 63D2
Tiptūr *India* 36B2
Tiquicheo *Mexico* 67B2
Tiranë *Alb* 23D2
Tirano *Italy* 17D1
Tiraspol *USSR* 25D6
Tir'at el Ismâilîya Canal *Egypt* 31A3
Tirchchirāppalli *India* 36B2
Tire *Turk* 23F3
Tirebolu *Turk* 30C1
Tiree I *Scot* 14B3
Tîrgovişte *Rom* 23F2
Tîrgu Jiu *Rom* 23E1
Tîrgu Mureş *Rom* 23E1
Tirich Mir Mt *Pak* 35C1
Tiris Region *Mor* 76A2
Tirlyanskiy *USSR* 24K5
Tîrnăveni *Rom* 23E1
Tírnavos *Greece* 23E3
Tirodi *India* 35D4
Tirol Province *Austria* 17D1
Tirso R *Sardegna* 22B2
Tiruchchendūr *India* 36B3
Tirunelveli *India* 36B3
Tirupati *India* 36B2
Tiruppattūr *India* 36B2
Tiruppur *India* 36B2
Tiruvannamalai *India* 36B2
Tishomingo *USA* 63C3
Tisīyah *Syria* 31D2
Tisza R *Hung* 21E3
Titlagarh *India* 37B3
Titograd *Yugos* 23D2
Titovo Užice *Yugos* 23D2
Titov Veles *Yugos* 23E2
Titule *Zaïre* 78C3
Titusville *USA* 61C3
Tiverton *Eng* 15D6
Tivoli *Italy* 22C2
Tixtla *Mexico* 67C2
Tiyeglow *Somalia* 78E3
Tizayuca *Mexico* 67C2
Tizimin *Mexico* 66D2
Tizi Ouzou *Alg* 77C1
Tiznit *Mor* 76B2
Tizpan el Alto *Mexico* 67B1
Tlacolula *Mexico* 67C2
Tlacotalpan *Mexico* 67C2
Tlalchana *Mexico* 67B2
Tlalnepantla *Mexico* 67C2
Tlalpan *Mexico* 67C2
Tlaltenago *Mexico* 67B1
Tlancualpicán *Mexico* 67C2
Tlapa *Mexico* 67C2
Tlapacoyan *Mexico* 67C2
Tlaquepaque *Mexico* 67B1
Tlaxcala *Mexico* 67C2
Tlaxcala State *Mexico* 67C2
Tlaxiaco *Mexico* 67C2
Tlell *Can* 56M5
Tlemcem *Alg* 77B2
Toamasina *Madag* 79E5
Toay *Arg* 72C3
Toba *Japan* 42C4
Toba and Kakar Ranges Mts *Pak* 35B2
Tobago I *Caribbean* 68E4
Tobelo *Indon* 45C2
Tobermory *Can* 58C1
Tobermory *Scot* 14B3
Tobi I *Pacific O* 39G6
Tobin,Mt *USA* 65C2
Tōbi-shima I *Japan* 42C3
Tobol R *USSR* 26H4
Toboli *Indon* 45B3
Tobol'sk *USSR* 26H4
Tobruk = Tubruq
Tobseda *USSR* 24J2
Tocantins R *Brazil* 71J4
Toccoa *USA* 61C2
Toce R *Italy* 17C1
Tocopilla *Chile* 69B2
Tocorpuri *Bol* 69C2
Tocorpuri Mt *Chile* 70E8
Tocuyo R *Ven* 70E1
Toda *India* 35D3
Todeli *Indon* 45B3
Tödi Mt *Switz* 17C1
Todong *S Korea* 42B3
Todos Santos *Mexico* 54B4
Tofua I *Tonga* 49H2
Togiak *USA* 56F4
Togiak B *USA* 56F4
Togian I *Indon* 45B3
Togni *Sudan* 32C3
Togo Republic *Africa* 77G4
Togtoh *China* 40C1
Tohamiyam *Sudan* 32C3
Tohatchi *USA* 62A2
Tojo *Indon* 45B3
Tok *USA* 56K3
Tokachi R *Japan* 41E3
Tokamachi *Japan* 42C3
Tokar *Sudan* 32C3
Tokara Retto Arch *Japan* 38F4
Tokat *Turk* 30C1
Tŏkchŏk-kundo Arch *S Korea* 41B4
Tok-do I *S Korea* 42B3
Tokelau Is *Pacific O* 49H1
Tokmak *USSR* 29F1
Tokomaru Bay *NZ* 51C1
Toku R *Can/USA* 56M4
Tokung *Indon* 44D3
Tokuno I *Japan* 38F4
Tokur *USSR* 41C1
Tokushima *Japan* 41C5
Tokuyama *Japan* 42B4

Tōkyō Uinta Mts

Tōkyō *Japan* 41D4
Tolaga Bay *NZ* 51C1
Toledo *Brazil* 71H8
Toledo *Chile* 72A1
Toledo *Spain* 19B2
Toledo *USA* 58C2
Toledo Bend Res *USA* 63D3
Tolentino *Italy* 17E3
Toliara *Madag* 79E6
Tolima *Colombia* 70C2
Toliman *Mexico* 67C1
Tolitoli *Indon* 45B2
Tolmezzo *Italy* 17E1
Tolmin *Yugos* 17E1
Tolocin *USSR* 21F2
Tolosa *Spain* 19B1
Tolsan-do I *S Korea* 42A4
Toltén *Chile* 72A3
Toltén R *Chile* 72A3
Toluca *Mexico* 67C2
Tol'yati *USSR* 24H5
Tom R *USSR* 41C1
Tomah *USA* 58A2
Tomahawk *USA* 58B1
Tomakomai *Japan* 41E3
Tomani *Malay* 44E2
Tomari *USSR* 41E2
Tomaszów Mazowiecka *Pol* 21E2
Tomatlán *Mexico* 67A2
Tombigbee R *USA* 61B2
Tomboco *Angola* 79B4
Tomboli *Indon* 45B3
Tombos *Brazil* 73D3
Tombouctou *Mali* 76B3
Tombstone *USA* 65E4
Tomé *Chile* 72A3
Tomelloso *Spain* 19B2
Tomer *Port* 19A2
Tomie *Japan* 42A4
Tomini *Indon* 45B2
Tomkinson Range Mts *Aust* 48B3
Tommot *USSR* 27O4
Tomorrit Mt *Alb* 23E2
Tomsk *USSR* 26K4
Toms River *USA* 60C3
Tonalá *Mexico* 66C3
Tonasket *USA* 64C1
Tonawanda *USA* 59D2
Tondano *Indon* 45C2
Tonga Is *Pacific O* 49H3
Tongatapu I *Tonga* 49H3
Tongatapu Group Is *Tonga* 49H3
Tonga Trench *Pacific O* 49H3
Tongbei *China* 41B2
Tongchang *N Korea* 42A2
Tongcheng *China* 40D3
Tongchuan *China* 40B2
Tongde *China* 40A2
Tongeren *Belg* 16C1
Tonggu Jiao I *China* 43E2
Tonghai *China* 40A5
Tonghe *China* 41B2
Tonghua *China* 41B3
Tongjiang *China* 41C2
Tongjosŏn-man *N Korea* 41B4
Tongkin,G of *Viet/China* 43D1
Tonglia *China* 40E1
Tongling *China* 40D3
Tongnae *S Korea* 42A3
Tongo *Aust* 50B2
Tongoy *Chile* 72A2
Tongren Guizhou *China* 40B4
Tongren Qinghai *China* 40A2
Tongsa *Bhutan* 37D2
Tongta *Burma* 43B1
Tongtian He R *China* 38C3
Tongue *Scot* 14C2
Tongue R *USA* 57A2
Tong Xian *China* 40D2
Tongxin *China* 40B2
Tongyu *China* 41A3
Tongzi *China* 40B4
Tonhil *Mongolia* 27L5
Tonich *Mexico* 54C4
Tonj *Sudan* 78C3
Tonk *India* 35D3
Tonkawa *USA* 63C2
Tonle Sap L *Camb* 43C3
Tonnerre *France* 16C3
Tono *Japan* 42D3
Tonopah *USA* 65C3
Tonsina *USA* 56J3
Tooele *USA* 64D2
Toogoolawah *Aust* 50D1
Toompine *Aust* 50B1
Toowoomba *Aust* 50D1
Topeka *USA* 63C2
Topolobampo *Mexico* 54C4
Toppenish *USA* 64B1
Toppock *USA* 65D4
Torbali *Turk* 23F3
Torbat-e-Heydarīyeh *Iran* 34D1
Torbat-e Jām *Iran* 34E1
Torbay *Eng* 15D6
Torbert,Mt *USA* 56H3
Tordesillas *Spain* 19A1
Torgau *E Germ* 20C2
Torhout *Belg* 16B1
Tori *Eth* 78D3
Tori I *Japan* 38H3
Torino *Italy* 17B2
Torit *Sudan* 78D3
Torixoreu *Brazil* 73B2
Tormes R *Spain* 19A1
Torne L *Sweden* 12J5
Torneträsk *Sweden* 12H5
Torngat Mts *Can* 53M4
Tornio *Fin* 12J5
Tornquist *Arg* 72C3
Torobuku *Indon* 45B3
Torodi *Niger* 77G3
Torom R *USSR* 41D1
Toronto *Can* 59D2
Toropets *USSR* 24E4
Tororo *Uganda* 78D3
Toros Dağlari Mts *Turk* 30B2
Torquato Severo *Brazil* 72E2
Torrance *USA* 65C4
Torrão *Port* 19A2
Torreblanca *Spain* 19C1
Torre del Greco *Italy* 22C2
Torrelavega *Spain* 19B1
Torremolinos *Spain* 19B2
Torrens,L *Aust* 50A2
Torrent *Arg* 72D1
Torreón *Mexico* 66B2
Torre Pellice *Italy* 17B2
Torres Is *Vanuatu* 49F2
Torres Str *Aust* 48D2
Torres Vedras *Port* 19A2
Torrington Connecticut *USA* 60D2
Torrington Wyoming *USA* 57B3
Torrón *Mexico* 54C4
Torshavn *Faroes* 12D3
Tortona *Italy* 17C2
Tortosa *Spain* 19C1
Torūd *Iran* 34D1
Toruń *Pol* 21D2
Tory I *Irish Rep* 13B2
Torzhok *USSR* 24E4
Tosa *Japan* 42B4
Tosa-shimizu *Japan* 41C5
Tosa-wan B *Japan* 41C5
Toscana Region *Italy* 17D3
To-shima I *Japan* 42C4
Tosmo *USSR* 12L7
Tosno *USSR* 24E4
Tostado *Arg* 72C1
Tosu *Japan* 42B4
Tosya *Turk* 30B1
Totala *Indon* 45B3
Tot'ma *USSR* 24G3
Totnes *Eng* 15D6
Totness *Suriname* 71G2
Totolapan *Mexico* 67C2
Totona *Spain* 19B2
Totoral *Chile* 72A1
Totoralejos *Arg* 72C1
Tottenham *Aust* 50C2
Tottori *Japan* 41C4
Touba *Ivory Coast* 76B4
Touba *Sen* 76A3
Toubkal Mt *Mor* 76B1
Toucy *France* 16B3
Tougan *U Volta* 77F3
Touggourt *Alg* 77D2
Tougué *Guinea* 76A3
Toul *France* 16C2
Toulon *France* 18D3
Toulouse *France* 18C3
Toumodi *Ivory Coast* 76B4
Toungoo *Burma* 43B2
Tourcoing *France* 16B1
Tourine *Maur* 76A2
Tournai *Belg* 16B1
Tourouvre *France* 16A2
Tours *France* 18C2
Towada *Japan* 41E3
Towada-ko L *Japan* 41E3
Towanda *USA* 60B2
Towner *USA* 57B2
Townsend *USA* 64D1
Townsville *Aust* 48D2
Towraghondi *Afghan* 34E1
Towson *USA* 60B3
Towy R *Wales* 15D6
Toyah *USA* 62B3
Toya-ko L *Japan* 42D2
Toyama *Japan* 41D4
Toyama-wan B *Japan* 42C3
Toygunen *USSR* 56D2
Toyohashi *Japan* 42C4
Toyonaka *Japan* 42C4
Toyooka *Japan* 42B3
Toyota *Japan* 41D4
Tozeur *Tunisia* 77D2
Traben-Trarbach *W Germ* 16D2
Trabzon *Turk* 30C1
Tracy Minnesota *USA* 57C3
Traiguén *Chile* 72A3
Trail *Can* 52G5
Tralee *Irish Rep* 13B3
Tramore *Irish Rep* 15B5
Tranås *Sweden* 12G7
Trang *Thai* 43B4
Trangan I *Indon* 39G7
Trangie *Aust* 50C2
Tranqueras *Urug* 72D2
Transalaskan Pipeline *USA* 56J2
Transantarctic Mts *Ant* 80E
Transcona *Can* 57C2
Transvaal Province *S Africa* 79C6
Transylvanian Alps = Muntii Carpaţii Meridionali
Trapani *Italy* 22C3
Traralgon *Aust* 50C3
Trarza Region *Maur* 76A3
Trat *Thai* 43C3
Travaillant L *Can* 56M2
Traveller's L *Aust* 50B2
Travemünde *W Germ* 20C2
Traverse City *USA* 58B2
Traverse Peak Mt *USA* 56G2
Travers,Mt *NZ* 51B2
Travis,L *USA* 62C3
Trebbia R *Italy* 17C2
Třebíč *Czech* 20D3
Trebinje *Yugos* 23D2
Trebon *Czech* 20C3
Treinta y Tres *Urug* 72E2
Trelew *Arg* 69C6
Trelleborg *Sweden* 12G7
Tremadog B *Wales* 15C5
Tremblant,Mt *Can* 59E1
Tremont *USA* 60B2
Tremonton *USA* 64D2
Trenčin *Czech* 21D3
Trenque Lauquén *Arg* 72C3
Trent R *Eng* 15E5
Trentino Region *Italy* 17D1
Trento *Italy* 17D1
Trenton *Can* 59D2
Trenton Missouri *USA* 63D1
Trenton New Jersey *USA* 60C2
Trepassey *Can* 53N5
Tres Arroyos *Arg* 72C3
Tres Corações *Brazil* 73C3
Três Lagoas *Brazil* 69F2
Tres Lomas *Arg* 72C3
Tres Passos *Brazil* 72E1
Tres Picos *Mexico* 67D2
Três Rios *Brazil* 73D3
Trets *France* 17A3
Treviglio *Italy* 17C2
Treviso *Italy* 17E2
Treysa *W Germ* 16E1
Trezzo *Italy* 17C2
Tribune *USA* 62B2
Trichūr *India* 36B2
Trida *Aust* 50C2
Trier *W Germ* 16D2
Trieste *Italy* 22C1
Triglav Mt *Yugos* 17E1
Trikomo *Cyprus* 31B1
Trim *Irish Rep* 15B5
Trincomalee *Sri Lanka* 36C3
Trinidad *Bol* 70F6
Trinidad *Urug* 72D2
Trinidad *USA* 62B2
Trinidad I *Arg* 72C3
Trinidad I *Caribbean* 68E4
Trinidade I *Atlantic O* 74G6
Trinidad & Tobago Is Republic *Caribbean* 68E4
Trinity *USA* 63C3
Trinity R *USA* 54D3
Trinity B *Can* 53N5
Trinity Is *USA* 56H4
Trion *USA* 61B2
Triora *Italy* 17B2
Tripoli *Leb* 31C1
Tripoli *Libya* 75A1
Trípolis *Greece* 23E3
Tripura State *India* 37D3
Tristan da Cunha Is *Atlantic O* 74H6
Trivandrum *India* 36B3
Trnava *Czech* 21D3
Trobriand Is *PNG* 48E1
Trois Pistoles *Can* 59F1
Trois-Riviéres *Can* 59E1
Troitsk *USSR* 26H4
Troitsko Pechorsk *USSR* 24K3
Troitskoye *USSR* 41D2
Troitzk *USSR* 24L5
Trollhättan *Sweden* 12G7
Trollheimen Mt *Nor* 12F6
Tromsø *Nor* 12H5
Trondheim *Nor* 12G6
Trondheimfjord Inlet *Nor* 12G6
Troödos Range Mts *Cyprus* 31B1
Troon *Scot* 14C4
Tropic of Cancer 74J3
Tropic of Capricorn 74K6
Troudenni *Mali* 76B2
Trout L Ontario *Can* 53J4
Trout Peak Mt *USA* 64E2
Trout Run *USA* 60B2
Trouville-sur-Mer *France* 16A2
Troy Alabama *USA* 61B2
Troy Montana *USA* 64C1
Troy New York *USA* 60D1
Troy Ohio *USA* 58C2
Troy Pennsylvania *USA* 60B2
Troyan *Bulg* 23E2
Troyes *France* 16C2
Troy Peak Mt *USA* 65C3
Trucial Coast Region *UAE* 33F2
Truckee R *USA* 65B3
Trujillo *Honduras* 66D3
Trujillo *Peru* 70C5
Trujillo *Spain* 19A2
Trujillo *Ven* 70D2
Trumbull,Mt *USA* 65D3
Trundle *Aust* 50C2
Truro *Can* 53M5
Truro *Eng* 15C6
Trust Territories of the Pacific Is *Pacific O* 39G6
Truth or Consequences *USA* 62A3
Tsagaan Nuur L *Mongolia* 38C2
Tsagan-Tologoy *USSR* 38C1
Tsaratanana *Madag* 79E5
Tsau *Botswana* 79C6
Tsavo *Kenya* 78D4
Tsavo Nat Pk *Kenya* 78D4
Tschida,L *USA* 57B2
Tselinograd *USSR* 26J4
Tses *Namibia* 79B6
Tsetserleg *Mongolia* 38C2
Tsetserleg *Mongolia* 38D2
Tsévié *Togo* 77G4
Tshabong *Botswana* 79C6
Tshane *Botswana* 79C6
Tshela *Zaïre* 78B4
Tshibala *Zaïre* 79C4
Tshikapa *Zaïre* 78C4
Tshuapa R *Zaïre* 78C4
Tsihombe *Madag* 79E6
Tsimlyanskoye Vodokhranilishche Res *USSR* 25G6
Tsinan = Jinan
Tsingtao = Qingdao
Tsiroanomandidy *Madag* 79E5
Tsna R *USSR* 21F2
Tsogt Ovoo *Mongolia* 40B1
Tsu *Japan* 42C4
Tsubata *Japan* 42C3
Tsuchira *Japan* 41E4
Tsugaru-kaikyō Str *Japan* 41E3
Tsumeb *Namibia* 79B5
Tsumis *Namibia* 79B6
Tsunugi *Japan* 42C3
Tsuruga *Japan* 41D4
Tsuruoka *Japan* 41D4
Tsushima *Japan* 42C3
Tsushima I *Japan* 41B5
Tsushima-Kaikyō = Korea Str
Tsuyama *Japan* 41C4
Tua R *Port* 19A1
Tuangku I *Indon* 44A2
Tuapse *USSR* 25F7
Tuatapere *NZ* 51A3
Tuba City *USA* 65D3
Tubarão *Brazil* 69G3
Tubas *Israel* 31C2
Tubbataha Reefs Is *Phil* 45E9
Tübingen *W Germ* 20B3
Tubruq *Libya* 75B1
Tuckerton *USA* 60C3
Tucson *USA* 65D4
Tucumán State *Arg* 69C3
Tucumcari *USA* 62B2
Tucunuco *Arg* 72B2
Tucupita *Ven* 70F2
Tudela *Spain* 19B1
Tudenet L *Can* 56N2
Tudmur *Syria* 30C3
Tuerto *Arg* 72C2
Tuggerah L *Aust* 50D2
Tugidak I *USA* 56H4
Tuguegarao *Phil* 45F7
Tugur *USSR* 27P4
Tugur R *USSR* 41D1
Tuhai He R *China* 40D2
Tui R *U Volta* 77F3
Tuktoyaktuk *Can* 56M2
Tukums *USSR* 21E1
Tukuyu *Tanz* 79D4
Tukzar *Afghan* 35B1
Tula *Mexico* 67C1
Tula *USSR* 24F5
Tulancingo *Mexico* 67C1
Tulangbawang R *Indon* 44B3
Tulare *USA* 65C3
Tularosa *USA* 62A3
Tulcán *Colombia* 70C3
Tulcea *Rom* 25D7
Tul'chin *USSR* 21F3
Tuli *Zim* 79C6
Tulia *USA* 62B3
Tulik V *USA* 56E5
Tulkarm *Israel* 31C2
Tullahoma *USA* 61B1
Tullarnore *Irish Rep* 15B5
Tulle *France* 18C2
Tullins *France* 17A2
Tullos *USA* 63D3
Tullow *Irish Rep* 15B5
Tully *USA* 60B1
Tulsa *USA* 63C2
Tulūl ash Shāmīyah Desert Region *Syria/S Arabia* 30C3
Tulun *USSR* 27M4
Tulungagung *Indon* 44D4
Tumaco *Colombia* 70C3
Tumany *USSR* 27R3
Tumbarumba *Aust* 50C3
Tumbes *Ecuador* 70B4
Tumby Bay *Aust* 50A2
Tumen *China* 41B3
Tumkūr *India* 36B2
Tump *Pak* 34E3
Tumpat *Malay* 43C4
Tumsar *India* 35D4
Tumu *Ghana* 77F3
Tumut *Aust* 50C3
Tumut R *Aust* 50C3
Tunapuna *Trinidad* 68L1
Tunceli *Turk* 30C2
Tunduma *Zambia* 79D4
Tunduru *Tanz* 79D5
Tundzha R *Bulg* 23F2
Tungabhadra R *India* 36B1
Tung-Chiang *Taiwan* 38E4
Tungnafellsjökull Mts *Iceland* 12B2
Tungsten *Can* 56N3
Tunguska R *USSR* 27M3
Tuni *India* 36C1
Tunis *Tunisia* 77E1
Tunja *Colombia* 70D2
Tunkhannock *USA* 60C2
Tuntutulik *USA* 56F3
Tununak *USA* 56F3
Tunuyán *Arg* 72B2
Tunuyán R *Arg* 72B2
Tunxi *China* 40D4
Tupā *Brazil* 73B3
Tupaciguara *Brazil* 73C2
Tupanciretа *Brazil* 72E1
Tupelo *USA* 63E3
Tupik *USSR* 21G1
Tupiza *Bol* 70E8
Tupper Lake *USA* 59E2
Tupungato *Arg* 72B2
Tupungato Mt *Arg* 69C4
Tura *India* 37D2
Tura *USSR* 27M3
Tura R *USSR* 24L4
Turabah *S Arabia* 32D2
Turān *Iran* 34D1
Turan *USSR* 27L4
Turayf *S Arabia* 30C3
Turbat *Pak* 34E3
Turbo *Colombia* 70C2
Turda *Rom* 23E1
Turfan Depression *China* 26K5
Turgay *USSR* 26H4
Turgen Uul Mt *Mongolia* 27L5
Turgutlu *Turk* 30A2
Turhal *Turk* 30C1
Türi *USSR* 12K7
Turia R *Spain* 19B2
Turin = Torino
Turinsk *USSR* 24L4
Turiy Rog *USSR* 41C2
Turkestan Region *C Asia* 28E1
Turkestan *USSR* 29E1
Turkey Republic *W Asia* 30C2
Turkmenskaya SSR Republic *USSR* 28D1
Turkmenskiy Zaliv B *USSR* 34C1
Turks Is *Caribbean* 68C2
Turku *Fin* 12J6
Turkwel R *Kenya* 78D3
Turlock *USA* 65B3
Turnagain,C *NZ* 51C2
Turneffe I *Belize* 66D3
Turners Falls *USA* 60D1
Turnhout *Belg* 16C1
Turnu Măgurele *Rom* 23E2
Turnu-Severin *Rom* 23E2
Turpan *China* 27K5
Turquino Mt *Cuba* 68B2
Turtkul' *USSR* 28E1
Turtle Creek Res *USA* 63C2
Turukhansk *USSR* 27K3
Turuntayevo *USSR* 38D1
Turvo R Goias *Brazil* 73B2
Turvo R São Paulo *Brazil* 73C3
Tur'ya R *USSR* 21E2
Tuscaloosa *USA* 63E3
Tuscany = Toscana
Tuscarora Mt *USA* 60B2
Tuscola Illinois *USA* 58B3
Tuscola Texas *USA* 62C3
Tuscumbia *USA* 61B2
Tusharīk *Iran* 34D2
Tussey Mt *USA* 60A2
Tuticorin *India* 36B3
Tutrakan *Bulg* 23F2
Tuttlingen *W Germ* 20B3
Tutulia I *American Samoa* 49H2
Tututepec *Mexico* 67C2
Tuul Gol R *Mongolia* 38D2
Tuvalu Is *Pacific O* 49G1
Tuvinskaya Republic *USSR* 27L4
Tuwayilel Haj Mt *Jordan* 31C4
Tuwwal *S Arabia* 32C2
Tuxpan Jalisco *Mexico* 67B2
Tuxpan Nayarit *Mexico* 67A1
Tuxpan Veracruz *Mexico* 67C1
Tuxtepec *Mexico* 67C2
Tuxtla Gutiérrez *Mexico* 66C3
Túy *Spain* 19A1
Tuy Hoa *Viet* 43D3
Tuz Gölü Salt L *Turk* 30B2
Tuz Khurmātū *Iraq* 30D3
Tuzla *Yugos* 23D2
Tweed R *Scot/Eng* 14D4
Tweed Heads *Aust* 50D1
Tweedsmuir Hills *Scot* 14D4
Twentynine Palms *USA* 65C4
Twillingate *Can* 53N5
Twin Bridges *USA* 64D1
Twin Buttes Res *USA* 62B3
Twin Falls *USA* 64D2
Twins,The Mt *NZ* 51B2
Two Harbours *USA* 58A1
Two Rivers *USA* 58B2
Tygda *USSR* 27O4
Tyler *USA* 63C3
Tymovskoye *USSR* 41E1
Tynda *USSR* 38F1
Tyne R *Eng* 14E4
Tyne and Wear Metropolitan County *Eng* 14E4
Tynemouth *Eng* 14E4
Tynset *Nor* 12G6
Tyonek *USA* 56H4
Tyr *Leb* 31C2
Tyre = Tyr
Tyrma *USSR* 41C1
Tyrma R *USSR* 41C1
Tyrone County *N Ire* 14B4
Tyrone New Mexico *USA* 62A3
Tyrone Pennsylvania *USA* 60A2
Tyrrell,L *Aust* 50B3
Tyrrhenian S *Italy* 22C2
Tyumen' *USSR* 26H4
Tyung R *USSR* 27O3
Tywyn *Wales* 15C5
Tzoumérka Mt *Greece* 23E3

U

Uarsciek *Somalia* 78E3
Ubá *Brazil* 73D3
Ubaí *Brazil* 73D2
Ubaitaba *Brazil* 73E1
Ubangi R *CAR* 78B3
Ubaye R *France* 17B2
Ube *Japan* 42B4
Ubeda *Spain* 19B2
Ubekendt Ejland I *Greenland* 53N2
Uberaba *Brazil* 73C2
Uberlândia *Brazil* 73C2
Ubon Ratchathani *Thai* 43D2
Ubort R *USSR* 21F2
Ubundi *Zaïre* 78C4
Ucayali R *Peru* 70D5
Uch *Pak* 35C3
Uchiura-wan B *Japan* 41E3
Uchur R *USSR* 27P4
Ucluelet *Can* 64A1
Uda R *USSR* 38C1
Udaipur *India* 35C4
Udaipur Garhi *Nepal* 37C2
Udaquiola *Arg* 72D3
Uddevalla *Sweden* 12G7
Uddjaur L *Sweden* 12H5
Udgir *India* 36B1
Udhampur *India* 35D2
Udine *Italy* 17E1
Udmurtskaya ASSR Republic *USSR* 24J4
Udon Thani *Thai* 43C2
Udskaya Guba B *USSR* 27P4
Udskoye *USSR* 41C1
Udupi *India* 36A2
Udzha *USSR* 27N2
Ueda *Japan* 42C3
Uele R *Zaïre* 78C3
Uelen *USSR* 27U3
Uelzen *W Germ* 20C2
Uere R *Zaïre* 78C3
Ufa *USSR* 24K5
Ufa R *USSR* 24K4
Ugab R *Namibia* 79B6
Ugaila R *Tanz* 78D4
Ugak B *USA* 56H4
Uganda Republic *Africa* 78D3
Ugashik B *USA* 56G4
Ugashik L *USA* 56G4
Ugine *France* 17B2
'Uglat as Suqūr *S Arabia* 32D1
Uglegorsk *USSR* 41E2
Uglich *USSR* 24F4
Uglovoye *USSR* 41C3
Ugra R *USSR* 24F5
Uig *Scot* 14B3
Uige *Angola* 79B4
Üijŏngbu *S Korea* 42A3
Uil *USSR* 25J6
Uinta Mts *USA* 64D2

Ŭiryŏng Villa Ahumada

Ŭiryŏng S Korea 42A3
Uisŏng S Korea 42A3
Uitenhage S Africa 79C7
Ujfehértó Hung 21E3
Uji Japan 42C4
Ujiji Tanz 78C4
Ujina Chile 69C2
Ujjain India 35D4
Ujung Indon 45B4
Ujung Pandang Indon 48A1
Ukerewe I Tanz 78D4
Ukhrul India 37D2
Ukhta USSR 24J3
Ukiah California USA 65B3
Ukiah Oregon USA 64C1
Ukiah USA 54A3
Ukmerge USSR 21E1
Ukrainskaya Republic USSR 25D6
Uku-jima I Japan 42A4
Ulaanbaatar Mongolia 38D2
Ulaangom Mongolia 38C2
Ulaan Uul Mongolia 40C1
Ulangar Hu L China 29G1
Ulansuhai Nur L China 53B1
Ulan Ude USSR 38D1
Ulan Ul Hu L China 38C3
Ulapes Arg 72B2
Ul'beya R USSR 27Q3
Ulchin S Korea 41B4
Ulcinj Yugos 23D2
Uldz Mongolia 38E2
Uliastay Mongolia 38C2
Ulla USSR 21F1
Ulladulla Aust 50D3
Ullapool Scot 14C3
Ullsfjorden Inlet Nor 12H5
Ullswater L Eng 15D4
Ullung-do I S Korea 41C4
Ulm W Germ 20C3
Uloowaranie,L Aust 50A1
Ulsan S Korea 41B4
Ulster Region N Ire 15B4
Ulu Indon 45C2
Ulungur He R China 26K5
Ulungur Hu L China 26K5
Ulva I Scot 14B3
Ulverston Eng 15D4
Ulverstone Aust 50E3
Ulya R USSR 27Q4
Ulyanovka USSR 21G3
Ul'yanovsk USSR 24H5
Ulysses USA 62B2
Uman USSR 25E6
Umanak Greenland 53N2
Umaria India 37B3
Umarkot Pak 35B3
Umaroona,L Aust 50A1
Umatilla USA 64C1
Umba USSR 24E2
Umba R Tanz 78D4
Umbertide Italy 17E3
Umboi I PNG 48D1
Ume R Sweden 12H6
Umea Sweden 12J6
Umiat USA 56H2
Umm al Qaiwain UAE 33G1
Umm as Samim Salt Marsh Oman 33G2
Umm Bell Sudan 78C2
Umm Hagar Eth 78D2
Umm Inderaba Sudan 32B3
Umm Keddada Sudan 78C2
Umm Lajj S Arabia 32C1
Umm Ruwaba Sudan 78D2
Umm Sa'id Qatar 33F2
Umm Saiyala Sudan 32B4
Umnaiti R Zim 79C5
Umnak I USA 56E5
Umpqua R USA 64B2
Umred India 35D4
Umtata S Africa 79C7
Umuarama Brazil 73B3
Una Brazil 73E2
Una R Yugos 22D1
Unadilla USA 60C1
Unadilla R USA 60C1
Unai Brazil 73C2
Unalakleet USA 56F3
Unalaska I USA 56E5
Unayzah S Arabia 32D1
Uncasville USA 60D2
Uncompahgre Plat USA 62A2
Underwood USA 57B2
Unecha USSR 24E5
Uneisa Jordan 31C3
Ungava B Can 53M4
União de Vitória Brazil 69F3
Unimak Bight USA 56F5
Unimak I USA 56F5
Unimak Pass USA 56E5
Unión Arg 72B3
Union Missouri USA 63D2
Union S Carolina USA 61C2
Union City Pennsylvania USA 59D2
Union City Tennessee USA 61B1
Union Springs USA 61B2
Uniontown USA 59D3
United Arab Emirates Arabian Pen 33F2
United States Range Mts Can 53K1
Unity USA 64C2
University Park USA 62A3
Unna W Germ 16D1
Unnão India 37B2
Unsan N Korea 42A2
Unst I Scot 14E1
Unuana I Indon 45B3
Ünye Turk 30C1
Unzha R USSR 24G4
Upata Ven 70F2
Upemba Nat Pk Zaïre 79C4
Upernavik Greenland 53N2
Upington S Africa 79C6
Upolu I Western Samoa 49H2
Upper Arlington USA 58C2
Upper Hutt NZ 51C2
Upper Klamath L USA 64B2
Upper L USA 64B2
Upper Laugh Erne L N Ire 15B4
Upper Manzanilla Trinidad 68L1
Upper Seal,L Can 53L4
Upperville USA 60B3
Upper Volta Republic Africa 76B3
Uppsala Sweden 12H7
Upsala Can 57D2
Upton USA 57B3
Urad Qianqi China 40B1
Urairah S Arabia 33E1
Urakawa Japan 42D2
Ural R USSR 25J5
Uralla Aust 50D2
Ural'sk USSR 25J5
Uralskiy Khrebet Mts USSR 26G4
Urandi Brazil 73D1
Uranium City Can 52H4
Urapunga Aust 39G8
Uravan USA 62A2
Urawa Japan 42C3
Uray USSR 24L3
Urbana Illinois USA 58B2
Urbana Ohio USA 58C2
Urbino Italy 17E3
Ure R Eng 15D4
Uren' USSR 24H4
Urfa Turk 30C2
Urgal USSR 41C1
Urgench USSR 28E1
Urgun Afghan 35B2
Urkan R USSR 41B1
Urla Turk 23F3
Urma USSR 41C1
Urmi R USSR 41C2
Uromi Nig 77H4
Uroševac Yugos 23E2
Uruaçu Brazil 71J6
Uruacu Brazil 73C1
Uruapan Mexico 67B2
Urucuia R Brazil 73C2
Uruguai R Brazil 72E1
Uruguaiana Brazil 72D1
Uruguay Republic S America 69E4
Uruguay R Urug 69E4
Urumīyeh Iran 34B1
Ürümqi China 29G1
Urup I USSR 38J2
'Urūq al Awārik Region S Arabia 33E3
Urusha USSR 41A1
Uruzgan Afghan 35B2
Uryū-ko L Japan 42D2
Uryupinsk USSR 25G5
Urzhum USSR 24J4
Urziceni Rom 23F2
Usa China 29G1
Usa Japan 42B4
Usa R USSR 24L2
Uşak Turk 30A2
Usakos Namibia 79B6
Ushashi Tanz 78D4
Ush Tobe USSR 26J5
Ushuaia Arg 69C8
Ushumun USSR 27O4
Usk R Wales 16E1
Üsküdar Turk 30A1
Uslar W Germ 16E1
Usogorsk USSR 24H3
Usol'ye Sibirskoye USSR 27M4
Uspallata Arg 72B2
Ussuri R USSR 41C2
Ussuriysk USSR 41C3
Ust'Belaya USSR 27T3
Ust'Bol'sheretsk USSR 27R4
Uster Switz 17C1
Ustica I Italy 22C3
Ústi nad Labem Czech 20C2
Ust'Ishim USSR 26J4
Ustka Pol 20D2
Ust'Kamchatsk USSR 27S4
Ust'-Kamenogorsk USSR 26K5
Ust'Kara USSR 24L2
Ust Karabula USSR 27L4
Ust'Katav USSR 24K4
Ust'-Kut USSR 27M4
Ust Labinsk USSR 25F6
Ust'Maya USSR 27P3
Ust'Nem USSR 24K3
Ust'Nera USSR 27Q3
Ust'Nyukzha USSR 27O4
Ust'Ordynskiy USSR 27M4
Ust'Tsil'ma USSR 24J2
Ust'Umal'ta USSR 27P4
Ust'ya R USSR 24G3
Ust' Yuribey USSR 24M2
Usuki Japan 42B4
Usumacinta R Guatemala/Mexico 66C3
Usvyaty USSR 21G1
Utah State USA 54B3
Utah L USA 65D2
Utara I Indon 45C2
Utena USSR 21F1
Uthal Pak 35B3
Utica USA 60C1
Utiel Spain 19B2
Utrecht Neth 20B2
Utrera Spain 19A2
Utsjoki Fin 12K5
Utsunomiya Japan 41D4
Uttaradit Thai 43C2
Uttar Pradesh State India 37B2
Utucuia R Brazil 73C2
Utukok R USA 56F2
Uval USSR 26H4
Uvéa I Nouvelle Calédonie 49F3
Uvinza Tanz 78D4
Uvira Zaïre 78C4
Uvkusigssat Greenland 53N2
Uvlade USA 62C4
Uvsikaupunki Fin 12J6
Uvs Nuur L China 38C1
Uwajima Japan 41C5
Uwak Indon 44A2
Uxin Qi China 40B2
Uyandina USSR 27Q3
Uyar USSR 27L4
Uyuni Bol 70E8
Uyûn Mûsa Well Egypt 31B4
Uzbekskaya S.S.R. Republic USSR 28E1
Uzerche France 18C2
Uzh R USSR 21F2
Uzhgorod USSR 21E3
Uzlovaya USSR 24F5
Uzunköprü Turk 30A1

V

Vaalwater S Africa 79C6
Vaasa Fin 12J6
Vác Hung 21D3
Vacaria Brazil 69F3
Vacaria R Mato Grosso Do Sul Brazil 73B3
Vacaria R Minas Gerais Brazil 73D2
Va Castell Arg 72B1
Vacaville USA 65B3
Vadodara India 35C4
Vadsø Nor 12K4
Vaduz Leichtenstein 17C1
Vaga R USSR 24G3
Va Gesell Arg 69E5
Vågø Faroes 12D3
Váh R Czech 21D3
Vahel Israel 31C3
Vaigai R India 36B2
Vaitupu I Tuvalu 49G1
Val USSR 41E1
Vâlcea Rom 25C6
Valcheta Arg 69C6
Valdagno Italy 17D2
Valday USSR 24E4
Valdayskaya Vozvyshennost' Upland USSR 24E4
Val de la Pascua Ven 70E2
Valdepeñas Spain 19B2
Valdez USA 56J3
Valdivia Chile 72A3
Val d'oise Department France 16B2
Val-d'Or Can 59D1
Valdosta USA 61C2
Vale USA 64C2
Valença Bahia Brazil 73E1
Valença Rio de Janeiro Brazil 73D3
Valence France 18C3
Valencia Region Spain 19B2
Valencia Spain 19B2
Valencia Ven 70E1
Valencia de Alcantara Spain 19A2
Valenciennes France 16B1
Valentine Nebraska USA 57B3
Valentine Texas USA 62B3
Valenza Italy 17C2
Valera Ven 70D2
Valga USSR 12K7
Valikiyo USSR 26E4
Valjevo Yugos 23D2
Valkeakoski Fin 12J6
Valla de Sannago Mexico 67B1
Valladolid Mexico 66D2
Valladolid Spain 19A1
Valle d'Aosta Region Italy 17B2
Valle de la Pascua Ven 68D5
Valle d'Isére France 17B2
Valledupar Colombia 70D1
Vallée de l'Azaouak V Niger 76C3
Vallée Tilemis V Mali 76C3
Valle Grande Bol 70F7
Vallejo USA 54A3
Vallenar Chile 72A1
Valle Pegueno V Brazil 73D1
Valletta Malta 77E1
Valley City USA 57C2
Valley Falls USA 64B2
Valleyfield Can 59E1
Valli di Comacchio Lg Italy 17E2
Valls Spain 19C1
Valmiera USSR 21F1
Valparaiso Brazil 73B3
Valparaiso Chile 72A2
Valparaiso Mexico 67B1
Valparaiso USA 61B2
Valsād India 35C4
Valuyki USSR 25F5
Valverde del Camino Spain 19A2
Vammala Fin 12J6
Van Turk 30D2
Vanavara USSR 27M3
Van Buren Arkansas USA 63D2
Van Buren Maine USA 59F1
Vancouleurs France 16C2
Vancouver Can 52F5
Vancouver USA 64B1
Vancouver,C USA 56E3
Vancouver I Can 52F5
Vancouver,Mt Can 56L3
Vandalia Illinois USA 58B3
Vandalia Ohio USA 58C3
Vanderhoof Can 52F4
Van Diemen,C Aust 39G8
Van Diemen G Aust 48C2
Vanegas Mexico 67B1
Vänern L Sweden 12G7
Vänersborg Sweden 12G7
Van Etten USA 60B1
Vangaindrano Madag 79E6
Van Gölü Salt L Turk 30D2
Vang Vieng Laos 43C2
Van Horn USA 62B3
Vanier Can 59D1
Vanikoto I Solomon Is 49F2
Vanino USSR 41E2
Vankarem USSR 27U3
Vännäs Sweden 12H6
Vannes France 18B2
Vanoise Mts France 17B2
Vanrhynsdorp S Africa 79B7
Vansittart I Can 53K3
Vanua Lava I Vanuatu 49F2
Vanua Levu I Fiji 49G2
Vanuatu Is Pacific O 47K5
Van Wert USA 58C2
Var R France 17B2
Vara R Italy 17C2
Varallo Italy 17C2
Varāmīn Iran 34C1
Vārānasi India 37B2
Varandey USSR 24K2
Varangerfjord Inlet Nor 12K4
Varangerhalvøya Pen Nor 12L4
Varazdin Yugos 22D1
Varazze Italy 17C2
Varberg Sweden 12G7
Varde Den 12F7
Vardø Nor 12L4
Varéna USSR 21E2
Varenna Italy 17C2
Varese Italy 17C2
Varginha Brazil 73C3
Varkaus Fin 12K6
Varna Bulg 23F2
Värnamo Sweden 12G7
Varnek USSR 24K2
Varnville USA 61C2
Várzea da Palma Brazil 73D2
Varzi Italy 17C2
Vasconcelos Brazil 72E2
Vascongadas Region Spain 19B1
Vāshīr Afghan 34E2
Vashka R USSR 24H3
Vasil'Kov USSR 25E5
Vassar USA 58C2
Västerås Sweden 12H7
Västervik Sweden 12H7
Vasto Italy 22C2
Vatnajökull Mts Iceland 12B2
Vatneyri Iceland 12A1
Vatra Dornei Rom 23F1
Vättern L Sweden 12G7
Vaughn USA 62A3
Va Unión Arg 72B1
Va Unión Coahuila Mexico 63F4
Va Unión Durango Mexico 67B1
Va Unión Sinaloa Mexico 67A1
Vaupés R Colombia 70D3
Vava'u Group Is Tonga 49H2
Vavunija Sri Lanka 36C3
Växjö Sweden 12G7
Vedia Arg 72C2
Vega USA 62B2
Vega I Nor 12G5
Vega Pt USA 56B6
Vejer de la Frontera Spain 19A2
Vejle Den 12F7
Velázquez Urug 72E2
Velebit Mts Yugos 22D2
Velenje Yugos 22D1
Velhas R Brazil 73D2
Velikaya R Rossiyskaya USSR 27T3
Velikaya R RSFSR USSR 21F1
Velikaya R USSR 12K7
Velikaya Kema USSR 41D2
Velikiye Luki USSR 24E4
Velikiy Ustyug USSR 24H3
Veliko Tŭrnovo Bulg 23F2
Vélingara Sen 76A3
Velizh USSR 21G1
Vella Lavella I Solomon Is 49E1
Vellore India 36B2
Velmerstat Mt W Germ 16E1
Vel'sk USSR 24G3
Velva USA 57B2
Vembanad L India 36B3
Vemor'ye USSR 41E2
Venado Tuerto Arg 69D4
Vençeslau Braz Brazil 73C3
Vendeuvre-sur-Barse France 16C2
Vendôme France 18C2
Venetie USA 56J2
Veneto Region Italy 17D2
Venezia Italy 17E2
Venezia Region Italy 17E2
Venezuela Republic S America 70E2
Vengurla India 36A1
Veniaminof V USA 56G4
Venice = Venezia
Venkatagiri India 36B2
Venlo Neth 20B2
Venta R USSR 21E1
Ventspils USSR 21E1
Ventuari R Ven 70E3
Ventura USA 65C4
Vepsovskaya Vozvyshennost' Upland USSR 24E3
Vera Arg 72C1
Vera Spain 19B2
Veracruz Mexico 67C2
Veracruz State Mexico 67C1
Verāval India 35C4
Verbania Italy 17C2
Vercelli Italy 17C2
Vercors Plat France 17A2
Vérde R Brazil 73A1
Verde R Goias Brazil 73B2
Verde R Jalisco Mexico 67B1
Verde R Mato Grosso do Sul Brazil 73B2
Verde R Oaxaca Mexico 67C2
Verde R USA 65D4
Verde,C = Cap Vert
Verde Grande R Brazil 73D2
Verde,Pen Arg 72C3
Verdon R France 18D3
Verdun France 16C2
Verdun-sur-le-Doubs France 17A1
Vereeniging S Africa 79C6
Vereshchagino USSR 24J4
Vereshchagino USSR 26K3
Verga,C Guinea 76A3
Vergara Arg 72D3
Vergara Urug 72E2
Vergato Italy 17D2
Verin Spain 19A1
Verissimo Sarmento Angola 79C4
Verkh Angara R USSR 27N4
Verkheimbatskoye USSR 26K3
Verkhneural'sk USSR 24K5
Verkhnevilyuysk USSR 27O3
Verkhnyaya Toyma USSR 24H3
Verkhoyansk USSR 27P3
Verkhoyanskiy Khrebet Mts USSR 27O3
Verkola USSR 24H3
Vermelho R Brazil 73B2
Vermenton France 16B3
Vermilion Can 52G4
Vermilion Bay Can 57D2
Vermillion USA 57C3
Vermillion L USA 57D2
Vermont State USA 55F2
Vernal USA 64E2
Verneuil France 16A2
Verneukpan Salt Pan S Africa 79C6
Vernon Can 52G4
Vernon France 16A2
Vernon USA 62C3
Vero Beach USA 61E4
Verola Greece 23E2
Verolanuova Italy 17D2
Verona Italy 17D2
Verónica Arg 72D3
Versailles France 16B2
Verviers Belg 16C1
Vervins France 16B2
Veselinovo USSR 21G3
Vesle R France 16C2
Vesoul France 18D2
Vesterålen Is Nor 12G5
Vestfjorden Inlet Nor 12G5
Vestmannaeyjar Iceland 12A2
Vesuvio Mt Italy 22C2
Veszprém Hung 21D3
Vetlanda Sweden 12H7
Vetluga R USSR 24G4
Veurne Belg 16B1
Vevey Switz 17B1
Vexin Region France 16B2
Veynes France 17A2
Vézelise France 16C2
Viana do Castelo Port 19A1
Viareggio Italy 17D3
Viborg Den 12F7
Vibo Valentia Italy 22D3
Vibraye France 16A2
Vice-commodoro Marambio Base Ant 80G2
Vicenza Italy 22C1
Vich Spain 19C1
Vichada R Colombia 70E3
Vichuga USSR 24G4
Vichy France 18C2
Vicksburg USA 63D3
Vicosa Brazil 73D3
Victor Harbor Aust 48C4
Victoria Arg 72C2
Victoria Cam 78A3
Victoria Chile 72A3
Victoria Hong Kong 40C5
Victoria Malay 44E1
Victoria State Aust 50B3
Victoria USA 63F4
Victoria R Aust 48C2
Victoria State Aust 48D4
Victoria de las Tunas Cuba 68B2
Victoria Falls Zambia/Zim 79C5
Victoria I Can 52G2
Victoria,L Aust 50B2
Victoria,L C Africa 78D4
Victoria Land Region Ant 80F7
Victoria,Mt Burma 37D3
Victoria,Mt PNG 39H7
Victoria Nile R Uganda 78D3
Victoria Range Mts NZ 51B2
Victoria River Downs Aust 48C2
Victoria Str Can 52H3
Victoriaville Can 59E1
Victoria West S Africa 79C7
Victorica Arg 72B3
Victorville USA 65C4
Vicuña Chile 72A2
Vicuña Mackenna Arg 72C2
Vidalia USA 61C2
Videle Rom 23F2
Vidin Bulg 23E2
Vidisha India 35D4
Vidzy USSR 21F1
Viedma Arg 69D6
Viéjo Costa Rica 68A4
Viella Spain 19C1
Vienna = Wien
Vienna Illinois USA 58B3
Vienna W Virginia USA 58C3
Vienne France 18C2
Vienne R France 18C2
Vientiane Laos 43C2
Vierwaldstätter See L Switz 17C1
Vierzon France 18C2
Vieste Italy 22D2
Vietnam Republic S E Asia 39D5
Vietri Viet 43D1
Vieux Fort St Lucia 68P2
Vif France 17A2
Vigan Phil 45F7
Vigevan Italy 17C2
Vignemale Mt France 18B3
Vigo Spain 19A1
Vijayawāda India 36C1
Vijosë R Alb 23D2
Vik Iceland 12B2
Vikhren Mt Bulg 23E2
Viking North Oilfield N Sea 15G5
Viking South Oilfield N Sea 15G5
Vikna I Nor 12G6
Vila da Maganja Mozam 79D5
Vila de Manatuto Indon 45C4
Vila de Salazar Indon 45C4
Vila Machado Mozam 79D5
Vilanculos Mozam 79D6
Vila Real Port 19A1
Vila Vasco da Gama Mozam 79D5
Vila Velha Brazil 73D3
Vilelas Arg 72C1
Vileyka USSR 21F2
Vilhelmina Sweden 12H6
Vilhena Brazil 71G6
Viljandi USSR 24D4
Vilkovo USSR 21F3
Villa Ahumada Mexico 62A3

Villa Angela
Waynesboro

Villa Angela Arg 72C1
Villa Atamisqui Arg 72C1
Villa Atuel Arg 72B2
Villaba Spain 19A1
Villa Carranza Mexico 67B2
Villach Austria 22C1
Villa Colon Arg 72B2
Villa Constitución Arg 72C2
Villa de Cos Mexico 67B1
Villa de Maria Arg 72C1
Villa de Reyes Mexico 67B1
Villa Dolores Arg 72B2
Villa Flores Mexico 67D2
Villafranca di Verona Italy 17D2
Villa General Mitre Arg 72C2
Villa General Roca Arg 72B2
Villa Gesell Arg 72D3
Villagran Mexico 67C1
Villaguay Arg 72D2
Villa Guillermina Arg 72D1
Villa Hayes Par 73A4
Villahermosa Mexico 66C3
Villa Hidalgo Mexico 67B1
Villa Huidobro Arg 72C2
Villa Iris Arg 72C3
Villa Maria Arg 72C2
Villa Montes Bol 70F8
Villa Neuva Mexico 67B1
Villa Nova de Gaia Port 19A1
Villanueva de la Serena Spain 19A2
Villanueva-y-Geltrú Spain 19C1
Villa Ojo de Agua Arg 72C1
Villa Regina Arg 72B3
Villarreal Spain 19B2
Villarrica Chile 72A3
Villarrica Par 69E3
Villarrobledo Spain 19B2
Villa San José Arg 72D2
Villa San Martin Arg 72C1
Villa Valeria Arg 72C2
Villavicencio Colombia 70D3
Villefranche France 18C2
Ville-Marie Can 53L5
Villena Spain 19B2
Villeneuve-St-Georges France 16B2
Villeneuve-sur-Lot France 18C3
Villeneuve-sur-Yonne France 16B2
Ville Platte USA 63D3
Villers-Cotterêts France 16B2
Villeurbanne France 18C2
Villingen-Schwenningen W Germ 16E2
Villupuram India 36B2
Vilnius USSR 21F2
Vilyuy USSR 27N3
Vilyuysk USSR 27O3
Vimoutiers France 16A2
Vina R Cam 77J4
Viña del Mar Chile 72A2
Vinaroz Spain 19C1
Vincennes USA 58B3
Vinchina Arg 72B1
Vindel R Sweden 12H5
Vindhya Range Mts India 35D4
Vineland USA 60C3
Vineyard Haven USA 60E2
Vinh Viet 43D2
Vinh Cam Ranh B Viet 43D3
Vinh Loi Viet 43D4
Vinh Long Viet 43D3
Vinita USA 63C2
Vinkovci Yugos 23D1
Vinnitsa USSR 21F3
Vinson Massif Upland Ant 80F3
Vinton USA 57D3
Vioolsdrift Namibia 79B6
Vipiteno Italy 17D1
Viqueque Indon 45C4
Virac Phil 45F8
Virddhāchalam India 36B2
Virden Can 57B2
Virei Angola 79B5
Virgem da Lapa Brazil 73D2
Virgin R USA 65D3
Virginia State USA 55F3
Virginia USA 57D2
Virginia Beach USA 59D3
Virginia City USA 65C3
Virgin Is Caribbean 68E3
Viroqua USA 58A2
Virovitica Yugos 22D1
Virton Belg 16C2
Virudunagar India 36B3
Vis I Yugos 22D2
Visalia USA 65C3
Visayan S Phil 45F8
Visby Sweden 12H7
Viscount Melville Sd Can 52H2
Višegrad Yugos 23D2
Viseu Port 19A1
Vishākhapatnam India 36C1
Vishera R USSR 24K3
Visp Switz 17B1
Vissingen Neth 18C1
Vista USA 65C4
Vistula = Wisla
Vitavia R Czech 20C3
Vite India 36A1
Vitebsk USSR 21G1
Viterbo Italy 22C2
Vitigudino Spain 19A1
Viti Levu I Fiji 55G2
Vitim R USSR 27N4
Vitora Spain 19B1
Vitória Brazil 71L8
Vitória da Conquista Brazil 71K6
Vitré France 18B2
Vitry-le-Francois France 16C2
Vittangi Sweden 12J5
Vittel France 16C2
Vittoria Italy 22C3
Vittorio Veneto Italy 17E2
Vityaz Depth Pacific O 38J2
Vivero Spain 19A1
Vivi R USSR 27L3
Vivorata Arg 72D3
Vizhne-Angarsk USSR 27N4
Vizianagaram India 36C1
Vizille France 17A2
Vizinga USSR 24J3
Vladeasa Mt Rom 23E1
Vladimir USSR 26F4
Vladimir Volynskiy USSR 21E2
Vladivostok USSR 41C3
Vlieland I Neth 20A2
Vlissingen Neth 16B1
Vlorë Alb 23D2
Vöcklabruck Austria 20C3
Vodnjan Yugos 17E2
Voeune Sai Camb 43D3
Vogel Peak Mt Nig 77J4
Vogelsberg Region W Germ 16E1
Voghera Italy 17C2
Vohibinany Madag 79E5
Vohimarina Madag 79F5
Voi Kenya 78D4
Voinjama Lib 76B4
Voiron France 18D2
Volborg USA 57A2
Volcán Baru Mt Panama 68A5
Volcán Citlaltepetl Mt Mexico 67C2
Volcán Lullaillaco Mt Chile 70E8
Volcáno Copahue Mt Chile 72A3
Volcáno Dumuyo Mt Arg 72A3
Volcano Is = Kazan Retto
Volcáno Lanin Mt Arg 72A3
Volcán Ollagüe Mt Chile 70E8
Volcáno Llaima Mt Chile 72A3
Volcáno Malpo Mt Arg 72B2
Volcáno Peteroa Mt Chile 72A3
Volcáno Tromen V Arg 72B3
Volcáno Villarrica Mt Chile 72A3
Volcán Paracutin Mt Mexico 67B2
Volcán Puraće Mt Colombia 70C3
Volcán Tinquiririca Mt Chile/Arg 72A2
Volchansk USSR 24K4
Volga R USSR 25H6
Volgodonsk USSR 25G6
Volgograd USSR 25G6
Volgogradskoye Vodokhranilishche Res USSR 25H5
Volkhov USSR 24E4
Volkhov R USSR 24E4
Volkovysk USSR 21E2
Volksrust S Africa 79C6
Volochanka USSR 27L1
Vologda USSR 24G4
Volognes France 18B2
Vólos Greece 23E3
Vol'sk USSR 25H5
Volta R Ghana 77G4
Volta Blanche R U Volta 77F3
Volta,L Ghana 77F4
Volta Noire R U Volta 77F3
Volta Redonda Brazil 73D3
Volta Rouge R U Volta 77F3
Volterra Italy 17D3
Voltri Italy 17C2
Volynskiy USSR 25D5
Volzhskiy USSR 25G6
Von Frank Mt USA 56H3
Vonguda USSR 24F3
Vopnafjörður Iceland 53R3
Voralberg Province Austria 17C1
Vorder Rhein R Switz 17C1
Vordingborg Den 20C1
Voriái I Greece 25C8
Vorkuta USSR 26H3
Vorma R Nor 12G6
Voronezh USSR 25F5
Voron'ya R USSR 12M5
Voroshilovgrad USSR 25F6
Võru USSR 12K7
Vosges Department France 16D2
Vosges Mts France 18D2
Voshnyy Saytocan Mts USSR 38C1
Voss Nor 12F6
Vostchnyy USSR 41E2
Vostochnyy USSR 41E1
Vostochnyy Sayan Mts USSR 27L4
Vostok Base Ant 80F9
Votkinsk USSR 24J4
Vouziers France 16C2
Voves France 16A2
Voy Vozh USSR 24K3
Voznesensk USSR 25E6
Vozvyshennost' Karabil' Desert Region USSR 34E1
Vranje Yugos 23E2
Vratsa Bulg 23E2
Vrbas Yugos 23D1
Vrbas R Yugos 22D2
Vrbovsko Yugos 22C1
Vreed en Hoop Guyana 71G2
Vrhnika Yugos 17F2
Vršac Yugos 23E1
Vrtoče Yugos 22D2
Vryburg S Africa 79C6
Vryheid S Africa 79D6
Vsevidof,Mt USA 56E5
Vukovar Yugos 23D1
Vuktyl' USSR 24K3
Vulcano I Italy 22C3
Vung Tau Viet 43D3
Vuollerim Sweden 12J5
Vyartsilya USSR 24E3
Vyatka R USSR 24J4
Vyazemskiy USSR 41C2
Vyaz'ma USSR 24E4
Vyazniki USSR 24G4
Vyborg USSR 24D3
Vym R USSR 24J3
Vyrnwy R Wales 15D5
Vyshiy Volochek USSR 24E4
Vyškov Czech 20D3
Vysokogornyy USSR 41D1
Vytegra USSR 24F3

W

Wa Ghana 77F3
Waal R Neth 16C1
Wabach USA 55E3
Wabasca R Can 52G4
Wabash USA 58B2
Wabash R USA 58B3
Wabatongushi L Can 58C1
Wabowden Can 52J4
Wabush Can 53M4
Waccasassa B USA 61C3
Wachusett Res USA 60E1
Waco USA 63C3
Wad Pak 35B3
Waddān Libya 75A2
Waddington,Mt Can 52F4
Wadena USA 57C2
Wadi Abu 'Amūd V Jordan 31D3
Wadi Abu Tarfa V Egypt 31B4
Wadi ad Dawāsin Watercourse S Arabia 32D2
Wadi Adhanah Watercourse Yemen 33E3
Wadi al Amilhayt Watercourse Oman 33F3
Wadi al Bātin Watercourse Iraq 30E4
Wadi al Ghudāf Watercourse Iraq 30D3
Wadi al Harīr V Syria 31D2
Wadi al Masīlāh Watercourse S Yemen 33F3
Wadi al Mirah Watercourse S Arabia/Iraq 30D3
Wadi al Ubayyid Watercourse Iraq 30D3
Wadi Aman Watercourse S Yemen 33F3
Wadi 'Araba V Israel 31C3
Wadi Ar'ar Watercourse S Arabia 30D3
Wadi as Hsabā' Watercourse S Arabia 33E2
Wadi as Sirhān V Jordan/S Arabia 30C3
Wadi ath Thamhar R Iraq 25G8
Wadi az Zaydi V Syria 31D2
Wadi Bishah Watercourse S Arabia 32D2
Wadi edh Dhab'i V Jordan 31D3
Wadi el'Aqaba V Egypt 31C4
Wadi el 'Arish V Egypt 31B3
Wadi el Brûk V Egypt 31B3
Wadi el Gafa V Egypt 31A3
Wadi el Ghadaf V Jordan 31D3
Wadi el Hasa V Jordan 31C3
Wadi el Higayib V Egypt 31B3
Wadi el Janab V Jordan 31D3
Wadi el Jeib V Israel/Jordan 31C3
Wadi el Khush Shah V Jordan 31D4
Wadi el Milk Watercourse Sudan 78C2
Wadi el Natrun Watercourse Egypt 30A3
Wadi el Saheira V Egypt 31B4
Wadi el Sîq Egypt 31B4
Wadi es Sir Jordan 31C3
Wadi Fidan V Jordan 31C3
Wadi Habawnāh Watercourse S Arabia 32D3
Wadi Haifa Sudan 32B2
Wadi Hareidin V Egypt 31C3
Wadi Hasana V Egypt 31B3
Wadi Hawrān R Iraq 30D3
Wadi Howa Watercourse Sudan 78C2
Wadi Ibra Watercourse Sudan 78C2
Wadi Jawf Watercourse Yemen 33E3
Wadi Luhfi Watercourse Jordan 31D2
Wadi Makhay Watercourse S Yemen 33E3
Wadi Mawr Watercourse Yemen 32D3
Wadi Mugshin Watercourse Oman 33F3
Wadi Mujib V Jordan 31C3
Wādi Mūsa Jordan 31C3
Wadi Ouena Watercourse Egypt 32B1
Wadi Qa'ash Shubyk V Jordan 31D4
Wadi Qinãb Watercourse S Yemen 33F3
Wadi Qîtaiya V Egypt 31C3
Wadi Ranyah Watercourse S Arabia 32D2
Wadi Ratiyah V Jordan 31D3
Wadi Ruweila V Jordan 31D4
Wadi Sha'it Watercourse Egypt 32B2
Wadi Shihan Watercourse Oman 33F3
Wadi Tathlith Watercourse S Arabia 32D2
Wadi Turabah Watercourse S Arabia 32D2
Wadi Ugeiqa V Jordan 31C3
Wad Medani Sudan 78D2
Waegwan S Korea 42A3
Wafra Kuwait 30E4
Wageningen Neth 16C1
Wager B Can 53K3
Wager Bay Can 53J3
Wagga Wagga Aust 50C3
Wagin Aust 48A4
Wagner USA 57C3
Waha Indon 45C3
Waha Libya 75A2
Wahoo USA 63C1
Wahpeton USA 57C2
Wai India 36A1
Waiau NZ 51B2
Waiau R NZ 51A3
Waiau R NZ 51B2
Waigama Indon 45C3
Waigeo I Indon 39G6
Waihi NZ 51C1
Waikabubak Indon 45A4
Waikaremoana,L NZ 51C1
Waikato R NZ 51C1
Waikelo Indon 45A4
Waikerie Aust 50A2
Waikouaiti NZ 51B3
Waimakariri R NZ 51B2
Waimate NZ 51B2
Waingapu Indon 48B1
Wainwright Can 52G4
Wainwright USA 56F1
Waipara NZ 51B2
Waipukurau NZ 51C2
Wairarapa,L NZ 51C2
Wairau R NZ 51B2
Wairoa NZ 51C1
Wairoa R NZ 51C1
Waitaki R NZ 51B2
Waitara NZ 51B1
Waitomo NZ 51C1
Waiuku NZ 51B1
Wajima Japan 42C3
Wajir Kenya 78E3
Wakasa-wan B Japan 42C3
Wakatipu,L NZ 51A3
Wakayama Japan 41D5
Wa Keeney USA 62C2
Wakefield Eng 15E5
Wakefield Jamaica 68H1
Wakefield Michigan USA 58B1
Wakefield Rhode Island USA 60E2
Wakema Burma 43B2
Wakkanai Japan 41E2
Wakool R Aust 50B3
Wakre Indon 45D3
Walbrzych Pol 20D2
Walcha Aust 50D2
Walcz Pol 20D2
Waldbröl W Germ 16D1
Walden USA 60C2
Waldia Eth 78E2
Waldshut W Germ 16E3
Wales Country U K 15D5
Wales USA 56E2
Wales I Can 53K3
Walewale Ghana 77F3
Walgett Aust 50C2
Walgreen Coast Region Ant 80F4
Walikale Zaïre 78C4
Walker USA 57D2
Walker L USA 65C3
Walkerton Can 58C2
Wall USA 57B3
Wallace USA 64C1
Wallaroo Aust 50A2
Walla Walla Aust 50C3
Walla Walla USA 64C1
Walldürn W Germ 16E2
Wallingford USA 60D2
Wallis and Futuna Is Pacific O 47K5
Wallowa USA 64C1
Wallowa Mts Mts USA 64C1
Wallumbilla Aust 50C1
Walnut Ridge USA 63D2
Walouru NZ 51C1
Walpole USA 60D1
Walsall Eng 15E5
Walsenburg USA 62B2
Walsenburgh USA 54C3
Walterboro USA 61C2
Walter F George Res USA 61B2
Walters USA 62C3
Waltham USA 60E1
Walton USA 60C1
Walvis Bay S Africa 79B6
Walvis Ridge Atlantic O 74J6
Wamba Nig 77H4
Wamba R Zaïre 78B4
Wamego USA 63C2
Wamsasi Indon 45C3
Wamsutter USA 64E2
Wana Pak 35B2
Wanaaring Aust 50B1
Wanaka NZ 51A2
Wanaka,L NZ 51A2
Wanapitei L Can 58C1
Wanda Shan Upland China 41C2
Wando S Korea 42A4
Wandoan Aust 50C1
Wanganella Aust 50B3
Wanganui NZ 49G4
Wanganui NZ 51B1
Wanganui R NZ 51C1
Wangaratta Aust 50C3
Wangiwangi I Indon 45B4
Wangkui China 41B2
Wango Fitini Ivory Coast 77F4
Wangqing China 41B3
Wanle Weyne Somalia 78E3
Wanning China 43E2
Wanpaca USA 58B2
Wanparti India 36B1
Wanxian China 40B3
Wanyuan China 40B3
Wappapello,L USA 63D2
Wappingers Falls USA 60D2
Wapsipinicon R USA 57D3
Wara Nat Pk Cam 77J3
Warangal India 36B1
Waratah Aust 50E3
Waratah B Aust 50C3
Warburg W Germ 16E1
Warburton Aust 50C3
Warburton R Aust 50A1
Ward R Aust 50C1
Warder Eth 78E3
Wardha India 35D4
Ward,Mt NZ 51A3
Ware Can 52F4
Ware USA 60D1
Wareham USA 60E2
Warendorf W Germ 16D1
Warialda Aust 50D1
Warin Chamrap Thai 43D2
Warmbad S Africa 79C6
Warminster USA 60C2
Warm Springs USA 65C3
Warnemünde E Germ 20C2
Warner Mts USA 64B2
Warner Robins USA 61C2
Warracknabeal Aust 50B3
Warrandirinna,L Aust 50A1
Warrego R Aust 48D3
Warren Arkansas USA 63D3
Warren Aust 50C2
Warren Massachusetts USA 60E2
Warren Minnesota USA 57C2
Warren Ohio USA 58C2
Warren Pennsylvania USA 59D2
Warrenpoint N Ire 15B4
Warrensburg USA 63D2
Warrenton S Africa 79C6
Warrenton USA 59D3
Warri Nig 77H4
Warrina Aust 50A1
Warrington Eng 15D5
Warrington USA 61B2
Warrior R USA 61B2
Warrnambool Aust 50B3
Warroad USA 57C2
Warsaw = Warszawa
Warsaw USA 60A1
Warszawa Pol 21E2
Warta R Pol 21D2
Warwick Aust 50D1
Warwick County Eng 15E5
Warwick Eng 15E5
Warwick New York USA 60C2
Warwick Rhode Island USA 60E2
Wasatch Range Mts USA 65D3
Wasco USA 65C3
Waseca USA 57D3
Washap Pak 34E3
Washburn USA 58A1
Washburn L Can 52H2
Washburn,Mt USA 64D2
Wāshīm India 35D4
Washington District of Columbia USA 55F3
Washington Georgia USA 61C2
Washington Indiana USA 58B3
Washington Iowa USA 57D3
Washington Missouri USA 63D2
Washington N Carolina USA 61D1
Washington New Jersey USA 60C2
Washington Pennsylvania USA 58C2
Washington State USA 54A2
Washington Utah USA 65D3
Washington Court House USA 58C3
Washington Land Can 53M1
Washington,Mt USA 59E2
Washita R USA 62C2
Wash,The Eng 15F5
Washuk Pak 35A3
Wasilla USA 56J3
Waspán Nic 68A4
Wassy France 16C2
Watampone Indon 45B3
Watansoppeng Indon 45A3
Waterbury USA 60D2
Waterford County Irish Rep 15B5
Waterford Irish Rep 13B3
Waterford Harbour Irish Rep 15B5
Waterloo Belg 16C1
Waterloo USA 57D3
Watersmeet USA 58B1
Waterton-Glacier Nat Pk USA 64D1
Watertown New York USA 59D2
Watertown S Dakota USA 57C3
Watertown Wisconsin USA 58B2
Waterville Maine USA 59F2
Waterville New York USA 60C1
Watervliet USA 60D1
Waterways Can 52G4
Watford Eng 15E6
Watford City USA 57B2
Watkins Bjerge Mt Greenland 53Q3
Watkins Glen USA 60B1
Watonga USA 62C2
Watrous Can 52H4
Watrous Can 54C1
Watrous USA 62B2
Watsa Zaïre 78C3
Watson Lake Can 56N3
Watsonville USA 65B3
Watukancoa Indon 45B3
Wau PNG 39H7
Wau Sudan 78C3
Waua Can 53K5
Wauchope Aust 50D2
Wauchula USA 61E4
Waukegan USA 58B2
Waukesha USA 58B2
Waupun USA 58B2
Waurika USA 63C3
Wausau USA 58B2
Wauwatosa USA 58B2
Wave Hill Aust 48C2
Waverey R Eng 15F5
Waverly Iowa USA 57D3
Waverly New York USA 60B1
Waverly Ohio USA 58C3
Wavre Belg 16C1
Wawa Can 58C1
Wawa Nig 77G4
Wāw Al Kabīr Libya 75A2
Wāw an Nāmūs Well Libya 75A2
Waxahachie USA 63C3
Wayabula Indon 45C2
Waycross USA 61C2
Wayne USA 57C3
Waynesboro Georgia USA 61C2
Waynesboro Mississippi USA 63E3
Waynesboro Pennsylvania USA 60B3

Waynesboro Yalalag

Waynesboro Virginia *USA* 59D3
Waynesville Missouri *USA* 63D2
Waynesville N Carolina *USA* 61C1
Wazi Khwa *Afghan* 35B2
Weald,The Upland *Eng* 15F6
Wear R *Eng* 14D4
Weatherford Oklahoma *USA* 62C2
Weatherford Texas *USA* 63C3
Weaverville *USA* 64B2
Webbwood *Can* 58C1
Webster New York *USA* 60B1
Webster S Dakota *USA* 57C2
Webster *USA* 60E1
Webster City Massachusetts *USA* 57D3
Webster Groves *USA* 58A3
Weda *Indon* 45C2
Weddell I *Falkland Is* 69D8
Weddell S *Ant* 80G2
Weed *USA* 64B2
Weedville *USA* 60A2
Wee Waa *Aust* 50C2
Weichang *China* 40D1
Weiden *W Germ* 20C3
Weifang *China* 40D2
Weihai *China* 40E2
Wei He R Henan *China* 40C3
Wei He R Shaanxi *China* 40C2
Weilmoringle *Aust* 50C1
Weinheim *W Germ* 16E2
Weining *China* 40A4
Weipa *Aust* 48D2
Weirton *USA* 58C2
Weiser *USA* 64C2
Weishan Hu L *China* 40D3
Weissenfels *E Germ* 20C2
Weiss L *USA* 61B2
Welch *USA* 58C3
Welkom *S Africa* 79C6
Welland *Can* 59D2
Welland R *Eng* 15E5
Wellesley Is *Aust* 48C2
Wellesley L *Can* 56L3
Wellfleet *USA* 60E2
Wellingborough *Eng* 15E5
Wellington *Aust* 50C2
Wellington Colorado *USA* 62B1
Wellington Kansas *USA* 63C2
Wellington *NZ* 51B2
Wellington Texas *USA* 62B3
Wellington Chan *Can* 53J2
Wells *Eng* 15D6
Wells Nevada *USA* 64D2
Wells New York *USA* 60C1
Wellsboro *USA* 60B2
Wellsford *NZ* 51B1
Wells,L *Aust* 48B3
Wellsville *USA* 60B1
Wels *Austria* 20C3
Welshpool *Wales* 15D5
Wenatchee *USA* 64B1
Wenatchee R *USA* 64C1
Wenchi *Ghana* 77F4
Wenden *China* 40E2
Wendover *USA* 64D2
Wenling *China* 40E4
Wenshan *China* 40A5
Wenthaggi *Aust* 48D4
Wentworth *Aust* 50B2
Wen Xian *China* 40A3
Wenzhou *China* 40E4
Wenzhu *China* 40C4
Wepener *Lesotho* 79C6
Wernecke Mts *Can* 56L2
Werra R *E Germ* 20C2
Werris Creek *Aust* 50D2
Wesel *W Germ* 16D1
Wesel *W Germ* 20B2
Weser R *W Germ* 20B2
Weskan *USA* 62B2
Weslaco *USA* 63F4
Wessel Is *Aust* 48C2
Wesser R *W Germ* 16E1
Wesserbergland Region *W Germ* 16E1
Wessington Spring *USA* 57C3
West Allis *USA* 58B2
West Australian Basin *Indian O* 46F5
West Australian Ridge *Indian O* 46F6
West B *USA* 63E3
West Bengal State *India* 37C3
West Branch Delaware R *USA* 60C1
West Branch Susquehanna R *USA* 60A2
West Bromwich *Eng* 15E5
Westbrook *USA* 59E2
Westby *USA* 58A2
West Chester *USA* 60C3
Westerburg *W Germ* 16D1
Westerland *W Germ* 20B2
Westerly *USA* 60E2
Western Australia State *Aust* 48B3
Western Ghats Mts *India* 36A1
Western Isles *Scot* 14B3
Western Sahara Region *Mor* 76A2
Western Samoa Is *Pacific O* 49H2
Westerschelde Estuary *Neth* 16B1
Westerwald Region *W Germ* 16D1
Westfalen Region *W Germ* 18D1
West Falkland I *Falkland Is* 69D8
Westfield Massachusetts *USA* 60D1
Westfield New York *USA* 59D2
Westfield Pennsylvania *USA* 60B2
West Frankfort *USA* 58B3
Westgate *Aust* 50C1
West Germany Federal Republic *Europe* 20B2
West Glamorgan County *Wales* 15D6
West Grand L *USA* 59F1
West Indies Is *Caribbean S* 74E4
West Liberty *USA* 58C3
West Lorne *Can* 58C2
Westmeath County *Irish Rep* 15B5
West Memphis *USA* 63D2
West Midlands County *Eng* 15E5
Westminster *Eng* 15E6
Westminster Maryland *USA* 60B3
Westminster S Carolina *USA* 61C2
Weston *Malay* 44E1
Weston *USA* 58C3
Weston-super-Mare *Eng* 15D6
West Palm Beach *USA* 61E4
West Plains *USA* 63D2
West Point Mississippi *USA* 63E3
West Point Nebraska *USA* 57C3
West Point New York *USA* 60D2
West Point Mt *USA* 56K3
Westport *NZ* 51B2
Westray I *Scot* 13C2
West Side Oilfield *N Sea* 15F5
West Virginia State *USA* 55E3
West Wyalong *Aust* 50C2
West Yellowstone *USA* 64D2
West Yorkshire County *Eng* 15E5
Wetar I *Indon* 45C4
Wetaskiwin *Can* 52G4
Wete *Tanz* 78D4
Wetter R *W Germ* 16E1
Wetzlar *W Germ* 16E1
Wevok = Cape Lisburne
Wewak *PNG* 48D1
Wewoka *USA* 63C2
Wexford County *Irish Rep* 15B5
Wexford *Irish Rep* 15B5
Weyburn *Can* 52H5
Weymouth *Eng* 15D6
Weymouth *USA* 60E1
Whakatane *NZ* 51C1
Whakatane R *NZ* 51C1
Whalsay I *Scot* 14E1
Whangarei *NZ* 51B1
Wharfe R *Eng* 15E5
Wharton *USA* 63C4
Whataroa *NZ* 51B2
Wheatland *USA* 57A3
Wheaton Maryland *USA* 60B3
Wheaton Minnesota *USA* 57C2
Wheeler Peak Mt Nevada *USA* 65D3
Wheeler Peak Mt New Mexico *USA* 62A2
Wheeling *USA* 58C2
Whitby *Can* 59D2
Whitby *Eng* 15E4
White R Arkansas *USA* 63D2
White R *Can* 56K3
White R Colorado *USA* 62A1
White R Indiana *USA* 58B3
White R S Dakota *USA* 57B3
White B *Can* 53N4
White Butte Mt *USA* 57B2
White Cliffs *Aust* 50B2
White Coomb Mt *Scot* 13C2
Whitefish *USA* 64D1
Whitefish Pt *USA* 58B1
Whitegull L *Can* 53M4
Whitehall New York *USA* 59E2
Whitehall Pennsylvania *USA* 60C2
Whitehall Wisconsin *USA* 58A2
Whitehaven *Eng* 15D4
Whitehorse *Can* 56L3
White I *NZ* 51C1
White L *USA* 63D4
Whitemark *Aust* 50E3
White Mountain Peak Mt *USA* 65C3
White Mts Alaska *USA* 56J2
White Mts New Hampshire *USA* 59E2
White Nile = Bahr el Abiad
White Nile R *Sudan* 78D2
White Plains *USA* 60D2
White River *Can* 53K5
White River *USA* 57B3
White S = Beloye More
White Salmon *USA* 64B1
White Sulphur Springs *USA* 64D1
Whiteville *USA* 61D2
White Volta R *Ghana* 77F4
Whitewater *USA* 58B2
Whithorn *Scot* 14C4
Whitmire *USA* 61C2
Whitney,Mt. *USA* 65C3
Whittier Alaska *USA* 56J3
Wholdia L *Can* 52H3
Whyalla *Aust* 50A2
Wiarton *Can* 58C2
Wiawso *Ghana* 77F4
Wibaux *USA* 57B2
Wichita *USA* 63C2
Wichita R *USA* 62C3
Wichita Falls *USA* 62C3
Wichita Mts *USA* 62C3
Wick *Scot* 14D2
Wickenburg *USA* 65D4
Wicklow County *Irish Rep* 15B5
Wicklow *Irish Rep* 15B5
Wicklow Mts *Irish Rep* 15B5
Widgeegoara R *Aust* 50C1
Wied R *W Germ* 16D1
Wielun *Pol* 21D2
Wien *Austria* 20D3
Wiener Neustadt *Austria* 20D3
Wieprz R *Pol* 21E2
Wiesbaden *W Germ* 16E1
Wiese R *W Germ* 16D3
Wigan *Eng* 15D5
Wiggins *USA* 63E3
Wigtown *Scot* 14C4
Wigtown B *Scot* 14C4
Wil *Switz* 17C1
Wilbur *USA* 64C1
Wilcannia *Aust* 50B2
Wildcat Peak Mt *USA* 65C3
Wildhorn Mt *Switz* 17B1
Wildspitze Mt *Austria* 17D1
Wildwood Florida *USA* 61C3
Wildwood New Jersey *USA* 60C3
Wiley *USA* 62B2
Wilhelm,Mt *PNG* 48D1
Wilhelmshaven *W Germ* 20B2
Wilkes-Barre *USA* 60C2
Wilkes Land *Ant* 80F8
Willamette R *USA* 64B2
Willandra R *Aust* 50B2
Willcox *USA* 65E4
Willemstad *Curaçao* 68D4
William Creek *Aust* 50A1
William,Mt *Aust* 50B3
Williams Arizona *USA* 65D3
Williams California *USA* 65B3
Williamsburg *USA* 59D3
Williams Lake *Can* 52F4
Williamson *USA* 58C3
Williamsport *USA* 60B2
Williamston *USA* 61D1
Williamstown Massachusetts *USA* 60D1
Williamstown W Virginia *USA* 58C3
Willimantic *USA* 60D2
Willingboro *USA* 60C2
Willis Group Is *Aust* 48E2
Williston Florida *USA* 61C3
Williston N Dakota *USA* 57B2
Williston *S Africa* 79C7
Willmar *USA* 57C2
Willoughby,C *Aust* 50A3
Willow Bunch *Can* 57A2
Willowmore *S Africa* 79C7
Willow Ranch *USA* 64B2
Willows *USA* 65B3
Willow Springs *USA* 63D2
Wilmington *Aust* 50A2
Wilmington Delaware *USA* 60C3
Wilmington N Carolina *USA* 61D2
Wilmington Vermont *USA* 60D1
Wilnona *USA* 53J5
Wilson Kansas *USA* 62C2
Wilson N Carolina *USA* 61D1
Wilson New York *USA* 60A1
Wilson *USA* 55F3
Wilson L *USA* 62C2
Wilson R *Aust* 50B1
Wilson,C *Can* 53K3
Wilson,Mt Colorado *USA* 62A2
Wilson,Mt Oregon *USA* 64B1
Wilsons Promontory Pen *Aust* 50C3
Wiltshire County *Eng* 15E6
Wiltz *Lux* 16C2
Wiluna *Aust* 48B3
Winamac *USA* 58B2
Winchendon *USA* 60D1
Winchester *Can* 59D1
Winchester *Eng* 15E6
Winchester Kentucky *USA* 58C3
Winchester New Hampshire *USA* 60D1
Winchester Virginia *USA* 59D3
Wind R *USA* 64E2
Windber *USA* 60A2
Windermere *Eng* 15D4
Windhoek *Namibia* 79B6
Windom *USA* 57C3
Windorah *Aust* 48D3
Wind River Range Mts *USA* 64E2
Windsor *Aust* 50D2
Windsor Connecticut *USA* 60D2
Windsor *Eng* 15E6
Windsor N Carolina *USA* 61D1
Windsor Nova Scotia *Can* 53M5
Windsor Ontario *Can* 58C2
Windsor Quebec *Can* 59E1
Windsor Forest *USA* 61C2
Windsor Locks *USA* 60D2
Windward Is *Caribbean* 68E4
Windward Pass *Caribbean* 68C3
Winfield Alabama *USA* 61B2
Winfield Kansas *USA* 63C2
Wingham *Aust* 50D2
Winifreda *Arg* 72C3
Winisk R *Can* 53K4
Winisk L *Can* 53K4
Winkana *Burma* 43B2
Winlock *USA* 64B1
Winneba *Ghana* 77F4
Winnebago *USA* 57D3
Winnebago,L *USA* 58B2
Winnemucca *USA* 64C2
Winner *USA* 57C3
Winnfield *USA* 63D3
Winnibigoshish L *USA* 57D2
Winnipeg *Can* 52J4
Winnipeg R *Can* 57C1
Winnipeg,L *Can* 52J4
Winnipegosis *Can* 52J4
Winnipesaukee,L *USA* 59E2
Winona Minnesota *USA* 57D3
Winona Mississippi *USA* 63E3
Winooski *USA* 59E2
Winslow *USA* 65D4
Winsted *USA* 60D2
Winston-Salem *USA* 61C1
Winterberg *W Germ* 16E1
Winter Gardens *USA* 61C3
Winter Park *USA* 61C3
Winterswijk *Neth* 16D1
Winterthur *Switz* 17C1
Winthrop *USA* 57D3
Winton *Aust* 48D3
Winton *NZ* 51A3
Wisbech *Eng* 15F5
Wisconsin State *USA* 55E2
Wisconsin R *USA* 58A2
Wisconsin Dells *USA* 58B2
Wisconsin Rapids *USA* 53K5
Wiseman *USA* 56H2
Wisla R *Pol* 21D2
Wismar *E Germ* 20C2
Wissembourg *France* 16D2
Witagron *Suriname* 71G2
Witchita Falls *USA* 54D3
Witham R *Eng* 15E5
Withernsea *Eng* 15F5
Witney *Eng* 15E6
Witten *W Germ* 16D1
Wittenberg *E Germ* 20C2
Wittenoom *Aust* 48A3
Wittlich *W Germ* 16D1
Wladyslawowo *Pol* 21D2
Włocławek *Pol* 21D2
Włodawa *Pol* 21E2
Wodonga *Aust* 50C3
Wohlen *Switz* 17C1
Wokam *Indon* 39G7
Woking *Eng* 15E6
Wolcott *USA* 60B1
Woleai I *Pacific O* 39H6
Wolf R *USA* 58B1
Wolfach *W Germ* 16E2
Wolf Creek *USA* 64B2
Wolf Creek P *USA* 62A2
Wolf Point *USA* 57A2
Wolfsberg *Austria* 20C3
Wolfsburg *W Germ* 20C2
Wollaston L. *Can* 52H4
Wollaston Lake *Can* 52H4
Wollaston Pen *Can* 52G3
Wollongong *Aust* 50D2
Wolmaranstad *S Africa* 79C6
Wolow *Pol* 20D2
Wolowaru *Indon* 45B4
Wolseley *Aust* 50B3
Wolverhampton *Eng* 15D5
Womelsdorf *USA* 60B2
Wondai *Aust* 50D1
Wŏnju *S Korea* 41B4
Wonominta R *Aust* 50B2
Wŏnsan *N Korea* 41B4
Wonthaggi *Aust* 50C3
Woocalla *Aust* 50A2
Woodbine *USA* 60C3
Woodbridge *USA* 59D3
Wood Buffalo Nat. Pk. *Can* 52G4
Woodburn *Aust* 50D1
Woodburn *USA* 64B1
Woodbury *USA* 60C3
Woodchopper *USA* 56K2
Woodland California *USA* 65B3
Woodland Washington *USA* 64B1
Woodlark I *PNG* 49E1
Woodmera *Aust* 48C4
Woodroffe,Mt *Aust* 48C3
Woods,L of the *Can* 57D2
Woodstock Illinois *USA* 58B2
Woodstock New Brunswick *Can* 59F1
Woodstock Ontario *Can* 58C2
Woodstock Virginia *USA* 60A3
Woodstown *USA* 60C3
Woodville *NZ* 51C2
Woodville *USA* 63D3
Woodward *USA* 62C2
Woomera *Aust* 50A2
Woonsocket *USA* 59E2
Wooster *USA* 58C2
Worcester *Eng* 15D5
Worcester *S Africa* 79B7
Worcester *USA* 60E1
Wörgl *Austria* 17E1
Workington *Eng* 15D4
Worland *USA* 64E2
Worms *W Germ* 16E2
Worms Head Pt *Wales* 15C6
Worthing *Eng* 15E6
Worthington *USA* 57C3
Wowoni I *Indon* 45B3
Wrangell *USA* 52E4
Wrangell *USA* 56M4
Wrangell,C *USA* 56A5
Wrangell I *USA* 56M4
Wrangell Mts *USA* 56K3
Wrath,C *Scot* 13B2
Wray *USA* 62B1
Wrexham *Wales* 15D5
Wrightson *USA* 65D4
Wrightsville *USA* 61C2
Wrigley *Can* 52F3
Wrocław *Pol* 20D2
Września *Pol* 21D2
Wuchang *China* 41B3
Wuchuan *China* 43E1
Wuda *China* 40E2
Wuday'ah *S Arabia* 33E3
Wudil *Nig* 77H3
Wuding He R *China* 40C2
Wudu *China* 40A3
Wugang *China* 40C4
Wuhai *China* 40B2
Wuhan *China* 40C3
Wuhu *China* 40D3
Wuhua *China* 40D5
Wŭjang *China* 35D2
Wujia He R *China* 40B1
Wu Jiang R *China* 40B4
Wukari *Nig* 77H4
Wuliaru I *Indon* 45D4
Wuling Shan Mts *China* 40B4
Wum *Cam* 77J4
Wumeng Shan Upland *China* 40A4
Wuntho *Burma* 37E3
Wuppertal *W Germ* 16D1
Wuqi *China* 40B2
Wuqing *China* 40D2
Würzburg *W Germ* 20B3
Wurzen *E Germ* 20C2
Wusuli Jiang R *China* 41C2
Wutai Shan Mt *China* 40C2
Wuvulu I *Pacific O* 39H7
Wuwei *China* 40A2
Wuxi *China* 40E3
Wuxing *China* 40E3
Wuyang *China* 40C2
Wuyiling *China* 41B2
Wuyi Shan Mts *China* 40D4
Wuyuan *China* 40B1
Wuyur He R *China* 41B2
Wuzhi Shan Mts *China* 43D2
Wuzhong *China* 40B2
Wuzhou *China* 40C5
Wyandotte *USA* 58C2
Wyandra *Aust* 50C1
Wye R *Eng* 15D6
Wylye R *Eng* 15D6
Wymondham *Eng* 15F5
Wyndham *Aust* 48B2
Wynne *USA* 63D2
Wynniatt B *Can* 52G2
Wynyard *Aust* 50E3
Wyoming State *USA* 54C2
Wyoming *USA* 58B2
Wyoming Peak Mt *USA* 64D2
Wyoming Range Mts *USA* 64D2
Wyong *Aust* 50D2
Wytheville *USA* 58C3

X

Xaidulla *China* 35D1
Xai Moron He R *China* 40D1
Xai Xai *Mozam* 79D6
Xaltinguis *Mexico* 67C2
Xangongo *Angola* 79B5
Xanten *W Germ* 16D1
Xánthi *Greece* 23E2
Xau,L *Botswana* 79C6
Xenia *USA* 58C3
Xiaguan *China* 38C4
Xiahe *China* 40A2
Xiamen *China* 40D5
Xi'an *China* 40B3
Xianfeng *China* 40B4
Xiangfan *China* 40C3
Xiang Jiang R *China* 40C4
Xiangtan Province *China* 40C4
Xianning *China* 40C4
Xianyang *China* 40B3
Xiao'ergou *China* 41A2
Xiao Shui R *China* 40C4
Xiapu *China* 40D4
Xichang *China* 40A4
Xicoténcatl *Mexico* 67C1
Xicotepec *Mexico* 67C1
Xieng Khouang *Laos* 43C2
Xifeng *China* 40B4
Xigazê *China* 37C2
Xi He R *China* 40A1
Xiji *China* 40B2
Xi Jiang R *China* 40C5
Xiliao He R *China* 40E1
Xilin *China* 40B5
Xilitla *Mexico* 67C1
Xinfeng *China* 40D4
Xinghe *China* 40C1
Xingkai Hu L *China/USSR* 41C2
Xingning *China* 40D5
Xingren *China* 40B4
Xingtai *China* 40C2
Xingu R *Brazil* 71H4
Xingxingxia *China* 38C2
Xingyi *China* 40A4
Xinhan *China* 41B3
Xining *China* 40A2
Xinjin Liaoning *China* 40E2
Xinjin Sichuan *China* 40A3
Xinkai He R *China* 41A3
Xinwen *China* 40D2
Xin Xian *China* 40C2
Xinxiang *China* 40C2
Xinyang *China* 40C3
Xinyi Guangdong *China* 40C5
Xinyi Jiangsu *China* 40D3
Xi Ujimqin Qi *China* 40D1
Xiuyan *China* 41A3
Xochimilco *Mexico* 67C2
Xuancheng *China* 40D3
Xuanhan *China* 40B3
Xuanhua *China* 40D1
Xuanwei *China* 40A4
Xuchang *China* 40C3
Xuddur *Somalia* 78E3
Xunhua *China* 40A2
Xun Jiang R *China* 40C5
Xunke *China* 41B2
Xunwu *China* 40D5
Xupu *China* 40C4
Xuwen *China* 43D2
Xuwen *China* 43E1
Xuyong *China* 40B4
Xuzhou *China* 40D3

Y

Ya'an *China* 40A4
Yaapeet *Aust* 50B3
Yabassi *Cam* 78B3
Yablochnyy *USSR* 41E2
Yablonovyy Khrebet Mts *USSR* 38D1
Yabrūd *Syria* 31D2
Yachats *USA* 64B2
Yacuiba *Bol* 70F8
Yādgīr *India* 36B1
Yafran *Libya* 75A1
Yagishiri-tō I *Japan* 42D2
Yagotin *USSR* 21G2
Yaguari R *Urug* 72D2
Yaguaron R *Urug* 72E2
Yahualica *Mexico* 67B1
Yahuma *Zaïre* 78C3
Yaita *Japan* 42C3
Yaizu *Japan* 42C4
Yajiang *China* 40A4
Yakataga *USA* 56K4
Yakima *USA* 64B1
Yakima R *USA* 64B1
Yako *U Volta* 77F3
Yakoma *Zaïre* 78C3
Yakujima-kaikyō Str *Japan* 41C5
Yakumo *Japan* 41E3
Yaku-shima I *Japan* 41C5
Yakutat *USA* 56L4
Yakutat B *USA* 56L4
Yakutsk *USSR* 27O3
Yakutskaya ASSR Republic *USSR* 27N3
Yala *Thai* 43C4
Yalalag *Mexico* 67C2

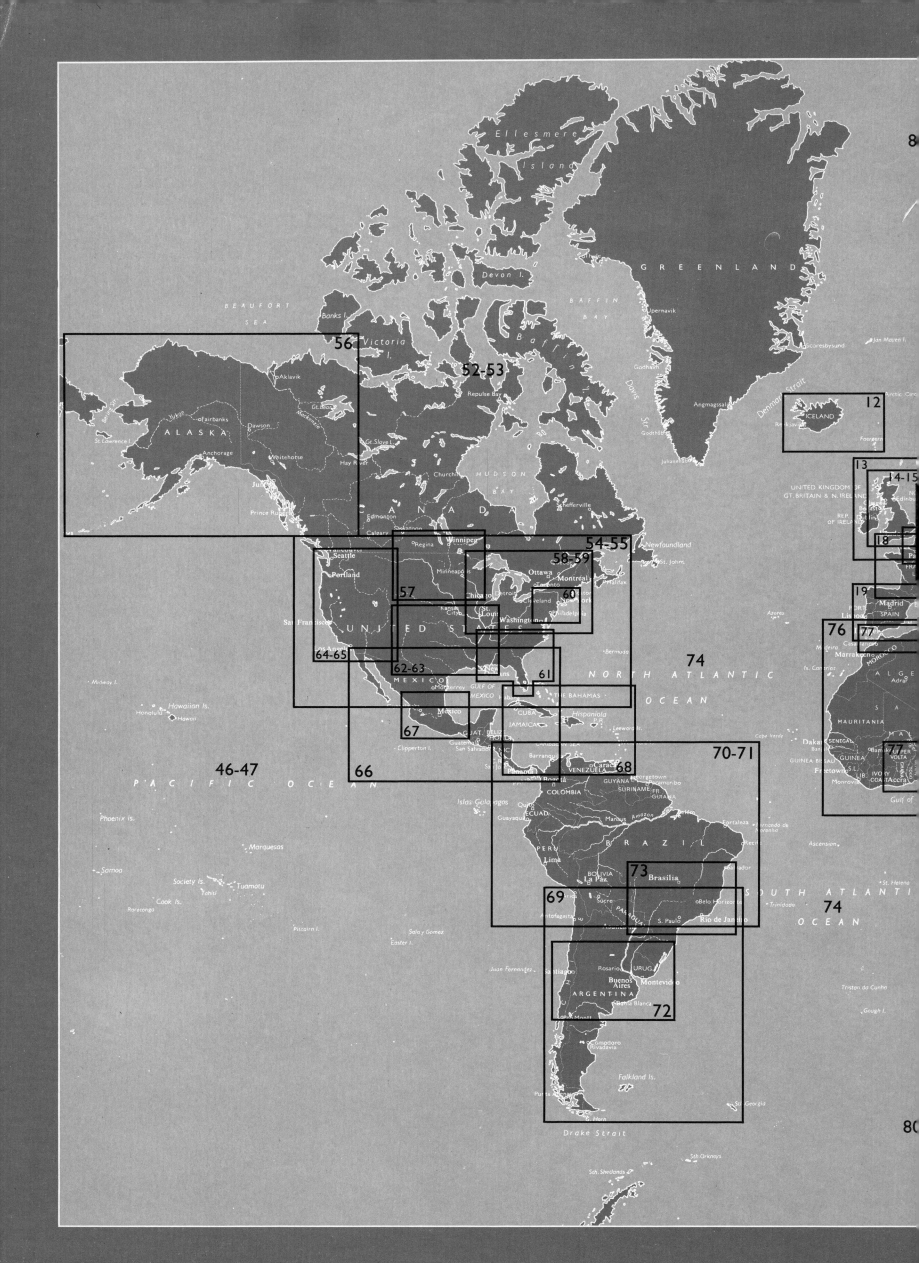